LDAP in the Solaris™ Operating Environment:
Deploying Secure Directory Services

Michael Haines
Tom Bialaski

Sun Microsystems Press
A Prentice Hall Title

Prentice Hall PTR offers excellent discounts on this book when ordered in quantity for bulk purchases or special sales. For more information, please contact: U.S. Corporate and Government Sales, 1-800-382-3419, corpsales@pearsontechgroup.com. For sales outside of the U.S., please contact: International Sales, 1-317-581-3793, international@pearsontechgroup.com.

Executive Editor: *Gregory G. Doench*
Production and Editorial Supervision: *Kathleen M. Caren*
Cover Design Director: *Jerry Votta*
Cover Designer: *Kavish & Kavish Digital Publishing and Design*
Manufacturing Manager: *Alexis R. Heydt-Long*
Marketing Manager: *Debby van Dijk*

Sun Microsystems Press:
Publisher: *Myrna Rivera*

First Printing
Text printed on recycled paper

ISBN 0-13-145693-8

Sun Microsystems Press
A Prentice Hall Title

Contents

Acknowledgments

This book is made possible through the generous support of many individuals. We sincerely appreciate the time and effort that everyone donated to bring this book to publication.

We would like to give a special thanks to the following people for their invaluable technical expertise and support, which contributed to technical quality and completeness of this book:

Ludovic Poitou – Sun™ ONE Product engineer

Neil A. Wilson – Sun ONE Product engineer

Jeff T. Moore – Solaris™ Naming Services engineer

We would also like to thank the following people for their invaluable technical contribution and support, which also contributed to technical quality and completeness of this book:

Michen Chang – Solaris Naming Services engineer

Joep Vesseur – Solaris Security Technology engineer

Unai Gaston Caminos – Sun ONE Products engineer

Sylvain Duloutre – Sun ONE Products engineer

John S. Howard – Sun Enterprise™ Engineering engineer

We would like to express our gratitude to those people who contributed to this book through their proficiencies in management and book development:

Cathy Miller	Lucy Ruble	Dany Gilgani
Peter Cunningham	Glenn Wright	Barb Jugo
Vicky Hardman	Gary Rush	Sue Blumenberg
Billie Markim	Wendy Werges	

Many thanks are owed to our families who provided encouragement and understanding when we needed it most. Thank you Jeanne Tringali, Bryony Haines, and Chris Ruble.

Finally, we want to thank the many readers of our first book, *Solaris and LDAP Naming Services, Deploying LDAP in the Enterprise.* After all, it was those readers who took the time to share their thoughts and experiences with the first book that provided the inspiration and motivation for this book.

Preface

LDAP in the Solaris™ Operating Environment – Deploying Secure Directory Services is one book in a growing collection of books that are part of the Sun BluePrints™ program.

This book describes best practices for planning and deploying naming services based on the Lightweight Directory Access Protocol (LDAP). Understanding general LDAP concepts and the specific Solaris implementation is key to successful deployment of resilient enterprise-wide naming services.

This book is a follow-up to the Sun BluePrints book titled *Solaris™ and LDAP Naming Service,* published in December 2000. The first book introduced LDAP concepts to Solaris system administrators who may not have been familiar with them. It also covered implementation details of the first generation of native LDAP in the Solaris™ Operating Environment (Solaris OE).

Much has changed since the first book was written. The directory server that ships with the Solaris OE has gone through a major revision and several minor ones. The Solaris OE LDAP client software has been significantly enhanced, especially in the area of security. New legacy naming service migration tools have been developed in addition to software that enables co-existence with Microsoft Windows environments.

So much new technology, and so many tools have been developed over the past two-and-a-half years, that a simple update to the first book did not make sense. Instead, the content is new. As with the first book, the focus is on how LDAP technology is integrated into the Solaris OE as a naming service, and not a comprehensive book on LDAP concepts and deployments. This book is not meant to replace the Sun product documentation, but rather to complement it by providing expert insight into how the technology works and how best to deploy it. The first book is not a prerequisite for this book.

The Solaris 9 Operating Environment delivers the second phase of Sun's vision for the naming service of the future, and because of the popularity of the Solaris 8 OE, many Solaris 9 OE features have been backported to Solaris 8 OE. New migration tools were included in the first Solaris 9 release and others are included in subsequent updates. The directory server software became integrated in Solaris 9 OE and newer versions are incorporated into Solaris updates.

This book is based primarily on the revisions or software that were available when it was written. Some comparison with older versions is included, so readers who are familiar with those versions can easily understand the differences. This book is based on the following Sun software:

- Solaris 9 4/03 OE

- Solaris 8 OE with Patch 108993-14 (or later version)

- Sun™ ONE Directory Server 5.2 (integrated Solaris OE version)

Many scripts and source code examples are referenced in this book. Rather than including them on a CD-ROM that could quickly become out-of-date, they are posted at http://www.sun.com/solutions/blueprints/tools/index.html. Readers can register, and freely download the examples. See "Obtaining the Downloadable Files for This Book" on page xxvii.

Who Should Use This Book

Three types of readers will find the information in this book useful.

- System architects who are responsible for defining enterprise-wide directory and naming service infrastructure.

- System administrators who are tasked with the actual deployment of directory and naming service technology.

- System programmers who must decide on the best way to implement custom features.

Before You Read This Book

You should be familiar with the basic administration and maintenance functions of the Solaris OE. You should also have an understanding of standard network protocols and topologies.

Because this book is designed to be useful to people with varying degrees of experience and knowledge about Solaris OE and LDAP technology, your experience and knowledge will determine the path you choose through this book.

How This Book Is Organized

This book is organized into the following chapters:

- Chapter 1 "Introducing LDAP in the Solaris Operating Environment" – Provides an overview of LDAP-based directory services, the methodologies used to successfully deploy LDAP, and describes terms and concepts commonly used throughout this book.

- Chapter 2 "Assessing Your Needs for Naming Service Transition and Consolidation" – Deals with issues of legacy naming services and reasons why you would move to LDAP-based naming services. This chapter presents business reasons for making the transition, and offers tips on migration planning.

- Chapter 3 "Defining Directory Service Security Architecture" – Discusses the Solaris OE security model for user authentication and naming service. An example of how to extend the security methods to match your company specific security policies is also provided.

- Chapter 4 "Deploying Solaris OE LDAP Naming Services" – Explains methodologies for deploying LDAP as a naming service along with deployment procedures. How to automate the installation and configuration is discussed with step-by-step examples provided.

- Chapter 5 "Migrating Legacy Data to LDAP" – Covers migration strategies and the tools that are available for migration. Emphasis is on how to import existing naming service data, and how to configure the directory services to co-exist with legacy naming services.

- Chapter 6 "Management Tools and Toolkits" – Provides a survey of tools available from several sources for managing your LDAP naming service data, and provides examples of how to use them effectively. This chapter also describes how to create your own customized tools for managing naming service data.

- Chapter 7 "Performing Administrative Tasks" – Presents tricks and tips for administering directory data. The topics covered in this chapter are topics that are not conventionally covered in product documentation.

- Chapter 8 "Selecting Storage for Optimum Directory Server Performance"– Describes how to choose the right computer hardware for directory server deployment based on performance characteristics.

- Chapter 9 "Performing Directory Server Benchmarks" – Describes the methods and tools used by the Sun Performance Group to characterize the performance of the Sun™ ONE Directory Server software.

- Chapter 10 "Emerging Directory Technologies" – Covers important new technologies. These include Directory Service Markup Language (DSML), Sun™ ONE Identity Synchronization for the Windows (ISW) platform and the NIS to LDAP (N2L) transition service.

The following appendices provide supporting material:

- Appendix A, "LDAP Standards Information" – Provides references to important documents such as RFCs.

- Appendix B, "LDAP v3 Result Codes" – Explains some of the common LDAP error codes that might be returned by your LDAP server.

- Appendix C, "Using snoop with LDAP" – Provides information and examples on how to use the snoop utility to debug network related LDAP problems.

- Appendix D, "Solaris OE 9 PAM Architecture" – Details the PAM application programming interface (API) and the PAM service provider interface (SPI). Also included are procedures on how to effectively write PAM modules when using the Solaris 9 OE.

- The Glossary – Provides a list of terms and acronyms used in this book.

Obtaining the Downloadable Files for This Book

A variety of files are available for use with this book. The files provide tools and files that are described throughout this book. These downloadable files are available to you free of charge, and by obtaining them, you'll be able to perform many of the best practices described in this book without having to reinvent the code.

We've made every attempt to provide code that is trouble free; however, because every compute environment is different, you should test the code thoroughly before using it in a production environment. As with most freely distributed code, these scripts and tools are provided to you with no support commitment on the part of Sun Microsystems, Inc.

What's Available for Download

TABLE P-1 lists the downloadable files and provides a description of what is included in each file. It is possible that the downloadable files will be updated over time, and those changes might not be listed in this book. In such cases, any changes will be described in a README file. Read any README files (if present) after unzipping the downloadable file.

TABLE P-1   Downloadable Files

Downloadable File Name	Description
ldap-schemas.tar.gz	Provides two LDIF files: • 99nisplusLDAPconfig.ldif – A schema definition for storing NIS+ to LDAP configuration information. See "Configuring the Sun ONE Directory Server Software as a Configuration Server for rpc.nisd" on page 326. • addSchema.ldif – Schema definition for storing additional NIS+ objects. See "Additional Schema Definitions" on page 329.
MakeLDIF-1.3.tar.gz	Provides all the files associated with the MakeLDIF utility. MakeLDIF is a template-based utility for generating LDIF files. The template file format allows for a great deal of flexibility when generating LDIF files. It is very useful for generating data if you want to use SLAMD for benchmarking an LDAP directory server. See "The MakeLDIF Program" on page 480.
SUNWmakeldif.tar.gz	Provides the same MakeLDIF files as described above, except these files are delivered in SVR4-package format. To install, use the pkgadd command after uncompressing and untarring this downloadable file. See "The MakeLDIF Program" on page 480.
SUNWmltempl.tar.gz	Provides template files that give you an automated way of generating your benchmarking data sets using MakeLDIF.
slamd-1.5.1.tar.gz	Contains the full SLAMD server distribution, including the main SLAMD server, the client application, and the documentation. Refer to the SLAMD Administrator's Guide for documentation on installing the SLAMD server. Also see "Installing the SLAMD Server" on page 510.
slamd_client-1.5.1.tar.gz	Contains the SLAMD client application by itself. See "SLAMD Clients" on page 514.
SOL9-PAM_Modules.class.gz	Java Installer (WSW) version of the PAM modules: • PAM Compare • PAM Crack • PAM Logon Times Provides the src code, make files (32/64-bit), and man pages. See "PAM Source Code" on page 611.
SOL9-PAM_Modules.tar.gz	Provides the same PAM Library modules as described above, except these files are in SVR4-package format. To install, use the pkgadd command after uncompressing and untarring the downloadable file. Packages: • SUNWspamc - PAM Compare Library module • SUNWspamck - PAM Crack Library module • SUNWspamlt - PAM Logon Times Library module See "PAM Source Code" on page 611.

Downloadable File Name	Description
LDAPSubtdel.tar.gz	The LDAPsubtdel program is written in Java and uses classes contained in LDAPJDK 4.1. The tool deletes a specified directory subtree including referrals. See "The LDAPsubtdel Program" on page 394

▼ To Download a File

1. **Go to the Sun BluePrints Scripts and Tools download site:**

   `http://www.sun.com/solutions/blueprints/tools/index.html`

2. **Select the software that you want to download.**

   See TABLE P-1 for downloadable file names.

Note – Not all software listed at this site pertains to this book.

---

3. **If you are not already registered at the Sun Download Center, register now.**

   You must be registered at the Sun Download Center before you can download the scripts and tools. If this is your first visit, select *Register now*. You only have to register once, and it's free. Whenever you come back to the Download Center, just enter your user name and password to log in.

4. **Log in to the Sun Download Center.**

5. **Accept the License Agreement.**

6. **Click on the package listed to download the compressed tar file.**

   Perform the download according to the download procedures presented by your browser.

7. **Uncompress and untar the file.**

```
# gunzip downloadable_file_name
# tar xvf file_name.tar
```

Sun BluePrints Program

The mission of the Sun BluePrints Program is to empower Sun's customers with the technical knowledge required to implement reliable, extensible, and secure information systems within the data center using Sun products. This program provides a framework to identify, develop, and distribute best practices information that applies across the Sun product lines. Experts in technical subjects in various areas contribute to the program and focus on the scope and usefulness of the information.

The Sun BluePrints Program includes books, guides, and online articles. Through these vehicles, Sun can provide guidance, installation and implementation experiences, real-life scenarios, and late-breaking technical information.

The monthly electronic magazine, Sun BluePrints OnLine, is located on the Web at http://www.sun.com/blueprints. To be notified about updates to the Sun BluePrints Program, please register on this site.

Accessing Sun Documentation Online

The docs.sun.com^{sm} web site enables you to access Sun technical documentation online. You can browse the docs.sun.com archive or search for a specific book title or subject. The URL is http://docs.sun.com/.

Typographic Conventions

The following table describes the typographic changes used in this book.

Typeface or Symbol	Meaning	Example
AaBbCc123	The names of commands, files, and directories; on-screen computer output	Edit your .login file. Use ls -a to list all files. machine_name% You have mail.
AaBbCc123	What you type, contrasted with on-screen computer output	machine_name% **su** Password:
AaBbCc123	Command-line placeholder: replace with a real name or value	To delete a file, type rm *filename*.
AaBbCc123	Book titles, new words or terms, or words to be emphasized	Read Chapter 6 in *User's Guide*. These are called *class* options. You *must* be root to do this.

Shell Prompts in Command Examples

The following table shows the default system prompt and superuser prompt for the C shell, Bourne shell, and Korn shell.

TABLE P-2

Shell	Prompt
C shell prompt	machine_name%
C shell superuser prompt	machine_name#
Bourne shell and Korn shell prompt	$
Bourne shell and Korn shell superuser prompt	#

## CHAPTER 1

Introducing LDAP in the Solaris Operating Environment

Information flow is a critical factor contributing to the success of any large-scale enterprise. This flow of information needs to be rapid, reliable, accessible, and consistent to achieve the maximum benefit. To meet this need, directory services are becoming very popular.

LDAP-based directory services provide a central repository for storing and managing identity profiles, access privileges, and application and network resource information. The information can be used for the authentication and authorization of users, to enable secure access to enterprise and Internet services and applications on a global basis.

Since directory technology is rapidly moving forward with terms and concepts introduced almost monthly, a detailed definition of terms used throughout this book is presented in this chapter with summarized definitions in the glossary for quick reference. Basic LDAP concepts are explained because they are referenced throughout the book.

This chapter is organized into the following sections:

- "Introduction" on page 2
- "The Big Picture" on page 3
- "LDAP Terms and Concepts" on page 6

Introduction

A great deal of progress in Solaris OE directory service technology has occurred since *Solaris and LDAP Naming Services* was published in December of 2000. More enhancements are on the way. This technology area is anything but static, which makes writing a meaningful yet timely book challenging. Because of the number of improvements over the past two years and imminent introduction of even more, we felt this was a good time to publish a follow-up book.

The Solaris 9 Operating Environment delivers the second phase of Sun's vision for the naming service of the future. Included in this release are technologies to securely access an LDAP server from a Solaris OE client and NIS+-to-LDAP migration tools. The LDAP installation and configuration process has also been greatly simplified.

Besides enhancements to Solaris OE naming services, early access to emerging technologies is available. A Directory Service-Markup Language version 2 (DSMLv2) interface is provided with the Sun ONE Directory Server 5.2 software. The Sun™ ONE Identity Synchronization for the Windows technology allows users to log in to both Solaris OE and Windows operating environments with the same user name and password. The NIS-to-LDAP transition service provides a way to begin your LDAP transition without disrupting Network Information Services (NIS) client software.

The Solaris OE authentication framework has been enhanced in Solaris 9 OE to allow incorporation of company-specific security policies. Tools and toolkits based on Java™ technology are available for creating your own customized LDAP management tools.

Drawing on personal experience with early adopters of Solaris OE LDAP naming services, common issues are addressed, as well as the following frequently asked questions:

- What new features does the Solaris 9 and Solaris 8 OE backport client have?
- How do I best deploy these new features?
- What LDAP technologies will be available in the future that might influence my deployment strategy today?
- How do I add functionality to meet my corporate requirements?
- What tools are available for managing LDAP directory data and what are the best practices for their usage?
- How do I integrate Sun's LDAP technology with Active Directory?

These are typical questions asked by IT architects who must define an enterprise-wide LDAP infrastructure, system programmers who need to perform customization, and system administrators who need to develop procedures for deploying and managing LDAP technology.

The Big Picture

You are an IT planner for a large multi-national corporation, or perhaps you are a systems manager responsible for a few hundred Solaris OE servers. In any case, you are aware of how critical a naming service is to the smooth operation of your data center. You may be deploying NIS, NIS+, or your own schema for updating naming service data by propagating text files around the network.

Your current naming service works okay, but you are not totally comfortable with the way it is deployed. Security is a concern and the proliferation of multiple data stores containing user and employee information is creating an administration nightmare. You have also learned that Sun is planning to stop supporting NIS+ in future releases and has similar plans for NIS. LDAP technology is clearly the direction Sun is moving towards as a replacement for NIS and NIS+, but it is not clear what you should be doing about it.

In a nutshell, the purpose of this book is to educate the you about Sun's LDAP implementations so a deployment plan can be established.

In Six Sigma terminology, the steps are:

1. Define

2. Measure

3. Analyze

4. Implement

5. Control

Whether your company is guided by Six Sigma methodology or not, you most likely perform similar activities. This book addresses these five activities in terms of planning and deploying LDAP technology.

Defining the Problem

Quantifying the problem is the first step to developing a solution. In some cases, you might not even be aware that a problem exists. To help in this phase, Chapter 2 "Assessing Your Needs for Naming Service Transition and Consolidation" provides a look at problems typical enterprises face and why they exist.

Measuring the Scope

Recognizing the problem is the first step, and measuring the scope of the problem is the second step. You might be surprised to find out how and where your naming service data is used, and what the authoritative source is. Chapter 2 "Assessing Your Needs for Naming Service Transition and Consolidation" provides a list of common uses and sources of naming service data and can be used as a guide to determining the impact a naming service transition can have.

Analyzing Alternative Solutions

Before you can make an informed deployment decision, you need to know what options are available. There are several chapters that address this activity. Chapter 3 "Defining Directory Service Security Architecture" discusses security options, including how to implement your own security policy. Knowledge about the default behavior of Solaris OE security mechanisms like the Pluggable Authentication Module (PAM) framework is important and included in this book.

Chapter 4 "Deploying Solaris OE LDAP Naming Services" discusses options for deploying a native version of the LDAP naming service client. The term *native* is used because the client uses LDAP operations to interact with the name service. This is in contrast to the Remote Procedure Call (RPC) interface used by NIS and NIS+ clients. Additional security options covered in Chapter 3 "Defining Directory Service Security Architecture" are specific to the Secured LDAP Client.

Another deployment option is to maintain your current NIS and NIS+ clients, but use an LDAP directory as the back end. The NIS+ migration tool for doing this is covered in Chapter 5 "Migrating Legacy Data to LDAP."

If you have a deployment of Windows 2000 Active Directory servers or Windows NT servers, you may want to visit Chapter 10 "Emerging Directory Technologies" to become familiar with the user account and password synchronization using the Sun ONE Identity Synchronization for the Windows technology.

Implementing

After you have decided on an approach that is right for your enterprise, you need to develop an implementation plan. Chapter 5 "Migrating Legacy Data to LDAP" provides the details on how to implement a native solution. Details on how to implement the NIS+ migration tool are discussed in Chapter 5 "Migrating Legacy Data to LDAP." Another aspect of deployment is converting your current naming service data to LDAP directory data. Techniques for doing this are discussed in Chapter 5 "Migrating Legacy Data to LDAP."

Deciding what hardware is right for your deployment is important. You want to make sure the servers can handle the current load and have headroom for anticipated loads in the future. However, you probably do not have an infinite budget to spend on hardware. Chapter 8 "Selecting Storage for Optimum Directory Server Performance" provides you with guidelines for server sizing and capacity planning.

Controlling

After your initial deployment, the directory data you imported for the LDAP naming service needs to be managed, and client access needs to be controlled. There are many tools and tool kits for doing this. Traditional ones are discussed in Chapter 6 "Management Tools and Toolkits." Emerging technology, namely DSML, for creating tools is covered in Chapter 10 "Emerging Directory Technologies."

LDAP Terms and Concepts

Readers who are new to LDAP technology might find some of the terminology confusing. In this section, common terms are defined in the context of LDAP services in the Solaris OE.

Directory Service versus Naming Service

The terms *directory service* and *naming service* are often used interchangeably. In a strict sense, a directory service implies that data is stored in a sophisticated structure, while a naming service generally uses a simpler data structure such as a two column table.

LDAP Server versus Directory Server

Often a *directory server* is mistakenly referred to as an *LDAP server* because the directory server uses LDAP technology to access information. In this book, the term directory server is used instead of LDAP server, not to be pedantic, but because there is a real difference between the two.

While file servers can be called NFS or SMB servers because of the underlying protocol they use, LDAP is more of an interface that a server uses than a specification of what the server is. A directory server refers to a product or a specific implementation that uses LDAP technology. While there are many directory servers out there, the one most referenced in this book is the Sun ONE Directory Server 5.2 software.

LDAP Models

LDAP is defined by the four models it supports as follows:

- Information Model
- Naming Model
- Functional Model
- Security Model

The following sections describe these models and how they are used in this book.

Information Model

Entries are arranged in a tree-like structure (FIGURE 1-1) called the directory information tree (DIT).

At the top of the DIT is the directory root, which is identified by the server name and port number on which the directory service is running. Multiple instances of the directory service can be running on the same server, with each instance having its own DIT.

Below the directory root is the directory suffix, of which there can be several for each DIT. Suffixes can be expressed as an organization (o=) or as an Internet-style domain component (dc=). The domain-based format typically mirrors a company's DNS domain address and is expressed as domain component (dc) entries.

Located below the suffix are organization unit (ou) entries. These entries can be nested, so an ou can contain other organization units. The name chosen for an ou only needs to be unique at the level at which it resides. The same ou can be used in a different portion of the DIT without creating a conflict. An ou entry called ou=people is created during the default Directory Server installation. This entry is the default location for storing user account information, but any ou can be used for that purpose.

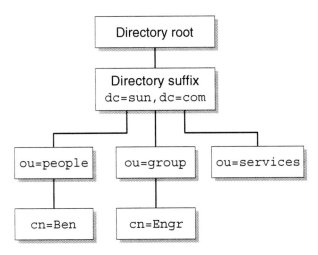

FIGURE 1-1   Sample Directory Information Tree (DIT)

If there are multiple directory servers in a network, they can be linked by LDAP referrals. A referral is a mechanism that instructs an LDAP client searching the directory to continue the search on another directory server. The referral accomplishes this instruction by passing a Uniform Resource Locator (URL) back to the client. Once the client receives the URL, the client can access the specified directory server.

Naming Model

LDAP is flexible, but at the same time provides enough structure that LDAP clients can access data in any LDAP-compliant directory. For comparison purposes, an LDAP directory is unlike a Solaris OE file system, where a search can always be initiated from the root file system (/). Instead, an LDAP directory search begins by specifying one specific entry, such as dc=blueprints, dc=com, as a search base. The entry name is specified as a distinguished name (DN), which is a series of relative distinguished names (RDNs).

Each directory server contains a single root directory-specific entry (DSE) which contains basic information about the LDAP server. The DSE contains a list of suffixes supported by the directory server. This entry can be read to determine what suffixes are present, and in turn, those suffixes can be searched.

Functional Model

Clients that need to access data on an LDAP server first perform a bind operation. The act of binding to the directory is analogous to logging in to a system. The bind operation requires, at a minimum, the DN of the user account entry with which the client wishes to bind. If the entry has a password, then, depending on the authentication method, the password is passed along with the DN. Alternatively, the client can perform an anonymous bind, which does not require a particular user name or password.

The bind operation specifies the type of authentication it is attempting to perform. The authentication method the client specifies must be supported by the directory server. The Simple Authentication and Security Level (SASL) interface provides a mechanism for deploying authentication methods that are not directory server specific. The DSE exposes a list of supported SASL mechanisms. The default is Simple authentication, which compares the password sent with the password stored for the specified DN. Because the Simple authentication method sends a clear text password, it is not secure unless combined with Transport Layer Security (TLS), such as SSL. However, other authentication methods (for example, DIGEST-MD5) work securely even without the use of TLS.

If the bind operation is successful, the client is considered authenticated. All subsequent client requests made on the established connection as a result of the bind are performed as the authenticated user. After the LDAP client requests are complete, an *unbind* operation is performed to release the connection.

Security Model

Access to LDAP entries on the server is protected by the rights established for the authenticated user. The rights can be assigned at the container, object, or attribute level. A portion of the DIT can be assigned stricter (or looser) control than other parts of the DIT. All entries of the same object class type can be assigned the same control. Control can also be established at the attribute level to protect certain information. For example, an employee's password might have restricted access, while other information is available to everyone.

The mechanism used to assign access rights is called the access control instruction (ACI). A single ACI can protect the entire DIT, or several can be used to provide finer-grained protection. When multiple ACIs are created, the ACIs that deny access take precedence. For example, if access is granted to everyone at the top level of the DIT but denied access to ou=Contractors, then the permission set for ou=Contractors is enforced.

ACIs are hierarchal. That is, an ACI set at any node of a DIT affects everything below it. Therefore you need to be aware of ACIs that may be set above the node or entry you are protecting.

Directory Objects and Attributes

The structure of a directory entry is defined by the object class to which it belongs. An object class defines a set of attributes that can be stored in a directory entry. LDAP object classes are extensible by creation of a new class that is a child of an existing one. All the attributes defined in the parent class are inherited by the child. The name of an object class must be unique within the directory server and can be registered as a standard LDAP object. These objects are assigned a numeric object identifier (OID) to ensure they will not conflict with another object class.

Attribute names are unique within the directory server and can be contained in more than one object class. The type of data that can be stored in an attribute and the way a search for data is handled is well defined. For example, searching for a string-valued attribute can be case sensitive or insensitive. Attributes can also contain more than one value and can have aliases.

To promote interoperability, a set of standard LDAP object classes and attributes have been defined. Definitions of these ship with most LDAP servers in the form of schema configuration files. If they do not exist on a server, you can add the content of these schema files to the LDAP configuration files.

Directory Schema

The information specified in a directory schema includes the object class name, required and allowed attributes, an OID number, and the allowable syntax. The following table shows the schema definition for the `posixAccount` object class attributes that stores Solaris OE user account information.

TABLE 1-1   `posixAccount` object Class Schema Definition

Attribute	Description	Syntax
cn (commonName)	Common Name of the POSIX account	DirectoryString (1-many)
gidNumber	Unique integer identifying group membership	Integer (single)
homePhone	The entry's home phone number	telephoneNumber (single)
uid (userID)	The user's login name	DirectoryString, (single)
uidNumber	An integer uniquely identifying a user	Integer (single)
description	A human-readable description of the object	DirectoryString (single)
gecos	GECOS comment field	DirectoryString (single)
loginShell	Path to the login shell	IA5String (single)
userPassword	Entry's password and encryption method	binary, (single)

In this example, `cn` is a case-insensitive string that can contain multiple values. The `gidNumber` and `uidNumber` are integers, and `homePhone` is represented by a special data type used for telephone numbers. The `loginShell` is represented by a case-exact string. Note that the LDAP `uid`, which is a string, is not the same as the numeric Solaris OE UID, which is represented by the LDAP attribute `uidNumber`.

Distinguished Names (DN)

A directory entry is identified by its DN, which is similar to a file system path name. Entries are composed of many attributes, some of which are the same as other entries. To distinguish between entries that may have the same values for some attributes, one attribute is usually singled out as being unique. For user account entries defined in the `posixAccount` object class, the unique attribute is `uid`.

To prevent duplicate values from being used, the Sun ONE Directory Server software is configured by default to enforce `uid` attribute uniqueness. Entries that do not have a `uid` attribute are typically identified by the `commonName (cn)` attribute, which is available in most object classes, but is not required by all object classes such as `organization (o)` and `organization unit (ou)`.

The form of a DN is as follows:

attribute=value,container,suffix

There can be multiple containers depending on the DIT topology.

The following is an example of a DN for a user account:

```
uid=cathy,ou=People,dc=example,dc=com
```

The RDN specifies the left-most portion of the DN, which uniquely identifies the entry relative to its parent. For example:

```
uid=cathy
```

In this case, `uid=cathy` has to be unique within the `ou=People` container.

Replication

Replication is the mechanism by which directory data is automatically copied from one directory server to another. Servers that can be updated are called *master servers* or *master replicas* and servers that cannot are called *read-only replicas*. The directory server that provides the data to other servers is called the *supplier server*. Servers that accept data from suppliers are called *consumers*. A directory server can be both a consumer and a supplier server. That is, it can receive updates from one server, then pass them on to one or more others.

The Sun ONE 5.2 Directory Server software supports three kinds of replication topologies:

- Single-Master Replication – The master copy of directory data is maintained on the supplier server. This server provides updates to consumer servers. All updates are performed on the master or supplier server.
- Multiple-Master Replication – Updates can be performed on up to four master servers. The masters keep in sync with each other by propagating updates to each other. In effect, the servers are both suppliers and consumers. A variation of this topology is the floating master. In this configuration, all updates are directed to a single master. If the master server fails, updates are then directed to another one.
- Cascading Replication – A server is set up as a hub that supplies updates to several consumers. The hub server receives updates from master servers then passes them on. The purpose of this configuration is to reduce the load on the master server.

Solaris OE LDAP Client

The term LDAP client has two connotations. In the traditional sense, any client that can perform LDAP operations is an LDAP client. This can be an LDAP-enabled browser like Netscape Communicator, or an operating environment that contains commands that are written to the LDAP API. The Solaris OE provides an LDAP API (see ldap(3LDAP)), and a number of tools, including ldapsearch(1), ldapadd(1), ldapdelete(1), ldapmodify(1), and ldapmodrdn(1) that are built directly on top of the API.

Another use of the term LDAP client is to identify a Solaris OE client that accesses an LDAP directory for its naming service data. The first generation of this client appeared in the Solaris 8 OE. This client is referred to as the *Native LDAP Client*. The second generation of the client appeared in Solaris 9 OE, and was later backported to Solaris 8 OE. This LDAP client is referred to as the *Secured LDAP Client*. In general, when the term LDAP client is used in this book, it refers to the Secured LDAP Client implementation.

## CHAPTER 2

Assessing Your Needs for Naming Service Transition and Consolidation

This chapter defines the problems businesses face, while making the case for transitioning from a legacy naming service to an LDAP-based directory service. Included are tips on how to identify issues that are commonly encountered in naming service transition and consolidation.

This chapter looks at how legacy naming services such as NIS and NIS+ are typically deployed in an enterprise today and why they were deployed the way they were.

Directory needs are as varied as the enterprises they serve. Because the transition to LDAP technology from legacy NIS/NIS+ naming services is not a one-to-one replacement, more than just naming service data needs to be addressed.

This chapter is organized into the following sections:

- "What Consolidation Means" on page 14
- "Understanding Legacy Naming Services" on page 20
- "Business Case for Transitioning to LDAP" on page 15
- "Migration Planning" on page 26

What Consolidation Means

For various reasons, operating environment data has become dispersed and fragmented within most enterprises. Often companies do not even know where all this operating environment data resides, let alone how to consolidate it to make it more manageable. Consolidation of naming service data is perhaps the most significant benefit of transitioning to an LDAP-based service.

Consolidation is the process of identifying all your data sources, reconciling conflicts, and creating a single authoritative data source. The process is not an easy one and requires careful planning. Sometimes data sources are used because of historical reasons, that is, we just do it that way. Other times, there are technical reasons such as application dependencies that determine which data sources are required.

There is a financial cost associated with consolidation, therefore tangible benefits must be derived to justify this cost. It is difficult to quantify this return on investment as it varies greatly in different enterprises. However, several factors can be used to evaluate the positive impact of the transition and consolidation.

Once a decision is made to embark on a consolidation or transition project, a number of planning steps are involved. You must first understand your current environment by knowing where data is stored and why it is stored there. See "Understanding Legacy Naming Services" on page 20. Next you must survey all your data sources and identify any overlap. This is discussed in "Migration Planning" on page 26.

Business Case for Transitioning to LDAP

Return on investment can be calculated by determining the cost of doing business the current way and the savings obtained by switching to a new process. Some of the savings are easier to quantify than others. For example, if it takes 50 system administrators to manage your current naming service, but only 25 after consolidation, the savings are obvious.

Some savings are harder to quantify, such as:

- Data loss, or compromise, caused by unauthorized access
- Loss of user productivity in the event that they cannot get access to needed resources due to naming service problems
- New opportunities for cost cutting by sharing data between applications

Identifying Potential Consolidation Problems

Before you can justify the expense of transitioning from your legacy naming service to LDAP, you need to understand what it buys you. The first step is to take a look at the problems encountered by staying with your legacy naming service. The following list highlights some of the pitfalls you might experience by not using a directory service:

- Fragmented data storage
- Duplicate data
- Loss of administration control
- Lack of extensibility
- Poor accessibility

Fragmented data can occur in a legacy naming service because there are autonomous organizations maintaining their own data or different applications requiring different data stores. Usually this is a result of how the organization evolved, and not the result of any conscious decision. At best, fragmented data is costly in terms of administrative costs. At worst, a security hole can be created if, for example, user accounts are unintentionally left enabled after the users have left the company.

Duplicate, unsynchronized data is the result of data fragmentation or poor data management. This situation usually occurs when data is not consistently updated across all data sources. For example, if an employee's phone number changes, but the change is not updated everywhere it is stored, you might retrieve the old number depending on which data source answers your request. A more serious problem can arise if user accounts are not synchronized. Users could be denied access to particular applications or resources if a change in the account is not propagated properly.

Loss of administrative control can be the result of decentralized data. If data is managed by disparate groups within an enterprise, it is difficult to enforce a consistent management policy. For example, some organizations may require passwords to be a certain length, while others may not see this as a necessity.

Lack of extensibility is the inability to add additional data fields to naming service data. This restricts its usefulness. It also makes creating new data stores a requirement to support new applications which require those extra fields.

Poor accessibility is the result of incompatibility between the numerous technologies that exist in the enterprise. The number of ways naming service data can be accessed enhances its usefulness. If data can be accessed through a variety of application programming interfaces (APIs) the cost of deploying new applications and tools to manage the data diminishes.

Identifying the Solution

The main reason to invest in a technology change is to either reduce your operation cost or make your company more competitive. Deploying LDAP in your enterprise offers the following benefits which help you meet these criteria:

- Consolidation of enterprise data
- Universal access
- Ease of management
- Ease of securing data

These benefits are described in the following sections.

Consolidation of Enterprise Data

The most common use of directories is to store information about users of enterprise computing resources. This information can reside in numerous places including:

- Human resource database
- Corporate phone book
- Email system
- Web services authentication
- Network Operating System (NOS) authentication

From a business point of view, maintaining duplicate information in multiple places creates extra overhead, loss of productivity, and possible security breaches. As employees are hired, fired, or leave voluntarily, entries need to be added or deleted in multiple places. Likewise, as changes, such as marital status data, entries in several locations needs to be updated. If applications require passwords, then users might be required to maintain several passwords, one each for each service they access.

Directory consolidation is usually the most frequently cited reason for moving to a new naming service. Because LDAP-based directories adhere to standards and have established a significant industry presence, this is the technology of choice for many consolidation projects.

Universal Access

Universal access means you can get to your data from a variety of clients in a variety of locations. Maintaining corporate data is useless unless it is easy to get to. Universal access to data reduces programming costs and allows employees access while at work or at home. It also provides a competitive edge because customers and partners can access the same data, or subset that you allow them to view.

Directories based on LDAP technology, such as the Sun ONE Directory Server 5.2 software, provide a variety of ways to access directory data, as follows:

- C library
- PerLDAP
- Java/Java Naming and Directory Interface™ (J.N.D.I.) API
- JavaServer Pages™ (JSP™) software/XML tag library
- DSML
- Command-line tools
- Netscape™ Communicator

There are many examples available in the Sun™ ONE Directory Server, Resource Kit (SDRK) software that can be downloaded for free from the http://www.sun.com web site. These examples illustrate how to take advantage of the universal access capabilities. Chapter 6 "Management Tools and Toolkits" provides useful tips on how to customize your own solutions based on these examples.

Ease of Management

Hidden in the cost of deploying new technology is the cost of training employees who must manage the new technology. Once data is consolidated, it is easier to manage. LDAP is a standard, so your investment in training is protected because the concepts are transferable to a wide range of applications and services.

A variety of tools and toolkits are available for managing directory data. Some are available from Sun, some from the public domain, and some are provided by third-party vendors. Chapter 6 "Management Tools and Toolkits" discusses many of these.

Ease of Securing Data

Maintaining user data in one type of data store, rather than several, makes the job of securing it easier because you only have to be concerned with one security mechanism for all your data stores. LDAP directories provide a flexible way of controlling access to data that provides a great deal of granularity. Encrypted data channels can be created to prevent unauthorized snooping.

Technical Benefits of LDAP Directories

This sections examines specific technological features that LDAP directories provide, and how these features result in business case benefits.

Extensible Schema

By extending the directory schema, you can create customized data entries that are still compatible with existing applications. This is significant because you can create an entry for a person, add company-specific attributes to that entry, and still have existing applications function properly. For example, an entry containing Solaris OE login information will work fine even though additional information about a person such as a department number, manager name, and work telephone number has been added to the user entry.

Scalability

Applications can scale either vertically or horizontally. Vertical scalability is the ability to take advantage of resources provided on a single large computer. Horizontal scalability is the ability to spread the application load among several smaller computers. The key technology behind horizontal scalability is the ability to distribute directory data across the enterprise. With Sun ONE Directory Server 5.2 software, this is accomplished with data replication and multiple databases.

Data replication was enhanced starting with the directory server 5.0 release by supporting the multi-master replication model. In this model, more than one server can master the same data. This allows updates to be performed on either system. Database distribution allows a large database to be broken up into smaller ones that can be distributed among several servers.

Directory servers generally require lots of RAM, disk, and network bandwidth in relation to CPU speed. Because the amount of RAM a computer can accommodate is finite, and network bandwidth across an enterprise may not be evenly distributed, horizontal scaling is usually more advantageous than vertical scaling.

Availability

Data replication in conjunction with load-balancing switches or LDAP proxy servers can provide high availability. Modern switches are capable of detecting the load on multiple LDAP servers and can direct LDAP operation to the least busy server. Alternatively, the LDAP client software can be designed to failover to alternate servers if the primary server fails.

Sun™ Cluster technology can be deployed to provide high availability without using LDAP data replication. Instead, a mirrored disk volume is shared among two or more systems, or nodes. Only one system controls the shared disk volume at any one time. If that system fails, control is transferred to one of the surviving nodes. The LDAP service is associated with a Virtual Internet Protocol (VIP) address that can also be transferred to a surviving node.

Future of NIS and NIS+

When the Solaris 9 OE was released, Sun announced the end of feature (EOF) of NIS+. While Sun will support NIS+ for some time in terms of minor bug fixes, there will be no new enhancements, and support will be dropped in some future Solaris release. It is also likely that a similar EOF announcement of NIS will be made at some time in the future.

To aid in the migration from NIS/NIS+ to LDAP, transition tools began shipping with the Solaris 9 OE. Deployment of these tools is discussed in Chapter 5 "Migrating Legacy Data to LDAP."

Understanding Legacy Naming Services

Network Information Services (NIS and NIS+) have served Sun customers well over the past years, but with the competitive landscape constantly changing, the evolution of technology, and heightened security concerns, a case can be made that legacy naming services are becoming outdated.

To understand why, you need to understand why naming services evolved the way they did. The next section presents a short history of NIS and NIS+ and the environments in which they were designed to operate. It is not meant to be comprehensive, but rather to highlight key points and illustrate the advantages that exist in the directory services available today.

Evolution of NIS

NIS, or Yellow Pages as it was originally called, was first introduced by Sun Microsystems, Inc. in 1985. It provided a centralized naming service that contained information about hosts on the network, users, groups, and other network related information. Centralized storage of this data was necessary due to a shift in the computing model as the timesharing of a single large computer was being replaced with separate, smaller, distributed computers.

Each of these smaller computers, or workstations, required access to information about network resources and users permitted access to them. The Berkeley Software Distribution (BSD) version of UNIX®, the basis for Sun's first operating system, had not provided a naming service, relying on the propagation of text files to all systems instead. This method became very cumbersome to administer as the number of workstations attached to a network began to grow.

To promote interoperability between heterogeneous systems, Sun published the Open Network Computing (ONC) specification. The ONC specification provides a means for any vendor to implement NIS. Over 100 vendors adopted ONC, making it a huge success.

The basic premise of NIS is to store naming data in binary files that contain key-value pairs. These binary files, called DBM files, are maintained on servers that are searched by clients specifying a key, and in return, receive the corresponding value. For example, on a client the login process specifies a user's name as a key to retrieve the corresponding password entry from the server.

The collection of computers that accessed the same NIS service were grouped in an NIS domain. The NIS domain generally only included systems located in close physical proximity. A domain consists of one master NIS server and one or more slave NIS servers. An NIS-specific protocol is used to propagate updated data from the master server to the slave servers.

Management of NIS information was performed by local system administrators who devised their own naming conventions for hosts, users, and groups. This was not an issue at the time, because the interaction of computers located at different locations was limited.

Clients interact with NIS servers by first binding to an NIS server. The bind operation takes place when the client boots, sending a broadcast packet and waiting for an NIS server to respond. That server is then used for all subsequent name service requests, unless the server fails to respond to a request. If that happens, the client rebinds to another server. The broadcast bind method was used in part for load balancing and for failover. Load balancing was achieved, in theory, because the client binds to the least busy server.

No client authentication is required with NIS. The client simply needs to have a domain name variable defined, and broadcast that name over the subnet on which it resides. If the name matches the domain the NIS server is serving, the bind operation is successful.

The simplicity of NIS made it very attractive, and it was widely deployed. Enhancements were made along the way to overcome some deficiencies. An alternative to the broadcast method was introduced which provided the means of specifying a list of NIS servers on the client. This enhancement allows a client to reach servers beyond their local subnet, but requires that clients know the addresses of such servers. Another added feature provides the ability for an NIS server to maintain a list of trusted clients that is used to accept or reject bind requests based on the IP address of the client. Although these enhancements were made, the basic structure of NIS has remained the same over the years.

Evolution of NIS+

Because of the deficiencies in NIS, a new name service called NIS+ was introduced. In retrospect, NIS+ was ahead of its time and was probably too aggressive in its implementation. For various reasons, it was not nearly as widely adopted as NIS. However, it did introduce some interesting concepts.

NIS+ was designed to replace NIS by providing a hierarchal structure that could span an entire enterprise, provide tighter security, and offer a more scalable replication model. The data structure used to store information was improved so it could be accessed by rows and columns, eliminating the need to store the same data in different maps as key-value pairs. Hierarchal trust relationships between domains and subdomains can be established, allowing administrative span of control to be tailored. For example, local system administrators can be allowed to update data in only one subdomain, where global system administrators can update data throughout the enterprise.

The security model is based on public key technology. Each principal, user, or computer, presents credentials in order to gain access to name service data. A network password is established for each NIS+ client, and the client uses it to log in to the naming service. This prevents someone with local root access from becoming an NIS+ client.

The replication model was improved by propagating incremental database updates instead of entire maps. This technique drastically reduces the amount of time and bandwidth required to keep maps synchronized. Instead of performing nightly updates of an entire database, NIS+ servers propagate changes as they occur.

Common Uses for NIS/NIS+

When NIS and NIS+ were developed, they provided critical services for enterprise environments of the time. NIS and NIS+ offered a centralized method for managing data related to user and group accounts, services, and augmented automated operating system installations.

Maintaining User and Group Data

Perhaps the most important use of NIS/NIS+ is to maintain user account and group membership data used during the authentication and authorization process. Whenever users log in to a system running NIS/NIS+, their profile data and credentials are retrieved along with authorization data in the form of a User Identifier (UID) and Group Identifier (GID). The netgroups database also plays a role in the authorization process by maintaining a list of users who can access particular hosts.

Maintaining System Data for Applications

The services, protocols, and rpc databases are important to enterprises deploying custom or non-standard network services. Without NIS/NIS+, local copies of text files on every client in the enterprise would have to be updated if a new service was deployed.

Applications based on secure RPCs require the storage of public and private keys. For security reasons and ease of access, NIS/NIS+ data is heavily used in enterprises deploying these types of applications.

Automating Installations

Another popular use of NIS/NIS+ is to aid in the use of network-based automated installations. Before a system has an operating system installed, it does not have a network identity in the form of an IP address. However, any networked computer has knowledge of its own Media Access Controller (MAC) address. By broadcasting its MAC address, a corresponding IP address is obtained from a server capable of performing this translation. This is accomplished using the Reverse Address Resolution Protocol (RARP). Because this mapping data needs to reside somewhere, and you might have numerous RARP servers in an enterprise, using a common data store makes sense. The NIS/NIS+ ethers database provides this mapping function.

To perform a hands-free installation, the installation server must be able to find information about the client. Specifically, it must know what software configuration to download. This information can be stored in the bootparams database. Because there might be many JumpStart™ servers that require this information throughout your enterprise, it makes sense to store and retrieve the data using NIS/NIS+. Client identification and bootparams information can also be stored in a DHCP server.

DNS and NIS/NIS+

As wide area network (WAN) bandwidth became cheaper, it became economical to communicate beyond the local area network (LAN). Access to computers throughout the enterprise and between different enterprises became part of normal operations. To facilitate finding systems outside your LAN, the Domain Name System (DNS) was developed as an industry standard and was widely adopted. Because DNS was only designed to assist in locating IP addresses of systems and email servers, it could not provide all the information that NIS could. This led to deployments with a combination of DNS and NIS.

Most enterprises these days deploy the DNS for translation of host names to IP addresses, and for identifying email servers. Some of this information is the same information that is stored in the NIS/NIS+ hosts database. Although you could replace the NIS/NIS+ hosts database with DNS, it is common practice to deploy both. Some applications, such as the Solaris OE `sysidtools` command (used by Solaris OE installation programs), communicate directly with NIS/NIS+, and therefore require the NIS/NIS+ `hosts` database. Administrators of some environments, such as computer labs, might find it more convenient to place their host names in the `hosts` database rather than DNS, because systems outside the lab do not need to access them.

DHCP

Dynamic Host Configuration Protocol (DHCP) servers, while technically not a naming service, do make use of naming services and potentially replace RARP as a mechanism for dynamically assigning or providing host information. DHCP has the advantage of working across subnets by setting up DHCP relay hosts. However, because of its simplicity, RARP remains a popular protocol used by Sun servers.

NIS Limitations

With the progression of technology, legacy naming services such as NIS and NIS+ are left with limitations, mainly due to the their architectural design which evolved under technological demands that are different than today. This section describes some of these limitations.

Architectural Limitations

An operating environment depends on naming service information being readily accessible, so it is critical that the naming service be highly available. To achieve availability, data must be replicated on multiple systems in case one server goes down. NIS replicates data by pushing entire NIS maps from master to slave servers. This means that a change in a single map entry can result in the entire map content being propagated even though the other entries are unchanged. For maps with a small number of entries, this might not be an issue. However, as more and more data is consolidated in single maps, this activity creates a significant amount of network traffic.

Security Issues

NIS clients do not have to authenticate their requests to look at data contained in NIS maps. This means that any system on the network can become an NIS client and have access to naming service data—a critical security concern. A workaround exists which allows you to specify a list of trusted systems and networks, then limit access to only them. However, this feature requires additional administration and it is not hard to spoof an IP address of a trusted system. Also, there is no convenient way to encrypt data sent to NIS clients from the server.

Naming Chaos

NIS domains were originally managed locally, so local administrators frequently created their own domain name scheme and way of naming users. The NIS domain name typically reflected the name or initials of an organization or a geographic location. With the advent of the Internet and the DNS global namespace, enterprises began to register their unique domain names. Depending on the size of your enterprise, you could subdivide the registered DNS domain name, typically along geographical lines. For example, a company like Sun Microsystems, Inc. would have a top-level DNS domain called `sun.com` and subdomains called `east.sun.com`, `uk.sun.com`, and so forth. NIS domain names began to be patterned after DNS domain names, but because of architectural limitations on the size of NIS maps, a further subdivision often became necessary.

NIS map entries need only be unique within an NIS domain, so there was no need to create a global user ID or login name. Likewise, group names only had to be unique within the domain. This led to the practice of allowing users to choose their own login names, or simplistic schemes like first name, first letter of last name. Because the allocation of user names was so casual, the likelihood of name collisions between different NIS domains was high.

Limitation Workarounds

To get around some of the limitations of NIS, some enterprises choose to generate `dbm` files from authoritative data sources other than NIS source files. For example data is stored and updated in a relational database management system (RDBMS) like Sybase or Oracle, then pushed out nightly to NIS servers. All updates are made on the RDBMS, that in turn updates the NIS master servers. This way the NIS servers are always kept in synchronization.

While this is one method of consolidation, it does have some drawbacks. Custom programs need to be created to generate the `dbm` files that NIS uses. There is also a lengthy propagation delay.

Migration Planning

The LDAP migration planning process consists of several tasks:

- Collecting data
- Analyzing the data
- Resolving conflicts
- Consolidating the data
- Choosing migration tools

This section provides tips on how to accomplish these steps.

Collecting Data and Resolving Conflicts

Identifying all sources of naming service data is one of the first steps you should perform. You should also identify what the authoritative source for the data is. The most obvious place to start is with your NIS and NIS+ databases. Other areas include:

- Electronic messaging system
- LDAP directory supporting web-based applications
- Lotus Notes/Domino
- Human Resource Database

If your enterprise is running multiple NIS/NIS+ domains, which is likely, you need to determine if all the domains use the same maps or if the maps vary among different domains. You also need to identify any custom NIS maps that you might be deploying. The following is a list of standard NIS/NIS+ maps, or databases, followed by descriptions of potential data consolidation issues to look out for.

- passwd and shadow
- group
- hosts
- ipnodes
- ethers
- bootparams
- netgroup
- networks
- netmasks

- `aliases`

- `services`

- `protocol`

- `rpc`

- `publickey`

- `automount`

- `user_attr`

- `audit_user`

- `auth_attr`

- `exec_attr`

- `prof_attr`

`passwd` *and* `shadow` *Databases*

The `passwd` and associated `shadow` database are arguably the most important and most used by the Solaris OE. The entry in this map has seven fields, each separated by colons, as shown in the example and described in TABLE 2-1.

Example `passwd` entry:

```
tb250:SnLaPR6XvcJV6:1250:10:Tom Bialaski, Enterprise
Engineer:/home/tb250:/bin/csh
```

TABLE 2-1   `passwd` and `shadow` Database Fields

Field	Description
`login_name`	A string composed of no more than eight alpha-numeric characters. The string is used as an index to locate a user's password. The login process searches the naming database until a match is found. There is nothing inherent in NIS or NIS+ to enforce login name uniqueness. The `pwck` command can be used to check for duplicates.
`password`	The password is actually obtained from the `shadow` database which contains one-for-one entries corresponding to the `passwd` database. In the `shadow` database the password is stored in UNIX crypt format, which is a one-way hash. Although the clear text password cannot be easily be determined, the hash string can be copied to another `passwd` database and used in the authentication process.
`uid`	A numeric value used in the Solaris OE authorization process. While the number should be unique within the namespace, there is nothing inherent to prevent duplicate `uid` numbers from being assigned. If duplicates exist, the first one found is used. When merging multiple NIS/NIS+ domains, you should verify that everyone has a unique `uid`. Most enterprises probably have already done this. However, merging databases from different companies can be problematical.
`gid`	A numeric value used to identify the user's primary group. Secondary groups are specified in the `groups` database. The `gid` is not expected to be unique and is usually assigned a name in the groups database. Like the `uid`, the `gid` is used for assigning and granting access rights. Issues with consolidated group membership information are discussed in the `group` database section.
`gecos`	Contains a free-form text field used to store descriptive information about a user. The information in the `gecos` field is used by some messaging applications to display the user's full name and title. Modern LDAP-based messaging systems provide several attributes for storing this information, which diminishes the importance of the `gecos` field. Because there are no guidelines for how to store data in this field, the format of the information varies widely between enterprises. Migrating this information to LDAP generally requires custom scripts.
`home_directory`	Specifies the directory where users are placed after a successful login. The directory specified here is usually an automount point. The common convention is to use the user login as the home directory name. Therefore, the same issues with login names apply here. Consolidation of automount tables is another issue which is discussed in the automount database section.
`user_shell`	Specifies the preferred shell to invoke after a successful login. Because there are no dependencies on the value of this field, there is no impact with consolidation.

group *Database*

The `group` database is used to either assign a name to a group, for example, `staff::10:`, or to assign secondary groups to a user. A numeric identifier called the `gid` is assigned to each group. By default, GID numbers 1-10, 12, and 14 are used by the Solaris OE. Group numbers should not be greater than 60000 (60001 and 60002 are reserved for `nobody` and `noaccess`). It is recommended that the GID for normal users be no less than 100. This is because some applications, such as PC NetLink, use group numbers under 100.

Group names and GID numbers have a high potential for collision when merging naming services because group names tend to be generic and GID numbers are usually assigned sequentially, starting from a boundary like 101 or 1001. There is also nothing inherent in NIS or NIS+ to prevent duplicate group names or undefined users being added to groups. The `grpchk` command can be used to check for these conditions. Sorting out group conflicts can represent the most challenging activity when consolidating naming service data.

The following is an example of what a group entry looks like:

```
lab:*:261:csdemo,carlab,waldo,adele,pj23592,riggs,ktegan,ann,
vella
```

hosts *Database*

The `hosts` database contains host names, host name aliases, and their associated IP address. While this information can also be stored in DNS, the Solaris OE `sysidtool` programs may make use of NIS or NIS+ to automatically configure Solaris OE systems. Host information is sometimes kept in both DNS and NIS/NIS+ databases so non-NIS/NIS+ clients can access the information. Most enterprises have already grappled with consolidating host names when they set up DNS. However, there might not be a one-to-one mapping between DNS domains and the LDAP namespace. For example, the U.S. might be split into east, central, and west DNS subdomains, but only have a single LDAP domain. This means there is a potential for host name conflicts when they are consolidated.

Systems that have multiple network interfaces, called multi-homed systems, have different LDAP representations than systems with single network interfaces. You will need to identify multi-homed systems, so they can be properly migrated.

ipnodes *Database*

This database is used to support Internet Protocol version 6 (IPv6). Because this protocol is relatively new and not widely adopted, there will be few consolidation problems. The issues here are the same with the hosts database, but might not apply to your environment.

ethers *Database*

The ethers database is used to map an Ethernet address to a host name and IP address. With most TCP/IP operations, this step is not necessary because the system sending or receiving a TCP/IP packet will already know its IP address and host name. However, to perform an automated installation using Solaris JumpStart software, the client does not have this knowledge, and must find out this information by broadcasting its MAC address. If JumpStart technology is used extensively throughout your enterprise, the ethers database may be quite large. The ethers database contains host names, so the same consolidation considerations apply as for the hosts database.

bootparams *Database*

The bootparams database is used to support Solaris OE JumpStart technology, network booting, and diskless client services. The entries it contains may reference NFS mount points by host name. If entries in the hosts database were modified to resolve conflicts, these entries need to be examined.

netgroup *Database*

The netgroup database is used to restrict access to network resources. The entries in the netgroup database include a domain name and, optionally, user names. If you have multiple domains that need to be collapsed into a single domain, the entries here need to be updated to reflect the new domain name.

networks *Database*

The networks database defines a name for a particular network number. It is referenced by some Solaris OE utilities like the netstat utility to display a meaningful name instead of just a number. Consolidation should have little effect unless there are name conflicts.

netmasks *Database*

The `netmasks` database defines a subnet mask for a particular network. It is referenced by `ifconfig(1m)` when configuring network interfaces. Because this information may be supplied through the JumpStart `sysidfg` file, it might not be used in your enterprise. If it is, consolidation should not be a problem because each entry would most likely be unique.

aliases *Database*

The `aliases` database is used to store email aliases used by the Sendmail facility. If you are not using Sendmail to forward messages, you do not have to worry about this database. If you are, then consolidation of NIS domains may have an impact. In most cases the same `aliases` database would be used throughout the enterprise, so consolidation would not be an issue. The `/usr/lib/sendmail -OCheckAliases` can be run to validate `aliases` before rebuilding the aliases database.

services *Database*

The `services` database is used to determine which port number a particular network service uses. For standard services with well known port numbers, consolidation is not an issue. However, for homegrown services, or services from different vendors, the potential for conflict exists.

protocol *Database*

The `protocol` database is used to map a protocol name to a protocol number. Because protocol names and numbers are industry standards, consolidation of this database should not be an issue.

rpc *Database*

The `rpc` database is used to map remote procedure calls (RPCs) to port numbers. If different parts of an enterprise developed their own unregistered RPC-based applications autonomously, it is likely there will be some conflicts here.

publickey *Database*

The `publickey` database is used to store public or secret keys typically used by secure RPC applications. If users' keys are being stored, you could have the same issues as with login names.

automount *Database*

The `automount` database actually consists of several databases. There is a top-level database called `auto_master` which contains a list of all other automount databases. Most organizations will have many `automount` databases defined. The potential for conflict is high, because common names such as `auto.tools` are used. Re-organizing your automount structure requires a fair amount of planning.

Role-Based Access Control (RBAC) Databases

To support new security features in the Solaris 8 OE, five new databases were introduced:

- `user_attr`
- `audit_user`
- `auth_attr`
- `exec_attr`
- `prof_attr`

If these are widely used in your enterprise, there is a possible conflict with `user_auth` because user names are stored here.

User-Defined (Custom) NIS Maps

The NIS and NIS+ naming services can be extended by creating your own NIS maps or NIS+ tables to hold data specific to your enterprise. To access this data, applications that use the Solaris OE naming service API are written. These applications generally communicate directly to the name service and not to the name service switch (the `nsswitch.conf` file).

There is a generic object class for specifying generic NIS maps in LDAP. However, unless your application consults the name service switch, converting it will not buy you much. Redesigning your application to access LDAP directories directly probably makes the most sense.

Establishing Unique IDs

Politically, one of the toughest migration decisions to make is establishing an enterprise-wide naming convention for assigning unique identifiers to all users. Employees who have worked for a growing company for a long time, or for a small company that has been absorbed, may be reluctant to change their simple login ID. For example, there may be a `tom@east`, `tom@central`, and `tom@west`. Obviously, at least two user IDs will have to change.

Choosing NIS/NIS+ Migration Tools

Once you have identified all your naming service data sources and resolved any conflicts, the next step is to decide what deployment approach works best for you. The two options are:

- Convert your clients to Secured LDAP Clients, eliminating NIS and NIS+
- Keep running NIS and NIS+ client, but use LDAP as a back-end store

With the first option, you can take advantage of the security features of the Secured LDAP Client, and you can use password storage schemes other than UNIX crypt. You can also take advantage of client failover and features such as Service Search Descriptors (SSDs). These features are explained in Chapter 4 "Deploying Solaris OE LDAP Naming Services."

The second option has the advantage of not having to modify client software. It also allows you to begin a migration including clients running earlier Solaris OE versions than Solaris 8 OE. The downside is that you still have the limitations of NIS and NIS+ and passwords are required to be stored in UNIX crypt. Descriptions of migration tools can be found in Chapter 5 "Migrating Legacy Data to LDAP" and in Chapter 10 "Emerging Directory Technologies."

It should be noted that the LDAP migration tools discussed in this book are designed to aid in the transition and not meant to be a permanent replacement for NIS and NIS+. If your clients support the Secured LDAP Client, you are encouraged to deploy it rather than the migration tools.

CHAPTER **3**

Defining Directory Service Security Architecture

This chapter discusses client-server directory service architectures and describes what you can and cannot do to secure data transfers and authentication. The focus is on the Secured LDAP Client, which is a core and integral component of the Solaris 9 Operating Environment.

This chapter starts by discussing the Sun ONE Directory Server software security features such as access control and authentication mechanisms, in particular SASL DIGEST-MD5 and the Generic Security Services Application Programming Interface (GSSAPI) authentication mechanisms, followed by Transport Layer Security (TLS), and the Start TLS functionality. The server side is discussed from a system administration and developer point of view. The final part of this chapter describes the PAM components and modules.

This chapter is organized into the following sections:

Understanding Directory Server Security

The Sun ONE Directory Server 5.2 software provides the foundation for the new generation of e-business applications and services.

Based on a highly advanced, carrier-grade architecture, the Sun ONE Directory Server software delivers a high-performance, highly scalable, and highly secure infrastructure that provides organizations with a secure directory service implementation.

Sun ONE Directory Server 5.2 Software Security Features

This section describes the following:

- "Access Control" on page 36
- "Authentication Mechanisms" on page 38

Access Control

One of the primary reasons for using an access control mechanism is to control and restrict access to information and to control the operations that can be performed by users and administrators of the directory server. Operations to control access to the directory server include the ability to restrict permissions for adding, deleting, and modifying directory entries.

Accessing the directory service requires that the directory client authenticate itself to the directory service. This means that the directory client must inform the directory server who is going to be accessing the directory data so that the directory server can determine what the directory client is allowed to view and what operations can be performed. A directory client first authenticates itself and then performs operations. The server decides if the client is allowed to perform the operation or not. This process is known as *access control*.

Prior to the release of the Sun ONE Directory Server 5.2 software, when a directory (LDAP) client or directory (LDAP) application authenticated to the directory server, the directory server would determine whether or not the directory (LDAP) client or directory (LDAP) application was in fact allowed to perform such operations (such as add, delete, or modify a particular directory entry).

Additional Security Features

The Sun ONE Directory Server 5.2 software provides additional security functionality. The following is an introduction to this new functionality.

- `GetEffectiveRights` - In addition to the access control framework that is currently used within the Sun ONE Directory Server 5.2 software version, a new feature has been added called `GetEffectiveRights` that addresses various needs. The `GetEffectiveRights` mechanism is used by clients to evaluate existing access control instructions (ACIs) and to report the effective rights that they grant for a given user on a given entry. The `GetEffectiveRights` feature is useful for various reasons:

  - Provides ACI management functionality that is used to verify that the current ACI's are really offering the intended access rights.

  - Aids the administration of users, and retrieves their rights to directory entries and attributes. However, note that though it can be used to determine if an operation would succeed or fail, it cannot be used to determine if an operation was successful.

  - Enables verification of the access control policy. You can retrieve the permissions list for a user on a given entry and its attributes.

  - Enables administrators to debug access control issues.

  - Allows directory-enabled applications to easily determine whether a user has permission to perform a particular operation (for example, not give the user the option to delete an entry if they don't actually have permission to delete it).

- Encrypted Attributes – Data in any directory service, needs to be protected. The Sun ONE Directory Server 5.2 software has many different ways and mechanisms for protecting access to directory data. In the context of *attribute encryption*, this feature is designed to provide data privacy or protection of physical access to data such as LDIF files, backup files, and database files. Thus, attribute encryption allows you to specify that certain attributes will be stored in an encrypted form. This feature is configured at a database level, and once you decide you want to encrypt an attribute, that particular attribute will be encrypted for every entry in the database.

- Start TLS – Start Transport Layer Security (Start TLS) is a LDAPv3 extended operation plug-in in the Sun ONE Directory Server software. This operation provides for TLS establishment in an LDAP association, which allows the client to initiate an encrypted connection over an existing (or opened LDAP connection.

Note – Start TLS now available on many platforms including the Windows platform.

- Scoped Password Policy – A password policy is a set of rules that control how passwords are used in the Sun ONE Directory Server software. To improve the security and make it difficult for password-cracking programs to break into the directory, it is desirable to enforce a set of rules on password usage. These rules are made to ensure that the users change their passwords periodically, the new password meets construction requirements, the reuse of old passwords is restricted, and to lock out users after a certain number of bad password attempts. In earlier versions of the directory server software, the password policy was limited in its functionality to one global policy for the entire directory. This limitation no longer exists in the Sun ONE Directory Server 5.2 software, which offers increased flexibility in that you can configure multiple password policies.

■ Dynamically Loadable SASL Library – The Simple Authentication and Security Layer (SASL) is a generic mechanism for providing authentication and, optionally, integrity and privacy support to connection-based protocols. In previous releases of the directory server software, there were two ways of thinking of how you could add a SASL security mechanism. One mechanism was to write a server plug-in that implemented the SASL mechanism in terms of a pre-bind operation. The other mechanism was to write a SASL mechanism plug-in that would be loaded by the SASL library itself. With this in mind, a shared library, libsasl, and associated plug-ins (GSSAPI, DIGEST-MD5, and CRAM-MD5) have been developed for both the Sun ONE Directory Server 5.2 software and Solaris OE. However, at the present time, the dynamically loadable SASL library is private to the Sun ONE Directory Server 5.2 software. When the integrated version of libsasl is introduced on the Solaris OE, the Dynamically Loadable SASL mechanisms will be supported. However, due to U.S. government regulations, there will only be support for authentication, but not encryption.

Authentication Mechanisms

This section discusses what authentication mechanisms are currently available, and how these authentication mechanisms can be used by directory (LDAP) clients.

The LDAPv3 standard which defines the LDAPv3 protocol was published in 1997, and originally proposed different mechanisms that could be used by directory (LDAP) clients to authenticate to directory (LDAP) servers (RFC 2251). RFC 3377 "The LDAPv3 Technical Specification" was published to list all RFC's that comprise the full specifications of LDAPv3. That is, RFC 2251-2256, RFC 2829 (authentication methods) and RFC 2830 (Extension for TLS). The Sun ONE Directory Server 5.2 software conforms to the LDAPv3 Technical Specification.

There are several authentication methods that can be used to authenticate to a LDAPv3 directory server:

■ None, no authentication, also known as anonymous – When using this method of authentication, a directory client will not be able to, or is not intended to, perform specific LDAP operations, such as modifications to directory entries or access to sensitive information. Using this method means that a directory client which has not authenticated or which has authenticated with its name but no password is anonymously authenticated. A client which failed to authenticate is not authenticated as anonymous but the following operations will be considered as anonymous. In addition to a client being unauthenticated by default until a successful bind has been performed, an anonymous bind can be performed by using Simple authentication with no password (and typically no DN) as per RFC 2251 section 4.2.2.

Note – While it is true that all directory server (LDAPv3) implementations must support anonymous authentication because LDAPv3 does not require a bind as the first operation, it is perfectly legal for a directory server to be configured in such a way that it rejects any attempt to perform an operation without first authenticating to the server.

- Simple, password-based authentication – When this method of authentication is used, the DN (distinguished name) and password are sent over the network in clear text (not encrypted). It should be noted however, that even with the inherent security vulnerabilities, it is possible to use Simple authentication with transport-layer security (like TLSv1/SSL or IPSec) in a secure manner.

- SASL authentication mechanisms – The Simple Authentication and Security Layer (SASL) is a specification and method used by the LDAPv3 protocol to support what is known as pluggable authentication. This mechanism is used by the directory server (LDAPv3) and directory client (LDAPv3) to identify the user, authenticate this user to the directory server (LDAPv3), and finally to negotiate an optional security layer for subsequent protocol interactions. The SASL (RFC 2222) mechanism is covered in more detail later in this chapter.

Note – The LDAP v2 protocol does not support the Simple Authentication and Security Layer (SASL).

- Certificate-based authentication – Using this method, it is possible with the Sun ONE Directory Server 5.2 software to require that when the client connects to the directory server, the client provides a digital certificate to the directory server as identification. Authenticating a client using a client certificate really falls under the SASL category because a client certificate will only be used to authenticate the client if that client performs a bind operation using the SASL EXTERNAL mechanism.

Understanding the SASL Mechanism

This section explains what the Simple authentication security layer (SASL) is, how this is implemented in Sun ONE Directory Server 5.2 software, and what authentication methods it supports.

The Simple Authentication and Security Layer (RFC 2222) is an Internet Specification (DRAFT standard like LDAPv3) and method for adding authentication support with an optional security layer to connection-based protocols, such as LDAPv3. SASL also describes a structure for authentication mechanisms. The result is an abstraction layer between protocols and authentication mechanisms such that any SASL-compatible authentication mechanism can be used with any SASL-compatible protocol.

Before going into any more detail, let's take a brief look at why SASL is so important. Before SASL was introduced, what happened when a new protocol was written that required authentication? The answer is similar to that of the Solaris Operating Environment before the Pluggable Authentication Module (PAM) feature was introduced. Developers of the protocol had to explicitly allow and define the individual authentication mechanism. You ended up with a protocol that was developed in such a way that it had a particular way of handling how a CRAM-MD5 login was handled, a particular way of handling how a Kerberos v4 login was handled, and so on.

One of the biggest concerns of this model was when a new authentication method was developed and the protocol needed to be modified to support this particular authentication mechanism. This led to a lengthy process before the new authentication mechanisms could be released, and if your application used more than one protocol, for example, an email client, the developer was required to support CRAM MD5 for IMAP and CRAM-MD5 for POP, which would potentially create many different authentication mechanisms to implement and support. This process, of course, was not desirable for the protocol or application developer in an ever-changing environment where new authentication mechanisms are always being developed.

What was needed was a mechanism whereby developers could simply have one framework to write to. This is where the Simple Authentication Security Layer (SASL) which is described in RFC 2222 comes in to its own and addresses some, but not all, of the above issues. As an example, not all forms of SASL mechanisms can be handled by simply linking with some external library. DIGEST-MD5 authentication is a very good example of this because while you can use an external library to handle all the negotiation and the work of verifying the password, it is necessary to establish some mapping between the identity provided by the user and an account in the directory server. SASL EXTERNAL is an even better example because in many cases it has to be handled entirely by the server.

The Simple Authentication and Security Layer (SASL), is a generic mechanism and framework for protocols to accomplish authentication. Applications such as the Sun ONE Directory Server software and Solaris OE Secured LDAP Clients use the SASL library as a means of informing the application how to accomplish the SASL protocol exchange, and what the results are.

SASL is a framework whereby SASL authentication mechanisms control the exact protocol exchange. For example, if you have two protocols (such as IMAP and POP) and a number of different ways of authenticating, SASL attempts to make it so that only *n* plus *m* different specifications need be written instead of *n* times *m* different specifications. With the Sun SASL library, the mechanisms need only be written once, and they'll work with all servers that use them.

FIGURE 3-1 shows the SASL components.

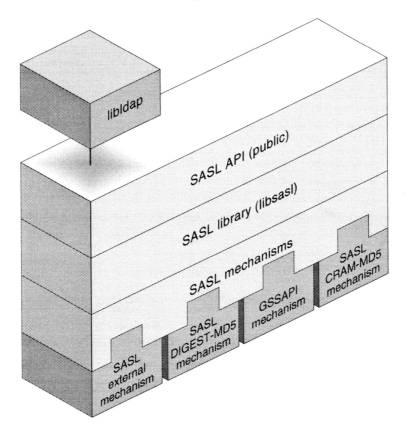

FIGURE 3-1   SASL Components

SASL DIGEST-MD5

The basic idea of the SASL DIGEST-MD5 mechanism is that both the client and server have a shared secret which is namely the user's password. Each side uses this secret together with nonces (defined on page 46) to prove to the other side that they do indeed know this shared secret without revealing the secret to the other side. If the client uses the wrong password, the server detects it. Similarly, if the server doesn't know the secret, the client detects that.

The Sun ONE Directory Server version 5.2 software integrates a new SASL library (libsasl), which is based on the Cyrus CMU implementation. Through this SASL framework, the directory server supports DIGEST-MD5 and the GSSAPI (which implements Kerberos v5).

Note – Currently the GSSAPI is only supported on the Solaris OE.

The SASL security feature is configurable through LDAP and is accessible through the entry cn=sasl, cn=security, cn=config. Using this entry, you can enable authentication mechanisms and also update the path where the SASL authentication mechanism is loaded by libsasl.

To solve the issue of mapping protocol identities to LDAP identities, there is a feature called *identity mapping* in the Sun ONE Directory Server 5.2 software. This feature maps from specific authentication protocols, such as DIGEST-MD5, GSSAPI, and HTTP, to an LDAP identity by applying mapping rules that are entirely customizable through LDAP. By default, there is an identity mapping for DIGEST-MD5 in the case where the client passes a dn as authid. It is possible to define as many mappings as you want. The identity mapping feature is described in the Sun ONE Directory Server 5.2 software documentation.

One of the important things to remember is that there is an authentication ID and an authorization (or proxy) ID. SASL also refers to the authorization ID as the user name. In the case when there is no proxy, the two identities are the same. Currently, the Sun ONE Directory Server 5.2 software does not support proxies through SASL.

The LDAPv3 Technical Specification (particularly RFC 2829), mandates the support of SASL DIGEST-MD5. Authenticating clients using the Digest authentication mechanism does not provide a strong authentication mechanism when compared to public key based mechanisms, but does prevent the much weaker and even more dangerous use of plain text passwords. In addition, the DIGEST-MD5 offers no confidentiality protection beyond protecting the actual password during the authentication phase. This means that the rest of the challenge and response, including the user's name and authentication realm, are available to an eavesdropper. However, the DIGEST-MD5 method can be used to provide integrity and confidentiality on the connection after the authentication process has been completed.

The MD5 message-digest algorithm is primarily used in three areas of the Solaris 9 Operating Environment. The Secured LDAP Client, the kernel (TCP and IPsec), and the User (SLP and PPP). Ronald Rivest, who was at the time working at the Laboratory for Computer Science at the Massachusetts Institute of Technology, published MD5 as an RFC (RFC 1321) in April 1992.

When you send data over the wire, you are concerned with three general issues: security, authenticity, and integrity. The *security* of your data ensures that no one else can read your data. This issue is important in many organizations that have information that cannot be exposed to external sources. *Authenticity* guarantees knowledge of the originator of the data; in other words, where the data source is from. This issue is important in areas such as the legal world where authentication issues (like digital signatures) are of great importance. Lastly, *integrity* guarantees that the data has not been tampered with in any way when it was transmitted, thus determining whether the data you received was the same data that was actually sent.

It is also very important to understand that MD5 hashing only guarantees the integrity of the data if it is possible to guarantee the integrity and/or authenticity of the MD5 digest itself. That is, if you use an MD5 digest to guarantee the integrity of a file, you should not store the digest with the file because if the file data is compromised it is very easy for a new MD5 digest to be generated. Alternately (and this is the way that DIGEST-MD5 works), all or part of the digest can include some shared secret that is known only by the originator and valid recipients, but not by untrusted third parties.

The MD5 algorithm guarantees the integrity of your data by taking a bit pattern of arbitrary but finite length and producing a 128-bit *fingerprint* or *message* digest of that pattern. This pattern is always 128-bit, regardless of the length of the bit pattern. It is extremely unlikely for two different files to produce the same fingerprint, but because an MD5 hash only consists of 128 bits, there are theoretically an infinite number of bit sequences that when hashed using MD5 will produce the same digest. The MD5 algorithm is not complex and does not require large substitution tables. Security experts estimate that the difficulty of finding two-bit patterns having the same digest is 2^{64} operations, and the difficulty of finding a bit pattern having predetermined digest is 2^{128} operations. It is computationally possible to determine a file based on its fingerprint, but it is not feasible based on current technology and techniques. This means that it is not possible for someone to figure out your data based on its MD5 fingerprint. Before we look at an example, we need to be aware that the Solaris 9 OE does not ship with the MD5 binary.

Take a look at an example of the output produced by MD5 on the binary file /usr/bin/crypt.

```
# md5-sparc /usr/bin/crypt
```

You should see output similar to the following:

```
MD5 (/usr/bin/crypt) = c54740de32d1903b78322a9be712a31d
```

In particular, the string `c54740de32d1903b78322a9be712a31d` is the fingerprint of `/usr/bin/crypt:`.

What happened in the above example is that the MD5 message-digest algorithm applied a mathematical algorithm to the binary `crypt` and produced the fingerprint. What you see is that you get the exact same fingerprint; if you do not, then you know that the binary has been altered in some way. Finally, since MD5 does not encrypt data, it is not restricted by any exportation laws, so you can distribute this tool freely anywhere in the world.

Note – In the Solaris 9 OE, there is no `md5` binary. What you will find is the `/platform/sun4u/kernel/misc/md5` and `/platform/sun4u/kernel/misc/sparcv9/md5` kernel modules, which export the standard MD5 calls to a user program. To obtain the `md5` binary, download the following file:
`http://sunsolve.Sun.COM/md5/md5.tar.Z`

Now that we have taken a look into what the MD5 message-digest is and how it works, it is time to apply this to how this actually translates and works in the Sun ONE Directory Server 5.2 software environment. This section introduces a new element that is discussed later in this chapter and called the *Secured LDAP Client*, which supports, and thus can be used to authenticate using DIGEST-MD5, to the Sun ONE Directory Server 5.2 software.

The following process describes how the Secured LDAP Client authenticates to the Sun ONE Directory Server 5.2 software using the SASL DIGEST-MD5 authentication mechanism.

1. Initial Authentication

   This process starts with the Secured LDAP Client sending a bind request with either the SIMPLE or SASL method. In this context, if it's SASL, the DIGEST-MD5 mechanism is specified. The DIGEST-MD5 authentication is a two-step bind operation.

   The Secured LDAP Client issues a SASL DIGEST bind request, as well as requesting a SASL DIGEST-MD5 bind. While it is possible to specify the bind DN in the initial request, the DN should not be sent, but if it is, if should be ignored. Rather, the authorization ID (which may be a DN, but may also be basically any other kind of ID provided that it can be uniquely resolved to a user entry using the directory server's identity mapping API) is provided by the client in the second stage of the bind request.

In this process, both sides can compute a shared secret, A1. A1 consists of a hash of the username, realm and password, which is concatenated with the directory server nonce and the directory client nonce. It is assumed that both the Secured LDAP client and directory server can obtain this hash, given the username and realm.

Note – Although the directory server does need to have access to the clear text password in order for the client to use DIGEST-MD5 authentication, the attribute encryption feature of the Sun ONE Directory Server 5.2 software can at least somewhat mitigate the risk of having clear text passwords in the server by ensuring that they are not stored on disk in clear text (and therefore would not show up clearly in most backups or LDIF exports).

---

2. Digest Challenge Stage

The directory server starts by sending a challenge, whereby the data encoded in the challenge contains a string formatted according to the rules for a digest-challenge which is shown in the following example:

```
# From RFC 2831 "Digest SASL Mechanism"
digest-challenge  =
        1#( realm | nonce | qop-options | stale | maxbuf | charset
algorithm | cipher-opts | auth-param )

        realm              = "realm" "=" <"> realm-value <">
        realm-value        = qdstr-val
        nonce              = "nonce" "=" <"> nonce-value <">
        nonce-value        = qdstr-val
        qop-options        = "qop" "=" <"> qop-list <">
        qop-list           = 1#qop-value
        qop-value          = "auth" | "auth-int" | "auth-conf" |
                             token
        stale              = "stale" "=" "true"
        maxbuf             = "maxbuf" "=" maxbuf-value
        maxbuf-value       = 1*DIGIT
        charset            = "charset" "=" "utf-8"
        algorithm          = "algorithm" "=" "md5-sess"
        cipher-opts        = "cipher" "=" <"> 1#cipher-value <">
        cipher-value       = "3des" | "des" | "rc4-40" | "rc4" |
                             "rc4-56" | token
        auth-param         = token "=" ( token | quoted-string )
```

As you can see in this example, there are various directives and values declared. The following is a short description of what each directive value means:

- `realm` – A string which enables users to know which user name and password to use, in the event that they have different ones for different servers. Conceptually, it is the name of a collection of accounts that might include the user's account. This string should contain at least the name of the host performing the authentication and might additionally indicate the collection of users who might have access. An example might be `registered_users@gotham.news.example.com`. This directive is optional; if not present, the client should solicit it from the user or be able to compute a default. A plausible default might be the realm supplied by the user when they logged in to the client system. Multiple realm directives are allowed, in which case the user or client must choose one as the realm for which to supply to `username` and password.

Note – In the Sun ONE Directory Server 5.2 software, the realm is always the FQDN host name of the server that appears in the value of the `nsslapd-localhost` attribute in the `cn=config` entry.

- `nonce` – The server's nonce is a random 32-byte (256-bit) random number, which is platform dependent. The server-specified data string which must be different each time a `digest-challenge` is sent as part of initial authentication. It is recommended that this string be base64 or hexadecimal data. Because the string is passed as a quoted string, the double-quote character is not allowed unless escaped. The contents of the `nonce` are implementation dependent. The security of the implementation depends on a good choice. It is recommended that it contain at least 64 bits of entropy. The `nonce` is opaque to the client. This directive is required and must appear exactly once; if not present, or if multiple instances are present, the client should abort the authentication exchange.

- `qop-options` – A quoted string of one or more tokens indicating the *quality of protection* values supported by the server. The value `auth` indicates authentication; the value `auth-int` indicates authentication with integrity protection; the value `auth-conf` indicates authentication with integrity protection and encryption. This directive is optional; if not present it defaults to `auth`. The client must ignore unrecognized options; if the client recognizes no option, it should abort the authentication exchange.

Note – At present, the Sun ONE Directory Server software only supports `auth` qop.

- `stale` – The `stale` directive is not used in initial authentication. This directive may appear at most once; if multiple instances are present, the client should abort the authentication exchange.

Note – At present, the Sun ONE Directory Server software does not support reauth, thus the server will not report a reauthentication stale because of a nonce timeout.

- maxbuf – A number indicating the size of the largest buffer the server is able to receive when using auth-int or auth-conf. If this directive is missing, the default value is 65536. This directive may appear at most once; if multiple instances are present, the client should abort the authentication exchange.

Note – maxbuf is only used if confidentiality or integrity is specified. The Sun ONE Directory Server software sets this to 65535.

- charset – This directive, if present, specifies that the server supports UTF-8 encoding for the username and password. If not present, the username and password must be encoded in ISO 8859-1 (of which US-ASCII is a subset). The directive is needed for backwards compatibility with HTTP Digest, which only supports ISO 8859-1. This directive may appear at most once; if multiple instances are present, the client should abort the authentication exchange.

Note – Only UTF-8 is supported. Any other charset will be rejected.

- algorithm – This directive is required for backwards compatibility with HTTP Digest, which supports other algorithms. This directive is required and must appear exactly once; if not present, or if multiple instances are present, the client should abort the authentication exchange.

Note – Only md5-sess is supported. Any other algorithm is rejected.

- cipher-opts – A list of ciphers that the server supports. This directive must be present exactly once if auth-conf is offered in the qop-options directive, in which case implementation of the 3des and des modes is mandatory. The client *must* ignore unrecognized options; if the client recognizes no option, it should abort the authentication exchange.
  - des – Data Encryption Standard (DES) cipher [FIPS] in cipherblock chaining (CBC) mode with a 56-bit key.
  - 3des – the *triple DES* cipher in CBC mode with EDE with the same key for each E stage (aka "two keys mode") for a total key length of 112 bits.
  - rc4, rc4-40, rc4-56 – the RC4 cipher with a 128-bit, 40-bit, and 5-bit key, respectively.

Note – No ciphers are currently offered by the Sun ONE Directory Server software because confidentiality is not yet supported.

■ `auth-param` – This construct allows for future extensions; it may appear more than once. The client *must* ignore any unrecognized directives. The size of a `digest-challenge` *must* be less than 2048 bytes.

Note – No `auth-param` is sent by Sun ONE Directory Server software at this time.

3. Digest Response Stage

The Secured LDAP Client makes note of the `digest-challenge` and responds with a string formatted and computed according to the rules for a `digest-response`. The Secured LDAP Client performs two MD5 hashes of the password with the challenge, and the realm. The challenge is the `nonce`; the realm is the realm containing the user's account. This directive is required if the server provided any realms in the `digest-challenge`, in which case it may appear exactly once and its value *should* be one of those realms. If the directive is missing, realm value is set to the empty string when computing. The way to understand this, is to think of A1 which is the shared secret, whereby A1 is not sent over the wire, but where just a one way hash of it is. Time is not used in the response, but it is possible to generate a random `nonce`. In the Solaris 9 OE, use `/dev/urandom`. For SASL, users are considered to be located in a realm. It is an organizational item. In this case, the server's specified realm (if there is one) is returned.

```
# From RFC 2831 "Digest SASL Mechanism"
digest-response  = 1#( username | realm | nonce | cnonce |
                       nonce-count | qop | digest-uri | response |
                       maxbuf | charset | cipher | authzid |
                       auth-param )

        username            = "username" "=" <"> username-value <">
        username-value      = qdstr-val
        cnonce              = "cnonce" "=" <"> cnonce-value <">
        cnonce-value        = qdstr-val
        nonce-count         = "nc" "=" nc-value
        nc-value            = 8LHEX
        qop                 = "qop" "=" qop-value
        digest-uri          = "digest-uri" "=" <"> digest-uri-value <">
        digest-uri-value    = serv-type "/" host [ "/" serv-name ]
        serv-type           = 1*ALPHA
        host                = 1*( ALPHA | DIGIT | "-" | "." )
        serv-name           = host
        response            = "response" "=" response-value
        response-value      = 32LHEX
        LHEX                = "0" | "1" | "2" | "3" |
                              "4" | "5" | "6" | "7" |
                              "8" | "9" | "a" | "b" |
                              "c" | "d" | "e" | "f"
        cipher              = "cipher" "=" cipher-value
        authzid             = "authzid" "=" <"> authzid-value <">
        authzid-value       = qdstr-val
```

In this example, there are various directives and values declared. Below is a short description of what each directive value means:

- username – The user's name in the specified realm, encoded according to the value of the charset directive. This directive is required and must be present exactly once; otherwise, authentication fails.

- realm – The realm containing the user's account. This directive is required if the server provided any realms in the digest-challenge, in which case it may appear exactly once and its value should be one of those realms. If the directive is missing, realm-value sets to the empty string when computing A1.

Note – If the same realm is not specified in the response as was in the challenge (the server's FQDN), then the authentication will fail.

- nonce – The server-specified data string received in the preceding `digest-challenge`. This directive is required and *must* be present exactly once; otherwise, authentication fails.

The following is an example of what would be returned in the digest response:

```
# From RFC 2831 "Digest SASL Mechanism"

HEX( KD ( HEX(H(A1)),
{ nonce-value, ":" nc-value, ":",
cnonce-value, ":", qop-value, ":", HEX(H(A2)) }))

This is where SASL digest-md5 will support authzid. NOTE: If the
userid and authzid do not match, then the Sun ONE Directory Server
policy is to refuse the authentication.

A1 = { H( { username-value, ":", realm-value, ":", passwd } ),
":", nonce-value, ":", cnonce-value }
```

Here the `username` (which must be UTF-8) is in the form that the directory server will map. For example: `dn`: *ldap_dn* or `u`: *username* or any other form for which you have matching rules defined.

The realm *must* be the FQDN of the directory server specified, which is sent to the client in the initial challenge stage, and the `passwd` would be the user's password. H(x) is the DIGEST-MD5 hash of the string, and `nonce` value is supplied by the directory server. The `cnonce` is a `nonce` generated by the Secured LDAP Client.

```
# From RFC 2831 "Digest SASL Mechanism"

A2        = { "AUTHENTICATE:", digest-uri-value }
Let { a, b, ... } be the concatenation of the octet strings a, b,
...

Let H(s) be the 16 octet MD5 hash [RFC 1321] of the octet string s.

Let KD(k, s) be H({k, ":", s}), i.e., the 16 octet hash of the
string k, a colon and the string s.
```

Let HEX(*n*) be the representation of the 16-octet MD5 hash *n* as a string of 32 hex digits (with alphabetic characters always in lower case, because MD5 is case sensitive).

Example: (S==Directory Server and C==Secured LDAP Client

```
S: realm="example.com",nonce="OA6MG9tEQGm2hh",qop="auth",
algorithm=md5-sess,charset=utf-8
```

This is the directory server reply, indicating `realm`, `nonce`, quality of protection it offers, mechanisms, and a specified character set.

Note – The Secured LDAP Client implementation only supports UTF-8.

```
C: charset=utf8,username="michaelh",realm="example.com",
nonce="OA6MG9tEQGm2hh",nc=00000001,cnonce="OA6MHXh6VqTrRk",
digest-uri="ldap/example.com",
response=d388dad90d4bbd760a152321f2143af7,qop=auth
```

We reconfirm a number of elements, and add additional ones, such as `cnonce` and `digest-uri`. These are needed by the directory server to confirm the Secured LDAP Client's password, which the directory server must know. The directory server has all the elements to be able to recompute the response.

The following step can be done if the directory server authentication is desired. However, The Secured LDAP Client currently does not check this, but instead retrieves this information from the server. Future versions of the Secured LDAP Client will check this.

```
S: rspauth=ea40f60335c427b5527b84dbabcdfff
```

The directory server calculates a new digest based on the above algorithm, to prove to the Secured LDAP Client that it knows the Secured LDAP Client password.

Note – The size of a `digest-response` is 2048 bytes, which is the limit for all authentication exchanges for DIGEST-MD5.

4. The authentication exchange is completed once the directory server has sent the `reauth` packet.

   Additionally, the DIGEST-MD5 authentication can be used for integrity and confidentiality. Currently neither the Sun ONE Directory Server 5.x software or the Secured LDAP Client supports this functionality.

It is important to understand that in the final exchange from the directory server to the client, the server is indicating that it too can calculate the shared secret A1. This will prove that this is a *trusted* server because it knows how to compute our shared secret.

Note – The DIGEST-MD5 details are buried deep in the underlying `libldap.so.5` library, which is used by the Secured LDAP Client (`libsldap.so.1`) library. In `libsldap`, we just call the LDAP client C API (which is currently a private Solaris OE interface), to bind. The rest is handled by the `libldap` library.

In summary, it is important to emphasize and understand that digests are one-way functions that are relatively easy to compute, but are extremely difficult to determine the possible inverses.

Setting up the SASL DIGEST-MD5 Authentication Mechanism

This procedure in this section uses the `ldapsearch` utility to authenticate against the Sun ONE Directory Server version 5.2 software, using the SASL DIGEST-MD5 authentication mechanism.

Before we get into the step-by-step instructions, it's worth discussing how SASL DIGEST-MD5 is configured because it can be a little tricky.

The DIGEST-MD5 authentication mechanism is now a loadable authentication plug-in in the Sun ONE Directory Server version 5.2 software. Now the LDAP tools (such as `ldapsearch`) rely on the LDAP C-SDK that relies on the `libsasl` to perform a SASL bind. This means that the `libsasl` has to be aware of where to load the DIGEST-MD5 plug-in. When you install the Sun ONE Directory Server version 5.2 software, the plug-ins are copied under *root_server*/`lib/sasl/libdigestmd5.so` (for 32-bit plug-ins), and *root_server*/`lib/sasl/64/libdigestmd5.so` (for 64-bit plug-ins). The directory server needs to be able to load these plug-ins, and know where to get the plug-ins. To achieve this, the directory server looks at the attribute value `dsSaslPluginsPath` under the config entry `cn=sasl,cn=security,cn=config` in the `dse.ldif`. By default, the `dsSaslPluginsPath` is set up to point to *root_server*/`lib/sasl`. You can update this multi-valued attribute if you want to load plug-ins that are stored in another location.

On the client side, it's a little bit different. First, a client might not be aware of where the directory server is installed. But the client needs to retrieve the SASL plug-ins anyway (at least the DIGEST-MD5 plug-in). In the Sun ONE Directory Server 5.2 software (on Solaris OE), the `sasl` library looks at `/usr/lib/mps/sasl2` (for 32-bit plug-ins) and `/usr/lib/mps/sparcv9` (for 64-bit plug-ins).

▼ To Set up the SASL DIGEST-MD5 Authentication Mechanism

> **Note –** This procedure refers to the installation of the unbundled version of the Sun ONE Directory Server 5.2 software. On future versions of Solaris OE, the Sun ONE Directory Server 5.2 software might include a set of SVR4 packages that you install using the pkgadd command, and configure using the directoryserver utility. If you are installing the directory server from SVR4 packages, your installation steps are different than those listed here. Refer to the product documentation, and to "Differentiating Server and Client Versions" on page 191 for details.

1. **Download the Sun ONE Directory Server version 5.2 software product from the** http://www.sun.com **web site.**

2. **Uncompress and extract the Sun ONE Directory Server software.**

   Extract in a directory other than the directory where you intend to install the server (not ServerRoot).

3. **Run the** idsktune **utility**

   The idsktune utility is located in the root of the directory server distribution. Apply any necessary patches and modifications that are reported by idsktune. Once this is done, rerun the idsktune utility to confirm that all is as it should be before running the setup command.

4. **Install and Configure the Sun ONE Directory Server version 5.2 software.**

   Refer to the product documentation for details.

5. **Create user accounts in the directory server.**

Use either the Sun ONE Directory Server Console or the MakeLDIF utility (this utility is available for download. See "Creating LDIF for Benchmarks" on page 479). This example uses the Java MakeLDIF utility.

```
# /usr/ccs/bin/make
Building...
Processed 1000 entries
1002 entries written to example-1k.ldif
Writing filters to example-1k-filter-file.ldif
Wrote 1000 equality filters for uid
Wrote 1000 equality filters for givenname
Wrote 1000 equality filters for sn
Wrote 2479 substring filters for cn
.
.
.
dn: employeeNumber=1000,ou=People,dc=example,dc=com
telephoneNumber: 1-510-315-4801
departmentNumber: 1000
sn: Ruble
employeeType: Employee
employeeNumber: 1000
objectclass: top
objectclass: person
objectclass: organizationalPerson
objectclass: inetOrgPerson
objectclass: mailRecipient
objectclass: nsCalUser
givenName: Lucille
mailDeliveryOption: mailbox
cn: Lucille Ruble
initials: LR
uid: lucyr
mail: Lucy.Ruble@example.com
userPassword: secret123
l: Menlo Park, United States
st: CA
description: This is the description for Lucille Ruble
mailhost: mailhost.example.com
nsCalHost: calhost.example.com
```

6. Add the newly created user accounts to the directory server.

Example using the `ldif2db` utility using the default database back end:

```
$ cd /var/Sun/mps/slapd-instance
$ ./stop-slapd
$ ./ldif2db -n userRoot -i LDIF_file
$ ./start-slapd
```

Example output from `ldif2db`:

```
importing data ...
[08/Jan/2003:15:46:27 +0000] - import userRoot: Index buffering
enabled with bucket size 16
[08/Jan/2003:15:46:27 +0000] - import userRoot: Beginning import
job...
[08/Jan/2003:15:46:27 +0000] - import userRoot: Processing file
"$(LDIF_FILE)"
[08/Jan/2003:15:46:32 +0000] - import userRoot: Finished scanning
file "$(LDIF_FILE)" (1002 entries)
[08/Jan/2003:15:46:33 +0000] - import userRoot: Workers finished;
cleaning up...
[08/Jan/2003:15:46:36 +0000] - import userRoot: Workers cleaned
up.
[08/Jan/2003:15:46:36 +0000] - import userRoot: Cleaning up
producer thread...
[08/Jan/2003:15:46:36 +0000] - import userRoot: Indexing complete.
Postprocessing...
[08/Jan/2003:15:46:36 +0000] - import userRoot: Flushing caches...
[08/Jan/2003:15:46:36 +0000] - import userRoot: Closing files...
[08/Jan/2003:15:46:37 +0000] - import userRoot: Import complete.
Processed 9002 entries in 10 seconds. (900.20 entries/sec)
```

Example using the `ldapmodify` utility:

Make sure that you use the `ldapmodify` command from the
`/var/Sun/mps/shared/bin` directory, or some of the options may not be
recognized because there are other versions of the `ldapmodify` command in the
Solaris OE.

```
$ cd /var/Sun/mps/shared/bin
$./ldapmodify -a -c -h directoryserver_hostname -p ldap_port
-D "cn=Directory Manager" -w "password" -f LDIF_file
-e /var/tmp/ldif.rejects 2> /var/tmp/ldapmodify.log
```

Note – If the `ldapmodify` command is not executed as `./ldapmodify` from the *server-root*/`shared/bin` directory, you must have `LD_LIBRARY_PATH` set to *server-root*/`lib` so that `ldapmodify` finds the appropriate dynamic libraries.

Note – In this example, the `-e /var/tmp/ldif.rejects 2>` `/var/tmp/ldapmodify.log` string is redirecting messages to a log file.

Example output from `ldapmodify`:

```
adding new entry employeeNumber=8995,ou=People,dc=example,dc=com

adding new entry employeeNumber=8996,ou=People,dc=example,dc=com

adding new entry employeeNumber=8997,ou=People,dc=example,dc=com

adding new entry employeeNumber=8998,ou=People,dc=example,dc=com

adding new entry employeeNumber=8999,ou=People,dc=example,dc=com

adding new entry employeeNumber=9000,ou=People,dc=example,dc=com
.
.
.
```

Example output from the access log:

```
[08/Jan/2003:14:57:49 +0000] conn=24 op=997 msgId=998 - ADD dn=
"employeeNumber=8995,ou=People,dc=example,dc=com"
[08/Jan/2003:14:57:49 +0000] conn=24 op=997 msgId=998 - RESULT
err=0 tag=105 nentries=0 etime=0
[08/Jan/2003:14:57:49 +0000] conn=24 op=998 msgId=999 - ADD dn=
"employeeNumber=8996,ou=People,dc=example,dc=com"
[08/Jan/2003:14:57:49 +0000] conn=24 op=998 msgId=999 - RESULT
err=0 tag=105 nentries=0 etime=0
[08/Jan/2003:14:57:49 +0000] conn=24 op=999 msgId=1000 - ADD dn=
"employeeNumber=8997,ou=People,dc=example,dc=com"
[08/Jan/2003:14:57:49 +0000] conn=24 op=1000 msgId=1001 - ADD dn=
"employeeNumber=8998,ou=People,dc=example,dc=com"
[08/Jan/2003:14:57:49 +0000] conn=24 op=999 msgId=1000 - RESULT
err=0 tag=105 nentries=0 etime=0
[08/Jan/2003:14:57:49 +0000] conn=24 op=1000 msgId=1001 - RESULT
err=0 tag=105 nentries=0 etime=0
[08/Jan/2003:14:57:49 +0000] conn=24 op=1001 msgId=1002 - ADD dn=
"employeeNumber=8999,ou=People,dc=example,dc=com"
[08/Jan/2003:14:57:49 +0000] conn=24 op=1001 msgId=1002 - RESULT
err=0 tag=105 nentries=0 etime=0
[08/Jan/2003:14:57:49 +0000] conn=24 op=1002 msgId=1003 - ADD dn=
"employeeNumber=9000,ou=People,dc=example,dc=com"
[08/Jan/2003:14:57:49 +0000] conn=24 op=1002 msgId=1003 - RESULT
err=0 tag=105 nentries=0 etime=0
[08/Jan/2003:14:57:49 +0000] conn=24 op=1003 msgId=1004 - UNBIND
[08/Jan/2003:14:57:49 +0000] conn=24 op=1003 msgId=-1 - closing -
U1
[08/Jan/2003:14:57:50 +0000] conn=24 op=-1 msgId=-1 - closed
.
.
.
```

7. **Confirm the current value of the** `passwordStorageScheme` **attribute value.**

The SASL DIGEST-MD5 authentication mechanism is a two-stage bind operation. In the first stage, the client issues a SASL DIGEST bind request (as previously mentioned, the bind DN is not typically included in the first request issued by the client when authenticating using DIGEST-MD5). The directory server returns a challenge. The client performs two DIGEST-MD5 hashes of the password with the Challenge, and the `Realm`. The client sends the result to the directory server. The directory server performs the same hashes and compares the results. Because the directory server must perform the hashes, the server requires a clear text password. Before changing the `passwordStorageScheme` attribute value, you can confirm the current value using the `ldapsearch` command.

Example output from `ldapsearch`:

```
$ cd /usr/sunone/servers/shared/bin
$ ./ldapsearch -h directoryserver_hostname -p ldap_port
-D "cn=Directory Manager" -w password
-b "cn=Password Policy,cn=config" "(objectclass=*)"
passwordStorageScheme
cn=Password Policy,cn=config
passwordStorageScheme=SSHA
```

8. **Run `ldapsearch` to verify the user, and to verify a successful bind.**

When you create directory user accounts, the passwords are stored in the default password storage mechanism (Salted Secure Hashing Algorithm (SSHA)). Using one of these accounts, you must change the userpassword to be in the clear. Before changing the `userpassword` of an entry, you should run `ldapsearch` to verify that the user exists in the directory server, (also note the format of the `userpassword` attribute value) and that you can bind successfully with the password.

Example running `ldapsearch` to verify a user entry:

```
$./ldapsearch -h directoryserver_hostname -p ldap_port
-b "dc=example,dc=com" uid=lucyr 1.1
dn: employeeNumber=1000,ou=People,dc=example,dc=com
```

Example of searching for the user entry `lucyr` and displaying the current `userpassword` attribute value:

```
$./ldapsearch -h directoryserver_hostname -p ldap_port
-b "dc=example,dc=com" -D "cn=Directory Manager" -w password uid=
lucyr userpassword
dn: employeeNumber=1000,ou=People,dc=example,dc=com
userpassword: {SSHA}zDGUDF2HHAMzheLjjXSNSem/NS2YSmItdXh8cQ==
```

Example of binding to the directory server as user `lucyr` using the correct credentials:

```
$./ldapsearch -h directoryserver_hostname -p ldap_port
-b "dc=example,dc=com" -D "employeeNumber=1000,ou=People,dc=
example,dc=com" -w password uid=lucyr 1.1
dn: employeeNumber=1000,ou=People,dc=example,dc=com
```

If the preceding `ldapsearch` was not successful, you will see something similar to the following output:

```
ldap_simple_bind: Invalid credentials
```

Note – The correct way in LDAPv3 to request that no attributes be returned is to specify an attribute list of `1.1` as specified in RFC 2251.

9. **Change the `passwordStorageScheme` attribute value to** `{CLEAR}`.

It is not necessary to set the default storage scheme to `clear` in the directory server in order to store passwords in clear text. Passwords can be stored in clear text regardless of the default password storage scheme by prefixing the clear text password with `{CLEAR}`. This can be beneficial if there are only a few special accounts in the server for which authentication will be performed using DIGEST-

MD5 and it is not desirable to store passwords for those other accounts in clear text. However, you will not be able to use pam_unix for authentication if you store passwords in clear text.

Example changing the passwordStorageScheme attribute value:

```
$ cd /usr/sunone/servers/shared/bin
$ ./ldapmodify -h directoryserver_hostname -p ldap_port
-D "cn=Directory Manager" -w password
```

You are now in the ldapmodify interactive mode. Enter the information, and when you are done, use Control-d to exit ldapmodify.

Example:

```
dn: cn=Password Policy,cn=config
changetype: modify
replace: passwordStorageScheme
passwordStorageScheme: clear
modifying entry cn=Password Policy,cn=config
```

10. **Confirm the** passwordStorateScheme **attribute value change.**

When you verify this attribute change, you see that an entry has been added to cn= # Password Policy,cn=config which looks like this:

```
$ ./ldapsearch -h directoryserver_hostname -p ldap_port
-D "cn=Directory Manager" -w password
-b "cn=Password Policy, cn=config" "(objectclass=*)"
passwordStorageScheme
cn=Password Policy,cn=config
passwordStorageScheme: clear
```

In this particular example, we loaded the directory user entries with the passwordStorageScheme attribute value set to {SSHA}. It is possible to make the modification to the passwordStorageScheme attribute prior to loading your directory entries, however, in practice this is never really the case.

11. **Change the `userpassword` attribute value to be in the clear for a user.**

Example:

```
$ ./ldapmodify -h directoryserver_hostname -p ldap_port
-D "cn=Directory Manager" -w password
dn: employeeNumber=1000,ou=People,dc=example,dc=com
changetype: modify
replace: userPassword
userPassword: password123
modifying entry employeeNumber=1000,ou=People,dc=example,dc=com
                      (Note: use contol-d to exit interactive mode)
```

12. **Verify that the password for the user is now in the clear.**

When you search the directory server for the user entry `lucyr` and return the
`userpassword` attribute value, you should see the clear text value of the password.

Example:

```
$./ldapsearch -h directoryserver_hostname -p ldap_port
-b "dc=example,dc=com" -D "cn=Directory Manager" -w password uid=
lucyr userpassword
dn: employeeNumber=1000,ou=People,dc=example,dc=com
userpassword: {clear}password123
```

Example of authenticating using SASL DIGEST-MD5:

```
$./ldapsearch -h directoryserver_hostname -p ldap_port -D "" -w password
-o mech=DIGEST-MD5 -o authid="dn:employeeNumber=1000,ou=
People,dc=example,dc=com" -o authzid="dn:employeeNumber=1000,ou=
People,dc=example,dc=com"
-b "dc=example,dc=com" -s base "(uid=lucyr)"
```

Note – Because of the way the Solaris OE packages install the SASL plug-ins, it is
necessary to specify a value for the `SASL_PATH` environment variable that points to
the *server-root*/`lib`/`sasl` directory.

GSSAPI Authentication and Kerberos v5

This section discusses the GSSAPI mechanism, in particular, Kerberos v5 and how this works in conjunction with the Sun ONE Directory Server 5.2 software and what is involved in implementing such a solution. Please be aware that this is not a trivial task.

It's worth taking a brief look at the relationship between the Generic Security Services Application Program Interface (GSSAPI) and Kerberos v5.

The GSSAPI does not actually provide security services itself. Rather, it is a framework that provides security services to callers in a generic fashion, with a range of underlying mechanisms and technologies such as Kerberos v5. The current implementation of the GSSAPI only works with the Kerberos v5 security mechanism. The best way to think about the relationship between GSSAPI and Kerberos is in the following manner: GSSAPI is a network authentication protocol abstraction that allows Kerberos credentials to be used in an authentication exchange. Kerberos v5 must be installed and running on any system on which GSSAPI-aware programs are running.

The support for the GSSAPI is made possible in the directory server through the introduction of a new SASL library, which is based on the Cyrus CMU implementation. Through this SASL framework, DIGEST-MD5 is supported as explained previously, and GSSAPI which implements Kerberos v5. Additional GSSAPI mechanisms do exist. For example, GSSAPI with SPNEGO support would be GSS-SPNEGO. Other GSS mechanism names are based on the GSS mechanisms OID.

Note – The Sun ONE Directory Server 5.2 software only supports the use of GSSAPI on Solaris OE. There are implementations of GSSAPI for other operating systems (for example, Linux), but the Sun ONE Directory Server 5.2 software does not use them on platforms other than the Solaris OE.

Understanding GSSAPI

The Generic Security Services Application Program Interface (GSSAPI) is a standard interface, defined by RFC 2743, that provides a generic authentication and secure messaging interface, whereby these security mechanisms can be plugged in. The most commonly referred to GSSAPI mechanism is the Kerberos mechanism that is based on secret key cryptography.

One of the main aspects of GSSAPI is that it allows developers to add secure authentication and privacy (encryption and or integrity checking) protection to data being passed over the wire by writing to a single programming interface. This is shown in FIGURE 3-2.

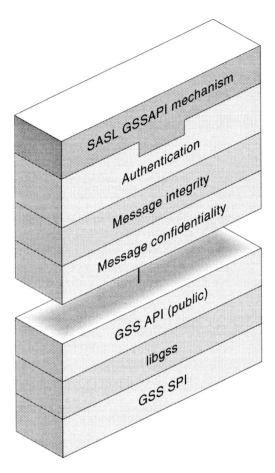

FIGURE 3-2 GSSAPI Layers

The underlying security mechanisms are loaded at the time the programs are executed, as opposed to when they are compiled and built. In practice, the most commonly used GSSAPI mechanism is Kerberos v5. The Solaris OE provides a few different flavors of Diffie-Hellman GSSAPI mechanisms, which are only useful to NIS+ applications.

What can be confusing is that developers might write applications that write directly to the Kerberos API, or they might write GSSAPI applications that request the Kerberos mechanism. There is a big difference, and applications that talk Kerberos directly cannot communicate with those that talk GSSAPI. The *wire* protocols are not compatible, even though the underlying Kerberos protocol is in use. An example is `telnet` with Kerberos is a secure `telnet` program that authenticates a `telnet` user and encrypts data, including passwords exchanged over the network during the `telnet` session. The authentication and message protection features are provided using Kerberos. The `telnet` application with Kerberos only uses Kerberos, which is based on secret-key technology. However, a `telnet` program written to the GSSAPI interface can use Kerberos as well as other security mechanisms supported by GSSAPI.

The Solaris OE does not deliver any libraries that provide support for third-party companies to program directly to the Kerberos API. The goal is to encourage developers to use the GSSAPI. Many open-source Kerberos implementations (MIT, Heimdal) allow users to write Kerberos applications directly.

Note – *On the wire*, the GSSAPI is compatible with Microsoft's SSPI and thus GSSAPI applications can communicate with Microsoft applications that use SSPI and Kerberos.

The GSSAPI is preferred because it is a standardized API, whereas Kerberos is not. This means that the MIT Kerberos development team might change the programming interface anytime, and any applications that exist today might not work in the future without some code modifications. Using GSSAPI avoids this problem.

Another benefit of GSSAPI is its pluggable feature, which is a big benefit, especially if a developer later decides that there is a better authentication method than Kerberos, because it can easily be plugged into the system and the existing GSSAPI applications should be able to use it without being recompiled or patched in any way.

Understanding Kerberos v5

Kerberos is a network authentication protocol designed to provide strong authentication for client/server applications by using secret-key cryptography. Originally developed at the Massachusetts Institute of Technology, it is included in the Solaris OE to provide strong authentication for Solaris OE network applications.

In addition to providing a secure authentication protocol, Kerberos also offers the ability to add privacy support (encrypted data streams) for remote applications such as `telnet`, `ftp`, `rsh`, `rlogin`, and other common UNIX network applications. In the Solaris OE, Kerberos can also be used to provide strong authentication and privacy support for Network File Systems (NFS), allowing secure and private file sharing across the network.

Because of its widespread acceptance and implementation in other operating systems, including Windows 2000, HP-UX, and Linux, the Kerberos authentication protocol can interoperate in a heterogeneous environment, allowing users on machines running one OS to securely authenticate themselves on hosts of a different OS.

The Kerberos software is available for Solaris OE versions 2.6, 7, 8, and 9 in a separate package called the Sun Enterprise Authentication Mechanism (SEAM) software. For Solaris 2.6 and Solaris 7 OE, Sun Enterprise Authentication Mechanism software is included as part of the Solaris Easy Access Server 3.0 (Solaris SEAS) package. For Solaris 8 OE, the Sun Enterprise Authentication Mechanism software package is available with the Solaris 8 OE Admin Pack.

For Solaris 2.6 and Solaris 7 OE, the Sun Enterprise Authentication Mechanism software is freely available as part of the Solaris Easy Access Server 3.0 package available for download from:
`http://www.sun.com/software/solaris/7/ds/ds-seas`.

For Solaris 8 OE systems, Sun Enterprise Authentication Mechanism software is available in the Solaris 8 OE Admin Pack, available for download from:
`http://www.sun.com/bigadmin/content/adminPack/index.html`.

For Solaris 9 OE systems, Sun Enterprise Authentication Mechanism software is already installed by default and contains the following packages listed in TABLE 3-1.

TABLE 3-1   Solaris 9 OE Kerberos v5 Packages

Package Name	Description
SUNWkdcr	Kerberos v5 KDC (root)
SUNWkdcu	Kerberos v5 Master KDC (user)
SUNWkrbr	Kerberos version 5 support (Root)
SUNWkrbu	Kerberos version 5 support (Usr)
SUNWkrbux	Kerberos version 5 support (Usr) (64-bit)

All of these Sun Enterprise Authentication Mechanism software distributions are based on the MIT KRB5 Release version 1.0. The client programs in these distributions are compatible with later MIT releases (1.1, 1.2) and with other implementations that are compliant with the standard.

How Kerberos Works

The following is an overview of the Kerberos v5 authentication system. From the user's standpoint, Kerberos v5 is mostly invisible after the Kerberos session has been started. Initializing a Kerberos session often involves no more than logging in and providing a Kerberos password.

The Kerberos system revolves around the concept of a *ticket*. A ticket is a set of electronic information that serves as identification for a user or a service such as the NFS service. Just as your driver's license identifies you and indicates what driving permissions you have, so a ticket identifies you and your network access privileges. When you perform a Kerberos-based transaction (for example, if you use `rlogin` to log in to another machine), your system transparently sends a request for a ticket to a Key Distribution Center, or KDC. The KDC accesses a database to authenticate your identity and returns a ticket that grants you permission to access the other machine. *Transparently* means that you do not need to explicitly request a ticket.

Tickets have certain attributes associated with them. For example, a ticket can be forwardable (which means that it can be used on another machine without a new authentication process), or postdated (not valid until a specified time). How tickets are used (for example, which users are allowed to obtain which types of tickets) is set by policies that are determined when Kerberos is installed or administered.

Note – You will frequently see the terms *credential* and *ticket*. In the Kerberos world, they are often used interchangeably. Technically, however, a credential is a ticket plus the session key for that session.

Initial Authentication

Kerberos authentication has two phases, an initial authentication that allows for all subsequent authentications, and the subsequent authentications themselves.

A client (a user, or a service such as NFS) begins a Kerberos session by requesting a ticket-granting ticket (TGT) from the Key Distribution Center (KDC). This request is often done automatically at login.

A ticket-granting ticket is needed to obtain other tickets for specific services. Think of the ticket-granting ticket as something similar to a passport. Like a passport, the ticket-granting ticket identifies you and allows you to obtain numerous "visas," where the "visas" (tickets) are not for foreign countries, but for remote machines or network services. Like passports and visas, the ticket-granting ticket and the other various tickets have limited lifetimes. The difference is that *Kerberized* commands notice that you have a passport and obtain the visas for you. You don't have to perform the transactions yourself.

The KDC creates a ticket-granting ticket and sends it back, in encrypted form, to the client. The client decrypts the ticket-granting ticket using the client's password.

Now in possession of a valid ticket-granting ticket, the client can request tickets for all sorts of network operations for as long as the ticket-granting ticket lasts. This ticket usually lasts for a few hours. Each time the client performs a unique network operation, it requests a ticket for that operation from the KDC.

Subsequent Authentications

The client requests a ticket for a particular service from the KDC by sending the KDC its ticket-granting ticket as proof of identity.

1. The KDC sends the ticket for the specific service to the client.

   For example, suppose user lucy wants to access an NFS file system that has been shared with krb5 authentication required. Since she is already authenticated (that is, she already has a ticket-granting ticket), as she attempts to access the files, the NFS client system automatically and transparently obtains a ticket from the KDC for the NFS service.

2. The client sends the ticket to the server.

   When using the NFS service, the NFS client automatically and transparently sends the ticket for the NFS service to the NFS server.

3. The server allows the client access.

   These steps make it appear that the server doesn't ever communicate with the KDC. The server does, though, as it registers itself with the KDC, just as the first client does.

Principals

A client is identified by its principal. A principal is a unique identity to which the KDC can assign tickets. A principal can be a user, such as joe, or a service, such as NFS.

By convention, a principal name is divided into three parts: the primary, the instance, and the realm. A typical principal could be, for example, lucy/admin@EXAMPLE.COM, where:

lucy is the primary. The primary can be a user name, as shown here, or a service, such as NFS. The primary can also be the word host, which signifies that this principal is a service principal that is set up to provide various network services.

admin is the instance. An instance is optional in the case of user principals, but it is required for service principals. For example, if the user lucy sometimes acts as a system administrator, she can use lucy/admin to distinguish herself from her usual user identity. Likewise, if Lucy has accounts on two different hosts, she can use two principal names with different instances (for example, lucy/california.example.com and lucy/boston.example.com).

Realms

A realm is a logical network, similar to a domain, which defines a group of systems under the same master KDC. Some realms are hierarchical (one realm being a superset of the other realm). Otherwise, the realms are non-hierarchical (or direct) and the mapping between the two realms must be defined.

Realms and KDC Servers

Each realm must include a server that maintains the master copy of the principal database. This server is called the master KDC server. Additionally, each realm should contain at least one slave KDC server, which contains duplicate copies of the principal database. Both the master KDC server and the slave KDC server create tickets that are used to establish authentication.

Understanding the Kerberos KDC

The Kerberos Key Distribution Center (KDC) is a trusted server that issues Kerberos tickets to clients and servers to communicate securely. A Kerberos ticket is a block of data that is presented as the user's credentials when attempting to access a Kerberized service. A ticket contains information about the user's identity and a temporary encryption key, all encrypted in the server's private key. In the Kerberos environment, any entity that is defined to have a Kerberos identity is referred to as a *principal*.

A principal may be an entry for a particular user, host, or service (such as NFS or FTP) that is to interact with the KDC. Most commonly, the KDC server system also runs the Kerberos Administration Daemon, which handles administrative commands such as adding, deleting, and modifying principals in the Kerberos database. Typically, the KDC, the admin server, and the database are all on the same machine, but they can be separated if necessary. Some environments may require that multiple realms be configured with master KDCs and slave KDCs for each realm. The principals applied for securing each realm and KDC should be applied to all realms and KDCs in the network to ensure that there isn't a single weak link in the chain.

One of the first steps to take when initializing your Kerberos database is to create it using the kdb5_util command, which is located in /usr/sbin. When running this command, the user has the choice of whether to create a stash file or not. The stash file is a local copy of the master key that resides on the KDC's local disk. The master key contained in the stash file is generated from the master password that the user enters when first creating the KDC database. The stash file is used to authenticate the KDC to itself automatically before starting the kadmind and krb5kdc daemons (for example, as part of the machine's boot sequence).

If a stash file is not used when the database is created, the administrator who starts up the krb5kdc process will have to manually enter the master key (password) every time they start the process. This may seem like a typical trade off between convenience and security, but if the rest of the system is sufficiently hardened and protected, very little security is lost by having the master key stored in the protected stash file. It is recommended that at least one slave KDC server be installed for each realm to ensure that a backup is available in the event that the master server becomes unavailable, and that slave KDC be configured with the same level of security as the master.

Currently, the Sun Kerberos v5 Mechanism utility, kdb5_util, can create three types of keys, DES-CBC-CRC, DES-CBC-MD5, and DES-CBC-RAW. DES-CBC stands for DES encryption with Cipher Block Chaining and the CRC, MD5, and RAW designators refer to the checksum algorithm that is used. By default, the key created will be DES-CBC-CRC, which is the default encryption type for the KDC. The type of key created is specified on the command line with the -k option (see the kdb5_util(1M) man page). Choose the password for your stash file very carefully, because this password can be used in the future to decrypt the master key and modify the database. The password may be up to 1024 characters long and can include any combination of letters, numbers, punctuation, and spaces.

The following is an example of creating a stash file:

```
kdc1 # /usr/sbin/kdb5_util create -r EXAMPLE.COM -s
Initializing database '/var/krb5/principal' for realm
'EXAMPLE.COM'
master key name 'K/M@EXAMPLE.COM'
You will be prompted for the database Master Password.
It is important that you NOT FORGET this password.
Enter KDC database master key: master_key
Re-enter KDC database master key to verify: master_key
```

Notice the use of the -s argument to create the stash file. The location of the stash file is in the /var/krb5. The stash file appears with the following mode and ownership settings:

```
kdc1 # cd /var/krb5
kdc1 # ls -l
-rw------- 1 root other 14 Apr 10 14:28 .k5.EXAMPLE.COM
```

Note – The directory used to store the stash file and the database should not be shared or exported.

Secure Settings in the KDC Configuration File

The KDC and Administration daemons both read configuration information from /etc/krb5/kdc.conf. This file contains KDC-specific parameters that govern overall behavior for the KDC and for specific realms. The parameters in the kdc.conf file are explained in detail in the kdc.conf(4) man page.

The kdc.conf parameters describe locations of various files and ports to use for accessing the KDC and the administration daemon. These parameters generally do not need to be changed, and doing so does not result in any added security. However, there are some parameters that may be adjusted to enhance the overall security of the KDC. The following are some examples of adjustable parameters that enhance security.

- kdc_ports – Defines the ports that the KDC will listen on to receive requests. The standard port for Kerberos v5 is 88. 750 is included and commonly used to support older clients that still use the default port designated for Kerberos v4. Solaris OE still listens on port 750 for backwards compatibility. This is not considered a security risk.

- max_life – Defines the maximum lifetime of a ticket, and defaults to eight hours. In environments where it is desirable to have users re-authenticate frequently and to reduce the chance of having a principal's credentials stolen, this value should be lowered. The recommended value is eight hours.

- max_renewable_life – Defines the period of time from when a ticket is issued that it may be renewed (using kinit -R). The standard value here is 7 days. To disable renewable tickets, this value may be set to 0 days, 0 hrs, 0 min. The recommended value is 7d 0h 0m 0s.

- default_principal_expiration – A Kerberos principal is any unique identity to which Kerberos can assign a ticket. In the case of users, it is the same as the UNIX system user name. The default lifetime of any principal in the realm may be defined in the kdc.conf file with this option. This should be used only if the realm will contain temporary principals, otherwise the administrator will have to constantly be renewing principals. Usually, this setting is left undefined and principals do not expire. This is not insecure as long as the administrator is vigilant about removing principals for users that no longer need access to the systems.

- `supported_enctypes` – The encryption types supported by the KDC may be defined with this option. At this time, Sun Enterprise Authentication Mechanism software only supports `des-cbc-crc:normal` encryption type, but in the future this may be used to ensure that only strong cryptographic ciphers are used.

- `dict_file` – The location of a dictionary file containing strings that are not allowed as passwords. A principal with any password policy (see below) will not be able to use words found in this dictionary file. This is not defined by default. Using a dictionary file is a good way to prevent users from creating trivial passwords to protect their accounts, and thus helps avoid one of the most common weaknesses in a computer network-guessable passwords. The KDC will only check passwords against the dictionary for principals which have a password policy association, so it is good practice to have at least one simple policy associated with all principals in the realm.

The Solaris OE has a default system dictionary that is used by the spell program that may also be used by the KDC as a dictionary of common passwords. The location of this file is: `/usr/share/lib/dict/words`. Other dictionaries may be substituted. The format is one word or phrase per line.

The following is a Kerberos v5 `/etc/krb5/kdc.conf` example with suggested settings:

```
# Copyright 1998-2002 Sun Microsystems, Inc. All rights reserved.
# Use is subject to license terms.
#
#ident   "@(#)kdc.conf   1.2     02/02/14 SMI"

[kdcdefaults]
        kdc_ports = 88,750

[realms]
        ___default_realm___ = {
                profile = /etc/krb5/krb5.conf
                database_name = /var/krb5/principal
                admin_keytab = /etc/krb5/kadm5.keytab
                acl_file = /etc/krb5/kadm5.acl
                kadmind_port = 749
                max_life = 8h 0m 0s
                max_renewable_life = 7d 0h 0m 0s
                default_principal_flags = +preauth
Needs moving -- dict_file = /usr/share/lib/dict/words
        }
```

Access Control

The Kerberos administration server allows for granular control of the administrative commands by use of an access control list (ACL) file (/etc/krb5/kadm5.acl). The syntax for the ACL file allows for wildcarding of principal names so it is not necessary to list every single administrator in the ACL file. This feature should be used with great care. The ACLs used by Kerberos allow privileges to be broken down into very precise functions that each administrator can perform. If a certain administrator only needs to be allowed to have read-access to the database then that person should not be granted full admin privileges. Below is a list of the privileges allowed:

- a – Allows the addition of principals or policies in the database.
- A – Prohibits the addition of principals or policies in the database.
- d – Allows the deletion of principals or policies in the database.
- D – Prohibits the deletion of principals or policies in the database.
- m – Allows the modification of principals or policies in the database.
- M – Prohibits the modification of principals or policies in the database.
- c – Allows the changing of passwords for principals in the database.
- C – Prohibits the changing of passwords for principals in the database.
- i – Allows inquiries to the database.
- I – Prohibits inquiries to the database.
- l – Allows the listing of principals or policies in the database.
- L – Prohibits the listing of principals or policies in the database.
- * – Short for all privileges (admcil).
- x – Short for all privileges (admcil). Identical to *.

Adding Administrators

After the ACLs are set up, actual administrator principals should be added to the system. It is strongly recommended that administrative users have separate /admin principals to use only when administering the system. For example, user Lucy would have two principals in the database - lucy@REALM and lucy/admin@REALM. The /admin principal would only be used when administering the system, not for getting ticket-granting-tickets (TGTs) to access remote services. Using the /admin principal only for administrative purposes minimizes the chance of someone walking up to Joe's unattended terminal and performing unauthorized administrative commands on the KDC.

Kerberos principals may be differentiated by the instance part of their principal name. In the case of user principals, the most common instance identifier is /admin. It is standard practice in Kerberos to differentiate user principals by defining some to be /admin instances and others to have no specific instance identifier (for example, lucy/admin@REALM versus lucy@REALM). Principals with the /admin instance identifier are assumed to have administrative privileges defined in the ACL file and should only be used for administrative purposes. A principal with an /admin identifier which does not match up with any entries in the ACL file will not be granted any administrative privileges, it will be treated as a non-privileged user principal. Also, user principals with the /admin identifier are given separate passwords and separate permissions from the non-admin principal for the same user.

The following is a sample /etc/krb5/kadm5.acl file:

```
# Copyright (c) 1998-2000 by Sun Microsystems, Inc.
# All rights reserved.
#
#pragma ident    "@(#)kadm5.acl   1.1     01/03/19 SMI"

# lucy/admin is given full administrative privilege
lucy/admin@EXAMPLE.COM *
#
# tom/admin user is allowed to query the database (d), listing
principals
# (l), and changing user passwords (c)
#
tom/admin@EXAMPLE.COM dlc
```

Note – It is highly recommended that the kadm5.acl file be tightly controlled and that users be granted only the privileges they need to perform their assigned tasks.

Creating Host Keys

Creating host keys for systems in the realm such as slave KDCs is performed the same way that creating user principals is performed. However, the -randkey option should always be used, so no one ever knows the actual key for the hosts. Host principals are almost always stored in the keytab file, to be used by root-owned processes that wish to act as Kerberos services for the local host. It is rarely necessary for anyone to actually know the password for a host principal because the key is stored safely in the keytab and is only accessible by root-owned processes, never by actual users.

When creating keytab files, the keys should always be extracted from the KDC on the same machine where the keytab is to reside using the ktadd command from a kadmin session. If this is not feasible, take great care in transferring the keytab file from one machine to the next. A malicious attacker who possesses the contents of the `keytab` file could use these keys from the file in order to gain access to another user or services credentials. Having the keys would then allow the attacker to impersonate whatever principal that the key represented and further compromise the security of that Kerberos realm. Some suggestions for transferring the `keytab` are to use Kerberized, encrypted `ftp` transfers, or to use the secure file transfer programs `scp` or `sftp` offered with the SSH package (`http://www.openssh.org`). Another safe method is to place the `keytab` on a removable disk, and hand-deliver it to the destination.

Hand delivery does not scale well for large installations, so using the Kerberized `ftp` daemon is perhaps the most convenient and secure method available.

Using NTP *to Synchronize Clocks*

All servers participating in the Kerberos realm need to have their system clocks synchronized to within a configurable time limit (default 300 seconds). The safest, most secure way to systematically synchronize the clocks on a network of Kerberos servers is by using the Network Time Protocol (NTP) service. The Solaris OE comes with an NTP client and NTP server software (`SUNWntpu` package). See the ntpdate(1M) and xntpd(1M) man pages for more information on the individual commands. For more information on configuring NTP, refer to the following Sun BluePrints OnLine NTP articles:

- "Using NTP to Control and Synchronize System Clocks – Part I: Introduction to NTP" (July 2001), `http://www.sun.com/blueprints/0701/NTP.pdf`

- "Using NTP to Control and Synchronize System Clocks – Part II: Basic NTP Administration and Architecture" (August 2001),
  `http://www.sun.com/blueprints/0801/NTPpt2.pdf`

- "Using NTP to Control and Synchronize System Clocks – Part III: NTP Monitoring and Troubleshooting" (September 2001),
  `http://www.sun.com/blueprints/0901/NTPpt3.pdf`

It is critical that the time be synchronized in a secure manner. A simple denial of service attack on either a client or a server would involve just skewing the time on that system to be outside of the configured clock skew value, which would then prevent anyone from acquiring TGTs from that system or accessing Kerberized services on that system. The default clock-skew value of five minutes is the maximum recommended value.

The NTP infrastructure must also be secured, including the use of server hardening for the NTP server and application of NTP security features. Using the Solaris Security Toolkit software (formerly known as JASS) with the `secure.driver` script to create a minimal system and then installing just the necessary NTP software is one such method. The Solaris Security Toolkit software is available at:

`http://www.sun.com/security/jass/`

Documentation on the Solaris Security Toolkit software is available at:

`http://www.sun.com/security/blueprints`

Establishing Password Policies

Kerberos allows the administrator to define password policies that can be applied to some or all of the user principals in the realm. A password policy contains definitions for the following parameters:

- Minimum Password Length – The number of characters in the password, for which the recommended value is 8.

- Maximum Password Classes – The number of different character classes that must be used to make up the password. Letters, numbers, and punctuation are the three classes and valid values are 1, 2, and 3. The recommended value is 2.

- Saved Password History – The number of previous passwords that have been used by the principal that cannot be reused. The recommended value is 3.

- Minimum Password Lifetime (seconds) – The minimum time that the password must be used before it can be changed. The recommended value is 3600 (1 hour).

- Maximum Password Lifetime (seconds) – The maximum time that the password can be used before it must be changed. The recommended value is 7776000 (90 days).

These values can be set as a group and stored as a single policy. Different policies can be defined for different principals. It is recommended that the minimum password length be set to at least 8 and that at least 2 classes be required. Most people tend to choose easy-to-remember and easy-to-type passwords, so it is a good idea to at least set up policies to encourage slightly more difficult-to-guess passwords through the use of these parameters. Setting the Maximum Password Lifetime value may be helpful in some environments, to force people to change their passwords periodically. The period is up to the local administrator according to the overriding corporate security policy used at that particular site. Setting the Saved Password History value combined with the Minimum Password Lifetime value prevents people from simply switching their password several times until they get back to their original or favorite password.

The maximum password length supported is 255 characters, unlike the UNIX password database which only supports up to 8 characters. Passwords are stored in the KDC encrypted database using the KDC default encryption method, DES-CBC-CRC. In order to prevent password guessing attacks, it is recommended that users choose long passwords or pass phrases. The 255 character limit allows one to choose a small sentence or easy to remember phrase instead of a simple one-word password.

It is possible to use a dictionary file that can be used to prevent users from choosing common, easy-to-guess words (see "Secure Settings in the KDC Configuration File" on page 70). The dictionary file is only used when a principal has a policy association, so it is highly recommended that at least one policy be in effect for all principals in the realm.

The following is an example password policy creation:

If you specify a kadmin command without specifying any options, kadmin displays the syntax (usage information) for that command. The following code box shows this, followed by an actual add_policy command with options.

```
kadmin: add_policy
usage: add_policy [options] policy
options are:
[-maxlife time] [-minlife time] [-minlength length]
[-minclasses number] [-history number]
kadmin: add_policy -minlife "1 hour" -maxlife "90 days"
-minlength 8 -minclasses 2 -history 3 passpolicy
kadmin: get_policy passpolicy
Policy: passpolicy
Maximum password life: 7776000
Minimum password life: 3600
Minimum password length: 8
Minimum number of password character classes: 2
Number of old keys kept: 3
Reference count: 0
```

This example creates a password policy called passpolicy which enforces a maximum password lifetime of 90 days, minimum length of 8 characters, a minimum of 2 different character classes (letters, numbers, punctuation), and a password history of 3.

To apply this policy to an existing user, modify the following:

```
kadmin: modprinc -policy passpolicy lucyPrincipal
"lucy@EXAMPLE.COM" modified.
```

To modify the default policy that is applied to all user principals in a realm, change the following:

```
kadmin: modify_policy -maxlife "90 days" -minlife "1 hour"
-minlength 8 -minclasses 2 -history 3 default
kadmin: get_policy default
Policy: default
Maximum password life: 7776000
Minimum password life: 3600
Minimum password length: 8
Minimum number of password character classes: 2
Number of old keys kept: 3
Reference count: 1
```

The Reference count value indicates how many principals are configured to use the policy.

Note – The default policy is automatically applied to all new principals that are not given the same password as the principal name when they are created. Any account with a policy assigned to it is uses the dictionary (defined in the `dict_file` parameter in `/etc/krb5/kdc.conf`) to check for common passwords.

Backing Up a KDC

Backups of a KDC system should be made regularly or according to local policy. However, backups should exclude the `/etc/krb5/krb5.keytab` file. If the local policy requires that backups be done over a network, then these backups should be secured either through the use of encryption or possibly by using a separate network interface that is only used for backup purposes and is not exposed to the same traffic as the non-backup network traffic. Backup storage media should always be kept in a secure, fireproof location.

Monitoring the KDC

Once the KDC is configured and running, it should be continually and vigilantly monitored. The Sun Kerberos v5 software KDC logs information into the /var/krb5/kdc.log file, but this location can be modified in the /etc/krb5/krb5.conf file, in the logging section.

```
[logging]
        default = FILE:/var/krb5/kdc.log
        kdc = FILE:/var/krb5/kdc.log
```

The KDC log file should have read and write permissions for the root user only, as follows:

```
-rw------ 1 root other 750 25 May 10 17:55 /var/krb5/kdc.log
```

Kerberos Options

The /etc/krb5/krb5.conf file contains information that all Kerberos applications use to determine what server to talk to and what realm they are participating in. Configuring the krb5.conf file is covered in the *Sun Enterprise Authentication Mechanism Software Installation Guide*. Also refer to the krb5.conf(4) man page for a full description of this file.

The appdefaults section in the krb5.conf file contains parameters that control the behavior of many Kerberos client tools. Each tool may have its own section in the appdefaults section of the krb5.conf file.

Many of the applications that use the appdefaults section, use the same options; however, they might be set in different ways for each client application.

Kerberos Client Applications

The following Kerberos applications can have their behavior modified through the user of options set in the appdefaults section of the /etc/krb5/krb5.conf file or by using various command-line arguments. These clients and their configuration settings are described below.

kinit

The kinit client is used by people who want to obtain a TGT from the KDC. The /etc/krb5/krb5.conf file supports the following kinit options: renewable, forwardable, no_addresses, max_life, max_renewable_life and proxiable.

telnet

The Kerberos telnet client has many command-line arguments that control its behavior. Refer to the man page for complete information. However, there are several interesting security issues involving the Kerberized telnet client.

The telnet client uses a session key even after the service ticket which it was derived from has expired. This means that the telnet session remains active even after the ticket originally used to gain access, is no longer valid. This is insecure in a strict environment, however, the trade off between ease of use and strict security tends to lean in favor of ease-of-use in this situation. It is recommended that the telnet connection be re-initialized periodically by disconnecting and reconnecting with a new ticket. The overall lifetime of a ticket is defined by the KDC (/etc/krb5/kdc.conf), normally defined as eight hours.

The telnet client allows the user to forward a copy of the credentials (TGT) used to authenticate to the remote system using the -f and -F command-line options. The -f option sends a non-forwardable copy of the local TGT to the remote system so that the user can access Kerberized NFS mounts or other local Kerberized services on that system only. The -F option sends a forwardable TGT to the remote system so that the TGT can be used from the remote system to gain further access to other remote Kerberos services beyond that point. The -F option is a superset of -f. If the Forwardable and or forward options are set to false in the krb5.conf file, these command-line arguments can be used to override those settings, thus giving individuals the control over whether and how their credentials are forwarded.

The -x option should be used to turn on encryption for the data stream. This further protects the session from eavesdroppers. If the telnet server does not support encryption, the session is closed. The /etc/krb5/krb5.conf file supports the following telnet options: forward, forwardable, encrypt, and autologin. The autologin [true/false] parameter tells the client to try and attempt to log in without prompting the user for a user name. The local user name is passed on to the remote system in the telnet negotiations.

rlogin *and* rsh

The Kerberos rlogin and rsh clients behave much the same as their non-Kerberized equivalents. Because of this, it is recommended that if they are required to be included in the network files such as /etc/hosts.equiv and .rhosts that the root users directory be removed. The Kerberized versions have the added benefit of using Kerberos protocol for authentication and can also use Kerberos to protect the privacy of the session using encryption.

Similar to telnet described previously, the rlogin and rsh clients use a session key after the service ticket which it was derived from has expired. Thus, for maximum security, rlogin and rsh sessions should be re-initialized periodically. rlogin uses the -f, -F, and -x options in the same fashion as the telnet client. The /etc/krb5/krb5.conf file supports the following rlogin options: forward, forwardable, and encrypt.

Command-line options override configuration file settings. For example, if the rsh section in the krb5.conf file indicates encrypt false, but the -x option is used on the command line, an encrypted session is used.

rcp

Kerberized rcp can be used to transfer files securely between systems using Kerberos authentication and encryption (with the -x command-line option). It does not prompt for passwords, the user must already have a valid TGT before using rcp if they wish to use the encryption feature. However, beware if the -x option is not used and no local credentials are available, the rcp session will revert to the standard, non-Kerberized (and insecure) rcp behavior. It is highly recommended that users always use the -x option when using the Kerberized rcp client.The /etc/krb5/krb5.conf file supports the encrypt [true/false] option.

login

The Kerberos login program (login.krb5) is forked from a successful authentication by the Kerberized telnet daemon or the Kerberized rlogin daemon. This Kerberos login daemon is separate from the standard Solaris OE login daemon and thus, the standard Solaris OE features such as BSM auditing are not yet supported when using this daemon. The /etc/krb5/krb5.conf file supports the krb5_get_tickets [true/false] option. If this option is set to true, then the login program will generate a new Kerberos ticket (TGT) for the user upon proper authentication.

ftp

The Sun Enterprise Authentication Mechanism (SEAM) version of the `ftp` client uses the GSSAPI (RFC 2743) with Kerberos v5 as the default mechanism. This means that it uses Kerberos authentication and (optionally) encryption through the Kerberos v5 GSS mechanism. The only Kerberos-related command-line options are -f and -m. The -f option is the same as described above for `telnet` (there is no need for a -F option). -m allows the user to specify an alternative GSS mechanism if so desired, the default is to use the `kerberos_v5` mechanism.

The protection level used for the data transfer can be set using the `protect` command at the `ftp` prompt. Sun Enterprise Authentication Mechanism software `ftp` supports the following protection levels:

- Clear unprotected, unencrypted transmission
- Safe data is integrity protected using cryptographic checksums
- Private data is transmitted with confidentiality and integrity using encryption

It is recommended that users set the protection level to `private` for all data transfers. The `ftp` client program does not support or reference the `krb5.conf` file to find any optional parameters. All `ftp` client options are passed on the command line. See the man page for the Kerberized `ftp` client, `ftp(1)`.

In summary, adding Kerberos to a network can increase the overall security available to the users and administrators of that network. Remote sessions can be securely authenticated and encrypted, and shared disks can be secured and encrypted across the network. In addition, Kerberos allows the database of user and service principals to be managed securely from any machine which supports the SEAM software Kerberos protocol. SEAM is interoperable with other RFC 1510 compliant Kerberos implementations such as MIT Krb5 and some MS Windows 2000 Active Directory services. Adopting the practices recommended in this section further secure the SEAM software infrastructure to help ensure a safer network environment.

Implementing the Sun ONE Directory Server 5.2 Software and the GSSAPI Mechanism

This section provides a high-level overview, followed by the in-depth procedures that describe the setup necessary to implement the GSSAPI mechanism and the Sun ONE Directory Server 5.2 software. This implementation assumes a realm of EXAMPLE.COM for this purpose. The following list gives an initial high-level overview of the steps required, with the next section providing the detailed information.

1. Setup DNS on the client machine. This is an important step because Kerberos requires DNS.

2. Install and configure the Sun ONE Directory Server version 5.2 software.

3. Check that the directory server and client both have the SASL plug-ins installed.

4. Install and configure Kerberos v5.

5. Edit the `/etc/krb5/krb5.conf` file.

6. Edit the `/etc/krb5/kdc.conf` file.

7. Edit the `/etc/krb5/kadm5.acl` file.

8. Move the `kerberos_v5` line so it is the first line in the `/etc/gss/mech` file.

9. Create new principals using `kadmin.local`, which is an interactive command-line interface to the Kerberos v5 administration system.

10. Modify the rights for `/etc/krb5/krb5.keytab`. This access is necessary for the Sun ONE Directory Server 5.2 software.

11. Run `/usr/sbin/kinit`.

12. Check that you have a ticket with `/usr/bin/klist`.

13. Perform an `ldapsearch`, using the `ldapsearch` command-line tool from the Sun ONE Directory Server 5.2 software to test and verify.

The sections that follow fill in the details.

Configuring a DNS Client

To be a DNS client, a machine must run the *resolver*. The resolver is neither a daemon nor a single program. It is a set of dynamic library routines used by applications that need to know machine names. The resolver's function is to resolve users' queries. To do that, it queries a name server, which then returns either the requested information or a referral to another server. Once the resolver is configured, a machine can request DNS service from a name server.

The following example shows you how to configure the `resolv.conf(4)` file in the server kdc1 in the `example.com` domain.

```
;
; /etc/resolv.conf file for dnsmaster
;
  domain              example.com
  nameserver          192.168.0.0
  nameserver          192.168.0.1
```

The first line of the `/etc/resolv.conf` file lists the domain name in the form:

`domain` *domainname*

Note – No spaces or tabs are permitted at the end of the domain name. Make sure that you press return immediately after the last character of the domain name.

The second line identifies the server itself in the form:

`nameserver` *IP_address*

Succeeding lines list the IP addresses of one or two slave or cache-only name servers that the resolver should consult to resolve queries. Name server entries have the form:

`nameserver` *IP_address*

IP_address is the IP address of a slave or cache-only DNS name server. The resolver queries these name servers in the order they are listed until it obtains the information it needs.

For more detailed information of what the `resolv.conf` file does, refer to the `resolv.conf(4)` man page.

▼ To Configure Kerberos v5 (Master KDC)

In the this procedure, the following configuration parameters are used:

- Realm name = `EXAMPLE.COM`
- DNS domain name = `example.com`
- Master KDC = `kdc1.example.com`
- admin principal = `lucy/admin`
- Online help URL =
  `http://example:8888/ab2/coll.384.1/SEAM/@AB2PageView/6956`

Note – This procedure requires that DNS is running.

Note – Before you begin this configuration process, make a backup of the /etc/krb5 files.

1. **Become superuser on the master KDC.** (kdc1, **in this example**)

2. **Edit the Kerberos configuration file** (krb5.conf).

Note – You need to change the realm names and the names of the servers. See the krb5.conf(4) man page for a full description of this file.

```
kdc1 # more /etc/krb5/krb5.conf
        [libdefaults]
                default_realm = EXAMPLE.COM

        [realms]
                                EXAMPLE.COM = {
                                kdc = kdc1.example.com
                                admin server = kdc1.example.com
                }

        [domain_realm]
                .example.com = EXAMPLE.COM

        [logging]
                default = FILE:/var/krb5/kdc.log
                kdc = FILE:/var/krb5/kdc.log

        [appdefaults]
            gkadmin = {
                help_url =
 http://example:8888/ab2/coll.384.1/SEAM/@AB2PageView/6956
                }
```

In this example, the lines for domain_realm, kdc, admin_server, and all domain_realm entries were changed. In addition, the line with ___slave_kdcs___ in the [realms] section was deleted and the line that defines the help_url was edited.

3. **Edit the KDC configuration file** (kdc.conf).

You must change the realm name. See the kdc.conf(4) man page for a full description of this file.

```
kdc1 # more /etc/krb5/kdc.conf
[kdcdefaults]
                kdc_ports = 88,750

        [realms]
                EXAMPLE.COM= {
                        profile = /etc/krb5/krb5.conf
                        database_name = /var/krb5/principal
                        admin_keytab = /etc/krb5/kadm5.keytab
                        acl_file = /etc/krb5/kadm5.acl
                        kadmind_port = 749
                        max_life = 8h 0m 0s
                        max_renewable_life = 7d 0h 0m 0s
Need moving ---------> default_principal_flags = +preauth
                }
```

In this example, only the realm name definition in the [realms] section is changed.

4. **Create the KDC database by using the** kdb5_util **command.**

The kdb5_util command, which is located in /usr/sbin, creates the KDC database. When used with the -s option, this command creates a stash file that is used to authenticate the KDC to itself before the kadmind and krb5kdc daemons are started.

```
kdc1 # /usr/sbin/kdb5_util create -r EXAMPLE.COM -s
Initializing database '/var/krb5/principal' for realm
'EXAMPLE.COM'
master key name 'K/M@EXAMPLE.COM'
You will be prompted for the database Master Password.
It is important that you NOT FORGET this password.
Enter KDC database master key: key
Re-enter KDC database master key to verify: key
```

Note – The -r option followed by the realm name is not required if the realm name is equivalent to the domain name in the server's name space.

5. **Edit the Kerberos access control list file** (kadm5.acl).

   Once populated, the /etc/krb5/kadm5.acl file contains all principal names that are allowed to administer the KDC. The first entry that is added might look similar to the following:

   ```
   lucy/admin@EXAMPLE.COM      *
   ```

   This entry gives the lucy/admin principal in the EXAMPLE.COM realm the ability to modify principals or policies in the KDC. The default installation includes an asterisk (*) to match all admin principals. This default could be a security risk, so it is more secure to include a list of all of the admin principals. See the kadm5.acl(4) man page for more information.

6. **Edit the** /etc/gss/mech **file.**

   The /etc/gss/mech file contains the GSSAPI based security mechanism names, its object identifier (OID), and a shared library that implements the services for that mechanism under the GSSAPI. Change the following from:

   ```
   # Mechanism Name           Object Identifier        Shared Library
   Kernel Module
   #
   diffie_hellman_640_0       1.3.6.4.1.42.2.26.2.4    dh640-0.so.1
   diffie_hellman_1024_0      1.3.6.4.1.42.2.26.2.5    dh1024-0.so.1
   kerberos_v5                1.2.840.113554.1.2.2     gl/mech_krb5.so
   gl_kmech_krb5
   ```

   To the following:

   ```
   # Mechanism Name           Object Identifier        Shared Library
   Kernel Module
   #
   kerberos_v5                1.2.840.113554.1.2.2     gl/mech_krb5.so
   gl_kmech_krb5
   diffie_hellman_640_0       1.3.6.4.1.42.2.26.2.4    dh640-0.so.1
   diffie_hellman_1024_0      1.3.6.4.1.42.2.26.2.5    dh1024-0.so.1
   ```

7. **Run the** `kadmin.local` **command to create principals.**

You can add as many admin principals as you need. But you must add at least one admin principal to complete the KDC configuration process. In the following example, `lucy/admin` is added as the principal.

```
kdc1 # /usr/sbin/kadmin.local
kadmin.local: addprinc lucy/admin
Enter password for principal "lucy/admin@EXAMPLE.COM":
Re-enter password for principal "lucy/admin@EXAMPLE.COM":
Principal "lucy/admin@EXAMPLE.COM" created.
kadmin.local:
```

8. **Create a** `keytab` **file for the** `kadmind` **service.**

The following command sequence creates a special `keytab` file with principal entries for `lucy` and `tom`. These principals are needed for the `kadmind` service. In addition, you can optionally add NFS service principals, host principals, LDAP principals, and so on.

Note – When the principal instance is a host name, the fully qualified domain name (FQDN) must be entered in lowercase letters, regardless of the case of the domain name in the `/etc/resolv.conf` file.

```
kadmin.local: ktadd -k /etc/krb5/kadm5.keytab
kadmin/kdc1.example.com
Entry for principal kadmin/kdc1.example.com with kvno 3,
encryption type DES-CBC-CRC
              added to keytab WRFILE:/etc/krb5/kadm5.keytab.
kadmin.local: ktadd -k /etc/krb5/kadm5.keytab
changepw/kdc1.example.com
Entry for principal changepw/kdc1.example.com with kvno 3,
encryption type DES-CBC-CRC
              added to keytab WRFILE:/etc/krb5/kadm5.keytab.
kadmin.local:
```

Once you have added all of the required principals, you can exit from `kadmin.local` as follows:

```
kadmin.local: quit
```

9. **Start the Kerberos daemons as shown:**

```
kdc1 # /etc/init.d/kdc start
kdc1 # /etc/init.d/kdc.master start
```

Note – You stop the Kerberos daemons by running the following commands:
```
kdc1 # /etc/init.d/kdc stop
kdc1 # /etc/init.d/kdc.master stop
```

10. **Add principals by using the SEAM Administration Tool.**

   To do this, you must log on with one of the admin principal names that you created earlier in this procedure. However, the following command-line example is shown for simplicity.

```
kdc1 # /usr/sbin/kadmin -p lucy/admin
Enter password: kws_admin_password
kadmin:
```

11. **Create the master KDC host principal which is used by Kerberized applications such as** klist **and** kprop.

```
kadmin: addprinc -randkey host/kdc1.example.com
Principal "host/kdc1.example.com@EXAMPLE.COM" created.
kadmin:
```

12. **(Optional) Create the master KDC root principal which is used for authenticated NFS mounting.**

```
kadmin: addprinc root/kdc1.example.com
Enter password for principal root/kdc1.example.com@EXAMPLE.COM:
password
Re-enter password for principal
root/kdc1.example.com@EXAMPLE.COM: password
Principal "root/kdc1.example.com@EXAMPLE.COM" created.
kadmin:
```

13. **Add the master KDC's host principal to the master KDC's** `keytab` **file which allows this principal to be used automatically.**

```
kadmin: ktadd host/kdc1.example.com
kadmin: Entry for principal host/kdc1.example.com with
->kvno 3, encryption type DES-CBC-CRC added to keytab
->WRFILE:/etc/krb5/krb5.keytab
kadmin:
```

Once you have added all of the required principals, you can exit from `kadmin` as follows:

```
kadmin: quit
```

14. **Run the** `kinit` **command to obtain and cache an initial ticket-granting ticket (credential) for the principal.**

This ticket is used for authentication by the Kerberos v5 system. `kinit` only needs to be run by the client at this time. If the Sun ONE directory server were a Kerberos client also, this step would need to be done for the server. However, you may want to use this to verify that Kerberos is up and running.

```
kdclient # /usr/bin/kinit root/kdclient.example.com
Password for root/kdclient.example.com@EXAMPLE.COM: passwd
```

15. **Check and verify that you have a ticket with the** `klist` **command.**

The `klist` command reports if there is a `keytab` file and displays the principals. If the results show that there is no `keytab` file or that there is no NFS service principal, you need to verify the completion of all of the previous steps.

```
# klist -k
Keytab name: FILE:/etc/krb5/krb5.keytab
KVNO Principal
---- -------------------------------------------------------------
3 nfs/host.example.com@EXAMPLE.COM
```

Note – The example given here assumes a single domain. The KDC may reside on the same machine as the Sun ONE directory server for testing purposes, but there are security considerations to take into account on where the KDCs reside.

With regards to the configuration of Kerberos v5 in conjunction with the Sun ONE Directory Server 5.2 software, you are finished with the Kerberos v5 part. It's now time to look at what is required to be configured on the Sun ONE directory server side.

Sun ONE Directory Server 5.2 GSSAPI Configuration

As previously discussed, the Generic Security Services Application Program Interface (GSSAPI), is standard interface that enables you to use a security mechanism such as Kerberos v5 to authenticate clients. The server uses the GSSAPI to actually validate the identity of a particular user. Once this user is validated, it's up to the SASL mechanism to apply the GSSAPI mapping rules to obtain a DN that is the bind DN for all operations during the connection.

The first item discussed is the new identity mapping functionality.

The identity mapping service is required to map the credentials of another protocol, such as SASL DIGEST-MD5 and GSSAPI to a DN in the directory server. As you will see in the following example, the identity mapping feature uses the entries in the `cn=identity` mapping, `cn=config` configuration branch, whereby each protocol is defined and whereby each protocol must perform the identity mapping. For more information on the identity mapping feature, refer to the Sun ONE Directory Server 5.2 Documents.

▼ To Perform the GSSAPI Configuration for the Sun ONE Directory Server Software

1. **Check and verify, by retrieving the `rootDSE` entry, that the GSSAPI is returned as one of the supported SASL Mechanisms.**

   Example of using `ldapsearch` to retrieve the rootDSE and get the supported SASL mechanisms:

   ```
   $./ldapsearch -h directoryserver_hostname -p ldap_port -b ""
   -s base "(objectclass=*)" supportedSASLMechanisms
   supportedSASLMechanisms=EXTERNAL
   supportedSASLMechanisms=GSSAPI
   supportedSASLMechanisms=DIGEST-MD5
   ```

2. **Verify that the GSSAPI mechanism is enabled.**

By default, the GSSAPI mechanism is enabled.

Example of using `ldapsearch` to verify that the GSSAPI SASL mechanism is enabled:

```
$./ldapsearch -h directoryserver_hostname -p ldap_port
-D"cn=Directory Manager" -w password -b "cn=SASL, cn=security,cn=
config" "(objectclass=*)"
#
# Should return
#
cn=SASL, cn=security, cn=config
objectClass=top
objectClass=nsContainer
objectClass=dsSaslConfig
cn=SASL
dsSaslPluginsPath=/var/Sun/mps/lib/sasl
dsSaslPluginsEnable=DIGEST-MD5
dsSaslPluginsEnable=GSSAPI
```

3. **Create and add the GSSAPI** identity-mapping.ldif.

Add the LDIF shown below to the Sun ONE Directory Server so that it contains the correct suffix for your directory server.

You need to do this because by default, no GSSAPI mappings are defined in the Sun ONE Directory Server 5.2 software.

Example of a GSSAPI identity mapping LDIF file:

```
#
dn: cn=GSSAPI,cn=identity mapping,cn=config
objectclass: nsContainer
objectclass: top
cn: GSSAPI

dn: cn=default,cn=GSSAPI,cn=identity mapping,cn=config
objectclass: dsIdentityMapping
objectclass: nsContainer
objectclass: top
cn: default
dsMappedDN: uid=${Principal},ou=people,dc=example,dc=com

dn: cn=same_realm,cn=GSSAPI,cn=identity mapping,cn=config
objectclass: dsIdentityMapping
objectclass: dsPatternMatching
objectclass: nsContainer
objectclass: top
cn: same_realm
dsMatching-pattern: ${Principal}
dsMatching-regexp: (.*)@example.com
dsMappedDN: uid=$1,ou=people,dc=example,dc=com
```

It is important to make use of the ${Principal} variable, because it is the only input you have from SASL in the case of GSSAPI. Either you need to build a dn using the ${Principal} variable or you need to perform pattern matching to see if you can apply a particular mapping. A principal corresponds to the identity of a user in Kerberos.

Note – You can find an example GSSAPI LDIF mappings files in *ServerRoot*/*slapd-server*/ldif/identityMapping_Examples.ldif.

The following is an example using ldapmodify to do this:

```
$./ldapmodify -a -c -h directoryserver_hostname -p ldap_port
-D "cn=Directory Manager" -w password -f identity-mapping.ldif
-e /var/tmp/ldif.rejects 2> /var/tmp/ldapmodify.log
```

4. **Perform a test using** ldapsearch.

   To perform this test, type the following ldapsearch command as shown below, and answer the prompt with the kinit value you previously defined.

   Example of using ldapsearch to test the GSSAPI mechanism:

```
$./ldapsearch -h directoryserver_hostname -p ldap_port -o mech=GSSAPI
-o authzid="root/hostname.domainname@EXAMPLE.COM" -b ""
-s base "(objectclass=*)"
```

The output that is returned should be the same as without the -o option.

Note – If you do not use the -h *hostname* option, the GSS code ends up looking for a localhost.*domainname* Kerberos ticket, and an error occurs.

TLSv1/SSL Protocol Support

This section discusses the Transport Layer Security (TLS) and how it provides the encrypted communications between two hosts, such as a directory server and client. The topic is covered in two categories:

- Server (directory server)
- Client (Secured LDAP Client)

To dispel any misunderstandings you might have, this section explains the differences between TLS and SSL.

SSL Background

The Secure Sockets Layer (SSL) was originally designed for the World Wide Web (WWW) environment to provide a secure channel between two machines. The SSL protocol has gone through various incarnations, beginning with version 1, and evolving into it's present state with its adoption be the Internet Engineering Task Force (IETF), which is now referred to as the Transport Layer Security (TLS) standard.

All the previous versions of the SSL protocol were developed by engineers who worked for Netscape Communications. Netscape's intention was to develop a security model whereby they could provide a single solution to address all the security issues around not only the Web, but also messaging, and news.

TABLE 3-2 shows the development cycle of SSL/TLS.

TABLE 3-2   SSL and TLS Development Cycle

SSL / TLS Protocol Version	Description
SSLv1	Developed by Netscape in 1994, but was never released.
SSLv2	Developed by Netscape in 1994, and the first release.
SSLv3	Developed by Netscape in 1995, and provided authentication only.
TLS	Adoption by the IETF in 1997. Provided new functionality such as a new MAC algorithm and new key expansion.

SSLv2

The goal of SSLv2 was to provide a secure channel between two hosts on the WWW environment. With this in mind, the SSL protocol needed to fit in well with the HTTP protocol, which is used by the Web. Netscape also wanted to provide a single security solution, which meant that this solution would have to work with other protocols and not just HTTP. Unfortunately, not all protocols use or require the same security properties.

SSLv3

There is no question that SSLv2 was widely adopted resulting in a great deal of popularity, thus ensuring that the design goals and principles of SSLv2 were carried forward into SSLv3. The main goal for SSLv3 was to fix a number of security problems found in SSLv2. This meant designing a more secure model that could negotiate multiple cryptographic algorithms. The end result is that SSLv3 supports many more multiple cryptographic algorithms.

TLS Background

In 1996 the IETF chartered the Transport Layer Security (TLS) working group to attempt to standardize an SSL-like protocol. It became apparent early on that there was very little support for changing the existing SSLv3 protocol, with the exception of a few minor bugs and enhancements. To this end, the new protocol just became a minor cleanup of SSLv3.

Understanding TLSv1 Transport Support

In your directory server (LDAP) deployment, it is highly likely that you have some form of security requirements that must be addressed. Specific security requirements are different from one organization to another. For example, a directory server (LDAP) that is available on the Internet has very specific security needs.

To provide secure communications over a network, your directory server (in particular, the Sun ONE Directory Server), includes and supports the LDAPS communications protocol. LDAPS (LDAP over SSL) is the standard LDAP protocol, which runs on top of the Secure Sockets Layer (SSL).

It is possible to not only use TLSv1 protocol to secure communications between a directory server (LDAP) and directory clients (LDAP), but also between directory servers (LDAP) that are bound by a replication agreement, or between a database link and a remote database. You can use TLSv1 with Simple authentication (bind DN and password), or with certificate-based authentication.

Two kinds of authentication mechanisms can be performed using TLSv1:

- Server authentication
- Client authentication

With server authentication, the client decides whether it trusts the certificate presented by the server. With client authentication, the client decides whether it trusts the certificate presented by the server, and the server decides whether it trusts the certificate presented by the client. In the case of server authentication, the client is not authenticated to the server at all. In the case of client authentication, the client may be authenticated to the server if it also performs a bind using the SASL EXTERNAL mechanism.

Using TLSv1 with the Simple authentication mechanism guarantees confidentiality and data integrity. One of the benefits of using a certificate to authenticate to the Directory Server (LDAP) instead of a bind DN and password is improved security.

The use of the certificate-based authentication mechanism is more secure than non-certificate bind operations. This is because certificate-based authentication uses public-key cryptography. As a result, bind credentials cannot be intercepted across the network.

The Sun ONE Directory Server software is capable of simultaneous TLSv1 and non-SSL communications. This means that you do not have to choose between TLSv1 or non-SSL communications for your directory server, because you can use both at the same time.

But one of the downsides to using TLSv1 is reduced efficiency.

The process of data encryption, with generally DES or RC4 does significantly reduce the throughput that can be achieved, and the initial negotiation and key agreement with RSA or DSA is even more expensive. There are potentially three cases for which you must be considered when dealing with the performance impact of TLSv1 in the Sun ONE Directory Server 5.2 software:

- Clients establish a connection over TLSv1 and maintain that connection for a number of operations (persistent connections). This is the best scenario for TLSv1 because the process of initializing the TLSv1-based connection is the most expensive part. In this case, using TLSv1 will introduce degradation over the performance when not using TLSv1.

- Clients establish a connection over TLSv1, perform one or two operations (for example, a bind and a search), close the connection, and then repeat. That is, the same system or set of systems are repeatedly used to establish short-lived TLSv1-based connections. This is much less efficient because as indicated above, the process of establishing TLSv1-based connections is rather expensive. However, it is not as bad as it could be because the same TLSv1 session (which is also expensive to set up) can be re-used across multiple TCP connections.

- Different client systems establish a connection over TLSv1, perform one or two operations (for example, a bind and a search), and then close the connection. That is, different systems are used to establish short-lived SSL-based connections. This is the least efficient of the three scenarios because the TLSv1 sessions cannot be reused across the different TCP connections, which means that the full negotiation process must be performed for each new connection. This case is a very uncommon scenario for real-world directory use.

Why Use TLSv1?

TLSv1 is used to protect sensitive information. Data that travels over a network is visible to a number of other machines on that network. This is especially of concern for information traveling over the Internet. Normally, the other machines simply ignore the information if it isn't intended for them, but that isn't necessarily the case. Most network interfaces support a feature known as promiscuous mode, in which they sue to pay attention to all traffic and not just information that pertains specifically to that machine. This can be a very helpful diagnostic feature for network administrators or even people that support a product that works in a networked environment. Applications like snoop (included in the Solaris OE) or the Network Monitor that comes with Windows NT, provide a mechanism for capturing and displaying that information. These applications are often called sniffers or protocol analyzers. More advanced protocol analyzers like Ethereal (available for free on a number of platforms, or as source code from http://www.ethereal.com) can even interpret the information that is captured so that it can be more easily understood by the user. This is helpful with text-based protocols like HTTP because it provides formatting for the request. It is invaluable for binary protocols like LDAP because otherwise the task of decoding the information and figuring out exactly what was going on between the client and the server is much more difficult.

Sniffers can be very helpful tools when trying to track down problems that are occurring in a networked environment. However, they can also be very helpful tools to those with less honorable intentions. They make it easy to see any information that is transferred over the network, so it is possible to capture sensitive information like credit card numbers being used to buy a product on the Web, passwords being used to bind to a directory server, or any other kind of information that would otherwise be protected. Using TLSv1 can thwart these attempts because the encrypted information is completely unintelligible except to the two machines that are having the conversation.

The layer of privacy provided by TLSv1 does not come without a price. Because TLSv1 is used to encapsulate information in another protocol, each machine must deal with the extra overhead of encrypting information before sending it over the network, and decrypting information received before attempting to interpret it. The primary form of overhead is in CPU utilization, but it is also necessary to transfer more information between the client and the server. For that reason, TLSv1 should generally be used only when it is necessary to ensure the privacy of the information that is being sent over the network.

How Does TLSv1 Work?

From a high level, TLSv1 works by encrypting information using data that is only available to the two machines having the encrypted conversation. The foundation of this set of information is the certificate. A certificate is a portion of binary data that can be used to establish proof of identity. There are two important parts of a certificate:

- The public key
- The private key

The public key is freely available and is used as the initial proof that the server is the system that the client believes it is. The private key is available only to the server and can be used to decrypt information that is encrypted using the server's public key.

Before information can be encrypted using TLSv1, a preliminary conversation must occur between the client and the server, known as the TLSv1 handshake, which is discussed in some detail later in this section. For now, this is what happens during the TLSv1 handshake:

1. The client sends some information to the server, including the TLSv1 version number that the client wants to use and some randomly generated data.

2. The server sends back some information that includes the TLSv1 version number the server will use, some randomly generated data, and the server's public key.

3. If the client decides to trust the server's certificate as proof of identification, it generates a shared secret. This shared secret is encrypted using the server's public key and sent to the server.

4. The server decrypts the data from the client using its private key to determine the shared secret.

5. All communication between the client and the server beyond that point is encrypted with that shared secret.

There is actually more that occurs during this TLSv1 handshake, but the above description is a good starting point.

Types of TLSv1

Two-types of TLSv1 are commonly used:

- Server authentication
- Client authentication

Server authentication is the most common form and is the most basic level of authentication that can be performed using TLSv1, and was explained in a brief description in the previous section. Essentially, server authentication is used to obtain enough information to get the shared secret to encrypt the information. It is called server authentication because the process involves a mechanism whereby the server sends proof of its identity to the client and the client is then able to decide whether to trust that information and continue its conversation with the server. In server authentication, the server automatically trusts the client, or trusts the client through some mechanism built into the encapsulated protocol (for example, the password used in an LDAP bind request). No proof of the client's identity is required in the TLSv1 handshake.

Client authentication extends the process of server authentication in that the server requires proof of the client's identity in addition to having to prove its identity to the client. In this case, the TLSv1 handshake is extended to include the server requesting that proof of identity from the client.

In this scenario, the client must have its own certificate, and send the public key to the server so that the server can determine whether to trust the identity of the client. The client does not require a certificate. This is only used when there is client authentication. There is also an additional step involved in the generation of the shared secret when client authentication is used.

FIGURE 3-3 shows that the TLS protocol runs above TCP/IP and below high-level application protocols.

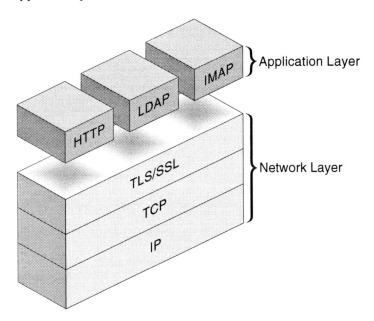

FIGURE 3-3   TLS Protocol in the Network Layer

TLS Protocol

The TLSv1 protocol is composed primarily of two subprotocols, which are:

- TLSv1 Record Protocol
- TLSv1 Handshake Protocol

The TLSv1 is the actual data transfer which is accomplished by the Record Protocol. This is achieved by breaking up the data stream to be transmitted into a series of fragments, with each fragment being independently protected and transmitted. Before any fragment can be transmitted, it must be protected against any potential attack. To provide the integrity protection, a message authentication code (MAC) is computed over the data, and is transmitted along with the fragment. This MAC is appended to the fragment and the concatenated data and MAC are encrypted to form the encrypted payload. A header is then attached to the payload. It is the concatenated header and encrypted payload that is referred as a *record*, which is then actually transmitted. FIGURE 3-4 shows the record protocol.

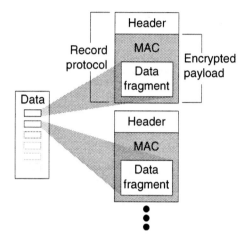

FIGURE 3-4   Composition of TLSv1 Record Protocol

The TLSv1 handshake protocol has various purposes, one of which includes the client and server negotiating on a set of algorithms which are used to protect the data. The client and server establish a set of cryptograhic keys which are used by these algorithms. The process works like this (also see FIGURE 3-5, and FIGURE 3-6 through FIGURE 3-10):

1. Server and client exchange hello messages

   a. Establish protocol version

   b. Set session ID

   c. Agree to use one of the following cipher suites, choosing the strongest cipher suite that is common between client and server:

      - Key Exchange Algorithm (public-key: RSA, DH)

      - Encryption Cipher

      - MAC Algorithm

   d. Establish compression method

   e. Exchange random values

2. Establish server authentication

a. Client confirms server's identity

b. Server sends certificate (necessary for KEA)

The TLS protocol supports a variety of different cryptographic algorithms, or ciphers, for use in operations such as authenticating the server and client to each other, transmitting certificates, and establishing session keys. Clients and servers can support different cipher suites, or sets of ciphers, depending on factors such as the version of TLS they support, company policies regarding acceptable encryption strength, and government restrictions on export of TLS-enabled software. The TLS handshake protocol determines how the server and client negotiate; which cipher suites they use, to authenticate each other, to transmit certificates, and to establish session keys. TABLE 3-3 describes the cipher suite algorithms.

TABLE 3-3   Cipher Suite Algorithms

DES	Data Encryption Standard, an encryption algorithm used by the U.S. Government
DSA	Digital Signature Algorithm, part of the digital authentication standard used by the U.S. Government
KEA	Key Exchange Algorithm, an algorithm used for key exchange by the U.S. Government
MD5	Message Digest algorithm developed by Rivest
RC2 and RC4	Rivest encryption ciphers developed for RSA Data Security
RSA	A public-key algorithm for both encryption and authentication. Developed by Rivest, Shamir, and Adleman
RSA key exchange	A key-exchange algorithm for SSL based on the RSA algorithm
SHA-1	Secure Hash Algorithm, a hash function used by the U.S. Government
SSHA	Salted Secure Hash Algorithm, a hash function used by the U.S. Government
SKIPJACK	A classified symmetric-key algorithm implemented in Fortezza-compliant hardware used by the U.S. Government
Triple-DES	DES applied three times

Key-exchange algorithms like KEA and RSA key exchange govern the way in which the server and client determine the symmetric keys they both use during a TLS session. The most commonly used TLS cipher suites use RSA key exchange.

c. Check certificate DN versus server's DN (used to protect against man-in-the-middle attack).

d. Premaster secret encrypted with server's public key (successful decryption by server provides additional authentication evidence)

e. Optionally check the host name used to connect to the server against the value of the CN attribute in the server certificate's subject DN. This is an optional step, whereby the host names are compared to host names and not to the DNs.

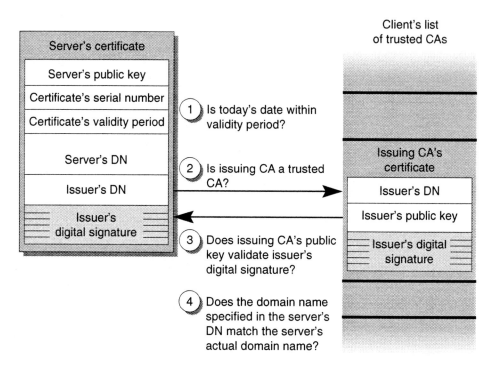

FIGURE 3-5   SSL Handshake Steps

3. Perform key exchange:

a. Generate Pre-master secret

b. Client and server share pre-master secret

c. Secret shared using KEA

d. RSA KEA example:

- Client creates pre-master secret

- Encrypt pre-master secret with server's public key

- Server decrypts pre-master secret with its own private key

4. Perform client authentication (optional) – For client authentication, it is up to the client whether it wishes to authenticate itself to the server. The client sends its certificate which contains the client's name (and possibly alternate names) and the client's public key and the CA – which the server should trust.

   a. Server confirms client's identity

   b. Client sends certificate at server's request with the following:

      - Client's identity

      - Client's public key

   c. Client authenticates identity/public key binding. The ability to encrypt using the private key proves that the client is the owner of the certificate based on the assumption that only that user knows the private key.

   d. Digital signature: random data encrypted with client's private key to validate signature with client's public key

   e. Verify certificate within client's LDAP entry to allow certificate revocation. This is only done after the TLSv1 negotiation is complete, and then only if the client sends a SASL bind request using the EXTERNAL mechanism and the server is configured to verify the certificate presented by the client against the certificate stored in the user's entry. If this is not the case, then the client certificate is not verified against anything in the user's entry, nor is any attempt made to associate the client certificate with any user entry during the TLSv1 negotiation process.

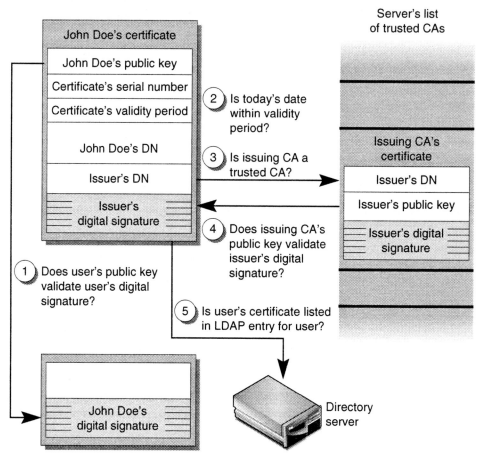

FIGURE 3-6   Client Authentication

5. Generate master secret (client and server)

    This is generated during first connection, and shared between connections.

6. Generate session keys (client and server, new for each connection)

7. Exchange cipher spec messages and finished messages

    a. Change cipher spec and announce start of encrypted message exchange

    b. Finished messages already encrypted with session key

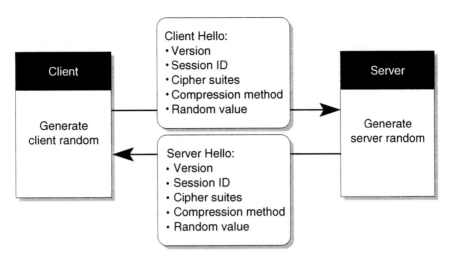

FIGURE 3-7 SSL Handshake Flow Chart (1 of 4)

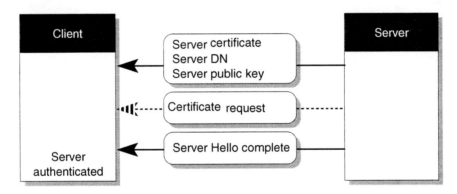

FIGURE 3-8 SSL Handshake Flow Chart (2 of 4)

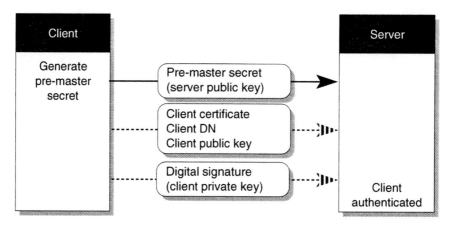

FIGURE 3-9   SSL Handshake Flow Chart (3 of 4)

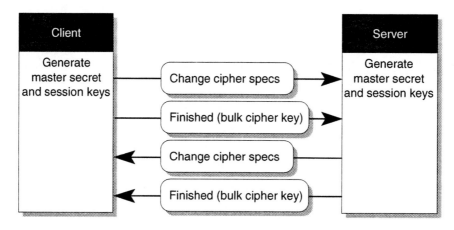

FIGURE 3-10 SSL Handshake Flow Chart (4 of 4)

TLSv1/SSL in the Sun ONE Directory Server 5.2 Software

The Sun ONE Directory server has the ability to support the TLSv1/SSL protocol in multiple areas, and can be enabled in the following situations:

- Both the administration server and DSML access are listening to HTTPS (HTTP over SSL). In this case HTTP over SSL refers to DSMLv2.
- Replication over SSL
- LDAP operations over SSL
- Chaining over SSL
- Console connected via SSL

The TLSv1/SSL Layer in the Sun ONE Directory Server 5.2 software is derived from the Network Security Services (NSS), and Netscape Portable Runtime (NSPR). NSS is a set of libraries designed to support cross-platform development of security-enabled server applications, and NSPR which provides low-level cross-platform support for operations such as threading and I/O. It is the Network Security Services that provides support for SSLv2, SSLv3, and TLSv1 and other security standards.

TABLE 3-4 lists the NSS and NSPR versions that are a component of the Sun ONE Directory Server 5.2 software and indicates where you can find more information.

TABLE 3-4   NSS and NSPR versions

Component	Version	Additional Information
Network Security Services (NSS)	3.3.4	`http://www.mozilla.org/projects/security/pki/nss`
Netscape Portable Runtime (NSPR)	4.1.4	`http://www.mozilla.org/projects/nspr`

FIGURE 3-11 shows a simplified view of the relationships between the NSS and NSPR shared libraries.

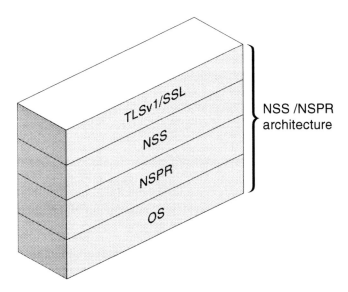

FIGURE 3-11 NSS/NSPR Architecture

The Network Security Services (NSS) has various security tools available, which may prove useful in the debugging and managing of your TLSv1/SSL implementation.

TLSv1/SSL Tools

Before we take a look at some of the TLSv1/SSL tools (TABLE 3-5), please be aware that these tools are not integrated into the Solaris 9 OE. You can get these tools from the Sun ONE Directory Server Resource Kit (SDRK) which is available from the Sun Download Center:

`http://wwws.sun.com/software/download/products/sunone`

Tools such as `ssltap` and many others can be obtained from:

`http://www.mozilla.org/projects/security/pki/nss/tools/`

This section describes some of the security certificate databases such as `cert7.db`, `key3.db`, and the `secmod.db`, which can list, generate, modify, or delete certificates within the `cert7.db` file and create or change the password, generate new public and private key pairs, display the contents of the key database, or delete key pairs within the `key3.db` file.

Security Databases

Public Key Cryptography Standard (PKCS) #11 specifies an API used to communicate with devices that hold cryptographic information and perform cryptographic operations. PKCS #11 supports a wide range of hardware and software devices intended for such purposes.

A PKCS #11 module (also referred to as a cryptographic module or cryptographic service provider) manages cryptographic services such as encryption and decryption through the PKCS #11 interface. PKCS #11 modules can be thought of as drivers for cryptographic devices that can be implemented in either hardware or software.

A PKCS #11 module always has one or more slots, which can be implemented as physical hardware slots in some form of a physical reader (for example, smart cards) or as conceptual slots in software. Each slot for a PKCS #11 module can contain a token, which is the hardware or software device that actually provides cryptographic services and optionally stores certificates and keys. The following is a brief explanation of the security databases:

- `cert7.db` – The database where the certificates (and therefore the public keys attached to them) are stored. Each certificate has a series of flags that account for the role that every certificate can take, as well as the uses for which that certificate is to be trusted. You can list, add, and modify the certificates within the database with `certutil`.

- `key3.db` – The database where the private keys associated to the public keys of the user certificates in `cert7.db` are kept. This file is protected by a password or pin.

- `secmod.db` – The file that keeps track of the available security modules. It lists each module with its slots and tokens, and specifies a default module. This is where an external module must be declared for the server to be able to detect it. By default, `secmod.db` manages two modules; the internal software module, and the built-in CA certificate module. `modutil` is the tool used to add, list, and modify modules to `secmod.db`.

TABLE 3-5 TLSv1/SSL Tools

Tool	Description
`certutil` 2.0	Manages certificate and key databases (`cert7.db` and `key3.db`).
`dbck` 1.0	Analyzes and repairs certificate databases.
`modutil` 1.1	Manages the database of PKCS#11 modules (`secmod.db`). The PKCS#11 modules refer to hardware encryption tokens like SSL accelerator cards or secure key storage mechanisms. Adds modules and modifies the properties of existing modules (such as whether a module is the default provider of some crypto service).
`pk12util` 1.0	Imports and exports keys and certificates between the cert/key databases and files in PKCS#12 format.
`ssltap` 3.2	Performs proxy requests for an SSL server and for contents of the messages exchanged between the client and server. The `ssltap` tool does not decrypt data, but it shows things like the type of SSL message (`clientHello`, `serverHello`, and so forth) and connection data (protocol version, cipher suite, and so forth). This tool is very useful for debugging.

Note – The Sun Crypto Accelerator 1000 card is the only PKCS#11 module that is officially supported in the Sun ONE Directory Server 5.2 software.

TLSv1/SSL Configuration Overview

Before implementing the TLSv1/SSL functionality, you need to be aware of the attributes and attribute values that are or may be required by the Sun ONE Directory Server 5.2 software for the following attributes:

- Certificate name
- Supported cipher suites
- Cryptographic token
- Optionally, secure port number

When using the Sun ONE Directory Server software, you also need to be aware of the following configuration entries:

- dn: cn=config

- dn: cn=encryption, cn=config

In the cn=config entry, pay particular attention to the nsslapd-security and nsslapd-secureport attributes. The nsslapd-security attribute enables the use of the security features (TLSv1/SSL and attribute encryption) in the Sun ONE Directory Server 5.2 software. If you require secure connections, or the use of the attribute encryption feature, this attribute must be set to on. With the nsslapd-secureport, you must select the TCP/IP port number that will be used for TLSv1/SSL communications. The default TCP/IP port number is 636, and is only used if the server has been configured with a private key and a certificate; otherwise the server does not listen on this port.

In the cn=encryption, cn=config entry, there are a number of attributes and attribute values to deal with such as specifying the support for a particular SSL version. The nsSSL2 attribute supports SSLv2, while the nsSSL3 attribute supports SSLv3. Both of these attributes can be set to on or off.

The nsSSLSessionTimeout specifies the session lifetime in the session cache (in seconds). The Default is 0 (zero), which results in the following:

- SSLv2 =100 sec

- SSLv3 =24 h

The nsSSLClientAuth attribute has the following values associated with a TLSv1/SSL connection:

- Off – no client authentication

- Allowed – request certificate, no error if no client certificate received

- Required – request certificate, error if no client certificate received

- Default – allowed

Next is the nsSSLServerAuth attribute, which stipulates the action that the TLSv1/SSL client should take on the server certificate sent by the TLSv1/SSL server in a TLSv1/SSL connection. The points of interest are:

- Weak – accept a server's certificate without checking the issuers CA

- Cert – accept server's certificate if the issuer CA is trusted

- cncheck – accept the server's certificate if:

  - The issuer CA is trusted

  - The certificate's cn matches the server's DNS host name

- Default – cert

The following is an example of the `cn=encryption,cn=config` entry.

```
# Example of using ldapsearch to show the cn=encryption,cn=config
# entry.
$./ldapsearch -h directoryserver_hostname -p ldap_port -b "cn=
encryption,cn=config" "(objectclass=*)"

#
# Should return
#

cn=encryption,cn=config
objectClass=top
objectClass=nsEncryptionConfig
cn=encryption
nsSSLSessionTimeout=0
nsSSLClientAuth=allowed
nsSSLServerAuth=cert
nsSSL2=off
nsSSL3=off
```

The `nsSSL3Ciphers` is a multi-valued attribute that specifies a set of encryption ciphers that the Sun ONE Directory Server 5.2 software will use during TLSv1/SSL communications. The following values are to be noted as interest:

- `enable/disable` – to enable and disable cipher suites
- `+all` – enable all cipher suites but `rsa_null_md5`
- `-all` – disable all cipher suites
- `cipher_suite` – enable or disable a cipher suite. Use the following syntax:
  `+cipher_suite1,-cipher_suite2,...`
- `Default` – all but `rsa_null_md5` enabled

The `nsKeyfile` attribute provides the following:

- Key database path relative to the SERVER_ROOT
- Key database usually in the alias directory (`alias/slapd-`*instancename*`-key3.db`)

The `nsCertfile` attribute provides the following:

- Certificate database path relative to the directory server installation directory (`/var/Sun/mps` by default)
- Certificate database usually in the alias directory (`alias/slapd-`*instancename*`-cert7.db`)

The nsSSLToken specifies where the certificate will be stored. In the vast majority of installations, this will be internal (software), which means that the certificate will be contained in the *cert7.db and *key3.db database files. However, it can be different if the certificate is stored elsewhere (it will be something like username@realm if you are using the Sun™ Crypto Accelerator 1000). The nsSSLToken attribute can have the following values:

- Token for the cryptograhic operations: internal / external
- Default: internal (software)

The nsSSLPersonalityssl attribute specifies the nickname of the certificate that is used as the TLSv1/SSL certificate for the directory server. It is generally something like server-cert. The nsSSLPersonalityssl attribute has the following values:

- Certificate name
- If external, token certname:tokenname - Even with external tokens, the format is still just the nickname of the certificate. This is true at least with the SCA 1000 card, which is the only external token supported in the 5.2 directory server. However, the nsSSLToken may be different for external tokens.

The nsSSLActivation attribute indicates whether the associated cipher family should be considered enabled for use. Given that there will generally only be a single cipher family (RSA), then it should be on if you want to use TLSv1/SSL in the directory server. Finally, the nsSSLActivation has the following values:

- on (the default)
- off

Now that we have covered the essential attributes and their values, we can now take a look at how we can now enable TLSv1/SSL in the Sun ONE Directory Server 5.2 software

Enabling TLSv1/SSL in the Sun ONE Directory Server 5.2 Software

This section describes the process of creating a certificate database, obtaining and installing a certificate for use with your Sun ONE Directory Server 5.2 software, and configuring the Sun ONE Directory Server 5.2 software to trust the certification authority's (CA) certificate. There are two methods you can use to perform these tasks. One method uses the Console, the other is through the command line. Both methods are covered in this chapter.

The following process is necessary before you can turn on TLSv1/SSL in the Sun ONE Directory Server software.

1. Obtain and install a certificate for your directory server, and configure the directory server to trust the certification authority's certificate. See "Obtaining and Installing Server Certificates" on page 113.

2. Turn on TLSv1/SSL in the Sun ONE Directory Server 5.2 software. See "Activating TLSv1/SSL in the Sun ONE Directory Server 5.2 Software" on page 126.

3. (Optional) Ensure that each user of the directory server obtains and installs a personal certificate for all clients that will authenticate using TLSv1/SSL. This procedure is not covered in this book.

Note – LDAPS implicitly requires you to have a secure port to listen to. With the Start TLS operation, this is no longer a requirement.

Obtaining and Installing Server Certificates

You must perform the following tasks to obtain and install server certificates.

- "Task 1: Generate a Certificate Request (Console)" on page 113
- "Task 2: Obtain the Certificate From a Certificate Authority (CA)" on page 118
- "Task 3: Install the Certificate" on page 121
- "Task 4: Trust the Certificate Authority" on page 123
- "Task 5: Confirm That Your New Certificates Are Installed" on page 124

These tasks use wizards where possible. You can accomplish the same objectives on the command line by performing the following procedure:

- "To Obtain and Install Server Certificates Using the Command-Line Interface" on page 124

For testing purposes, you can generate a self-signed certificate as described in:

- "To Generate a Self-Signed Certificate Request" on page 125

▼ Task 1: Generate a Certificate Request (Console)

1. **On the Sun ONE Directory Server Console, select the Tasks tab and click Manage Certificates.**

   If this is the first time that you've opened this window, you are asked to assign a password to protect the key db as shown in FIGURE 3-12. This password is required to start the directory server when TLSv1/SSL is enabled.

   The Manage Certificates window is displayed (FIGURE 3-13).

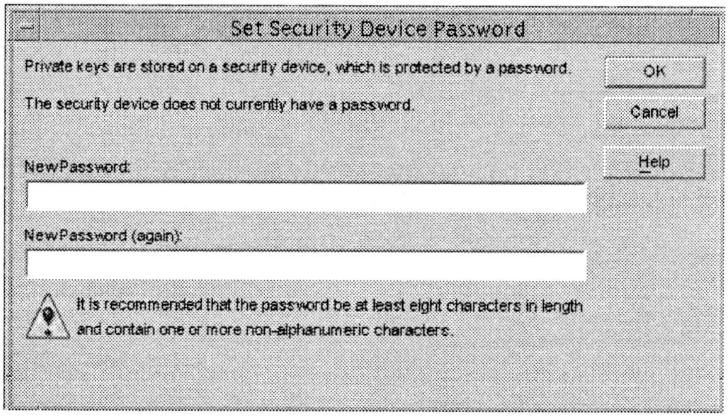

FIGURE 3-12 Console Security Device Password Window

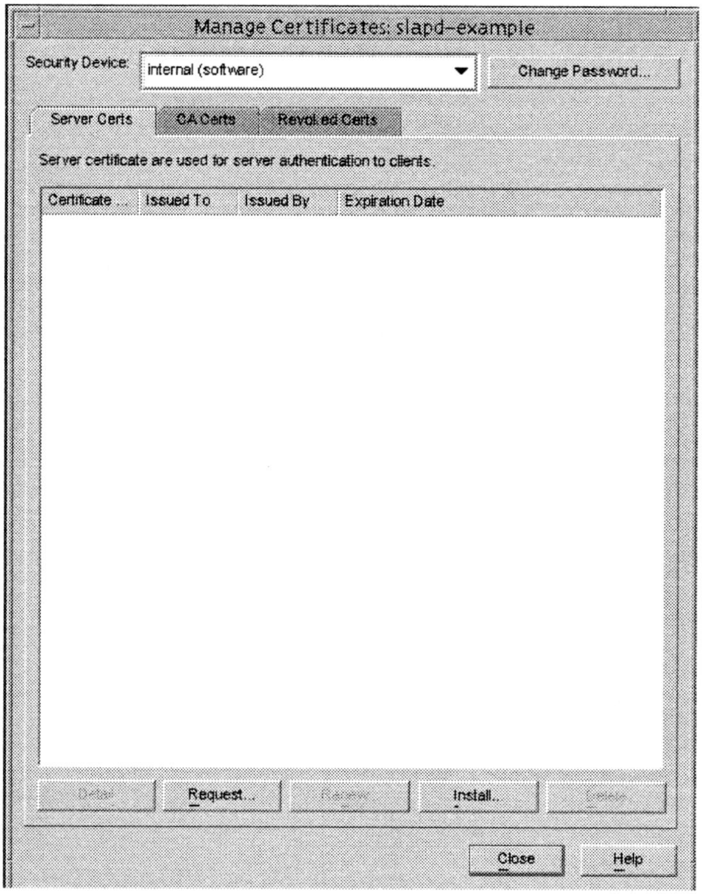

FIGURE 3-13 Manage Certificates Window

2. **Select the Server Certs tab, and click the Request button.**

The Certificate Request Wizard is displayed (FIGURE 3-14).

3. **Click Next.**

4. **Enter the Requestor Information in the text fields (FIGURE 3-14), then click Next.**

The following information is required:

- Server Name – Enter the fully qualified host name of the directory server as it is used in DNS lookups, for example, `blueprints.example.com`.

- Organization – Enter your organization name.

- Organizational Unit – Enter your organizational unit information.

- City/locality – Enter your city name.

- State/province – Enter the full name of your state or province (no abbreviations).

- Country/region – Select the two-character abbreviation for your country's name (ISO format). The country code for the United States is US, Great Britain is GB, Holland is NL, Singapore is SG, and so on.

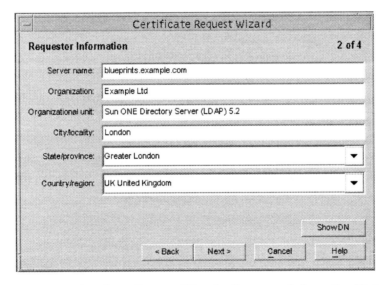

FIGURE 3-14 Certificate Request Wizard – Requestor Information Dialog Box

5. In the Token Password dialog box (FIGURE 3-15), enter the password that will be used to protect the private key, and click Next.

Note – The Next button is greyed out until you supply a password. When you click Next, the Request Submission dialog box is displayed.

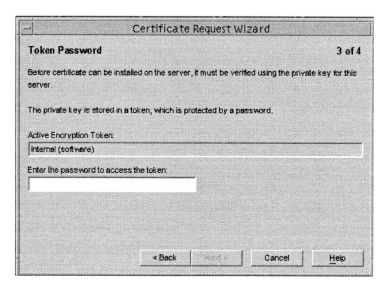

FIGURE 3-15 Certificate Request Wizard – Token Password Dialog Box

6. In the Request Submission dialog box (FIGURE 3-16), select Copy to Clipboard to copy the certificate request information that you will send to the Certificate Authority.

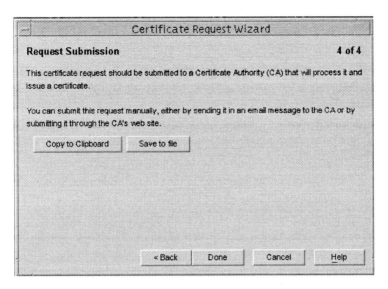

FIGURE 3-16 Certificate Request Wizard – Request Submission Dialog Box

Example of the PKCS #10 Request:

```
# Example PKCS #10 Request
-----BEGIN NEW CERTIFICATE REQUEST-----
MIIB3jCCAUcCAQAwgZ0xCzAJBgNVBAYTAkdCMRcwFQYDVQQIEw5HcmVhdGVyIExv
bmRvbjEPMA0GA1UEBxMGTG9uZG9uMRgwFgYDVQQKEw9CbHVlUHJpbnRzIEluYy4x
KDAmBgNVBAsTH1N1biBPTkUgRGlyZWN0b3J5IChMREFQKSBTZXJ2ZXIxIDAeBgNV
BAMTF3Npcm9lLnVrLmJsdWVwcmludHMuY29tMIGfMA0GCSqGSIb3DQEBAQUAA4GN
ADCBiQKBgQDFSPHLHPJaFXDIiLphKhaDOBB4QAOUr4oo8QIVB4gzsRVtPxeGUuy8
o+mGprCpgXpu0fNG5v8tgjiv4pzFL+r1UjJrTWQTLWMO6znGuAufR35B//nO2e6d
GQQvvYAPcxQFTOcfXcmJuoDyfR38DkGbVUdHFpa3ELADTnd2HGW/NQIDAQABoAAw
DQYJKoZIhvcNAQEEBQADgYEAeITbrpLpG0ODyJmLh1eQMCM1ZgD2A7v9I5q1eDWz
xiWZVMPXPzmMFXjA+YOnfBd/UGBCHF6cmNCoTugolsGhir3dTIjACsoStcNf8x1P
IfCkUZ0C6pQBOIbb1ochcojU8Al6jd2s26vhC+6xmEwf9Z3vfLcI/1mevQ8HCC8n
uBM=
-----END NEW CERTIFICATE REQUEST-----
```

You use this generated request to request a certificate from a certificate authority (the next task).

▼ Task 2: Obtain the Certificate From a Certificate Authority (CA)

In this task you have a couple of options:

- Send the previously generated certificate request to a certificate authority in email, or
- Go to a Certificate Authority web site and paste your request.

The outcome should be the same with either choice. That is, the CA will send you a certificate through e-mail. It is worth noting that the way to request a certificate from a CA varies depending on the CA.

The Sun ONE Certificate Manager software can be used to manage and sign digital certificates. This procedure uses the Sun ONE Certificate Manager as the CA. For small organizations, self-signed certificates are acceptable. However, for enterprise configurations, using an established CA is recommended.

Note – Sun ONE Certificate Manager version 4.7 is used in this procedure.

---

1. **Using a browser, go to the Sun ONE Certificate Manager secure URL.**

   This example uses `https://example.blueprints.com:443/`

2. **Select SSL Application Server under the Enrollment tab.**

3. **Copy the certificate request from the directory server, and paste it into the certificate manager system (in the TLSv1/SSL Server PKCS#10 request area, as shown in** FIGURE 3-17**):**

Note – It is advisable to have multiple Registration Authorities (RA) that you can select from, for example, BluePrints Inc. CA for production systems, and BluePrints Inc. TEST CA for development and test systems.

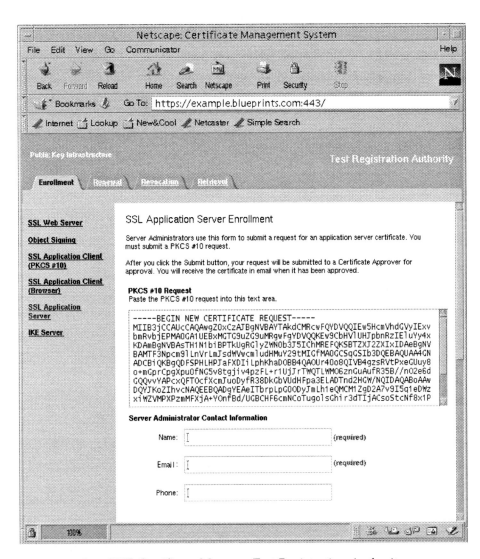

FIGURE 3-17 Sun ONE Certificate Manager Test Registration Authority

Note – Be sure to Include the "-----BEGIN CERTIFICATE-----" and "-----END CERTIFICATE-----" tags in the information pasted into the certificate install wizard.

4. **Fill out all the other information required by the Certificate Authority (CA) as described in** TABLE 3-6.

TABLE 3-6 Information Required by the CA

Name	Enter your name here
Email	Enter your email address.
Additional Comments	Enter your request details here. As an example, your request may be for enabling TLSv1/SSL on your own Enterprise Directory Service Infrastructure.
Revocation Password	Enter the database PIN for this system

The revocation password is needed if a certificate holder wants the certificate revoked, but does not have access to the private key in order to sign the revocation request.

5. **Click Submit at the bottom of the page.**

The Certificate Request Result screen appears (FIGURE 3-18), confirming that the request has been submitted. Note the request ID provided in the response message in the example below (You can use it later to retrieve the certificate, once the certificate has been issued).

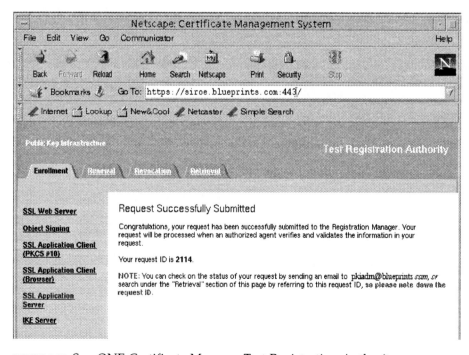

FIGURE 3-18 Sun ONE Certificate Manager Test Registration Authority

Next, your request gets added to the agent queue of the Certificate Manager for approval by that Certificate Manager's agent. If you have permissions to access that Certificate Manager's Agent interface, you can issue the certificate. Otherwise, you should wait for the other agent to approve the request you submitted and issue the certificate.

The Sun ONE Certificate Manager administrator must approve the request by going to the services URL. Example: `http://example.blueprints.com:8100`

Once you are in the Certificate Request Approval Page, you can perform the following to view that status of your request:

1. On the Certificate Management Retrieval Services menu, click Check Request Status.

2. Enter the request ID that was given to you when you submitted the initial request.

The following is an example of the information returned to you:

Request: 2114
Submitted on: 4/8/2003 12:38:59
Status: pending

▼ Task 3: Install the Certificate

This task is dependent on receiving an email from your CA with instructions on how to pick up your certificate (usually the CA provides you with a URL).

1. **Using a browser, go to the URL that was provided by the CA.**

2. **In the Sun ONE Directory Server Console, select the Tasks tab and click Manage Certificates.**

   The Manage Certificates window is displayed.

3. **Select the Server Certs tab, and click Install.**

   The Certificate Install Wizard is displayed.

4. **Select In the following encoded text block.**

5. **Copy and Paste the base-64 formatted certificate.**

   See FIGURE 3-19 for an example of entering the certificate into the Certificate Wizard.

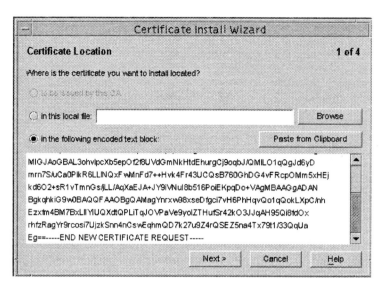

FIGURE 3-19 Certificate Install Wizard

6. **Check that the certificate information you have pasted is displayed correctly, and click Next.**

   The new TLSv1/SSL server certificate appears in the list of Server Certs in the Certificate Manager Window (FIGURE 3-20).

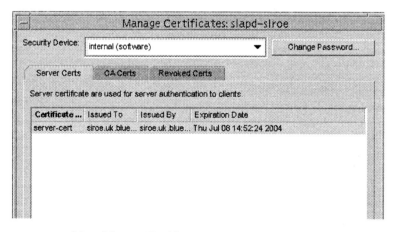

FIGURE 3-20 List of Server Certificates

▼ Task 4: Trust the Certificate Authority

Configuring the Sun ONE Directory Server 5.2 software to trust the certificate authority consists of obtaining your CA's certificate and installing it into your server's certificate database. Once you have the CA certificate, you can use the Certificate Install Wizard to configure the Sun ONE Directory Server software to trust the Certificate Authority.

1. **On the Sun ONE Directory Server 5.2 Console, select the Tasks tab and click Manage Certificates.**

   The Manage Certificates window is displayed.

2. **For each of the CA certs, go to the CA Certs tab, and click Install.**

   The Certificate Install Wizard is displayed.

3. **Locate the CA certificate (or CA certificate chain in its base-64 encoded format), and select Retrieval and then Import CA Certificate Chain.**

4. **Select Display Certificates in the CA Certificate Chain for Importing Individually into a Server and then click Submit.**

5. **Copy the text of the base 64 cert.**

   Copy the section between "-----BEGIN CERTIFICATE-----" and "-----END CERTIFICATE-----" and paste it into the window.

   Note – Repeat this install for each of the Certificates (sections between "-----BEGIN CERTIFICATE-----" and "-----END CERTIFICATE-----") present on the page.

   ---

6. **Check that the certificate information that is displayed is correct, and click Next.**

7. **Select both of the following as the purpose of trusting this Certificate Authority:**

   Accepting connections from clients (Client Authentication). The server checks that the client's certificate has been issued by a trusted Certificate Authority.

   Accepting connections to other servers (Server Authentication). The server checks that the directory to which it is making a connection (for example, for replication updates) has a certificate that has been issued by a trusted Certificate Authority.

8. **Click Done to dismiss the wizard.**

   Once you have installed your certificate and trusted the CA's certificate, you are ready to activate TLSv1/SSL. However, before proceeding, you should first make sure that the certificates have been installed correctly.

▼ Task 5: Confirm That Your New Certificates Are Installed

1. **On the Sun ONE Directory Server Console, select the Tasks tab and click Manage Certificates.**

   The Manage Certificates window is displayed.

2. **Select the Server Certs tab.**

   A list of all the installed certificates for the server are displayed.

3. **Scroll through the list. You should find the certificates that you have installed.**

   The Sun ONE Directory Server software is now ready for TLSv1/SSL activation.

Using the Command Line to Obtain and Install Server Certificates

The following steps are performed on the command line instead of through a GUI. The five steps listed here have the same results as all the tasks that use the GUI.

▼ To Obtain and Install Server Certificates Using the Command-Line Interface

1. **If you do not have** `certutil` **in you current PATH, you must either change directory to** *server-root*/`shared/bin` **or set the** `LD_LIBRARY_PATH` **shell variable to** *server-root*/`lib`.

2. **Run the** `certutil` **command to generate a Certificate Signing Request (CSR) as shown:**

   The `certutil` binary is located in *server-root*/`shared/bin`.

   ```
   $cd server-root/shared/bin
   $./certutil -R -s subject -a -d cert-dir -P "slapd-instancename-"
   ```

3. **Take this output and provide it to a third-party CA to be signed (just like you would with the request generated through the Sun ONE Directory Server Console).**

4. **To install the certificate once it has been signed use the** `certutil` **command as shown:**

```
$cd server-root/shared/bin
$./certutil -A -n server-cert -t Pu,Pu,Pu -a -i certfile -D cert-dir -P
"slapd-instancename-"
```

5. **Import the CA certificate withe the** `certutil` **command:**

```
$cd server-root/shared/bin
$./certutil -A -n ca-cert -t CT,CT,CT -a -i ca_certfile -D cert-dir -P
"slapd-instancename-"
```

▼ To Generate a Self-Signed Certificate Request

Use this procedure when you want to test TLSv1/SSL without using a real CA.

1. **If you do not have** `certutil` **in you current PATH, you must either change directory to** *server-root*/shared/bin **or set the** LD_LIBRARY_PATH **shell variable to** *server-root*/lib.

2. **Issue the** `certutil` **command as shown:**

```
$cd server-root/shared/bin
$ ./certutil -N -d <serveroot>/alias -P "slapd-example -"
```

Running the above command will request that a password is given to protect the key db.

Note – The password must be at least eight characters long, and must contain at least one non-alphabetic character.

You are prompted for a password to protect the private key store, which you should provide, and then it will create a new certificate database in the *server-root*/alias directory.

3. **Issue the following command:**

```
$cd server-root/shared/bin
$ ./certutil -S -n "server-cert" -s subject -t CTPu,CTPu,CTPu -x -v
12 -d <serveroot>/alias -P "slapd-example -" -5
```

The -t option specifies the trust attributes to modify in an existing certificate or to apply to a certificate when creating it or adding it to a database. In this example, we used CTPu, where C is the trusted CA to issue server certificates (SSL only), where T is the trusted CA to issue the client certificates to, where P is the trusted peer, and u is the certificate that can be used for authentication or signing. For more information on certutil, refer to:

http://www.mozilla.org/projects/security/pki/nss/tools/certutil.html

4. **Respond as prompted.**

You are asked to randomly enter a text until the progress meter is full, then asked for the password for the private key store (the one you just used above). You receive a list of options for certificate extensions. Enter a 1 to indicate that it is an SSL server, followed by a 9 to indicate that there are no more extensions. Say y to indicate that it is a critical extension.

After completing the above successfully, you can use the certificate in this database for your directory server. It is self-signed, and nothing will trust it by default, so you must use that newly-created database as the trust store as well.

The following databases are also created:

- slapd-example-cert7.db
- slapd-example-key3.db

Activating TLSv1/SSL in the Sun ONE Directory Server 5.2 Software

Before you can activate TLSv1/SSL, you must create a certificate database, obtain and install a server certificate, and trust the CA's certificate as described in "Obtaining and Installing Server Certificates" on page 113.

Once those tasks are complete, you can then enable the TLSv1/SSL capabilities of the Sun ONE Directory Server software. This process is simple, but involves a few tasks. The first task is to configure the directory server to use TLSv1/SSL.

▼ To Configure the Directory Server to Use TLSv1/SSL

1. **Select the Configuration tab from the Sun ONE Directory Server Console** (FIGURE 3-21).

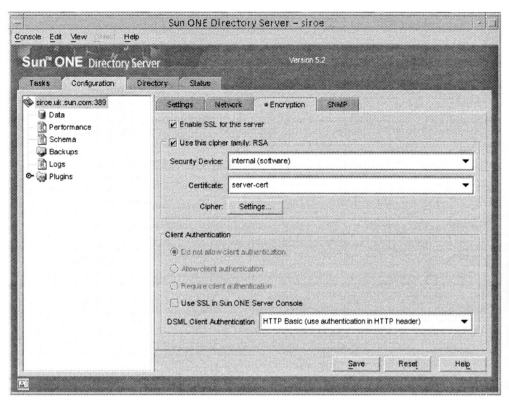

FIGURE 3-21 Encryption Tab in the Configuration Window in the Sun ONE Directory Console

2. **Select the Encryption tab from the right pane, and choose:**

   ■ Security Device (token)
   ■ Certificate

3. **Choose Cipher family preferences by clicking the corresponding check box and clicking on the Settings button next to "Cipher:".**

   FIGURE 3-22 is an example of the Cipher Preferences for the Sun ONE Directory Server 5.2 software.

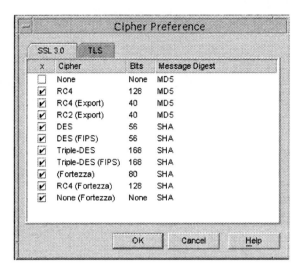

FIGURE 3-22 Cipher Preference Panel

4. **Set the client authentication policy.**

5. **Check Enable SSL for this server.**

6. **Select the server certificate by name.**

7. **(Optional) Choose to connect the Sun ONE Server Console to Directory Server over TLSv1/SSL.**

   It is strongly recommended that you do not select Use SSL in Sun ONE Server Console while initially enabling SSL in the server. If you do this and there is a problem with the way that TLSv1/SSL has been configured, it will not be possible to administer the server through the console without manually editing information under o=NetscapeRoot. If you want to administer the directory server through the admin console using TLSv1/SSL, then you should enable that after you have confirmed that TLSv1/SSL has been properly configured.

8. **(Optional) Configure and set the Secure Port for the Sun ONE Directory Server software.**

   a. **Go to the Configuration➤Network Tab as shown in** FIGURE 3-23.

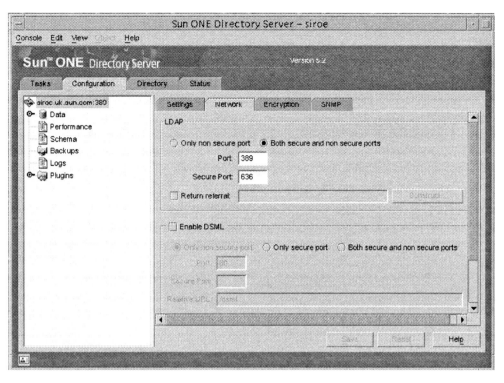

FIGURE 3-23 Network Tab in the Sun ONE Directory Console

b. Specify in the bottom of this pane whether you wish to disable, allow, or require client authentication.

In most cases, the default of Allow client authentication is acceptable.

Note – It is possible to require client authentication for TLSv1/SSL-based connections and still be able to use the admin console, as long as the admin console is not communicating with the directory server over TLSv1/SSL. Therefore, if you want to require client authentication, one possibility is to set `nsslapd-listenhost` to `127.0.0.1` so that it only listens for non-secure connections on the loopback interface, and run the admin console from the directory server machine itself, connecting over LDAP rather than LDAPS.

---

9. Click Save.

After clicking Save, the Console shows a dialog box telling you changes do not take affect until the server is restarted. You must use the command line for this, because the command line provides a means of entering a password.

10. Stop and restart the directory server.

Example:

```
# directoryserver_install_dir/slapd-instancename/stop-slapd
# directoryserver_install_dir/slapd-instancename/start-slapd
Enter PIN for Internal (Software) Token:
#
```

Note – If you configure the directory server to verify the client certificate against a certificate stored in the user's entry, then you can use either a binary or an ASCII representation of the certificate to add the data to the user's entry. Usually it's easier to use the ASCII version because it is easier to include in an LDIF file.

Additional Information about TLSv1/SSL in the Sun ONE Directory Server Software

By default, the Sun ONE Directory Server software uses port 636 for encrypted communication because this is the standard LDAPS port. If this port is already in use, or if you would like to use a different port, you can also specify that in the administration server. Under the Configuration tab, click on the Settings tab in the right pane instead of the Encryption tab. The port to use for LDAPS communications is specified in the text field labeled Encrypted port in the Network Settings section. Enter the correct value, and click the Save button to update the configuration.

Alternatively, you can specify the port to use for TLSv1/SSL communication with the secure-port directive (nsslapd-secureport) in the dse.ldif configuration file.

Although you can use the nsslapd-listenhost parameter in the dse.ldif configuration file to specify the IP address on which the directory server will listen, this applies only to unencrypted LDAP traffic. If you wish to restrict LDAPS communication to a single IP address, you can do so with the nsslapd-securelistenhost directive.

When all of the TLSv1/SSL-related configuration of the Sun ONE Directory Server software is complete, you must restart the server in order for the changes to take effect and cause the directory server to actually listen for LDAPS requests. This introduces a problem, however, because the directory server must be able to access the private key on startup, but this is stored in the certificate database key store, which is password-protected. You will be prompted for this password when the directory server starts, either on the command line (on UNIX systems) or in a dialog box (on Windows NT). On UNIX systems, the fact that the password will be requested from the command line means that you will not be able to use the

administration console to restart the directory server. It also means that the directory server will not automatically start when the machine boots on either UNIX or Windows NT systems. To remedy this, you can create a file that contains the password so that you will not be prompted for the password when the server is restarted. This file should be stored in the `alias` directory under the directory server install root and should be called
`slapd-`*instancename*`-pin.txt`, where *instancename* is the name of the directory server instance for which you have installed the certificate. You will also see files named `slapd-`*instancename*`-cert7.db` and `slapd-`*instancename*`-key3.db` in that directory, which are the certificate trust and key stores, respectively. The text that should be placed in your file is `Internal (Software) Token:`*password*, where *password* is the password for the certificate key store (there should not be any spaces on either side of the colon). Permissions on that file should be configured so that they are identical to the permissions of the certificate trust and key store, respectively.

At this point, you can restart the directory server and you should not be asked for a password. Use the command `netstat -an` to look at the network sockets that are in use on the machine. You should be able to see that the directory server is listening on both ports 389 and 636 (or whatever LDAP and LDAPS ports you have chosen). If you do not, then there is likely a problem with the TLSv1/SSL configuration, and you should check the directory server's error log for more information.

Using TLSv1/SSL in the Sun ONE Server Console

The Sun ONE Administration Server Console is actually a web server that uses the HTTP protocol to communicate with the administration console and LDAP to communicate with the configuration directory with the use of CGI. However, it doesn't have to be that way. The administration server can use HTTPS to communicate with the administration console and LDAPS to communicate with the configuration directory. In order to do the former, it needs a server certificate, and the latter requires that the certificate used by the configuration directory is trusted by the administration server. This section describes how to do each of these.

The process of requesting and installing certificates in the administration server is almost exactly the same as requesting and installing certificates in the directory server. The only difference is that you do it in the administration server configuration of the Administration Server console instead of in one of the directory server instances. Upon opening the Sun ONE Server Console for the Administration Server, click on the Configuration tab and then the Encryption tab (FIGURE 3-24). You will see what is essentially the same interface as the Encryption tab in the directory server console.

Note – In the Sun ONE Server Console (5.2) there are now options to either Disable Client Authentication, or Require Client Authentication.

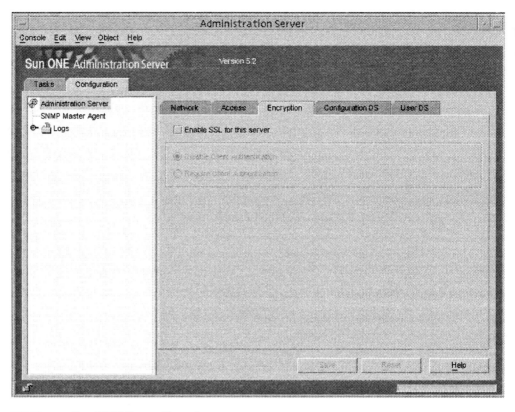

FIGURE 3-24 Sun ONE Server Console

To request and install a server certificate, and to install CA certificates and trusted certificate chains, use the certificate setup wizard exactly as you would use it to perform those functions if the certificates were for the directory server.

Similarly, the process of enabling TLSv1/SSL in the Sun ONE Administration Server Console is virtually identical to enabling TLSv1/SSL in the Sun ONE Directory Server software. Simply check the Enable SSL for this Server checkbox. At that point, it is necessary to restart the administration server. This should be done on the command line in UNIX systems because you will be prompted for the key store password. You cannot use a PIN file to automate this process as you can with the directory server, however a simple workaround exists. Because the `start-admin` program is simply a shell script that sets up the appropriate environment to invoke the `ns-httpd` executable to start the administration server, and because the TLSv1/SSL password is read from STDIN, you can pipe the password to the process when it is started.

Enabling TLSv1/SSL in the Sun ONE Administration Server Console

Unlike the directory server, which has the ability to listen for both LDAP and LDAPS requests at the same time, the administration server can only listen for HTTP or HTTPS traffic, but not both. Therefore, once TLSv1/SSL is enabled in the administration server, the console must use TLSv1/SSL to communicate with it. The change required to do this is simple, but is often overlooked, and might be a source of confusion when you can no longer log in to the administration console once the administration server is using TLSv1/SSL.

The change that needs to be made is in the Administration URL, which is typically `http://servername:port`. Once TLSv1/SSL is enabled for the administration server, the URL must change from `http` to `https`, as shown in FIGURE 3-25:

FIGURE 3-25 Using TLSv1/SSL in the Sun ONE Administration Server Console With an `https` URL

Understanding and Using TLSv1/SSL LDAP Client Architecture

This section describes the LDAP operations using both the `ldapsearch` and `ldapmodify` commands over TLSv1/SSL and the Secured LDAP Client implementation in the Solaris OE. Before processing, the following requirements must be meet. The following is only given as an outline with the details discussed later:

- Certificate database:
  - Install the server cert's issuer CA cert – trust for server authentication (trust flag: C)
- If cert-based client authentication is required:
  - Key database
  - Request and install user certificate in cert db

- Install user cert's issuer CA cert in server's cert db - trust for client authentication (trust flag: T)

Once a certificate has been installed in the directory server and TLSv1/SSL has been enabled, you should test this functionality to ensure that everything is working properly. The easiest and most convenient way to do this is by using the ldapsearch command-line utility. This utility is located in the shared/bin directory under the directory server root and has the ability to communicate with the directory server using TLSv1/SSL using either server or client authentication.

Note – This is not the Solaris 9 OE integrated version of the ldapsearch command-line tool.

First, it is necessary to understand the syntax for the ldapsearch utility without TLSv1/SSL enabled. The basic syntax for the ldapsearch command is as follows:

```
$./ldapsearch options query attributes-to-return
```

The options described in TABLE 3-7 are the most commonly used:.

TABLE 3-7 Common ldapsearch Options

Command-line Options	Comment
-h	The DNS host name or IP address of the directory server. If this parameter is not specified, the default localhost (127.0.0.1) is used.
-p	The port on which the directory server is listening. If this parameter is not specified, the default 389 is used.
-D	The DN to use to bind to the directory server. If this parameter is not specified, the search will be performed anonymously.
-w	The password to use for the bind DN. If a bind DN is specified, the password is required.
-b	The DN of the entry to use as the search base. This parameter is required.
-s	The search scope. It must be one of the following: • base • one • onelevel • sub • subtree If this parameter is not specified, then a default of subtree is used.

The easiest way to test connectivity to the directory server using ldapsearch is to retrieve the root DSE. This entry is available anonymously (so no bind credentials are required), and it is known to exist in the directory server no matter how the administrator has configured the server. The root DSE has a null DN, which you can specify in ldapsearch as "", and you must perform a base-level search to get any results. Assuming that the directory server is listening on 127.0.0.1:389, the correct syntax for the search is:

```
$./ldapsearch -h 127.0.0.1 -p 389 -b "" -s base "(objectclass=*)"
```

You will see the root DSE in LDIF format returned. This is returned using the unencrypted LDAP protocol, but confirms that the directory server is up and responding properly.

Look at the ldapsearch operational arguments for the ldapsearch command over TLSv1/SSL as shown in TABLE 3-8.

TABLE 3-8   Common Command-line Options to ldapsearch with TLSv1/SSL

Command-line Options	Comment
Simple Authentication:	
-p	Secure port
-Z	TLSv1/SSL encrypted connection
-P	cert-db-path
Certificate-based client authentication:	
-K	key-db-path
-W	key-db-pwd
-N	certificate-name
-3	cn check in server authentication

Note – Earlier versions of the directory server did not require the -K argument to ldapsearch if you were only using TLSv1/SSL server authentication. However, starting with version 5.1, and still applicable to version 5.2, it is necessary to provide the path to the private-key store even if client authentication is not going to be used. This is because of a change in the underlying LDAP SDK for C used to build tools like ldapsearch and ldapmodify.

To test the TLSv1/SSL capabilities of the Sun ONE Directory Server software, you must add a couple more parameters to the search request. The -Z parameter, as mentioned above, indicates that you are using TLSv1/SSL to make an LDAPS connection, and the -P *path-to-trust-db* parameter specifies the location of the certificate trust database. The easiest certificate trust database to use is the directory server's own certificate database, which is the slapd-*instancename*-cert7.db file in the *server-root*/alias directory, because we know that the directory server's own certificate is included in that trust database and is trusted by default.

Additionally, you must change the port from the *insecure* LDAP port to the TLSv1/SSL-enabled LDAPS port of the directory server. With the above changes, the following command should be able to retrieve the root DSE of the directory server using LDAPS, (assuming that the directory is listening for LDAPS requests on 127.0.0.1:636 and the instance name of the server is example).

```
$./ldapsearch -h 127.0.0.1 -p 636 -b "" -s base -Z
-P ../../alias/slapd-example-cert7.db "(objectclass=*)"
```

Note – The above command should all be on one line.

In the above example, you can see exactly the same results as in the previous search, but the search is done using LDAPS instead of LDAP. If so, then the directory server is responding properly to TLSv1/SSL requests using server authentication.

The ldapsearch utility can also be configured to make LDAPS requests using client authentication. This process is significantly more complex than server authentication and carries a few additional requirements. Those requirements include:

- The public and private keys of the client certificate must exist in the certificate database that is used.

- The client certificate must exist in the directory server in the usercertificate;binary attribute of the entry with which you are binding. This is only true if the certmap.conf file has been configured to verify the certificate (verifycert set to on).

- The certificate mapping mechanism must be used to uniquely map the certificate subject DN to an entry in the database. There are a number of ways of establishing this mapping if the DN of the user does not match the subject DN of the certificate (and it is not very common for a user certificate's subject DN to match the DN of the user's entry in the directory). But unless the subject of the client certificate exactly matches the DN of the directory entry containing the certificate, you must provide the -D parameter that contains the DN of the user entry as whom you wish to bind. The certmap.conf allows some flexibility here.

The mechanism for fulfilling these requirements is discussed in the next section of configuring an LDAP Client to use TLSv1/SSL. It must be noted, however, that if you want to use client authentication, it is recommended that you use a Netscape Communicator (any browser can be used that supports certificate and key databases) certificate database (this is shown in our example) rather than the directory server's certificate database. Once you have met those requirements, then you must specify the additional parameters, as shown in TABLE 3-8, for the ldapsearch command.

All of the examples in this section used the ldapsearch command-line utility to interact with the Sun ONE Directory Server software using LDAPS. The same functionality exists in the ldapmodify utility, which can be used to add, delete, or modify entries in the directory server. The use of the ldapmodify command is not discussed here, but all of theTLSv1/SSL related options are exactly the same for ldapmodify as for ldapsearch. Therefore, if you can use ldapsearch to search the directory using an TLSv1/SSL-encrypted connection, then you can use those same options with ldapmodify to modify the directory server data.

▼ To Generate a TLSv1/SSL Client Certificate

In this procedure showing an example of using client authentication, all of the users on a client that wish to use TLSv1/SSL when connecting to a Sun ONE directory server using LDAP client applications, must generate a TLSv1/SSL client certificate. To create a certificate we need to follow these steps listed below:

1. **Request a signed certificate from the CA using the Netscape browser.**

   This example in FIGURE 3-26 uses the Sun ONE Certificate Server URL to request a client certificate (`https://blueprints.example.com:443`):

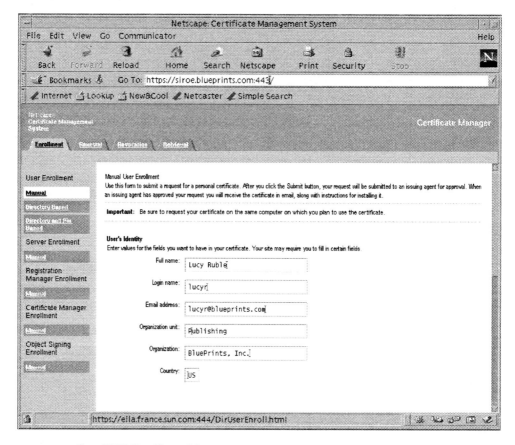

FIGURE 3-26 Sun ONE Certificate Manager

2. **Fill in all the necessary information.**

3. **Select the Submit button at the bottom of the request page.**

   The browser generates a keypair and sends the public part of this keypair to the Sun ONE Certificate Server in our example. The Sun ONE Certificate Server software then signs the key together with the additional information that you previously provided.

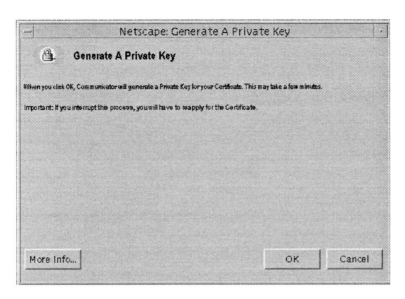

FIGURE 3-27 Key Generation Dialog Box

4. **Click OK (**FIGURE 3-27**).**

5. **Enter a password to protect your private key (**FIGURE 3-28**).**

FIGURE 3-28 Password Request Dialog Box

After you enter your password, the private key is generated. If you are using Netscape Communicator or the Mozilla browser, you should see `cert7.db`, `key3.db` and `secmod.db` under your browser's directory (for example, the `.netscape` or `.mozilla` directories). The Netscape browser uses the security database files in the `~/.netscape` directory. Therefore, it is already set up to query the Sun ONE directory server using TLSv1/SSL. The `secmod.db` is the file where Network Security Services (NSS) lists the different PCKS#11 modules available to you. Each module can have several slots, each slot being usually based on a token or security device.

For instance, the NSS library delivers an internal module by default, which consists of a couple of slots (you can see this by using `modutil` on the `secmod.db/secmodule.db`):

- Slot NSS Internal Cryptographic Services -> Token "NSS Generic Crypto Services"

- Slot NSS User Private Key and Certificate Services -> Token "NSS Certificate DB"

This file is also where you plug in your external modules, such as accelerator cards.

If you experience a message like the following:

```
Please enter the password of pin for the Communicator
Certificate DB
```

Then it assumes you have already provided a password the first time you accessed your browser's certificate/key databases. If you don't remember the password, there is nothing you can do, and you will have to generate a new cert/key database pair.

The Sun ONE Certificate software presents a request ID to you. Before you can import the certificate, the Certificate Server Administrator must approve your request. You can receive the request notification by email or verbally.

Example of a Certificate Request being sent by email:

```
<html>
<body>
<h2>An automatically generated notification from <i>ca</i></h2>
Your certificate request has been processed successfully.
<p>
SubjectDN= <b>E=lucy.ruble@example.com,CN=Lucy Ruble,UID=
lucyr,OU=Publishing,O=Example,C=US</b><br>
IssuerDN= <b>CN=Certificate Manager,O=Example,Inc,C=us</b><br>
notAfter= <b>09-Jan-04 9:28:59 PM</b><br>
notBefore= <b>10-Jan-03 9:28:59 PM</b><br>
Serial Number= <b>153</b><p>
<p>
To get your certificate, please follow this
<A HREF="https://cms.blueprints.com:444/displayBySerial?op=
displayBySerial&serialNumber=153">URL</A>

Please contact your admin if there is any problem.
</body>
</html>
```

Example of a Request that has been successfully submitted is shown in FIGURE 3-29.

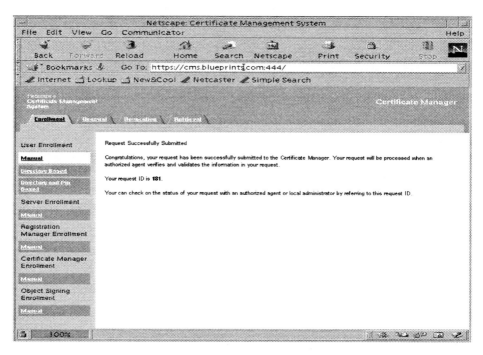

FIGURE 3-29 Example of a Successfully Submitted Request

The following examples show actual signed certificate components.

This is the certificate section:

```
# Example certificate
Certificate   0x099


 Certificate contents


    Certificate:
        Data:
            Version:   v3
            Serial Number: 0x99
          Signature Algorithm: MD5withRSA - 1.2.840.113549.1.1.4
            Issuer: CN=Certificate Manager,O=blueprints, C=us
            Validity:
                Not Before: Thursday, April 10, 2003 9:28:59 PM
                Not  After: Friday, April 9, 2004 9:28:59 PM
```

```
                    Subject: E=lucy.ruble@sun.com,CN=Lucy Ruble,UID=
lucyr,OU=Publishing,O=Example, Inc,C=US
                    Subject Public Key Info:
                        Algorithm: RSA - 1.2.840.113549.1.1.1
                        Public Key:
                        30:81:89:02:81:81:00:AE:1D:D5:23:20:AC:F7:BD:B8:
                        44:42:77:BE:23:AA:FD:32:46:41:CA:D1:F0:F2:24:94:
                        43:71:ED:63:22:84:DB:EC:68:2B:FF:32:D1:FC:F6:B4:
                        98:39:7C:B4:ED:B7:A7:12:89:EE:C2:DF:8D:71:D3:35:
                        07:56:0E:33:F0:F5:A6:EE:6B:DD:43:92:FD:90:31:8B:
                        0B:B9:DD:5A:8E:05:79:15:F4:21:87:FC:DC:81:73:49:
                        03:32:78:D2:AA:13:0F:32:D5:E4:C1:88:92:B7:B3:B5:
                        B6:CF:2B:AF:68:C8:A4:8C:D6:1B:02:74:81:45:93:D1:
                            8F:E8:A5:C9:59:ED:85:02:03:01:00:01
                    Extensions:
                    Identifier: Certificate Type - 2.16.840.1.113730.1.1
                        Critical: no
                        Certificate Usage:
                            SSL Client
                            Secure Email
                        Identifier: Key Type - 2.5.29.15
                        Critical: yes
                        Key Usage:
                            Digital Signature
                            Non Repudiation
                            Key Encipherment
                    Identifier: Authority Key Identifier - 2.5.29.35
                        Critical: no
                        Key Identifier:

DB:6B:27:D7:93:90:3B:68:BB:41:10:12:AB:36:D8:95:
                            02:60:F0:6C
            Signature:
                    Algorithm: MD5withRSA - 1.2.840.113549.1.1.4
                    Signature:
                        94:5B:04:2D:0B:82:A6:FD:C9:C0:49:95:B1:C1:8D:09:
                        67:7C:AA:E0:A1:ED:4D:CF:4A:2F:FF:66:87:B1:88:D0:
                        FA:B0:AA:EB:68:15:7F:92:87:52:FD:7E:A1:2B:0C:AA:
                        D6:FE:BE:05:B4:09:97:E9:6D:CC:27:7A:88:4D:87:09
```

The following is the certificate fingerprint section:

```
# Example certificate fingerprint

Certificate fingerprints


    MD2:    4F:22:38:50:E2:C4:A4:09:95:06:E0:E4:A0:1F:9B:3F
    MD5:    9E:8F:5F:ED:9F:FB:D2:14:2D:AF:74:E0:62:90:60:CE
    SHA1:
2D:8E:33:90:19:CE:18:7E:B3:9B:5C:4D:DC:AE:B5:05:3A:FD:F8:87
```

These are the details on how to install the certificate:

```
# Example of how to install the certificate

The following format can be used to install this certificate into
a Netscape server.

-----BEGIN CERTIFICATE-----
MIICVjCCAgCgAwIBAgICAJkwDQYJKoZIhvcNAQEEBQAwOTELMAkGA1UEBhMCdXMx
DDAKBgNVBAoTA3N1bjEcMBoGA1UEAxMTQ2VydGlmaWNhdGUgTWFuYWdlcjAeFw0w
MzA0MTAxNjU4NTlaFw0wNDA0MDkxNjU4NTlaMIGgMQswCQYDVQQGEwJVSzEeMBwG
A1UEChMVU3VuIE1pY3Jvc3lzdGVtcywgSW5jMRgwFgYDVQQLEw9TdW4gRW5naW5l
ZXJpbmcxFzAVBgoJkiaJk/IsZAEBEwdtaDEzNzQ5MRcwFQYDVQQDEw5NaWNoYWVs
IEhhaW5lczElMCMGCSqGSIb3DQEJARYWbWljaGFlbC5oYWluZXNAc3VuLmNvbTCB
nzANBgkqhkiG9w0BAQEFAAOBjQAwgYkCgYEArh3VIyCs9724REJ3viOq/TJGQcrR
8PIklENx7WMihNvsaCv/MtH89rSYOXy07benEonuwt+NcdM1B1YOM/D1pu5r3UOS
/ZAxiwu53VqOBXkV9CGH/NyBc0kDMnjSqhMPMtXkwYiSt7O1ts8rr2jIpIzWGwJ0
gUWT0Y/opclZ7YUCAwEAAaNGMEQwEQYJYIZIAYb4QgEBBAQDAgWgMA4GA1UdDwEB
/wQEAwIF4DAfBgNVHSMEGDAWgBTbayfXk5A7aLtBEBKrNtiVAmDwbDANBgkqhkiG
9w0BAQQFAANBAJRbBCOLgqb9ycBJlbHBjQlnfKrgoe1Nz0ov/2aHsYjQ+rCq62gV
f5KHUv1+oSsMqtb+vgW0CZfpbcwneohNhwk=
-----END CERTIFICATE-----
```

6. **Once you receive a signed certificate, import the signed certificate.**

   With the signed certificate, it is now possible to import the signed client certificate. To perform this, scroll down to the end of the page, and look for:

   ```
   Importing this certificate
   ```

   To import the certificate into your client, select the Import Your Certificate button.

7. **Enter the password for the Communicator Certificate Database** (FIGURE 3-30).

FIGURE 3-30 Password Dialog Box for the Communicator Certificate Database

Once you have successfully typed in the correct password, you will have a new private key stored in ~/.netscape/key3.db, and a new certificate stored in ~/.netscape/cert7.db.

You must make sure that the certificate of the CA that signed our TLSv1/SSL-client certificate is trusted.

8. **Verify and set up the appropriate trust relations.**

   a. **From the Netscape browsers menu select Communicator ➤ Tools ➤ Security Info.**

   b. **Under the Certificates, select Your certificate.**

   You should see the certificate you just imported from the Certificate Server.

   c. **Select the certificate and click the Verify button.**

   The browser shows you a dialog box (FIGURE 3-31) showing that the certificate is not trusted.

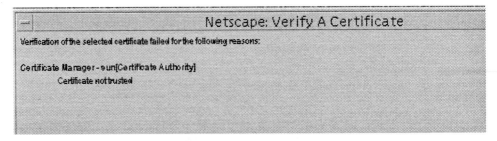

FIGURE 3-31 Netscape Verify a Certificate Dialog Box Showing Failed Verification

d. Go to the Security Info window, select Signers in the navigation frame and select the certificate signer from the list in the right frame.

This changes the certificate so that it is trusted.

The CA that signed the certificate must have the appropriate trust relations. To accomplish this task from the Netscape Browser.

e. Click the Edit button.

The Edit Certification Authority dialog box appears (FIGURE 3-32).

f. Modify the trust relation by checking each Accept option (FIGURE 3-32).

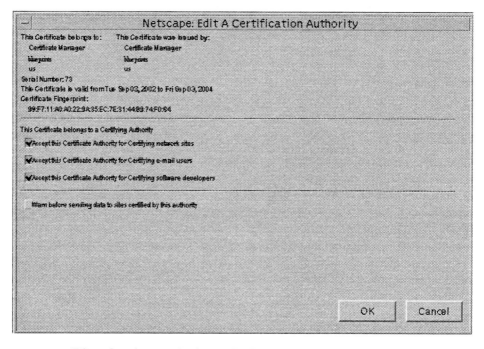

FIGURE 3-32 Edit a Certification Authority Dialog Box

g. Verify the client certificate again, as you did previously.

The browser shows that the certificate is now trusted (FIGURE 3-33).

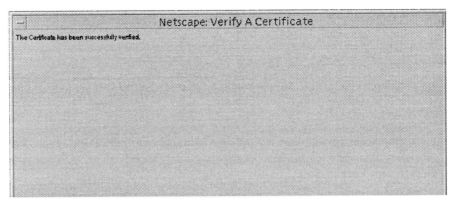

FIGURE 3-33 Verify a Certificate Dialog Box

Initializing the Secured LDAP Client

When you initially created your client certificate, you chose to use the manual option from the certificate management system (CMS). Remember, however, that by selecting this option, you end up having your client certificate in your browser's certificate/key database pair, so these are the databases that you have to use with the Secured LDAP client application.

To use the TLSv1/SSL security databases (cert7.db and key3.db), these databases must be placed in the directory defined by the clients certificatePath attribute. This is required because the Secured LDAP Client library (libsldap.so.1) uses the ldapssl_client_init API from libldap to initialize itself to connect to a secure LDAP server over TLsv1/SSL. This call requires the path to the database containing certificates and the database must be a cert7.db certificate database.

You can use the NS_LDAP_HOST_CERTPATH parameter in the Secured LDAP Client profile to specify the path. If you don't, the path by default is the /var/ldap directory. So copy the database files and give read access as shown in the following example:

```
# /usr/bin/cp /.netscape/cert7.db /var/ldap
# /usr/bin/cp /.netscape/key3.db /var/ldap
# /usr/bin/chmod 400 /var/ldap/cert7.db /var/ldap/key3.db
```

Note – The Netscape browser uses the security database files in the ~/.netscape directory. Therefore, it is already set up to query the Sun ONE Directory Server software using TLSv1/SSL.

The Solaris OE version of the `libldap` library and TLSv1/SSL require mutual authentication. Therefore, the servers IP address that the client uses must resolve to the same name that is contained in the servers certificate. Because the servers certificate uses its fully qualified domain name, `example.com` for example, if you are using the Secured LDAP client, the address must resolve to the name in the certificate.

Note – The LDAP name service cannot be used to resolve the address to the LDAP server. DNS can be used for host resolution. If you add the host to the `/etc/hosts` file, be sure to add it so that the host name resolves to the same name that is in the certificate.

First add the full host name and address of the server to the `/etc/hosts` file. Edit the `/etc/nsswitch.ldap` file to use `files` and then `LDAP` for hosts resolution. The modified `nsswitch.ldap` file should have an entry as follows:

```
hosts: files ldap
```

You must modify the `/etc/nsswitch.ldap` file because when you run the `ldapclient init` command, it is copied to the `/etc/nsswitch.conf` file.

The TLSv1/SSL support in the Secured LDAP Client is implemented as a library, and it is `libldap.so.5` that actually implements the client side of it. This works in the following way.

In the Secured LDAP client profile, the `authenticationMethods` that you can specify are:

- NONE
- SIMPLE
- SASL/DIGEST-MD5
- SASL/CRAM-MD5
- TLS:NONE
- TLS:SIMPLE
- TLS:SASL/CRAM-MD5
- TLS:SASL/DIGEST-MD5

Those that start with `TLS:` indicate that a TLSv1/SSL session is required. When the `libsldap` library sets up the connection to the Sun ONE Directory (LDAP) Server (or any directory server for that matter), it first calls a private interface in `libldap.so.5` to initialize the client application for TLSv1/SSL (open the certificate database), then calls the private interface again to initialize an LDAP session with the secure directory server. After this, everything is performed in the same way as a non-TLS session.

In the Secured LDAP Client, there is a list of encryption types with encryption strengths of TLSv1/SSl certificates that can be used by the Solaris OE Secured LDAP Client.

The Secured LDAP client informs the directory server which cipher suites it supports (in preferential order – see below). The directory server replies with the subset of mechanisms it supports (in preferential order). The policy is to allow all of these cipher suites, except those that are not enabled. The following cipher suites are present by default:

- `SSL 3.0:`
- `SSL_RSA_EXPORT_WITH_RC2_CBC_40_MD5`
- `SSL_RSA_WITH_RC4_128_MD5`
- `SSL_RSA_WITH_3DES_EDE_CBC_SHA`
- `TLS_RSA_EXPORT1024_WITH_RC4_56_SHA`
- `TLS_RSA_EXPORT1024_WITH_DES_CBC_SHA`
- `SSL_RSA_EXPORT_WITH_RC4_40_MD5`
- `SSL_RSA_FIPS_WITH_3DES_EDE_CBC_SHA`
- `SSL_RSA_FIPS_WITH_DES_CBC_SHA`
- `SSL_RSA_WITH_DES_CBC_SHA`

These may work (see Note):

- `SSL_FORTEZZA_DMS_WITH_NULL_SHA`
- `SSL_FORTEZZA_DMS_WITH_FORTEZZA_CBC_SHA`
- `SSL_FORTEZZA_DMS_WITH_RC4_128_SHA`

Note – The three Fortezza cases listed above require other things installed, such as cards, boards, and tokens. Sun does not currently support them at this time.

For SSL2:

- `SSL_CK_RC4_128_WITH_MD5`
- `SSL_CK_RC4_128_EXPORT40_WITH_MD5`
- `SSL_CK_RC2_128_CBC_WITH_MD5`
- `SSL_CK_RC2_128_CBC_EXPORT40_WITH_MD5`
- `SSL_CK_IDEA_128_CBC_WITH_MD5`
- `SSL_CK_DES_64_CBC_WITH_MD5`
- `SSL_CK_DES_192_EDE3_CBC_WITH_MD5`

▼ To Verify That TLSv1/SSL Is Working

This procedure verifies that TLSv1/SSL is working on the directory server and that the client profile is set up.

1. **Use the `ldapsearch` command as shown in the following examples.**

```
$ ./ldapsearch -h directoryserver_hostname -p ldap_port
-D "cn=Directory Manager" -w password
-b "cn=encryption,cn=config" cn=*
objectClass=top
objectClass=nsEncryptionConfig
cn=encryption
nsSSLSessionTimeout=0
nsSSLClientAuth=allowed
nsSSLServerAuth=cert
nsSSL2=off
nsSSL3=on
```

```
$ ./ldapsearch -h directoryserver_hostname -p ldap_port
-b "ou=profile,dc=example,dc=com" "cn=default"
cn=default,ou=profile,dc=example,dc=com
objectClass=top
objectClass=DUAConfigProfile
defaultServerList=blueprints.example.com
defaultSearchBase=dc=example,dc=com
authenticationMethod=tls:simple
followReferrals=FALSE
defaultSearchScope=one
searchTimeLimit=30
profileTTL=43200
cn=default
credentialLevel=proxy
bindTimeLimit=10
```

2. **Initialize the Secured LDAP client with the** `ldapclient init` **command using the name of the server instead of the address.**

Example:

```
$ ./ldapclient init -a proxydn=cn=proxyagent, ou=profile,dc=
example,dc=com -a proxypassword=proxy -a domainname=example.com
example.com
#
$ ldapclient list
NS_LDAP_FILE_VERSION= 2.0
NS_LDAP_BINDDN= cn=proxyagent,ou=profile,dc=example,dc=com
NS_LDAP_BINDPASSWD= {NS1}ecc423aad0
NS_LDAP_SERVERS= blueprints.example.com
NS_LDAP_SEARCH_BASEDN= dc=example,dc=com
NS_LDAP_AUTH= tls:simple
NS_LDAP_SEARCH_REF= FALSE
NS_LDAP_SEARCH_SCOPE= one
NS_LDAP_SEARCH_TIME= 30
NS_LDAP_PROFILE= default
NS_LDAP_CREDENTIAL_LEVEL= proxy
NS_LDAP_BIND_TIME= 10
```

3. **(Optional) Verify the encrypted traffic.**

It is good practice to verify the encrypted traffic. Out of the standard Solaris OE command-line tools, only the `ldaplist` and `ldapaddent` commands access the Sun ONE Directory (LDAP) server using TLSv1/SSL. The command-line tools (`ldapsearch`, `ldapmodify` and `ldapdelete`) that are provided with the Sun ONE Directory software distribution are enhanced to use TLSv1/SSL. These are located in the *path/directory-server-instance/*`shared/bin` directory.

Here is an example of verifying the encrypted traffic with TLSv1/ SSL using the `ldapsearch` command:

```
$ ./ldapsearch -h directoryserver_hostname -p ldap_port 636 -Z
-P /var/ldap/cert7.db -b "dc=example,dc=com" "cn=*"
```

To actually verify that the traffic is encrypted, use something like the Solaris 9 OE `/usr/sbin/snoop` command (see Appendix C, "Using `snoop` with LDAP). The more advanced protocol analyzers like Ethereal (available for free for a number of platforms, and as source code from `http://www.ethereal.com`) can even interpret the information that is captured so that it can be more easily understood. This is helpful with text-based protocols like HTTP because it provides formatting for the request. It is invaluable for binary protocols like LDAP because the task of decoding the information and figuring out exactly what is going on between the client and the server is much more difficult.

Note – Ethereal is available on the Solaris 8 and 9 OE Companion Software CDs. However, support for this utility is not provided by Sun.

Start TLS Overview

The TLS Protocol Version 1.0 is defined in RFC 2246. Before deciding to use the Start TLS functionality, it is worth taking the time to understand what TLS actually offers. The primary use of the TLS protocol with LDAP is to ensure connection confidentiality and integrity, and to optionally provide for authentication. Be aware that using the Start TLS operation on its own does not provide any additional security because the security element is accomplished through the use of TLS itself.

The level of security provided though the use of TLS is dependent directly on both the quality of the TLS implementation used and the style of usage of that implementation.

Note – The Start TLS extended operation in the Sun ONE Directory Server 5.2 software is available on all platforms. This was not the case with version 5.1, where NT is not supported.

The Start TLS operation is an extended operation defined by the LDAPv3 protocol that is initiated by a client starting the TLS protocol over an already established LDAP connection. What actually happens is that the client transmits an LDAP PDU (protocol data unit) containing the LDAPv3 `ExtendedRequest`, and specifying the OID for the Start TLS operation. The OID is:

`1.3.6.1.4.1.1466.20037`

This extended operation enables the ability of securing a connection that was not secure, based on a client's demand.

This extended operation is forwarded to the directory server in terms of an LDAP extended request that contains a specific OID as referenced above, identifying the Start TLS operation. It is up to the directory server to decide whether or not the request should be accepted or rejected. The server sends an extended LDAP PDU containing a Start TLS extended response back to the client with either a successful or a non-successful answer as to whether the directory server is willing and able to negotiate TLS. If the `ExtendedResponse` contains a result code indicating success, then the directory server is willing and able to negotiate TLS. If, on the other hand, the `ExtendedResponse` contains a result code other than success, this indicates that the directory server is unwilling or unable to negotiate TLS. If the Start TLS extended request is not successful, the result code will be one of:

- `operationsError` – TLS already established.
- `protocolError` – TLS is not supported or incorrect PDU structure.
- `referral` – The directory server does not support TLS.
- `unavailable` – There is a serious problem with TLS, or the directory server is down.

In the case that a successful response is returned, the directory server initializes TLSv1/SSL (initializes both the certificate and key databases, and sets the cipher policy), imports the current socket into a TLSv1/SSL-socket, and configures it in order to behave as a TLSv1/SSL server.

In the Sun ONE Directory Server 5.2 software, the Start TLS extended operation is implemented as an internal extended operation plug-in. The implementation itself is based on the IETF RFC 2830 "Lightweight Directory Access Protocol (v3): Extension for Transport Layer Security" (`ftp://ftp.rfc-editor.org/in-notes/rfc2830.txt`).

When the Sun ONE directory server receives a Start TLS extended operation request, it performs a series of checks as specified in the above document (such as checking whether there are other operations still pending on the connection, whether security is enabled on the directory server, and so on). If successful, it performs the TLSv1/SSL handshake and uses a secure connection.

As to the configuration of the Sun ONE directory server, no specific configuration has to be taken into account except for the Windows platforms, where you must add the `ds-start-tls-enabled: on` attribute to the `cn=config` entry. This is necessary because on Windows, the server handles connections differently depending on whether they are secured or non-secured; secured connections need to be handled using NSPR (as NSS is built upon NSPR), whereas non-secured ones benefit from the Windows I/O completion ports architecture, which turns out to be more efficient. So, if you want to convert a non-secured connection into a secured one (perform Start TLS operation), you must know beforehand so that the server can also handle non-secured connections using NSPR right from the start-up.

For Start TLS to work, the security must be enabled in the server, with all the necessary configuration (certificate and key databases, server certificate available, cipher preferences set, client authentication policy specified, and so forth).

Note – You don't need to have a dedicated secure port open. That is, in fact, one of the strong points of Start TLS— it allows you to have secure connections on the non-secure LDAP port.

In summary, the complexity of setting up TLSv1/ SSL is mainly on the Sun ONE directory server-side, and is categorized in the following main points:

1. Find a CA. You can use an existing one, or you will have to set up something like the Sun ONE/iPlanet™ Certificate Server.

2. The Sun ONE Directory (LDAP) server has to get a server certificate from the CA, and has to activate TLSv1/SSL afterwards.

3. The Secured LDAP Client has to get a CA certificate from the same CA.

4. You must copy $HOME/cert7.db and $HOME/key3.db to /var/ldap. The path /var/ldap can be overwritten by setting up certificatepath with ldapclient -a certificatepath *path*

Note – Currently the Secured LDAP does not use Start TLS.

---

5. If you want to test an LDAP client authentication, the server has to get a CA certificate and the client has to get a client certificate from the same CA. But it's not required by the Secured LDAP Client.

Enhanced Solaris OE PAM Features

The Pluggable Authentication Module (PAM) feature is an integral part of the authentication mechanism for the Solaris 9 OE. PAM provides you with the flexibility to choose any authentication service available on a system to perform end-user authentication. Other PAM implementations are Linux-PAM and OpenPAM.

By using PAM, applications can perform authentication regardless of what authentication method is defined for a given client.

PAM enables you to deploy the appropriate authentication mechanism for each service throughout the network. You can also select one or multiple authentication technologies without modifying applications or utilities. PAM insulates application developers from evolutionary improvements to authentication technologies, while at the same time, allows deployed applications to use those improvements.

PAM employs run-time pluggable modules to provide authentication for system entry services. PAM offers a number of benefits, including:

■ Offers flexible configuration policy by enabling each application or service to use its own authentication policy. PAM provides the ability for you to choose a default authentication mechanism. By using the PAM mechanism to require multiple passwords, protection is enhanced on high-security systems. For example, you might want users to be authenticated by Kerberos, and to bind to a directory server using SASL/DIGEST-MD5.

- Provides ease-of-use for end users. Password usage is easier using PAM. If users have the same passwords for different mechanisms, they do not need to retype the password. Configured and implemented properly, PAM offers a way to prompt the user for passwords for multiple authentication methods without having the user enter multiple commands. For example, a site may require certificate-based password authentication for `telnet` access, while allowing console login sessions with just a UNIX password.

- Enhances security and provides ease-of-use of the Solaris 9 OE in an extensible way. The security mechanisms accessible through PAM are implemented as dynamically loadable, shared software modules that are installed by system administrators in a manner that is transparent to applications. By increasing overall security, users enjoy greater service levels and lower cost of ownership.

Traditional Solaris OE Authentication and PAM

Traditional Solaris OE authentication is based on the method developed for early UNIX implementations. This method employs a one-way encryption hashing algorithm called `crypt(3c)`. The encrypted password is stored either in a file or in a Solaris OE naming service, from which it is retrieved during the user login process. The traditional UNIX method of the Solaris OE authentication, using `crypt`, is very popular and has been enhanced to use an LDAP directory as its data store.

Before proceeding with the details on authentication, you must have a good understanding of what `crypt` is. There is some confusion because of a naming conflict with an *application* named *crypt*. This is a standard tool that ships with the Solaris OE, and is a program for encrypting and decrypting the contents of a file. (This program is located in `/usr/bin/crypt`.)

However, when the term *crypt* is referred to in authentication, it is normally cited as `crypt(3c)` and refers to the standard UNIX password hashing algorithm (`crypt(3c)`), available to C programmers in the `libc.so` library.

A more sophisticated authentication method based on public key technology was introduced with the Network Information System (NIS+) naming service (now rebranded as the Sun OS™ 5.0 Network Information Service). The NIS+ naming service method does not replace `crypt(3c)`, but rather provides an additional security layer by introducing the concept of a network password. When users access network services through the secure remote procedure call (RPC) mechanism, the network password is required.

Originally developed by Sun Microsystems and adopted by the Open Software Foundation (OSF) for inclusion in Common Desktop Environment (CDE)/Motif, PAM provides a mechanism for dynamic system authentication and related services such as password, account, and session management. Realizing that new authentication models continue to be developed, Sun created the PAM architecture that allows additional methods to be added without disturbing existing ones. PAM was introduced in the Solaris 2.6 OE to overcome having to recode system entry services such as, login, passwd, dtlogin, telnet, and rlogin when a new authentication mechanism was introduced.

The PAM architecture and alternatives to traditional Solaris OE authentication are discussed in Appendix D, "Solaris OE 9 PAM Architecture."

UNIX Passwords

Passwords are created with the Solaris OE passwd command. This command prompts the user for a (new) password, which the user enters as a text string. In the Solaris OE, this text string is hashed—or one-way encrypted—using the crypt(3c) algorithm. The result is stored either in /etc/shadow, or in the passwd.byname and passwd.byuid NIS maps. If the NIS+ naming service is used, the results are stored in the Passwd and Cred table type. The crypt(3c) algorithm is provided with a random seed, known technically as a *salt string*, so that the result is different each time the passwd command is run, even if the same text string is used.

When a user logs in, the Solaris OE login program challenges the user to provide a password. This password is hashed in the same manner as the passwd command. If the output from this process matches the output that is stored in the password database, the user is authenticated.

FIGURE 3-34 illustrates how the UNIX password process works.

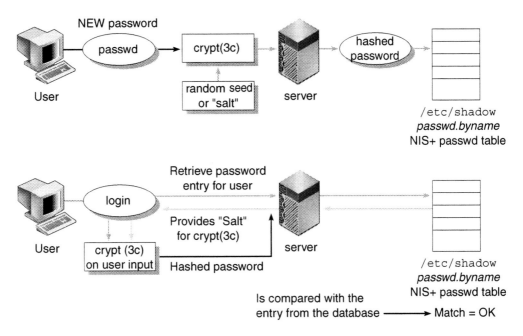

FIGURE 3-34 Login Program Text String Converting to a Hashed String

Benefits and Drawbacks of crypt(3c)

The major benefit of crypt(3c) is that it is easy to implement in a closed environment. Authentication takes place on the host that the user logs in to, so an authentication server is not required. In the case of local logins, the clear text passwords are never stored or sent over the network, so there is no reason to be concerned about eavesdroppers intercepting the password. However, when authenticating over a network using telnet or rlogin, passwords are sent in clear text.

Because crypt(3c) uses a one-way encryption algorithm, it is difficult to decrypt passwords stored on the server. Only the user knows what the actual password is. This means that there is no way to convert passwords stored in crypt to another format required by a different authentication method.

When the crypt(3c) function is called, it takes the first eight characters and returns its computation. This computation is then injected with a randomly generated value called the *salt*. In conventional crypt, the salt is stored as the first two characters. This salt value is then added, resulting in a sequence of 13 characters. The result is that the salt is actually an important part of the password string that is stored in the specific naming service.

As CPUs and storage capabilities increase, the `crypt(3c)` algorithm becomes vulnerable to attack. The `crypt(3c)` mechanism shipping with the Solaris 9 OE, along with PAM authentication, is exactly the same implementation that has been in the Solaris OE for many years now, and could one day change.

Introduction to Flexible `crypt(3c)`

The Solaris OE `crypt(3c)` mechanisms work well for authenticating local Solaris OE clients, but they are not the only methods used by applications and services running in the Solaris OE. This can make it difficult for system developers and system administrators, who must work with multiple password systems, and for users who must remember multiple passwords.

In the Solaris 9 12/02 OE, Sun updated the `crypt(3c)` API to allow different algorithms to be used for encrypting the users login password, this is known as *flexible crypt(3c)* for passwords.

The reason this feature was extended is because since the Solaris 2.6 OE, the Solaris OE has supported a `getpassphrase()` routine, which is identical to `getpass(3C)` routine, except it reads and returns a string of up to 256 characters in length. However, the `crypt(3c)` algorithm which it typically provides input to, is still limited to receiving only 8 ASCII characters.

The existing `crypt(3c)` API has been be preserved to provide applications that verify a user's password by calling `crypt(3c)` and using `strcmp(3c)` with the value returned by `getpwnam(3c)` so that they continue to work without any source code change or a recompile. This is obviously a very important aspect when adding any new or enhanced feature.

Functionally, a plug-in framework has been added to `crypt(3c)` to allow the changing of the underlying password hashing algorithm. Currently this ships with two new password hashing algorithms that use the Blowfish and MD5 hashes (for compatibility with BSD / Linux).

By default, the behavior of this new feature that provides extended `crypt(3c)` and adds `crypt_gensalt(3c)` is to use the old UNIX `crypt(3c)` on the password change, unless the user already has a new style password. This feature is turned on and used by changing the settings in the `/etc/security/policy.conf` file, which is the configuration file used for the security policy. For more information refer to `policy.conf(4)`.

The PAM interface in the Solaris 9 OE makes it easier for you to deploy different authentication technologies without modifying administrative commands such as `login`, `telnet`, and other administrative commands. Administrators are able to select one or multiple authentication technologies, without modifying applications or utilities. PAM can also be an integral part of a single sign-on system. The PAM APIs provide a flexible mechanism that increases overall system security. The PAM APIs are described in Appendix D, "Solaris OE 9 PAM Architecture."

Solaris 9 OE PAM Framework

The PAM framework enables new authentication technologies to be plugged in without the need to change commands such as login, dtlogin, rsh, su, ftp, and telnetd. PAM is also used to replace the UNIX login with other security mechanisms, such as Kerberos and LDAP authentication. Mechanisms for account, session, and password management can also be plugged in through this framework.

This framework consists of four specific components:

- PAM API presented to the application programs
- PAM framework responsible for implementing the API
- PAM service provider interface (SPI) implements the back-end functionality for the PAM API
- Configuration file pam.conf specifies which service providers are used for the various programs

PAM allows you to choose any combination of services to provide authentication. These include a flexible configuration policy that enables a per-application authentication policy, choice of a default authentication mechanism for non-specified applications, and multiple passwords on high security systems. Another valuable service is the ease of use for the end user that enables no retyping of user passwords if the passwords are the same, and optional parameters passed to the services.

With the introduction of the new PAM framework in the Solaris 9 OE, the LDAP service module for PAM has been extended to support the account service, which checks a user's password and account status by binding to the directory (LDAP) server. The directory server returns the password status to pam_ldap, which in turn maps the status to the PAM error codes. A user might be rejected when logging in with an expired password, or might see a warning message after logging in when the password is about to expire.

The pam_ldap module has also been updated to support password syntax checking, which is performed through the Sun™ Open Net Environment (Sun ONE) Directory Server 5.1 and greater (formerly known as the iPlanet™ Directory Server software) password policy engine. When changing the password (using the passwd command), the user might see error messages such as password too short, password in history, and so forth. In addition, it adds mechanisms for account lockout after too many failed attempts, forced password change after reset (if reset by root DN in the directory server), minimum password ages, and different password policies for different groups of users.

Note – The pam_ldap account management feature is not supported with iPlanet Directory Server software version 5.0.

PAM Types

The PAM framework currently provides four different types of service modules, which are implemented by dynamic loadable module types to provide authentication related services. These modules are categorized based on the function they perform:

- Authentication (auth) – Provides authentication for users and enables credentials to be set, refreshed, or destroyed.
- Account management (account) – Checks for password aging, account expiration, and access hour restrictions. Once the user is identified by the authentication modules, the account management modules determine whether the user can be given access.
- Session management (session) – Manages the opening and closing of a session. The modules can log activity, or clean up after the session is over. For example, the unix_session module updates the lastlog file.
- Password management (password) – Contains functionality that enables the user to change an authentication token (usually a password).

Stacking

PAM enables authentication by multiple methods through stacking. When a user is authenticated through PAM, multiple methods can be selected to fully identify the user. Depending on the configuration, the user can be prompted for passwords for each authentication method. This means that the user need not execute another command to be fully authenticated. The order in which the methods are used is determined through the configuration file, /etc/pam.conf.

Note – Stacking has the potential of increased security risk because the security of each mechanism could be subject to the least secure password method used in the stack.

PAM Operation

The PAM software consists of a library, several modules, and a configuration file. The PAM library, /usr/lib/libpam.so, provides the framework to load the appropriate modules and manage stacking. It provides a generic structure for all of the modules to plug into.

FIGURE 3-35 illustrates the PAM framework.

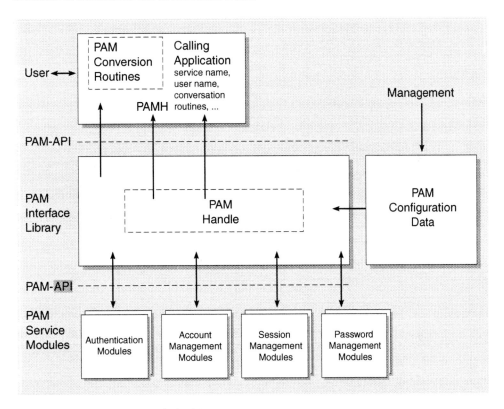

FIGURE 3-35 PAM Framework Architecture

FIGURE 3-36 illustrates the relationship between the applications, the library, and the modules. The login, passwd, and su applications use the PAM library to access the appropriate module. The pam.conf file defines which modules are used with each application. Responses from the modules are passed back through the library to the application.

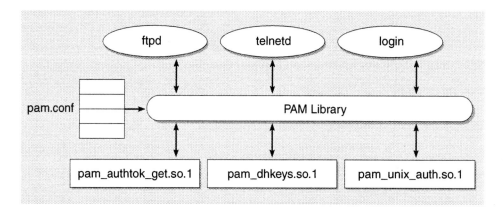

FIGURE 3-36 PAM and the Relationship Between Applications, Library, and Modules

Pluggable Authentication Service Modules

Each module provides the implementation of a specific mechanism. More than one module type (auth, account, session, or password) can be associated with each module, but each module needs to manage at least one module type. The following is a description of the modules that are part of the Solaris 9 OE.

- pam_authtok_get – Supports authentication and password management. This module takes care of obtaining (old or new) passwords from the user, so that other modules on the stack can concentrate on their task, and not worry about obtaining information from the user.

- pam_authtok_check – This module provides functionality to the password management stack. Specifically, it performs a number of checks on the construction of the newly entered password. See pam_authtok_check(5) man page for a description of the checks it performs.

- pam_authtok_store – Provides functionality to the PAM password management stack. When invoked with flags set to pam_update_authtok, this module updates the authentication token for the user specified by pam_user.

- pam_dhkeys – Supports authentication and password management. This module specifically deals with the establishment and modification of the Diffie-Hellman keys which are used, for example, for secure RPC calls (NIS+ and Secure NFS).

- pam_passwd_auth – Provides authentication functionality to the password service as implemented by passwd(1). It differs from the standard PAM authentication modules in its prompting behavior.

- pam_unix_account – Provides functionality to the PAM account management stack, as the PAM account management module for UNIX. The pam_acct_mgmt(3PAM) function retrieves password aging information from the repositories specified in nsswitch.conf(4) and verifies that the user's account and password have not expired.

- `pam_unix_auth` – Verifies the password that the user has entered against any password repository specified in the `nsswitch.conf` using normal UNIX `crypt(3c)` style password encryption, and can only be used for authentication.

- `pam_unix_session` – Provides functions to initiate and to terminate session as the session management PAM module for UNIX.

- `pam_ldap` – Implements the functions that provide functionality for the PAM authentication, account management, and password management stacks. (new in Solaris 9 12/02 OE). `pam_ldap` has also been updated in Solaris 9 OE 12/02 to support password syntax checking, which is done through the Sun ONE Directory Server password policy engine.

In addition to the above `pam_ldap` service module, a new `server_policy` option can be specified with the `pam_unix_auth`, `pam_unix_account`, `pam_passwd_auth`, and `pam_authtok.store` modules. This option instructs these modules to ignore a user if the user is only found in the directory server (LDAP) repository, and let the stacked below `pam_ldap` module to process the user according to the password policy set in the Sun ONE Directory Server software.

For security, these files must be owned by `root` and have their permissions set so that the files are *not* writable through `group` or `other` permissions. If the file is not owned by `root`, PAM will not load the module. This requirement on permissions and owner for the modules is not documented anywhere, and might change in future releases.

Note – In FIGURE 3-36, pam_unix is not layered entirely on the LDAP server. The pam_unix module sits on the Name Service Switch (NSS) layer and the NSS back ends that could be files, NIS, NIS+, or LDAP.

PAM Configuration File Update

The PAM configuration file, `/etc/pam.conf`, determines what authentication services are used and in what order. Edit this file to select the desired authentication mechanisms for each system entry application.

Configuration File Syntax

The PAM configuration file consists of entries with the following syntax:

service_name module_type control_flag module_path module_options

TABLE 3-9 explains the functions of the syntax.

TABLE 3-9   Configuration File Syntax

Syntax	Description
service_name	Name of the service (for example, `ftp`, `login`, `telnet`)
module_type	Module type for the service (`auth`, `account`, `session`, `password`)
control_flag	Determines the continuation or failure semantics for the module (see note below)
module_path	Pathname of the module
module_options	Specific options passed to the service modules

Comments can be added to the `pam.conf` file by starting the line with a pound sign (#). Use white space to delimit the fields.

Note – An entry in the PAM configuration file is ignored if one of the following conditions exists: the line has fewer than four fields, an invalid value is given for *module_type* or *control_flag*, or the named module is not found.

TABLE 3-10 summarizes PAM configurations.

TABLE 3-10   PAM Configurations

Service Name	Daemon or Command	Module Type
`cron`	`/usr/sbin/cron`	`account`
`dtlogin`	`/usr/dt/bin/dtlogin`	`auth, account, session`
`ftp`	`/usr/sbin/in.ftpd`	`auth, account, session`
`init`	`/usr/sbin/init`	`session`
`login`	`/usr/bin/login`	`auth, account, session, password`
`passwd`	`/usr/bin/passwd`	`auth, account, password`
`ppp`	`/usr/bin/pppd`	`auth, account, session`
`rexecd`	`/usr/sbin/in.rexecd`	`auth, account`
`rexd`	`/usr/sbin/rpc.rexd`	`account, session`
`rlogin`	`/usr/sbin/in.rlogind`	`auth, account, session, password`
`rsh`	`/usr/sbin/in.rshd`	`auth, account`

TABLE 3-10 PAM Configurations *(Continued)*

Service Name	Daemon or Command	Module Type
sac	/usr/lib/saf/sac	session
sshd	/usr/lib/ssh/sshd	auth, account, session, password
su	/usr/bin/su	auth, account
telnet	/usr/sbin/in.telnetd	auth, account, session, password
ttymon	/usr/lib/saf/ttymon	session
uucp	/usr/sbin/in.uucpd	auth, account

Control Flags

To determine continuation or failure behavior from a module during the authentication process, you must select one of four control flags for each entry. Successful or failed attempts are indicated through control flags. Even though these flags apply to all module types, the following explanation assumes that the flags are being used for authentication modules. The control flags are as follows:

required – This module must return success in order to have an overall successful result. If all of the modules are labeled as required, authentication through all modules must succeed for the user to be authenticated. If some of the modules fail, an error value from the first failed module is reported. If a failure occurs for a module flagged required, all modules in the stack are still tried but failure is returned. If none of the modules are flagged required, at least one of the entries for that service must succeed for the user to be authenticated.

requisite – This module must return success for additional authentication to occur. If a failure occurs for a module flagged requisite, an error is immediately returned to the application and no additional authentication is done. If the stack does not include prior modules labeled required that failed, the error from this module is returned. If a earlier module labeled required has failed, the error message from the required module is returned.

optional – If this module fails, the overall result can be successful if another module in this stack returns success. The optional flag should be used when one success in the stack is enough for a user to be authenticated. This flag should only be used if it is not important for this particular mechanism to succeed. If your users need to have permission associated with a specific mechanism to get their work done, you should not label it optional.

`sufficient` – If this module is successful, skip the remaining modules in the stack, even if they are labeled `required`. The `sufficient` flag indicates that one successful authentication is enough for the user to be granted access. More information about these flags is provided in the next section, which describes the default `/etc/pam.conf` file.

`binding` – This is a new control flag that has been added to the PAM framework in Solaris 9 12/02 OE. The control flag `binding` has a meaning of *terminate processing upon success, and report the failure if unsuccessful*. This option effectively provides a local account overriding remote (LDAP) account functionality.

Generic `pam.conf` File

The following is an example of a generic `pam.conf` file:

```
# PAM configuration
# Authentication management
#
login    auth requisite pam_authtok_get.so.1
login    auth sufficient pam_unix_auth.so.1
login    auth required pam_ldap.so.1
#
rlogin   auth sufficient pam_rhosts_auth.so.1
rlogin   auth required   pam_authtok_get.so.1
rlogin   auth sufficient pam_unix_auth.so.1
#
dtlogin auth required   pam_authtok_get.so.1
dtlogin auth required   pam_unix_auth.so.1
#
rsh      auth sufficient pam_rhosts_auth.so.1
rsh      auth required   pam_unix_auth.so.1
#
dtsession auth required pam_authtok_get.so.1
dtsession auth required pam_unix_auth.so.1
#
other    auth required   pam_authtok_get.so.1
other    auth required   pam_unix_auth.so.1
#
# Account management
#
login    account requisite        pam_roles.so.1
login    account required         pam_projects.so.1
login    account required         pam_unix_account.so.1
#
dtlogin account requisite        pam_roles.so.1
dtlogin account required         pam_projects.so.1
```

```
dtlogin account required        pam_unix_account.so.1
#
cron    account required        pam_projects.so.1
#
cron    account required        pam_unix_account.so.1
#
other   account requisite       pam_roles.so.1
other   account required        pam_projects.so.1
other   account required        pam_unix_account.so.1
# Session management
#
other   session required        pam_unix_session.so.1
#
# Password management
#
other   password requisite      pam_authtok_get.so.1
other   password requisite      pam_authtok_check.so.1
other   password sufficient     pam_authtok_store.so.1
other   password required       pam_ldap.so.1
```

This generic pam.conf file specifies the following behavior:

- When running login, authentication must succeed for the pam_authtok_get module and for either the pam_unix_auth or the pam_ldap module.

- For rlogin, authentication through the pam_authtok_get and pam_unix_auth modules must succeed if authentication through pam_rhost_auth fails.

- The sufficient control flag for rlogin's pam_rhost_auth module indicates that if the authentication performed by the pam_rhost_auth module is successful, the remainder of the stack is not executed, and a success value is returned.

- Most of the other commands requiring authentication require successful authentication through the pam_unix_auth module.

Note – With the above configuration, pam_unix is tried first, and if the userPassword attribute is readable, and the password is correct, then the pam_ldap module is not called. As a result, the pam_ldap password management is not used.

The other service name allows a default to be set for any other commands requiring authentication that are not included in the file. The other option makes it easier to administer the file because many commands that use the same module can be covered by only one entry. Also, the other service name, when used as a catchall, can ensure that each access is covered by one module. By convention, the `other` entry is included at the bottom of the section for each module type. The rest of the entries are in the file control account management, session management, and password management.

Normally, the entry for the `module_path` is root relative. If the file name entered for `module_path` does not begin with a slash (/), the path `/usr/lib/security/$ISA` is added to the file name, where `$ISA` is expanded by the framework to contain the instruction set architecture of the executing machine (refer to the `isainfo(1)` man page for additional information).

A full path name must be used for modules located in directories other than the default. The values for the `module_options` can be found in the man pages for the module (for example, `pam_unix_auth(5)`).

If `login` specifies authentication through both `pam_unix_auth` and `pam_ldap`, the user is prompted to enter a password for each module. Example:

```
# Authentication management
#
login auth required pam_authtok_get.so.1
login auth sufficient pam_unix_auth.so.1
login auth required pam_ldap.so.1
```

PAM and LDAP Password Management Extensions

It is important to provide a quick overview to clarify the difference between PAM Password Management Extensions and the new `pam_ldap` password management.

PAM Password Management Extensions provide the same functionality as the existing `pam_unix` module. The only difference is *how* the module is packaged. What used to be a single module is now split up into multiple components, known as *service modules*, each performing a separate function. This modular construction makes implementing custom password management policies easier.

The new `pam_ldap` password management facility includes two new account management features: *password aging* and *account expiration*. Because the directory server provides its own mechanism for account management, a conflict can occur if you want `pam_ldap` to implement a different password policy than what is set for the directory-wide policy. For example, the directory might force all users to change passwords after 60 days, but you might want some special user accounts to be able to keep their current password for a longer period of time.

To support this flexibility, the PAM framework has been enhanced by the addition of a new control flag called `binding`. The primary reason this *control* flag was introduced was the fact that prior to Solaris 9 12/02 OE, the PAM framework lacked sufficient control flags to provide functionality needed to return the appropriate failure semantics for service modules which should return immediately upon success, but report its error upon failure. In particular, `pam_ldap` depends on this change to correctly provide failure semantics for a mixture of local and server controlled accounts on the same machine. Effectively, this control flag allows you to override the password policy that the directory server enforces.

A `server_policy` option has been added to instruct `pam_unix` to allow users that only have LDAP accounts to be processed by the password policy set on the directory server. This option can be used to instruct the `pam_unix_account`, `pam_unix_auth`, and `pam_passwd_auth` service modules to ignore the user being authenticated and let the `pam_ldap` module stacked below them process the user according to the password policy established in the directory server. This effectively allows you to override the local `pam_unix` password policy.

Note – The `pam_authtok_store` module handles this option differently.

The `server_policy` option was introduced to solve a problem found when stacking the `pam_unix_account` and `pam_ldap` modules together. When used, it tells the module to rely on the policy specified on the LDAP server and not to apply a local policy.

Because the `pam_unix_account` receives incomplete information from the LDAP server, it might inadvertently decide that an active account has expired, or that an expired account is still active. Specifying `server_policy` in `/etc/pam.conf` tells `pam_unix_account` not to guess an account's status but to leave the decision to the LDAP server. The LDAP server keeps accurate current status of each account and can draw the correct conclusion about its expiration status.

Because this feature enables the `pam_ldap` module to fully support the account management, it is reasonable to use the following PAM configuration for account management.

```
other   account   requisite  pam_roles.so.1
other   account   required    pam_projects.so.1
other   account   binding pam_unix_account.so.1 server_policy
other   account   required    pam_ldap.so.1
```

Note – In this configuration, note the binding control flag for `pam_unix_account.so.1`.

This configuration specifies that the pam_unix_account should check the user's local account first. Because of the binding control flag, the stack succeeds or fails depending on the values returned by the pam_unix_account. If only the LDAP account exists for the user, the pam_unix_account does nothing and allows pam_ldap to determine the stack's success or failure.

Customer feedback indicated that the PAM functionality in the Solaris OE needed some enhancements. The requested changes included improving the mechanism used to validate password structures, adding the ability to change numbers of characters, total password length, and so forth.

In previous versions of the Solaris OE, this functionality was tightly coupled in a single monolithic module (pam_unix) and local extensions could not be incorporated in the module.

Only with a great deal of effort could you extend part of the operations performed by this module. Because of this, the pam_unix(5) functionality has been replaced with a new set of modular PAM service modules that are listed in this section. The functionality of pam_unix has been entirely replaced in the Solaris 9 OE. New PAM modules are now provided that replace a specific piece of pam_unix. This makes it easier to customize the PAM behavior by inserting or replacing individual modules. The Solaris 9 OE no longer uses pam_unix by default. During upgrades, any existing instances of pam_unix in pam.conf are replaced by the new modules.

In the Solaris 9 OE, the functionality provided by the old pam_unix module has been split over a number of small modules, each performing a well-defined task, that can be easily extended or replaced by modifying the pam.conf file.

These new modules are:

- pam_authtok_get(5)
- pam_authtok_check(5)
- pam_authtok_store(5)
- pam_unix_auth(5)
- pam_dhkeys(5)
- pam_unix_account(5)
- pam_unix_session(5)

You no longer have to replace the pam_authtok_check module to extend or replace the standard password strength checks. Just list the module in the /etc/pam.conf file right before, after, or instead of the pam_authtok_check file.

▼ To Add a PAM Module

1. **Determine the control flags and other options you want to use.**

2. **Become superuser.**

3. **Copy the new module to /usr/lib/security.**

> **Note –** If you have a 64-bit version of the module, you should place that version in `/usr/lib/security/sparcv9`.

4. **Set the permissions so that the module file is owned by** `root` **and the permissions are** `755`.

5. **Edit the PAM configuration file,** `/etc/pam.conf`, **to add this module to the appropriate services.**

▼ To Verify the Configuration

It is essential to do some testing before logging out, in case the configuration file is misconfigured.

1. **Test the modified service or the other configuration.**

2. **Run** `rlogin`, `su`, **and** `telnet` **(if these services have been changed).**

   If the service is a daemon spawned only once when the system is booted, it might be necessary to reboot the system before you can verify that the module has been added, however it might be possible to restart the daemon using the appropriate `/etc/init.d/` script.

▼ To Disable `.rhosts` Access With PAM From Remote Systems

A common use of the `.rhosts` file is to simplify remote logins between multiple accounts owned by the same user. For example, if you have multiple accounts on more than one system, you might need to perform specific tasks, and using the `.rhosts` file is ideal.

However, using the `.rhosts` file as an authentication mechanism is a weak form of security and should be avoided.

● **Remove the** `rlogin` **and** `rsh` (`pam_rhosts_auth.so.1`) **entries from the PAM configuration file.**

   This prevents reading the `~/.rhosts` files during an `rlogin` session, and therefore, prevents unauthenticated access to the local system from remote systems. All `rlogin` access requires a password, regardless of the presence or contents of any `~/.rhosts` or `/etc/hosts.equiv` files.

Note – To prevent other unauthenticated access to the ~/.rhosts file, remember to disable the rsh service. The best way to disable a service is to remove the service entry from /etc/inetd.conf. The remote shell server, rshd, and the remote login server, rlogind, only use PAM; they do not call the ruserok() function themselves.

PAM Error Reporting

Diagnostic messages generated by the PAM modules or the PAM framework are output using syslog(3c). They are logged to the facility that was specified at the time the application (login, telnet, sshd) called openlog(3c), so the exact location of these messages depends upon whether the application uses PAM. The facility indicates the application or system component generating the message. As an example, here are a few possible facility values:

- LOG_KERN – Messages generated by the kernel. These cannot be generated by any user processes.
- LOG_USER – Messages generated by random user processes. This is the default facility identifier if none is specified.
- LOG_MAIL – The mail system.

For example, login sends its messages to the LOG_AUTH facility, while rlogind sends its messages to the LOG_DAEMON facility. Other daemons might use a configurable facility (sshd, ftpd, and so forth) which can be set in the configuration file of the particular service.

Depending on the severity of the diagnostic message, the PAM module directs the message to one of the eight available log priorities.

Note – For additional details on the syslog() function and priorities, refer to the syslog(3c) and syslog.conf(4) man pages.

Debug messages are logged with:

```
syslog(LOG_DEBUG, "...")
```

Critical messages are logged with:

```
syslog(LOG_CRIT, "...")
```

For example, a general error message (LOG_ERR) from PAM, used by login, is directed to auth.crit and ends up in a log file as:

```
Jul 22 22:11:43 host login: [ID 887986 auth.error]
ACCOUNT:pam_sm_acct_mgmt: illegal option debuf
```

▼ To Initiate Diagnostics Reporting for PAM

1. **Back up the** syslog.conf **file before editing it.**

2. **Determine the** syslog **facility used by the application you want to receive diagnostic reports from.**

   The facility that we are going to use in this example is auth.

3. **Edit the** /etc/syslog.conf **to add a line describing where the message with the intended facility and priority will be logged.**

   Example of line added:

```
auth.debug /var/adm/authlog
```

   Note that these message levels are part of a hierarchy:

```
High -----------------------------------Low
EMERG ALERT CRIT ERR WARNING NOTICE INFO DEBUG
```

   Due to this hierarchical ordering, a syslog channel specified to log debug messages also logs messages at all higher levels (for example, logs messages with priority debug *and up*).

4. **Make sure that the log file specified in the previous step actually exists.**

   If it doesn't exist, create it now.

   Example:

```
# touch /var/adm/authlog
```

5. **Make** syslogd **re-read the configuration file by sending it a HUP signal:**

```
# pkill -HUP syslogd
```

▼ To Initiate PAM Error Reporting

The following example displays all alert messages on the console. Critical messages are mailed to `root`. Debug messages are added to `/var/log/pamlog`.

```
auth.alert /dev/console
auth.crit root
auth.debug /var/log/pamlog
```

Each line in the log file contains a timestamp, the name of the system that generated the message, and the message itself. Be aware that a large amount of information may be written to the `pamlog` file.

The log format was changed in the Solaris 8 OE and subsequent releases, and now includes a hash-value of the message generating string for example—`user %s not found`. It now contains the message facility and severity.

● **Add the `debug` flag to a PAM module to enable diagnostics reporting of that module.**

Example:

```
# PAM Module Debugging
#
login    auth requisite        pam_authtok_get.so.1
login    auth required         pam_dhkeys.so.1          debug
login    auth required         pam_unix_auth.so.1       debug
login    auth required         pam_dial_auth.so.1
```

This configuration example enables debugging information from `pam_dhkeys.so.1` and `pam_unix_auth.so.1`.

What gets logged might vary quite a bit, because there is no standard describing the information that needs to be output in response to this option. It is a good practice for module developers to recognize this `debug` flag and enable some form of debugging when the flag is specified in `/etc/pam.conf`.

PAM LDAP Module

The PAM LDAP module (`pam_ldap`) was introduced in the Solaris 8 OE for use in conjunction with `pam_unix` for authentication and password management with an LDAP server. This module was written to support stronger authentication methods such as CRAM-MD5, in addition to the other UNIX authentication capabilities provided by `pam_unix`.

Note – The pam_ldap module must be used in conjunction with the modules supporting the UNIX authentication, password and account management, because pam_ldap is designed to be stacked directly below these modules.

With the release of Solaris 9 12/02 OE, pam_ldap provides support for authentication, account management, and password management.

The pam_ldap module should be stacked directly below the pam_unix module in the configuration file /etc/pam.conf. If there are other modules that are designed to be stacked in this manner, they could be stacked *under* the pam_ldap module. This design must be followed in order for authentication and password management to work when pam_ldap is used. The following is a sample of /etc/pam.conf file with pam_ldap stacked under pam_unix:

```
# Authentication management for login service is stacked.
# If pam_unix succeeds, pam_ldap is not invoked.
login    auth sufficient /usr/lib/security/pam_unix.so.1
login    auth required /usr/lib/security/pam_ldap.so.1
# Password management
other    password sufficient /usr/lib/security/pam_unix.so.1
other    password required /usr/lib/security/pam_ldap.so.1
```

It is important to note that the control flag for pam_unix is sufficient. This flag means that if authentication through pam_unix succeeds, then pam_ldap is not invoked. Also, other service types, such as dtlogin, su, telnet, and so forth can substitute for login. See FIGURE 3-37.

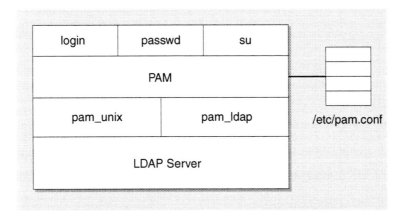

FIGURE 3-37 pam_ldap Structure

The options supported by pam_ldap are:

- debug – If this option is used with pam_ldap, debugging information is output to the syslog(3C) files.
- nowarn – This option turns off warning messages.

How PAM and LDAP Work

Before discussing the details of how PAM and LDAP work, it is important to provide a quick overview to distinguish between how the password is stored and how the authentication mechanism is used to authenticate to the LDAP server. The password can be stored in a variety of formats in the directory server, such as salted secure hash algorithm (SSHA), secure hash algorithm (SHA), CRYPT, and so forth.

The authentication mechanisms currently used and supported in the Solaris 8 OE LDAP Client, are NONE, SIMPLE, and CRAM-MD5 authentication. Simple authentication requires the client to pass a distinguished name (DN) and password to the server in clear text. Currently, the Sun ONE Directory Server 5.x software does not support the authentication mechanism CRAM-MD5, which sends only the digest over the wire. CRAM-MD5 is implemented as a Simple authentication and security layer (SASL) mechanism, and both the client and server must use it. What happens is the client request authentication is based on SASL/CRAM-MD5 and the server must support this to complete the authentication. In general, very few clients use CRAM-MD5, now that RFC 2829 mandates the use of DIGEST-MD5, which is intended to be an improvement over CRAM-MD5.

Note – DIGEST-MD5 as an authentication mechanism for LDAPv3 directory servers is mandated in RFC 2829. RFC 2831 provides information about DIGEST-MD5 as a SASL mechanism, but is not LDAP specific.

With the introduction of the Sun ONE Directory Server 5.2 software, support for SASL/DIGEST-MD5 has also been added as an authentication mechanism. This feature was initially introduced in the Sun ONE Directory Server 5.1 software release.

With SASL/DIGEST-MD5, a digest is created and sent across the wire to authenticate to the directory server. The directory server then compares the digest that was sent with the digest created by itself with the stored password and returns success if it matches. In this case, the password is *not* sent in clear text. To address the absence of a security model in the Solaris 8 OE LDAP Client, the Solaris 9 OE now incorporates the Sun ONE Directory Server 5.1 software and Solaris 9 OE Secured LDAP Client, addressing the security issues found in the LDAP Client.

To use SASL/DIGEST-MD5, the Sun ONE Directory Server software requires that the password is stored in the directory in the clear. In the Sun ONE Directory Server 5.2 software, you need to make sure that you enable the SASL mechanism that you wish to use. Also there is support for identity mapping which was covered previously. The identity mapping allows for quite a bit of flexibility. For the Sun ONE Directory Server 5.1 release, two forms are supported, which are dn: and u: as specified in the RFC. This has built-in rules to handle the identity mapping.

Note – With identity mapping, you must map to one, and only one, identity.

Note – In the current release of the Solaris 9 OE, the extended Start TLS operation is not supported.

Authentication With pam_unix

In authentication with pam_unix, depending on how the client is configured, the client retrieves the password that is stored in the server by making a call to the getspnam function. This function binds to the LDAP server with the proxy agent account (the reason the proxy passwd is sent across the wire in clear text). The proxy agent password is stored in the userPassword attribute in the directory server. This proxy agent account can reside anywhere in the directory server, but must contain the userPassword attribute.

Note that the ACIs of the proxy agent allow this account to have read access to all user passwords, which you may not want to do if you are using pam_ldap. ACIs are instructions that are stored in the directory server itself. Every entry can have a set of rules that define an ACI for that entry. An ACI appears as an attribute in the entry so it can be retrieved by using LDAP search, or it can be added, updated, or deleted with an LDAP modify operation.

An entry may have one ACI, many ACIs, or none. ACIs allow or deny permissions to entries. When the directory server processes an incoming request for that entry, the server uses the ACIs specific to that entry to determine whether or not the LDAP client has permission to perform the requested operation.

Note – LDAP stores data as entries. An entry has a distinguished name (DN) to uniquely identify it within the directory server

---

The encrypted password is sent to the client side and compared with the encrypted password supplied by the user at the password prompt. If there is a match, pam_unix returns success. The following tables illustrate the authentication mechanisms currently used.

TABLE 3-11 lists the PAM abbreviations used in this section.

TABLE 3-11   PAM Abbreviations

Abbreviation	Description
UP	User password
PP	Proxy agent password
NP	New password
NO*	Not applicable (at present)

TABLE 3-12 illustrates if the user password and proxy password are transmitted in the clear during PAM authentications.

TABLE 3-12   PAM Authentication

Authentication Mechanisms	pam_unix		pam_ldap	
SIMPLE	UP-No	PP-Yes	UP-Yes	PP-Yes
DIGEST-MD5	UP-NO*	PP-No	UP-No	PP-No
TLS: SIMPLE	UP-No	PP-No	UP-No	PP-No
TLS: DIGEST-MD5	UP-No	PP-No	UP-No	PP-No

Note – In TABLE 3-11 and TABLE 3-12 the reason for "NO*" as the value of the DIGEST-MD5 UP column is because the Sun ONE Directory Server version 5.1 software requires that passwords be stored in the server in clear text for DIGEST-MD5 to work.

For updating passwords in `pam_unix`, the same comparison as for authentication takes place (because the user has to bind as the `dn`); then the new password is encrypted and *not* passed over the wire in clear text (TABLE 3-13).

TABLE 3-13 PAM Update of Password

Authentication Mechanisms	pam_unix			pam_ldap		
SIMPLE	UP-No	PP-Yes	NP-No	UP-Yes	PP-Yes	NP-Yes
DIGEST-MD5	UP-NO*	PP-No	NP-NO*	UP-No	PP-No	NP-Yes
TLS: SIMPLE	UP-No	PP-No	NP-No	UP-No	PP-No	NP-No
TLS: DIGEST-MD5	UP-No	PP-No	NP-No	UP-No	PP-No	NP-No

The matrices are easier to understand when you distinguish between how the password is stored and how the authentication mechanism is used to authenticate to the LDAP server. The password can be stored in a variety of formats, such as SSHA, SHA, crypt, clear text, and so forth. The authentication mechanisms that are currently supported are NONE, SIMPLE, SASL/CRAM-MD5, SASL/DIGEST-MD5, TLS:NONE, TLS:SIMPLE, TLS:SASL/CRAM-MD5, and TLS:SASL/DIGEST-MD5.

`pam_ldap` *Authentication*

In authentication that uses `pam_ldap`, the user password is passed to the server in an `auth` structure in clear text because authentication is being attempted with the user `dn` and `password`. If Simple authentication is used, and the password matches, then `success` is returned. Using `pam_ldap` in the Solaris 9 OE Secured LDAP Client now provides SASL/DIGEST-MD5 authentication, privacy, and data integrity with SSL/TLS. If you require stronger authentication mechanisms such as DIGEST-MD5; then you must use `pam_ldap`. In addition, `pam_ldap` is designed to be extended for future authentication mechanisms that will be supported in future Solaris OE releases. One of the benefits of using `pam_ldap`, is that it does not require passwords to be stored in any specific format, so you can store passwords using SSHA, SHA, or CRYPT formats.

For additional information, see the `pam_ldap` man page for the correct way to stack the authentication management for login service, and password management modules in the `/etc/pam.conf` configuration file.

Note – CRAM-MD5 is supported by the Secured LDAP Client, but not by the Sun ONE Directory Server software. However, DIGEST-MD5 is supported by both.

Secured LDAP Client Backport to the Solaris 8 OE

Now that we have touched on the Solaris 9 OE Secured LDAP clients, which have the option to use TLSv1 and SASL/DIGEST-MD5 for authentication, we can discuss what has been done with the Solaris 8 OE LDAP clients. Initially as previously discussed, the Solaris 8 OE LDAP clients relied on clear text passwords or the less secure SASL/CRAM-MD5 for authentication. This is obviously not desirable for customers that wanted to deploy a secure naming service, and also maintain equal and matching functionality in both the Solaris 8 and 9 OE.

Note – The Sun ONE directory server does not support SASL/CRAM-MD5.

With this in mind, Sun backported the Secured LDAP Client found in the Solaris 9 OE to the Solaris 8 OE to provide TLSv1/ and SASL/DIGEST-MD5 support for the LDAP client. The following lists what functionality has been backported:

- The configuration of the directory server (LDAP) setup has been simplified with the use of idsconfig.
- A more robust security model that supports strong authentication and Transport Layer Security (TLS) encrypted sessions. A client's proxy credentials are no longer stored in a client s profile on the directory server.
- The ldapaddent command allows you to populate and dump data onto the server.
- Service search descriptors and attribute mapping
- New profile schema
- PAM Framework including account management
- Updated man pages include:
  - ldaplist(1)
  - ldapaddent(1)
  - pam_authok_check(5)
  - pam_authok_get(5)
  - pam_authok_store(5)
  - pam_passwd_auth(5)
  - pam_unix_auth(5)
  - pam_conf(4)

You can obtain the Secured LDAP Client Backport for the Solaris 8 OE from:

`http://sunsolve.sun.com/pub-cgi/show.pl?target=patches/patch-access`

In the Enter a Patch ID field, enter one of the following patches:

- 108993-xx (SPARC™ systems)
- 108994-xx (x86 systems)

## CHAPTER 4

Deploying Solaris OE LDAP Naming Services

In Chapter 2 "Assessing Your Needs for Naming Service Transition and Consolidation," preliminary steps required when planning a transition to LDAP based naming services were discussed. Chapter 3 "Defining Directory Service Security Architecture" provided insight into how the directory server and Solaris OE authentication mechanisms worked and discussed how to extend PAM functions. In this chapter, the actual deployment steps are detailed for both server and client. This chapter provides both an examination of the components that make up the deployment, and step-by-step procedures for implementing them.

This chapter is organized into the following sections:

Understanding the DIT

One of the most important decisions to make when transitioning to an LDAP name service is determining how your directory information tree (DIT) should be organized. This is important because it is difficult, and potentially disruptive, to redesign your DIT after it is implemented. Questions to ask are:

- Is the directory suffix name meaningful?
- Are there particular security policies you need to implement?
- Will the DIT be shared with other applications?

Other considerations indirectly affecting the DIT are:

- What will your user entries look like?
- Do you plan to create custom attributes and object classes?
- How large will the directory need to scale to?
- Will the deployment be departmental or enterprise-wide?

The following sections discuss these considerations, explain what the defaults are, and offer advice for alternatives:

- "Understanding the Directory Suffix" on page 184
- "Creating Containers" on page 186
- "Using ACIs to Support Security Policies" on page 189
- "Co-Existence with Other LDAP-Aware Applications" on page 190

Understanding the Directory Suffix

The directory suffix is the top node of your DIT and last component of an entry's distinguished name (DN). In some respects it resembles the root (/) directory in a UNIX file system. Unlike the root directory, there is no single predefined name for the top of the tree. Instead, there may be several suffixes defined for a DIT. However, in virtually all cases, user data is only contained under one of the suffixes. Other suffixes are used to store items such as configuration data.

To determine what suffixes a DIT contains, you can perform a base-level search of the directory server entry (DSE) of the directory service instance you are interested in. The supported suffixes are returned as namingContexts attribute values. To find out what data is contained beneath a suffix, you can perform subsequent searches on each suffix.

There are no hard and fast rules for choosing a suffix name. However, because the suffix is specified as part of the search base that is used to locate entries, it makes sense to choose a suffix name that is meaningful and easy to remember. For example, many companies choose a suffix that resembles their registered DNS name. Besides making the name easy to remember, this technique provides you with a unique name, which could be important if you plan to share directory data with a business partner. Unlike DNS, there are no registration authorities for issuing directory suffix names.

Choosing a Suffix Name

Suffix names can be constructed by specifying one of three naming conventions:

1. organization (o=)

2. country code (C=)

3. domain component (dc=)

The first two naming conventions come from the X.500 and X.509 specifications that predated the wide use of the Internet. At the time there was no global DNS infrastructure that included nearly all companies like the one that exists today. To establish unique names, X.500 specified elements like the country of origin and name of a corporation. The country attribute represented the country where the enterprise is based and the organization attribute represented the name of the corporation. The country naming attribute is not recommended because it is not suited for international corporations.

The second naming convention takes advantage of the fact that practically every corporation has a registered DNS address. This name is generally recognizable by everyone within the enterprise, which make it a practical choice.

The organization *Attribute*

The organization attribute can contain a DNS domain name like: o=sun.com, or simply the name of your enterprise like o=sun. The organization attribute is sometimes used to identify components that are not related to the name of an enterprise, for example, o=internet. Using the o= attribute in this manner might be alright to support internal applications, but should be avoided if possible.

The dc *Attribute*

The domain component (dc) attribute is typically specified more than once to form a DNS address. For example:

```
dc=example,dc=com
```

If you choose, you can specify additional subdomains. For example:

```
dc=uk,dc=example,dc=com
```

Either the `dc=` or `o=` convention work just fine. By default, Sun ONE Directory Server 5.2 software uses the `dc=` notation set to your DNS domain as the main suffix. For example, if you are in the `uk.example.com` domain, the default main suffix is `dc=uk,dc=example,dc=com`.

Creating a Suffix

Directory suffixes can be created either during the initial directory server installation and setup, or after the directory server is configured. As described in "Configuring Sun ONE Directory Servers and Clients" on page 214, you are prompted for a main suffix. The default that is displayed is the domain of the system you are installing it on, expressed using the `dc=` format.

Accepting the default is perfectly reasonable, although you might not want to map the directory suffix to the full DNS domain name of the system you are installing the directory server on. This is because the directory service scales much better than DNS, so you might choose to place all your naming data under the same suffix. For example, even though your DNS domains are split up into `east.example.com`, `central.example.com`, `west.example.com`, and so forth, you might choose to only use the two trailing components. For example, `example.com`. If you do not split your DNS domains internal to your company, this is not an issue.

Creating Containers

Below the suffix, containers are created where your naming service data will be placed. Containers are usually denoted by specifying the organizational unit (`ou`) object class. By default, the directory server installation creates the following three containers:

- `ou=People`
- `ou=Groups`
- `ou=Special Users`

The following additional containers are needed to support the Secured LDAP Client:

- `ou=group`
- `ou=services`
- `ou=protocols`
- `ou=rpc`

- `ou=hosts`
- `ou=networks`
- `ou=netgroup`
- `ou=printers`
- `ou=profiles`
- `ou=projects`
- `ou=solarisauthattr`
- `ou=solarisprofattr`
- `automountMapName=auto_*`

The names of the containers can be changed from the default names, but this is not recommended because you would have to explicitly supply the names of the containers to your clients. One exception might be the `ou=People` container where user entries are stored. If you choose to split up your users into different categories, you might wish to create additional containers such as `ou=SalesPeople`.

Notice that there is an `ou=group` container present. Do not confuse this with the `ou=Groups` container. The former is applicable only to POSIX-defined groups, while the latter is used for directory user groups.

The containers where automap entries are stored are not designated as organizational units (ou) like the other containers. Instead, the `autoMapName` attribute that is contained in an `automountmap` entry is used. These are shown in bold in FIGURE 4-1.

When the `idsconfig` script (discussed on page 225) is run to configure your directory server, a DIT similar to the one shown in the following diagram is created.

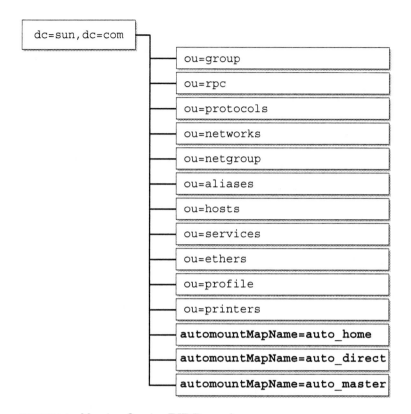

FIGURE 4-1   Naming Service DIT Example

Additional containers are created when the directory is populated with the
ldapaddent(1M) or smattrpop(1M) commands. Use of these commands and
procedures for creating additional containers is described in Chapter 5 "Migrating
Legacy Data to LDAP."

Using ACIs to Support Security Policies

Access Control Instructions (ACIs) are the mechanism used by the directory server to control access to directory data. To implement LDAP as a Solaris OE name service, some default ACIs need to be overwritten. The nicknames of three ACIs that are often created, or modified, are:

- LDAP_Naming_Services_deny_write_access
- VLV Request Control
- LDAP_Naming_Services_proxy_password_read

The first ACI overwrites the default behavior of the directory server. The default allows the owner of an entry to modify the values in that entry. Because a user entry stores information contained in the passwd and shadow databases, there are some passwd and shadow attributes that users should not be able to modify. For example, you do not want users to be able to change their uidnumber (UNIX UID), which could effectively give them root privileges. However, you might want them to be able to change other attributes such as gecos and description. This ACI usually appears at the top node of your DIT. The ACI that is created when the idsconfig command is run, looks like this:

```
(targetattr =
"cn||uid||uidNumber||gidNumber||homeDirectory||shadowLastChange|
|shadowMin||shadowMax||shadowWarning||shadowInactive||shadowExpi
re||shadowFlag||memberUid")(version 3.0; acl
LDAP_Naming_Services_deny_write_access; deny (write) userdn =
"ldap:///self";)
```

The second ACI is a modification of the default for virtual list view (VLV) access. This type of access is used by the Secured LDAP Client for some requests for performance reasons. The default allows access to all, which means all users have entries (credentials) in the directory. This presents a dilemma because the client does not have credentials to bind to the directory until the client is initialized. To become initialized, an anonymous bind is performed to retrieve a client profile. To permit anonymous binds that use the VLV control mechanism, permission must be granted to anyone, which sounds similar to all, but does not require the existence of an account. The ACI is located at dn:oid=2.16.840.1.113730.3.4.9,cn= features,cn=config and looks like this:

```
(targetattr != "aci") (version 3.0; acl "VLV Request Control";
allow(read,search,compare) userdn = "ldap:///anyone";)
```

The third ACI is optional and is only required if pam_unix style authentication is being deployed. This is because pam_unix authentication takes place on the client which must be able to retrieve the password of the user who is logging in. The directory server default only allows the `RootDN` (`cn=directory manager`) the ability to read passwords, so this access control must be overwritten to grant that access to the `proxyagent` account that the Secured LDAP Client uses to bind to the directory. The ACI is usually located at the top node of your DIT and looks like this:

```
(target="ldap:///dc=example,dc=com")(targetattr=
"userPassword")(version 3.0; acl
LDAP_Naming_Services_proxy_password_read; allow
(compare,read,search) userdn = "ldap:///cn=proxyagent,ou=
profile,dc=example,dc=com";)
```

Note – This ACI is inherently insecure and should be avoided if possible. Support of `pam_unix` style authentication should only be used for transition purposes and removed once all your clients can use `pam_ldap`.

Details on how to add and modify existing ACIs are described in Chapter 6 "Management Tools and Toolkits."

Co-Existence with Other LDAP-Aware Applications

Another consideration when designing a DIT is whether the DIT will be shared with other applications and whether those applications require a particular DIT structure. There is such a wide range of applications that use LDAP for data storage and user authentication it is impossible to provide details on how to develop a corresponding DIT.

The NIS+ Gateway application is covered in this book. Refer to Chapter 5 "Migrating Legacy Data to LDAP" if you are planning to deploy NIS+ along with the Secured LDAP Client. In general, the `idsconfig` script creates an appropriate DIT for using LDAP as a naming service. However, password read access and storage schemes are important considerations because the NIS+ Gateway requires password storage to be in crypt format and readable by the application.

Differentiating Server and Client Versions

Providing installation and configuration instructions for deploying Secured LDAP clients is a challenging task because Sun supports several different versions of directory servers and clients. This section explains what the differences are, how to identify what version you are using, and which tools to use with each client version. The topics covered are:

- "Directory Server Versions" on page 191
- "LDAP Name Service Client Versions" on page 197
- "Mixing Client and Server Versions" on page 214

Directory Server Versions

Over the years, the name of the directory server and how it is packaged have changed. Most of the name changes have been due to marketing preferences or trademark constraints. No matter what the reason, the name changes have been a source of confusion. The packaging changes are primarily a result of integrating the directory server into the Solaris OE, while at the same time supporting multiple platforms that do not have the same software installation mechanism as the Solaris OE.

The following directory server versions are discussed in this chapter:

- Netscape Directory Server 4.1x software (bonus software)
- iPlanet Directory Server 5.1 software (bundled in Solaris 9 OE, initial release)
- Sun ONE Directory Server 5.1 software (compressed tar file)
- Sun ONE Directory Server 5.2 software (compressed tar file)
- Sun ONE Directory Server 5.2 software (SVR4 packages)

Netscape Directory Server 4.1x (Bonus Software)

The Netscape Directory Server 4.1x version was co-packaged with the Solaris 8 OE in the Bonus Pack CD. No integrated setup scripts like `idsconfig` were provided in 4.1, but an equivalent script was made available on the `www.sun.com/blueprints` web site.

The End of Life (EOL) of this product has been announced by Sun, so its deployment is discouraged. Besides the support issue, this version is missing a couple of key features and therefore deployment is undesirable. The missing features are:

- Multi-Master Replication (MMR)
- SASL DIGEST-MD5 Authentication
- SASL GSSAPI

MMR capability is key to deploying a cost effective high-availability architecture. SASL/DIGEST-MD5 authentication allows passwords to be encrypted before they are sent to the server. A complete description of SASL/DIGEST-MD5 and SASL/GSSAPI can be found in Chapter 3 "Defining Directory Service Security Architecture.

The Netscape Directory Server 4.1x software came packaged as a single compressed tar file that you would extract from the Bonus CD or download from the iPlanet web site. A free 200K user license for this version of the directory server is included with the Solaris 8 OE.

iPlanet Directory Server 5.1 (Bundled)

The iPlanet Directory Server 5.1 software shipped as part of the Solaris 9 OE distribution media, and for the first time was available in SVR4 package format. These packages are:

- `IPLTadcon` – Administration Server Console
- `IPLTadman` – Administration Server Documentation
- `IPLTadmin` – Administration Server
- `IPLTcons` – Console Client Base
- `IPLTdscon` – Directory Server Console
- `IPLTdsman` – Directory Server Documentation
- `IPLTdsr` – Directory Server (`root`)
- `IPLTdsu` – Directory Server (`usr`)
- `IPLTjss` – Network Security Services for Java software
- `IPLTnls` – Nationalization Languages and Localization Support
- `IPLTnspr` – Portable Runtime Interface
- `IPLTnss` – Network Security Services
- `IPLTpldap` – PerLDAP

These packages are installed when the Full Distribution (`SUNWCall`) or Full Distribution+OEM (`SUNWCXall`) package cluster is selected during the installation of Solaris 9 OE. Besides the simplified installation, other enhancements are provided in the initial Solaris 9 OE release, such as the following:

- `/usr/bin/directoryserver` wrapper script – Takes away the path dependencies inherent in previous directory server versions. This allows you to run directory administration commands without having to know where the directory server software is loaded. The directory server setup program was modified to place the software in a fixed location rather than an arbitrary one. It also automatically creates a startup file called `/etc/init.d/directory` for you.

- `idsconfig` script – Used to make the necessary configuration changes to support LDAP as a name service.

- `ldapaddent` program – Used to populate LDAP entries with data from name service databases in `files` format. There is no equivalent functionality in the previous version, although the `dsimport` command that was part of the NIS Extensions software could be tweaked to import LDAP name service data.

Sun ONE Directory Server 5.1 Software (compressed tar file)

This version is almost identical to the iPlanet Directory Server 5.1 bundled version, although the name has changed because the directory server is an integral component of the Sun Open Network Environment (Sun ONE). This software can be downloaded from the `sun.com` web site and configured with the `idsconfig` script to support LDAP as a name service. The `ldapaddent` utility can be used to populate the directory.

This version is not integrated with the `/usr/sbin/directoryserver` wrapper, so you must specify where to install the software. Another key difference is the update delivery mechanism. Updated versions of the unbundled directory server are provided as Service Packs that contain an entire image of the software, while updates to the bundled version are provided as patches.

Note – Service Pack 1 contained changes to the RFC 2307 schema files that caused `idsconfig` to fail. This problem can be fixed by manually editing the `11rfc2307.ldif` schema file. The problem is fixed in Service Pack 2.

Sun ONE Directory Server 5.2 Software (SVR4 packages)

Like the iPlanet Directory Server 5.1 version, the Sun ONE Directory Server 5.2 software is distributed as SVR4 packages. However, the package names have changed and the number of packages has increased. Some of the packages contain updates to packages in the Solaris OE distribution, some are required to run the Directory Server in 64-bit mode, and some are only required with the Solaris 8 OE.

A complete list of all packages in alphabetical order is:

- SUNWasha – Sun ONE Administration Server component for Sun™ Cluster software
- SUNWasvc – Sun ONE Administration Console
- SUNWasvcp – Sun ONE Administration Server Console Plug-in
- SUNWasvr - Sun ONE Administration Server (Root)
- SUNWasvu – Sun ONE Administration Server (Usr)
- SUNWdsha – Sun One Directory Server Component for Sun Cluster software
- SUNWdsvcp – Sun ONE Directory Server Console Plug-in
- SUNWdsvh – Sun ONE Directory Server Heap Allocator
- SUNWdsvhx – Sun ONE Directory Server Heap Allocator (64-bit)
- SUNWdsvpl – Sun ONE Directory Server PerLDAP modules
- SUNWdsvr – Sun ONE Directory Server (Root)
- SUNWdsvu – Sun ONE Directory Server (Usr)
- SUNWdsvx – Sun ONE Directory Server (64-bit)
- SUNWicu – International Components for Unicode User Files
- SUNWicux – International Components for Unicode User Files (64-bit)
- SUNWjss – Network Security Services for Java (JSS) software
- SUNWldk – LDAP C SDK
- SUNWldkx – LDAP C SDK (64-bit)
- SUNWpr – Netscape Portable Runtime
- SUNWprx – Netscape Portable Runtime (64-bit)
- SUNWsasl – Simple Authentication and Security Layer
- SUNWsaslx – Simple Authentication and Security Layer (64-bit)
- SUNWtls – Network Security Services
- SUNWtlsx – Network Security Services (64-bit)

These packages are designed to support both the Solaris 8 and the Solaris 9 OE and both the 32-bit and 64-bit mode of the directory server. Some are not specific to the Directory Server and are used by other applications. The Administration Server and Sun ONE Server Console applications are also included among these packages.

To understand the role each package plays it is helpful to group them in the following way.

Shared Packages, 32-bit

Shared packages are those that are not unique to the Directory Server, Administration Server, or Console. These include:

- SUNWicu
- SUNWtls
- SUNWsasl
- SUNWjss
- SUNWldk
- SUNWpr

Shared Packages, 64-bit

These packages are layered on top of the previous one to enable 64-bit operations of applications. They include:

- SUNWicux
- SUNWtlsx
- SUNWsaslx
- SUNWldkx
- SUNWprx

Sun ONE Server Console Packages

This is contained in a single package, which is:

- SUNWasvc

Sun ONE Administration Server

These include:

- SUNWasvu
- SUNWasvr
- SUNWasvcp
- SUNWdsvcp

Note – There is no 64-bit version of the Administration Server

---

Directory Server Packages, 32-bit

These include:

- `SUNWdsvpl`
- `SUNWdsvu`
- `SUNWdsvr`

Directory Server Packages, 64-bit

This is contained in a single package, which is:

- `SUNWdsvx`

Solaris 8 OE Specific Packages

These packages help increase Directory Server performance:

- `SUNWdsvh`
- `SUNWdsvhx`

Sun Cluster HA Agents

Separate agents for the Directory and Administration Servers are included as:

- `SUNWasha`
- `SUNWdsha`

Sun ONE Directory Server 5.2 Software (compressed tar file)

This is essentially the same release as the SVR4 package version, but the delivery mechanism is quite different. It is distributed as a compressed tar file rather than SVR4 packages and there is no `/usr/sbin/directoryserver` wrapper program.

The unbundled version of the directory server does have some features that might interest system administrators. These include:

- Can be installed by a non-root user.
- More than one installation can be performed on the same system. This can be useful for separating test and production versions of the software.
- Consistency with other operating environments. For example, there aren't any SVR4 packages for Linux and Windows.
- More flexibility on where to install the software.
- Combines installation and configuration.

LDAP Name Service Client Versions

There are two distinctly different Solaris OE LDAP naming service clients available, commonly referred to as:

- Native Solaris OE LDAP Client
- Secured LDAP Client

Sometimes they are referred to as the Phase 1 and Phase 2 implementation respectively. The Secured LDAP Client was introduced in the Solaris 9 OE and later backported to the Solaris 8 OE. It is a superset of the Phase 1 implementation, and available on the same platforms, so there are no compelling reasons to deploy Phase 1.

For completeness, and for the benefits of those who are familiar with Phase 1, both are discussed in the following sections so that feature and implementation differences can be highlighted.

Phase 1 - Native Solaris OE LDAP

From a deployment view, the key differences between the Phase 1 and Phase 2 implementation are the structure of the client profiles and the tools used to manage them. The client profile that supports Phase 1 is easily identified by its version number of 1.0 and its object class of SolarisNamingProfile. The tool used to generate this profile is the ldap_gen_profile utility.

The following sections describe the attributes defined for the SolarisNamingProfile object class and how they are created using the ldap_gen_profile utility.

Version 1 Client Profile

The schema definition of the Version 1.0 profile is contained in the user99.ldif file under the server root for your directory server instance. The location of the schema files is dependent on the version of the directory server you are using. This client profile can be used by the Secured LDAP Client (Phase 2), but would not support the new features described in the Phase 2 section.

Not all of the attributes defined by the SolarisNamingProfile object class are used. For example, the SolarisCertificatePath and SolarisCertificatePassword attributes were never used, and have been replaced in the Version 2.0 client profile. Also, although the SolarisTransportSecurity attribute can be set to SSL, this feature was never implemented.

The following code box shows the schema definition for the
`SolarisNamingProfile`. Note the readable format used to represent the schema

```
objectclass SolarisNamingProfile
    oid
        1.3.6.1.4.1.42.2.27.5.2.7
    superior
        top
    requires
        objectclass,
        cn,
        SolarisLDAPServers,
        SolarisSearchBaseDN
    allows
        SolarisAuthMethod,
        SolarisBindDN,
        SolarisBindPassword,
        SolarisCacheTTL
        SolarisCertificatePassword,
        SolarisCertificatePath,
        SolarisDataSearchDN,
        SolarisPreferredServer,
        SolarisPreferredServerOnly,
        SolarisSearchReferral,
        SolarisSearchScope,
        SolarisSearchTimeLimit,
        SolarisTransportSecurity
```

definition. The actual format Sun ONE Directory Server 5.2 software uses can be
found in the `99user.ldif` file in the schema directory.

Version 1.0 client profile templates should always be initially generated by the
Solaris OE `ldap_gen_profile` utility. This assures that only the supported
attributes are used and the appropriate values are entered. Once a template is
created, you can change the attribute values for different profiles.

Note – The `ldap_gen_profile` utility is not available in the Solaris 9 OE release.
Therefore, to generate Version 1.0 profiles you need to run the `ldap_gen_profile`
utility on a system running the Solaris 8 OE. If the Solaris OE 8 Enhanced LDAP
Naming Services feature patch is installed, there may be an issue with the generation
of Version 1.0 profiles. Check `sunsolve.sun.com` for the latest status on this issue.

The following shows a Version 1.0 profile in LDAP Data Interchange Format (LDIF) representation.

```
dn: cn=416default,ou=profile,dc=example,dc=com
SolarisBindDN: cn=proxyagent,ou=profile,dc=example,dc=com
SolarisBindPassword: {NS1}4a3788e8c053424f
SolarisLDAPServers: 129.148.181.130
SolarisSearchBaseDN: dc=example,dc=com
SolarisAuthMethod: NS_LDAP_AUTH_SIMPLE
SolarisTransportSecurity: NS_LDAP_SEC_NONE
SolarisSearchReferral: NS_LDAP_FOLLOWREF
SolarisSearchScope: NS_LDAP_SCOPE_ONELEVEL
SolarisSearchTimeLimit: 30
SolarisCacheTTL: 43200
cn: v1default
objectClass: top
objectClass: SolarisNamingProfile
```

The `ldap_gen_profile` *Utility*

To generate LDIF that can be imported into your directory server, use the `ldap_gen_profile` command. There are two versions of this command:

- The original version that shipped with the Solaris 8 OE
- The updated version that is installed with the enhanced naming services feature patch (108993-18)

The command syntax for the first version is shown below and described in TABLE 4-1. Refer to the patch documentation for the syntax of the second version.

```
/usr/sbin/ldap_gen_profile -P profile_name [-O] [ -a none | simple
| cram_md5 ] [ -b baseDN ] [ -B alternate_search_dn ] [ -d domainname ]
[ -D Bind_DN ] [ -e   client_TTL ] [  -o   timeout_value ] [  -p server_preference
] [ -r  follow_referrals ]   [  -w client_password ] LDAP_server_addr
```

TABLE 4-1   `ldap_gen_profile` Utility Options

Options	Description
`-a none	simple	cram_md5`	Specifies the authentication method. Multiple values can be specified, separated by commas. the default value is none. If simple or `cram_md5` is specified, a password must be provided. Note: The `cram_md5` authentication method is not supported by the Sun ONE Directory Server 5.1 or 5.2 software versions.
`-b baseDN`	Specifies the search `baseDN` (for example `dc=example,dc=com`.) The default is the root naming context on the first server specified.
`-B alternate_search_dn`	Overrides the *baseDN* for LDAP searches for any of the databases defined in the `/etc/nsswitch.conf` file.
`-d domainname`	Specifies the domain name (which becomes the default domain for the machine). The default is the current domain name.
`-D Bind_DN`	Specify the Bind Distinguished Name (for example, `cn=proxyagent,ou=profile,dc=example,dc=com`).
`-e client_TTL`	Specifies the TTL value for the client information. This is only relevant if the machine was initialized with a client profile. Set *client_TTL* to 0 (zero) if you do not wish for `ldap_cachemgr` to attempt an automatic refresh from the servers. The times are specified with either a 0 (zero, for no expiration) or a positive integer and either d for days, h for hours, m for minutes or s for seconds. The default is 12h.
`-o timeout_value`	Specifies LDAP operation timeout value. The default is three minutes.
`-O`	Informs the client to contact only the servers on the preferred list. The default is FALSE.
`-p server_preference`	Specifies the server preference list (for example, `129.123.123.1:8080, 129.123.123.2:386`) The preferred servers can be defined either by the server specific address or by the subnet on which the server resides. To remove the server preference, specify `""` for the -p option. The default preference is the local subnet.

TABLE 4-1 `ldap_gen_profile` Utility Options *(Continued)*

Options	Description
-P *profile_name*	Specifies a profile that is downloaded from the server and sets all the entries automatically. This option also sets an expiration time that `ldap_cachemgr` can use to automatically update the file if needed. The default *profile_name* is `default` and is stored in the `ou=profile` container.
-r *follow_referrals*	The default is to follow referrals. Enter a value of `noref` to override the default.
-v	Specifies verbose mode. Recommended for troubleshooting.
-w *client_password*	Specifies client password for `SIMPLE` and `cram_md5` authentication modes. This option is not required if authentication mode is `none`.

`ldap_gen_profile` example:

```
ldap_gen_profile -P eng -a simple -d eng.example.com -w test123 \
-b dc=eng,dc=example,dc=com -B ou=people,dc=lab,dc=eng,dc=\
example,dc=com -D cn=proxyagent,ou=profile,cd=eng,dc=example,dc=\
com -r noref -e 1h -O -p 129.123.123.1 -o 30s 129.123.200.7 \
129.123.00.1 129.123.5.6 > myprofile.ldif
```

Adding the `SolarisBindLimit` *Attribute*

When the `ldap_gen_profile` command is run to create a client profile, the attribute `SolarisBindTimeLimit` is specified in the resulting LDIF with a value of 30. This attribute was created to fix a problem in the Phase 1 native implementation that prevented LDAP server failover to work properly. By specifying the attribute and a value in seconds, you can direct the LDAP client to try a secondary server after a defined period of time. The `SolarisNamingProfile` schema was not updated in the Sun ONE Directory Server 5.1 release, so you needed to add it manually.

Note – The failover mechanism was fixed in Phase 2, so this is no longer an issue.

How Parameter Values are Stored

After the Phase 1 client is initialized, the parameter values specified in the client profile are placed in two files:

- `/var/ldap/ldap_client_file`
- `/var/ldap/ldap_client_cred`

The parameters are stored as `NS_LDAP_*` values instead of the attribute names. This allows different attributes to be used to provide the same information. For example, the version 2.0 profile schema defines different attribute names, but the `NS_LDAP_*` parameters names are the same.

The following example shows a sample `ldap_client_file` file.

```
# more ldap_client_file
#
# Do not edit this file manually; your changes will be lost.Please
use ldapclient (1M) instead.
#
NS_LDAP_FILE_VERSION= 1.0
NS_LDAP_SERVERS= 128.100.100.1
NS_LDAP_SEARCH_BASEDN= dc=example,dc=com
NS_LDAP_AUTH= NS_LDAP_AUTH_SIMPLE
NS_LDAP_SEARCH_REF= NS_LDAP_FOLLOWREF
NS_LDAP_SEARCH_SCOPE= NS_LDAP_SCOPE_ONELEVEL
NS_LDAP_SEARCH_TIME= 30
NS_LDAP_PROFILE= default
```

The following example shows a sample `ldap_client_cred` file.

```
# more ldap_client_cred
#
# Do not edit this file manually; your changes will be lost.Please
use ldapclient (1M) instead.
#
NS_LDAP_BINDDN= cn=proxyagent,ou=profile,dc=example,dc=com
NS_LDAP_BINDPASSWD= {NS1}4a3788e8c053424f
```

Note – The `ldap_cachemgr` daemon in Phase 1 updated both of these files which is considered a security hole. In Phase 2, only the information contained in `ldap_client_file` is updated.

Phase 2 - Secured LDAP Client

The Phase 2 implementation emphasis is on security, so Phase 2 has been dubbed *Secured LDAP Client*. The distinguishing features of this client are:

- Runs on Solaris 8 and 9 OE (Solaris 8 OE requires a patch).
- Works with both Version 1.0 and Version 2.0 profiles
- Runs over the TLS/SSL secure transport.
- Supports SASL/DIGEST-MD5 authentication.
- Supports sophisticated searches though the Service Search Descriptor (SSD) mechanism.
- Allows for a flexible DIT with object class and attribute mapping.
- Stores proxy credentials locally.
- Password management through shadow database parameters (requires patch).
- Supports the new automount object class.

To take advantage of these enhancements, you need to create and deploy Version 2.0 client profiles. The ldap_gen_profile command has been replaced in Solaris 9 OE with an enhanced version of ldapclient. The following sections provide details on both the content and generation of Version 2.0 profiles.

Version 2 Client Profile

The Version 2.0 is easily identified by the defining object class of DUAConfigProfile. A new set of attributes has been defined for use with this object class, although some serve the same purpose. Notice that the Solaris prefix has been removed from both the object class and its attributes. This is because the client profile has been adopted for platforms other than those running the Solaris OE.

Below is the schema for the Version 2 client profile.

```
objectclass DUAConfigProfile
    oid
        1.3.6.1.4.1.11.1.3.1.2.4
    superior
        top
    requires
        cn
    allows
        attributeMap,
        authenticationMethod,
        bindTimeLimit,
        credentialLevel,
        defaultSearchBase,
        defaultSearchScope,
        defaultServerList,
        defaultSearchScope,
        followReferrals,
        objectclassMap,
        preferredServerList,
        profileTTL,
        searchTimeLimit,
        serviceAuthenticationMethod,
        serviceCredentialLevel,
        serviceSearchDescriptor
```

TABLE 4-2 provides an alphabetical listing of the attributes with descriptions.

TABLE 4-2   Version 2 Profile Attributes

Attribute	Default Value	Description
attributeMap	none	Specifies a mapping from an attribute defined by a service to an attribute in an alternative schema. This can be used to change the default schema used for a given service. The syntax of attributeMap is defined in the profile IETF draft. This option can be specified multiple times. Example: attributeMap: passwd:uid=NTuserName In this example, the LDAP client uses the LDAP attribute NTuserName rather than the default uid for the passwd service.
authenticationMethod	none	Specifies the default authentication method used by all services unless overridden by the serviceAuthenticationMethod attribute. Multiple values can be specified using a comma-separated list. The following methods are available: SIMPLE, SASL/DIGEST-MD5, TLS:SIMPLE, and TLS:SASL/DIGEST-MD5 If credentialLevel is set to anonymous, this attribute is ignored. However, services such as pam_ldap may use this attribute, even if credentialLevel is anonymous.
bindTimeLimit	30	Specifies the maximum time in seconds that a client should spend performing a bind operation. Set this to a positive integer.
certificatePath	/var/ldap	Specifies the certificate path for the location of the certificate database. The value is the path where security database files reside. This is used for TLS support, which is specified in the authenticationMethod and serviceAuthenticationMethod attributes. This is a local attribute.
credentialLevel	No default value	Specifies the credential level the client should use to contact the directory. The credential levels supported are either anonymous or proxy. If a proxy credential level is specified, then the authenticationMethod attribute must be specified to determine the authentication mechanism. Further, if the credential level is proxy and at least one of the authentication methods require a bind DN, the proxyDN and proxyPassword attribute values must be set.

TABLE 4-2   Version 2 Profile Attributes *(Continued)*

Attribute	Default Value	Description
defaultSearchBase	No default value	Specifies the default search base DN. The serviceSearchDescriptor attribute can be used to override the defaultSearchBase for given services. There is no default.
defaultServerList	No default value	Specifies the default list of directory servers to search. Uses same semantics as the preferredServerList attribute.
defaultSearchScope=one | sub	one	Specifies the default search scope for the client's search operations. This default can be overridden for a given service by specifying a serviceSearchDescriptor.
domainName	*current_ domainname*	Specifies the DNS domain name. This becomes the default domain for the machine. This attribute is only used during client initialization and is only local.
followReferrals=true | false	true	Specifies the referral setting. A setting of true implies that referrals will be automatically followed, and false results in referrals not being followed.
objectclassMap	none	Specifies a mapping from an object class defined by a service to an object class in an alternative schema. This can be used to change the default schema used for a given service. The syntax of objectclassMap is defined in the profile IETF draft. Example: objectclassMap: passwd:posixAccount= unixAccount In this example, the LDAP client uses the LDAP object class of unixAccount rather than the posixAccount for the passwd service. This is a multi-valued attribute.
preferredServerList	No default value	Specifies a space-separated list of preferred server IP addresses to be contacted before servers specified by the defaultServerList attribute. The port number is optional. If not specified, the default LDAP server port number 389 is used, except when TLS is specified in the authentication method. In this case, the default LDAP server port number is 636. Fully qualified host names might also be used. If fully qualified host names are used, you must configure nsswitch.conf to use files or DNS, not ldap, to resolve host lookups. If you fail to configure nsswitch.conf properly, then your system or certain processes might hang if they use a hostname value.

TABLE 4-2   Version 2 Profile Attributes *(Continued)*

Attribute	Default Value	Description
profileName	default	Specifies a profile name. For ldapclient init, this attribute is the name of an existing profile which might be downloaded periodically depending on the value of the profileTTL attribute. For ldapclient genprofile, this is the name of the profile to be generated.
profileTTL	43200	Specifies the TTL value in seconds for the client information. This is only relevant if the machine was initialized with a client profile. If you do not want ldap_cachemgr(1M) to attempt to refresh the LDAP client configuration from the LDAP server, set profileTTL to 0 (zero). Valid values are either 0 (zero, for no expiration) or a positive integer in seconds. The default value of 43200 seconds results in 12 hours.
proxyDN	No default value	Specifies the Bind Distinguished Name (bindDN) for the proxy identity. This option is required if the credential level is proxy, and at least one of the authentication methods requires a bindDN. This is a local attribute. There is no default value.
proxyPassword	No default value	Specifies the client proxy password. This option is required if the credential level is proxy, and at least one of the authentication methods requires a bindDN. This is a local attribute. There is no default.
searchTimeLimit	30	Specifies the maximum number of seconds allowed for an LDAP search operation. Note: The server might have its own search time limit.

TABLE 4-2   Version 2 Profile Attributes *(Continued)*

Attribute	Default Value	Description
serviceAuthenticationMethod	No default value	Specifies the authentication methods used by a service. Multiple values can be specified by a comma-separated list. The default value is no service authentication methods, in which case, each service would default to the authenticationMethod value. The supported authentications are listed under the AuthenticationMethod attribute. Three services support this feature: • passwd-cmd – used to define the authentication method used by passwd(1) to change the user's password and other attributes. • keyserv – used to identify the authentication method used by the chkey(1) and newkey(1M) utilities. • pam_ldap – defines the authentication method to be used for authenticating users when pam_ldap(5) is configured. If the serviceAuthenticationMethod attribute is not set for any of these services, the authenticationMethod attribute is used to define the authentication method. This is a multi-valued attribute.
serviceCredentialLevel	None	Specifies the credential level used by a service. Multiple values can be specified in a space-separated list. The supported credential levels are anonymous or proxy. At present, no service uses this attribute. This is a multi-valued attribute.
serviceSearchDescriptor	None	Overrides the default base DN for LDAP searches for a given service. The format of the descriptors also allows overriding the default search scope and search filter for each service. The syntax of serviceSearchDescriptor is defined in the profile IETF draft. This is a multi-valued attribute. Example: serviceSearchDescriptor: passwd:ou=people,dc=a1,dc=example,dc=com?one In this example, the LDAP client performs a one-level search in ou=people,dc=a1,dc=example,dc=com rather than ou=people,defaultSearchBase for the passwd service.

Generating Version 2 Profiles

The ldapclient command in Solaris 9 OE and ldap_gen_profile command in the Solaris 8 OE naming services patch were enhanced to accept additional command-line arguments. If the genprofile argument is specified, version 2.0 profiles are generated in LDIF format. The ldap_gen_profile command was removed in Solaris 9 OE, with the new ldapclient command taking its place.

Use the following syntax of ldapclient to generate profiles.

/usr/sbin/ldapclient [-v | -q] **genprofile -a profileName=**
profileName [**-a attrName=***attrVal*]

Example:

```
ldapclient genprofile -a profileName=eng \
-a credentialLevel=proxy -a authenticationMethod=sasl/DIGEST-MD5 \
-a bindTimeLimit=20 \
-a defaultSearchBase=dc=eng,dc=example,dc=com \
-a "serviceSearchDescriptor=passwd:ou=people,dc=a1,dc=example,dc=com?one" \
-a serviceAuthenticationMethod=pam_ldap:tls:simple \
-a defaultSearchScope=sub \
-a attributeMap=passwd:uid=employeeNumber \
-a objectclassMap=passwd:posixAccount=unixAccount \
-a followReferrals=false \
-a profileTTL=6000 \
-a preferredServerList=129.100.100.30 \
-a searchTimeLimit=30 \
-a "defaultServerList=128.100.200.1 129.100.100.1 204.34.5.6" > eng.ldif
```

The following LDIF is produced by the previous example.

```
dn: cn=profileName,ou=profile,dc=eng,dc=example,dc=com
ObjectClass: top
ObjectClass: DUAConfigProfile
defaultServerList: 29.100.200.1 129.100.100.1 204.34.5.6
defaultSearchBase: dc=eng,dc=example,dc=com
authenticationMethod: sasl/DIGEST-MD5
followReferrals: FALSE
defaultSearchScope: sub
searchTimeLimit: 30
preferredServerList: 129.100.100.30
profileTTL: 6000
cn: profileName
credentialLevel: proxy
serviceSearchDescriptor: passwd:ou=people,dc=a1,dc=example,dc=
com?one
bindTimeLimit: 20
attributeMap: passwd:uid=employeeNumber
objectClassMap: passwd:posixAccount=unixAccount
serviceAuthenticationMethod: pam_ldap:tls:simple
```

The following is a sample ldap_client_file generated from a Version 2.0 profile.

```
# cd /var/ldap
# more ldap_client_file
#
# Do not edit this file manually; your changes will be lost.Please
use ldapclient(1M) instead.
#
NS_LDAP_FILE_VERSION= 2.0
NS_LDAP_SERVERS= 129.100.181.98
NS_LDAP_SEARCH_BASEDN= dc=example,dc=com
NS_LDAP_AUTH= tls:simple
NS_LDAP_SEARCH_REF= FALSE
NS_LDAP_SEARCH_SCOPE= one
NS_LDAP_SEARCH_TIME= 30
NS_LDAP_CACHETTL= 43200
NS_LDAP_PROFILE= ssl
NS_LDAP_CREDENTIAL_LEVEL= proxy
NS_LDAP_BIND_TIME= 10
```

The version can be easily identified from the value of NS_LDAP_FILE_VERSION. As with the Phase 1 implementation, the parameters listed in the file contain the NS (name service) prefix. Although some of the parameter names might be the same, the actual attribute in the profile is different. A mapping of parameter names to attributes is shown in TABLE 4-3.

When you run the idsconfig command, the ldapclient genprofile command runs to create a profile. See Chapter 7 "Performing Administrative Tasks" for procedures on creating additional profiles.

The following code box shows an example of the ldap_client_cred file generated by ldapclient init.

```
# cd /var/ldap
# more ldap_client_cred
#
# Do not edit this file manually; your changes will be lost. Please
use ldapclient (1M) instead.
#
NS_LDAP_BINDDN= cn=proxyagent,ou=profile,dc=example,dc=com
NS_LDAP_BINDPASSWD= {NS1}4a3788e8c053424f
NS_LDAP_HOST_CERTPATH= /certs/ldap
```

The contents of this file look similar to the Phase 1 file except for the optional NS_LDAP_HOST_CERTPATH parameter. This parameter is used to specify an alternative to the /var/ldap directory for storing the client's certificate database. However, unlike Phase 1, the information contained here is not kept in the client profile. To change it, use the ldapclient mod command.

Example:

```
# ldapclient mod -a certificatePath=/newpath
```

More information on updating the local configuration files is contained in Chapter 7 "Performing Administrative Tasks."

TABLE 4-3   File Parameter Mappings

Parameter	Phase 2 Attribute	Phase 1 Attribute
NS_LDAP_FILE_VERSION	none	none
NS_LDAP_SERVERS	defaultserverlist	solarisldapservers
NS_LDAP_SEARCH_BASEDN	defautlsearchbase	solarissearchbasedn
NS_LDAP_AUTH	authenticationmethod	solarisauthmethod
NS_LDAP_SEARCH_REF	followreferrals	solarissearchreferral
NS_LDAP_SEARCH_SCOPE	defaultsearchscope	solarissearchscope
NS_LDAP_SEARCH_TIME	searchtimelimit	solarissearchtimelimit
NS_LDAP_CACHETTL	profilettl	solariscacheTTL
NS_LDAP_PROFILE	cn	cn
NS_LDAP_CREDENTIAL_LEVEL	credentiallevel	none
NS_LDAP_BIND_TIME	bindTimeLimit	solarisbindtimelimit
NS_LDAP_BINDDN	none	solarisbinddn
NS_LDAP_BINDPASSWD	none	solarisbindpassword
NS_LDAP_HOST_CERTPATH	none	solariscertificatepath

Note – The NS_LDAP_BIND_TIME, NS_LDAP_BINDDN, NS_LDAP_BINDPASSWD, and NS_LDAP_HOST_CERTPATH parameters are stored in local files and not in a client profile.

Defining Authentication Methods

The Phase 2 implementation provides several ways to set up authentication for both the proxy account and for users. These options are:

- none
- SIMPLE
- SASL/DIGEST-MD5
- TLS:SIMPLE
- TLS:SASL/DIGEST-MD5

These options are covered in Chapter 3 "Defining Directory Service Security Architecture" in detail. Before you configure the directory server as a name server, you need to decide what level of authentication is appropriate for your environment. Available levels include:

- Proxy authentication – This is recommended for most configurations. With this method, accesses to the naming server are made as a proxy user. A password is required.

- "Proxy anonymous" authentication – If clients do not have proxy credentials, they can still gain access as anonymous users. To implement this, set up ACIs that allow anonymous access for certain data. For example, the `hosts` container could be public while the `passwd` container requires proxy credentials.

You must also decide on the type of user authentication you want to support. The options here are:

- `pam_unix`
- `pam_ldap`

As described in Chapter 4 "Deploying Solaris OE LDAP Naming Services," the type of authentication you choose will dictate the format in which passwords are stored.

Note – You can mix and match the proxy access authentication by setting the `serviceAuthenticationMethod` attribute.

Mixing Client and Server Versions

In general, you can set up a directory server that supports Phase 1 and Phase 2 clients on either the Solaris 8 or 9 OE. The main difference is the way the software is packaged. In the Solaris 9 OE, the Sun ONE Directory Server software is part of the SUNWCall and SUNWCXall package clusters, so will automatically get loaded when you choose to install everything. To load the Sun ONE Directory Server 5.2 software on Solaris 8 OE, you must download the applicable software from the www.sun.com web site.

Besides installing the directory server software on the Solaris 8 OE, you need the updated ldapclient, ldapaddent, and ldap_gen_profile commands to create Version 2 client profiles and to populate the directory server with naming service data. These utilities are available with the 108993-18 and later versions of the patch.

A single DIT can be configured to support both Phase 1 and Phase 2 clients. However, to share automaps, the old schema definition that defines automaps must be used, and the Phase 2 client needs to map the new schema definition into the old one. More information on this topic can be found in Chapter 5 "Migrating Legacy Data to LDAP." Because there is no technical reasons to maintain Phase 1 clients, it is advisable to upgrade your Phase 1 clients to Phase 2, rather than supporting both.

Configuring Sun ONE Directory Servers and Clients

This section discusses various ways that you can install and configure Sun ONE Directory servers and clients. The topics covered are:

- "Configuring the Directory Server" on page 215
- "Enabling TLS/SSL on the Directory Server" on page 232
- "Configuring the Clients" on page 237

Configuring the Directory Server

The Sun ONE Directory Server 5.2 software is designed so that the installation process is separate from the configuration process. What this means is that all the packages can be installed without any configuration required. You may choose to install all the packages and only configure the components you are interested in running. The caveat here is that if the 64-bit packages are loaded, the Directory Server will be configured to run in 64-bit mode by default. This section describes the following tasks required to perform these activities:

- "To Verify the Installation of the Sun ONE Directory Server 5.2 Packages" on page 215
- "To Configure the Directory Server Software" on page 219
- "Enabling TLS/SSL on the Directory Server" on page 232
- "To Verify the TLS/SSL Configuration on the Server" on page 237

▼ To Verify the Installation of the Sun ONE Directory Server 5.2 Packages

1. **Verify that the Sun ONE Directory Server 5.2 packages are installed on the systems that you plan to configure as directory servers.**

   You can verify the installation of packages in one of two ways:

   - Use the pkginfo command:

   ```
   # pkginfo SUNWdsvh SUNWdsvhx SUNWdsvpl . . .
   ```

   - Check for the existence of the v5.2 directory and the setup files that are created when the Sun ONE Directory Server software is installed:

   ```
   vipivot# cd /usr/ds/v5.2
   vipivot# ls -l
   total 14
   drwxr-xr-x    4 root bin 512 Feb 11 15:42 bin
   drwxr-xr-x    4 root bin 1024 Feb 11 15:43 lib
   drwxr-xr-x    3 root bin 512 Feb 11 15:42 nsPerl5.005_03
   drwxr-xr-x    3 root bin 512 Feb 11 15:42 nsPerl5.006_01
   drwxr-xr-x    4 root bin 512 Feb 11 15:43 plugins
   drwxr-xr-x    2 root bin 12 Feb 11 15:42 sbin
   drwxr-xr-x    4 root bin 512 Feb 11 15:43 setup
   ```

2. **If the directory server packages are not installed, install the packages from the Sun ONE Directory Server 5.2 software distribution.**

Check the Sun ONE Directory Server 5.2 Installation and Tuning Guide for the correct order to load the packages.

Correct Installation Order (64-bit version) for Solaris 9 OE.

```
# pkgadd -d . SUNWicu
# pkgadd -d . SUNWicux
# pkgadd -d . SUNWpr
# pkgadd -d . SUNWprx
# pkgadd -d . SUNWtls
# pkgadd -d . SUNWtlsx
# pkgadd -d . SUNWtls
# pkgadd -d . SUNWsasl
# pkgadd -d . SUNWsaslx
# pkgadd -d . SUNWjss
# pkgadd -d . SUNWldk
# pkgadd -d . SUNWldkx
# pkgadd -d . SUNWasvc
# pkgadd -d . SUNWasvu
# pkgadd -d . SUNWasvr
# pkgadd -d . SUNWasvcp
# pkgadd -d . SUNWdsvcp
# pkgadd -d . SUNWdsvpl
# pkgadd -d . SUNWdsvu
# pkgadd -d . SUNWdsvr
# pkgadd -d . SUNWdsvx
# pkgadd -d . SUNWasha
# pkgadd -d . SUNWdsha
```

Note – The packages that have an "x" at the end of their names are required to run the 64-bit version of the directory server. To load a 32-bit version, do not install those packages.

▼ To Run the idsktune Command

The idsktune program checks for current patches and recommends Solaris OE parameter settings that help optimize performance. You should run this command and make the recommended changes before continuing with the configuration. The following shows an invocation of idsktune and the suggested parameter changes it recommends.

● Run the idsktune **command as shown.**

```
# cd /usr/ds/v5.2/bin/slapd/server
# ls
64          ldif        ns-ldapagt  pwdhash
idsktune    mmldif      ns-slapd    sparcv9
# ./idsktune
Sun ONE Directory Server system tuning analysis version 15-JAN-
2003.
Copyright 2002 Sun Microsystems, Inc.
.....
```

Sample output:

```
NOTICE: System is usparc-SUNW,Ultra-5_10solaris 5.9_s9s_u2wos_10
(1 processor).
NOTICE: Patch 112601-05 (SunOS 5.9: PGX32 Graphics) is not
installed.
NOTICE: Patch 112902-07 is present, but 112902-08 (SunOS 5.9:
kernel/drv/ip Patch) is a more recent version.
NOTICE: Patch 112963-03 is present, but 112963-05 (SunOS 5.9:
linker patch) is a more recent version.
NOTICE: Patch 113023-01 (SunOS 5.9: Broken preremove scripts in
S9 ALC packages) is not installed.
NOTICE: Patch 113033-02 is present, but 113033-03 (SunOS 5.9:
patch /kernel/drv/isp and /kernel/drv/sparcv9/isp) is a more
recent version.
NOTICE: Patch 113277-03 is present, but 113277-04 (SunOS 5.9: sd
and ssd Patch) is a more recent version
NOTICE: Patch 113333-01 is present, but 113333-02 (SunOS 5.9:
libmeta Patch) is a more recent version.
NOTICE: Patch 113923-02 (X11 6.6.1: security font server patch)
is not installed.
NOTICE: Solaris patches can be obtained from
http://sunsolve.sun.com or your Solaris support representative.
Solaris patches listed as required by the JRE are located at
http://www.sun.com/software/solaris/jre/download.html or can be
obtained from your Solaris support representative.
WARNING: Only 512MB of physical memory is available on the system.
1000MB is the recommended minimum.
NOTICE: /etc/system does not have a setting for
tcp:tcp_conn_hash_sizeThe default is 256.
NOTICE : The tcp_conn_req_max_q value is currently 128, which
will limit the value of listen backlog which can be configured.
It can be raised by adding to /etc/init.d/directory a line similar
to: ndd -set /dev/tcp tcp_conn_req_max_q 1024
```

```
NOTICE: The tcp_keepalive_interval is set to 7200000 milliseconds
(120 minutes).This might cause temporary server congestion from
lost client connections.
NOTICE: The tcp_keepalive_interval can be reduced by adding the
following line to /etc/init.d/directory: ndd -set /dev/tcp
tcp_keepalive_interval 600000
NOTICE: The NDD tcp_ip_abort_cinterval is currently set to 180000
milliseconds (180 seconds).This might cause long delays in
establishing outgoing connections if the destination server is
down.
NOTICE: If the directory service is intended only for LAN or
private high-speed WAN environment, this interval can be reduced
by adding to /etc/init.d/directory: ndd -set /dev/tcp
tcp_ip_abort_cinterval 10000
NOTICE: The NDD tcp_ip_abort_interval is currently set to 180000
milliseconds (180 seconds).This might cause long delays in
detecting connection failure if the destination server is down.
NOTICE: If the directory service is intended only for LAN or
private high-speed WAN environment, this interval can be reduced
by adding to /etc/init.d/directory: ndd -set /dev/tcp
tcp_ip_abort_interval 60000
NOTICE: The TCP initial sequence number generation is not based
on RFC 1948. If this directory service is intended for external
access, add the following to /etc/init.d/directory: ndd -set
/dev/tcp tcp_strong_iss 2
NOTICE: The NDD tcp_smallest_anon_port is currently 32768.  This
allows a maximum of 32768 simultaneous connections.  More ports
can be made available by adding a line to /etc/init.d/directory:
ndd -set /dev/tcp tcp_smallest_anon_port 8192
WARNING: tcp_deferred_ack_interval is currently 100
milliseconds. This will cause Solaris to insert artificial delays
in the LDAP protocol.It should be reduced during load testing.
This line can be added to the /etc/init.d/directory file: ndd -
set /dev/tcp tcp_deferred_ack_interval 5
NOTICE: / partition has less space available, 433MB, than the
largest allowable core file size of 1362MB.  A daemon process
which dumps core could cause the root partition to be filled.
```

▼ To Configure the Directory Server Software

Before you configure your directory server as an LDAP name server, you need to do a little preparation work. The following is a checklist of information you should have in hand.

- Storage volume partition and file system where the directory database will reside – By default, the database is installed in the /var/mps/serverroot directory.

- Solaris OE user and group in which to run the directory server – You can specify nobody, but for added security it is best to create a separate user and group from which to run the directory server. This gives you better control over how the user account will be used.

- Server certificate – If you plan to run the server in secure mode (TLS/SSL) you need a signed server certificate. This part of the configuration is performed after the initial installation and configuration, and can be done later.

- LDAP Domain name – This is the domain that clients specify during initialization.

A directory server can be configured either in interactive mode or in an automated fashion using Jumpstart. The following sections describe both methods.

▼ To Set up the Directory Server (Interactive Mode)

1. **Run the** directoryserver **command as shown.**

```
# /usr/sbin/directoryserver configure -nodisplay
```

By specifying the -nodisplay option, the directoryserver command runs on the command line, and not through a GUI. This is an efficient way to set up a directory server when you are running the command remotely, or when you aren't using a graphics-capable monitor.

2. **Provide the requested information when prompted.**

The following example is an abbreviated list of questions that are asked. Typical responses are shown in bold, and comments in italics.

```
Choose the type of installation you prefer from the following
choices:
1. Express
2. Typical
3. Custom
What would you like to do [2] 2
Typical is sufficient for most cases.
Choose the system user and group names under whose identity
the Sun ONE server will run.
    System User [root] ds5user
    System Group [other] ds5group
You must create this user and group before you start the configuration.
You can store Sun ONE server configuration information in another
Sun ONE directory server.
If you have already prepared a configuration server, you can
configure the new server to use that existing one.
1. The new instance will be the configuration directory server
2. Use existing configuration directory server
What would you like to do [1] 1
The assumption here is that this is your first directory server instance.
You might already have a directory server where you store user
and group information.
1. Store data in the new directory server
2. Store data in an existing directory server
What would you like to do [1] 1
Again the assumption is this is the first directory server instance.
Settings the new directory will use for basic operation
Server Identifier [hostname] myldap
Server Port [389] 389
Suffix [dc=example, dc=com] dc=example, dc=com
This is where you can specify a suffix of your choice. See the beginning of this chapter for
details. The other defaults are common choices.
The configuration server administrator is the LDAP identity
typically used to log in to the Sun ONE Console.

    Configuration server administrator ID [admin]: admin
    Password: *******
    Password: *******
Enter a descriptive, unique name for the administration domain,
such as the name of the organization responsible for managing the
domain.
    Administration Domain [ ] example.com
```

> *Any name can be specified here. The name becomes significant when other administration*
> *servers are configured.*
> ```
> Enter a Distinguished Name (DN) for the Directory Manager and a
> password at least 8 characters long.
> Directory Manager DN [ ]: cn=Directory Manager
> Password: *******
> Password (again): *******
> ```
> *You can choose a different name, but this might lead to confusion for other administrators and*
> *support personnel who expect that name.*

▼ To Set Up the Administration Server (Interactive Mode)

1. Run the `mpsadmserver` **command as shown.**

```
# /usr/sbin/mpsadmserver configure -nodisplay
```

By specifying the `-nodisplay` option you configure the server on the command line, and not through a GUI.

2. Provide the requested information when prompted.

The following example is an abbreviated list of questions that are asked. Typical responses are shown in bold, and comments in italics.

```
Enter the fully qualified domain name of the computer
Fully Qualified Name [myldap.domain.com] myldap.example.com

Choose the type of installation you prefer from the following
choices:
1. Express
2. Typical
What would you like to do [2] ? 2
Administration Port [7871] : 20000
```
The value 20000 is chosen because it is easy to remember. Be careful not to choose a port that is already in use because the configuration will fail.
```
Choose the system user and group names under whose identity the
Sun ONE server will run.
System User [root] root
System Group [other] other
```
If you want to be able to start and stop the directory server you need a user who has those permissions.
```
Configuration Directory Server
Host [] : myldap.example.com
Port [] : 389
```
This information must match what was used to configure the directory server instance that contains the configuration data.It is recommended to enter the FQN of the LDAP server here to avoid access problems later.
```
Configuration Directory Server Administrator
Administrator Id [admin] : admin
Password [] : *******
```
The ID and password must match with the account created on the configuration server.
```
Administration Domain [example.com]: example.com
```
This must match the administration domain specified in the directory server.

▼ To Set Up the Directory Server (Silent Mode)

Silent mode installations are particularly useful when combined with automated installations that use Jumpstart technology.

1. **Edit a copy of the** /usr/ds/v5.2/setup/typical.ins **file.**

   The bold text in the following example shows the file entries that were changed.

   ```
   # Wizard Statefile section for Sun ONE Directory Distribution

   [STATE_BEGIN Sun ONE Directory Distribution
   dfc8280d7b940d1acc9e411ed388f11685a1ae8e]

   # This is the Fully Qualified Name of the computer in the
   # form <hostname>.<domainname> (e.g., host.domain.com).
   # Replace token FullMachineName
   FullMachineName = myldap.example.com
   # Unix user and group to run the Sun One server
   # Replace tokens UserID and GroupID
   ServerUser = ds5user
   ServerGroup = ds5group
   # This server is the Configuration Directory Server
   UseExistingConfigDirectory = 0 (See the following example)
   # User Data will be stored in this server
   UseExistingUserDirectory = 0 (See the following example)
   # Directory Settings for this server
   # Replace tokens InstanceName, LDAPPort and BaseSuffix
   DirectoryIdentifier = myldap
   DirectoryPort = 389
   DirectorySuffix = dc=example,dc=com
   # Admistrator Identifier and Password
   # Replace tokens AdminUserID and AdminUserPasswd
   ConfigDirectoryAdminID = admin
   ConfigDirectoryAdminPwd = admin
   # Administration Domain
   # Replace token AdministrationDomain
   AdminDomain = example.com
   # Directory Manager Identifier and Password
   # Replace tokens DirectoryManagerDN and DirectoryManagerPasswd
   DirectoryManager = cn=Directory Manager
   DirectoryManagerPwd = dirmanager

   [STATE_DONE Sun ONE Directory Distribution
   dfc8280d7b940d1acc9e411ed388f11685a1ae8e]
   ```

Note – The checksum lines at the start and end of the file are used to check if the file was created with the same version of the directory server you are installing.

The installation file assumes you are using the same directory server instance for both configuration and user data. Configuration data can be shared among several servers and is only referenced when the directory server starts. Sharing configuration data enables updates to be performed in only one place. If you have a directory server already set up as a configuration server, specify the name of it as shown here.

```
# This server is the Configuration Directory Server
UseExistingConfigDirectory = mycfgserver.example.com
# User Data will be stored in this server
UseExistingUserDirectory = 0
```

If you are setting up a configuration server that contains no user data, specify the name of a server that contains user data as shown here.

```
# This server is the Configuration Directory Server
UseExistingConfigDirectory = 0
# User Data will be stored in this server
UseExistingUserDirectory = myldapserver.example.com
```

2. **Run the** `directoryserver` **command as shown.**

```
# /usr/sbin/directoryserver -noconsole -nodisplay -state myfile.ins
```

The directory server will be installed without prompting you with questions. You can combine a silent mode installation with Jumpstart to perform a fully automated installation, as described in "Automating Installations" on page 244.

▼ To Set Up the Administration Server (Silent Mode)

1. **Run** `mpsadmserver` **as shown.**

```
# /usr/sbin/mpsadmserver -nodisplay -noconsole -saveState filename
```

A generic instruction file is created that you modify in the next step.

2. **Edit the administration state file that was created in the previous step.**

Make changes so that the parameters specified in this file correspond to your configuration.

```
# vi filename
# Install Wizard Statefile section for Sun ONE Administration
Distribution
#
#
[STATE_BEGIN Sun ONE Administration Distribution
0268835a2e5c475b4e526cd711ddfe114ea7c1a3]
FullMachineName = myldap.example.com
AdminPort = 20000
ServerUser = root
ServerGroup = other
ConfigDirectoryHost = myldap.example.com
ConfigDirectoryPort = 389
ConfigDirectoryAdminID = admin
ConfigDirectoryAdminPwd = admin
AdminDomain = example.com
AdminSysUser = root
AdminSysGroup = other
 [STATE_DONE Sun ONE Administration Distribution
0268835a2e5c475b4e526cd711ddfe114ea7c1a3]
```

3. **Run the** mpsadmserver **command as shown.**

```
# /usr/sbin/mpsadmserver configure -nodisplay -noconsole -state
filename
```

▼ To Run the idsconfig Command (Interactive Mode)

This command creates the object classes, containers, ACIs, and client profiles required before you can run native Solaris OE LDAP.

1. **Run the** `/usr/lib/ldap/idsconfig` **command as shown.**

   Note that the `domainname` to be served is independent of your DNS domain name.

```
# cd /usr/lib/ldap
# ./idsconfig
Enter the iPlanet Directory Server's (iDS) hostname to setup:
myldap.example.com
Enter the port number for iDS (h=help): [389]
Enter the directory manager DN: [cn=Directory Manager]
Enter passwd for cn=Directory Manager :
Enter the domainname to be served (h=help): [dc=example,dc=com]
Enter LDAP Base DN (h=help): [dc=example,dc=com]
Enter the profile name (h=help): [default]
Default server list (h=help): [128.100.100.1]
Preferred server list (h=help):
Choose desired search scope (one, sub, h=help): [one]
The following are the supported credential levels:
  1  anonymous
  2  proxy
  3  proxy anonymous
Choose Credential level [h=help]: [1] 2
The following are the supported Authentication Methods:
  1  none
  2  simple
  3  sasl/DIGEST-MD5
  4  tls:simple
  5  tls:sasl/DIGEST-MD5
Choose Authentication Method (h=help): [1] 4
Do you want the clients to follow referrals (y/n/h)? [n]
Do you want to modify the server timelimit value (y/n/h)? [n]
Do you want to modify the server sizelimit value (y/n/h)? [n]
Do you want to store passwords in "crypt" format (y/n/h)? [n]
Do you want to setup a Service Authentication Methods (y/n/h)? [n]
Client search time limit in seconds (h=help): [30]
Profile Time To Live in seconds (h=help): [43200]
Bind time limit in seconds (h=help): [10]
Do you wish to setup Service Search Descriptors (y/n/h)? [n] y
  A  Add a Service Search Descriptor
  D  Delete an SSD
  M  Modify an SSD
  P  Display all SSD's
  H  Help
  X  Clear all SSD's
  Q  Exit menu
Enter menu choice: [Quit] a
Enter the service id: passwd
Enter the base: ou=people2
```

```
Enter the scope: one
              Summary of Configuration
   1  Domain to serve              : example.com
   2  Base DN to setup             : dc=example,dc=com
   3  Profile name to create       : default
   4  Default Server List          : 128.100.100.1
   5  Preferred Server List        :
   6  Default Search Scope         : sub
   7  Credential Level             : proxy
   8  Authentication Method        : tls:simple
   9  Enable Follow Referrals      : FALSE
  10  iDS Time Limit               :
  11  iDS Size Limit               :
  12  Enable crypt password storage : FALSE
  13  Service Auth Method pam_ldap :
  14  Service Auth Method keyserv  :
  15  Service Auth Method passwd-cmd:
  16  Search Time Limit            : 30
  17  Profile Time to Live         : 43200
  18  Bind Limit                   : 10
  19  Service Search Descriptors Menu

Enter config value to change: (1-19 0=commit changes) [0]
Enter DN for proxy agent: [cn=proxyagent,ou=profile,dc=
example,dc=com]
Enter passwd for proxyagent:
Re-enter passwd:
```

2. As `idsconfig` **runs, the steps performed are displayed as they are completed. Observe the following:**

```
1. Schema attributes have been updated.
2. Schema objectclass definitions have been added.
3. NisDomainObject added to dc=example,dc=com.
4. Top level "ou" containers complete.
5. automount maps: auto_home auto_direct auto_master auto_shared
        processed.
6. ACI for dc=example,dc=com modified to disable self modify.
7. Add of VLV Access Control Information (ACI).
8. Generated client profile and loaded on server.
9. Processing eq,pres indexes:
        ipHostNumber (eq,pres)   Finished indexing.
        uidNumber (eq,pres)   Finished indexing.
        ipNetworkNumber (eq,pres)   Finished indexing.
        gidnumber (eq,pres)   Finished indexing.
        oncrpcnumber (eq,pres)   Finished indexing.
        automountKey (eq,pres)   Finished indexing.
10. Processing eq,pres,sub indexes:
        membernisnetgroup (eq,pres,sub)   Finished indexing.
        nisnetgrouptriple (eq,pres,sub)   Finished indexing.
11. Processing VLV indexes:
        example.com.gethostent vlv_index   Entry created
        example.com.getnetent vlv_index   Entry created
        example.com..getpwent vlv_index   Entry created
        example.com.getrpcent vlv_index   Entry created
        example.com.getspent vlv_index   Entry created

idsconfig: Setup of iDS server myldap.example.com is complete.
```

Note – The assumption is that `idsconfig` is run right after the directory server installation and configuration. Therefore, the indexes get created quickly. With a populated directory, indexing can be quite lengthy, during which time the directory is placed in read-only mode.

3. **Set up the VLV Indexes as described by the output of** `idsconfig`.

Creating VLV indexes is a two-part process. The first part is done by the `idsconfig` script. The second part requires the directory server to be halted, so must be performed separately as shown below.

```
Note: idsconfig has created entries for VLV indexes. Use the
      directoryserver(1m) script on vipivot to stop
      the server and then enter the following vlvindex
      sub-commands to create the actual VLV indexes:

  directoryserver -s <server-instance> vlvindex -n userRoot -T
example.com.getgrent
  directoryserver -s <server-instance> vlvindex -n userRoot -T
example.com.gethostent
  directoryserver -s <server-instance> vlvindex -n userRoot -T
example.com.getnetent
  directoryserver -s <server-instance> vlvindex -n userRoot -T
example.com.getpwent
  directoryserver -s <server-instance> vlvindex -n userRoot -T
example.com.getrpcent
  directoryserver -s <server-instance> vlvindex -n userRoot -T
example.com.getspent
```

▼ To Run the `idsconfig` Command (Silent Mode)

1. **Create an output file.**

```
# /usr/lib/ldap/idsconfig -o my_conf_file
```

By specifying the `-o` option, a configuration file is created that can be used for subsequent installations.

Example:

```
# /tmp/idsconfig.ins - This file contains configuration
# information for Native LDAP. Use the idsconfig tool to load it.

#
# WARNING: This file was generated by idsconfig, and is intended
#  to be loaded by idsconfig as is.  DO NOT EDIT THIS FILE!
#
IDS_SERVER="myldap.example.com"
IDS_PORT=389
IDS_TIMELIMIT=
```

```
IDS_SIZELIMIT=
LDAP_ROOTDN="cn=Directory Manager"
LDAP_ROOTPWD=dirmanager
LDAP_DOMAIN="example.com"
LDAP_TREETOP="dc=example,dc=com"

# Internal program variables that need to be set.
NEED_PROXY=0
NEED_TIME=0
NEED_SIZE=0
NEED_CRYPT=FALSE

# LDAP PROFILE related defaults
LDAP_PROFILE_NAME="default"
DEL_OLD_PROFILE=1
LDAP_BASEDN="dc=example,dc=com"
LDAP_SERVER_LIST="128.100.100.1"
LDAP_AUTHMETHOD=""
LDAP_FOLLOWREF=FALSE
LDAP_SEARCH_SCOPE="one"
NEED_SRVAUTH_PAM=0
NEED_SRVAUTH_KEY=0
NEED_SRVAUTH_CMD=0
LDAP_SRV_AUTHMETHOD_PAM=""
LDAP_SRV_AUTHMETHOD_KEY=""
LDAP_SRV_AUTHMETHOD_CMD=""
LDAP_SEARCH_TIME_LIMIT=30
LDAP_PREF_SRVLIST=""
LDAP_PROFILE_TTL=43200
LDAP_CRED_LEVEL="proxy"
LDAP_BIND_LIMIT=10
# Proxy Agent
LDAP_PROXYAGENT="cn=proxyagent,ou=profile,dc=example,dc=com"
LDAP_PROXYAGENT_CRED="test1234"

# Export all the variables (just in case)
export IDS_HOME IDS_PORT LDAP_ROOTDN LDAP_ROOTPWD
LDAP_SERVER_LIST LDAP_BASEDN
export LDAP_DOMAIN LDAP_TREETOP LDAP_PROXYAGENT
LDAP_PROXYAGENT_CRED
export NEED_PROXY
export LDAP_PROFILE_NAME LDAP_BASEDN LDAP_SERVER_LIST
export LDAP_AUTHMETHOD LDAP_FOLLOWREF LDAP_SEARCH_SCOPE
LDAP_SEARCH_TIME_LIMIT
export LDAP_PREF_SRVLIST LDAP_PROFILE_TTL LDAP_CRED_LEVEL
LDAP_BIND_LIMIT
export NEED_SRVAUTH_PAM NEED_SRVAUTH_KEY NEED_SRVAUTH_CMD
export LDAP_SRV_AUTHMETHOD_PAM LDAP_SRV_AUTHMETHOD_KEY
LDAP_SRV_AUTHMETHOD_CMD
```

```
export LDAP_SERV_SRCH_DES SSD_FILE

# Service Search Descriptors start here if present:

# End of /tmp/idsconfig.ins
```

As described in"Automating Installations" on page 244, you can create an
idsconfig output file, then use it to perform an automated installation using
JumpStart technology.

idsconfig *Tips and Observations*

The following tips and observations might clear up questions you have.

- The directory server you are configuring must be running when you run the
  idsconfig command because idsconfig uses LDAP to make the changes

- The name of the domain to be served is independent of your DNS domain. While
  it can have the same name, it doesn't need to.

- Anonymous credential level does not work with pam_unix authentication. This is
  because user passwords need to be readable by some identity, which is normally
  a proxy account. Unless you make passwords readable by anonymous, pam_unix
  will not work.

- The BaseDN specified does not have to be a root suffix. If you specify a container,
  such as ou=nsmaps,dc=example,dc=com, the ou=nsmap container is created
  for you (if it does not already exist).

- Only one client profile is created. See Chapter 7 "Performing Administrative
  Tasks" for details on creating additional profiles.

- At the Preferred Servers prompt, you must enter the IP address and not the host
  name. This is because a name service might not be running at the time the
  information is needed.

- Choosing an authentication method only creates an attribute in the profile. For
  example, if you specify tls:simple you still need to configure TLS/SSL on both the
  server and client. You can generate the profile before TLS/SSL is configured, but
  must configure it before clients are initialized using the profile.

- The default for the profile time to live is 12 hours. This means if you modify
  the profile in the directory, clients will not see the changes until the cache is
  refreshed, by default, in 12 hours.

- While Service Search Descriptors (SSDs) can be specified, they will be very
  rudimentary. If you want to deploy SSDs, see Chapter 7 "Performing
  Administrative Tasks" for more details.

Enabling TLS/SSL on the Directory Server

To take advantage of the ability to encrypt name service data, you need to perform the following tasks:

- Enable TLS/SSL on the directory server.
- Create a client profile that specifies TLS as an authentication method.
- Provide the client with a certificate database containing the Certificate Authority (CA) certificate.

These tasks are described in the following sections.

Enabling SSL

To enable SSL on the directory server, you need to have a signed server certificate available. The certificate must be signed by a trusted Certificate Authority (CA). The CA can be a commercial one or one you set up for company use. Alternatively, you can self-sign a certificate. In either case, you will need access to the signer's certificate so it can be stored in the client's certificate database.

For web browsers such as Netscape Communicator, obtaining the signer's certificate is as simple as pointing your browser at a URL and accepting the certificate. For an LDAP client, there is no way to duplicate this procedure. However, the same certificate database created for Communicator can also be used by the LDAP client.

The process of requesting a certificate to be signed and then installing it on your directory server consists of several steps that include:

1. Create a Certificate Signing Request (CSR) by invoking the directory server certificate wizard or generating one with another tool.

2. Send the CSR to a Certificate Authority (CA). This can be through email, a web interface, or simply transferring the CSR file to the CA.

3. Retrieve the signed certificate from the CA. This can be received through email, retrieved from a web site, or obtained by a file transfer.

4. Import the certificate into the directory server. This can be through the certificate wizard or performed manually.

The way these steps are performed varies depending on the type of CA you use. For the examples presented here, self-signed certificates are used. That is, you become the CA that signs the certificate. This method is useful for testing and for organizations that do not have access to a CA. Chapter 3 discusses how to use the certutil and keyutil utilities for creating your own CA, generating certificate requests, and then generating a certificate.

Enabling SSL on the Directory Server

The Sun ONE Directory Server provides a wizard that will generate a CSR and install the signed certificate for you. Essentially what this does is create `cert7.db` and `key3.db` databases. If you configure these using `certutil` as described in Chapter 3, you can bypass the wizard by copying them to the appropriate location. The names need to change to reflect the name of the directory server instance in which they will be used.

```
# cp cert7.db slapd-myserver-cert7.db
# cp key3.db slapd-myserver-key3.db
# cp slapd-myserver-cert7.db /var/mps/serverroot/alias
# cp slapd-myserver-key3.db /var/mps/serverroot/alias
```

Once the `slapd-myserver-cert7.db` and `slapd-myserver-key3.db` databases are in place, you can enable SSL from the directory console. To do this, go to the Configuration tab and highlight the first line (your server instance). Click on the Encryption tab and observe the screen shown in FIGURE 4-2.

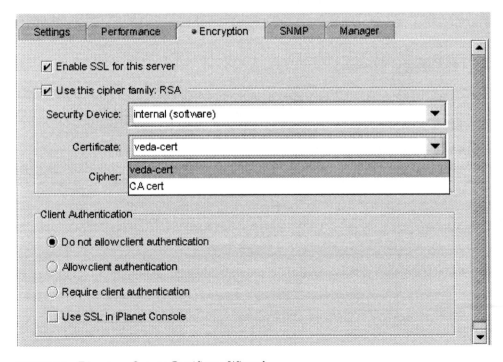

FIGURE 4-2 Directory Server Certificate Wizard

To enable SSL, check the Enable SSL for this server and Use this cypher family: RSA boxes. You should also see the server certificate you created under the Certificate: pull-down menu. When you click on the Save button, you are instructed to restart the directory server. When you manually restart the directory server you see the following output.

```
# directoryserver stop
# directoryserver start
Enter PIN for Internal (Software) Token: *******
```

This is the same PIN used when the cert7.db and key3.db databases were created. At this point, the directory server is listening on port 636 for TLS/SSL requests.

Automatic Startup of SSL

Because there might be cases where the directory server is restarted without an administrator present, it is desirable to have the server start without querying for a password. This can be accomplished by creating a file that contains the key3.db database password. Usually, this file resides in the alias directory under the directory server root. The following example shows how the password file is created.

```
# cd /var/mps/serverroot/alias
# ls -l
-rw------- 1 root other 196608 Sep  5 16:49 slapd-myserver-cert7.db
-rw------ 1 root other 32768 Sep  5 16:49 slapd-myserver-key3.db
-rw------- 1 root other 32768 Sep 10 11:32 secmod.db
# vi slapd-myserver-pin.txt
<insert text>
Internal (Software) Token:mysecret
<exit>
#
```

The permissions shown assume the Directory Server is started and run as root. If this is not the case, the ownership of the files must be adjusted. The permission and ownership of the password file should be set so only the user starting the directory server can read it.

▼ To Configure TLS/SSL From the Command Line

LDIF provides an alternative to the Sun ONE Directory Console for configuring TLS/SSL. LDIF can be created and imported to generate the same configuration. There are three tasks to create this configuration:

1. Create an entry that will contain TLS/SSL information.

2. Modify some default directory data.

3. Turn on TLS/SSL.

1. Create LDIF representation that looks like this and import it.

```
dn: cn=RSA,cn=encryption,cn=config
changetype: add
objectclass: top
objectclass: nsEncryptionModule
cn: RSA
nsSSLToken: internal (software)
nsSSLPersonalitySSL: server-cert
nsSSLActivation: on
```

The nickname `server-root` matches the name given to the certificate created for the `slapd-myserver-cert7.db` database.

2. **Create LDIF representation that looks like this and import it.**

```
dn: cn=encryption,cn=config
changetype: modify
replace: nsSSL2
nsSSL2: on
-
replace: nsSSL3
nsSSL3: on
-
replace: nsSSLClientAuth
nsSSLClientAuth: allowed
-
replace: nsSSL3Ciphers
nsSSL3Ciphers: -rsa_null_md5,-rsa_fips_3des_sha,-rsa_fips_des_s
ha,+rsa_3des_sha,+rsa_rc4_128_md5,+rsa_des_sha,+rsa_rc4_40_md5
-
replace: nsCertFile
nsCertFile: alias/slapd-myserver-cert7.db
-
replace: nsKeyFile
nsKeyFile: alias/slapd-myserver-key3.db
```

The names of the database files, `slapd-myserver-cert7.db` and `slapd-myserver-key3.db`, match the ones that were placed there.

3. **Create LDIF representation that looks like this and import it.**

```
dn: cn=config
changetype: modify
replace: nsslapd-secureport
nsslapd-secureport: 636
-
replace: nsslapd-security
nsslapd-security: on
```

▼ To Verify the TLS/SSL Configuration on the Server

1. **Make sure there is a process listening to port 636.**

```
# netstat -an | grep 636 | grep LISTEN
*.636 *.*                       0     0 24576      0 LISTEN
...
#
```

2. **Access the directory server in one of the following two ways:**

   - From Netscape Communicator, go to

     `ldaps:///myserver:636/`

   - From the command line, enter:

```
# ./ldapsearch -h ipivot -p 636 -Z -P /var/ldap/cert7.db -K
/var/ldap/key3.db -s base -b "" objectclass=\*
 . . .
```

This output displayed on the screen where the command was entered should be the Directory Server Entry (DSE), which looks like this:

```
dn:
objectClass: top
namingContexts: dc=example,dc=com
namingContexts: o=NetscapeRoot
supportedExtension: 2.16.840.1.113730.3.5.7
supportedExtension: 2.16.840.1.113730.3.5.8
supportedExtension: 2.16.840.1.113730.3.5.3
supportedExtension: 2.16.840.1.113730.3.5.5
supportedExtension: 2.16.840.1.113730.3.5.6
supportedExtension: 2.16.840.1.113730.3.5.4
...
```

Configuring the Clients

There are three versions of Solaris LDAP clients:

- Solaris 8 OE (Phase 1) – is the original version that shipped with Solaris 8 OE. This client is overwritten when you install patch 108993-18 (or later version).

- Solaris 8 OE patch client (Phase 2) – is loaded when you install patch 108993-16 (or later).

- Solaris 9 OE client – installed as a core component of the Solaris 9 OE. To take advantage of password aging, you must install patch 112960-03 (or later).

The first version of the client has been made obsolete by the introduction of the 108993-16 patch.

Solaris LDAP Client Initialization

Secured LDAP Clients are initialized either by the sysidtools program when the Solaris OE is installed, or by running the ldapclient command after the client has been configured with another name service. A description of sysidtools is provided in "Automating Installations" on page 244 because it is a key component of achieving automated installations. You can run the ldapclient command with or without client profiles. However, use of profiles is highly recommended for ease of administration, so this is the only method discussed.

Client initialization consists of the following tasks that are performed as the result of running the ldapclient command.:

1. Creating the ldap_client_file and ldap_client_cred files in the /var/ldap directory.

2. Modifying the /etc/nsswitch.conf file to include the ldap tag.

3. Starting the /usr/lib/ldap/ldap_cachemgr process.

Other files that may be modified include:

- /etc/defaultdomain
- /etc/.rootkey
- /var/nis/NIS_COLD_START
- /var/nis/.NIS_PRIVATE_DIRCACHE
- /var/nis/client-info

The ldap_client_file file is created from data contained in the client profile. The ldap_client_cred file is created from command-line arguments.

Example:

```
# ldapclient init -a proxyDn=cn=proxyagent,ou=profile,dc=\
example,dc=com -a domainname=example.com -a profilename=default\
-a proxypassword=test1234 128.100.100.1
```

In this example, the proxyDn and proxypassword arguments result in the creation of the following content:

```
# cat /var/ldap/ldap_client_cred
# Do not edit this file manually; your changes will be lost.Please
use ldapclient (1M) instead.
#
NS_LDAP_BINDDN= cn=proxyagent,ou=profile,dc=example,dc=com
NS_LDAP_BINDPASSWD= {NS1}4a3788e8c053424f
```

The following is a compressed example of the default nsswitch.ldap file. This file is copied to /etc/nsswitch.conf when the client is initialized. Notice that the ldap string is added as a tag along with the files tag.

```
# cat /etc/nsswitch.ldap
passwd:      files ldap
group:       files ldap

hosts:       ldap [NOTFOUND=return] files
ipnodes:     files

networks:    ldap [NOTFOUND=return] files
protocols:   ldap [NOTFOUND=return] files
rpc:         ldap [NOTFOUND=return] files
ethers:      ldap [NOTFOUND=return] files
netmasks:    ldap [NOTFOUND=return] files
bootparams:  ldap [NOTFOUND=return] files
publickey:   ldap [NOTFOUND=return] files

netgroup:    ldap

automount:   files ldap
aliases:     files ldap

services:    files ldap
sendmailvars:   files

printers:       user files ldap

auth_attr: files ldap
prof_attr: files ldap

project:     files ldap
```

The `ldap_cachemgr` process is started when the `/etc/init.d/ldap.client` script is run. It is also started by the `ldapclient` command when it is run to initialize a client. The `ldap_cachemgr` process is started automatically if the `ldap_client_file` exists as shown in bold in the `ldap.client` script below.

```
#!/sbin/sh
# Copyright (c) 1999,2001 by Sun Microsystems, Inc.
#ident   "@(#)ldap.client        1.3       01/10/29 SMI"
case "$1" in
start)
        [ -f /var/ldap/ldap_client_file ] && \
            [ -f /usr/lib/ldap/ldap_cachemgr ] || exit 0
        /usr/lib/ldap/ldap_cachemgr
        ;;
stop)
        [ -f /usr/lib/ldap/ldap_cachemgr ] &&
/usr/lib/ldap/ldap_cachemgr -K
        ;;
*)
        echo "Usage: $0 { start | stop }"
        exit 1
        ;;
esac
exit 0
```

▼ To Configure pam_ldap

By default, the /etc/pam.conf file is configured for pam_unix authentication. While this form of authentication works with LDAP as a name service, pam_ldap is recommended, as discussed in Chapter 3 "Defining Directory Service Security Architecture.

● **To enable** pam_ldap **for all services, add the bolded lines to the** pam.conf **file as shown in the following code box.**

```
# login service (explicit because of pam_dial_auth)
login    auth sufficient         pam_unix_auth.so.1
login    auth required           pam_ldap.so.1 try_first_pass
# rlogin service (explicit because of pam_rhost_auth)
rlogin   auth required           pam_unix_auth.so.1
rlogin   auth required            pam_ldap.so.1 try_first_pass
# rsh service (explicit because of pam_rhost_auth,
# and pam_unix_auth for meaningful pam_setcred)
rsh      auth required           pam_unix_auth.so.1
rsh      auth required           pam_ldap.so.1 try_first_pass
# PPP service (explicit because of pam_dial_auth)
ppp      auth required           pam_unix_auth.so.1
ppp      auth required           pam_dap.so.1 try_first_pass
# Default definitions for Authentication management
# Used when service name is not explicitly mentioned for
authenctication
other    auth required           pam_unix_auth.so.1
other    auth required           pam_ldap.so.1 try_first_pass
# passwd command (explicit because of a different authentication
# module)
passwd   auth required           pam_passwd_auth.so.1
passwd   auth required           pam_ldap.so.1 try_first_pass
# Default definition for  Password management
# Used when service name is not explicitly mentioned for password
# management
other    password requisite          pam_authtok_get.so.1
other    password requisite          pam_authtok_check.so.1
other    password sufficient pam_authtok_store.so.1
other    password required pam_ldap.so.1 try_first_pass
```

Running DNS and LDAP Name Services

Unlike NIS, there is no DNS forwarding capability built into the LDAP name service. In many cases, it is desirable to be able to resolve fully qualified DNS names in addition to simple host names. This is important when configuring clients to accept server certificates that have DNS names defined. For security reasons, the client must be able to resolve the DNS name, or else it assumes the certificate is not valid.

▼ To Enable DNS With LDAP

● **Modify two files as shown:**

```
# vi /etc/resolv.conf
.
.
.
nameserver 125.148.172.14


# vi /etc/nsswitch.conf
.
.
.
hosts:        dns ldap [NOTFOUND=return] files
```

The IP address 125.148.172.14 should be replaced with an address of one of your DNS servers and the dns tag should be placed before the ldap tag for the hosts entry in /etc/nsswitch.conf as shown.

Enabling TLS/SSL on the Client

The authentication method the Secured LDAP Client uses to connect with the name service is determined by the authenticationMethod attribute specified in the client profile. This attribute can be overridden to use another authentication method like the pam_ldap authentication and password management by adding the serviceAuthenticationMethod attribute. If this attribute is not specified, the same method is used for all services including proxy authentication.

▼ To Configure the Client to Use TLS/SSL as a Transport

1. **Insert the** `tls:simple` **tag as the value of the** `authenticationMethod` **attribute in the client profile as shown here in LDIF representation.**

```
dn: cn=sslProfile,ou=profile,dc=example,dc=com
objectClass: top
objectClass: DUAConfigProfile
defaultServerList: 128.100.100.1
defaultSearchBase: dc=example,dc=com
authenticationMethod: tls:simple
followReferrals: FALSE
defaultSearchScope: one
searchTimeLimit: 30
profileTTL: 43200
cn: sslProfile
credentialLevel: proxy
bindTimeLimit: 10
```

2. **Create a client certificate database.**

   To complete the configuration, the client must have a certificate database contained in the signer certificate that the directory server uses. Although it can be empty, a `key3.db` file is also required. The same `cert7.db` file used on the directory server can be used by the client.

   Example:

```
# cp cert7.db /var/ldap/cert7.db
# chmod 444 /var/ldap/cert7.db
# touch /var/ldap/key3.db
# chmod 444 /var/ldap/key3.db
```

Note – Make sure the client can resolve DNS names, because the certificate that was created specifies the fully qualified directory server name in the `cn=` field.

Automating Installations

The installation of both the client and server can be automated using JumpStart technology. To accomplish an automated installation, scripts need to be developed. In this section, the basic steps for setting up a JumpStart environment for both the directory server and clients are discussed including tips for creating scripts. You will find the following sections:

- "Automating the Directory Server Installation" on page 244
- "Automating LDAP Client Installations" on page 248
- "Hands-off Installation of an LDAP Client" on page 253

Automating the Directory Server Installation

Overview

To set up a directory server to support Secured LDAP Clients (whether through automation or not), a number of steps are required:

1. Load the Solaris OE on the directory server.

2. If the Sun ONE Directory Server 5.2 packages are not included, load them.

3. Install applicable patches.

4. Set up DNS as a name service.

5. Set up tuning parameters.

6. Configure the Directory Server (basic).

7. Configure TLS/SSL on the server.

8. Configure the Directory Server to support LDAP as a name service.

9. Populate the Directory Server with name service data.

Steps 1–5 can be accomplished before a system reboot. Steps 6–8 must be performed after the system reboots. Sample Jumpstart finish scripts are discussed in the following sections. Additional details on JumpStart finish scripts and how to run them following a system reboot can be found in the Sun BluePrints book *JumpStart Technology: Effective Use in the Solaris Operating Environment*.

▼ To Prepare a JumpStart Server to Install and Configure a Directory Server

The directions here assume you are familiar with Jumpstart basics. Refer to the *Advanced Installation Guide* if you are not.

1. **Create an install server with the Solaris OE.**

   The install server can be created either from the Solaris 8 or Solaris 9 OE distribution.

2. **Load the Sun ONE Directory Server 5.2 packages.**

   To add packages that are not part of the Solaris OE distribution, a JumpStart finish script is required. You can create one with your favorite editor.

A sample JumpStart finish script to install the packages might look like this:

```sh
#!/bin/sh
BASE=/a
MNT=/mnt
ADMIN_FILE=/tmp/admin
mount -f nfs jsserver:/jumpstart/Packages/ds52 ${MNT}
cat >${ADMIN_FILE} <<DONT_ASK
mail=root
instance=overwrite
partial=nocheck
runlevel=nocheck
idepend=nocheck
rdepend=nocheck
space=ask
setuid=nocheck
conflict=nocheck
action=nocheck
basedir=default
DONT_ASK
/usr/sbin/pkgadd -a ${ADMIN_FILE} -d ${MNT} -R ${BASE} SUNWasha
/usr/sbin/pkgadd -a ${ADMIN_FILE} -d ${MNT} -R ${BASE} SUNWasvc
/usr/sbin/pkgadd -a ${ADMIN_FILE} -d ${MNT} -R ${BASE} SUNWasvcp
/usr/sbin/pkgadd -a ${ADMIN_FILE} -d ${MNT} -R ${BASE} SUNWasvu
/usr/sbin/pkgadd -a ${ADMIN_FILE} -d ${MNT} -R ${BASE} SUNWdsha
/usr/sbin/pkgadd -a ${ADMIN_FILE} -d ${MNT} -R ${BASE} SUNWdsvcp
/usr/sbin/pkgadd -a ${ADMIN_FILE} -d ${MNT} -R ${BASE} SUNWdsvh
/usr/sbin/pkgadd -a ${ADMIN_FILE} -d ${MNT} -R ${BASE} SUNWdsvhx
/usr/sbin/pkgadd -a ${ADMIN_FILE} -d ${MNT} -R ${BASE} SUNWdspl
/usr/sbin/pkgadd -a ${ADMIN_FILE} -d ${MNT} -R ${BASE} SUNWdsvr
/usr/sbin/pkgadd -a ${ADMIN_FILE} -d ${MNT} -R ${BASE} SUNWdsvu
/usr/sbin/pkgadd -a ${ADMIN_FILE} -d ${MNT} -R ${BASE} SUNWdsvx
/usr/sbin/pkgadd -a ${ADMIN_FILE} -d ${MNT} -R ${BASE} SUNWicu
/usr/sbin/pkgadd -a ${ADMIN_FILE} -d ${MNT} -R ${BASE} SUNWicux
/usr/sbin/pkgadd -a ${ADMIN_FILE} -d ${MNT} -R ${BASE} SUNWjss
/usr/sbin/pkgadd -a ${ADMIN_FILE} -d ${MNT} -R ${BASE} SUNWldk
/usr/sbin/pkgadd -a ${ADMIN_FILE} -d ${MNT} -R ${BASE} SUNWldkx
/usr/sbin/pkgadd -a ${ADMIN_FILE} -d ${MNT} -R ${BASE} SUNWpr
/usr/sbin/pkgadd -a ${ADMIN_FILE} -d ${MNT} -R ${BASE} SUNWprx
/usr/sbin/pkgadd -a ${ADMIN_FILE} -d ${MNT} -R ${BASE} SUNWsasl
/usr/sbin/pkgadd -a ${ADMIN_FILE} -d ${MNT} -R ${BASE} SUNWsaslx
/usr/sbin/pkgadd -a ${ADMIN_FILE} -d ${MNT} -R ${BASE} SUNWtls
/usr/sbin/pkgadd -a ${ADMIN_FILE} -d ${MNT} -R ${BASE} SUNWtlsx
umount ${MNT}
```

3. **Install patches.**

   In general, you want to install the recommended patches that correspond to the OE installed on the server. Directory Server-specific patches should also be installed.

4. **Set up DNS.**

   The system that the Directory Server is installed on should be configured for DNS before it is configured as a directory server. One way to do this is to have a `sysidcfg` file that specifies `dns`.

5. **Configure tuning parameters.**

   Depending on your anticipated load, you might want to change some of the TCP parameter defaults.

   Example:

```
#!/bin/sh
echo "set tcp:tcp_conn_hash_size 1024" >> /a/etc/system
( cat <<EOF
ndd -set /dev/tcp tcp_conn_req_max_q 1024
ndd -set /dev/tcp tcp_keepalive_interval 600000
ndd -set /dev/tcp tcp_ip_abort_cinterval 10000
ndd -set /dev/tcp tcp_ip_abort_interval 60000
ndd -set /dev/tcp tcp_strong_iss 2
ndd -set /dev/tcp tcp_smallest_anon_port 8192
ndd -set /dev/tcp tcp_deferred_ack_interval 5
EOF
) >> /a/etc/init.d/inetinit
```

6. **Configure the basic directory server parameters.**

   The directory server needs to be configured after the system reboots. One way to trigger a script to run after it boots is to copy a script to the `/etc/rc*` directory. After it runs, you can delete it. For example:

```
#!/bin/sh
cp ${SI_CONFIG_DIR}/Files/S98dirconfig /a/var/ldap
```

   The content of `S98dirconfig` might look like this:

```
#!/bin/sh
DIR=/net/jsserver/jumpstart/Files
/usr/sbin/directoryserver configure -nodisplay -state \
${DIR}/typical.ins
```

> **Note –** See "To Set Up the Directory Server (Silent Mode)" on page 222 for instructions on how to generate the `typical.ins` file

7. **Configure TLS/SSL.**

See "Enabling TLS/SSL on the Directory Server" on page 232 for instructions on how to manually configure TLS/SSL. The `cert7.db` and `key3.db` databases can be copied over with a JumpStart finish script.

Example:

```
#!/bin/sh
cp ${SI_CONFIG_DIR}/Files/cert7.db /a/var/mps/serverroot/alias
/slapd-myserver-cert7.db
cp ${SI_CONFIG_DIR}/Files/key3.db /a/var/mps/serverroot/alias
/slapd-myserver-key3.db
```

8. **Configure Directory Server support for Secured LDAP clients.**

See "To Run the `idsconfig` Command (Silent Mode)" on page 229 for instructions on how to perform a silent installation. The script might look something like this:

```
#!/bin/sh
DIR=/net/jsserver/jumpstart/Files
/usr/lib/ldap/idsconfig -i ${DIR}/idsconfig.ins
```

9. **Populate the directory server with name service data.**

Because the `ldapaddent` command can only be run on an LDAP name service client and a directory server cannot be its own client, you will not be able to use the `ldapaddent` command for an automated installation. Alternatively, you can use other data migration scripts as described in Chapter 5 "Migrating Legacy Data to LDAP."

Automating LDAP Client Installations

In some respects, configuring a client for LDAP is similar to any other name service like NIS or NIS+. The following section is a review of how name services are configured for clients, and how the LDAP name service fits in.

How a Solaris OE Client Is Configured

A Solaris OE client is configured by a suite of five programs collectively known as sysidtool(1M). The five programs are:

- /usr/sbin/sysidnet
- /usr/sbin/sysidns
- /usr/sbin/sysidsys
- /usr/sbin/sysidroot
- /usr/sbin/sysidpm

These programs are executed when the following two events occur:

- The Solaris OE is installed
- During the first reboot following the execution of the sys-unconfig(1M) command

TABLE 4-4 shows what information is obtained from each of the five utilities.

TABLE 4-4   sysidtool Information

Command	Information Obtained
sysidnet	host name, IP address, console type, locale
sysidns	name service, IP subnet mask, domain name, host name and IP address of name server(s), LDAP client profile
sysidsys	time zone, data, time
sysidroot	root password
sysidpm	power management
sysidconfig	controls use of sysidcfg(4)

This information can be obtained from any of the following sources:

- The system console (interactively)
- A name service
- A sysidcfg file

The first two sources are used to obtain the information during system installation or following a reboot after the sys-unconfig command is run. The third source is used for automatic hands-off installation. During installation, sysidtool attempts to find an NIS+ server on the local subnet where the system installation is taking place. If no NIS+ server is found, a search is performed for an NIS server. If either an NIS+ or NIS server is located, configuration data is extracted from its NIS maps or NIS+ tables. If neither is found, sysidtool prompts the user for the required information.

During a hands-off installation, `sysidtool` searches for a file called `sysidcfg` whose location is specified in the `/etc/bootparams` file on the boot server. Information contained in the `sysidcfg` file can be used instead of obtaining the data from a name service. An example of a `sysidcfg` file is provided in "The `sysidcfg` File" on page 253.

Information Required to Configure an LDAP Client

A Solaris OE LDAP client requires much of the same configuration information that an NIS+ or NIS client does. This common information includes:

- Host name
- IP address
- Netmask
- Root password
- Locale
- Time zone

Beside this information, an LDAP client requires several additional pieces of information:

- The name of the domain it belongs to (equivalent to an NIS+ or NIS domain name)
- The IP address of an LDAP server that serves that domain and contains LDAP client profiles set up for the client
- The name of the LDAP client profile to download
- Optionally, the credentials the client uses to bind to the directory

The domain name is similar to the NIS domain name except that it is present in an entry on an LDAP directory server instead of an NIS server configuration file. LDAP client profiles are entries that are created on an LDAP server configured to support Solaris OE native LDAP clients. The LDAP profile server does not have to be the same LDAP server (or servers) that the LDAP client will ultimately access for name service data, but it is a common practice to use the same server.

Note – Installation of an LDAP client through `sysidtool` requires that an `ipHost` entry containing the host name and IP address of the client be created on the LDAP server specified in the LDAP client profile. The name service configuration will fail if a host entry matching the client's host name cannot be found on the LDAP server.

The following two examples show the dialogue that takes place when LDAP is specified as the name service during an interactive installation. For brevity, only the portion that pertains to name service configuration is shown.

Example of the dialog during an interactive installation of a Solaris Native LDAP:

```
Available name services:

1. NIS+
2. NIS
3. DNS
4. LDAP
5. None

Please enter the number corresponding to the type of name service
you would like [2]: 4

Please specify the domain where this system resides. Make sure you
enter the name correctly including capitalization and punctuation.

Enter this system's domain name [example.com]:example.com

Please enter the name of the LDAP profile being used to configure
this system as an LDAP client. You must also enter the IP address
of the server that contains the profile.

Enter the name of the profile [default]: myprofile
Enter the address of the profile server []: 128.0.0.7
```

Note – The default domain name that is displayed is obtained from an NIS or NIS+ server. This domain name is only displayed if one is found on the subnet that the client is attached to. A search for LDAP servers on the subnet is not performed, so a domain name cannot be determined by examining one.

Example of the output from an interactive installation of a Solaris Native LDAP Client:

```
You have entered the following values:

Host Name:                    ldapclient
IP Address:                   128.0.0.10
System part of a subnet:   Yes
Netmask:                      255.255.255.0
Enable IPv6:                  No
Name Service:                 LDAP
Domain Name:                  example.com
Profile Name:                 myprofile
Profile Server Address:    128.0.0.7
Time Zone:                    Eastern
Power Management: Turn Power Management Off
Do not ask about Power Management at reboot.
```

Client Post-Installation Issues

- When the client reboots, you will notice a console message similar to the following:

```
NIS domainname is example.com
```

This message is misleading, because it implies you are running NIS. The domain name refers to the nisdomain attribute set on the LDAP server that the client is binding to. Unlike an NIS client, there is no ypbind process running on a native LDAP client.

- For user authentication, pam_unix is the only authentication method specified in the /etc/pam.conf file. If you want to authenticate users using pam_ldap, additional lines need to be added to the pam.conf file.

- Unless your LDAP server is populated with rpc map data, you will get errors when the system boots. To eliminate these errors, edit the following line in the /etc/nsswitch.conf file.

```
#rpc:         ldap [NOTFOUND=return] files
rpc:          files ldap
```

The next section walks you through a complete hands-off installation.

Hands-off Installation of an LDAP Client

This section describes how to use a JumpStart server to automatically install native LDAP clients. This procedure assumes you already have an LDAP server configured to support native LDAP clients. Before attempting an automatic installation, you should make sure an interactive client installation works with the LDAP server you have configured.

The `sysidcfg` File

Unlike the NIS and NIS+ name services, `sysidtool` cannot use LDAP as a name service to obtain configuration information. Instead, the only option for a hands-off installation is the creation of a `sysidcfg` file for the client that is read by the JumpStart installation utilities. How to create and where to place `sysdicfg` files is explained in the *Advanced Installation Guide*.

`sysidcfg` file syntax:

```
name_service=LDAP
{domain_name=domain_name
profile=profile_name
profile_server=ip_address
proxyDN=proxy_account_DN
proxyPassword=password}
```

The following is a sample of a complete `sysidcfg` file for a group of LDAP clients.

```
system_locale=en_US
timezone=US/Eastern
terminal=sun-cmd
timeserver=localhost
name_service=LDAP
{domain_name=example.com
profile=myprofile
profile_server=128.100.100.7
proxyDN="cn=proxyagent,ou=profile,dc=example,dc=com"
proxyPassword=mysecret}
root_password=m4QPOWNY
```

Note – To use the `proxyDN` and `proxyPassword` parameters, Solaris 9 12/02 OE release or greater is required.

Note – The variable `profile_server` refers to the LDAP directory server that contains the LDAP profile specified with the `profile` variable. Do not confuse this terminology with the JumpStart profiles or profile servers.

▼ To Prepare a JumpStart Server to Install Solaris LDAP Clients

This procedure assumes you have already set up a JumpStart boot, install, and profile server.

1. **Add the client's host name, IP address, and Ethernet address to the** `/etc/hosts` **and** `/etc/ethers` **files on the JumpStart boot server, or to the name service the boot server is using.**

Note – The JumpStart boot server that supports LDAP clients can use LDAP as a name service. However, a `sysidcfg` file must still be created on the JumpStart server for the client because the LDAP client cannot use LDAP as a naming service until the client is fully installed.

2. **Create a** `sysidcfg` **file specifying LDAP as the name service.**

   A `sysidcfg` file can be shared among several clients. However, if you want to specify a different root password or LDAP profile, you need to create separate `sysidcfg` files.

Note – Only one `sysidcfg` file can appear in a directory. If you want to set up different configuration parameters for different clients, a separate directory needs to be created for each client or group of clients.

3. **Run the** `add_install_client` **command, specifying the** `-c` **and the** `-p` **options.**

   Example:

   ```
   # ./add_install_client -c jumpserv:/jumpstart -p
   jumpserv:/jumpstart/ldapclient1/sysidcfg ldapclient1 sun4u
   ```

4. (Optional) Create JumpStart finish scripts to handle modifications.

To make any additional modifications, such as specifying pam_ldap authentication and changing the default database search path in the nsswitch.conf file, you need to add a JumpStart finish script. For example, the following script replaces the system default pam.conf and nsswitch.conf files with preconfigured ones.

```
cp /a/etc/pam.conf /a/etc/pam.conf.orig
cp ${SI_CONFIG_DIR}/Files/pam.conf /a/etc/pam.conf
cp /a/etc/nsswitch.conf /a/etc/nsswitch.conf.orig
cp ${SI_CONFIG_DIR}/ldapfiles/nsswitch.conf /a/etc/nsswitch.conf
```

This example assumes you have a directory named ldapfiles on the JumpStart server and have preconfigured the pam.conf and nsswitch.conf files.

5. To enable TLS/SSL, create a finish script similar to the following example:

```
cp ${SI_CONFIG_DIR}/Files/cert7.db /a/var/ldap
cp ${SI_CONFIG_DIR}/Files/key3.db /a/var/ldap
```

6. On the client, run the boot **command from the PROM monitor prompt.**

```
ok> boot net - install
```

Choosing High-Availability Options

There are essentially two options to make your directory service highly available. The first option is to deploy the built-in data replication facility of the Sun ONE Directory Server software. The second option is to deploy Sun Cluster technology.

The replication facility has been available for some time and is well documented, therefore this section only focuses on a new feature in Sun ONE Directory Server software that allows replication over a wide area network (WAN). Replication by itself, does not provide client failover capability, so failover techniques are discussed. Finally, sample deployments of the LDAP data agent for Sun Cluster 3 software are provided.

Wide Area Network (WAN) Replication

Performing reliable and consistent data replication over a WAN presents challenges. This is because WAN links typically operate at much slower speeds than local area network (LAN) speeds that are 100 Mbyte/second or greater. The slower speed produces greater latency that can prevent multi-master replication from working properly, as is the case with the Sun ONE Directory Server 5.1 implementation.

The problem occurs because the supplier needs to wait for an acknowledgement from the consumer to assure that the update was received. While this is not an issue over high speed LANs, the longer latency time over WANs make this implementation unworkable. To get around this problem, Sun ONE Directory Server 5.2 allows you to group changes before they are sent, and to compress the data.

Grouping allows you to specify a certain number of requests that can be sent to the consumer without the supplier having to wait for an acknowledgement from the consumer before continuing. You use the ds5ReplicaTransportGroupSize attribute to specify the number of changes that can be grouped into a single update request and the ds5ReplicaTransportWindowSize attribute to specify the number of sendUpdate requests that can occur before consumer acknowledgement is required. The default group size is 1 and the default window size is 10, which means that unless otherwise specified, default replication behavior will not group requests, but will allow ten sendUpdate requests to be sent before consumer acknowledgement is required.

The correct window size will depends on the latency and bandwidth of your WAN connection. You should analyze these factors. The group and window sizes are based on the number of entries, not the size of the entries. Therefore, it may be difficult to tune these parameters if your entry sizes vary greatly.

Client Failover

Once you have set up data replication, you need some mechanism to direct your LDAP clients to access an alternative LDAP server if the current one fails. The LDAP specification does not define how client failover should happen, so it is up to you to decide to include client failover and how it should be implemented. The Secured LDAP Client was designed to allow specification of a list of potential servers to contact in case of a problem.

There are three attributes that affect how client failover takes place. These are;

- `preferredServerList`
- `defaultServerList`
- `bindTimeLimt`

The `preferredServerList` attribute is a list of servers specified in the order you want to contact them. Contact to these servers is attempted before those listed in the `defaultServerList` attribute. The servers can be listed as IP addresses or fully qualified host names. IP addresses are preferable because they do not rely on a name service.

The `defaultServerList` attribute contains a list of servers. The default action for Version 1.0 clients is to choose servers on the local subnet first, not by the order specified. This does not apply to Version 2.0 clients.

The `bindTimeLimit` attribute specifies the amount of time to wait until a connection to an alternate server is attempted. Once it is determined that the primary server is not responding, the alternate is used for subsequent operations. The client occasionally tries the primary server again to see if it is back online.

Note – If you are using SSL server certificates that contain the LDAP server's fully qualified DNS name, the client will have to be able to resolve it. You can still specify the IP address, but need to have DNS running or the FQN specified in `/etc/hosts`.

An alternate method of client failover is to use an external device or mechanism such as:

- DNS round-robin
- Load-balancing switch
- LDAP proxy server

DNS round-robin is a technique often used to balance the load access to web sites. The way it works is to have multiple IP addresses listed for a particular DNS host name. When a DNS lookup is performed, the requestor is sent back one of the IP addresses in the list. The next requester is sent to the next IP address in the list, and so on. The problem with using DNS round-robin with Secured LDAP Clients is that the client will cache the IP address returned by DNS and use that one instead of performing additional lookups. You can disable caching, but this can have undesirable side effects.

Load-balancing network switches are very popular. The way they work is to create a virtual internet protocol (VIP) that references a list of real IP addresses. The client always connects to the VIP address, which directs it to one on the list. If a server on the list fails to respond, client requests are not sent to it.

An alternative to using hardware switches is to deploy a software solution like the Sun ONE Directory Proxy Server 5.2 software. This solution provides much more flexibility than load balancing switches and provides complex LDAP filtering. Additional benefits are:

- Provides automatic LDAP referral following that makes it possible to balance across both masters and consumers and have referrals automatically followed if a client writes to a consumer.

- Provides LDAP protocol validation, which prevents malformed requests from reaching the directory servers. This can prevent intentional or unintentional server crashes.

- Detects certain types of denial of service (DoS) attacks and prevents clients from having a significant impact from these attacks.

Note – If you are deploying TLS/SSL with Directory Proxy Server 5.2 software, the server certificate for each LDAP server should contain the DNS name of the VIP, rather than the real DNS name of the LDAP server. Also, TLS/SSL Client Authentication cannot be used.

Sun Cluster 3 Software LDAP Data Services

Sun Cluster 3 technology provides a framework for creating highly available data services. The way this technology works is to place all the application or service data on a shared disk volume and create a VIP that can be transferred to any node in the cluster. Clients access the data service by specifying the VIP instead of the server's real IP address. Data replication is performed at a low levels, mirroring the data disks. A probe is continually run to monitor the health of the server that owns the VIP. If it fails, the VIP is transferred to a healthy server.

To create a cluster that supports the Sun ONE Directory Server, two components are required:

- Sun Cluster 3 core components
- Sun Cluster 3 LDAP data services

The core components provide the software required to perform the hardware failover and the framework for handling generic data services. The LDAP Data Services provide the probe and specific instructions on how to failover the LDAP service. The installation and configuration of Sun Cluster 3 core components is well documented, so it is not covered here. Instead, the focus is on the LDAP Data Service.

The Sun Cluster 3 LDAP data services are contained in two SVR4 packages:

- SUNWasha – Administration Server component
- SUNWdsha – Directory Server component

The software for these components is placed in /usr/ds/v5.2/bin/cluster. Instructions on how to configure these services can be found in Appendix C of the *Sun ONE Directory Server Installation and Tuning Guide.*

Troubleshooting Tips

Murphy's law states that whatever can go wrong, will go wrong. While it is impossible to anticipate every conceivable misconfiguration or malfunction that can cause LDAP failures, there are common pitfalls, and the following sections offer some suggestions on how to recognize and correct these common problems:

- "Directory Server Configuration Problems" on page 260
- "Sun ONE Console Problems" on page 263
- "Server Configuration Problems" on page 266
- "Secured LDAP Client Problems" on page 268
- "Authentication Problems" on page 270

The suggestions describe how to use the following tools:

- Directory server access and error logging
- The Solaris OE `snoop` command
- Process tracing
- Solaris OE `ldapclient` and `ldaplist` commands

A detailed discussion on the use of these tools appears in Chapter 6 "Management Tools and Toolkits" and Appendix C, "Using `snoop` with LDAP." If you are unfamiliar with the tools discussed here, consult that chapter first.

Directory Server Configuration Problems

Directory server installation is not a common area in which to experience trouble, especially if you are installing the bundled version. However, there are four common problems that you might encounter:

1. The Solaris OE is missing a critical patch.

2. The DNS Fully Qualified Name (FQN) specified during the setup procedure is not resolvable by the host it is being installed on.

3. The directory server port that was selected is already in use.

4. The 64-bit version is being installed on a system running a 32-bit kernel.

These problems usually result in error messages during the installation or during the final step when the directory server is started for the first time. To diagnose these problems, perform the following procedures. After you fix the problem you should run `setup` or `configure` again.

▼ To Troubleshoot a Missing Solaris OE Patch

1. **Watch for possible errors displayed during the installation.**

   The errors might also be observed by examining the directory server error log, either through the Directory Console, or the `/var/mps/serverroot/slapd-`*instance*`/logs/error` file. Directory Server errors have numbers associated with them so they can be cross-referenced.

2. **Rerun the `idsktune` program on the system where the directory server is being installed.**

   Before installing the directory server, you should run the `idsktune` command and make sure all the required patches are applied. The command does not actually modify anything, so it can be rerun after the installation to verify that the required patches were indeed applied. More details on `idsktune` are in "To Run the `idsktune` Command" on page 216.

3. **Check SunSolve^{sm} services for the latest patches.**

   If you are running the bundled Solaris 9 OE directory server, a missing patch should not be an issue. However, if you have downloaded an older version of the directory server, it is conceivable that the version of `idsktune` you run will not be aware of newer required patches. You can always download the latest version of `idsktune` from the directory product page on the `sun.com` web site if you are unsure of the version you are running. The Solaris™ Patch Manager Tool and PatchPro utility are also useful for managing patches. Information on these utilities can be found at `http://sunsolve.sun.com`.

▼ To Troubleshoot DNS FQN Failures

1. **When the directory server is started for the first time (at the end of the setup program), watch for errors.**

   A common error looks like the following example:

   ```
   Start Slapd  Starting Slapd server configuration.
   ERROR: Ldap authentication failed for url
   ldap://myserver.example.com:389/o=NetscapeRoot user id admin
   (151:Unknown error.)
   Fatal Slapd Did not add Directory Server information to
   Configuration Server.
   ERROR. Failure installing iPlanet Directory Server. Do you want to
   continue [n]?
   ```

   Notice the third line where the FQN is shown (`myserver.example.com`, in this example).

2. **Make sure you can ping the FQN as a default for the host name during setup.**

Example:

```
# ping -s myserver.example.com 56 1
PING example: 56 data bytes
64 bytes from myserver.example.com (129.148.181.98): icmp_seq=0.
time=0. ms

----example PING Statistics----
1 packets transmitted, 1 packets received, 0% packet loss
round-trip (ms)  min/avg/max = 0/0/0
```

If you get a response such as `ping: unknown host myserver.example.com`, check the `/etc/nsswitch.conf` file to see if it is set up to search DNS. You can also add the FQN as an alias in the local `/etc/hosts` file, then rerun `setup`.

▼ What to Do When the Directory Server Port Is Already in Use

This situation usually exhibits itself during `setup` when the default port number of the directory server is displayed. If the displayed number in brackets is not [389], chances are there is another directory instance running on that port. Another reason that port 389 may not listed as the default is if the installation is being performed as a non-root user. In this case, only ports above 1024 are available for configuration.

1. **Check to see if another directory service instance is running.**

Run the following command:

```
# ps -elf | grep ns-slapd
8 R root 2039 1804 . . . . . ./ns-slapd -D /opt/iplanet/servers/
```

If a process is running, the abbreviated output shows you the installation directory. The pathname to the right of the output pinpoints the process from which it was started. You can then go to that location and issue the appropriate `stop-slapd` command to stop the other instance.

2. **Check to see if a process is running on the port you wish to use for the directory server.**

For example, to check port 389:

```
# netstat -an | grep 389
. . .
*.389 *.* 0 0 24576 0 LISTEN
192.9.200.1.33611 192.9.200.1.389   32768 0 32768 ESTABLISHED
```

The output of the netstat command shows you if the port number is listening to, or has a connection to, the port you specified. You can also use this check to make sure the directory server you are running is really listening on the port you think it is. If another process is already listening on the port, you can use the open source lsof utility to identify the process using that port.

▼ To Recognize an Incompatible Installation of the 64-Bit Version on a 32-Bit System

This problem presents itself when the package dependencies are checked. If you ignore the messages and proceed with the installation, the directory configuration fails.

● **Remove all the packages you just installed and only install the packages without a trailing** x **in their name.**

Sun ONE Console Problems

The Sun ONE Console can fail to start for several reasons. Problems in this area often have to do with the Console having dependencies on other processes. If the Console is started from a window shell that is logged in as a different user than the desktop, the user must be granted permission (with xhost +) to access the display. In addition, the administration and directory servers must be running before the Console can start.

Some of the potential problems are:

■ You are invoking the console on a display you do not have permission to access.

■ The administration server is not running, or the address or port number is not correct.

■ The directory server is not running or having problems.

▼ To Invoke `startconsole` on a Protected Display

The console is an X-based application and the X-server must permit access. This situation is a common one because it is typical to log in, then switch to another user, (for example, root) to perform administrative functions. When you try to start the Console, you receive the following error:

```
# /usr/sbin/directoryserver startconsole &
Xlib: connection to ":0.0" refused by server
Xlib: Client is not authorized to connect to Server
Console: Can't connect to X11 window server using ':0.0' as the
value of the DISPLAY variable.
```

To fix this problem, type the following command as the user to which the desktop display belongs.

```
$ xhost +
access control disabled, clients can connect from any host
```

Note – For production use, you should not use just the "+" sign. Instead, specify the IP address of the system you are granting access to or connect to the system running the Console with Secure Shell (SSH).

▼ To Troubleshoot Console Login Rejections

1. **Run the** `startconsole` **command.**

   You should see this screen:

2. **Check the address in the Administration URL field to make sure it is correct.**

   The address that appears by default is obtained from the `Console.4.0.Login.preferences` file located in the `.mcc` directory in your home directory. This file is not removed when you uninstall the directory server, so the file might exist from an earlier directory server installation. If you type in the correct address, the console preference file is automatically updated.

3. **Make sure the administration server is running.**

```
# ps -elf | grep ns-httpd
8 S root 580 579 . . .0:01 ns-httpd -d /var/mps/serverroot/adm
```

By specifying the -el options, the command path name (or at least part of it) is displayed.

4. **View the parameters the administration server is using by looking at the** adm.conf **file.**

```
# cd /var/mps/serverroot/admin-serv/config
# cat adm.conf
ldapHost: myserver.example.com
ldapPort:    389
sie:   cn=admin-serv-myserver, cn=Netscape Administration Server,
cn=Server Group, cn=myserver.example.com, ou=example.com,
o=NetscapeRoot
siepid:    admin
isie:    cn=Netscape Administration Server, cn=Server Group, cn=
myserver.example.com, ou=example.com, o=NetscapeRoot
port:    20000
ldapStart:    slapd-veda/start-slapd
```

You can see from this file that the LDAP host containing the required configuration data is myserver.example.com on port 389. It also shows that the administration server is running on port 20000.

5. **Make sure the directory server is running.**

```
# ps -ef | grep slapd
root  6329 1 0 Feb 27 ? 0:34 ./ns-slapd -D /var/mps/serverroot/
slapd-myserver -i /var/mps/serverroot/slapd-my
```

6. **Verify the URL used to connect with begins with** https **if the administration server is set up to listen on a secure port** (FIGURE 4-3).

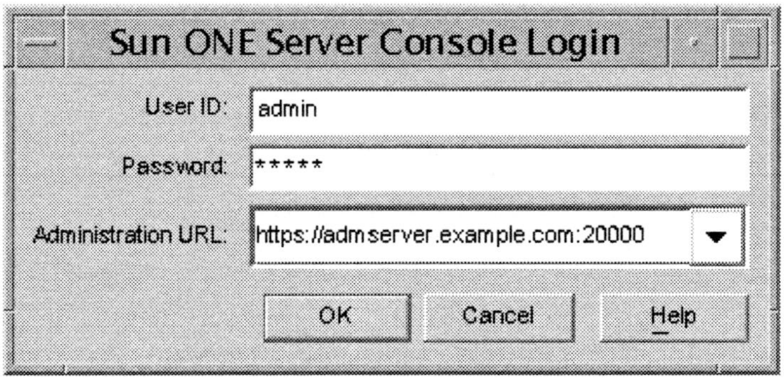

FIGURE 4-3 Sun ONE Server Console Login Dialog Box

Server Configuration Problems

▼ To Troubleshoot `idsconfig` Failures

If the `idsconfig` script is run after the `directoryserver configure` command provided with Sun ONE Directory Server 5.2, you should not encounter problems. However, if you run the script against an unbundled version of the Sun ONE Directory Server, you might have a problem. One known issue is with the 5.1sp1 release. For example, you might see the error message:

```
ERROR: update of schema attributes failed!
```

1. **If you see this error, add a comment symbol (#) to the lines shown below in the schema files located in the** `./config/schema/10rfc2307.ldif` **directory.**

```
# attributeTypes: ( 1.3.6.1.1.1.1.25 NAME 'automountInformation'
DESC 'Standard LDAP attribute type' SYNTAX 1.3.6.1.4.
1.1466.115.121.1.26 X-ORIGIN 'RFC 2307' )

# objectClasses: ( 1.3.6.1.1.1.2.9 NAME 'automount' DESC 'Standard
LDAP objectclass' SUP top MUST ( cn $ automountInfo
rmation ) MAY ( description ) X-ORIGIN 'RFC 2307' )
```

2. **After the changes are made, stop, then restart the directory server.**

▼ To Diagnose Other `idsconfig` Problems

- **Watch for the following database-related problem.**

  The following error is usually caused by using a back-end database name other than `userRoot`. The problem can be fixed by modifying the `idsconfig` script and commenting out the check database back ends. Contact Sun service for additional information.

  ```
  ERROR: Cannot determine the top of the tree
  ```

  Other script failures can be debugged by running the `idsconfig` script with the `-x` option and observing the commands that were being run at the point where the `idsconfig` script failed.

  ```
  # vi /usr/lib/ldap/idsconfig
  .
  .
  .
  #!/bin/sh  -x
  .
  .
  .
  ```

Secured LDAP Client Problems

These client problems might exhibit any of the following symptoms:

- Client fails to initialize.
- Client initializes, but cannot access data.
- Client can see data, but users cannot log in.

▼ To Troubleshoot Client Initialization Problems

1. **Watch for profile or domain name errors.**

   A common problem is that either the profile name entered on the command line or the domain name the client is set to does not match the server setting. A common error message might look like this:

   ```
   NOTFOUND:Could not find the nisDomainObject for DN dc=example,dc=
   com
   findDN: __ns_ldap_list(NULL, "(&(objectclass=
   nisDomainObject)(nisdomain=foo))"
   ```

   In this example, the client either had its /etc/defaultdomain value set to foo or foo was specified with the ldapclient -d argument.

2. **Check the value set in the directory with the ldapsearch command.**

   Example:

   ```
   # ldapsearch -h myserver -b dc=example,dc=com nisdomain=\*
   dc=example
   objectClass=top
   objectClass=organization
   objectClass=nisDomainObject
   dc=example
   nisDomain=notfoo
   ```

   The problem can be fixed by specifying notfoo as the domain name or by modifying the value of the nisDomain attribute on the directory server.

▼ To Troubleshoot Client Data Access Problems

If an initialized Solaris LDAP client cannot access naming service, check the following.

● **Check the name service containers with the** `ldaplist` **command.**

If the client is set up correctly, you should be able to see the name service containers as shown in the following example:

```
# ldaplist
dn: cn=Directory Administrators,dc=example,dc=com
dn: ou=People,dc=example,dc=com
dn: ou=Special Users,dc=example,dc=com
dn: ou=group,dc=example,dc=com
dn: ou=Groups,dc=example,dc=com
dn: ou=rpc,dc=example,dc=com
.
.
.
```

You might see this instead:

```
# ldaplist
ldaplist:Object not found(Session error no available conn.)
```

This indicates the client is unable to access the data using the authentication method defined for it. Even though the client might have initialized without problems, the following misconfigurations could exist:

- The `proxyDN` or `proxypassword` entered on the command line could be wrong.
- The directory server certificate might contain a DNS address that the client is unable to resolve.

To verify the `proxyDN` and associated `proxypassword`, try to bind to the directory server using a command like `ldapsearch`.

```
# ldapsearch -D "cn=proxyagent,ou=profile,dc=example.com" -w
mysecret -b dc=example,dc=com objectclass=\*
```

If the `ldapsearch` command fails, make sure the password is what you think it is. If it succeeds, check the content of `/var/ldap/ldap_client-cred` for misspelling. For clients using the TLS:SIMPLE authentication method, check the server certificate header for the address of the directory server and make sure you can ping that address.

Authentication Problems

▼ To Troubleshoot Password Authentication Problems

After the client is successfully initialized, users might not be able to log in. This is a common problem that can be caused by a variety of configuration errors.

If users cannot get authenticated, the first thing to do is to verify the entry for the user who is trying to log in. You can do this with either the `ldapsearch` or `ldaplist` command as shown below.

1. **Use the** `ldaplist` **command to verify the user's entries.**

```
# ldaplist -l passwd tom
dn: uid=tom,ou=people,dc=example,dc=com
objectClass: posixAccount
objectClass: shadowAccount
objectClass: account
objectClass: top
uid: tom
cn: tom
uidNumber: 12050
gidNumber: 10
gecos: Tom Bialaski - Enterprise Engineer
homeDirectory: /home/tom
loginShell: /bin/csh
userPassword: {crypt}SnLaPR6XvcJV6
shadowLastChange: 11892
shadowFlag: 0
#
```

By specifying the `-l` option and the `uid` of the user, the entire entry for that user is displayed. The number of attributes and object classes will depend on your environment, but the entry must contain both the `posixAccount` and `shadowAccount` object classes. The `userPassword` attribute must contain a non-NULL value for authentication to work with pam_unix.

In this example, the `userPassword` attribute and its value is displayed. This is because the directory server is configured to support `pam_unix` style authentication. What this means is the proxy agent account that was created by the `idsconfig` setup script has read and search privileges for that attribute. This is not a requirement for `pam_ldap` style authentication.

The format of how the password is stored helps determine how authentication is performed. If pam_unix is used, the `userpassword` attribute is prefixed with `{crypt}`. If pam_ldap is used, the `userpassword` attribute might show up as a different hash format like {SSHA}. If it does, this could indicate a security hole by allowing read access to the proxy agent's userPassword attribute. Note that the Directory Manager will always be able to read passwords.

2. **(Alternative) Use the** ldapsearch **command to verify the user's entries.**

An alternative way to check the user entry is with the ldapsearch command, as shown below.

```
# ldapsearch -D "cn=directory manager" -w mysecret -b \
ou=people,dc=example,dc=com uid=michael
uid=michael,ou=people,dc=example,dc=com
objectClass=posixAccount
objectClass=shadowAccount
objectClass=account
objectClass=top
uid=michael
cn=michael
uidNumber=2505
gidNumber=10
gecos=Michael Haines - Professional Services
homeDirectory=/home/michael
loginShell=/bin/csh
userPassword={SSHA}irwM5kV7M5zNFuJgpYJEd+SF6YIbfEBNeiVJfQ==
shadowLastChange=11892
shadowFlag=0
```

In this example, the password is stored in the Salted Secure Hashing Algorithm (SSHA) format and can only be used with pam_ldap authentication.

3. **Use the** snoop **command to monitor communication between the client and server.**

If the user entry looks correct, the next step is to monitor the handshake activity that takes place while the client is attempting to access the server. An easy way to do this is to run the snoop command while authentication is attempted.

In the following example, no data encryption is used, so everything comes across the network in clear text. An alternative for debugging data-encrypted communication is to turn on process tracing, which is discussed later. You may wish to verify that everything works first before turning encryption on.

The following partial snoop trace shows the initial bind that takes place when a client using proxy credentials first contacts the server.

```
# snoop -v ldap | grep LDAP
LDAP:    ----- Lightweight Directory Access Protocol Header -----
LDAP:      *[LDAPMessage]
LDAP:        [Message ID]
LDAP:        Operation *[APPL 0: Bind Request]
LDAP:          [Version]
LDAP:          [Object Name]
LDAP:              cn=proxyagent,ou=profile,dc=example,dc=com
LDAP:          Authentication: Simple  [0]
LDAP:              test1234
LDAP:        Operation *[APPL 0: Bind Response]
LDAP:          [Result Code]
LDAP:            Success
```

The key here is the distinguished name (DN), which is cn=proxyagent,ou=profile,dc=example,dc=com, and the associated password of test1234. These are the credentials the client attempted to bind with. Assuming they match, a Success result code is returned.

Authentication Examples

The method used to authenticate users is determined by how the pam.conf file is constructed on the client system. For the examples, the following Solaris 9 OE configuration file is used.

```
# cat /etc/pam.conf
# Authentication management
#
# login service (explicit because of pam_dial_auth)
#
login   auth requisite          pam_authtok_get.so.1
login   auth required           pam_dhkeys.so.1
login   auth sufficient         pam_unix_auth.so.1
login   auth required           pam_ldap.so.1 try_first_pass
login   auth required           pam_dial_auth.so.1
```

This is the recommended stacking of PAM modules as discussed in Chapter 3 "Defining Directory Service Security Architecture." With a file set up like this one, pam_unix authentication is tried first, and if it succeeds, the user is authenticated. If it fails, pam_ldap is tried. The following sections show traces of how this is done.

Authentication with `pam_unix`

In this example a user called `tom` logs in. The user's password is stored in {crypt} format (highlighted in bold text).

```
LDAP:       Operation *[APPL 4: Search Request]
LDAP:          [Base Object]
LDAP:             ou=people,dc=example,dc=com
.....
LDAP:             Equality Match *[3]
LDAP:                [Attr Descr]
LDAP:                   objectClass
LDAP:                [Value]
LDAP:                   shadowAccount
LDAP:             *[3]
LDAP:                [OctetString]
LDAP:                   uid
LDAP:                [OctetString]
LDAP:                   tom
```

The trace shows that a search is performed in the `ou=people` container for an entry that contains the `shadowAccount` object class and an `uid` attribute equal to `tom`. The search base of `ou=people,dc=example,dc=com` is determined by values set in the client profile that the client is configured to use. The following trace shows the result of this search.

```
LDAP:       Operation *[APPL 4: Search ResEntry]
LDAP:          [Object Name]
LDAP:             uid=tom,ou=people,dc=example,dc=com
LDAP:          *[Partial Attributes]
LDAP:             *[Attribute]
LDAP:                [Type]
LDAP:                   uid
LDAP:                *[Vals]
LDAP:                   [Value]
LDAP:                      tom
LDAP:             *[Attribute]
LDAP:                [Type]
LDAP:                   userpassword
LDAP:                *[Vals]
LDAP:                   [Value]
LDAP:                      {crypt}SnLaPR6XvcJV6
```

The search in this case finds an entry with a DN of uid=tom,dc=sun,dc=com that matches the search criteria. The value of the userpassword attribute is then retrieved. If the value matches the password that the user entered, the authentication criteria is satisfied so pam_ldap is never invoked. If the value does not match, then pam_ldap is invoked as shown in the next example.

Authentication with pam_ldap

In the following example, a user called michael attempts to log in. In this case the password for the account is not stored in {crypt} format so the attempt at pam_unix authentication fails. The try_first_pass option is specified in pam.conf, so the user is not prompted to enter an LDAP password. Instead, the first password entered is tried. If, however, the password entered was mistyped, the user is prompted for an LDAP password. In this example, it is assumed that the password entered the first time is correct.

```
LDAP:        Operation * [APPL 3: Search Request]
LDAP:           [Base Object]
LDAP:               ou=people,dc=example,dc=com
LDAP:           [Scope]
LDAP:            singleLevel
LDAP:           [DerefAliases]
LDAP:            derefAlways
LDAP:           [SizeLimit]
LDAP:           [TimeLimit]
LDAP:           [TypesOnly]
LDAP:          And * [0]
LDAP:             Equality Match * [3]
LDAP:                 [Attr Descr]
LDAP:                     objectclass
LDAP:                 [Value]
LDAP:                     posixAccount
LDAP:             * [3]
LDAP:                 [OctetString]
LDAP:                  uid
LDAP:                 [OctetString]
LDAP:                     michael
```

In this example, a search is made for an entry that contains the posixAccount object class and has a uid attribute value equal to michael. This search is somewhat different than the one performed for pam_unix in that the posixAccount object class is specified instead of the shadowAccount object class, and the userpassword attribute value is not requested.

If the search is successful, the DN of the entry is returned, which is used in the next example to bind to the directory.

```
LDAP:   ----- Lightweight Directory Access Protocol Header -----
LDAP:     * [LDAPMessage]
LDAP:       [Message ID]
LDAP:       Operation * [APPL 0: Bind Request]
LDAP:         [Version]
LDAP:         [Object Name]
LDAP:             uid=michael,ou=people,dc=example,dc=com
LDAP:         Authentication: Simple  [0]
LDAP:             mysecret
.....
LDAP:       Operation * [APPL 1: Bind Response]
LDAP:         [Result Code]
LDAP:           Success
```

In this example, the entry found that satisfied the search criteria has a DN of uid=michael,ou=people,dc=example,dc=com. Using this DN along with the password, the bind request is attempted. If the request is successful, the user is authenticated. A key difference between pam_unix authentication (discussed in the previous example) is that the password entered by the user is sent to the directory server. In the example, no data encryption is used, so the password is sent in clear text. In production use, you would want to use data encryption, but for debugging purposes, sending it in clear text is helpful. If it works with clear text, then data encryption can be turned on.

Authentication Problem Summary

The following is a summary of possible symptoms and corrective actions for common authentication problems.

pam_unix *Problems*

■ Proxy agent bind fails

This problem can be caused by having an incorrect DN specified in the ldap_client_cred or password. This can be checked by trying to bind to the directory with the same credentials the client is using.

Example:

```
# ldapsearch -D "cn=proxyagent,ou=profile,dc=example,dc=com" -b \
dc=east, dc=sun,dc=com objectclass=\*
Bind Password:wrong_password
ldap_simple_bind_s: Invalid credentials
```

or

```
# ldapsearch -D cn=proxyagent,ou=profile,dc=example,dc=com -b \
dc=sun,dc=com objectclass=\*
Bind Password:
ldap_simple_bind_s: No such object
```

- User entry not found

  This could be caused by the entry missing the shadowAccount attribute, a bad search base, or a wrong value for the uid attribute.

- Password is not retrieved

  This can be caused by not having the correct ACI set. You can check it by running the following command and observing the output.

```
# ldapsearch -D "cn=directory manager" -b dc=example,dc=com \
aci=\* aci
Bind Password:*******
    .
    .
    .
dc=example,dc=com
aci=(targetattr =
"cn||uid||uidNumber||gidNumber||homeDirectory||shadowLastChange|
|shadowMin||shadowMax||shadowWarning||shadowInactive||shadowExpi
re||shadowFlag||memberUid")(version 3.0; acl
LDAP_Naming_Services_deny_write_access; deny (write) userdn =
"ldap:///self";)
aci=(target="ldap:///dc=east,dc=sun,dc=com")(targetattr=
"userPassword")(version 3.0; acl
LDAP_Naming_Services_proxy_password_read; allow
(compare,read,search) userdn = "ldap:///cn=proxyagent,ou=
profile,dc=example,dc=com";)
    .
    .
    .
```

If this ACI does not exist or has wrong information, the proxyagent account will not be able to search for and read the password. This ACI should have been set up by the idsconfig script, but might be missing if it failed or if it was manually configured and another configuration process was used.

■ No RPC Credentials warning message

This message might appear on some Solaris 8 OE clients. It usually occurs when the user's password cannot be retrieved by pam_unix. If this happens, pam_unix attempts to obtain RPC credentials to authenticate against, but cannot find any. A notification of this is mistakenly sent, even though this is normal behavior if pam_unix is stacked before pam_ldap and the directory does not allow the password to be read. This message can be ignored.

Automounter Problems

The Solaris OE automounter relies heavily on a naming service to obtain the information it requires to function properly. If the information cannot be obtained or is incorrect, the automounter will fail to work. Identifying the source of the problem can be tricky because you might only see a message like this:

```
# cd /home/tom
/home/tom: No such file or directory
```

The first step in diagnosing the problem is to determine where the automounter is looking for the information it needs. You can start by looking at the /etc/nsswitch.conf file that the client is using.

```
# cat /etc/nsswitch.conf
.
.
.
hosts:      ldap [NOTFOUND=return] files
. . . .
automount:  files ldap
.
.
.
# cat /etc/auto_master
/net            -hosts          -nosuid,nobrowse
/home           auto_home       -nobrowse
/xfn            -xfn
/tools          auto_tools      -nobrowse
+auto_master
```

The two key entries here are `hosts` and `automount`. The hosts entry is used to resolve the address of the NFS server specified in the `autofs` mount entry, and the `automount` entry is used to determine where to look for the `auto_master` entry. In this example, `files` is searched first, so the `/etc/auto_master` file is consulted to identify `autofs` mount points. The `+auto_master` notation instructs `autofs` to consult a name service if the mount point is not found in the file.

To see the entry on the directory server, run the following command:

```
# ldaplist -l auto_home tb250
dn: cn=tb250,nisMapName=auto_home,dc=example,dc=com
        objectClass: nisObject
        objectClass: top
        cn: tb250
        nismapentry: nfsserver:/export/home7/tb250
        nismapname: auto_home
```

From the output, you can see an old style notation specifying `nisObject` to define automount objects. This definition does not work with the Phase 2 clients unless `objectclass` mapping is implemented.

```
# ldaplist -l auto_home tb250
dn: automountKey=tb250,automountMapName=auto_home,dc=example,dc=
com
        objectClass: automount
        objectClass: top
        automountKey: tb250
        automountInformation: nfsserver:/export/home7/tb250
#
```

This output shows the Phase 2 definition for the automount object is used. These objects do not work with Phase 1 clients or Phase 2 clients using Version 1.0 client profiles.

To see what the automounter is doing, you can turn on debugging as shown in this example.

```
# /etc/init.d/autofs stop
# /usr/lib/autofs/automountd -vTT
# /usr/sbin/automount -v
automount: /net mounted
automount: /home remounted
automount: /xfn mounted
automount: no unmounts
# cd /home/tom
LOOKUP REQUEST: Thu Aug 22 08:46:39 2002
name=tb250[] map=auto_home opts=nobrowse path=/home direct=0
getmapent_ldap: key=[ tom ]
ldap_match: ldapkey =[ tom ]
ldap_match: searchfilter =[ (&(objectClass=nisObject)
(nisMapName=auto_home)(cn=tom)) ]
ldap_match: __ns_ldap_list OK
mapline: nfsserver:/export/home7/tom
do_mount1:(nfs,nfs) /home/tom -nobrowse
nfsserver:/export/home7/tom penalty=0
nfsmount: standard mount on /home/tom :
nfsserver:/export/home7/tom
ping: nfsserver timeout=15 request vers=3 min=2
pingnfs OK: nfs version=3
nfsmount: Get mount version: request vers=3 min=3
nfsmount: mount version=3
mount nfsserver:/export/home7/tom /home/tom ()
mount nfsserver:/export/home7/tom dev=3a40003 rdev=0 OK
MOUNT REPLY    : status=0, AUTOFS_DONE
```

In this example, the search is made for an nisObject object. This means that is was performed on a Phase 1 client. The next example shows what the output on a Phase 2 client would look like.

```
# cd /home/tb250
t1      LOOKUP REQUEST: Fri Aug 23 08:49:24 2002
t1         name=tb250[] map=auto_home opts=nobrowse path=/home
direct=0
t1         PUSH /etc/auto_home
t1      getmapent_ldap called
t1      getmapent_ldap: key=[ tb250 ]
t1      ldap_match called
t1      ldap_match: key =[ tb250 ]
t1      ldap_match: ldapkey =[ tb250 ]
t1         ldap_match: Requesting list for (&(objectClass=
automount)(automountKey=tb250)) in auto_home
t1         ldap_match: __ns_ldap_list OK
t1         ldap_match: found: nfsserver:/export/home7/tb250
```

Debugging SASL DIGEST-MD5 Problems

If SASL/DIGEST-MD5 authentication is used, a snoop trace will look something like this (bold text indicates the information to look for):

```
LDAP:   ----- Lightweight Directory Access Protocol Header -----
LDAP:    *[LDAPMessage]
LDAP:      [Message ID]
LDAP:      Operation *[APPL 0: Bind Request]
LDAP:        [Version]
LDAP:        [Object Name]
LDAP:        Authentication: SASL *[3]
LDAP:          [OctetString]
LDAP:            DIGEST-MD5
LDAP:
LDAP:   ----- LDAP:    -----
LDAP:
LDAP:    ""
LDAP:
LDAP:   ----- Lightweight Directory Access Protocol Header -----
LDAP:    *[LDAPMessage]
LDAP:      [Message ID]
LDAP:      Operation *[APPL 1: Bind Response]
LDAP:        [Result Code]
LDAP:        SASL Bind In Progress
LDAP:        [Matched DN]
LDAP:        [Error Message]
LDAP:      SASL Credentials   [7]
LDAP:          realm="myserver.example.com",no
LDAP:          nce="PXZxIw/DacrytK",qop="auth",
LDAP:          algorithm=md5-sess,charset=utf-8
LDAP:
```

If you are having SASL/DIGEST-MD5 problems, check the directory server access log for errors, make sure SASL/DIGEST-MD5 is enabled and that passwords are stored in clear text.

TLS/SSL Errors

TLS/SSL problems can be tricky to debug because the data transfer is encrypted. If you have problems connecting, check the system log (syslog) and the directory server access log for error messages.

Example:

```
# cat /var/adm/messages
...
Sep  5 10:23:29 eelab14 ldaplist[9626]: [ID 605618 user.error]
libldap: CERT_VerifyCertName: cert server name 'myldap' does not
match 'myserver.example.com': SSL connection denied
.
.
.
```

In this example, there is a mismatch between the fully qualified directory server name and the name contained in the server certificate header.

If the system log fails to provide sufficient information, check the directory server access log for clues. You can get additional information by turning on error log tracing as shown in FIGURE 4-4.

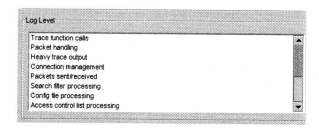

FIGURE 4-4   Error Log Properties

Password Problems

Problems can occur if the password is not stored in the expected format, or the password is not what you expect. To generate a hashed password, use the pwdhash command as shown.

```
# directoryserver pwdhash -D /var/mps/serverroot/slapd-vipivot \
-s crypt hello
{crypt}VfHh.ESyoKX0U
# directoryserver pwdhash -D /var/mps/serverroot/slapd-vipivot \
-s ssha hello
{SSHA}3Kvdi0z6hIfQUCWGBvhGyo4rCOdRENccR0OPXQ==
```

To change a password and store it in UNIX crypt format:.

```
dn: uid=tb250,ou=people,dc=example,dc=com
changetype: modify
replace: userpassword
userpassword: {crypt}VfHh.ESyoKX0U
```

To change a password and store it in Sated Secure Hash Algorithm (SSHA):

```
dn: cn=proxyagent,ou=profile,dc=example,dc=com
changetype: modify
replace: userpassword
userpassword: {SSHA}3Kvdi0z6hIfQUCWGBvhGyo4rCOdRENccR0OPXQ==
```

To change a password and store it in clear text.

```
dn: uid=test,ou=people,dc=example,dc=com
changetype: modify
replace: userpassword
userpassword: {clear}hello
```

CHAPTER **5**

Migrating Legacy Data to LDAP

This chapter covers migration tools available for transitioning from your current NIS or NIS+ environment to an LDAP-based one.

As discussed in Chapter 2 "Assessing Your Needs for Naming Service Transition and Consolidation," there are two approaches that you can take to transition from legacy naming services to LDAP-based services. One approach is to replace your NIS/NIS+ clients with the Secured LDAP Client. The second approach is to keep your current NIS/NIS+ clients and deploy a transition tool to gain access to LDAP naming service data.

The first approach is covered in Chapter 4 "Deploying Solaris OE LDAP Naming Services." The second approach, using the NIS+ to LDAP Gateway, is discussed in this chapter. A similar transition tool that was in beta test when this book was written, is discussed in Chapter 10 "Emerging Directory Technologies."

In either deployment scenario, the LDAP directory needs to be populated with your naming service data. There are several tools available to accomplish this:

- The ldapaddent command
- Public domain migration scripts
- Homegrown migration scripts
- The NIS+ Gateway upload tool

All these tools perform the same function. That is, each tool takes input in the from the /etc files or NIS/NIS+ maps and converts them to LDAP entries. To understand how this translation takes place, the following topics are covered in this chapter:

The focus of this chapter is on using the ldapaddent command to populate your directory. Some migration scripts are available on the http://www.padl.com web site. These are written in Perl and can be modified and redistributed as long as the copyrights in the source files are maintained.

Mapping Naming Service Data to LDAP Entries

The mapping for naming service data to LDAP is defined in three Internet Engineering Task Force (IETF) schemas. These are:

- RFC 2307 bis Network Information Service Schema
- LDAP Mailgroups Internet Draft Schema
- Internet Print Protocol Draft Schema

In addition to these, there are two Solaris OE schemas. These are:

- Solaris OE Project Schema
- Roles-Based Access Control (RBACK) Schema

The schema definitions are provided in the *System Administration Guide: Naming and Directory Services (DNS, NIS, and LDAP*. This book is part of Solaris 9 9/02 OE release).

It should be noted that schema definitions only define object classes and attributes that are either required or allowed. They do not specify how the corresponding entries are created. That is, they do not specify a distinguished name (DN), which is used to identify entries. The next section discusses the significance of DNs.

Entry Formats

Entries are identified by a DN which is analogous to a path name in a Solaris OE file system, only in reverse order. The left most component of the DN is called the Relative Distinguished Name (RDN) and consists of one or more naming attributes and their values. The naming attribute can be any attribute contained in the entry. The components to the right of the RDN identify the tree or subtree where the entry resides. The RDN only needs to be unique within a container, although in most cases you would want to make it unique within the entire directory. For example, you may want to separate users in different subtrees, but you would want to give each one a unique uid attribute value. The following is an example of an entry's DN:

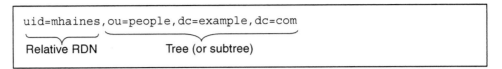

The component uid=mhaines is the RDN, and the components ou=people, dc= example, dc=com represent where in the directory information tree (DIT) the entry is stored. The attribute uid is used as the naming attribute, although another attribute like cn would work. The reason uid is commonly used is that most enterprises have established unique user identifiers for all their computer users.

RDNs can also be multivalued. In this case, you would have more than one naming attribute. While multivalued RDNs are not common, they are used to represent Solaris hosts entries because the same IP address can be associated with multiple host names. By specifying both the host name and IP address in the RDN, unique entries can be created.

How Clients Use Entry DNs

Most LDAP clients do not reference an entry DN directly. Instead, a search is made specifying some attribute, like uid, as part of a filter and requesting the DN to be returned. The DN can then be used for authentication by attempting an LDAP bind operation with the returned DN as the bind DN. For example, if a Solaris OE user logs in using pam_ldap, the following sequence occurs:

1. The user's uid is sent to the directory server as part of a search filter that includes a search base.

2. Starting at the specified search base, a search is performed for an entry that has a uid value matching the one sent to it.

3. The user's entry is returned to the client.

4. The client binds to the directory with the DN of that entry.

LDAP client programs such as ldapaddent actually create entries. When an entry is created, a DN must be specified. To create the DN, predetermined default naming attributes are chosen. While the Secured LDAP Client can work with entries created that use a different naming attribute, for compatibility it is best to stick with this convention. The next section describes how to use the ldapaddent command to create LDAP entries.

Running `ldapaddent`

Before you can start using LDAP as your naming server, you need to populate it with your current NIS or NIS+ data. Solaris 9 OE and the Solaris 8 OE backport provides a utility for doing this called `ldapaddent(1M)`. Before running this command, you should make sure your source files are cleaned up as described in Chapter 2 "Assessing Your Needs for Naming Service Transition and Consolidation." You also need to be a native LDAP client of the server for which you are importing data. This is so you can use the authentication methods and encrypted data channel you have set up for clients.

A system running the directory service cannot be its own client; therefore, two systems are required to run `ldapaddent`. One system would run the directory service and the other system that is configured as a client uses the directory service. This might be inconvenient because you may want to configure your clients after the server is populated.

You can cheat a little by temporarily configuring your directory server as its own client, then reverting back to the original configuration. A word of caution: It is very important that a reboot does not occur while the server is configured as its own client, because the server will hang. You should also be aware that after the server is initialized as an LDAP naming service client, you will not be able to access the previous naming service data. For example, if you are using DNS to resolve host addresses, you need to re-initialize DNS.

Supported Databases

The command `ldapaddent` creates entries in LDAP containers from their corresponding /etc files. This operation is customized for each of the standard databases that are used in the administration of Solaris OE systems. The databases include:

- `aliases`
- `auto_*`
- `bootparams`
- `ethers`
- `group`
- `hosts`
- `netgroup`
- `netmasks`

- networks
- passwd
- shadow
- protocols
- publickey
- rpc
- services

By default, ldapaddent reads from the standard input, then adds this data to the LDAP container associated with the database specified on the command line. An input file from which data can be read is specified using the -f option.

The entries are stored in the directory based on the client's configuration, thus the client must be configured to use LDAP naming services. The location where entries are to be written can be overridden by using the -b option. If the entry to be added exists in the directory, the command displays an error and exits, unless the -c option is used.

Even though there is a shadow database, there is no corresponding shadow container. Both the shadow and the passwd data is stored in the ou=people container. Similarly, data from the networks and netmasks databases is stored in the networks container.

You must add entries from the passwd database before you attempt to add entries from the shadow database. The addition of a shadow entry that does not have a corresponding passwd entry will fail.

For better performance, the recommended order in which the databases should be loaded is as follows:

1. passwd database, followed by shadow database

2. networks database, followed by netmasks database

3. bootparams database, followed by ethers database

Note – Only the first entry of a given type that is encountered will be added to the LDAP server. The ldapaddent command skips any duplicate entries.

Authentication Options

The `ldapaddent` command supports a wide range of authentication options when the -a switch is specified. These include:

- simple
- SASL DIGEST-MD5
- TLS SIMPLE
- TLSv1 SASL/DIGEST-MD5

Selecting `simple` causes passwords to be sent over the network in clear text, and therefore its use is strongly discouraged. Additionally, if the client is configured with a profile which uses no authentication, that is, either the `credentialLevel` attribute is set to `anonymous` or `authenticationMethod` is set to `none`, the user must use this option to provide an authentication method.

Binding to the Directory Server

The -b *baseDN* option creates entries in the `baseDN` directory. `baseDN` is not relative to the client's default search base, but rather, it is the actual location where the entries will be created. If this parameter is not specified, the first search descriptor defined for the service, or the default container will be used.

The -D `bindDN` creates an entry which has write permission to the baseDN. When used with the -d option, this entry only requires read permission. The -w *bind_password* option is used for authenticating the `bindDN`. If this parameter is missing, the command will prompt for a password. NULL passwords are not supported in LDAP. When you use -w *bind_password* to specify the password for authentication, the password is visible to other users of the system by means of the `ps` command, in script files, and in shell history.

Examples Using `ldapaddent`

Example 1: Adding password entries to the directory server:

```
# ldapaddent -a simple -D "cn=directory manager" -w mysecret -f
/etc/passwd passwd
```

Example 2: Adding group entries:

The following example shows how to add group entries to the directory server using sasl/DIGEST-MD5 as the authentication method.

```
# ldapaddent -D "cn=directory manager" -w mysecret -a
"sasl/DIGEST-MD5" -f /etc/group group
```

Example 3: Adding auto_master entries:

The following example shows how to add auto_master entries to the directory server:

```
# ldapaddent -a simple -D "cn=directory manager" -w mysecret -f
/etc/auto_master auto_master
```

Example 4: Dumping password entries from the directory to a file:

The ldapaddent command can be used to extract LDAP entries and to create equivalent /etc file format by specifying the -d option. The following example shows how to dump password entries from the directory to a file called passwd.file.

```
# ldapaddent -d passwd > passwd.file
```

Default Entry Formats

The following are examples of entries created by the ldapaddent command.

passwd *and* shadow *Database Entry Example*

```
dn: uid=tsmith,ou=people,dc=example,dc=com
objectClass: posixAccount
objectClass: shadowAccount
objectClass: account
objectClass: top
uid: tsmith
cn: Tom Smith
uidNumber: 31932
gidNumber: 10
gecos: Tom Smith
homeDirectory: /home/tsmith
loginShell: /bin/csh
userPassword: {crypt}1QfftqDbJHUQQ
shadowLastChange:
shadowMin:
shadowMax:
shadowWarning:
shadowInactive:
shadowExpire:
shadowFlag:
description:
```

In this example the entry was created from a file generated from existing NIS maps. For example:

```
# ypcat passwd > passwd.file
```

The -p option is specified with the ldapaddent command to instruct it to get the password from the input file and not the /etc/shadow file. This is why the shadow* attributes are blank. If the shadow database was used, the shadow* attributes would look like this:

```
shadowLastChange: 12138
shadowMin: 30
shadowMax: 180
shadowWarning: 10
shadowInactive: 90
shadowExpire: 12157
shadowFlag: 0
```

From these examples you can see that uid is used as the naming attribute and account is used as a structural object class to which the posixAccount and shadowAccount auxiliary object classes were added. The gecos attribute is populated from the GECOS field, but there are no commonName(cn) or description attribute values assigned. The password is always stored in UNIX crypt.

It is very likely you would want to extend the user entries beyond what ldapaddent creates for you. Instructions for doing so can be found in Chapter 7 "Performing Administrative Tasks."

group *Database Entry Example*

```
dn: cn=einsteins,ou=group,dc=example,dc=com
objectClass: posixGroup
objectClass: top
cn: einsteins
gidNumber: 8199
memberUid: rperry
memberUid: dmahoney
memberUid: dam
userPassword: {crypt}XT0vcJvEWY
```

The DN for these entries uses the cn attribute that defines the name of the group. The password for the group is defined by the userPassword attribute. If the password field contains an asterisk (*), it is stored in the password storage scheme for which the directory server is set.

hosts *Database Entry Example*

```
dn: cn=xer33a4b+ipHostNumber=10.10.181.22,ou=Hosts,dc=example,dc=
com
objectClass: ipHost
objectClass: device
objectClass: top
cn: xer33a4b
cn: np-ubur03-11
cn: ubur03-11
cn: bur311
cn: bur313
ipHostNumber: 10.10.181.22
```

The DN for hosts entries contains two naming attributes: cn and ipHostNumber. The reason for this is that a system that has multiple network interfaces, sometimes referred to as multi-homed, might use the same host name with different IP addresses for different interfaces. If only the cn attribute that defines the canonical host name was used, conflict would occur. If a hosts entry has one or more aliases defined, they are specified by additional cn attributes.

automount *Database Entry Examples*

```
dn: cn=tcool,nismapname=auto_home,dc=example,dc=com
objectClass=nisObject
objectClass=top
cn=tcool
nisMapEntry=hosta:/export/home/tcool2
```

This entry was created by running ldapaddent on a client that was initialized with a Version 1 profile (objectclass=SolarisNamingProfile). You can tell this because the nisObject object class is specified in the entry. If the client running ldapaddent was configured with a Version 2 profile (objectclass= DUAconfigProfile), the automountMap object class would be specified in the entry.

The following examples assume the client is configured with a Version 2 profile.

```
dn: automountMapName=auto_home,dc=example,dc=com
automountMapName: auto_home
objectClass: top
objectClass: automountMap

dn: automountMapName=auto_direct,dc=example,dc=com
automountMapName: auto_direct
objectClass: top
objectClass: automountMap

dn: automountMapName=auto_master,dc=example,dc=com
automountMapName: auto_master
objectClass: top
objectClass: automountMap

dn: automountMapName=auto_shared,dc=example,dc=com
automountMapName: auto_shared
objectClass: top
objectClass: automountMap
```

These entries represent the top-level containers for the standard automount maps. The following examples show what the entries look like below one of the top-level containers. In this case, the auto_master container is examined.

```
dn: automountKey=/net,automountMapName=auto_master,dc=example,dc=
com
objectClass: automount
objectClass: top
automountKey: /net
automountInformation: -hosts  -nosuid,nobrowse

dn: automountKey=/home,automountMapName=auto_master,dc=
example,dc=com
objectClass: automount
objectClass: top
automountKey: /home
automountInformation: auto_home -nobrowse

dn: automountKey=/xfn,automountMapName=auto_master,dc=example,dc=
com
objectClass: automount
objectClass: top
automountKey: /xfn
automountInformation: -xfn

dn: automountKey=/tools,automountMapName=auto_master,dc=
example,dc=com
objectClass: automount
objectClass: top
automountKey: /tools
automountInformation: auto_tools          -intr,nosuid,nobrowse
```

This example defines the standard /net, /home, and /xfn automaps. In addition, a custom map called /tools is shown. The /tools map contains entries that look like this:

```
dn: automountKey=pricebooks,automountMapName=auto_tools,dc=
example,dc=com
objectClass: automount
objectClass: top
automountKey: pricebooks
automountInformation: salesdesk:/home1/hardware_data/pricebooks

dn: automountKey=networker,automountMapName=auto_tools,dc=
example,dc=com
objectClass: automount
objectClass: top
automountKey: networker
automountInformation: sundries:/export/home3/networker

dn: automountKey=upgrades,automountMapName=auto_tools,dc=
example,dc=com
objectClass: automount
objectClass: top
automountKey: upgrades
automountInformation: crimson-tide:/upgrades
```

ethers *Database Entry Example*

```
dn: cn=eelab14,ou=ethers,dc=example,dc=com
objectClass: ieee802Device
objectClass: top
cn: eelab14
macAddress: 8:0:20:1:2:3
```

Note – The cn attribute used by ldapaddent to create this entry has been removed from the RFC 2307 schema defined in the Sun ONE Directory Server 5.2 software 11rfc2307.ldif file.

bootparams *Database Entry Example*

```
dn: cn=hostb,ou=ethers,dc=example,dc=com
objectClass: bootableDevice
objectClass: top
cn: hostb
bootParameter: hostb
bootParameter: root=
hosta:/export/home/s9_1202/Solaris_9/Tools/Boot
bootParameter: install=hosta:/export/home/s9_1202
bootParameter: boottype=:in
bootParameter: rootopts=:rsize=32768
```

Note – The cn attribute used by ldapaddent to create this entry has been removed from the RFC 2307 schema defined in the Sun ONE Directory Server 5.2 software 11rfc2307.ldif file.

alias *Database Entry Example*

```
dn: cn=postmaster,ou=aliases,dc=example,dc=com
objectClass: mailGroup
objectClass: top
mail: postmaster
mgrpRFC822MailMember: root
cn: postmaster
```

`publickey` *Database Entry Example*

```
dn: cn=eelab14+ipHostNumber=129.148.181.216,ou=Hosts,dc=
example,dc=com
objectClass: ipHost
objectClass: device
objectClass: top
objectClass: NisKeyObject
cn: eelab14
ipHostNumber: 129.148.181.216
nisPublickey: {DES}c8d350d3dbb0fd2c3a00c512572706656e9feb0d5647d
354
nisSecretkey: {DES}4c099ef5f415947efd1cbb3da6a4939425f8bc1db5cfc
c30722c735ba9ca101c
```

This is an example of what a public key for a computer would look like. In this case the `NisKeyObject` object class is added to the host entry.

In the following example, a public key is added to a user entry.

```
dn: uid=tsmith,ou=people,dc=example,dc=com
objectClass: posixAccount
objectClass: shadowAccount
objectClass: account
objectClass: top
objectClass: NisKeyObject
uid: tsmith
cn: Tom Smith
uidNumber: 3193
gidNumber: 10
gecos: Tom Smith
homeDirectory: /home/tsmith
loginShell: /bin/csh
shadowLastChange:
shadowMin:
shadowMax:
shadowWarning:
shadowInactive:
shadowExpire:
shadowFlag:
description:
nisPublickey: {dh192-0}36253a65eca 220c00c4db49d2dbc994919cba07
0512984f7
nisSecretkey: {dh192-0}f9c50e98c03f58999aeeb55086868a67bdd8c559
49d72538e69da24a07f2de6d
```

The public key could also be added with the `newkey` command:

```
# newkey -u tsmith -s ldap
Adding new key for unix.3193@example.com
Enter tsmith's password: *******
#
```

Note – The authentication method used by the `newkey` command is the same as login, unless it is overridden with the `serviceAuthenticationMethod` attribute.

Importing Other Databases

Some databases are not handled by the `ldapaddent` command. These include:

- Projects
- RBAC-related databases
- Printers

`projects` Database

The default projects defined in `/etc/project` can be expressed in LDIF like this:

```
dn: solarisprojectname=system,ou=projects,dc=example,dc=com
objectClass: top
objectClass: solarisproject
SolarisProjectID: 0
SolarisProjectName: system

dn: solarisprojectname=user.root,ou=projects,dc=example,dc=com
objectClass: top
objectClass: solarisproject
SolarisProjectID: 1
SolarisProjectName: user.root

dn: solarisprojectname=noproject,ou=projects,dc=example,dc=com
objectClass: top
objectClass: solarisproject
SolarisProjectID: 2
SolarisProjectName: noproject

dn: solarisprojectname=default,ou=projects,dc=example,dc=com
objectClass: top
objectClass: solarisproject
SolarisProjectID: 3
SolarisProjectName: default
```

As discussed in Chapter 6 "Management Tools and Toolkits," the Solaris
Management Console (smc(1M)) can be used to manage project data. Below is an
LDIF representation of a new project created through smc.

```
dn: SolarisProjectName=testproj,ou=projects,dc=example,dc=com
objectClass: SolarisProject
objectClass: top
SolarisProjectName: testproject
SolarisProjectID: 100
memberUid: tomb,mhaines
memberGid: operator
SolarisProjectAttr:
description: Test Project
```

RBAC-Related Databases

To use LDAP as a naming service for role-based access control (RBAC) data, there must be a defined mapping between the field names specified in the /etc files and LDAP object classes and attributes. TABLE 5-1 shows the mapping between RBAC databases and LDAP object classes.

TABLE 5-1   Object class Mapping

RBAC Database	LDAP Container	object class
usr_attr	ou=People	SolarisUserAttr
prof_attr	ou=SolarisProfAttr	SolarisProfAttr SolarisExecAttr
auth_attr	ou=SolarisAuthAttr	SolarisAuthAttr
exec_attr	ou=SolarisProfAttr	SolarisProfAttr SolarisExecAttr

TABLE 5-2 shows the attributes defined for the four RBAC-related object classes.

TABLE 5-2   LDAP Attributes

object class	Supported Attributes
SolarisUserAttr	SolarisUserQualifier SolarisAttrReserved1 SolarisAttrReserved2 SolarisAttrKeyValue
SolarisProfAttr	cn SolarisAttrReserved1 SolarisAttrReserved2 SolarisAttrLongDesc SolarisAttrKeyValue
SolarisExecAttr	SolarisKernelSecurityPolicy SolarisProfileType SolarisAttrReserved1 SolarisAttrReserved2 SolarisProfileID SolarisAttrKeyValue
SolarisAuthAttr	cn SolarisAttrReserved1 SolarisAttrReserved2 SolarisAttrShortDesc SolarisAttrLongDesc SolarisAttrKeyValue

TABLE 5-3 and TABLE 5-4 show the mapping between fields in the RBAC databases and their equivalent LDAP attributes.

TABLE 5-3   Database Fields

Database Name	Fields
user_attr	user:qualifier:res1:res2:attr
prof_attr	profname:res1:res2:desc:attr
exec_attr	name:policy:type:res1:res2:id:att r
auth_attr	name:res1:res2:short_desc:long_de sc:attr

TABLE 5-4   Equivalent LDAP Attributes

RBAC Database:field	LDAP Attribute
usr_attr:username	uid
usr_attr:qualifier	SolarisUserQualifier
usr_attr:res1	SolarisAttrReserved1
usr_attr:res2	SolarisAttrReserved2
usr_attr:attr	SolarisAttrKeyValue
prof_attr:profname	cn
prof_attr:res1	SolarisAttrReserved1
prof_attrres2	SolarisAttrReserved2
prof_attr:attr	SolarisAttrKeyValue
prof_attr:desc	SolarisAttrLongDesc
exec_attr:name	cn
exec_attr:policy	SolarisKernelSecurityPolicy
exec_attr:type	SolarisProfileType
exec_attr:res1	SolarisAttrReserved1
exec_attr:res2	SolarisAttrReserved2
exec_attr:attr	SolarisAttrKeyValue
exec_attr:id	SolarisProfileID
auth_attr:name	cn
auth_attr:res1	SolarisAttrReserved1

TABLE 5-4   Equivalent LDAP Attributes *(Continued)*

RBAC Database:field	LDAP Attribute
auth_attr:res2	SolarisAttrReserved2
auth_attr:attr	SolarisAttrKeyValue
auth_attr:short_desc	SolarisAttrShortDesc
auth_attr:long_desc	SolarisAttrLongDesc

Creating RBAC Entries with LDIF

Two additional containers need to be added to your DIT. These are:
`ou=SolarisAuthAttr` and `ou=SolarisProfAttr`.

To add the `SolarisAuthAttr` and `SolarisProfAttr` Containers, create an LDIF
file and import the file with `ldapmodify`:

```
dn: ou=SolarisAuthAttr,dc=example,dc=com
changetype: add
ou: SolarisAuthAttr
objectclass: top
objectclass: organizationalUnit

dn: ou=SolarisProfAttr,dc=example,dc=com
ou: SolarisProfAttr
objectclass: top
objectclass: organizationalUnit
```

Adding Extended User Attributes to Existing Users

The extended user attributes that are contained in `user_attr` can be added to a
user's LDAP entry. This can be done either at the time the user entry is created or
applied to an entry that already exists. The following example shows LDIF for
adding the extended attributes to an existing user entry.

Contents of `user_attr`

```
# cat /etc/user_attr
tom::::auths=solaris.*,solaris.grant;profiles=All
.
.
.
#
```

Modifying the user entry:

To add the extended user attributes to a user's LDAP entry, create an LDIF file and import it with the `ldapmodify` command.

```
dn: uid=tom,ou=people,dc=example,dc=com
changetype: modify
replace: objectclass
objectClass: top
objectClass: account
objectClass: person
objectClass: posixAccount
objectClass: shadowAccount
objectClass: SolarisUserAttr
-
replace: SolarisAttrKeyValue
SolarisAttrKeyValue: auths=solaris.*,solaris.grant;profiles=All
```

In this example, the `SolarisUserAttr` object class is added to the entry and the data contained in `user_attr` is specified in the `SolarisAttrKeyValue` attribute. Similar LDIF can be used to modify the extended attributes later.

Adding Profile Descriptions

The standard profile attributes are defined in the /etc/security/prof_attr file.

```
# cat /etc/security/pro_attr
System Administrator:::Can perform most non-security
administrative tasks:profiles=Audit Review,Printer
Management,Cron Management,Device Management,File System
Management,Mail Management,Maintenance and Repair,Media
Backup,Media Restore,Name SZZervice Management,Network
Management,Object Access Management,Process Management,Software
Installation,User Management,All;help=RtSysAdmin.html
.
.
.
#
```

The standard profile attributes can be converted to LDIF representation as shown.

```
dn: cn=System Administrator,ou=SolarisProfAttr,dc=example,dc=com
changetype: add
cn: System Administrator
objectclass: top
objectclass: SolarisProfAttr
SolarisAttrKeyValue: profiles=Audit Review,Printer Management,
Cron Management,Device Management,File System Management,Mail
Management,Maintenance and Repair,Media Backup,Media Restore,
Name Service Management,Network Management,Object Access
Management,Process Management,Software Installation,User
Management,All;help=RtSysAdmin.html
SolarisAttrLongDesc:Can perform most non-security administrative
tasks
```

Adding Authorization Descriptions

In this example, an LDAP entry for one line in the authorization description database is created.

Contents of `auth_attr` file:

```
# cat /etc/security/auth_attr
solaris.admin.diskmgr.read:::View Disks::help=AuthDiskmgrRead.html
  .
  .
  .
```

LDIF can be used to create an entry:

```
dn: cn=solaris.admin.diskmgr.read,ou=SolarisAuthAttr,dc=example,
dc=com
changetype: add
cn: solaris.admin.diskmgr.read
objectclass: top
objectclass: SolarisAuthAttr
SolarisAttrShortDesc: View Disks
SolarisAttrKeyValue:help=AuthDiskmgrRead.html
```

Adding Execution Profiles

In this example, an LDAP entry for one line in the `exec_attr` file is created.

Content of `exec_attr` file:

```
# cat /etc/security/exec_attr
Network Management:suser:cmd:::/usr/bin/setuname:euid=0
  .
  .
  .
```

LDIF to create an entry:

```
dn: cn=Network Management+SolarisKernelSecurityPolicy=
suser+SolarisProfileType=cmd+SolarisProfileId=
/usr/bin/setuname,ou=SolarisProfAttr,dc=example,dc=com
changetype:add
cn: Network Management
SolarisKernelSecurityPolicy: suser
SolarisProfileType: cmd
SolarisProfileId: /usr/bin/setuname
SolarisAttrKeyValue: euid=0
objectclass: SolarisProfAttr
objectclass: top
```

Note – The DN contains all the fields with values, separated by the + (plus) sign.

Printer Entries

Printer entries are created using the lpset command, as shown.

```
# lpset -n ldap -D "cn=directory manager" -w mypassword -h
ldapserver -a bsdaddr=printhost,myprinter,Solaris myprinter
```

Note – This command should be run for a shell script to avoid the password from appearing in the output of ps -ef.

The printer defined here is a networked printer that supports a Berkeley Software Distribution (BSD) print spooler. The entry in LDIF format looks like this:

```
dn: printer-uri=myprinter,ou=printers,dc=example,dc=com
objectClass: top
objectClass: printerService
objectClass: printerAbstract
objectClass: sunPrinter
printer-name: myprinter
sun-printer-bsdaddr: printhost,myprinter,Solaris
printer-uri: myprinter
```

LDAP to NIS+ Gateway

What Is a Gateway?

A gateway is a service that provides a mapping of one type of data to another. In respect to naming services, a gateway is used to map NIS+ data to LDAP data. The NIS+ gateway maintains a copy of NIS+ data most of which is stored in a LDAP directory. The copy of the data is updated whenever the corresponding LDAP entries are updated. It can also be updated using the native naming service tools.

To function transparently to clients, a modified version of the native server rpc.nisd, is used to service the clients. The modified server references a mapping file to determine how to store the native naming service data in LDAP and how to retrieve it so it can be presented to the client. The modified server is also responsible for maintaining cache consistency.

The advantage of the new gateway over the previous NIS Extensions implementation is that the service is decoupled from any particular LDAP server. The NIS Extensions were implemented partly as a directory plug-in that only worked with a specific directory server version (Netscape Directory Server 4.1x). The process that provided the native naming service (dsypservd) had to run on the same system as the directory server.

The new gateway technology uses a Solaris OE process that is a standalone process from the directory server process. This allows the gateway to run on a different server than the directory server, although you can run them on the same server if you want to. The only dependency is the operating environment. FIGURE 5-1 depicts what a gateway deployment might look like.

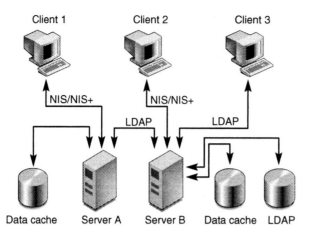

Client 1   Client 2   Client 3

NIS/NIS+   NIS/NIS+

LDAP   LDAP

Data cache   Server A   Server B   Data cache   LDAP

FIGURE 5-1   Gateway Deployment

In FIGURE 5-1, Client 1 is a native NIS+ client that communicates to Server A which is running the gateway software. In this case, only cached data is maintained on the server. When data updates occur, the cache is refreshed from the directory server that resides on Server B. The native NIS+ client called Client 2 communicates directly to a server where the directory server resides. The third client, Client 3, is running native LDAP and is accessing the same information the other clients are.

NIS+ Gateway Components

FIGURE 5-1 shows how the gateway was implemented. The software for this service is contained in the following packages:

- SUNWnisr
- SUNWnisu

These packages also contain the software for native NIS and NIS+. They are loaded as part of the core installation, so should be available. However, to run the NIS+ Gateway software, a directory server must exist somewhere on the network. In theory, any LDAP v3-compliant directory server should work, but only the bundled Sun ONE directory Server software is discussed here. This is because several additional configuration steps are required to configure other directory servers, and those steps are beyond the scope of this book.

There are only three visible components of the NIS+ Gateway software:

- /usr/sbin/rpc.nisd
- /etc/default/rpc.nisd
- /var/nis/NIS+LDAPmapping

The same rpc.nisd process is used whether you are running the gateway or running native NIS+ without the gateway. The rpc.nisd process determines the configuration by the presence of the NIS+LDAPmapping file in the /var/nis directory. If a file with that exact name does not exist, the rpc.nisd process will not use the directory server as a back-end store.

The /etc/default/rpc.nisd file contains information about what directory server to use and where to search for information it contains. There are many parameters that can be configured in this file, as described in a following section.

The NIS+LDAPmapping file describes how the NIS+ data is mapped to LDAP attributes and object classes. The mapping file is quite complex, but in most deployments, only a slight modification is required. For reference, all the relevant parameters are described.

Using the Gateway as a Transition Tool

The following tasks are recommended:

1. The Solaris 9 OE rpc.nisd(1M) can be configured to use an LDAP server as its data repository. In this way, the normal NIS+ database becomes a cache for the LDAP data, with configurable time to live (TTL) values. The cache improves performance, and enables the rpc.nisd to serve NIS+ data even if communication with the LDAP server is interrupted temporarily.

2. Two configuration files, rpc.nisd(4) and NIS+LDAPmapping(4), control communication between rpc.nisd and the LDAP server, and the way that NIS+ table entries are mapped to LDAP entries. A template configuration file, /var/nis/NIS+LDAPmapping.template, covers all standard NIS+ tables, and can be used as a basis when creating a customized NIS+ to LDAP mapping.

3. A test utility, nisldapmaptest(1M), can be used to try out mapping configurations without affecting NIS+ data.

4. The NIS+ passwd.org_dir table stores passwords in the UNIX crypt format, so the LDAP server must be set up to use crypt format for the userPassword attribute for those accounts that are shared with NIS+.

5. In general, migration from NIS+ to LDAP starts by installing and configuring one or more LDAP servers to support the Solaris OE name service clients.

6. Install the Solaris 9 OE on the NIS+ master, and configure `rpc.nisd` on the NIS+ master to map NIS+ data to and from LDAP. The `rpc.nisd` has options that enable uploading all NIS+ data to LDAP.

7. Only the NIS+ master needs to run the Solaris 9 OE. All other NIS+ servers and clients can remain on earlier Solaris OE releases (or whatever OS they are currently using).

8. Once a complete LDAP name service environment exists, conversion of NIS+ clients to LDAP clients can start. While this conversion is going on, NIS+ and LDAP name service clients share the same data, and the NIS+ master `rpc.nisd` keeps the data in sync.

NIS+ servers remain NIS+ clients until their NIS+ server role is decommissioned, at which time they can be converted to be LDAP name service clients. Once the NIS+ master is the only remaining NIS+ client, it can be converted to be an LDAP client and the conversion is complete.

The following sections examine the configuration files and the parameters they contain.

`rpc.nisd` - Configuration File for NIS+ Service Daemon

The `/etc/default/rpc.nisd` file specifies configuration information for the `rpc.nisd` server. Configuration information can come from a combination of three places (listed in order of precedence):

1. From the `rpc.nisd` command line

2. From the `/etc/default/rpc.nisd` file

3. From information stored in an LDAP directory

Although many configuration parameters can be set, in most cases the defaults will work fine.

Most of the parameters used in the `/etc/default/rpc.nisd` file have the same names as the corresponding LDAP attributes. Some of the initialization parameters do not have equivalents because they are used to locate and connect to the LDAP server to retrieve the configuration data.

The parameters can be placed in three categories:

- Initialization parameters
- Parameters used to retrieve data
- Parameters to initiate some type of action

Each of these types is described in the following sections.

Initialization Parameters

The following attributes are not part of the `nisplusLDAPconfig` object class and can only be set locally, either in `rpc.nisd(4)`, or from the command line. These are used only for loading configuration data from the LDAP server. If all the configuration data is set in `NIS+LDAPmapping(4)` and `rpc.nisd(4)`, these parameters need not be set.

Note – If the LDAP service is unavailable, `rpc.nisd(1M)` will wait until it can successfully read the configuration data before offering the NIS+ service.

- `nisplusLDAPconfigDN` – The DN for configuration information. If empty, all other `nisplusLDAPConfig*` values are ignored with the expectation that all attributes are specified in this file or on the command line. When `nisplusLDAPConfigDN` is not specified at all, the DN is derived from the NIS+ domain name by default. If the domain name is `x.y.z.`, the default `nisplusLDAPconfigDN` is:

  `nisplusLDAPconfigDN=dc=x,dc=y,dc=z`

- `nisplusLDAPconfigPreferredServerList` – The list of servers to use for the configuration phase. There is no default. The following is an example of a value for `nisplusLDAPconfigPreferredServerList`:

  `nisplusLDAPconfigPreferredServerList=127.0.0.1:389`

- `nisplusLDAPconfigAuthenticationMethod` – The authentication method used to obtain the configuration information. The recognized values for `nisplusLDAPconfigAuthenticationMethod` are:

  - `none` – No authentication attempted.
  - `simple` – Password of proxy user sent in the clear to the LDAP server.
  - `sasl/cram-md5` – Use SASL/CRAM-MD5 authentication. This authentication method may not be supported by all LDAP servers. A password must be supplied.
  - `sasl/digest-md5` – Use SASL/DIGEST-MD5 authentication. This authentication method may not be supported by all LDAP servers. A password must be supplied.

There is no default value. The following is an example of a value for `nisplusLDAPconfigAuthenticationMethod`:

`nisplusLDAPconfigAuthenticationMethod=simple`

- `nisplusLDAPconfigTLS` – The transport layer security used for the connection to the server. The recognized values are:
  - `none` – No encryption of transport layer data. This is the default value.
  - `ssl` – SSL encryption of transport layer data. The directory server must be configured for SSL and a certificate database is required.

  Export and import control restrictions may limit the availability of transport layer security.

- `nisplusLDAPconfigTLSCertificateDBPath` – The name of the file containing the certificate database. The default path is `/var/nis`, and the default file name is `cert7.db`. The certificate database is set up the same way as with the Secured LDAP Client. See Chapter 3 "Defining Directory Service Security Architecture" for more details.

- `nisplusLDAPconfigProxyUser` – The proxy user used to obtain configuration information. There is no default value. If the value ends with a comma, the value of the `nisplusLDAPconfigDN` attribute is appended. For example:

`nisplusLDAPconfigProxyUser=cn=nisplusAdmin,ou=People,`

- `nisplusLDAPconfigProxyPassword` – The password that should be supplied to LDAP for the proxy user when the authentication method requires one. In order to avoid having this password publicly visible on the machine, the password should only appear in the configuration file, and the file should have an appropriate owner, group, and file mode. There is no default value.

Data Retrieval Parameters

- `preferredServerList` – The list of servers to use when reading or writing mapped NIS+ data from or to LDAP. There is no default value. Example:

`preferredServerList=127.0.0.1:389`

- `authenticationMethod` – The authentication method to use when reading or writing mapped NIS+ data from or to LDAP. For recognized values, see the `LDAPconfigAuthenticationMethod` attribute. There is no default value. Example:

`authenticationMethod=simple`

- `nisplusLDAPTLS` – The transport layer security to use when reading or writing NIS+ data from or to LDAP. For recognized values, see the `nisplusLDAPconfigTLS` attribute. The default value is none. Note that export and import control restrictions may limit the strength of encryption available to the transport layer security.

- `nisplusLDAPTLSCertificateDBPath` – The name of the file containing the certificate DB. For recognized and default values see the `nisplusLDAPconfigTLSCertificateDBPath` attribute.

- `defaultSearchBase` – The default portion of the DN to use when reading or writing mapped NIS+ data from or to LDAP. The default is derived from the value of the `baseDomain` attribute, which in turn usually defaults to the NIS+ domain name. If `nisplusLDAPbaseDomain` has the value x.y.z, the default `defaultSearchBase` is dc=x,dc=y,dc=z. Sample attribute value:

  `defaultSearchBase=dc=somewhere,dc=else`

- `nisplusLDAPbaseDomain` – The domain to append when NIS+ object names are not fully qualified. The default is the domain the `rpc.nisd` daemon is serving, or the first such domain, if there is more than one candidate.

- `nisplusLDAPproxyUser` – Proxy user used by the `rpc.nisd` to read or write from or to LDAP. There is no default value. If the value ends in a comma, the value of the `defaultSearchBase` attribute is appended. Example:

  `nisplusLDAPproxyUser=cn=nisplusAdmin,ou=People,`

- `nisplusLDAPproxyPassword` – The password that should be supplied to LDAP for the proxy user when the authentication method so requires. In order to avoid having this password publicly visible on the machine, the password should only appear in the configuration file, and the file should have an appropriate owner, group, and file mode. There is no default value.

- `nisplusLDAPbindTimeout`
- `nisplusLDAPsearchTimeout`
- `nisplusLDAPmodifyTimeout`
- `nisplusLDAPaddTimeout`
- `nisplusLDAPdeleteTimeout`

  Establish timeouts for LDAP bind, search, modify, add, and delete operations, respectively. The default value is 15 seconds for each one. Floating point values are allowed.

- `nisplusLDAPsearchTimeLimit` – Establish a value for the `LDAP_OPT_TIMELIMIT` option, which suggests a time limit for the search operation on the LDAP server. The server may impose its own constraints on possible values. Refer to LDAP server documentation. The default is the `nisplusLDAPsearchTimeout` value. Only integer values are allowed.

  The `nisplusLDAPsearchTimeout` limits the amount of time the client `rpc.nisd` waits for completion of a search operation, so setting the `nisplusLDAPsearchTimeLimit` larger than the `nisplusLDAPsearchTimeout` is not recommended.

- `nisplusLDAPsearchSizeLimit` – Establish a value for the `LDAP_OPT_SIZELIMIT` option, which suggests a size limit, in number of entries, for the search results on the LDAP server. The server may impose its own constraints on possible values. Refer to LDAP server documentation. The default is zero, which means unlimited. Only integer values are allowed.

- `nisplusLDAPfollowReferral` – Determines if the `rpc.nisd` should follow referrals or not. Recognized values are `yes` and `no`. The default value is `no`.

- `nisplusNumberOfServiceThreads` – Sets the maximum number of RPC service threads that the `rpc.nisd` may use. Note that the `rpc.nisd` can create additional threads for certain tasks, so that the actual number of threads running can be larger than the `nisplusNumberOfServiceThreads` value.

  The value of this attribute is a decimal integer from zero to (2**31)-1, inclusive. Zero, which is the default, sets the number of service threads to three plus the number of CPUs available when the `rpc.nisd` daemon starts. Example:

  `nisplusNumberOfServiceThreads=16`

Action-Related Parameters

The following attributes specify the action to be taken when some event occurs. The values are all of the form event=action. The default action is the first one listed for each event.

Note – A complete list of parameters is provided, although only the ones with `*LDAP*` in their names are directly related to the NIS+ to LDAP gateway.

- `nisplusLDAPinitialUpdateAction` – Provides the optional capability to update all NIS+ data from LDAP, or vice versa, when the `rpc.nisd` starts. Depending on various factors such as both NIS+ and LDAP server and network performance, as well as the amount of data to be uploaded or downloaded, these operations can consume significant CPU and memory resources. During upload and download, the `rpc.nisd` has not yet registered with `rpcbind`, and provides no NIS+ service. When data is downloaded from LDAP, any new items added to the `rpc.nisd`'s database get a TTL for an initial load. See the description for the `nisplusLDAPentryTtl` attribute on `NIS+LDAPmapping`(4).

  - `none` – No initial update in either direction. This is the default.

  - `from_ldap` – Causes the `rpc.nisd` to fetch data for all NIS+ objects it serves, and for which mapping entries are available, from the LDAP repository.

  - `to_ldap` – The `rpc.nisd` writes all NIS+ objects for which it is the master server, and for which mapping entries are available, to the LDAP repository.

- `nisplusLDAPinitialUpdateOnly` – Use in conjunction with `nisplusLDAPinitialUpdateAction`.

`no` – Following the initial update, the `rpc.nisd` starts serving NIS+ requests. This is the default.

`yes` – The `rpc.nisd` exits after the initial update. This value is ignored if specified together with `nisplusLDAPinitialUpdateAction=none`.

- `nisplusLDAPretrieveErrorAction` – If an error occurs while trying to retrieve an entry from LDAP, one of the following actions can be selected:
  - `use_cached` – Action according to `nisplusLDAPrefreshError` below. This is the default.
  - `retry` – Retry the retrieval the number of times specified by `nisplusLDAPretrieveErrorAttempts`, with the `nisplusLDAPretrieveErrorTimeout` value controlling the wait between each attempt.
  - `try_again`
  - `unavail`
  - `no_such_name`
  - `Return` – with `NIS_TRYAGAIN`, `NIS_UNAVAIL`, or `NIS_NOSUCHNAME`, respectively, to the client.

    Note that the client code may not be prepared for this and can react in unexpected ways.

- `nisplusLDAPretrieveErrorAttempts` – The number of times a failed retrieval should be retried. The default is unlimited. The `nisplusLDAPretrieveErrorAttempts` value is ignored unless `nisplusLDAPretrieveErrorAction=retry`.

- `nisplusLDAPretrieveErrorTimeout` – The timeout (in seconds) between each new attempt to retrieve LDAP data. The default is 15 seconds. The value for `nisplusLDAPretrieveErrorTimeout` is ignored unless `nisplusLDAPretrieveErrorAction=retry`.

- `nisplusLDAPstoreErrorAction` – An error occurred while trying to store data to the LDAP repository.
  - `retry` – Retry operation `nisplusLDAPstoreErrorAttempts` times with `nisplusLDAPstoreErrorTimeout` seconds between each attempt. Note that this might tie up a thread in the `rpc.nisd` daemon.
  - `system_error` – Return `NIS_SYSTEMERROR` to the client.
  - `unavail` – Return `NIS_UNAVAIL` to the client. Note that the client code may not be prepared for this and can react in unexpected ways.

- `nisplusLDAPstoreErrorAttempts` – The number of times a failed attempt to store should be retried. The default is unlimited. The value for `nisplusLDAPstoreErrorAttempts` is ignored unless `nisplusLDAPstoreErrorAction=retry`.

- `nisplusLDAPstoreErrortimeout` – The timeout, in seconds, between each new attempt to store LDAP data. The default is 15 seconds. The `nisplusLDAPstoreErrortimeout` value is ignored unless `nisplusLDAPstoreErrorAction=retry`.

- `nisplusLDAPrefreshErrorAction` – An error occurred while trying to refresh a cache entry.

  - `continue_using` – Continue using expired cache entry, if one is available. Otherwise, the action is retry. This is the default.

  - `retry` – Retry operation `nisplusLDAPrefreshErrorAttempts` times with `nisplusLDAPrefreshErrorTimeout` seconds between each attempt. Note that this may tie up a thread in the `rpc.nisd` daemon.

  - `cache_expired`

  - `tryagain`

  - `Return` – `NIS_CACHEEXPIRED` or `NIS_TRYAGAIN`, respectively, to the client. Note that the client code may not be prepared for this and can react in unexpected ways.

- `nisplusLDAPrefreshErrorAttempts` – The number of times a failed refresh should be retried. The default is unlimited. This applies to the `retry` and `continue_using` actions, but for the latter, only when there is no cached entry.

- `nisplusLDAPrefreshErrorTimeout` – The timeout (in seconds) between each new attempt to refresh data. The default is 15 seconds. The value for `nisplusLDAPrefreshErrorTimeout` applies to the `retry` and `continue_using` actions.

- `nisplusThreadCreationErrorAction` – The action to take when an error occurred while trying to create a new thread. This only applies to threads controlled by the `rpc.nisd` daemon not to RPC service threads. An example of threads controlled by the `rpc.nisd` daemon are those created to serve `nis_list`(3NSL) with callback, as used by `niscat`(1) to enumerate tables.

  - `pass_error` – Pass on the thread creation error to the client, to the extent allowed by the available NIS+ error codes. The error might be `NIS_NOMEMORY`, or another resource shortage error. This action is the default.

  - `retry` – Retry operation `nisplusThreadCreationErrorAttempts` times, waiting `nisplusThreadCreationErrorTimeout` seconds between each attempt. Note that this might tie up a thread in the `rpc.nisd` daemon.

- `nisplusThreadCreationErrorAttempts` – The number of times a failed thread creation should be retried. The default is unlimited. The value for `nisplusThreadCreationErrorAttempts` is ignored unless the `nisplusThreadCreationErrorAction=retry`.

- `nisplusThreadCreationErrorTimeout` – The number of seconds to wait between each new attempt to create a thread. The default is 15 seconds. Ignored unless `nisplusThreadCreationErrorAction=retry`.

- `nisplusDumpError` – An error occurred during a full dump of an NIS+ directory from the master to a replica. The replica can:
  - `retry` – Retry operation `nisplusDumpErrorAttempts` times waiting `nisplusDumpErrorTimeout` seconds between each attempt. Note that this may tie up a thread in the `rpc.nisd`.
  - `rollback` – Try to roll back the changes made so far before retrying per the retry action. If the rollback fails or cannot be performed due to the selected `ResyncServiceAction` level, the `retry` action is selected.
- `nisplusDumpErrorAttempts` – The number of times a failed full dump should be retried. The default is unlimited. When the number of retry attempts has been used up, the full dump is abandoned, and will not be retried again until a resync fails because no update time is available.
- `nisplusDumpErrorTimeout` – The number of seconds to wait between each attempt to execute a full dump. The default is 120 seconds.
- `nisplusResyncService` – Type of NIS+ service to be provided by a replica during resync, that is, data transfer from NIS+ master to NIS+ replica. This includes both partial and full resyncs.
  - `from_copy` – Service is provided from a copy of the directory to be resynced while the resync is in progress. Rollback is possible if an error occurs. Note that making a copy of the directory might require a significant amount of time, depending on the size of the tables in the directory and available memory on the system.
  - `directory_locked` – While the resync for a directory is in progress, it is locked against access. Operations to the directory are blocked until the resync is done. Rollback is not possible.
  - `from_live` – The replica database is updated in place. Rollback is not possible. If there are dependencies between individual updates in the resync, clients might be exposed to data inconsistencies during the resync. In particular, directories or tables might disappear for a time during a full dump.
- `nisplusUpdateBatching` – How updates should be batched together on the master.
  - `accumulate` – Accumulate updates for at least `nisplusUpdateBatchingTimeout` seconds. Any update that comes in before the timeout has occurred will reset the timeout counter. Thus, a steady stream of updates less than `nisplusUpdateBatchingTimeout` seconds apart could delay pinging replicas indefinitely.
  - `bounded_accumulate` – Accumulate updates for at least `nisplusUpdateBatchingTimeout` seconds. The default value for timeout is 120 seconds. Incoming updates do not reset the timeout counter, so replicas will be informed once the initial timeout has expired.

- none – Updates are not batched. Instead, replicas are informed immediately of any update. While this should maximize data consistency between master and replicas, it can also cause considerable overhead on both master and replicas.
- `nisplusUpdateBatchingTimeout` – The minimum time (in seconds) during which to accumulate updates. Replicas will not be pinged during this time. The default is 120 seconds.
- `nisplusLDAPmatchFetchAction` – An NIS+ match operation, that is, any search other than a table enumeration, will encounter one of the following situations:
  - Table believed to be entirely in cache, and all cached entries are known to be valid. The cached tabled data is authoritative for the match operation.
  - Table wholly or partially cached, but there may be individual entries that have timed out.
  - No cached entries for the table. Always attempt to retrieve matching data from LDAP. When the table is wholly or partially cached, the action for the `nisplusLDAPmatchFetchAction` attribute controls whether or not the LDAP repository is searched:

    `no_match_only` – Only go to LDAP when there is no match at all on the search of the available NIS+ data, or the match includes at least one entry that has timed out.

    `always` – Always make an LDAP lookup.

    `never` – Never make an LDAP lookup.
- `nisplusMaxRPCRecordSize` – Sets the maximum RPC record size that NIS+ can use over connection-oriented transports. The minimum record size is 9000, which is the default. The default value will be used in place of any value less than 9000. The value of this attribute is a decimal integer from 9000 to 2**31, inclusive.

Storing Configuration Attributes in LDAP

Most attributes previously described, as well as those from the `NIS+LDAPmapping(4)` man page, can be stored in LDAP. In order to do so, you must add definitions to your LDAP server, which are described here in LDIF format, suitable for use by `ldapadd(1)`. The attribute and object class OIDs are examples only.

Using LDAP to Store Configuration Data

Except for the information required to locate and search an LDAP configuration server, the NIS+ Gateway configuration parameters can be stored in an LDAP directory. Most of the information is stored in the `nisplusLDAPconfig` object class, which is shown below.

The `nisplusLDAPconfig` Object Class:

```
NAME 'nisplusLDAPconfig'
DESC 'NIS+/LDAP mapping configuration'
MUST
cn
MAY
preferredServerList
defaultSearchBase
authenticationMethod
nisplusLDAPTLS
nisplusLDAPTLSCertificateDBPath
nisplusLDAPproxyUser
nisplusLDAPproxyPassword
nisplusLDAPinitialUpdateAction
nisplusLDAPinitialUpdateOnly
nisplusLDAPretrieveErrorAction
nisplusLDAPretrieveErrorAttempts
nisplusLDAPretrieveErrorTimeout
nisplusLDAPstoreErrorAction
nisplusLDAPstoreErrorAttempts
nisplusLDAPstoreErrorTimeout
nisplusLDAPrefreshErrorAction
nisplusLDAPrefreshErrorAttempts
nisplusLDAPrefreshErrorTimeout
nisplusNumberOfServiceThreads
nisplusThreadCreationErrorAction
nisplusThreadCreationErrorAttempts
nisplusThreadCreationErrorTimeout
nisplusDumpErrorAction
nisplusDumpErrorAttempts
nisplusDumpErrorTimeout
nisplusResyncService
nisplusUpdateBatching
nisplusUpdateBatchingTimeout
nisplusLDAPmatchFetchAction
nisplusLDAPbaseDomain
nisplusLDAPdatabaseIdMapping
nisplusLDAPentryTtl
nisplusLDAPobjectDN
nisplusLDAPcolumnFromAttribute
nisplusLDAPattributeFromColumn
```

Most of the attributes that the `nisplusLDAPconfig` object class can contain are not included in any Sun ONE Directory Server schema files. The following attributes are also used by the `DUAconfigProfile` object class and are included when you run the `idsconfig` script to set up the directory server to support native LDAP clients.

- `preferredServerList`
- `defaultSearchBase`
- `authenticationMethod`

The last six attributes shown in bold type in the example do not equate to configuration parameters in the `/etc/default/rpc.nisd` file. These are used to map data from NIS+ to LDAP and are described in "How NIS+ Data is Mapped to LDAP" on page 328.

The following are the schema definitions for the attributes used in the `nisplusLDAPconfig` object class. These are included for reference only. If you choose to use LDAP to store configuration parameters, follow the instructions in "Configuring the Sun ONE Directory Server Software as a Configuration Server for `rpc.nisd`" on page 326.

Attributes shared by `DUAconfigProfile`:

```
NAME 'defaultSearchBase'
DESC 'Default LDAP base DN used by a DUA'
EQUALITY distinguishedNameMatch
SYNTAX SINGLE-VALUE )

NAME 'preferredServerList'
DESC 'Preferred LDAP server host addresses used by DUA'
EQUALITY caseIgnoreMatch \
SYNTAX SINGLE-VALUE

NAME 'authenticationMethod' \
DESC 'Authentication method used to contact the DSA'
EQUALITY caseIgnoreMatch \
SYNTAX SINGLE-VALUE )
```

Attributes Requiring Configuration:

```
NAME nisplusLDAPTLS
DESC Transport Layer Security
SYNTAX SINGLE-VALUE

NAME nisplusLDAPTLSCertificateDBPath
DESC Certificate file
SYNTAX SINGLE-VALUE

NAME 'nisplusLDAPproxyUser'
DESC 'Proxy user for data store/retrieval'
SYNTAX SINGLE-VALUE

NAME 'nisplusLDAPproxyPassword'
DESC 'Password/key/shared secret for proxy user'
SYNTAX SINGLE-VALUE

NAME 'nisplusLDAPbaseDomain'
DESC 'Default domain name used in NIS+/LDAP mapping'
SYNTAX SINGLE-VALUE
```

Note – These attributes can be set locally in /etc/default/rpc.nisd.

Attributes Generally Not Requiring Configuration:

```
NAME 'nisplusNumberOfServiceThreads'
DESC 'Max number of RPC service threads'
SYNTAX SINGLE-VALUE

NAME 'nisplusThreadCreationErrorAction' \
DESC 'Action when a non-RPC-service thread creation fails' \
SYNTAX SINGLE-VALUE

NAME 'nisplusThreadCreationErrorAttempts'
DESC 'Number of times to retry thread creation'
SYNTAX SINGLE-VALUE

NAME 'nisplusThreadCreationErrorTimeout'
DESC 'Timeout between each thread creation attempt'
SYNTAX SINGLE-VALUE

NAME 'nisplusDumpErrorAction'
DESC 'Action when a NIS+ dump fails'
SYNTAX SINGLE-VALUE

NAME 'nisplusDumpErrorAttempts'
DESC 'Number of times to retry a failed dump'
SYNTAX SINGLE-VALUE

NAME 'nisplusDumpErrorTimeout'
DESC 'Timeout between each dump attempt'
SYNTAX SINGLE-VALUE

NAME 'nisplusResyncService'
DESC 'Service provided during a resync'
SYNTAX SINGLE-VALUE

NAME 'nisplusUpdateBatching'
DESC 'Method for batching updates on master'
SYNTAX SINGLE-VALUE

NAME 'nisplusUpdateBatchingTimeout'
DESC 'Minimum time to wait before pinging replicas'
SYNTAX SINGLE-VALUE )
```

Error Action Attributes:

```
NAME 'nisplusLDAPinitialUpdateAction'
DESC 'Type of initial update'
SYNTAX SINGLE-VALUE

NAME 'nisplusLDAPinitialUpdateOnly'
DESC 'Exit after update ?'
SYNTAX SINGLE-VALUE

NAME 'nisplusLDAPretrieveErrorAction' \
DESC 'Action following an LDAP search error'
SYNTAX SINGLE-VALUE )

NAME 'nisplusLDAPretrieveErrorAttempts'
DESC 'Number of times to retry an LDAP search'
SYNTAX SINGLE-VALUE

NAME 'nisplusLDAPretrieveErrorTimeout'
DESC 'Timeout between each search attempt'
SYNTAX SINGLE-VALUE

NAME 'nisplusLDAPstoreErrorAction'
DESC 'Action following an LDAP store error'
SYNTAX 26 SINGLE-VALUE

NAME 'nisplusLDAPstoreErrorAttempts'
DESC 'Number of times to retry an LDAP store'
SYNTAX SINGLE-VALUE

NAME 'nisplusLDAPstoreErrorTimeout'
DESC 'Timeout between each store attempt'
SYNTAX SINGLE-VALUE

NAME 'nisplusLDAPrefreshErrorAction'
DESC 'Action when refresh of NIS+ data from LDAP fails'
SYNTAX SINGLE-VALUE

NAME 'nisplusLDAPrefreshErrorAttempts'
DESC 'Number of times to retry an LDAP refresh'
SYNTAX SINGLE-VALUE

NAME 'nisplusLDAPrefreshErrorTimeout'
DESC 'Timeout between each refresh attempt'
SYNTAX SINGLE-VALUE
```

Attributes Used for Mapping Data:

```
NAME 'nisplusLDAPmatchFetchAction'
DESC 'Should pre-fetch be done ?'
SYNTAX SINGLE-VALUE

NAME 'nisplusLDAPdatabaseIdMapping'
DESC 'Defines a database id for a NIS+ object'
SYNTAX

NAME 'nisplusLDAPentryTtl'
DESC 'TTL for cached objects derived from LDAP'
SYNTAX

NAME 'nisplusLDAPobjectDN'
DESC 'Location in LDAP tree where NIS+ data is stored'
SYNTAX

NAME 'nisplusLDAPcolumnFromAttribute'
DESC 'Rules for mapping LDAP attributes to NIS+ columns'
SYNTAX

NAME 'nisplusLDAPattributeFromColumn'
DESC 'Rules for mapping NIS+ columns to LDAP attributes'
SYNTAX
```

Configuring the Sun ONE Directory Server Software as a Configuration Server for `rpc.nisd`

The basic tasks for configuring the Sun ONE Directory Server software are:

1. Update the directory schema.

2. Create an LDAP entry that contains the `nisplusLDAPconfig` object class and associated parameters.

3. Modify the `/etc/default/rpc.nisd` file.

▼ Task 1 – To Update the Schema

1. **Obtain the** `99nisplusLDAPconfig.ldif` **file from the downloadable file called** `ldap-schemas.tar.gz`.

   See "Obtaining the Downloadable Files for This Book" on page xxvii.

2. Copy the schema file to your directory server config directory.

```
# cp 99nisplusLDAPconfig.ldif
/var/mps/serveroot/instance/config/schema
```

3. Stop and restart the directory server.

```
# directoryserver stop
# directoryserver start
```

▼ Task 2 – To Create a Configuration Entry

1. Create an LDIF file with the appropriate parameters.

```
# vi nisplusConfig.ldif
dn: cn=example.com,dc=example,dc=com
cn: domain
objectClass: top
objectClass: nisplusLDAPconfig
nisplusLDAPproxyUser: cn=proxyagent,ou=profile,dc=example,dc=com
nisplusLDAPproxyPassword: mysecret
nisplusLDAPbaseDomain: example.com
nisplusNumberOfServiceThreads: 32
  .
  .
  .
```

2. Import the LDIF file.

```
# ldapmodify -a -D "cn=directory manager" -w mypassword -f \
nisplusConfig.ldif
```

▼ Task 3 – To Modify `rpc.nisd`

● **At a minimum, change the following parameters:**

```
# vi /etc/default/rpc.nisd
nisplusLDAPconfigDN=dc=example,dc=com
nisplusLDAPconfigPreferredServerList=125.148.181.130
nisplusLDAPconfigAuthenticationMethod=simple
nisplusLDAPconfigProxyUser=cn=proxyagent,ou=profile,dc=
example,dc=com
nisplusLDAPconfigProxyPassword=mysecret
```

Note – The example shown here uses a simple LDAP bind. This is only recommended if `rpc.nisd` and the directory server are running on the same server.

How NIS+ Data is Mapped to LDAP

To be able to access the same data from both NIS+ clients and LDAP clients, the data NIS+ tables need to be represented as LDAP object classes and attributes. The object classes for the most part have been defined in RFC 2307, which is the same data structure used to map NIS data. However, because you may wish to store NIS+ data that does not have an NIS counterpart, additional object classes and attributes might need to be defined.

The mapping of NIS+ data to LDAP is not a one-to-one relation. That is, the rows and columns of NIS+ tables are not translated directly into LDAP attributes. If this were the case, a generic LDAP representation of NIS+ tables could be used for all data. Implementing mapping that way would not leverage the power of LDAP, because one of its strengths is the ability to deal with complex data.

In most cases, the default mappings work fine. Default mappings are defined in a file called `/var/nis/NIS+LDAPmapping.template`. The defaults can be overwritten by configuration data stored in LDAP, or by command-line arguments specified when `rpc.nisd`(1M) is started. To start the mapping function, `rpc.nisd` looks for the presence of a `/var/nis/NIS+LDAPmapping` file. An alternative file can be referenced by specifying the `-m` switch.

Not all NIS+ table entry mappings are defined in the RFC 2307bis specification, so additional schema definitions must be added to your directory server. These schema definitions include:

■ `timezone` attributes and object classes

■ `client_info` attributes and object classes

- NIS+ object data
- Principals and netnames
- Non-standard data

Additional Schema Definitions

In this section, sample schema definitions are provided in LDIF format that you can import into the Sun ONE Directory Server software using `ldapmodify` or `ldapadd`. You can obtain the sample schemas from the `addSchema.ldif` file available from the `ldap-schemas.tar.gz` downloadable file (see "Obtaining the Downloadable Files for This Book" on page xxvii).

If you choose not to deploy these additional schema definitions, it does not mean they will not be available to NIS+ clients. The information will still be available in the data cache, but it will not be stored in LDAP.

`timezone` Schema

If you choose to maintain time zone information in LDAP, your directory server needs to be configured with an additional schema definition. After the schema definition is added, you must uncomment the lines referring to `timezone` in the `NIS+LDAPmapping` file to activate LDAP storage of the information. Below is the LDIF representation of the `nisplusTimeZone` attribute and the `nisplusTimeZoneData` object class.

```
dn: cn=schema
changetype: modify
add: attributetypes
attributetypes: ( 1.3.6.1.4.1.42.2.27.5.42.42.15.0
    NAME 'nisplusTimeZone'
    DESC 'tzone column from NIS+ timezone table'
    SYNTAX 1.3.6.1.4.1.1466.115.121.1.26 SINGLE-VALUE )

dn: cn=schema
changetype: modify
add: objectclasses
objectclasses:  ( 1.3.6.1.4.1.42.2.27.5.42.42.16.0
    NAME 'nisplusTimeZoneData'
    DESC 'NIS+ timezone table data'
    SUP top STRUCTURAL MUST ( cn )
    MAY ( nisplusTimeZone $ description ) )
```

Below is a sample LDIF to create the container for the time zone data.

```
dn: ou=Timezone,dc=example,dc=com
ou: Timezone
objectClass: top
objectClass: organizationalUnit
```

client_info Schema

If you wish to store the client_info table in LDAP, you need to update your directory server schema files. After you update the schema, you need to uncomment the lines referring to client_info in the NIS+LDAPmapping file to activate the LDAP storage of this information. The schema for client_info attributes and object classes in LDIF format is:

```
dn: cn=schema
changetype: modify
add: attributetypes
attributetypes: ( 1.3.6.1.4.1.42.2.27.5.42.42.12.0 \
NAME 'nisplusClientInfoAttr' \
DESC 'NIS+ client_info table client column' \
SYNTAX 1.3.6.1.4.1.1466.115.121.1.15 SINGLE-VALUE )
attributetypes: ( 1.3.6.1.4.1.42.2.27.5.42.42.12.1 \
NAME 'nisplusClientInfoInfo' \
DESC 'NIS+ client_info table info column' \
SYNTAX 1.3.6.1.4.1.1466.115.121.1.26 SINGLE-VALUE )
attributetypes: ( 1.3.6.1.4.1.42.2.27.5.42.42.12.2 \
NAME 'nisplusClientInfoFlags' \
DESC 'NIS+ client_info table flags column' \
SYNTAX 1.3.6.1.4.1.1466.115.121.1.26 SINGLE-VALUE )

dn: cn=schema
changetype: modify
add: objectclasses
objectclasses: ( 1.3.6.1.4.1.42.2.27.5.42.42.13.0 \
NAME 'nisplusClientInfoData' \
DESC 'NIS+ client_info table data' \
SUP top STRUCTURAL MUST ( cn ) \
MAY (nisplusClientInfoAttr $ nisplusClientInfoInfo $ \
nisplusClientInfoFlags))
```

Sample LDIF to create the container.

```
dn: ou=ClientInfo,dc=example,dc=com
ou: ClientInfo
objectClass: top
objectClass: organizationalUnit
```

NIS+ Object Data and Entry Data

The NIS+ naming service stores information about the NIS+ objects themselves, in addition to the entries they contain. This information can be used to set ownership and access rights of the objects. LDAP provides its own mechanism for defining object access rights, so the information is not applicable in LDAP. You might wish to replicate this information to another NIS+ Gateway over LDAP, so storing the information in LDAP might be useful.

The default NIS+LDAPmapping(4) file assumes that NIS+ objects will be mapped, so no additional steps are required to activate it. However, as the sample deployment illustrates, you need to comment out lines in NIS+LDAPmapping to avoid having to add the additional schema definition. The following is an LDIF representation for adding the NIS+ object schema.

```
dn: cn=schema
changetype: modify
add: attributetypes
attributetypes: ( 1.3.6.1.4.1.42.2.27.5.42.42.1.0 \
NAME 'nisplusObject' \
DESC 'An opaque representation of a NIS+ object' \
SYNTAX 1.3.6.1.4.1.1466.115.121.1.5 SINGLE-VALUE )

dn: cn=schema
changetype: modify
add: objectclasses
objectclasses: ( 1.3.6.1.4.1.42.2.27.5.42.42.2.0 \
NAME 'nisplusObjectContainer' \
SUP top STRUCTURAL DESC 'Abstraction of a NIS+ object' \
MUST ( cn $ nisplusObject ) )
```

The following is an LDIF representation that can be imported to create the container.

```
dn: ou=nisPlus,dc=example,dc=com
ou: nisPlus
objectClass: top
objectClass: organizationalUnit
```

Associated with object data is information about ownership, access rights and time to live. The NIS+ Gateway makes assumptions about what this data should be based on the information stored about the object itself. In most cases, it is not necessary to change this behavior.

The following shows the LDIF representation of the nisplusEntryData object class and its associated attributes.

```
dn: cn=schema
changetype: modify
add: attributetypes
attributetypes: ( 1.3.6.1.4.1.42.2.27.5.42.42.4.0 \
NAME 'nisplusEntryOwner' \
DESC 'Opaque representation of NIS+ entry owner' \
SYNTAX 1.3.6.1.4.1.1466.115.121.1.26 SINGLE-VALUE )
attributetypes: ( 1.3.6.1.4.1.42.2.27.5.42.42.4.1 \
NAME 'nisplusEntryGroup' \
DESC 'Opaque representation of NIS+ entry group' \
SYNTAX 1.3.6.1.4.1.1466.115.121.1.26 SINGLE-VALUE )
attributetypes: ( 1.3.6.1.4.1.42.2.27.5.42.42.4.2 \
NAME 'nisplusEntryAccess' \
DESC 'Opaque representation of NIS+ entry access' \
SYNTAX 1.3.6.1.4.1.1466.115.121.1.26 SINGLE-VALUE )
attributetypes: ( 1.3.6.1.4.1.42.2.27.5.42.42.4.3 \
NAME 'nisplusEntryTtl' \
DESC 'Opaque representation of NIS+ entry TTL' \
SYNTAX 1.3.6.1.4.1.1466.115.121.1.26 SINGLE-VALUE )

dn: cn=schema
changetype: modify
add: objectclasses
objectclasses: ( 1.3.6.1.4.1.42.2.27.5.42.42.5.0 \
NAME 'nisplusEntryData' \
SUP top STRUCTURAL DESC 'NIS+ entry object non-column data' \
MUST ( cn ) MAY ( nisplusEntryOwner $ nisplusEntryGroup $ \
nisplusEntryAccess $ nisplusEntryTtl ) )
```

Principal Names and Netnames

Principal names and the secure RPC equivalent netnames are used by NIS+ for authentication. While the RFC 2307 specification provides a mapping for public and private keys, there is no provision for storing principal or netnames. This information is maintained in the NIS+ `cred.org_dir` table, for which there is no standard LDAP counterpart.

To get around this issue, the NIS+ Gateway makes some assumptions about how principal names and netnames should be constructed. Basically, the name is constructed by appending the domain name to either the user UID or host nodename. In most cases this works fine. The schema definition for principled names and netnames is shown below.

```
dn: cn=schema
changetype: modify
add: attributetypes
attributetypes: ( 1.3.6.1.4.1.42.2.27.5.42.42.7.0 NAME
'nisplusPrincipalName' \
DESC 'NIS+ principal name' \
EQUALITY caseIgnoreIA5Match SINGLE-VALUE \
SYNTAX 1.3.6.1.4.1.1466.115.121.1.15 )
attributetypes: ( 1.3.6.1.4.1.42.2.27.5.42.42.9.0 NAME
'nisplusNetname' \
DESC 'Secure RPC netname' \
EQUALITY caseIgnoreIA5Match SINGLE-VALUE \
YNTAX 1.3.6.1.4.1.1466.115.121.1.15 )

dn: cn=schema
changetype: modify
add: objectclasses
objectclasses: ( 1.3.6.1.4.1.42.2.27.5.42.42.10.0\
NAME 'nisplusAuthName' \
SUP top AUXILLIARY DESC 'NIS+ authentication identifiers' \
MAY ( nisplusPrincipalName $ nisplusNetname ) )
```

NIS+ to LDAP Mapping

The `/var/nis/NIS+LDAPmapping` file controls how NIS+ data is mapped to LDAP attributes and how LDAP attributes are mapped to NIS+ data. At first glance, the syntax of the file can be quite daunting. In practice, however, usually only minor changes are required. In this section, the syntax of the file is examined to give you a better understanding of how the mapping takes place.

The `NIS+LDAPmapping` file contains five directives, which are:

- `nisplusLDAPdatabaseIdMapping`
- `nisplusLDAPentryTtl`
- `nisplusLDAPobjectDN`
- `nisplusLDAPattributeFromColumn`
- `nisplusLDAPcolumnFromAttribute`

`nisplusLDAPdatabaseIdMapping` Directive

This is an identifier the NIS+ Gateway uses to establish a relationship between an NIS+ object and a label the gateway uses internally. In some cases, the label is used to identify more than one NIS+ object, such as a table object and directory object. All the standard NIS+ objects have IDs assigned. Example:

```
nisplusLDAPdatabaseIdMapping       passwd:passwd.org_dir
nisplusLDAPdatabaseIdMapping       group:group.org_dir
nisplusLDAPdatabaseIdMapping       auto_master:auto_master.org_dir
nisplusLDAPdatabaseIdMapping       auto_home:auto_home.org_dir
nisplusLDAPdatabaseIdMapping       bootparams:bootparams.org_dir
```

`nisplusLDAPentryTtl` Directive

This parameter specifies the time-to-live (TTL) for the `rpc.nisd` cache. There are three values associated with each database ID. The first two values represent a range of time in seconds that `rpc.nisd` randomly picks from when the object is initialized. The third value is used for subsequent cache refreshes. A random time is selected to prevent all objects from refreshing at the same time.

The following are examples:

```
nisplusLDAPentryTtl          passwd:1800:3600:3600
nisplusLDAPentryTtl          group:1800:3600:3600
nisplusLDAPentryTtl          auto_master:1800:3600:3600
nisplusLDAPentryTtl          auto_home:1800:3600:3600
nisplusLDAPentryTtl          bootparams:1800:3600:3600
nisplusLDAPentryTtl          ethers:1800:3600:3600
nisplusLDAPentryTtl          hosts:1800:3600:3600
```

nisplusLDAPobjectDN Directive

This parameter specifies where in the DIT NIS+ object data resides. If the DN ends with a trailing comma, the value of the defaultSearchBase parameter (set in the rpc.nisd configuration) is appended to it. There are three action fields that determine:

- Where to read data from
- Where to write data to
- What to do if the LDAP data is deleted

If the third action field is left out, the default action is to delete the entire entry. Below is an example.

Example:

```
nisplusLDAPobjectDN     hosts:ou=Hosts,?one?objectClass=ipHost:\
ou=Hosts,?one?objectClass=ipHost,\
objectClass=device,objectClass=top
```

Note – Because where to read the data from and where to write it to is the same, the write location can be omitted as long as the colon is present.

The action is shown as an LDAP search filter. The hosts:ou=Hosts,?one?objectClass=ipHost is read as follows (assuming the domain is example.com):

1. Start the search as ou=Hosts,dc=example,dc=com

2. Perform a one-level search (do not search below ou=Hosts).

3. Search only for entries that contain the object class of ipHost.

The write action is the same as the read. The delete action is the default. That is, delete the entire entry.

nisplusLDAPattributeFromColumn Directive

This directive is used to specify rules for mapping NIS+ data to LDAP. For example:

```
nisplusLDAPattributeFromColumn \
hosts: dn=("cn=%s+ipHostNumber=%s,", cname, addr), \
cn=cname, \
cn=name, \
ipHostNumber=addr, \
description=comment
```

In this example, the relative distinguished name (RDN) of the LDAP entry would be the cn= attribute with the value of the NIS+ cname (canonical name) attribute, followed by the string +ipHostNumber=, then the value of the NIS+ addr attribute. The entry contains a cn attribute with the value of cname and if the host name has an alias, another cn attribute with the alias name. The IP address is assigned to the ipHostNumber attribute and if a comment field exists, the value of it is assigned to the description attribute. For example, if the NIS+ entry looks like this:

```
# niscat -h hosts.org_dir
# cname name addr comment
localhost localhost 127.0.0.1
esso mailserver 10.10.9.12 #Mail server for Bldg 1
  .
  .
  .
```

The corresponding LDAP entry looks like this:

```
dn: cn=esso+ipHostNumber=10.10.9.12,\
ou=Hosts,dc=example,dc=com
objectClass: ipHost
objectClass: device
objectClass: top
cn: esso
cn: mailserver
ipHostNumber: 10.10.9.12
description:Mail server for Bldg 1
```

`nisplusLDAPcolumnFromAttribute` Directive

This directive performs the opposite action of the
`nisplusLDAPattributeFromColumn` directive. That is, it defines the rules to map
LDAP data to NIS+. For example:

```
nisplusLDAPcolumnFromAttribute \
hosts: cname=cn, \
(name)=(cn), \
addr=ipHostNumber, \
comment=description
```

Using the Default Configuration Files

In most cases you will want to change some of the default configuration parameters.
However, you can run the NIS+ Gateway without any modifications to the
configuration files. A list of assumptions is presented here to help you gauge how
much modification will be required to fit your environment.

Assumptions

- The directory server is running on the same server as the NIS+ Gateway. That is,
  the server IP address is set to `127.0.0.1` and the port number is `389`.
- The NIS+ standard directories and tables are to be mapped, with the exception of
  `timezone.org_dir` and `client_info.org_dir`. This implies that the schema
  to hold the NIS+ table objects (`nisObjectContainer`) needs to be defined on
  the directory server. The schema definitions for `timezone` and `client_info` do
  not need to be defined.
- The mapping is two way—that is, from NIS+ to LDAP and from LDAP to NIS+.
  This configuration allows updates to be made from either service.
- The authentication method defined is `none`. This implies anonymous access to the
  directory and there is no transport layer security.
- The directory server supports the RFC2307bis schema. This is the default
  configuration for the Sun ONE Directory Server software.
- Only the entry values are mapped. Information contained in pseudo-columns
  such as table owner and group is not mapped.
- The default NIS+ credentials are sufficient.
- The configuration data will not be maintained in LDAP.

Common Configuration Changes

The following is a list of changes that you probably will want to make.

1. Directory Server address and port number.

   In the `rpc.nisd` file, change: `preferredServerList=127.0.0.1:389`

2. Authentication Method:

   `nisplusLDAPproxyUser`

3. The bind-DN to use for authentication:

   `nisplusLDAPproxyPassword`

4. Transport Security:

   To use transport layer security, set `nisplusLDAPconfigTLS` or
   `nisplusLDAPTLS` to `ssl`, and set
   `nisplusLDAPconfigTLSCertificateDBPath` or
   `nisplusLDAPTLSCertificateDBPath` to the file containing the certificate
   database. In order to successfully use authentication and transport layer security,
   the server must also support the chosen values.

5. Time-to-Live Parameters

   To change the TTLs, edit the `nisplusLDAPentryTtl` for the appropriate
   database ID. To change LDAP container locations or object classes, edit the
   `nisplusLDAPobjectDN` value for the appropriate database ID.

6. NIS+ Table Object Support

   The `nisplusObjectContainer`, `nisplusObject`, and `ou=nisPlus` labels are
   suggestions. If you change `nisplusObjectContainer`, or `ou=nisPlus`, edit the
   mapping file to reflect this. To change `nisplusObject`, for example, to
   `myObject`, add `nisplusObject=myObject` to the `filterAttrValList` and
   `attrValList` portions of the `readObjectSpec` and `writeObjectSpec` of the
   `nisplusLDAPobjectDN` value for the mapping. See the description of
   `nisplusLDAPobjectDN` below.

NIS+ to LDAP Migration Example

The NIS+ Gateway is very flexible, providing many different ways to configure it to meet your needs. Providing examples that cover all the different possible configurations would be very long and would be more confusing than beneficial. Therefore, the following assumptions are made about the environment where the NIS+ Gateway is run.

- The target directory server is Sun ONE Directory Server 5.x software.
- The `idsconfig` script is run on the directory server.
- The directory server is set up to store passwords in crypt format.
- The current NIS+ service consists of a single domain with one NIS+ master server.
- The `timezone` and `client_info` tables are not mapped. This eliminates the need to update the directory server schema.
- Table objects are not mapped. This eliminates the need to update the directory server schema.
- The LDAP structure is empty and will be populated by running `rpc.nisd`.

▼ To Migrate Your Data From NIS+ to LDAP

Before proceeding, make sure you backup all NIS+ data; see `nisbackup(1M)`.

1. **Upgrade your NIS+ master server to run the Solaris 9 OE.**

2. **Install the Sun ONE Directory Server software, and run the `idsconfig` script.**

   The sample deployment assumes the Sun ONE Directory Server software is running on the same system as the NIS+ Gateway, but this is not necessary. If you choose not to run them on the same system, the server IP address and port number must be defined in `rpc.nisd`.

3. **Obtain the password for the `cn=directory` manager account.**

   The sample deployment uses this account as the proxy user for accessing data stored in the LDAP directory. For a real production environment you should create a separate account for this purpose and grant that account read and write access privileges.

4. **Edit the following lines in `/etc/default/rpc.nisd`.**

   - `preferredServerList=127.0.0.1:389` – You do not have to edit this line if the directory server is running on the same system as NIS+ Gateway.
   - `defaultSearchBase=dc=example,dc=com` - You do not have to edit this line if the directory server DIT equates to your NIS+ domain name.
   - `authenticationMethod=simple`
   - `nisplusLDAPproxyUser=cn=directory manager` – If you choose not to use this account, specify the DN of an existing account.

- `nisplusLDAPproxyPassword=dirmanager` – Make sure you read protect the `rpc.nisd` file to protect the password.

5. **Create a copy of the** `/var/nis/NIS+LDAPmapping.template` **file.**

   The copy should be created in the `/var/nis` directory and can be called anything except `NIS+LDAPmapping`. For this example, we assume the copy of the mapping file is `/var/nis/nlm`.

6. Edit the `/var/nis/nlm` **file to disable directory and group objects.**

```
# Standard NIS+ directories
#nisplusLDAPdatabaseIdMapping    basedir:
#nisplusLDAPdatabaseIdMapping    orgdir:org_dir
#nisplusLDAPdatabaseIdMapping    groupsdir:groups_dir

# Standard NIS+ groups.
#nisplusLDAPdatabaseIdMapping    admin:admin.groups_dir

# Standard NIS+ directories
#nisplusLDAPentryTtl             basedir:21600:43200:43200
#nisplusLDAPentryTtl             orgdir:21600:43200:43200
#nisplusLDAPentryTtl             groupsdir:21600:43200:43200
#nisplusLDAPentryTtl             admin:21600:43200:43200

# Standard NIS+ directories
#nisplusLDAPobjectDN    basedir:cn=basedir,ou=nisPlus,?base?\
# objectClass=nisplusObjectContainer:\
# cn=basedir,ou=nisPlus,?base?\
# objectClass=nisplusObjectContainer,\
# objectClass=top

#nisplusLDAPobjectDN    orgdir:cn=orgdir,ou=nisPlus,?base?\
# objectClass=nisplusObjectContainer:\
# cn=orgdir,ou=nisPlus,?base?\
# objectClass=nisplusObjectContainer,\
# objectClass=top

#nisplusLDAPobjectDN
#groupsdir:cn=groupsdir,ou=nisPlus,?base?\
# objectClass=nisplusObjectContainer:\
# cn=groupsdir,ou=nisPlus,?base?\
# objectClass=nisplusObjectContainer,\
# objectClass=top

#nisplusLDAPobjectDN    admin:cn=admin,ou=nisPlus,?base?\
# objectClass=nisplusObjectContainer:\
# cn=admin,ou=nisPlus,?base?\
# objectClass=nisplusObjectContainer,\
# objectClass=top
```

7. **Edit the** `/var/nis/nlm` **file to remove all references to table objects.**

Any entry containing `_table` needs to be commented out. Example (not all entries shown for brevity):

```
#nisplusLDAPdatabaseIdMapping   passwd_table:passwd.org_dir
#nisplusLDAPdatabaseIdMapping   group_table:group.org_dir
#nisplusLDAPdatabaseIdMapping
auto_master_table:auto_master.org_dir
  .
  .
  .

nisplusLDAPentryTtl passwd_table:21600:43200:43200
#nisplusLDAPentryTtl group_table:21600:43200:43200
#nisplusLDAPentryTtl auto_master_table:21600:43200:43200
  .
  .
  .

#nisplusLDAPobjectDN    #passwd_table:cn=passwd,ou=
nisPlus,?base?\
#objectClass=nisplusObjectContainer:\
# cn=passwd,ou=nisPlus,?base?\
# objectClass=nisplusObjectContainer,\
# objectClass=top
  .
  .
  .
```

8. **Test the mapping you created using the** `nisldapmaptest` **utility with the** `im` **option specifying the mapping file** `nlm`.

See the instructions in the next section that explain how to perform the testing.

Note – Make sure you remove the test data entries before performing the next step.

---

9. **Upload all NIS+ data to LDAP using** `rpc.nisd`.

Example:

```
# pkill rpc.nisd
# /usr/sbin/rpc.nisd -D \
-x nisplusLDAPinitialUpdateAction=to_ldap \
-x nisplusLDAPinitialUpdateOnly=yes
```

10. **Verify that the LDAP entries were created.**

See the instructions in the next section that explain how to perform the verification.

11. **Rename** /var/nis/nlm to /var/nis/NIS+LDAPmapping **and restart**
rpc.nisd.

```
# cd /var/nis
# cp nlm NIS+LDAPmapping
# /usr/sbin/rpc.nisd
```

Testing and Troubleshooting the NIS+ Gateway

Before uploading all your NIS+ data to the LDAP server, it is wise to test out the
mapping you established. This should be done before you rename the configuration
file to NIS+LDAPmapping and restart rpc.nisd, which activates the NIS+
Gateway.

The following assumes you have a group in your NIS+ database called gem. The
nisldapmaptest command is run in the verbose mode to give you a clearer idea of
what the command is doing.

```
# nisldapmaptest -v -r -m nls -t group.org_dir name=gem
createQuery: NIS+ query: [name=gem] group.org_dir.example.com.
mapToLDAP: group.org_dir.example.com.: 1 * 1 potential updates
mapToLDAP: group.org_dir.example.com.: 1 update requested
controlSupported: 127.0.0.1: 1.2.840.113556.1.4.319: disabled
controlSupported: 127.0.0.1: 2.16.840.1.113730.3.4.9: enabled
mapToLDAP: group.org_dir.example.com.: 1 update performed
```

As you can observe from the last line the update was performed. To verify this, you
can run the ldapsearch command as shown in the following example.

```
# ldapsearch -b dc=example,dc=com cn=gem
cn=gem,ou=Group,dc=example,dc=com
cn=gem
gidNumber=2292
objectClass=posixGroup
objectClass=top
```

To remove test entries:

```
# ldapsearch -b dc=example,dc=com cn=gem dn
cn=gem,ou=Group,dc=example,dc=com
# ldapdelete -D "cn=directory manager" -w mypass cn=gem,ou=
Group,dc=example,dc=com
```

Once the NIS+ Gateway is activated, you can test it by creating an entry in LDAP and see if it appears in NIS+.

```
# vi /tmp/hosts.ldif
dn: cn=test1+ipHostNumber=10.10.9.12,ou=Hosts,dc=example,dc=com
cn: test1
ipHostNumber: 10.10.9.12
objectClass: ipHost
objectClass: device
objectClass: top

# ldapmodify -a -D "cn=directory manager" -f /tmp/hosts.ldif
Bind Password:
adding new entry cn=test1+ipHostNumber=10.10.9.12,ou=Hosts,dc=
example,dc=com
#
```

After a few seconds, you should be able to see the new entry from NIS+ as shown in this example.

```
# niscat hosts.org_dir | grep test1
test1 test1 10.10.9.12
```

Troubleshooting Tips

Most errors are the result of misconfigured rpc.nisd or NIS+LDAPmapping files. If you encounter problems, follow these steps:

- Check for syslog messages in /var/adm/messages that are generated from rpc.nisd.
- Restart rpc.nisd with the verbose (-v) option for more detailed error messages.
- Run the nisldapmaptest(1M) utility for entries that fail, observing error messages.
- Run snoop if the directory server is on a separate system. See Appendix C, "Using snoop with LDAP."

Common Problems

- The directory server is missing necessary schema definitions. This will occur if you fail to comment out the directory, group, and table entries in `NIS+LDAPmapping(4)` file and do not add the `nisObjectContainer` object class and associated attributes.

- The naming service containers, for example `ou=hosts`, have not been created. To avoid this, run the `idsconfig` command before uploading NIS+ data.

- The proxy user account specified does not have sufficient write permissions. For test purposes you can choose `cn=directory manager` to avoid this issue.

- The NIS+ tables being imported have duplicate entries. While this is allowed in NIS+, you will get an LDAP object class violation error when they are imported because it will be interpreted as a multi-value attribute.

## CHAPTER 6

Management Tools and Toolkits

After your directory server is installed and configured as described in Chapter 4 "Deploying Solaris OE LDAP Naming Services," you need to start managing your directory data. A variety of tools and toolkits are available for this purpose.

The good news about tools and techniques to manage LDAP directories is that there are so many to choose from. The bad news is that because there are so many, you have the daunting task of having to determine which tools are best suited for your environment. The tools you choose depends on a variety of factors. These include:

- System administrator's level of experience

- Frequency of tasks

- Uniqueness of your environment

- Availability of tool developers

To know what tools are the right fit, you need to know the capabilities and limitations of each tool. To present this information in a manageable fashion, this chapter presents the tools in the following categories:

- "Using the JDGW" on page 386
- "Creating a Program With the LDAP SDK for Java" on page 393

Command-Line Tools

This section describes four categories of tools that can be run from the command line to manage LDAP data and the directory configuration. These categories are:

- Standard LDAP Utilities
- Solaris OE Secured LDAP client specific tools
- Sun ONE Directory Server administration tools

The standard LDAP utilities are used to search for, and to update data in the directory. Updates can be performed by importing LDAP Data Interchange Format (LDIF) or specifying data on the command line. Besides being able to manipulate data entries, most directory configuration changes can be made by importing LDIF. You will see many examples of this later.

Solaris OE specific tools are those that interface directly with the bundled directory server or directly with naming service data. The Solaris OE ldaplist command, for example, performs a search of the directory using parameters for which the Secured LDAP Client is configured, to locate naming service data.

Sun ONE Directory Server administration tools are scripts or programs that perform routine maintenance. Some of these tools ship with the Sun ONE Directory Server software while others are available by downloading the Sun ONE Directory Server, Resource Kit (SDRK) software. Examples are scripts to start and stop the server and to backup data. The bundled Solaris 9 OE directory server provides a wrapper script called /usr/sbin/directoryserver that performs the same functions as the unbundled version of the directory server utilities without having to know where the actual utilities reside.

Standard LDAP Utilities

Standard LDAP utilities are tools that use LDAP to interact with a directory server and are available on multiple platforms. Standard LDAP utilities communicate over the LDAP v3 protocol, so the commands can be run anywhere. These tools perform the following tasks:

- Creation and deletion of entries
- Modification of entries
- Renaming entries

- Searching for or reading entries

In general, the following information is supplied depending on what operation is being performed:

- Host name and port number of the directory server
- Bind DN and password
- Search base or entry name
- Name of file containing LDIF statements

Two sets of standard LDAP utilities can exist on a Solaris OE system. One set is installed when the SUNW11dap package for Solaris 8 and 9 OE is loaded. The other is contained in the Sun ONE Directory Server software distribution and is installed when the directory server is configured.

Although the two sets of utilities look similar and perform similar functions the supported features and command syntax are significantly different. Therefore it is important to know which set of standard LDAP utilities you are running when following the examples in this book.

Note – The examples referenced in this book assume you are using the Sun ONE Directory Server software version of the standard LDAP utilities unless otherwise specified.

Differences Between Standard LDAP Utilities

You may be asking why two sets of utilities exist that do basically the same thing. The reason for this is more historical than technical. Prior to the Sun/AOL/Netscape Alliance, Sun had produced its own directory server which included its own version of the standard LDAP utilities. These versions eventually shipped as part of the Solaris 2.6 OE. After the Alliance was formed, Sun decided to discontinue their original directory server and adopt the Netscape version because it was the market leader.

However, the Netscape version of the utilities relied on software libraries that did not ship with the Solaris OE. Therefore, the Netscape utilities could not ship as part of the Solaris OE. Legal restrictions at the time prevented Sun from shipping the libraries.

To determine which utilities you are using, it is helpful to know where the utilities are installed. The following lists show where to find the utilities.

Solaris 8 and 9 OE with `SUNWlldap` loaded:

- `/usr/bin/ldapsearch`
- `/usr/bin/ldapmodify`
- `/usr/bin/ldapadd`
- `/usr/bin/ldapdelete`
- `/usr/bin/ldapmodrdn`

Bundled Sun ONE Directory Server 5.1 software (Solaris 9 OE):

- `/usr/iplanet/ds5/shared/bin/ldapsearch`
- `/usr/iplanet/ds5/shared/bin/ldapmodify`
- `/usr/iplanet/ds5/shared/bin/ldapdelete`

Unbundled version of Sun ONE Directory Server 5.1 software:

- *install-root*`/shared/bin/ldapsearch`
- *install-root*`/shared/bin/ldapmodify`
- *install-root*`/shared/bin/ldapdelete`

Sun ONE Directory Server 5.2 software, compressed tar file (default location):

- `/var/Sun/mps/shared/bin/ldapsearch`
- `/var/Sun/mps/shared/bin/ldapmodify`
- `/var/Sun/mps/shared/bin/ldapdelete`
- `/var/Sun/mps/shared/bin/ldapcompare`

Sun ONE Directory Server 5.2 software, SVR4 packages:

- `/var/mps/serverroot/shared/bin/ldapsearch`
- `/var/mps/serverroot/shared/bin/ldapmodify`
- `/var/mps/serverroot/shared/bin/ldapdelete`
- `/var/mps/serverroot/shared/bin/ldapcompare`

You can see that there are five Solaris OE commands (the first five listed above), but only three Sun ONE Directory Server commands (the rest of the list). TABLE 6-1 describes how they map to each other.

TABLE 6-1   Sun ONE Directory Server Software versus Solaris OE Commands

Solaris OE Command	Sun ONE Directory Server Software Equivalent
ldapadd	Run ldapmodify -a which has the same effect. In fact, the ldapadd command is actually a hard link to the Sun ldapmodify command
ldapmodrdn	Same effect as specifying changetype: modrdn in LDIF, then importing it using ldapmodify.

The Sun ONE Directory Server utilities are usually preferred over the Solaris OE utilities because the Sun ONE Directory Server utilities offer:

- More detailed failure messages
- Output in LDIF
- SSL support
- SASL support
- Additional controls – server-side sort, VLV search
- Character set conversion

The downside to the Sun ONE Directory Server commands is they are only available on systems that have the directory server installed and configured. You also need to run the commands in the directory for which they are installed, or set your LD_LIBRARY_PATH shell variable (see ld.so.1(1) for details). For example:

```
# LD_LIBRARY_PATH=/var/Sun/mps/lib;export LD_LIBRARY_PATH
```

Even though the differences between the two sets of utilities are subtle, they are especially important when used in scripts. For example, look at the following two code boxes.

Solaris OE version:

```
# ldapsearch -b "(dc=example,dc=com)" cn=test2
cn=test2+ipHostNumber=10.10.25.22,ou=Hosts,dc=example,dc=com
cn=test2
ipHostNumber=10.10.25.22
objectClass=ipHost
objectClass=device
objectClass=top

# ldapsearch -L -b "(dc=example,dc=com)" cn=test2
dn: cn=test2+ipHostNumber=10.10.25.22,ou=Hosts,dc=example,dc=com
cn: test2
ipHostNumber: 10.10.25.22
objectClass: ipHost
objectClass: device
objectClass: top
```

Sun Directory Server version:

```
# ldapsearch -b "(dc=example,dc=com)" cn=test2
version: 1
dn:cn=test2+ipHostNumber=10.10.25.22,ou=Hosts,dc=example,dc=com
cn: test2
ipHostNumber: 10.10.25.22
objectClass: ipHost
objectClass: device
objectClass: top
```

While the output looks similar, the default Sun ONE Directory Server command output is in a format suitable for importing as LDIF because it includes a dn: directive and uses : as a delimiter instead of = . To get the same output with the Solaris OE version of the command, the -L switch is required. The reason this is significant is that a convenient way to create LDIF is to extract existing entries, then modify them as explained later.

Another obvious difference is how the absence of a bindDN password is handled. The Solaris OE version prompts you for a password if a bindDN is specified and no password is supplied. The Sun ONE Directory Server version defaults to an anonymous bind if the password is omitted.

Note – See ldapsearch(1) for details on the bundled version of the tool and the Sun ONE Directory Server 5.2 software documentation for the second version.

Specific Tools for the Secured LDAP Client

In addition to the standard LDAP commands, Solaris OE provides LDAP-aware commands that can be run on a Secured LDAP Client. The advantage of these commands is that they are simple to use. This is because they make use of the same configuration data the client uses. This means you do not have to be aware of the directory server name or IP address and what base suffix is defined to hold naming service data.

These commands include:

- `ldaplist`
- `ldapaddent`
- `ldapclient`
- `idsconfig`

The `ldaplist` command can be used to search for Solaris OE naming service information instead of `ldapsearch` and is discussed in the following sections. The `ldapaddent`, `ldapclient`, and `idsconfig` commands are discussed in Chapter 4 "Deploying Solaris OE LDAP Naming Services" in the context of Secured LDAP Client initialization. In the following sections, additional uses of these commands are discussed.

ldaplist

The `ldaplist` command can be thought as a user-friendly version of the `ldapsearch` command used to search for Solaris OE naming service information. Unlike `ldapsearch`, the `ldaplist` command can only be run on a Secured LDAP Client. This is because information contained in the Secured LDAP Client profile is used as defaults. Therefore you do not have to enter a directory server IP address, search base, or bind DN, because these are defined in the profile. You can specify either the LDAP container name (ou=) or the naming service database name.

The `ldaplist` command is easy to use for beginners, and can also be a useful tool for advanced users. For those who are familiar with the standard LDAP search command, it is helpful to understand the defaults that `ldaplist` uses.

Issuing the command without any arguments results in a list of container DNs in the default search base. This includes both the standard containers that `idsconfig` creates, along with any containers you may have created. For example:

```
# ldaplist
dn: cn=Directory Administrators, dc=example,dc=com

dn: ou=People, dc=example,dc=com
 .
 .
 .
```

To see an entire entry, the `-l` switch is specified. For example:

```
# ldaplist -l
dn: cn=Directory Administrators, dc=example,dc=com
        objectClass: top
        objectClass: groupofuniquenames
        cn: Directory Administrators

dn: ou=People, dc=example,dc=com
        objectClass: top
        objectClass: organizationalunit
        ou: People
 .
 .
 .
```

The -h switch displays the default mappings used for the databases along with the object class used to define the entry and default attribute. For example:

```
# ldaplist -h
database            default type          objectclass
=============       =================      =============
auto_*              automountKey          automount
automount           automountMapName      automountMap
publickey           uidnumber             niskeyobject
publickey           cn                    niskeyobject
bootparams          cn                    bootableDevice
ethers              cn                    ieee802Device
group               cn                    posixgroup
hosts               cn                    iphost
ipnodes             cn                    iphost
netgroup            cn                    nisnetgroup
netmasks            ipnetworknumber       ipnetwork
networks            ipnetworknumber       ipnetwork
passwd              uid                   posixaccount
protocols           cn                    ipprotocol
rpc                 cn                    oncrpc
services            cn                    ipservice
aliases             cn                    mailGroup
project             SolarisProjectID      SolarisProject
printers            printer-uri           sunPrinter
#
```

The database column equates to a database listed in the /etc/nsswitch.conf file. The default type column is the default attribute that is searched on. The objectclass column specifies that only entries containing those object classes are searched.

The following example illustrates how these mappings work along with other command features.

Example showing the LDAP search filter

```
# ldaplist -v -1 hosts "test*"
+++ database=hosts
+++ filter=(&(objectclass=iphost)(cn=test*))
+++ template for merging SSD filter=(&(%s)(cn=test*))
dn: cn=test2+ipHostNumber=129.250.25.22, ou=Hosts, dc=example,dc=
com
        cn: test2
        ipHostNumber: 129.250.25.22
        objectClass: ipHost
        objectClass: device
        objectClass: top

dn: cn=test3+ipHostNumber=129.250.181.98,ou=Hosts,dc=example,dc=
com
        cn: test3
        ipHostNumber: 129.250.181.98
        objectClass: ipHost
        objectClass: device
        objectClass: top
#
```

The -v switch is specified on the command line to show the LDAP search filter, which is represented by the lines beginning with "+++":

```
+++ database=hosts
+++ filter=(&(objectclass=iphost)(cn=test*))
+++ template for merging SSD filter=(&(%s)(cn=test*))
```

The database being searched is hosts. This could also be represented by the container ou=hosts on the command line instead. The search filter specifies entries that contain the object class iphost (the default for this database) and a cn attribute that contains the string test as the first four characters. The example uses the wild card * to shown that these types of searches are possible. Since no attribute was specified on the command line, the default cn= was assumed.

The last line specifies how to incorporate the Service Search Descriptor (SSD) filter if one is defined in the client profile for the database hosts. In this case no SSD is defined, so the template passes the specified string test without modification.

ldapaddent

The `ldapaddent` command is used to load data into the LDAP server. Use of this command is described in Chapter 5 "Migrating Legacy Data to LDAP." However, it can also be used to add new entries after the directory is initialized. This can be useful if you are merging data from an NIS or NIS+ domain after your directory server is already configured and loaded with data from another domain.

Note – If you attempt to import a file that contains entries that already exist in the directory (that is, have the same DN), the `ldapaddent` command will abort. If you wish to skip over duplicate entries, specify the `-c` switch on the command line.

The `ldapaddent` can be used to extract entries from the directory in `files` format. However, you can accomplish the same result with `getent(1M)`. To do this with ldapaddent, specify the `-d` option. For example, to extract a user account from the directory with the user ID of `jsmith`, perform the following command:

```
# ldapaddent -d passwd | grep jsmith
jsmith:g0HKYO511jUHE:87317:40:John Smith:/home/jsmith:/bin/csh:
#
```

Similarly, you could use the `getent` command, which is more efficient:,

```
# getent passwd | grep jsmith
jsmith:g0HKYO511jUHE:87317:40:John Smith:/home/jsmith:/bin/csh:
#
```

Note – The user password is only extracted if the LDAP client where the command is run is configured with a proxy user that has password read permission. Otherwise you would need to bind to the directory with a DN that does have password read permission, such as `cn=directory manager`.

---

ldapclient

The `ldapclient` command is primarily used to initiate a Secured LDAP Client. However, it can also be used to perform the following tasks:

- List the current client configuration
- Create additional client profiles
- Update local client parameters
- Uninitialize a client

Note – All the above tasks except for creating client profiles require root privileges.

The following code boxes provide examples of performing these tasks.

- List the current settings:

```
# ldapclient list
NS_LDAP_FILE_VERSION= 2.0
NS_LDAP_BINDDN= cn=proxyagent,ou=profile,dc=example,dc=com
NS_LDAP_BINDPASSWD= {NS1}4a3788e8c053424f
NS_LDAP_SERVERS= 129.100.200.1
NS_LDAP_SEARCH_BASEDN= dc=example,dc=com
NS_LDAP_AUTH= simple
NS_LDAP_SEARCH_REF= FALSE
NS_LDAP_SEARCH_SCOPE= one
NS_LDAP_SEARCH_TIME= 30
NS_LDAP_PROFILE= default
NS_LDAP_CREDENTIAL_LEVEL= proxy
NS_LDAP_BIND_TIME= 10
#
```

- Create a new profile specifying all attributes:

```
# ldapclient genprofile -a profileName=eng \
-a credentialLevel=proxy \
-a authenticationMethod=sasl/DIGEST-MD5 \
-a bindTimeLimit=20 \
-a defaultSearchBase=dc=example,dc=com \
-a "serviceSearchDescriptor=passwd:ou=people,dc=a1,dc=
example,dc=com?one" \
-a serviceAuthenticationMethod=pam_ldap:tls:simple \
-a defaultSearchScope=sub \
-a attributeMap=passwd:uid=employeeNumber \
-a objectclassMap=passwd:posixAccount=unixAccount \
-a followReferrals=false -a profileTTL=6000 \
-a preferredServerList=129.100.100.30 \
-a searchTimeLimit=30 \
-a "defaultServerList=29.100.200.1 129.100.100.1 \
204.34.5.6" > eng.ldif
```

- Change the proxy password on a client:

```
# ldapclient mod -a proxyPassword=newpassword
```

- Revert back to the old naming service:

```
# ldapclient uninit
System successfully recovered
#
```

Note – Only one redo is possible. That is, you can only revert back to the previous configuration state.

---

idsconfig

The idsconfig script is primarily used to configure a new directory server to support Secured LDAP Clients. However, the script can be rerun on an already configured system without any ill effects. No data will be deleted, and if a configuration change was already made, it is simply skipped.

The idsconfig script can be run to create additional profiles or to configure the directory server to support proxy authentication.

The idsconfig script can create an output file that can be used as input for subsequent runs. This is useful when setting up a JumpStart infrastructure.

Other LDAP-Aware Commands

Commands that use the name service switch like gentent and smattrpop, can work with LDAP data. The command getent is useful because it displays all the data in your search path and the order in which data is found.

Tricks and Tips Using LDAP Commands

This section shows how LDAP commands can be used to perform useful functions.

> **Note –** The examples assume you are running the LDAP commands on the same system the directory server is running on. Therefore, the `-h` option is omitted.

Deleting Multiple Entries

As a system administrator, you might have a need to remove several entries at the same time. Removing them one at a time would be tedious, but the process can be easier using simple LDAP commands in combination. In this example, all users who belong to the group with the GID of 20 are removed.

▼ To Delete Multiple Entries

1. Search for the users for which you are interested.

```
# ldapsearch -b ou=people,dc=example,dc=com gidnumber=20 dn
uid=tb135994,ou=People,dc=example,dc=com

uid=tbanzi,ou=People,dc=example,dc=com

uid=tb95209,ou=People,dc=example,dc=com

uid=tb127286,ou=People,dc=example,dc=com

uid=dm88477,ou=People,dc=example,dc=com

uid=cs99346,ou=people,dc=example,dc=com

uid=dustin,ou=people,dc=example,dc=com
#
```

2. Write the list to a file and use it as input to the `ldapdelete` command.

```
# ldapsearch -b ou=people,dc=example,dc=com gidnumber=20 dn\ >
/tmp/del.list
# ldapdelete -D "cn=directory manager" -w mysecret -f
/tmp/del.list
# ldapsearch -b ou=people,dc=example,dc=com gidnumber=20 dn
#
```

Identifying Secondary Groups That a User Belongs To

An easy way to determine which groups a user belongs to is to search for the user's group membership ID and return the DN of the groups in which they appear.

● **To search for groups that user ID** dam **belongs to:**

```
# ldapsearch -b ou=group,dc=example,dc=com memberuid=dam dn
cn=einsteins,ou=group,dc=example,dc=com

cn=quasars,ou=group,dc=example,dc=com

cn=rsc,ou=group,dc=example,dc=com

cn=labrats,ou=group,dc=example,dc=com

cn=fw-sqa,ou=group,dc=example,dc=com

cn=wgweb,ou=group,dc=example,dc=com

cn=rsi,ou=group,dc=example,dc=com

cn=excaliburs,ou=group,dc=example,dc=com

cn=wgs-sqa,ou=group,dc=example,dc=com

cn=bluemoon,ou=group,dc=example,dc=com
#
```

Sun ONE Directory Server Administration Tools

Most of the administration commands are located in the slapd-*instance* directory under the server-root where the directory server software was installed. For example:

/var/mps/serverroot/slapd-*instance*

The commands found here are either shell or Perl scripts that invoke other programs. The reason for this organization is that the actual commands executed have complicated syntaxes and it is easier to create a script that passes the proper parameters to the program than to remember the numerous parameters.

The scripts are generated when the directory server is configured, and are tailored to work with only a single instance of the directory. The following is a list of scripts:

- `bak2db` – restores backup while offline
- `bak2db.pl` – restores backup while online
- `db2bak` – offline or online backup
- `db2bak.pl` – online backup
- `db2index.pl` – builds an index while online
- `db2ldif` – dumps a database in LDIF while offline or online
- `db2ldif.pl` – dumps a database in LDIF while online
- `getpwenc` – creates a password hash
- `ldif2db` – restores a database from LDIF while offline
- `ldif2db.pl` – restores a database from LDIF while online
- `ldif2ldap` – simple restore using `ldapmodify`
- `monitor` – displays content of `cn=monitor`
- `ns-accountstatus.pl` – displays status of an account
- `ns-activate.pl` – activates one or several accounts
- `ns-inactivate.pl` – inactivates one or several accounts
- `restart-slapd` – stops, then starts the directory server
- `restoreconfig` – restores `o=NetscapeRoot`
- `saveconfig` – saves `o=NetscapeRoot`
- `schema_push.pl` – offline tool that forces the schema to be replicated when the server starts
- `start-slapd` – starts a directory server instance
- `stop-slapd` – stops a directory server instance
- `suffix2instance` – adds a directory suffix
- `vlvindex` – adds a VLV index

Using the `directoryserver` Wrapper

The `/usr/sbin/directory` wrapper script, that is part of the Solaris 9 OE bundled directory server software, can be used to perform many useful administration commands. The wrapper script executes Sun ONE Directory Server commands and scripts for you. The advantage of using the wrapper is that you do not need to know where the instances of directory servers are installed.

Note – When you install the Sun ONE Directory Server 5.2 software SVR4 packages, the Solaris 9 OE version of `/usr/sbin/directoryserver` script is overwritten with an updated version.

`directoryserver` *Command Basics*

There are many options the `directoryserver` command supports, so it is easy to get confused about how to use it. Examples are provided in the Chapter 7 "Performing Administrative Tasks." However, it is helpful to keep a few principles in mind. These are:

- You can only run it against the local host.
- You must run it as `root` to start and stop the directory and admin servers.
- You must supply the `cn=directory manager` or equivalent credentials when performing an operation on the directory that requires it.
- Most operations require that you provide the server instance name. The default name of the first instance you install is the host name of the system you install the directory server software on. For some operations, like `start` and `stop`, all instances are acted upon as defaults.
- Some of the operations require the directory server to be running and some require that it be stopped.

`directoryserver` *Command Operations*

Here is a list of functions that can be performed through `directoryserver`:

- Start and stop server instances
- Start and stop the administration server
- Start the Sun ONE Console
- Backup and restore the directory configuration data
- Import and export LDIF
- Backup and restore a database
- Map a suffix

GUI-based Tools

Graphical User Interface (GUI) tools are an alternative to command-line tools and are useful for administrators who are new to LDAP. In general, you would use GUI tools to perform tasks requiring few changes, or as learning tools. For repetitive tasks or tasks requiring many updates to directory data, you would want to create scripts.

GUI tools provide a visual way of looking at the directory hierarchy. However, if the number of entries is large, displaying them in a readable format becomes problematical.

While there are many third-party graphical tools for displaying and manipulating LDAP data, this section only focuses on three:

- Sun ONE Directory Console
- Sun Management Console
- The LDAP Browser/Editor

The first tool is part of the directory server software distribution. The second tool is part of the Solaris OE, and the third is a public domain tool.

Sun ONE Directory Console

The Sun ONE Directory Console is a Java-based application that can be installed along with, or separate from, the directory server. The Directory Console can also be displayed through the X protocol on a remote system. Most common administration functions can be performed through the Directory Console, although some may be cumbersome.

The Sun ONE Directory Server documentation does a good job at detailing how to perform most procedures. The intent of this section is not to repeat those procedures, although some similar examples are provided for educational purposes.

In general, command-line tools and scripts built around them are recommended over use of the Sun ONE Directory Console because of their flexibility and repeatability. However, the Console can be a valuable learning tool, and at times can be more convenient for some tasks. All operations that are performed by the Console can be captured in a form suitable for used with `ldapmodify` by enabling the directory server audit log.

Sample Tasks Using the Directory Console

The following are examples of how the Directory Console can be used to perform useful tasks.

▼ To View the DIT With the Directory Console

1. **Run directoryserver startconsole and log in.**

   The default login account is the admin account that was set up when the Administration Server software was configured.

2. **Under Server Group, double-click Directory Server.**

   The directory view in the Directory Console provides you with a graphical display of data in the DIT. While the same information can be gathered from the output of the ldapsearch command, users who are not familiar with LDAP command syntax will find viewing the DIT in this manner convenient. FIGURE 6-1 shows what a DIT might look like after the idsconfig command is run and naming service data is imported. Information about individual entries can be displayed by double clicking on them. The DN of the highlighted entry is displayed on the bottom bar and there is a search facility for locating entries.

   One drawback of viewing entries through the Directory Console is that performance can become sluggish when there are a large number of entries. Another problem is that there is no way to dump the LDIF representation of a single entry.

Note – Newly created entries do not immediately appear in the view. You may have to perform a Refresh of the view to see new entries.

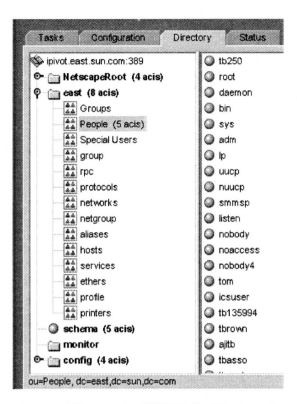

FIGURE 6-1   Viewing the DIT With the Directory Console

▼ To Add New Entries With the Directory Console

Entries can be created, modified, or deleted from the Directory Console. However, creating entries is not always a one-step process. This is because the Directory Console is a general-purpose tool that makes assumptions about how entries should be constructed. In the case of entries defining a Solaris OE user profile, the entry you create will require additional object classes and attributes that are not created by the Directory Console.

FIGURE 6-2 is an example of creating a user account through the Directory Console that can be used to log in to a Solaris OE system.

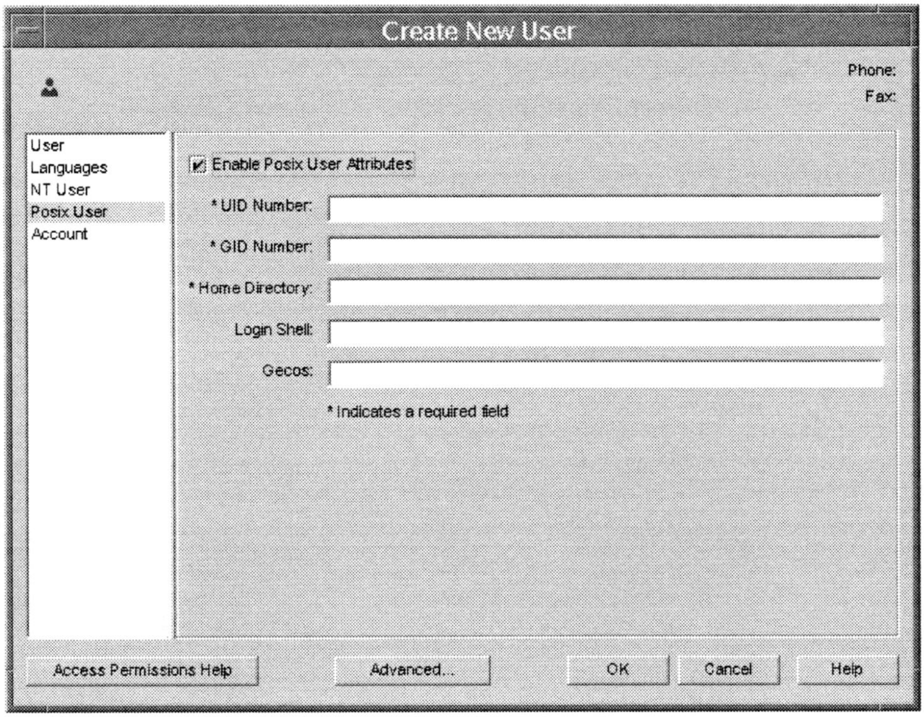

FIGURE 6-2 Directory Console New User Form

In this example, the POSIX User account option is chosen from the New➤User pull-down menu. The screen allows you to enter attributes that are required by the `posixAccount` object class. However, the entry created is incomplete for use with the Secured LDAP Client because it does not contain the `shadowAccount` object class.

To complete the entry, you need to manually add the `shadowAccount` object class by following these steps:

1. **Click on the Advanced button.**

2. **Click on the Object class field.**

3. **Click on Add Value**

4. **Choose shadowAccount from the list.**

FIGURE 6-3 shows what the Directory Console display should look like following these steps.

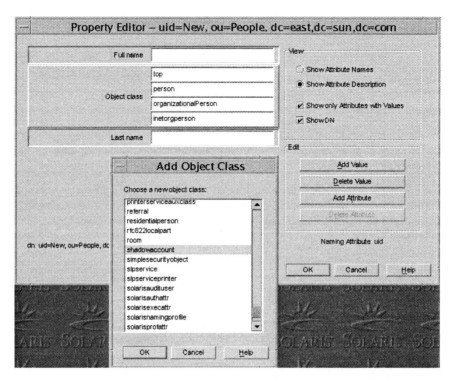

FIGURE 6-3 Adding Shadow Account Attributes With the Property Editor

---

Note – The Sun ONE Directory Server 5.2 software uses the Edit with Generic Editor pull-down menu option rather than the Advanced button.

▼ To Add Non-User Entries With the Directory Console

The Directory Console can be used to create other RFC 2307 defined entries besides the `posixAccount` entries described previously.

1. **Right click on the container where you want to create the new entry (`ou=hosts` for example).**

2. **Choose New▸Other from the pull-down menu.**

   You should see the New Object window, which appears similar to the Add Object Class window that was shown in the previous example.

3. **From the window, choose one of the object classes that are defined in RFC 2307.**

   In FIGURE 6-4, the `ipHost` object class is chosen.

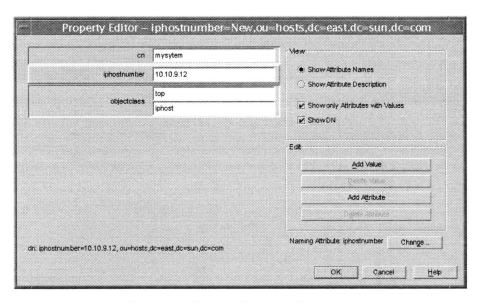

FIGURE 6-4 Adding a Host name With the Property Editor

The only two required attributes are the host name, represented by `cn` and the IP address, represented by `ipHostNumber`. While an `ou=host` entry can be created this way, it is not in the same format that `ldapaddent` and the NIS/NIS+ Gateways use by default. For example, the device object class is not included and the RDN uses the `ipHostNumber` attribute in place of `cn`.

Sun Management Console

The Sun Management Console (smc) is essentially a container for GUI-based system administration tools. The tools are stored in collections called toolboxes. By default, a toolbox for managing local databases, that is, `/etc` files, is created. Toolboxes for managing naming service data can be created as described later in this section.

Once a toolbox is created for your LDAP naming service, management tools, such as user management tools, can be installed in the toolbox. The definition for the toolbox and the tools it contains can be stored in a file and loaded once smc is started.

FIGURE 6-5 shows how users stored in an LDAP naming service would appear in smc.

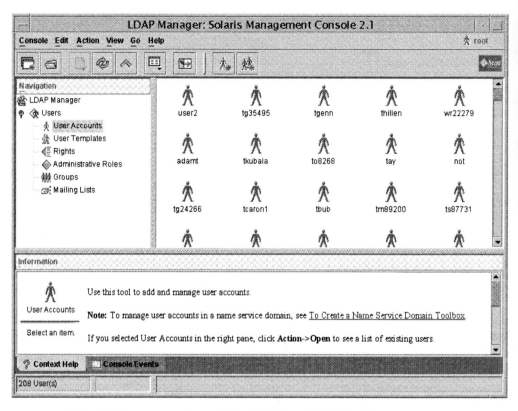

FIGURE 6-5   Solaris Management Console (smc) With an LDAP Toolbox

To add new users, the Add User Wizard can be used as shown in FIGURE 6-6.

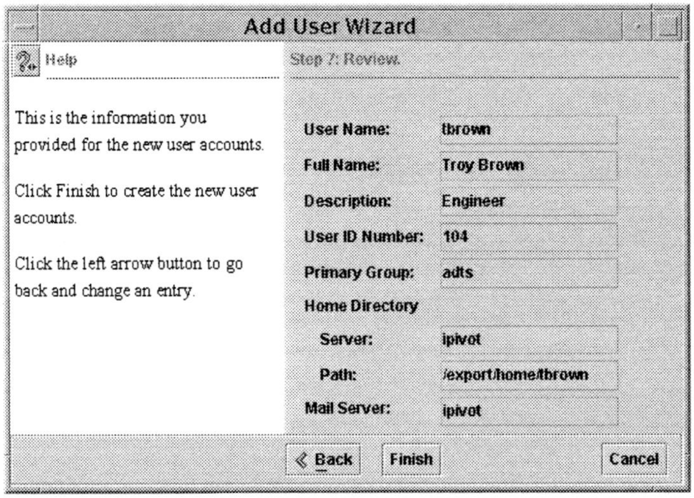

FIGURE 6-6   Adding a User Through smc

▼ To Set Up an LDAP Name Service Domain Toolbox

Before setting up an LDAP toolbox, you should have a configured and populated directory server. You can set up the toolbox either on the same system as the directory server, or on a different system.

1. **On the system running the directory server, verify that smc recognizes the server.**

```
# /usr/sadm/bin/dtsetup scopes
Getting list of manageable scopes...
Scope 1 file:/hosta/hosta
Scope 2 ldap:/hosta/dc=example,dc=com
#
```

In the above example, notice that two scopes are present. The first one refers to the local system and appears on all systems running smc. The second one is discovered when the web-based enterprise management (wbem) server is initialized.

2. **On the system where you plan to create the toolbox, add the credentials necessary to bind to the directory server with read and write access.**

```
# /usr/sadm/bin/dtsetup storeCred
Administrator DN:cn=Directory Manager
Password:*******
Password (confirm):*******
#
```

3. Launch the smc toolbox editor.

```
# /usr/sadm/bin/smc edit &
```

The editor is displayed.

4. Click on the Toolbox URL line in the left pane.

This is the line directory under Management Tools.

5. From the Action pull-down menu, choose Properties.

This brings up the Toolbox URL Wizard (FIGURE 6-7).

6. Accept the defaults by clicking Next until the Save As option appears.

7. Click on Override, and fill in Server and Domain as shown below.

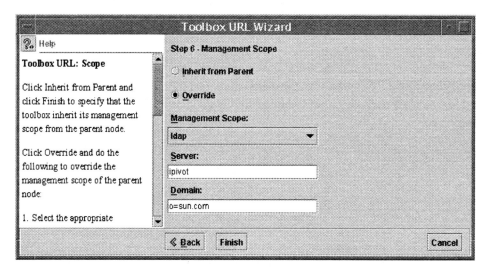

FIGURE 6-7   Toolbox Wizard

8. Click on Finish.

9. Choose the Save As option from the Toolbox pull-down menu and specify a path name where the configuration file will be stored.

10. Exit the editor and bring up smc.

```
# /usr/sadm/bin/smc &
```

11. From the Console pull-down menu, choose Open Toolbox.

12. Choose the Local Toolbox tab and select the configuration file you saved.

If all goes well, you can view user data as in FIGURE 6-8.

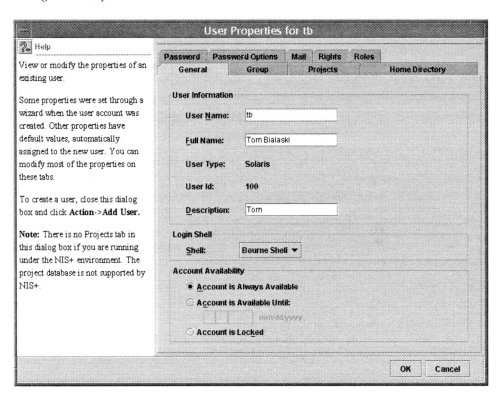

FIGURE 6-8   User Property Sheet

LDAP Browser/Editor (LBE)

The LDAP Browser/Editor (LBE) is public domain software developed at the University of Michigan that can be downloaded from various web sites. The following instructions use LBE version 2.8.2.

▼ To Install and Configure the LBE

1. Extract the LBE tar file.

```
# tar xf Browser282b2.tar
# cd ldapbrowser
# ls
CHANGES.TXT
LICENSE.ICONS
LdapBrowser.lnk
applet
attributes.config.sample
faq.html
help
hosta.cfg:      ascii text
lbe.jar:        ZIP archive
lbe.sh:         executable shell script
lib:            directory
readme.html:    ascii text
relnotes.html:  ascii text
templates:      directory
#
```

2. Invoke the LBE.

```
# export JAVA_HOME=/usr/j2se
# sh ./lbe.sh &
```

3. After the LBE starts, create a new connection by choosing Connect, then New.

FIGURE 6-9 is displayed.

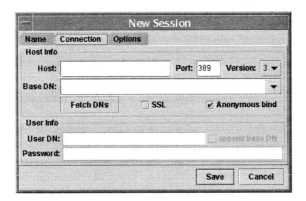

FIGURE 6-9   Creating a New LDAP Session

4. Fill in all the information.

You can assign a name to the connection, which creates a configuration file. The next time you want to connect, you pick the connection name and the configuration file is read.

The FIGURE 6-10 shows what an entry in a directory tree might look like.

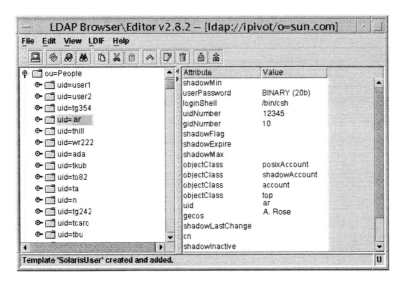

FIGURE 6-10   LBE Representation of a User Entry

5. Add entries by creating a template.

Templates can be created from existing entries by highlighting an entry, then choosing Create Template. You can create entries from a template by choosing Add-Entry, then picking the template you want.

FIGURE 6-11 shows what a template for a `posixUser` entry might look like:

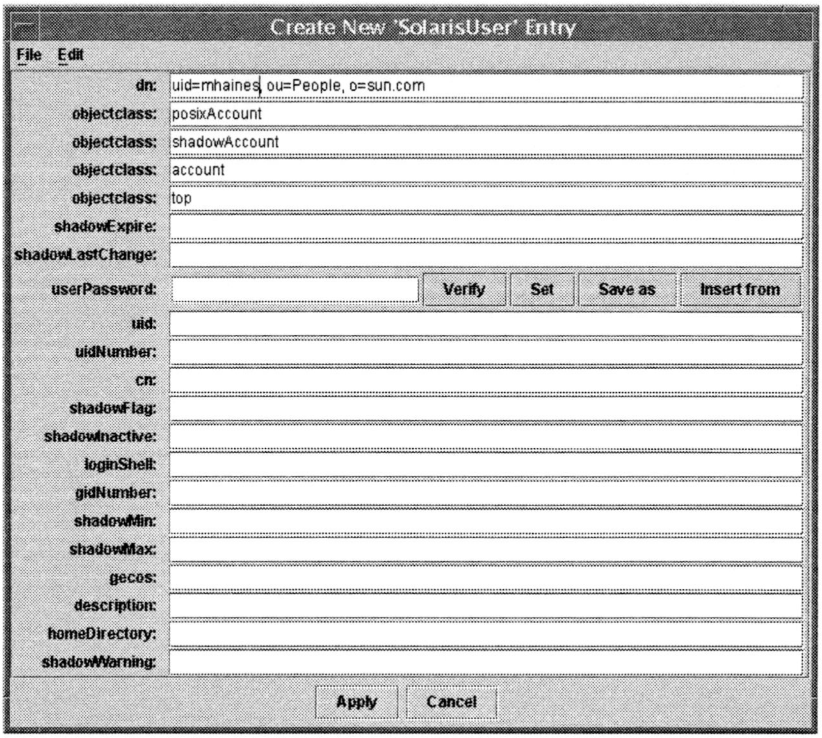

Create New 'SolarisUser' Entry

File Edit

dn:	uid=mhaines ou=People, o=sun.com
objectclass:	posixAccount
objectclass:	shadowAccount
objectclass:	account
objectclass:	top
shadowExpire:	
shadowLastChange:	
userPassword:	[ ] Verify Set Save as Insert from
uid:	
uidNumber:	
cn:	
shadowFlag:	
shadowInactive:	
loginShell:	
gidNumber:	
shadowMin:	
shadowMax:	
gecos:	
description:	
homeDirectory:	
shadowWarning:	

Apply   Cancel

FIGURE 6-11 LBE Template for a New User

Toolkits and LDAP APIs

Although a multitude of general purpose LDAP tools are available, you may want to develop your own customized tools that reflect the way you do business. The good news is that there are many toolkits and application programming interfaces (APIs) to choose from. The bad news is that you need to decide which ones are best for you.

Consider the following factors when choosing a toolkit:

- Programming experience
- Performance requirements
- Portability, platform support
- Ease of programming
- Compatibility with other tools you developed

Providing an exhaustive list of tools and their capabilities would be a subject of another book. For example the Mark Wilcox book, *Implementing LDAP*, goes into detail on several of the LDAP APIs. The intent of this section is to introduce you to some of the most common toolkits, and to provide simple examples of how to implement them.

The toolkits discussed are:

- PerLDAP
- JSP Directory Gateway (JDGW)

The APIs discussed are:

- LDAP C Software Development Kit (SDK)
- Directory SDK for Java software
- Java Naming and Directory Interface (J.N.D.I.) API

PerLDAP

PerLDAP is an interface to the Sun ONE LDAP C SDK. Two types of interfaces are provided:

- Object oriented
- Direct

The object-oriented interface provides a set of Perl modules that perform common LDAP operations. The direct interface uses the C library calls directly.

The object-oriented interface is easier to use and will do most, if not all, of what you want it to do. The examples provided here are based on the object-oriented Perl modules.

Why Use PerLDAP?

Perl is the programming language of choice for many system administrators. While you could create Perl scripts that call the standard LDAP commands like, `ldapsearch` and `ldapmodify`, you would not have the same level of control. One example where you would use PerLDAP instead of Perl+LDAP commands, is to create a CGI gateway. This is useful if you want to build tools that can be accessed through web pages and you are already familiar with creating CGI scripts with Perl.

There are some limitations of PerLDAP that should be noted. These include:

- Limited support of LDAPv3 protocol features
- Open-source effort has been discontinued

LDAP Perl Modules

These include:

- `Mozilla::LDAP::Conn` – The main interface to LDAP functions. It includes creating a connection, searching for and modifying data.
- `Mozilla::LDAP::Entry` – Class is used to create new entries, get and set attributes, and other functions pertaining to directory entries.
- `Mozilla::LDAP::LDIF` – Provides routines for manipulating LDIF.
- `Mozilla::LDAP::Utils` – Provides general purpose LDAP routines.
- `Mozilla::LDAP::API` – Provides wrappers around C functions in the LDAP C SDK.

▼ To Set Up PerLDAP

1. **Obtain the following:**
   - PerLDAP modules – These are located in:
     `/usr/ds/v5.2/nsPerl5.006_01/lib/site/Mozilla/LDAP`
   - LDAP C SDK – this can be downloaded from:
     `http://www.sun.com/software/download/developer/`

2. **Copy the LDAP Perl modules to a location specified in your @INC search path.**

```
# perl -e 'print "@INC"'
/usr/perl5/5.6.1/lib/sun4-solaris-64int /usr/perl5/5.6.1/lib
/usr/perl5/site_perl/5.6.1/sun4-solaris-64int
/usr/perl5/site_perl/5.6.1 /usr/perl5/site_perl
/usr/perl5/vendor_perl/5.6.1/sun4-solaris-64int
/usr/perl5/vendor_perl/5.6.1 /usr/perl5/vendor_perl .
# cd /usr/ds/v5.2/nsPerl5.006_01/lib/site
# cp -r Mozilla /usr/site_perl5/5.6.1
```

Note that the example shown here assumes you are running Solaris 9 OE 12/02, which includes Perl 5.6.1. Other OE releases may have different Perl versions, so the path names would be different.

3. **Install the LDAP C SDK as shown.**

```
# gunzip ldapcsdk5.10-SunOS5.8_OPT.OBJ.tar.gz
# tar xf ldapcsdk5.10-SunOS5.8_OPT.OBJ.tar
# pwd
/ldapcsdk
# ls
README                              lib
docs                                redist.txt
etc                                 release.gif
examples                            relnotes_41.htm
include                             relnotes_5x.htm
ldapcsdk5.06-SunOS5.8_OPT.OBJ.tar   tools
```

4. **Set the** LD_Library_PATH **variable:**

```
# LD_LIBRARY_PATH=/ldapcsdk/lib
# export LD_LIBRARY_PATH
```

5. Perform a simple user search.

This example Perl script does a search for entries that match the `uid` entered on the command line.

```
# cat getentry.pl
#!/usr/bin/perl

use Mozilla::LDAP::Conn;

my $host = "localhost";
my $port = 389;
my $dn = "";
my $passwd = "";

my $base = "ou=people,dc=example,dc=com";
my $filter = "uid=$ARGV[0]";
my $scope = "subtree";
#
my $conn = new Mozilla::LDAP::Conn($host,$port,$dn,$passwd);
die "Could't connect to LDAP server $host" unless $conn;

my $entry = $conn->search($base, $scope, $filter);

while($entry)
    {
      $entry->printLDIF();
      $entry = $conn->nextEntry;
    }
  print "\n";

$conn->close if $conn;
```

▼ To Build an LDAP Gateway Using PerLDAP

As described in the next section, the JSP Directory Gateway is available for creating web-based interfaces for updating data in the directory. However, you may feel more comfortable writing a CGI interface with Perl. In this section, creating a bare bones CGI program for creating entries in a directory is described. The assumption is that you are familiar with Perl and the CGI interface, so the emphasis is on how to use PerLDAP to create your interface.

The following assumptions are made:

- The PerLDAP Perl Modules are installed.
- The `CGI.pm` module is installed.
- The LDAP C SDK is installed and the `libldap50.so` library is located where the PerLDAP modules can find it.
- The Solaris OE bundled Apache server is used.

1. **Enable the Apache Web Server:**

   a. **Create a** `/etc/apache/http.conf` **file.**

   An easy way to create this file is to make a copy of the `httpd.conf-example` file, calling the new file `/etc/apache/http.conf`.

   b. **Review the** `http.conf` **file, and make changes as needed.**

   The defaults work in most cases.

   c. **Start the** `httpd` **process.**

   ```
   # /usr/apache/bin/httpd&
   ```

2. **Create a PerLDAP script:**

a. **Using your favorite editor, create the following** `adduser.pl` **script.**

```
#!/usr/bin/perl
use strict;
use CGI; # CGI library
use CGI::Carp qw(fatalsToBrowser);
#use URI::URL;
use Mozilla::LDAP::Conn;
use Mozilla::LDAP::Utils;

# Name of LDAP server, port, container for user accounts,
# and default user password
my $ldap_host = "localhost";
my $ldap_port = 389;
my $ldap_base = "ou=people,dc=example,dc=com";
my $upasswd = "secret";

# Credentials used to create new user account entries
my $dn = "cn=directory manager";
my $pwd = "netscape";

my $query = new CGI;

# Print headers for HTML returned
print $query->header;
print $query->start_html(-title=>'New User');

# Retrieve parameters from form
my $loginid = $query->param('loginid');
my $uidnumber = $query->param('uidnumber');
my $gidnumber = $query->param('gidnumber');
my $homedir = $query->param('homedir');
my $cn = $query->param('cn');
my $shell = $query->param('shell');

my $ldap = new
Mozilla::LDAP::Conn($ldap_host,$ldap_port,$dn,$pwd) ||
    die("Failed to open LDAP connection.\n");
my $entry = $ldap->newEntry();
$entry->setDN("uid=$loginid,$ldap_base");
$entry->{objectclass} = ["top", "account", "posixaccount",
"shadowaccount" ];
$entry->{uid} = [ "$loginid" ];
$entry->{uidnumber} = [ "$uidnumber" ];
$entry->{gidnumber} = [ "$gidnumber" ];
$entry->{homedirectory} = [ "$homedir" ];
```

```
$entry->{cn} = [ "$cn" ];
$entry->{loginshell} = [ "$shell" ];
$entry->{userpassword} = [ "$upasswd" ];
if (! $ldap->add($entry)) {
    die ("Can't create account for $loginid");
}

# Check to see if the entry was created and print it
my $filter = "uid=$loginid";
my $entry = $ldap->search($ldap_base, "subtree",$filter);
if (! $entry) {
    print "Can't find user entry";
}
else {
print $query->h1("The following user account entry was
created...");
print "Account created for $entry->{cn}[0]";
print "<PRE>";
$entry->printLDIF();
}
print "</PRE>";
print $query->end_html();
```

b. **Place the script in** /var/apache/cgi-bin.

3. To Create HTML for an Input Form

a. Create some HTML that represents your input form.

```html
<html>
<body>
Add New User Form
<br><form method=POST action="/cgi-bin/adduser.pl">
<br>
Enter loginID:<br>
<input name="loginid" size=20><br>
Enter Full Name:<br>
<input name="cn" size=40><br>
Enter uidNumber:<br>
<input name="uidnumber" size=10><br>
Enter gidNumber:<br>
<input name="gidnumber" size=10><br>
Enter Home Directory:<br>
<input name="homedir" size=20><br>
Enter Login shell:<br>
<input name="shell" size=10><br>
<input type=submit VALUE="Submit">
<input type=reset VALUE="Clear Form"><p>
</form>
</body>
</html>
```

b. Place the HTML in /var/apache/htdocs.

4. Test the script:

a. In a browser, go to http://*myserver/myform.html*.

b. Fill in the form and click submit.

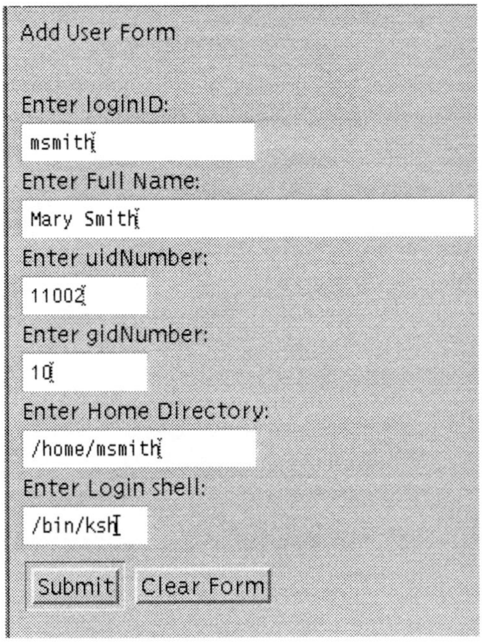

```
Add User Form

Enter loginID:
┌─────────────────────────┐
│ msmith                  │
└─────────────────────────┘
Enter Full Name:
┌───────────────────────────────────────┐
│ Mary Smith                            │
└───────────────────────────────────────┘
Enter uidNumber:
┌─────────────────────┐
│ 11002               │
└─────────────────────┘
Enter gidNumber:
┌─────────────────────┐
│ 10                  │
└─────────────────────┘
Enter Home Directory:
┌─────────────────────────┐
│ /home/msmith            │
└─────────────────────────┘
Enter Login shell:
┌─────────────────────┐
│ /bin/ksh            │
└─────────────────────┘

┌─────────┐ ┌──────────────┐
│ Submit  │ │ Clear Form   │
└─────────┘ └──────────────┘
```

FIGURE 6-12 Add User Form

c. Observe the output.

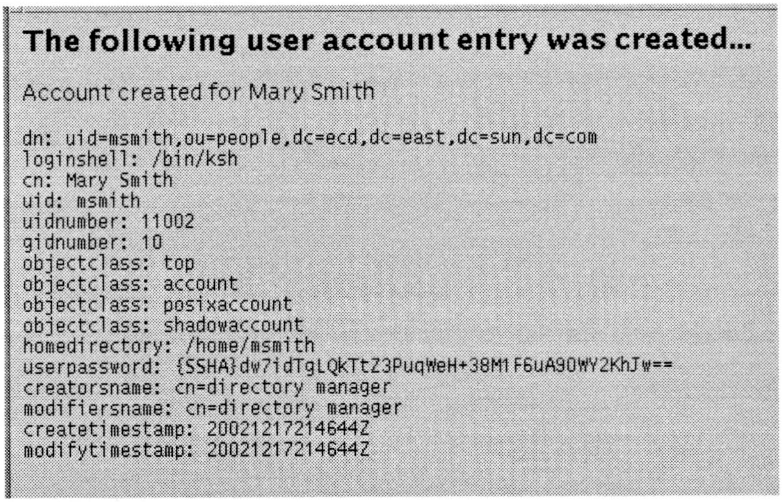

The following user account entry was created...

Account created for Mary Smith

```
dn: uid=msmith,ou=people,dc=ecd,dc=east,dc=sun,dc=com
loginshell: /bin/ksh
cn: Mary Smith
uid: msmith
uidnumber: 11002
gidnumber: 10
objectclass: top
objectclass: account
objectclass: posixaccount
objectclass: shadowaccount
homedirectory: /home/msmith
userpassword: {SSHA}dw7idTgLQkTtZ3PuqWeH+38M1F6uA9OWY2KhJw==
creatorsname: cn=directory manager
modifiersname: cn=directory manager
createtimestamp: 20021217214644Z
modifytimestamp: 20021217214644Z
```

FIGURE 6-13 Example of Output

Using the JDGW

The JSP Directory Gateway (JDGW) is a sample phone book application that ships as part of the Sun ONE Directory Server Resource Kit 5.1 software. This application is based on JavaServer Pages (JSP) technology and can be customized to fit your environment. This section explains what the JDGW does, how it works, and how to customize it.

Note – The instructions provided in this chapter are based on the Sun ONE Directory Server Resource Kit version 5.1. Please check the instructions for the version of the resource kit that you are using.

What Does It Do?

The JDGW application creates HTML that can be displayed in any web browser. The HTML presents a form that can be used to initiate a directory search and forms to edit directory entries. While the sample application can be useful as is stands, you will probably want to customize it to include data fields particular to your organization.

How Does It Work?

The major components are shown in FIGURE 6-14:

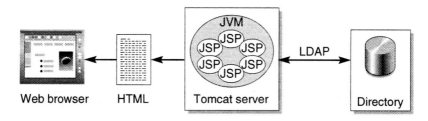

Web browser   HTML   Tomcat server   Directory

FIGURE 6-14 Major JDGW Components

The web server used is the Tomcat server which, provides a JSP framework. This includes tags that are XML-like structures containing logic to create HTML pages. The Sun ONE Directory Server Resource Kit contains tag libraries that are used to access LDAP directories.

Setting It Up

The following components are required:

- Sun ONE Directory Server Resource Kit
- Tomcat v4.0 or later
- Java™ 2 Platform v1.3.1 software
- Sun ONE Directory Server, configured with user entries

▼ To Install the Software

1. **Download the JDK from** `java.sun.com/2je/1.3/`

   Install the JDK software in a directory such as `/files/JDK`.

2. **Download the Tomcat server from**
   `http://jakarta.apache.org/site/binindex.html`

3. **Unzip and untar the** `jakarta-tomcat-4.1.12.tar.gz` **file.**

   Use a directory such as `/files/TOMCAT`.

4. **Set the** `CATALINA_HOME` **and** `JAVA_HOME` **shell variables.**

   ```
   # export CATALINA_HOME=/files/TOMCAT/jakarta-tomcat-4.1.12
   # export JAVA_HOME=/files/JDK
   ```

5. **Run the** `startup.sh` **command.**

   ```
   # $CATALINA_HOME/bin/startup.sh
   ```

6. **Edit the phone book properties sheet.**

   Add information that is specific to your environment.

   ```
   # cd /opt/iPlanet/jdgw/phonebook-app
   # ls
   WEB-INF build.xml   jsp ldif lib properties
   # cd /opt/iPlanet/jdgw/phonebook-app/WEB-INF/classes
   # more lookmeup.properties
   hostname=myserver.example.com
   port=389
   base=ou=people,dc=example,dc=com
   country=US
   language=en
   ```

7. **Edit the** `server.xml` **file.**

Add the lines shown in the example.

```
# cd /files/TOMCAT/jakarta-tomcat-4.1.12/conf
# vi server.xml
<Context path="/jdgw" docBase="/opt/iPlanet/jdgw/phonebook-app"
debug="0" reloadable="true">
<Logger className="org.apache.catalina.logger.FileLogger"
prefix="jdgw_log." suffix=".txt" timestamp="true"/>
```

▼ To Customize LookMeUp

FIGURE 6-15 shows how the LookMeUp application is structured.

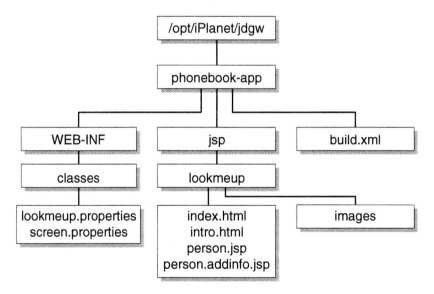

FIGURE 6-15 LookMeUp Application Structure

The easiest customization is to add additional attributes. In the example, `posixAccount` attributes are added under the Additional Information section header. Modifications are made to the following files:

- `screen.properties`
- `person.jsp`
- `person.addinfo.jsp`

In this example, the application is expanded to retrieve the homedirectory, uidnumber, and gidnumber attributes from the entries searched.

1. **Edit the** screen.properties **file.**

   This should be done while the application is not running because the changes take effect the next time the application is accessed. This file is referenced when the HTML of the search return screen is rendered. It defines the label written for the field corresponding to the attribute that is retrieved.

   screen.properties example:

```
# cd /opt/iPlanet/jdgw/phonebook-app/WEB-INF/classes
# vi screen.properties
.
.
.
person-head.title=Person Entry -
person-addinfo.title=Additional Information
person-addinfo.description=Description:
person-addinfo.seealso=See Also:
person-addinfo.homedirectory=Home Directory:
person-addinfo.uidnumber=UID Number:
person-addinfo.gidnumber=GID Number:
person-addinfo.url=URL:
.
.
.
```

2. **Edit the** person.jsp **file.**

   This file defines the attributes that are retrieved.

`person.jsp` example:

```
# cd /opt/iPlanet/jdgw/phonebook-app/jsp/lookmeup
# vi person.jsp
...
<ldap:search
        host="$app:hostname"
        srchScope="base"
        base="$request:dn"
        var="results"
        port="$app:port"
        filter="(objectclass=*)"
        attrs=
"cn|sn|givenname|telephonenumber|mail|postofficebox|uid|facsimil
etelephonenumber|pager|homephone|mobile|postaladdress|roomnumber
|physicaldeliveryofficename|businesscategory|title|ou|manager|de
partmentnumber|carlicense|description|seealso|labeleduri|homedir
ectory|uidnumber|gidnumber|employeenumber|modifytimestamp|modifi
ersname"
        response="srchresp"/>
...
```

3. **Edit the** `person-addinfo.jsp` **file.**

This file creates the HTML table where the retrieved attribute values are placed.

person-addinfo.jsp example:

```
# cd /opt/iPlanet/jdgw/phonebook-app/jsp/lookmeup
# vi person-addinfo.jsp
...
<TR>
<TD VALIGN="TOP"><B><util:prop prps="screen" key="person-
addinfo.seealso" lang="$app:language" cntry=
"$app:country"/></B></TD>
<TD VALIGN="TOP" NOWRAP>
<ldap:attr default=" " entry="$entry" name="seealso"> 
</TR>

<TR>
<TD VALIGN="TOP"><B><util:prop prps="screen" key="person-
addinfo.homedirectory" lang="$app:language"cntry=
"$app:country"/></B></TD>
<TD VALIGN="TOP" NOWRAP>
<ldap:attr default=" " entry="$entry" name="homedirectory"
> 
</TD></TR>

<TR>
<TD VALIGN="TOP"><B><util:prop prps="screen" key="person-
addinfo.uidnumber" lang="$app:language" cntry=
"$app:country"/></B></TD>
<TD VALIGN="TOP" NOWRAP>
<ldap:attr default=" " entry="$entry" name="uidnumber"
> 
</TR>

<TR>
<TD VALIGN="TOP"><B><util:prop prps="screen" key="person-
addinfo.gidnumber" lang="$app:language" cntry=
"$app:country"/></B></TD>
<TD VALIGN="TOP" NOWRAP>
<ldap:attr default=" " entry="$entry" name=
"gidnumber"/> 
</TR>
  .
  .
  .
```

4. Stop and restart the Tomcat server.

This is required so that the JSPs will be read.

```
# cd /files/TOMCAT/jakarta-tomcat-4.1.12/bin
# ./shutdown.sh
Using CATALINA_BASE:   /files/TOMCAT/jakarta-tomcat-4.1.12
Using CATALINA_HOME:   /files/TOMCAT/jakarta-tomcat-4.1.12
Using CATALINA_TMPDIR: /files/TOMCAT/jakarta-tomcat-4.1.12/temp
Using JAVA_HOME:       /files/JDK/j2sdk1_3_1_06
# ./startup.sh
Using CATALINA_BASE:   /files/TOMCAT/jakarta-tomcat-4.1.12
Using CATALINA_HOME:   /files/TOMCAT/jakarta-tomcat-4.1.12
Using CATALINA_TMPDIR: /files/TOMCAT/jakarta-tomcat-4.1.12/temp
Using JAVA_HOME:       /files/JDK/j2sdk1_3_1_06
#
```

Note – You need to set the CATALINA_BASE and JAVA_HOME shell variables before running the shutdown.sh and startup.sh scripts.

5. Check to see if you can retrieve data.

Bring up the user information. You should see additional fields that were added. FIGURE 6-16 shows an example.

Additional Information	
Description:	
See Also:	
Home Directory:	/home/tb250
UID Number:	1250
GID Number:	10
URL:	

FIGURE 6-16 New User Fields

LDAP APIs

In addition to the scripting languages and toolkits mentioned earlier in this chapter, the C and Java programming languages can be used to develop directory enabled applications. The Application Programming Interfaces (APIs) that support these languages include:

- C LDAP API
- J.N.D.I. API
- Java™ API

The C LDAP Software Development Kit (SDK) provides examples, documentation, header files, and pre-compiled libraries. The C LDAP SDK is available for different platforms including Windows, HP-UX, and AIX. You will have to download a version that matches your target platform. Updates to the SDK are continually made available to fix bugs and to provide access to LDAPv3 extensions. If binary portability between platforms is not your top priority, the C LDAP SDK is a good choice for creating directory enabled applications.

The Java Naming and Directory Interface (J.N.D.I.) API is a Java extension that provides Java applications with a unified interface to multiple naming and directory services. J.N.D.I. API Service Providers are available for NIS, LDAP, DNS, and CORBA. By writing to the J.N.D.I. API, the programmer does not need to know the underlying interfaces for those services.

The Java API differs from the J.N.D.I. API in that the interface performs LDAP operations directly. This provides greater control and allows the programmer to take advantage of LDAP features not accessible through the J.N.D.I. API. The following section provides details on how to create a program using the Java™ 2 SDK.

Creating a Program With the LDAP SDK for Java

Another way to develop your own administrative tools is to write them in Java programming language. In this section, a sample program is examined as a guide to creating Java programs that access LDAP directories. It is not meant to be a programming guide. There are many good books available on that topic.

To write a Java-based tool, you need:

- A recent version of the Java 2 SDK (can be downloaded from `http://wws.sun.com/software/download/developer`)
- The LDAP Java SDK

To perform an LDAP operation on a server, you need to perform these tasks:

1. Create a new `LDAPConnection` object.

2. Use the `connect` method to connect to the LDAP server.

3. Perform the LDAP operation.

4. Use the `disconnect` method to disconnect from the server when done.

To illustrate how a Java program can be written, the `LDAPsubtdel` program, available in the Sun ONE Directory Server Resource Kit 5.2 software, is used.

The `LDAPsubtdel` Program

The `LDAPsubtdel` program is written in Java and uses classes contained in LDAPJDK 4.1. The tool deletes a specified directory subtree including referrals.

The source files for `LDAPsubtdel` are available from the Directory Server Resource Kit version 5.2 software. This program is also available for download. See "Obtaining the Downloadable Files for This Book" on page xxvii.

There are two source files:

- `LDAPBase.java`
- `LDAPSubtdel.java`

The `LDAPBase.java` file gathers parameters entered on the command line and performs some error checking. The LDAP-related operations are performed in `LDAPSubtdel.java`. The header for the file looks like this:

```
import java.util.*;
import netscape.ldap.*;
import netscape.ldap.util.*;
```

These directives cause the following packages to be imported:

- `netscape.ldap`
- `netscape.ldap.beans`
- `netscape.ldap.ber.stream`
- `netscape.ldap.controls`
- `netscape.ldap.factory`
- `netscape.ldap.util`

The code that creates an LDAP connection structure and bind to the directory looks like this:

```
/* perform an LDAP client connection operation */
        try {
                client = new LDAPConnection();
                client.connect( ldaphost, ldapport );
        } catch(Exception e) {
            System.err.println("Error: client connection \
failed!");
            System.exit(0);
        }

        /* perform an LDAP bind operation */
        try {
            client.authenticate( version, binddn, ldappasswd );
        } catch (Exception e) {
            System.err.println( e.toString() );
            System.exit(0);
        }
```

In the following code sample, the connect and authenticate methods associated with the LDAPConnection object are used to bind to the directory server.

```
LDAPSearchResults res =
  client.search( dn,
      client.SCOPE_ONE,
      "(|(objectclass=*)(objectclass=ldapSubEntry))",
      new String[] {LDAPv3.NO_ATTRS},
      false,
      cons );
```

In this code sample, a directory search is performed by the `search` method. The object class `ldapSubEntry`, is included in the search filter so all entries including those with CoS and roles definitions will be returned. The entries found are stored in the `LDAPSearchResults` object.

```
// Recurse on entries under this entry
   while ( res.hasMoreElements() ) {
       try {
// Next directory entry
           LDAPEntry entry = res.next();
           theDN = entry.getDN();
           // Recurse down
           if (! delete( theDN, client, doSubtreeDelete ))
             allChildrenDeleted = false;
           } catch ( LDAPReferralException e ) {
   // Do not follow referrals, just list them
   System.out.println( "Search reference: " );
   LDAPUrl refUrls[] = e.getURLs();
   for ( int i = 0; i < refUrls.length; i++ ) {
   System.out.println(
   "   " + refUrls[i].getUrl() );
   }
   allChildrenDeleted = false;
   continue;
   } catch ( LDAPException e ) {
   System.out.println( e.toString() );
   continue;
   }
}
```

The `LDAPentry` object is used to hold the entries as they are examined.

The actual deletion looks like the following:

```
// At this point, the DN represents a leaf node,
           // so stop recursing and delete the node
           try {
               if ( doSubtreeDelete ) {
                   if ( allChildrenDeleted ) {
                       if ( !dn.equals(basedn) || removebasedn ) {
                           if ( verbose && doSubtreeDelete )
                               System.err.println("Deleting entry
"+dn+"\n");

                           client.delete(dn, delcons);
                       }
```

The delete method is called to remove the entry specified by the DN. LDAP constraints are specified in delcons as shown below.

```
LDAPSearchConstraints cons = client.getSearchConstraints();
LDAPConstraints delcons = client.getConstraints();
```

## CHAPTER 7

Performing Administrative Tasks

Now that you are aware of the tools and techniques available for managing your LDAP directory data, as covered in Chapter 6 "Management Tools and Toolkits," you are ready to start administering your directory data.

Most of the routine administration tasks are covered in the Sun ONE Directory Server software documentation. This chapter does not repeat the procedures for performing those tasks, but instead presents tricks and tips that are not conventionally covered in standard documentation.

This chapter is organized into the following sections:

- "Identifying Directory Management Tasks" on page 400
- "Directory Data Backup and Recovery" on page 406
- "Managing Client Profiles and Proxy Agent Accounts" on page 412
- "Managing Directory Data Replication" on page 417
- "Monitoring Directory Services" on page 424
- "Managing Users and Groups" on page 432
- "Extending the Directory Schema" on page 440

The focus of the chapter is on administering the Sun ONE Directory Server 5.2 software and the Secured LDAP Client. However, some examples are provided for previous versions and mixed environments.

Identifying Directory Management Tasks

The skills and techniques required to manage an LDAP-based naming server are a combination of those of an experienced Solaris OE system administrator and database administrator. Some of the tasks are routine, such as adding and deleting users, while others are less frequently performed, such as setting up replication. The following is a list of common tasks that you are likely to perform:

- Directory Data Backup and Recovery
- Provisioning Users and Groups
- Managing Client Profiles
- Restricting User Access
- Managing Replica Servers
- Monitoring the Directory Service
- Extending the Directory Schema
- Troubleshooting Problems

Directory Data Backup and Recovery

Your directory server contains both configuration and user data. Configuration data is consulted by the directory server when the directory server initializes, by the administration server, and possibly by other Sun ONE applications that might be running. User data is placed in one or more directory databases and is referenced by your LDAP-aware applications. Both types of data should be backed up regularly.

Although you might be deploying directory data replication, there is a potential that corrupted data can be propagated from one server to another. Accidental deletion of data can occur, in which case the data would be deleted on replicas as well. Therefore, it is prudent to back up your directory data regularly.

The frequency of backups depends on how frequently your data changes. Configuration data tends to be relatively static and does not require as frequent backups as user data. If the directory is used solely for naming service data, most updates would likely occur when users are added or removed, and when passwords are changed. The frequency of this activity depends on how dynamic or stable your user population is.

Directory data backups can occur while the directory server is online or offline. Offline backups are faster, but directory data is not accessible while the backup is performed. Online backups do not require the directory server be taken offline, but are slower and can only take a snapshot of what the directory data looks like at a single point of time. If updates are performed while an online backup is being performed, they may or may not be backed up.

Data recovery can either be performed offline or online. As for backups, the offline method is faster. The online recovery is slower, but does not have a significant impact on overall directory server performance.

The Sun ONE Directory Server 5.2 software ships with tools for doing both offline and online data backup and recovery. These procedures are described in "Directory Data Backup and Recovery" on page 406.

Provisioning Users and Groups

Managing users and groups is perhaps the most common task for system administrators. New user accounts need to be created and deleted when a user joins or leaves the organization. Users are typically placed in groups so they can share resource access rights with other similar users. Likewise, they need to be added or removed from groups when they join or leave.

Provisioning users and groups in an NIS or NIS+ environment is relatively straightforward. This is because user account data is consistent for all users. Only the POSIX-defined fields need to be addressed. These are:

- Login name
- Password
- User Identifier (UID)
- Group Identifier (GID)
- GECOS
- Home directory
- User shell

Because of the extensibility of LDAP, it is likely that much more information about users will be maintained in the directory. For example, an LDAP entry for a user at Sun might look like this:

Sample User Entry

```
cn=A Rose (5550),ou=people,dc=example,dc=com
inetuserstatus=active
manager=cn=Billy Smith (11350),ou=people,dc=example,dc=com
seaprincipalid=FYYMqeyCWAN777mm5aIW
seaprincipaltype=H
mailhost=bonzo.example.com
sn=Rose
employeetype=Employee
nickname=Ave
employeenumber=5555
datasource=NetAdmin
telephonenumber=x51212/+1 978 555 1212
objectclass=top
objectclass=person
objectclass=organizationalPerson
objectclass=inetOrgPerson
objectclass=emailPerson
objectclass=NameViewPerson
objectclass=mailRecipient
givenname=Avery
departmentnumber=0123456
host=uday.example.com
maildeliveryoption=mailbox
roomnumber=10
globallocation=usa100
l=BURLINGTON, UNITED STATES
countrycode=US
cn=A Rose
cn=Avery Rose
cn=Avery S. Rose
cn=A Rose (5555)
reportsto=12345
```

There is so much more user information stored than what POSIX defines, so standard Solaris OE provisioning tools are not adequate because the tools are not aware of site-specific attributes that might have been added. In most cases you will want to create your own user provisioning scripts or tools. Tips for doing so are presented in "Managing Users and Groups" on page 432. Details on how to add custom or site-specific attributes can be found in "Extending the Directory Schema" on page 440.

Another aspect of provisioning users is creating a home directory for them. In most cases this will be an NFS-mounted directory that is mounted using the automounter. The automounter depends on a naming service for data, so home directory mount points need to be specified in LDAP.

The notion of group membership takes on a new meaning with LDAP as a naming service because two types of groups exist:

- POSIX groups
- LDAP groups

The POSIX groups are used to determine file access rights, and work the same way as if they were maintained in NIS or NIS+. LDAP groups only pertain to directory resources. That is, access to data maintained by the directory. While the Solaris OE does not care about LDAP groups, you might want to take advantage of LDAP groups for administrative purposes. For example, you could assign LDAP group membership to system administrators responsible for managing naming service data. There is no relationship between POSIX and LDAP groups, so provisioning tools must treat these as separate entities.

Password Management

Another aspect of user management is managing the password policy of users. That is, establishing policies such as how often users are required to change their passwords. Password management can be set on the directory server or by setting the attribute values defined in the `shadowAccount` object class. In the latter case, password management works the same as with NIS/NIS+.

Managing Client Profiles

Client profiles are the mechanism you use to modify how a particular client host interacts with the LDAP naming service. You can group several hosts together by furnishing them with the same profile. There are several parameters that can be adjusted to affect the behavior of a naming service client. These include:

- Listing of preferred and alternate servers
- Search path for naming service data
- Timeout limits
- Object class and attribute mapping
- Service Search Descriptors (SSDs)
- Authentication method

A single client profile is created when you run `idsconfig` to configure your directory server. In many cases you will want to create additional profiles to take advantage of the flexibility they provide. "Managing Client Profiles and Proxy Agent Accounts" on page 412 discusses how to create new profiles and propagate them to clients.

Managing Proxy Agent Credentials

Related to client profiles are the credentials used to authenticate a client to a directory server. This information is kept in the local /var/ldap/ldap_client_cred file. If the proxyagent password is changed, the file needs to be updated. See "Managing Client Profiles and Proxy Agent Accounts" on page 412 for details.

Restricting User Access

For security reasons, it is often desirable to limit user access to particular systems. For example, you might only want certain users or groups of users to be able to log in to mission-critical servers. There are several ways to do this with the LDAP naming service. These include:

- Implementing netgroups
- Implementing client profiles containing Service Search Descriptors (SSDs)
- Object class and attribute mapping
- Setting directory server access control instructions (ACIs)

Another aspect of restricting access to systems is controlling what functions can be performed by a particular user. This is done through Role-Based Access Control (RBAC). While this is not unique to LDAP, the data that RBAC relies on must be mapped to specific LDAP object classes and attributes.

"Deploying RBAC with LDAP" on page 439 describes procedures for restricting actions and deploying RBAC.

Managing Replica Servers

After you set up and configure your initial directory server, you will want to create replicas. Besides the initial setup of replicas, there are several other management issues. These include:

- Enabling SSL
- Changing Replication Agreements
- Monitoring Replication Status
- Decommissioning Replicas
- Rebuilding Replicas

There are several tools and techniques for managing replicas, covered in "Managing Directory Data Replication" on page 417.

Directory Server Monitoring

To assure your directory service is running smoothly, it is wise to monitor it to detect problems before your users encounter them. There are several tools and technologies available that do this to varying degrees. These include:

- Service Availability Manager (SAM) add-on to Sun™ Management Center 3.0 (SunMC)
- BMC Patrol
- Java™ Management Extensions (JMX) agent
- Simple Network Management Protocol (SNMP)
- Directory Console Performance Counters
- Access Log Viewer

Monitoring tools can be used to send alarms if malfunctions are detected, or to monitor resource usage. The SAM add-on to SunMC periodically performs a pre-defined search on the directory and measures the response time. If the response time exceeds a pre-established value, an alarm is sent to SunMC where it is processed.

SNMP agents work in a similar fashion except they communicate using the SNMP protocol. More sophisticated monitoring can be accomplished with third-party tools such as BMC Patrol.

Another aspect of monitoring is making sure the directory is tuned properly and that clients are not having problems connecting. Lots of useful information can be obtained from the Directory Console performance counters. Information about access issues, such as permission problems, can be obtained by examining the directory server access log.

Procedures and techniques for using these tools is found in "Using `logconv.pl`" on page 427.

Extending the Directory Schema

A major enhancement of an LDAP-based naming service over NIS and NIS+ is the ease of extending the data stored in it. One of your goals of migrating to LDAP is probably to consolidate information about users, so you will most likely want to add user data that goes beyond the basic information contained in the `passwd` NIS maps and NIS+ tables. To do this, you can use standard LDAP object classes or create your own.

The standard LDAP schema defines object classes such as `inetOrgPerson` that defines many attributes that describe information about an employee. However, with the rapid communication technology changes that are occurring, more and more information needs to be stored. For example, an employee might now have a mobile phone, home ISP email address and pager number in addition to their home phone number and office phone and email address.

Details on what schema definitions are available and how update the schema is fairly well documented in the Sun ONE Directory Server software documentation. A quick overview and tips on how to update the schema is provided in "Extending the Directory Schema" on page 440.

Troubleshooting Directory Server Problems

Tied in with monitoring your directory server, is how to isolate problems once they are detected. Programs like `snoop` are useful, but cannot be used if data encryption is used. Log files are helpful and can be enhanced by turning on process tracing. Troubleshooting tips are presented in "Troubleshooting Tips" on page 260, and error codes likely to be encountered are described in Appendix B, "LDAP v3 Result Codes". Appendix C, "Using `snoop` with LDAP" provides guidance on how to effectively use snoop to diagnose problems.

Directory Data Backup and Recovery

There are two types of data that need to be backed up. These are:

- Directory configuration data
- Directory user data

Directory configuration data can be shared among several directory servers, so only needs to be backed up on the directory server instance that contains the configuration data. In most cases, the configuration data is fairly static and does not need to be backed up repeatedly.

Directory data is contained in databases other than `o=NetscapeRoot`. By default, a `UserRoot` database is created during the directory server installation. Additional databases might also exist. Backups can either be done online or offline.

Note – The examples shown in this section are for use with the SVR4 packages version of Sun ONE Directory Server 5.2 software. To run them on the compressed tar file version, run the commands shown directly from the slapd-*instance* instead of using the `directoryserver` wrapper script.

Configuration Data Backup and Restore

The `directoryserver` wrapper can be executed with the `saveconfig` sub-command, as shown below.

```
# /usr/sbin/directoryserver -s hosta saveconfig
/var/mps/serverroot/slapd-hosta/saveconfig
saving configuration ...
ldiffile: /var/mps/serverroot/slapd-
hosta/confbak/2002_11_11_091333.ldif
[11/Nov/2002:09:13:35 -0500] - export NetscapeRoot: Processed 94
entries (100%).
#
```

The `saveconfig` subcommand actually invokes the `saveconfig` shell script located in the `/var/mps/serverroot/slapd-`*instance* directory. The command can be run with the directory server running or stopped. You must be logged in as `root` to run the command.

To restore the configuration, the directory server must be stopped. The following example shows how a saved configuration is restored.

```
# directoryserver stop
/var/mps/serverroot/slapd-hosta/stop-slapd
# directoryserver -s hosta restoreconfig
/var/mps/serverroot/slapd-hosta/restoreconfig
Restoring /var/mps/serverroot/slapd-
hosta/confbak/2002_11_11_091333.ldif
[11/Nov/2002:09:26:10 -0500] - import NetscapeRoot: Index
buffering enabled with bucket size 15
[11/Nov/2002:09:26:10 -0500] - import NetscapeRoot: Beginning
import job...
[11/Nov/2002:09:26:11 -0500] - import NetscapeRoot: Processing
file "/var/mps/serverroot/slapd-
hosta/confbak/2002_11_11_091333.ldif"
[11/Nov/2002:09:26:11 -0500] - import NetscapeRoot: Finished
scanning file "/var/mps/serverroot/slapd-
hosta/confbak/2002_11_11_091333.ldif" (94 entries)
[11/Nov/2002:09:26:11 -0500] - import NetscapeRoot: Workers
finished; cleaning up...
[11/Nov/2002:09:26:14 -0500] - import NetscapeRoot: Workers
cleaned up.
[11/Nov/2002:09:26:14 -0500] - import NetscapeRoot: Cleaning up
producer thread...
[11/Nov/2002:09:26:14 -0500] - import NetscapeRoot: Indexing
complete.  Post-processing...
[11/Nov/2002:09:26:14 -0500] - import NetscapeRoot: Flushing
caches...
[11/Nov/2002:09:26:14 -0500] - import NetscapeRoot: Closing
files...
[11/Nov/2002:09:26:14 -0500] - import NetscapeRoot: Import
complete.  Processed 94 entries in 4 seconds. (23.50 entries/sec)
# directoryserver start
/var/mps/serverroot/slapd-hosta/start-slapd
#
```

Note – The saveconfig command only backs up data used by the Administration Server and Sun ONE Console. Other data such as dse.ldif and changes to schema files should also be backed up regularly.

Directory Data Backup and Restore

The db2bak subcommand is used to back up all your databases while the directory server is offline or online. You must be logged in as root to run this command. The default location for backups is /var/mps/serverroot/slapd-*instance*/bak. Backups can grow to a large size, so it is wise to place them on a separate partition.

The following example shows backing up a database using db2bak.

```
# directoryserver stop
/var/mps/serverroot/slapd-hosta/stop-slapd
# directoryserver -s hosta db2bak
/var/mps/serverroot/slapd-hosta/db2bak
[11/Nov/2002:09:36:45 -0500] - Backing up file 1
(/var/mps/serverroot/slapd-
hosta/bak/2002_11_11_09_36_43/userRoot/id2entry.db3)
[11/Nov/2002:09:36:45 -0500] - Backing up file 2
(/var/mps/serverroot/slapd-
hosta/bak/2002_11_11_09_36_43/userRoot/entrydn.db3)
...
[11/Nov/2002:09:36:47 -0500] - Backing up file 24
(/var/mps/serverroot/slapd-
hosta/bak/2002_11_11_09_36_43/DBVERSION)
# directoryserver start
```

To restore the database that was backed up in the previous example, run the bak2db command.

```
# directoryserver stop
# directoryserver -s hosta bak2db /var/mps/serverroot/slapd-
hosta/bak/2002_11_11_09_36_43
/var/mps/serverroot/slapd-hosta/bak2db /var/mps/serverroot/slapd-
hosta/bak/2002_11_11_09_36_43
[11/Nov/2002:09:49:26 -0500] - Restoring file 1
(/var/mps/serverroot/slapd-hosta/db/userRoot/id2entry.db3)
[11/Nov/2002:09:49:26 -0500] - Restoring file 2
(/var/mps/serverroot/slapd-hosta/db/userRoot/entrydn.db3)
. . .
[11/Nov/2002:09:49:27 -0500] - Restoring file 24
(/var/mps/serverroot/slapd-hosta/db/DBVERSION)

[11/Nov/2002:09:49:28 -0500] - libdb: warning:
/var/mps/severroot/slapd-hosta/db/NetscapeRoot/uniquemember.db3:
No such file or directory
[11/Nov/2002:09:49:28 -0500] - libdb: warning:
/var/mps/serverroot/slapd-hosta/db/NetscapeRoot/uid.db3: No such
file or directory
. . .
# directoryserver start
/var/mps/serverroot/slapd-hosta/start-slapd
#
```

Note – The warning messages can be ignored because the o=netscaperoot does
not contain the default index files.

As an alternative to backing up the directory while it is online or offline, you can use
the db2bak-task command which invokes the db2bak.pl Perl script. The
command extracts the database data, then creates an LDIF file. The backup runs in
the background. To enable you to synchronize your backup with commands that
need to run after the backup is finished, a temporary directory entry can be created
to flag the fact that the backup is in progress. When the backup finishes, the entry is
deleted. The following example shows commands that will create this temporary
directory.

```
# directoryserver -s hosta db2bak-task -D "cn=directory manager"
-w netscape
/var/mps/serverroot/slapd-hosta/db2bak.pl -D cn=directory manager
-w netscape
adding new entry cn=backup_2002_11_11_10_1_56, cn=backup, cn=
tasks, cn=config
# ldapsearch -D "cn=directory manager" -w netscape -b cn=
backup,cn=tasks,cn=config objectclass=\*
cn=backup, cn=tasks, cn=config
objectClass=top
objectClass=extensibleObject
cn=backup
# ls -l bak
total 4
drwx------    4 nobody    nobody         512 Nov 11 09:36
2002_11_11_09_36_43
drwx------    4 nobody    nobody         512 Nov 11 10:01
2002_11_11_10_1_56
#
```

Note – The command requires that you provide credentials with appropriate access rights. Only Simple authentication is supported, which requires you to supply a password. Be aware that if you supply the password on the command line, it will be visible in the ps output. To prevent this, the password can be placed in a file and the -j option can be used to read it.

To restore the backup from the previous example, run the bak2db-task command as shown in the following example.

```
# directoryserver -s hosta bak2db-task -D "cn=directory manager"
-w netscape -a /var/mps/severroot/slapd-
hosta/bak/2002_11_11_10_1_56
/var/mps/severroot/slapd-hosta/bak2db.pl -D cn=directory manager
-w netscape -a /var/mps/serverroot/slapd-
hosta/bak/2002_11_11_10_1_56
adding new entry cn=restore_2002_11_11_10_25_37, cn=restore, cn=
tasks, cn=config
#
```

Managing Client Profiles and Proxy Agent Accounts

A client profile and proxy agent account are set up automatically when the idsconfig command is run to initialize the directory. While the environment created is a good starting point, you will most likely want to create additional client profiles and proxy agent accounts after the initial configuration.

Reasons for doing this include:

- To implement access and security policies on a per client or group of clients basis.
- To improve security by establishing separate passwords for different client systems to use when they bind to the LDAP server to obtain naming service data.

Creating too many profiles can result in increased management cost and complexity. You should take this into consideration when deciding how you want to implement client profiles.

Two client profile features are especially useful for implementing access policies. These are:

1. Service Search Descriptors (SSDs)

2. Attribute mapping

SSDs provide a great deal of flexibility and have many uses. Basically, they let you control which naming service data that a particular system is permitted to access. For example, you may set up an SSD that only allows a certain group of users to log in to a system or only auto-mounts a limited number of directories.

Attribute mapping can also be used to deny or allow access to a particular system based on the value of a particular attribute in the user's entry. It can also be used to change user profile data based on the system they log in to. For example, a different login shell or home directory can be set based on which client system a user logs in to.

The credentials that a system uses to bind to the directory server with are maintained in a file located in /var/ldap on the system the user logs in to. These credentials consist of a proxy DN and password contained in the proxyDN entry. Any directory object that can bind to the directory server can be used for a proxy DN, but for administration control, it is best to have dedicated proxy accounts for that purpose. While a single proxy DN and password can be used for all client systems, it might make sense to use different accounts for different sets of systems. The access rights of the proxy account can also be used to control access to naming service data.

The following sections explain the mechanics for managing client profiles and proxy agent accounts. Examples are provided to show how they can be deployed.

Creating Additional Profiles

When the idsconfig command is run, you are prompted for a profile name. The following examples show the prompts used to gather information to create a profile.

```
Enter the profile name (h=help): [default] newprofile
Default server list (h=help): [129.100.100.1] 129.100.100.1
Preferred server list (h=help):
Choose desired search scope (one, sub, h=help):  [one] one
The following are the supported credential levels:
   1   anonymous
   2   proxy
   3   proxy anonymous
Choose Credential level [h=help]: [1] 2
The following are the supported Authentication Methods:
   1   none
   2   simple
   3   sasl/DIGEST-MD5
   4   tls:simple
   5   tls:sasl/DIGEST-MD5
Choose Authentication Method (h=help): [1] 2

Current authenticationMethod: simple

Do you want to add another Authentication Method? n
Do you want the clients to follow referrals (y/n/h)? [n] n
Do you want to modify the server timelimit value (y/n/h)? [n] n
Do you want to modify the server sizelimit value (y/n/h)? [n] n
Do you want to store passwords in "crypt" format (y/n/h)? [n] n
Do you want to setup a Service Authentication Methods (y/n/h)? n
Client search time limit in seconds (h=help): [30] 30
Profile Time To Live in seconds (h=help): [43200] 43200
Bind time limit in seconds (h=help): [10] 10
```

In this section of the example, the SSD parameter is set.

```
Do you wish to setup Service Search Descriptors (y/n/h)? [n] y
   A  Add a Service Search Descriptor
   D  Delete a SSD
   M  Modify a SSD
   P  Display all SSD's
   H  Help
   X  Clear all SSD's
   Q  Exit menu
Enter menu choice: [Quit] a
Enter the service id: passwd
Enter the base: ou=contractors,dc=example,dc=com
Enter the scope: sub
```

The last section of the example shows where information about a proxyagent
account is gathered.

```
Enter config value to change: (1-19 0=commit changes) [0] 0
Enter DN for proxy agent: [cn=proxyagent,ou=profile,dc=example,dc=
com] cn=proxyagent1,ou=profile,dc=example,dc=com
Enter passwd for proxyagent: passwd
Re-enter passwd: passwd
```

While you can rerun the idsconfig command to create additional client profiles or
additional proxy agent accounts, this approach is not recommended because other
parameters besides those in the client profile are set. If you are not careful, you can
unintentionally overwrite other parameters. It should be noted that idsconfig will
generate Version 2 client profiles. The Solaris 8 OE ldap_gen_profile command
must be run to generate Version 1 profiles.

Another method is to run the ldapclient genprofile command. This command
assumes a number of defaults when it is run. You can overwrite any of the defaults
as shown in the following example.

```
# ldapclient genprofile -a profileName=newprofile \
-a credentialLevel=proxy \
-a authenticationMethod=sasl/DIGEST-MD5 \
-a bindTimeLimit=20 \
-a defaultSearchBase=dc=example,dc=com \
-a "serviceSearchDescriptor=passwd:ou=temps,dc=sun,dc=com?one" \
-a serviceAuthenticationMethod=pam_ldap:tls:simple \
-a defaultSearchScope=sub \
-a attributeMap=passwd:uid=employeeNumber \
-a objectclassMap=passwd:posixAccount=unixAccount \
-a followReferrals=false \
-a profileTTL=6000 \
-a preferredServerList=129.100.100.30 -a searchTimeLimit=30 \
-a "defaultServerList=29.100.200.1 129.100.100.1 204.34.5.6"
```

The `ldapclient genprofile` command does not update the directory. Instead it simply generates LDIF that can be imported into the directory as shown in the following example.

```
dn: cn=newprofile,ou=profile,dc=example,dc=com
ObjectClass: top
ObjectClass: DUAConfigProfile
defaultServerList: 29.100.200.1 129.100.100.1 204.34.5.6
defaultSearchBase: dc=example,dc=com
authenticationMethod: sasl/DIGEST-MD5
followReferrals: FALSE
defaultSearchScope: sub
searchTimeLimit: 30
preferredServerList: 129.100.100.30
profileTTL: 6000
cn: eng
credentialLevel: proxy
serviceSearchDescriptor: passwd:ou=people,dc=example,dc=com?one
bindTimeLimit: 20
attributeMap: passwd:uid=employeeNumber
objectClassMap: passwd:posixAccount=unixAccount
serviceAuthenticationMethod: pam_ldap:tls:simple
```

This method allows more flexibility in the creation of client profiles than `idsconfig`. For example, complex filters can be specified in the SSD and attribute and object class mapping can be used.

Note – No error checking is performed by ldapclient genprofile. If you mistype a value for a parameter, the value will be used whether it is correct or not.

The third method of generating a new profile is to generate LDIF from an existing profile in the directory and edit it with new values. For example:

```
# ldapsearch -L -b dc=example,dc=com \
objectclass=DUAConfigProfile > profile.ldif
# vi profile.ldif
dn: cn=default,ou=profile,dc=example,dc=com
objectClass: top
objectClass: DUAConfigProfile
defaultServerList: 129.100.100.1
defaultSearchBase: dc=example,dc=com
authenticationMethod: simple
followReferrals: FALSE
defaultSearchScope: one
searchTimeLimit: 30
profileTTL: 43200
cn: default
credentialLevel: proxy
bindTimeLimit: 10
# ldapmodify -a -D "cn=Directory Manager" -f profile.ldif
password:
#
```

This might be the best method because you can easily create new profiles by making a copy, then performing a few edits.

Adjusting the Client Cache

The parameter profileTTL sets the cache refresh time. This parameter is kept in the /var/ldap/ldap_client_file file. To get the client to refresh its cache, perform the following command:

```
# pkill -HUP ldap_cachemgr
```

Managing Directory Data Replication

Sun ONE Directory Server 5.2 software provides replication management tools that allow you to monitor replication between servers. Monitoring replication activity assists in troubleshooting the causes of replication problems. All of the Directory Server replication monitoring tools can be used when the TLS/SSL transport is used for replication traffic.

The three replication management tools are:

- `insync`
- `entrycmp`
- `repldisc`

The `insync` tool indicates the state of synchronization between a master replica and one or more consumer replicas. Being aware of the degree of synchronization is vital when it comes to managing potential conflicts.

The `entrycmp` tool allows you to compare the same entry on two or more servers. An entry is retrieved from the master replica, and the entry's `unique ID` is used to retrieve the same entry from a given consumer. All of the entries attributes and values are compared, and if everything is identical, the entries are considered to be the same.

The `repldisc` tool allows you to discover a replication topology. Topology discovery starts with one server and builds a graph of all known servers within the topology. The `repldisc` tool then prints an adjacency matrix describing the topology. This replication topology discovery tool is useful for large, complex deployments where it might be difficult to recall the global topology.

Creating Replication Agreements from Scripts

Replication can be set up and managed through the Sun ONE Directory Console. It can also be set up and managed from the command line or scripts. As with most directory configuration procedures, LDIF is used. In this section, example LDIF is presented to illustrate how tasks are performed. Once created, the LDIF is imported using the `ldapmodify` command.

Multi-Master Replication Example

The first step is to create a new database instance on each server if the one you want to replicate does not already exist. This is necessary because the unit of replication is a database instance.

The following example shows the LDIF used for creating a new database instance.

```
dn: cn=example,cn=ldbm database,cn=plugins,cn=config
changetype: add
objectclass: top
objectclass: extensibleObject
objectclass: nsBackendInstance
cn: example
nsslapd-cachesize: -1
nsslapd-cachememsize: 2097152
nsslapd-suffix: dc=example,dc=com

dn: cn="dc=example,dc=com", cn=mapping tree, cn=config
changetype: add
objectclass: top
objectclass: extensibleobject
objectclass: nsmappingtree
cn: dc=example,dc=com
nsslapd-state: backend
nsslapd-backend: example
nsslapd-parent-suffix: dc=example,dc=com
```

The next step is to configure the new database instance for replication. This requires:

1. Creating a replication account.

2. Defining the type of replication for which the server will partake.

3. Specifying a location for the change log.

The following example shows setting up a database instance for multi-master replication.

```
dn: cn=Replication Manager, cn=replication, cn=config
changetype: modify
add: userpassword
userpassword: secret12

dn: cn=replica, cn="dc=example,dc=com", cn=mapping tree, cn=config
changetype: add
objectclass: top
objectclass: nsds5replica
objectclass: extensibleObject
cn: replica
nsds5replicaroot: dc=example,dc=com
nsds5replicaid: 2
nsds5replicatype: 3
nsds5flags: 1
nsds5replicabinddn: cn=Replication Manager, cn=replication, cn=
    config
nsds5ReplicaPurgeDelay: 86400
nsds5ReplicaTombstonePurgeInterval: 1800

dn: cn=changelog5,cn=config
changetype: add
objectclass: top
objectclass: extensibleobject
nsslapd-changelogdir: /var/mps/serverroot/slapd-hosta/cl5db
```

Note – The replica ID number, `nsds5replicaid`, needs to be unique on each system. Also, this step needs to be completed before you can initialize replicas.

The next step is to set up a replication agreement that will determine how changes are propagated. The following example sets up a replication agreement on a system called `ldaphost1` with a replication partner called `ldaphost2`.

Replication Agreement for `ldaphost1`:

```
dn: cn=agmt1, cn=replica, cn="dc=example,dc=com", cn=mapping tree,
  cn=config
changetype: add
objectclass: top
objectclass: nsDS5ReplicationAgreement
cn: agmt1
nsDS5ReplicaHost: ldaphost2
nsDS5ReplicaPort: 389
nsDS5ReplicaBindDN: cn=Replication Manager, cn=replication, cn=
  config
nsDS5ReplicaCredentials: secret12
nsDS5ReplicaBindMethod: SIMPLE
nsDS5ReplicaRoot: dc=example,dc=com
description: A sample replication agreement.
```

Finally, you can initiate replication with the following example on `ldaphost1`.

Consumer Initiation:

```
dn: cn=agmt1, cn=replica, cn="dc=example,dc=com", cn=mapping tree,
  cn=config
changetype: modify
replace: nsds5BeginReplicaRefresh
nsds5BeginReplicaRefresh: start
```

Test the configuration by creating an entry on `ldaphost1` and see if it propagates to `ldaphost2`.

To complete the process, set up a replication on `ldaphost2`.

Note – Online replication initialization as shown in these examples is best suited for directories with small amounts of data. For large directories offline initialization is recommended.

Replication Agreement for `ldaphost2`

```
dn: cn=agmt1, cn=replica, cn="dc=example,dc=com", cn=mapping tree,
cn=config
changetype: add
objectclass: top
objectclass: nsDS5ReplicationAgreement
cn: agmt1
nsDS5ReplicaHost: ldaphost1
nsDS5ReplicaPort: 389
nsDS5ReplicaBindDN: cn=Replication Manager, cn=config
nsDS5ReplicaCredentials: secret12
nsDS5ReplicaBindMethod: SIMPLE
nsDS5ReplicaRoot: dc=example,dc=com
description: A sample replication agreement.
```

Replication Management

There are a number of useful functions that can be performed through the command line or scripts. These are:

- Displaying replicas
- Displaying replication agreements
- Forcing replication from a consumer
- Stopping replication
- Restarting replication

Displaying Replicas

The following example shows how to display replication agreements that have already been established on a directory server.

```
# ldapsearch -L -D "cn=directory manager" -w netscape -b "cn=
mapping tree, cn=config" objectclass=nsds5replica
dn: cn=replica, cn="dc=example,dc=com", cn=mapping tree, cn=config
objectClass: top
objectClass: nsds5replica
objectClass: extensibleObject
cn: replica
nsDS5ReplicaRoot: dc=example,dc=com
nsDS5ReplicaId: 1
nsDS5ReplicaType: 3
nsDS5Flags: 1
nsDS5ReplicaBindDN: cn=Replication Manager, cn=config
nsds5ReplicaPurgeDelay: 86400
nsds5ReplicaTombstonePurgeInterval: 1800
nsState:: AAEAAD35/CoAAAAAAAAAAABAAA=
nsDS5ReplicaName: 999c2182-1dd111b2-801ff648-85a3fef3
nsds5ReplicaChangeCount: 2
#
```

Removing Replicas

The following example shows a shell script for removing replicas and agreements:

```
#! /bin/sh

ldapsearch -h ldaphost1 -D "cn=directory manager" -w mysecret\
 -b "cn=replica,cn='dc=example,dc=com',cn=mapping tree, \
cn=config" "(objectclass=*)" dn | ldapdelete -h ldaphost1\
-D "cn=directory manager" -w mysecret
```

Checking Replication Status

This example of the `replcheck.pl` tool shows the output containing the comparison of the internal attribute, called the replication update vector, that stores the replication status.

In this scenario, the sample command checks the replication status for the entire replicated tree under the `dc=example,dc=com` suffix, between a supplier replica hosted by master and a read-only consumer hosted by `ro-hub`.

```
$ perl -IinstallDir replcheck.pl -w password -b "dc=example,dc=
com" \ master:1389 ro-hub:1389
Connected to masterConnected to ro-hub
Getting replication update vector for master replica of dc=
example,dc=com
=> {replica 1 ldap://master.example.com:1389}
3c63e0b0000000010000
3c63f44b000100010000
=> {replica 3 ldap://ro-hub.example.com:1389}
=> {replicageneration} 3c63da79000000030000
Getting replication update vector for ro-hub replica of dc=
example,dc=com
=> {replica 1 ldap://master.example.com:1389}
3c63e0b0000000010000
3c63f443000100010000
=> {replica 3 ldap://ro-hub.example.com:1389}
=> {replicageneration} 3c63da79000000030000
****
<{replica 1 ldap://master.example.com:1389} 3c63e0b0000000010000
3c63f44b000100010000>
----
<{replica 1 ldap://master.example.com:1389} 3c63e0b0000000010000
3c63f443000100010000>
****************
Replication Update Vector for ro-hub doesn't match with master
Servers are not in sync
$ echo $?    ## show return value
1
```

The first part of the output up to the **** separator displays the replication update vector in each replica. The second part compares all vector elements for each pair of replicas being considered and displays those that do not match. These elements encode information about the latest replication operations, and any differences in this pair of values indicates that the replicas are not up to date.

In this example, the two elements differ slightly, and the tool displays the unmatched vector elements and human-readable explanation. Finally, the return value shows that the `replcheck.pl` tool reported that the second host on the command line, ro-hub, is out-of-date.

Monitoring Directory Services

The most obvious reason to monitor the health of your directory service is to detect a failure as soon as it occurs so it can be fixed quickly. Another reason is to make sure the directory service is running efficiently. Failures can be detected and reported by running agents on the directory server that report back to some central management console. These include:

- Service Availability Manager add-on to Sun™ Management Center (SunMC) 3.0 software
- Java Management Extensions (JMX) framework
- BMC Patrol

Tools to analyze the behavior of your directory service include:

- Sun ONE Directory Console Performance Counters
- `logconv.pl` – access log analyzer.

This section provides an overview of these tools.

Sun Management Center 3.0 Software

The Sun Management Center (SunMC) software provides a framework to simplify management of Sun systems. It is based on a three-tier architecture, as shown in FIGURE 7-1.

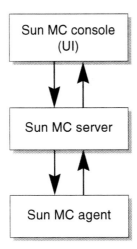

FIGURE 7-1 SunMC Components

In this architecture, agents report back to a server that interfaces to the SunMC console. The console displays status information and provides an operator interface. The agent can reside on the system running the service or on a remote system. To monitor an LDAP service you need to install an additional piece of software (SunMC add-on) called the Service Availability Manager (SAM). The SAM provides Synthetic Transaction Modules (STMs), that mimic clients accessing the service.

The STM for LDAP is configured with an LDAP server IP address, port number, and search base. A predefined search is periodically performed against the configured directory servers. The agent running the LDAP STM reports back to the SunMC server if the search exceeds a pre-defined threshold.

FIGURE 7-2 shows how this can be deployed.

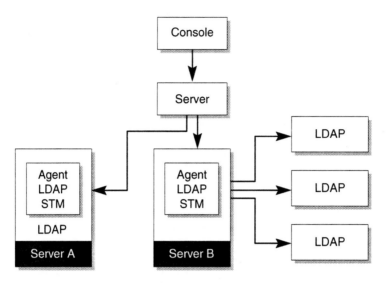

FIGURE 7-2   SunMC With the SAM Add-on

In this diagram, System A is running the LDAP STM on the same server as the LDAP server. System B is running the LDAP STM, but is not running an LDAP server. Instead, it is monitoring three other LDAP servers.

Sun ONE Directory Server 5.2 Software Performance Counters

Useful data pertaining to cache hits can be obtained from the Status Display under Suffixes. FIGURE 7-3 shows output from a directory server with two suffixes.

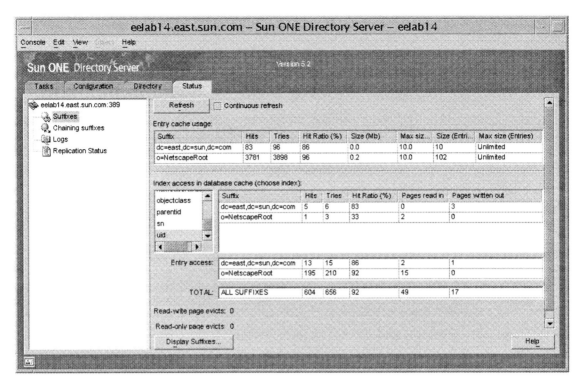

FIGURE 7-3 Sun ONE Directory Console Showing the Directory Server Status Screen

Unlike the previous version, you can choose which attribute you want to monitor.

Using `logconv.pl`

The Directory Server Resource Kit software includes a Perl script called `logconv.pl` for examination of directory server access logs. This is a very helpful tool because log files can become quite large making them difficult to interpret without automated tools. The `logconv.pl` program provides the summarized information. It is a static tool that uses the directory server access log for input.

The `logconv.pl` command syntax:

```
./logconv.pl [-h] [-d rootDN] [-s size_limit] [-X ipaddress] [-E error_code]
[-N] [-v] [-V] [-efcibaltnxgju] [ access_log_file ]
```

Using the following `logconv.pl` options, the following data can be extracted:

```
e        Error Code stats
f        Failed Login Stats
c        Connection Code Stats
i        Client Stats
b        Bind Stats
a        Search Base Stats
l        Search Filter Stats
t        Etime Stats
n        Nentries Stats
x        Extended Operations
r        Most Requested Attribute Stats
g        Abandoned Operation Stats
j        Recommendations
u        Unindexed Search Stats
```

`logconv.pl` example:

```
# ./logconv.pl -V /files/public/access*
iPlanet Access Log Analyzer 4.31

Initializing Variables...
Processing 1 Access Log(s)...

  /files/public/access.20021218-091516   (Total Lines: 9964)

Restarts:               0

Total Connections:      1184
Total Operations:       3206
Total Results:          3206
Overall Performance:    100.0%

Searches:               1472
Modifications:          0
Adds:                   0
Deletes:                0
Mod RDNs:               0

5.x Stats
Persistent Searches:    0
Internal Operations:    0
Entry Operations:       0
Extended Operations:    576
Abandoned Requests:     0
```

```
Smart Referrals Received:        0

VLV Operations:                  0
VLV Unindexed Searches:          0
SORT Operations:                 0
SSL Connections:                 0

Entire Search Base Queries:      0
Unindexed Searches:              0


FDs Taken:                       1184
FDs Returned:                    1184
Highest FD Taken:                69

Broken Pipes:                    0
Connections Reset By Peer:       0
Resource Unavailable:            0
Binds:                           1158
Unbinds:                         1184


 LDAP v2 Binds:                  0
 LDAP v3 Binds:                  1158
 Expired Password Logins:        0
 SSL Client Binds:               0
 Failed SSL Client Binds:        0
 SASL Binds:                     0

 Directory Manager Binds:        0
 Anonymous Binds:                0
 Other Binds:                    1158


----- Errors -----

err=0                   3206    Successful Operations

----- Total Connection Codes -----

U1                      1184    Cleanly Closed Connections


----- Top 20 Clients -----

Number of Clients:  2

896    129.148.181.216
                 896 -  U1   Cleanly Closed Connections
```

```
288    129.148.181.130
                    288 -  U1    Cleanly Closed Connections

----- Top 20 Bind DN's -----

Number of Unique Bind DN's: 2

870           cn=proxyagent,ou=profile,dc=example,dc=com
288           cn=replication manager, cn=config
----- Top 20 Search Bases -----

Number of Unique Search Bases: 6

765           ou=people,dc=example,dc=com
314           root dse
288           cn=schema
101           ou=hosts,dc=example,dc=com
2             ou=profile,dc=example,dc=com
2             dc=example,dc=com


----- Top 20 Search Filters -----

Number of Unique Search Filters: 11

602           (objectclass=*)
153           (&(objectclass=posixaccount)(uid=user2))
153           (&(objectclass=posixaccount)(uid=user12345678))
153       (&(objectclass=posixaccount)(uidnumber=123456789))
153           (&(objectclass=posixaccount)(uidnumber=101))
153           (&(objectclass=posixaccount)(uid=user123456789))
33            (&(objectclass=iphost)(iphostnumber=
129.148.181.216))
33            (&(objectclass=iphost)(cn=eelab14))
33            (&(objectclass=iphost)(iphostnumber=
129.148.181.130))
4             (nisdomain=*)
2         (&(|(objectclass=solarisnamingprofile)(objectclass=
duaconfigprofile))(cn=default))


----- Top 20 Most Requested Attributes -----

864       cn
765       uidNumber
765       homeDirectory
765       description
```

765	gecos
765	loginShell
765	uid
765	gidNumber
314	supportedControl
288	supportedExtension
288	nsSchemaCSN
99	ipHostNumber
26	supportedSASLMechanisms
4	nisDomain
2	All Attributes

Managing Users and Groups

Unlike accounts set up in NIS and NIS+, you probably have additional information that you want to store about users. The `ldapaddent` command can be used to create user entries from `/etc/passwd` and `/etc/shadow`, but chances are it would not contain all the attributes you want stored.

One way to create customized user entries is to write a script that helps automate the process. The following is an example of a shell script that creates user entries from the command line.

Part 1 - Get the parameters:

```
#!/bin/sh
USHELL=/bin/sh
PWORD=secret
COMMENT=""
HOMEDIR=""
UID=""
GID="10"
CN=""
USERID=""
LDAPSERVER=hosta
DMPASSWD=mysecret
STARTUID=100
ENDUID=1000

parse_arg()
{
    while getopts "w:c:d:g:u:s:" ARG
    do
        case $ARG in
            w)      PWORD=$OPTARG;;
            c)      COMMENT=$OPTARG;;
            d)      HOMEDIR=$OPTARG;;
            g)      GID=$OPTARG;;
            u)      UID=$OPTARG;;
            s)      USHELL=$OPTARG;;
            *)  echo "**ERROR: Supported option missing handler!"
                    exit 1;;
        esac
    done
    return `expr $OPTIND - 1`
}
```

Part 2 - Create the entry:

```
parse_arg $*
shift $?
USERID=$1

if [ -z "$USERID" ]; then
        echo "User ID must be entered"
        exit 1
fi

CN="$2 $3"
if [ -z "$2" ]; then
        CN="$USERID"
fi

if [ -z "$HOMEDIR" ]; then
        HOMEDIR=/home/$USERID
fi
if [ -z "$UID" ]; then
    find_uid
fi

( cat <<EOF
uid=$USERID,ou=people,dc=example,dc=com
objectClass=posixAccount
objectClass=shadowAccount
objectClass=account
objectClass=top
uid=$USERID
cn=$CN
uidNumber=$UID
gidNumber=$GID
gecos=newuser
homeDirectory=$HOMEDIR
loginShell=$USHELL
userPassword=$PWORD

EOF
) > lusr.ldif
ldapmodify -a -h $LDAPSERVER -D "cn=directory manager" -w
$DMPASSWD -f lusr.ldif
```

Password Management

Directory server password management can be easily performed through the Directory Console. This is a convenient way to change the default password storage scheme and set password aging. FIGURE 7-4 shows an example.

Note – The password-aging attributes stored in the directory are operational attributes that are not stored in the user entry.

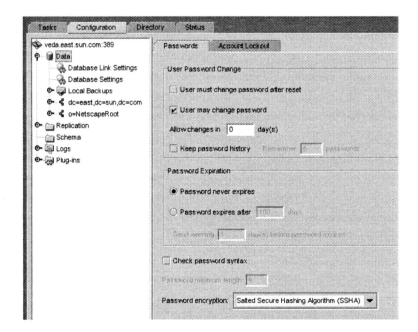

FIGURE 7-4   Password Management in the Directory Console

Limiting User Access to a Client System

There are a number of ways you can restrict access to particular client systems using LDAP. These include:

- netgroups
- Alternate search paths with SSDs

The method for limiting access by deploying netgroups with LDAP is the same method used with NIS. The basics steps are:

1. Modify the local /etc/passwd and /etc/shadow file.

2. Modify the local /etc/nsswitch.conf file.

3. Create and populate an entry in ou=netgroup.

Modifying /etc/passwd

The way netgroups works is to direct the user and password search to look in a naming service for a list of users allowed to log in. The directive used is the +@ symbol followed by a netgroup name. The following is an example of what the /etc/passwd and /etc/shadow files would look like specifying a netgroup called *ldap-users*.

The passwd file

```
# cat /etc/passwd
root:x:0:1:Super-User:/:/sbin/sh
daemon:x:1:1::/:
bin:x:2:2::/usr/bin:
sys:x:3:3::/:
.
.
.
ldaptest:x:137850:1::/home/ldaptest:/bin/sh
+@ldap-users:x:::::
#
```

The shadow file

```
# cat /etc/shadow
root:GNIWbjOoY1P2g:6445::::::
daemon:NP:6445::::::
bin:NP:6445::::::
sys:NP:6445::::::
ldaptest:KW25kt7gvYupk:11892::::::
.
.
.
+@ldap-users::::::
```

Modifying `nsswitch.conf`

The `nsswitch.conf` file needs to be modified so it will be accessed in the compatibility mode. Prior to the introduction of the Name Service Switch (NSS), a plus (+) sign was used in the `/etc/passwd` file to direct the search to NIS. With the NSS, the + was no longer necessary because you could specify your search path in the `nsswitch.conf` file. However, to use `netgroups`, the old style is required. The following is an example of what the applicable portion of an `nsswitch.conf` file might look like.

```
# cat /etc/nsswitch.conf
.....
passwd:        compat
passwd_compat: ldap [tryagain=continue]
......
netgroup:    ldap [tryagain=continue]
......
```

Creating `Netgroup` Entries

Entries can be created using `ldapaddent` or by creating your own LDIF.

Example of a `netgroup` entry:

```
# ldaplist -l netgroup
dn: cn=ldap-users,ou=netgroup,dc=example,dc=com
        objectClass: nisNetgroup
        objectClass: top
        cn: ldap-users
        nisNetgroupTriple: (,user1,)
        nisNetgroupTriple: (,user3,)
        nisNetgroupTriple: (,user2,)
        nisNetgroupTriple: (,user5,)
#
```

Setting an Alternate Search Path

You can specify where in the DIT the client system is allowed to search.

```
# ldapclient list
NS_LDAP_FILE_VERSION= 2.0
NS_LDAP_BINDDN= cn=proxyagent,ou=profile,dc=example,dc=com
NS_LDAP_BINDPASSWD= {NS1}4a3788e8c053424f
NS_LDAP_SERVERS= 100.100.100.1
NS_LDAP_SEARCH_BASEDN= dc=example,dc=com
NS_LDAP_AUTH= simple
NS_LDAP_SEARCH_REF= FALSE
NS_LDAP_SEARCH_SCOPE= one
NS_LDAP_SEARCH_TIME= 30
NS_LDAP_PROFILE= newprofile
NS_LDAP_CREDENTIAL_LEVEL= proxy
NS_LDAP_SERVICE_SEARCH_DESC= passwd:ou=temps,dc=example,dc=
com?one
NS_LDAP_BIND_TIME= 10
#
```

The DIT is arranged with two branches as shown in FIGURE 7-5.

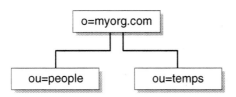

FIGURE 7-5 Two Branches of the DIT

In this configuration, users are placed in two different branches of the DIT. If you want to designate some systems that only people in the temps branch can log into, you can create a client profile that would look in the ou=temps container.

Restricting automount Access on Client Systems

Another use of SSD is to restrict what file systems a particular system is allowed to mount. This can be done by setting the search path of the automount database. It should be noted that the restriction set in this case would be per system and not per user.

Changing User Login Parameters

Client profiles can be used to pass different login parameters to users depending on what system they log in to. For example, you might want a different login shell for restrictive and non-restrictive systems.

To change users shells based on what system they log into, you can specify the `AttributeMap` attribute in the client profile. Before you do this you need to create custom attributes that store the alternate shells. For example:

```
attribute: ushell
Type: DirectoryString

attribute: rshell
Type: DirectoryString

objectclass: shelluser
requires: ushell, rshell
```

Note – The section "Extending the Directory Schema" on page 440 explains how to do this.

Next, you need to add the new attributes to the user's entry:

```
dn: uid=user2,ou=people,dc=example,dc=com
        objectClass: posixAccount
        objectClass: shadowAccount
        objectClass: account
        objectClass: top
        objectClass: shelluser
        uid: user2
        cn: user2
        uidNumber: 101
        gidNumber: 10
        gecos: newuser
```

Next, you need to create client profiles that map the `loginShell` attribute:

```
dn: cn=newprofile,ou=profile,dc=example,dc=com
objectClass: top
objectClass: DUAConfigProfile
defaultServerList: 129.100.100.1
defaultSearchBase: dc=example,dc=com
authenticationMethod: simple
followReferrals: FALSE
defaultSearchScope: one
searchTimeLimit: 30
profileTTL: 600
cn: newprofile
credentialLevel: proxy
bindTimeLimit: 10
attributeMap: passwd:loginShell=rshell
```

Deploying RBAC with LDAP

Role-Based Access Control (RBAC) was introduced in the Solaris 8 OE to address the problem of how to delegate system administration responsibility. Prior to RBAC, administrators were provided with the superuser (root) password or `setuid` scripts were written with group permissions granted to specific administrators. Granting root permissions to a large population of administrators is dangerous because the `root` user can do intentional or unintentional damage to a server in addition to breaching security. Custom `setuid` scripts are insecure and are difficult to manage.

The concept behind RBAC is that a subset of administrative functions can be assigned to a particular user. What these functions are and who is permitted to perform them are controlled by four databases. These are:

- `user_attr(4)`
- `auth_attr(4)`
- `prof_attr(4)`
- `exec_attr`

The databases can be stored locally in files under `/etc` or in a naming service. The `/etc` files are:

- `/etc/user_attr`
- `/etc/security/auth_attr`
- `/etc/security/prof_attr`
- `/etc/security/exec_attr`

The precedence of local files versus naming service is set in the
/etc/nsswitch.conf file. However there is not a one-to-one relationship.
TABLE 7-1 shows the relationship between the database and a tag contained in the
nsswitch.conf file.

TABLE 7-1   nsswitch.conf Tag Mapping

RBAC Database	Relevant nsswitch.conf Tag
user_attr	Set by the precedence for passwd
prof_attr	Set by prof_attr
auth_attr	Set by auth_attr
exec_attr	Set by prof_attr

Refer to Chapter 5 "Migrating Legacy Data to LDAP" for details on how to import
RBAC data.

Extending the Directory Schema

The Sun One Directory Server 5.2 software maintains schema definitions in LDIF.
These definitions reside in several files located in /var/mps/serverroot/slapd-
instance/config/schema by default. These files are read when the directory server
is initialized. Adding your own schema definitions is usually done by creating an
LDIF representation and either importing it under cn=schema or appending it to
the 99user.ldif file located in the directory previously mentioned.

In most cases, scripts like idsconfig will automatically update the schema for you.
However, if you want to create your own definitions, you must update the directory
server somehow. This can be done either by importing LDIF or through the
Directory Console.

To create your own attributes and object classes using the Directory Console, go to
the Configuration tab and click on Schema. FIGURE 7-6 shows the Schema display.

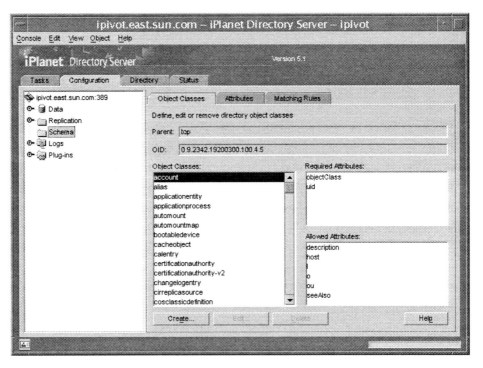

FIGURE 7-6 Directory Server Console Schema Display

This screen is also useful for browsing the schema definitions already established on your directory server. If you encounter object class violations while configuring your directory server, check the error log for details, and use the Directory Console to determine which attributes are required and which ones are allowed. You can also view the matching rules that apply.

To create your own schema definitions, start by clicking on the Attribute tab, then the Create button. You must always create the attributes that your object class will use first. Once all you attributes are defined, you can create a new object class and include the attributes in your new object class.

Once the new definitions are completed, the `99user.ldif` file is automatically updated. You can extract the LDIF representation created, and import it into other servers.

Example of Script to Update the Schema

```
#!/bin/sh
( cat <<EOF
dn: cn=schema
changetype: modify
add: attributetypes
attributeTypes: ( sunaccessSmradip-oid NAME 'sunaccessSmradip'
SYNTAX 1.3.6.1.4.1.1466.115.121.1.15 X-ORIGIN 'user defined' )
attributeTypes: ( sunaccessSmradonlinestatus-oid NAME 'sunacce
ssSmradonlinestatus'  SYNTAX 1.3.6.1.4.1.1466.115.121.1.15 X-O
RIGIN 'user defined' )
EOF
) > attr.ldif
# ldapmodify -D "cn=directory manager" -w mysecret -f attr.ldif
```

Note – The text following the directive `attributeTypes:` is shown wrapped.

## CHAPTER 8

Selecting Storage for Optimum Directory Server Performance

Providing detailed directory server sizing information is difficult because of the many ways that directory services can be deployed. There are, however, some general guidelines for choosing the appropriate Sun hardware that can be helpful. The most significant hardware factors affecting directory server performance are:

- Disk storage subsystem
- CPU
- Memory

Network bandwidth is a consideration, but with speeds of 1Gbit/second, it is difficult for a directory server to saturate the network. In this chapter, the focus is on choosing the correct disk storage subsystem and the right class of Sun systems to provide optimum performance for directory services.

To choose the correct disk storage subsystem, you need to understand the performance characteristics of the available subsystems and how they relate to directory server performance. Choosing the server platform is tricky because the load you put on the directory server can vary greatly between different environments.

To address the disk storage subsystem, a detailed look into Sun storage technology is presented as follows:

Note – Storage products described in this chapter are for products available at the time of this writing. It is likely that the storage products you have to choose from have changed as new models are introduced. Nevertheless, the same concepts and performance principles apply.

Software Characteristics

Before delving into the details of how hardware affects directory server performance, it is helpful to understand what performance capabilities are needed in terms of directory server software.

As your e-business infrastructure becomes more complex and mission critical, the directory services must scale vertically and horizontally to meet your needs of today and the future.

Vertical scalability is achieved by adding additional RAM and disks to an existing machine to improve performance and to minimize data center sprawl. The scalability of the directory server can also be observed as you add additional CPUs. Although the server performance does improve with each additional CPU (up to about 12), adding the thirteenth CPU yields a much smaller improvement than adding the second or third. Directory services software must be designed to take advantage of vertical scalability. It should also be noted that the above information about the number of CPUs is for the Sun ONE Directory Server 5.2 software. Other versions of the directory server will likely have different levels of scalability. For instance, we know this is true for version 5.1, which only scales to about 8 CPUs.

Horizontal scalability of reads and writes through the directory server can be achieved through adding more replicas, but the ability to have more master servers does not significantly improve write performance because all the changes must still be applied on all masters.

The Sun ONE Directory Server software provides these vertical and horizontal scalability requirements. Some of the key performance features of the Sun ONE Directory Server 5.2 software are:

- Multi-processor support, with near-linear scalability up to about 7 or 8 CPUs, with diminishing returns for each additional CPU added after that up to around 13 CPUs.

- 64-bit caching that allows in-RAM caches of databases sizes of currently up to 576 Gbytes of memory (Solaris OE SPARC systems). This is largely due to the fact that performance issues are found in systems with more than this.

- Multiple database technology allows tuning and deployment of multiple disk subsystems for a single directory instance
- Four-way multi-master replication across local area networks (LANs) and wide area networks (WANs) for always-on, highly available service, which also includes the capability of *compression* of changes during transport (useful only over a WAN)

Survey of Sun Storage Subsystems

Sun provides a range of storage options ranging from local SCSI disks to the highly resilient and performant Sun™ StorEdge 9900 series. Given such a large range, decisions have to be made as to which systems are the most appropriate to deploy for the Sun ONE Directory Server 5.2 software. Please note, however, that network-attached storage is not a supported configuration for the Sun ONE Directory Server software and should not be used. In addition to providing relatively poor performance compared to the other possibilities, network file systems like NFS and AFS also do not support the kinds of locking required by the directory server database, so when using them you run the risk of corrupting the directory server database.

The Sun™ StorEdge T3b storage array is widely deployed and is seen as the mainstay for the Sun™ ONE Directory Server 5.2 software to achieve maximum performance. For this reason, a large portion of this section is devoted to its configuration.

Local SCSI Disks, Internal FC-AL Disks, High-End Storage

As an example, Sun has a broad family of Sun StorEdge Solutions, including the Sun StorEdge™ 3310 SCSI array which is the only SCSI array; the Sun StorEdge D1000 array, which is a host-based software RAID device; the Sun StorEdge A1000 array, which is a hardware RAID device; and the Sun StorEdge D2 Array, which is ideal in a workgroup array.

Even though the Sun StorEdge A1000 array is still available, it should be disregarded and probably not used with the Sun™ ONE Directory Server 5.2 software because it is probably coming to the end of its life, and has relatively slow SCSI disks and a small cache size of only 64 Kbytes.

For lower-end systems such as the Sun Fire™ E280R and Sun Fire v880 systems, it is feasible to use these disk subsystems in conjunction with the Sun™ ONE Directory Server 5.2, in particular when deploying in an enterprise environment. In general, using internal SCSI disks is possible with systems such as the Sun Fire E280R and Sun Fire v880 systems with disk subsystems such as the Sun StorEdge 3310 array and above, as they do warrant a disk array with read/write caching and hardware RAID controllers.

Storage Arrays with Cache

Sun offers a wide range of storage arrays which includes the Sun StorEdge 3310 array and above that have cache and hardware RAID controllers. In all cases, they can be configured with dual controllers and mirrored storage.

The latest incarnation of the Sun StorEdge T3 array is the T3b, which has a 100 Mbyte/sec fibre controller, 1-Gbyte cache, and fast fibre-channel arbitrated loop (FC-AL) disks. Management of hardware RAID within the array is accomplished using the simple onboard UNIX-like interface to its operating system (for example, you can use the telnet command to communicate with the array and configure it through a set of simple commands). Scalability, which equates to more disk space and more controllers for more I/O operations and throughput, is achieved by adding more Sun StorEdge T3b arrays. There are no licensing issues or additional cabinets to purchase, so the Sun StorEdge T3b array is a relatively inexpensive path to follow. As needs grow, you simply add a new array. The Sun StorEdge T3b array is a mid-priced storage device, and is therefore a good price/performance fit for machines with 2-24 processors.

Note – The Sun StorEdge T3b arrays can be clustered, but doing so requires additional infrastructure such as fiber switches or hubs.

High-End Storage Subsystems

The high-end storage subsystems currently available include all of the Sun StorEdge 9900 range of products. These provide very high levels of availability, using software to predict and automatically swap and replace disks that are likely to fail. High levels of performance are provided by virtue of large caches and multiple paths to fast disks. Furthermore, these subsystems readily support multi-hosting, which is an advantage in a clustered Sun™ ONE Directory Server 5.2 environment. The disadvantages of the Sun StorEdge 9900 range of products are the price and the initial complexity in setup and implementation.

Introduction to the Sun StorEdge T3b Storage Array

While much is known about standard SCSI disks, knowledge of Sun StorEdge T3b arrays is less common. This section aims to address this issue. The Sun StorEdge T3b array is the second release of the Sun StorEdge T3 array. Upon release, it became known as the Sun StorEdge T300 array, and soon changed to the Sun StorEdge T3 array. The Sun StorEdge T3b array is a mid-life upgrade to the Sun StorEdge T3 line. It consists of a new controller and an increase in the size of its cache from 256 Mbytes to 1 Gbyte.

Sun StorEdge T3b Array Architecture

Sun StorEdge T3b arrays can be deployed in two ways.

- As a standalone workgroup array
- In a partner-pairs configuration

The standalone workgroup array is more performant than partner-pairs but this is at the expense of resiliency. Regardless of deployment method, the basic hardware architecture is the same. The Sun StorEdge T3b array has the following characteristics:

- Must have a full compliment of similar sized disks. Currently, disk sizes are either 36 Gbytes or 72 Gbytes.
- One fiber channel arbitrated loop (FC-AL) controller capable of a maximum throughput of 100 Mbytes/sec.
- A serial port and an Ethernet interface. Either can be used to configure the Sun StorEdge T3b array's hardware RAID controller and to manage the array (for example, check system logs, load firmware, and so on).
- A 1-Gbyte cache. In partner-pair mode, these caches can be mirrored between the partners. To do this, a pair of communicating cables connect the pair. In the event of a controller failure on one of the partners, I/O requests can be diverted across these cables.
- The ability to enable or disable volume slicing on the Sun StorEdge T3b arrays. If volume slicing is disabled, then a maximum of two logical units (LUNs) are configurable. A LUN in the context of a Sun StorEdge T3b array is an abstraction that allows one or more of the physical disks to be considered as a single logical volume. The Sun StorEdge T3b array only allows access to its disks through this abstraction; a host operating system cannot address the Sun StorEdge T3b array's individual disks.

LUN RAID Configuration

A Sun StorEdge T3b array LUN must be configured as a hardware RAID volume. RAID levels are discussed in "RAID Explained for Directory Administrators" on page 459, but for now, it is only necessary to be aware of the basics of RAID, and what levels can be configured on a Sun StorEdge T3b array's LUNs. The following levels can be used:

- RAID 0 is known as a stripe. The first block of the volume will be on one hard disk drive, the second on another, the third on another, and so on until all drives in the LUN are used, whereupon the pattern begins again from the first drive. Striping effectively spreads and balances the load of read and write operations across multiple disks to improve performance. The capacity of a RAID 0 volume is equal to the sum of the capacities of all the disks in the LUN. It could be mistakenly read that the capacity of a RAID 0 volume is equal to the size of a single drive. Although RAID 0 can provide high performance at low cost, it is potentially dangerous, because the loss of any single drive means that you effectively lose all the data.

- RAID 1 is defined as a mirror, although the way the Sun StorEdge T3b array implements RAID 1 really results in RAID 1+0. For example, if four disks are in the LUN, a RAID 0 stripe will be made across two disks, as described above, and then the blocks that make up that stripe will be mirrored in the same manner to the other two disks. Thus, the total capacity of the four disks is halved, but if one of the mirrored pairs fail, the data is still available and usable. Mirroring (RAID 1) increases resiliency.

- RAID 5 is when data is striped across the drives in the LUN, along with parity information. If a disk fails, the parity and data on the other disks is used to calculate the value of the data on the failed disk. Two disk failures results in all data to be lost. As a consequence, a RAID 5 volume has a capacity of one disk less than the number of disks in the LUN. RAID 5 is more resilient than RAID 0, and less resilient but cheaper to implement than RAID 1.

Given that a Sun StorEdge T3b array can have up to two LUNs, the combinations of volumes shown in TABLE 8-1 can be used.

TABLE 8-1 Sun StorEdge T3 Array Volumes

LUN/Volume 1	LUN/Volume 1	Hot Spare
9-disk RAID 5	None	
8-disk RAID 5	None	X
9-disk RAID 1	None	
8-disk RAID 1	None	X
2-disk RAID 1	7 disk RAID 5	
2-disk RAID 1	6 disk RAID 5	X

TABLE 8-1   Sun StorEdge T3 Array Volumes *(Continued)*

LUN/Volume 1	LUN/Volume 1	Hot Spare
2- disk RAID 1	7 disk RAID 1	
2-disk RAID 1	6 disk RAID 1	X
4-disk RAID 0	5 disk RAID 1	
2-disk RAID 0	6 disk RAID 5	X

Note – The hot spare is only applicable to RAID 5 and RAID 1 volumes. It provides further resiliency over and above that already provided by these RAID levels. Should a disk fail, the hot spare will automatically be swapped into the volume and populated with data and parity information (RAID 5 only) to bring the volume up to its full complement of disks.

LUN Block Size Configuration

To create a volume, a blocksize must be set. The Sun StorEdge T3b array has three possible block sizes: 16 Kbytes, 32 Kbytes and 64 Kbytes. To determine the best block size, consideration must be given to the type of I/O the application performs. For example, if the application performs many small read and write operations, the 16-Kbytes size is probably most appropriate, whereas for very large read and writes (for example, data warehousing) a 64-Kbytes block size might be a better fit.

As far as the Sun ONE Directory Server software is concerned, the internal database page size is 8 Kbytes. This is the size of I/O to and from the disk. The data values passed between the directory server and database is arbitrary, and the database tries to fit as many values onto a page as it can, or if a value is greater than 8 Kbytes, it uses overflow pages, again, 8 Kbytes in size. This basically means that whenever any write is made to the database, it is therefore done in an 8-Kbyte chunk. Having said this, in the index files (all except `id2entry`) the data values are at or below 8 Kbytes by splitting them into blocks of approximately 8 Kbytes. This is the `idlist` block size which is a tunable configuration parameter. The parameter in the directory server that controls the page size used by the database is `nsslapd-db-page-size` in the entry `cn=config,cn=ldbm database,cn=plugins,cn=config`. Note, however, that if you want to change this, you must first export the database to LDIF, make the change, and re-import from LDIF. Furthermore, any binary backups you previously had will be invalid. Therefore, you should only change this if you have an extremely good reason to do so.

Note – `Blocksize` is a system-wide parameter. This means that all LUNs and volumes on the Sun StorEdge T3b array, or in the case of a partner-pairs, both arrays, must have the same block size.

Other LUN Parameters

Other parameters that need to be considered are:

- Cache mode
- Read ahead policy
- LUN reconstruction rate
- Cache mirroring and multi-pathing support

The latter two parameters only affect partner-pair configurations. LUN reconstruction rate only impacts performance when a hot spare is swapped in. Read ahead policy is either `on`, meaning reads can be cached, or `off`, meaning no data is brought into cache early for future retrieval. The cache mode can be set to one of four modes: `auto`, `writebehind`, `writethrough` or `none`. If set to `auto`, the Sun StorEdge T3b array intelligently decides on-the-fly whether the cache should be used in `writebehind` or `writethrough` mode. `Writebehind` results in writes that are made into the cache and then de-staged to physical disk at a time of the Sun StorEdge T3b array's choosing. `Writethrough` provides that a write will go straight through the cache to disk. Setting the mode to `writebehind` or `writethrough` forces the cache to always behave in the chosen manner. Cache mode can affect resiliency.

Sun StorEdge T3 Array Configuration Considerations

FIGURE 8-1 shows a Sun StorEdge T3b workgroup array in its recommended default configuration of eight disks in a single RAID 5 LUN with a hot spare. This is sometimes confusingly referred to as a 7+1+1 RAID 5 layout, presumably to identify that one disk will be lost to parity, although the parity is amortized over all of the eight disks.

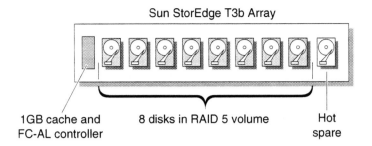

Sun StorEdge T3b Array

1GB cache and   8 disks in RAID 5 volume   Hot
FC-AL controller   spare

FIGURE 8-1   Basic Sun StorEdge T3b Array Setup

When a Sun StorEdge T3b array is configured as shown in FIGURE 8-1 and connected to a server, its hardware volume, or LUN, presents itself to the server's operating system as if it were a very large disk. FIGURE 8-2 helps explain how a host machine's operating system views a Sun StorEdge T3b array LUN.

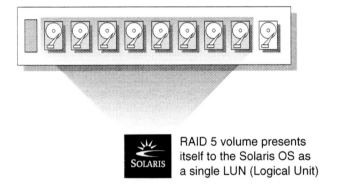

RAID 5 volume presents itself to the Solaris OS as a single LUN (Logical Unit)

FIGURE 8-2   Solaris OS View of the Sun StorEdge T3b Array Volume

Sun StorEdge T3b Array High-Availability Considerations

Certain resiliency features are common to both workgroup arrays and partner-pair arrays. These features include a hot-spare disk (assuming LUNs are configured with one), redundant power supplies, and batteries. If any of these items fail, the array will keep serving I/O requests, but if the cache mode was set to auto, its data is de-staged to disk, and the mode will be set to writethrough. This way, the Sun StorEdge T3b array can guarantee that all future requests are immediately written to disk and the data is less susceptible to corruption after another failure. If the cache mode had been forced to writebehind, the Sun StorEdge T3b array would remain in this mode even after a failure, and therefore, be more susceptible to corruption following a subsequent failure.

Partner-pairing provides greater resilience. If a controller or the path to a controller on one of the Sun StorEdge T3b arrays becomes disabled, I/O requests are automatically redirected through interconnecting cables. FIGURE 8-3 conceptually shows how this happens.

Note – For redirection to work, alternate pathing software must be installed on the host.

On Solaris OE platforms, alternate pathing software is provided by either Veritas DMP (part of the Veritas Volume Manager software), or mpxio which is part of the Solaris Operating Environment. The multi-pathing system parameter on the Sun StorEdge T3b array must also be enabled for controller and fiber path failover to work correctly.

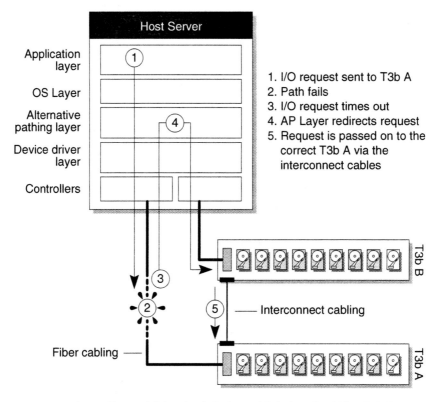

FIGURE 8-3   Controller and Fiber Path Failover With Sun StorEdge T3b Partner Pair Arrays

On a pathing or controller failure, the cache mode is set to writethrough if it was initially set to auto. To protect caches from power failures and memory errors, cache mirroring is usually set to on in partner-pair deployments. This means that every write is copied to the partner's cache, so if a cache fails, data integrity is preserved. There is overhead associated with cache mirroring; where copying and routing over the interconnect takes time, and the amount of cache available is reduced, so the likelihood of flooding increases. Thus, performance might decrease.

In summary, partner-pairing does provide resilience by giving all components a level of redundancy, assuming the use of hot spare disks. In most cases, however, data integrity and Sun StorEdge T3b array availability cannot be guaranteed should a further similar failure occur. Multiple levels of redundancy are the domain of high-end storage solutions such as the Sun StorEdge 9900 range, as is predictive fault analysis and repair.

Recommended Configurations for the Sun ONE Directory Server 5.2 Software

One of the main considerations when architecting a directory solution is in providing a performant solution while not completely ignoring resiliency or what would be reasonable to deploy in a production environment. If you are architecting an enterprise directory solution, the default single RAID 5 LUN layout of eight disks and one hot spare can be used with the Sun StorEdge T3b arrays configured as workgroup arrays. This provides protection against disk failures, which are the most likely failure, but not against controller failures. This configuration further allows the use of odd numbers of arrays, which on smaller directory server implementations may be something desirable For example, you might not want the expense of purchasing two Sun StorEdge T3b arrays, given a small directory data size and budget. Using the workgroup array configuration instead of partner-pairs means that cache mirroring and its overhead do not have to be considered.

RAID 0 over the nine disks of an array is possibly the most performant layout, but the only way to add resiliency is to use a software mirror on another array. Doing this is the most expensive solution available. RAID 5's read performance is not that much worse than RAID 0's, given that no parity calculations have to be made (an eight-disk RAID 5 layout would approximate a seven-disk RAID 0 stripe), and may be considered a good choice when using data that is mostly read and seldom written.

Using RAID 1 (1+0) layouts with nine disks would buy very little advantage, because the stripe only goes over four disks, assuming that the mirror would be on the other four, with the last disk being used as a hot spare. Directory server performance tests at Sun have shown that RAID 5 over eight disks has better performance than a 4+4 RAID 1 layout, although the latter is slightly more resilient.

Sun ONE Directory Server 5.2 Enterprise and Software Volume Managers

Volume management provides a logical view of the disks under its control. Volume management can create volumes smaller than a physical disk and partition, or larger than a physical disk by combining disks into a volume. A volume manager can also provide resiliency by mirroring volumes, or by using algorithms that allow the rebuilding of data should a disk in a volume fail. Thus, volume management provides an easy, flexible way to manage storage. Volume management is synonymous with RAID levels (see "RAID Explained for Directory Administrators" on page 459).

Solaris™ Volume Manager (formerly known as Solstice DiskSuite) software, and Veritas Volume Manager are the volume management products available for use with the Sun™ ONE Directory Server 5.2 software.

Traditionally, the Solaris Volume Manager software was considered a good volume manager for a small numbers of disks, but it became more difficult to use and administer with larger numbers of disk subsystems. This manageability gap, coupled with advanced features implemented by Veritas, such as importing and exporting volumes and dynamic multi-pathing, led to Veritas becoming the de facto standard for Sun's customers.

Veritas software might still be a viable choice for use in some Sun™ ONE Directory Server 5.2. environments. However, in new deployments, you should weigh the pros and cons carefully because the latest releases of the Solaris Volume Manager software now compares very favorably with Veritas software.

Sun StorEdge T3b Array and Veritas Volume Manager

In the previous section we described how a hardware volume or LUN is viewed as a disk by the operating system. Here is example output from the `format` utility:

```
# format
Searching for disks...done

AVAILABLE DISK SELECTIONS:
       0. c0t0d0 <SUN18G cyl 7506 alt 2 hd 19 sec 248>
          /ssm@0,0/pci@18,700000/pci@1/SUNW,isptwo@4/sd@0,0
       1. c0t1d0 <SUN18G cyl 7506 alt 2 hd 19 sec 248>
          /ssm@0,0/pci@18,700000/pci@1/SUNW,isptwo@4/sd@1,0
       2. c0t6d0 <SUN18G cyl 7506 alt 2 hd 19 sec 248>
          /ssm@0,0/pci@18,700000/pci@1/SUNW,isptwo@4/sd@6,0
       3. c16t1d0 <SUN-T300-0200 cyl 34530 alt 2 hd 224 sec 64>

/ssm@0,0/pci@1b,700000/pci@2/SUNW,qlc@4/fp@0,0/ssd@w50020f230000
096b,0
       4. c17t1d0 <SUN-T300-0200 cyl 34530 alt 2 hd 224 sec 64>

/ssm@0,0/pci@1b,600000/pci@1/SUNW,qlc@4/fp@0,0/ssd@w50020f230000
0947,0
       5. c18t1d0 <SUN-T300-0200 cyl 34530 alt 2 hd 224 sec 64>
Specify disk (enter its number): ^D
```

Note – T300 is a legacy name for T3/T3b.

Note – The operating system has no idea what the underlying volume is. For example, it could be RAID 0, RAID 5, or no RAID configuration at all.

Before Veritas can use the Sun StorEdge T3b array LUNs attached to the host, it must add them to a logical construct called a *disk group*. Once added, the LUNs are known as Veritas disks (FIGURE 8-4). These logical disks can then be carved up or combined to form volumes. Here is an example of a command line to create a stripe over two Veritas disks:

```
# vxassist  -g blueprints make vol1 20g layout=striped
stripeunit=128 ncolumn=2 alloc="disk1 disk2"
```

To explain what this means, `blueprints` is the Veritas disk group, `vol1` is the
volume being made, `ncolumn` is the number of Veritas disks being used, and `alloc`
is a list of the logical disks being used. The `stripeunit` is the number of Veritas
blocks. A Veritas block is 512 bytes, and so 128 equates to a stripe width of
64 Kbytes. This means that the first 64 Kbytes of the stripe will be on `disk1`, the
second 64 Kbytes on `disk2`, the third 64 Kbytes on `disk1`, and so on until the
requested size of the volume, (20 Gbytes) is reached.

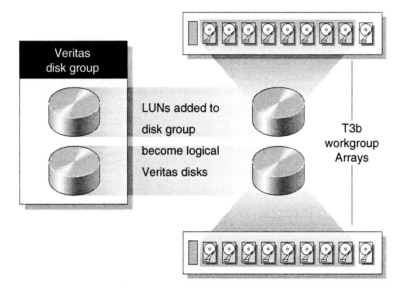

FIGURE 8-4 Veritas View of the LUNs

Once a volume is created, it is added to the host's device tree, can have a file system
applied to it, and can be mounted in the normal way.

Note – The path takes into account the Veritas abstractions. TABLE 8-2 contrasts the
device paths for a partition (slice) of a standard SCSI disk and a Veritas volume.

TABLE 8-2 Device Paths

Raw (character) device	Logical (block) device
/dev/rdsk/c0t0d0s6	/dev/dsk/c0t0d0s6
/dev/vx/rdsk/blueprints/vol1	/dev/vx/dsk/sunone/vol1

As discussed in the previous sections, striping over disks (physical and logical) improves performance. Striping over controllers further improves performance because the number of I/O operations and data throughput is aggregated (for example, a single fiber controller can handle 100 Mbytes/sec transfers, but two controllers can handle 200 Mbytes/sec).

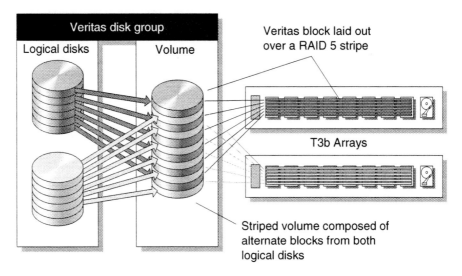

FIGURE 8-5   Plaiding Striped Software Volumes Over RAID 5 Hardware Volumes

FIGURE 8-5 shows how the blocks that make up the software stripe are laid out on the hardware RAID 5 stripe. Conceptually, the software stripe can be thought of as running vertically and the hardware RAID 5 stripe as running horizontally, forming a weave which is known as *plaiding*. Therefore, when a write is made to the file system mounted on the software stripe (for example, /dev/vx/dsk/blueprints/vol1) the underlying software and hardware spreads this write over two 100-Mbytes/sec controllers and sixteen disks. Similarly, when a read is made, both controllers and all the disks are involved. Even without the use of the caches of the two Sun StorEdge T3b arrays, this parallelism greatly increases the I/O speed when compared to serialized I/O on single disks. Plaiding can be advantageous when architecting and deploying the Sun ONE Directory Server software.

File Systems: UFS versus Veritas File System (VxFS)

Historically, the choice between using UFS (the default file system type on Solaris OE) and VxFS was clear cut. If a file system was relatively static, extent sizes could be easily calculated and deployed. Performance gains over UFS would be made by using VxFS because seeks to data blocks could be more easily calculated and take less time than inode traversal in UFS. The other major reason for using VxFS was that its metadata was written to a special area on disk known as a journal. Should the system crash causing damage to the file system, the file system could be quickly repaired using this journal. For a UFS-type file system, such a crash would result in a tedious, time-consuming file system check (fsck(1M)).

The major disadvantage with VxFS is the management required to properly maintain the extents on a file system that are continually updated. If this work is ignored, performance can quickly degrade. The other disadvantage is that license fees are required for its use.

Since Solaris 2.6 Operating Environment, Sun Microsystems has invested much time in improving UFS. Indeed, tests done by Rich McDougal and Jim Mauro of Sun Microsystems have shown that UFS performance on Solaris 8 OE approximates very closely with optimally tuned VxFS. Given that UFS does not require any real maintenance and does not cost any money, it seems advantageous to use it in lieu of VxFS. The only other advantage of VxFS, journalling, has also been negated as of the Solaris 7 OE, where UFS can be mounted with the logging option. This performs the same function as journalling, and therefore obviates the need for file system checks, and allows quick rebuilds in the event of a crash. Thus, from a performance, availability, and cost perspective, UFS should be chosen for directory server deployments.

However, the UNIX File System (UFS) performance improvements that were made in the Solaris 9 12/02 OE release change the storage management outlook. Veritas might have been a better choice than UFS in previous versions of the Solaris OE, but this is no longer the case.

A recent study conducted by Sun Microsystems compared the performance of the UFS (Sun's integrated and preferred file system for general purpose Solaris OE software installations) against the Veritas Foundation Suite 3.5 software (Veritas File System, VxFS 3.5 on Veritas Volume Manager, VxVM 3.5). The results of the study reveal the following.

- Logging UFS significantly outperformed VxFS 3.5 in the Solaris 9 12/02 OE release, with no special tuning required on either product.

- The performance stability of Logging UFS and Solaris Volume Manager software is unmatched by the Veritas Foundation Suite 3.5.

- The predictable scalability of Logging UFS and Solaris Volume Manager software could not be duplicated by the Veritas Foundation Suite 3.5

While there was once a compelling reason to use Veritas for performance and feature reasons, nearly all of those reasons are now eliminated, either directly in the UFS, or through the use of other Sun technologies such as Sun StorEdge™ QFS (Quick File System) software and SAMFS (Storage and Archive Manager File System) software.

In addition to the above points, there are a few additional reasons to favor the UFS over VxFS.

- UFS is available at no cost, VxFS is not.

- No VxVM (volume manager) volume needs to be configured as a dump device.

- By default, some VxFS file systems are configured with large file support turned off, which can cause problems in the case of directory server customers when any of their database files hit the 2-Gbyte size limit.

Veritas software might still be a viable choice for use in some Sun™ ONE Directory Server 5.2. environments. However, in new deployments, you should weigh the pros and cons carefully because the latest releases of the Solaris Volume Manager software now compares very favorably with Veritas software.

RAID Explained for Directory Administrators

If you are new to RAID and think that RAID might be an appropriate technology for your directory services environment, the following sections describe RAID technology in further detail.

RAID is an acronym derived from "redundant array of inexpensive disks," although today it is sometimes referred to as "redundant array of *independent* disks" to eliminate the cost element. As either version of the name suggests, RAID's primary purpose is to provide resiliency. Typically, if one disk in the array fails, the data on that disk will not be lost, but still be available on one or more of the other disks in the array. In order to implement this resiliency, RAID has to provide an abstraction that allows multiple disk drives to be configured into a larger virtual disk, usually referred to as a *volume*. This is achieved by concatenating, mirroring, or striping physical disks. Concatenation is where the blocks of one disk logically follow those of another disk. For example, disk 1 has blocks 0-99, disk 2 has blocks 100-199, and so forth. Mirroring is where the blocks of one disk are copied to another and are kept in continuous synchronization. Striping takes the virtual disk layout and, using algorithms, places blocks of data on two or more physical disks. Before considering these methods further it is worth discussing how RAID can be implemented.

Software RAID versus Hardware RAID

RAID is implemented using either software or a hardware RAID manager device. There are advantages and disadvantages for each method:

- Hardware RAID is usually considered more performant because it is implemented using logic gates and hence does not have to make the calculations that software RAID does. Furthermore, hardware RAID is dissociated from the host machine, leaving the host free to get on with the execution of its applications.

- Hardware RAID is generally more expensive than software RAID.
- Software RAID can be more flexible than hardware RAID. For example, a hardware RAID manager is usually associated with a single array of disks or with a prescribed set of arrays, whereas software RAID can encapsulate any number of arrays of disks, or, if desired, just certain disks within an array.

RAID Levels

The following sections discuss RAID configurations, known as levels. The most common RAID levels, 0, 1, 1+0 and 5 are covered in detail, with brief descriptions of the more esoteric levels (RAID 2, 3, and 4).

RAID 0, Striped Volume

Striping (FIGURE 8-6) spreads data across multiple physical disks. The logical disk, or volume is divided into chunks or stripes and then distributed in a round-robin fashion onto physical disks. A stripe is always one or more disk blocks in size, with all stripes of equal size.

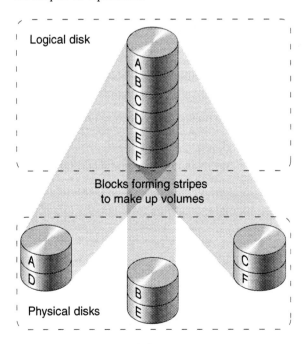

FIGURE 8-6   RAID 0 Disk Striping

The purpose of striping is to gain performance. For example, random writes can be dealt with very quickly because it is likely that the data being written is destined for more than one of the disks in the striped volume; hence, the disks will be able to work in parallel. The same applies to random reads. For large sequential reads and writes, the case might not be quite so clear. However, it has been seen that sequential I/O performance can be improved. For example, when Oracle writes redo logs to disk, it generates many I/O requests which can swamp a single disk controller. If each disk in the striped volume has its own dedicated controller, swamping is far less likely to occur and performance is improved.

The name RAID 0 is a contradiction inasmuch as, on its own, there is no redundancy. If any disk fails in a RAID 0 stripe, the entire logical volume is lost. However, it is worth noting that RAID 0 is the most economical of all RAID levels because all of the disks are used to store data.

RAID 1, Mirrored Volume

The purpose of mirroring (FIGURE 8-7) is to provide redundancy. If one of the disks in the mirror fails, data is still available and processing can continue.

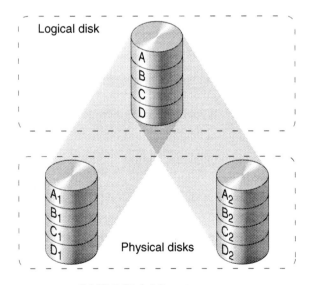

FIGURE 8-7 RAID 1 Disk Mirroring

Disk writes are made to the logical disk volumes are written to both physical disks). Reads made from the logical disk come from one or the other physical disk. Reads are often round-robined between physical disks for performance.

RAID 1+0

RAID 1+0, which is also sometimes referred to as RAID 10, provides the highest levels of performance and resiliency. As a consequence, it is the most expensive level of RAID to implement. FIGURE 8-8 illustrates the RAID 1+0 layout. The data is available with up to three disk failures, as long as each of those disks is from different mirrors.

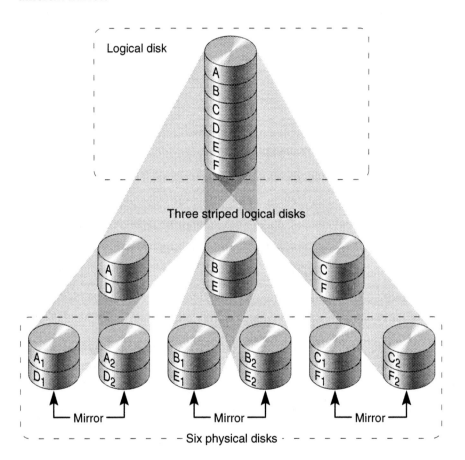

FIGURE 8-8   RAID 1+0 Layout

RAID 0+1

RAID 0+1 is a slightly less resilient version of RAID 1+0. A stripe is created and mirrored. If one or more disks fails on the same side of the mirror, then the data is still available. However, if a disk fails on the other side of the mirror, then the logical volume is lost. This is subtly different than RAID 1+0 because disks on either side can fail simultaneously and data is still available.

RAID 5

RAID 5 is not as resilient as mirroring but still provides redundancy inasmuch as data is still available after a single disk failure. This is accomplished by using a parity stripe and by logically XORing the bytes of the corresponding stripes on the other disks. For example, the parity value for each byte on the '0' stripes in FIGURE 8-9 equals A0 XOR B0 XOR C0 XOR D0 and the parity for the '3' stripes equals A3 XOR C3 XOR D3 XOR E3. Should disk 3 fail, the data for stripes C0, C1, C3 and C4 are recalculated using the data and parity in the corresponding stripes in the remaining disks. Because this calculation is performed on the fly, performance is degraded from that normally achieved with RAID 5.

In normal operation, RAID 5 is less performant than RAID 0, 1+0, and 0+1. This is because a RAID 5 volume must perform four physical I/O operations for every logical write. The old data and parity must be read, two XOR operations must be performed, and the new data and parity must be written. Read operations do not suffer the same and are slightly less performant than a standard stripe using the same number of disks (the RAID 5 volume effectively has one less disk in its stripe because it is given over to parity).

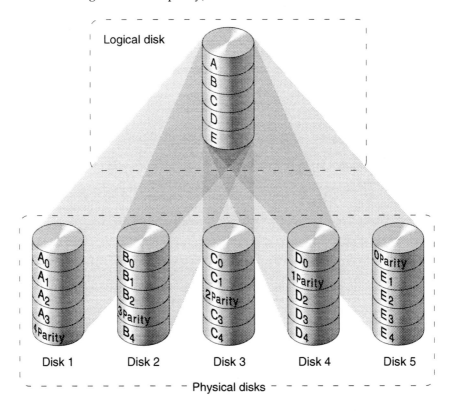

FIGURE 8-9 RAID 5

Given the performance issues of RAID 5, it is generally not a good idea to implement it with software unless the data is read only (or unless there are very few writes to the volume). Disk arrays, such as the Sun StorEdge T3b array which have write caches and fast XOR logic engines mitigate these performance issues, making RAID 5 a cheaper, viable alternative to mirroring.

RAID Levels 2, 3, and 4

RAID levels 2 and 3 are good for large sequential transfers of data (for example, video streaming). Both levels only process one I/O cycle at time, making them inappropriate for applications demanding random access. RAID 2 is implemented using Hamming error correction coding (ECC). This means that three physical disk drives are required to store the ECC data, making it more expensive than RAID 5, but less expensive than RAID 1+0 (so long as more than three disks are in the stripe). RAID 3 uses a bitwise parity method to achieve redundancy. Parity is not distributed as with RAID 5 (FIGURE 8-9), but written to a single dedicated disk.

Unlike RAID levels 2 and 3, RAID 4 uses an independent access technique where multiple disk drives can be accessed simultaneously. It uses parity in a manner similar to RAID 5, except that parity is written to a single disk. As such, the parity disk often becomes a bottleneck because it is accessed for every write and effectively serializes multiple writes.

## CHAPTER 9

Performing Directory Server Benchmarks

This chapter describes the methods and tools used by the Sun Performance Group to characterize the performance of the Sun ONE Directory Server software running on different classes of Sun servers by placing various loads on them, then measuring response time.

We do not publish any benchmark numbers in this chapter. There are too many variables, so we provide the techniques and leave the benchmark results for you to perform, tailored to your environment.

It is also important to note that we do not cover all aspects of a performance benchmark because doing so would consume a book all of its own. Instead, this chapter provides a framework from which you can develop a benchmark testing strategy that best suits your unique environment. The good news is that a recently completed document called *Benchmarking the Sun ONE Directory Server 5.2 with SLAMD and MakeLDIF* is part of the SLAMD documentation set (available for download). Refer to this document for additional Benchmarking information.

This chapter is organized into the following sections:

- "Why Benchmark?" on page 466
- "Creating a Benchmark Configuration" on page 469
- "Creating LDIF for Benchmarks" on page 479
- "Using SLAMD, the Distributed Load Generation Engine" on page 507
- "Directory Server Performance Tuning" on page 541

Why Benchmark?

Before you can identify the ideal hardware and software configuration for your directory services environment, you need to have a general idea, or baseline, of how your hardware and software work together. Benchmarking involves running a set of standard tests in a controlled environment. In this controlled environment, you can manipulate individual components (hardware and software) to see what enhances and what degrades performance, and thereby establish what works best in your environment. Periodic benchmark measurements also keep you apprised of the ongoing performance of your directory services so you can make sure everything is running optimally.

As you will find out as you go through this chapter, performance analysis of the Sun ONE Directory Server software is an immense task, that involves not only throughput and availability but could also include replication, backup and recovery considerations, and many other tasks.

Before we get into the specific details, be aware that this chapter provides one example of performing a benchmark, and that any actual benchmarking should be strongly based on the usage patterns you expect in a production environment.

Directory Server Benchmark Objectives

It is important in any performance benchmark to fully understand what you are testing. With this in mind, let's define some of the performance characteristics of the Sun ONE Directory Server software, and describe the acceptance criteria for performance.

The benchmark testing environment comprises a set of generation programs simulating real-world user interactions with the Sun™ ONE Directory Server. The main objectives are the measurement of the following:

- Vertical scalability of the directory server:

  Identifies when the performance of one instance of the Directory Server reaches a plateau, even when the number of CPUs is increased.

- General scalability of the directory server is identified by:

  - How many SEARCH LDAP operations the Directory Server can handle on the same node. Here, the LDAP client will create a persistent, anonymous connection to the directory server. Entries are then selected based on the approach, which is to use weighted operations that target some entries more frequently than others across the entire set of data in the directory server and retrieved with either a subtree, or substring search on the userid. This is a much closer approximation to real-world usage patterns and can have a significant impact on performance, particularly when the data set is too large to fit entirely in the cache. The search will return the user's email address based on their userid. This is measured in queries per second.

- How many ADD LDAP operations the Directory Server can handle on the same node. The LDAP Client creates a persistent, authenticated connection to the directory server. Whole entries are added to the DIT. This is measured in operations per second.

- How many DELETE LDAP operations the Directory Server can handle on the same node. The LDAP client creates a persistent, authenticated connection to the directory server. Whole entries are deleted in the DIT. This is measured in operations per second.

- How many MODIFY LDAP operations the Directory Server can handle on the same node. The LDAP client creates a persistent, authenticated connection to the directory server. A single attribute is updated in the entries selected across the entire set of data in the directory server. The attribute is indexed with an equality index. This is measured in updates per second.

- How many AUTHENTICATE operations the Directory Server can handle on the same node. The LDAP Client creates a persistent, anonymous connection to the directory server. User authentication involves first performing a search to find the user's entry and then a bind to verify the credentials they have provided. There may also be an additional step whereby a determination is made about whether the user is in a particular group or role. This is measured in authentications per second.

- How many RANDOM LDAP operations the Directory Server can handle on the same node. The LDAP client will create a persistent, anonymous connection to the directory server. A set of the above operations are performed against the entire set of data in the directory server. This is measured in queries per authentications per updates per second.

- How many SEARCH, ADD, DELETE, MODIFY, AUTHNETICATE, RANDOM LDAP operations the directory server can handle on the same node over TLSv1/SSL.

- How many IMPORTs which is measured in the number of entries per second, using the LDIF2DB utility the Directory Server can handle on the same node. An LDAP data interchange format (LDIF) file containing the test entry records is generated by the MakeLDIF file generator application (discussed in detail later) and imported using the Sun™ ONE Directory Server LDIF2DB program.

The acceptance criteria are really determined by the success or failure of a particular test that is described in performance benchmark. Depending upon the performance benchmark test, the success criteria can include: receipt of a particular return code from a server (often expressed as an error message), getting a response from the directory server, or displaying search results correctly on the requesting LDAP client. If the criteria are not met for a given performance test, it is deemed to have failed.

Benchmark Test Harness Description

This section describes the test harness (required functionality addressed by the benchmark tests) for the benchmark performance validation test, so that testing conditions can be distinctly characterized and performance numbers obtained from one run to another are comparable.

Overview of Benchmark Tasks

There are many approaches you can take in performing a benchmark for your directory services. The next few sections of this chapter describe the benchmark process using various tools that Sun has developed to simplify this difficult endeavor. A high-level outline of the process using these tools is as follows:

1. Set up and configure the hardware in your test environment (select, install, and configure the hardware, network and so on).

2. Install and patch the operating system.

3. Use idsktune to ensure that the necessary patches and tuning are performed.

4. Configure and tune your systems (storage, in particular).

5. Install the Sun ONE Directory Server software in your test environment. This includes areas such as directory server configuration, DIT Structure and Database Topology, Data Structure, Indexing, Access Control Structure, and so on.

6. Load directory server data. This chapter uses the MakeLDIF program (covered later in this chapter) to simplify this task.

7. Pretest. The preliminary testing phase consists of verifying that the directory server testing process does indeed work as expected and that it produces valid results. You also need to consider the expected length of each test when computing the time required for this testing.

8. Perform the benchmark testing and tuning. This chapter uses the SLAMD application to quickly and conveniently run various test scenarios.

9. Collect and analyze the benchmark results. This chapter does not list the numerous ways in which the data can be analyzed. In some cases, you might need to experiment with different hardware and software configurations, or different test scenarios, rerunning the benchmark tests until you've reached an optimum configuration. Take throughput, latency and utilization into account.

Creating a Benchmark Configuration

This section describes in detail a sample benchmark configuration. This configuration was actually built and used for testing in our labs at Sun, so you can use it knowing it works. Even if your systems and configuration differ, the following specifications provide an idea of the kinds of things you need to consider when setting up a directory server performance benchmark environment.

Note – The performance benchmark tests are not designed to verify full LDAPv3 protocol conformance.

System Hardware Details

When it comes to selecting your hardware, there are obviously many permutations. The following Sun systems were used in our benchmark configuration:

Benchmark Directory Server

- System Model: Sun Fire™ V880 server
- CPU Type: 900-MHz UltraSPARC® III
- Number of CPUs: 8
- Memory: 48 Gbytes
- Disk Array Type: Four 36-Gbyte 7200-rpm SCSI disks (non RAID) / Eight 36-Gbyte 7200-rpm StorEdge T3 disk subsystem (RAID 1/0)

Benchmark Client

It is possible that when performing a benchmark to run the load generation process, that a single client system will not be sufficient, because the client itself will be the bottleneck rather than the server. Running the load generation process on multiple client systems at the same time will make it possible to generate higher levels of load than can be achieved using only a single client system This can be used to more accurately simulate a production environment that may need to deal with large numbers of clients.

- System Model: Sun Fire 420R system
- CPU Type: 400-MHz UltraSparc II

- Number of CPUs: 4
- Memory: 4 Gbytes

System Software Details

- Standard Solaris 9 OE installation, with the latest operating system patches.
- Solaris kernel and TCP/IP parameters tuned based on tuning recommendations in the Sun™ ONE Directory Server 5.x product documentation, and as recommend by the `idsktune` utility provided with the Sun™ ONE Directory Server 5.x product.
- For a non-RAID volume configuration, the Solaris OE UFS was used.
- For a RAID 1/0 (mirroring and striping) volume configuration, the file system used was Veritas software.

Storage Architecture and Configuration

As discussed in "Selecting Storage for Optimum Directory Server Performance" on page 443, the storage you choose and the way you configure your storage plays a big part in the performance of your directory services.

Given that the Sun StorEdge T3b storage array is the mainstay of the Sun™ ONE Directory Server 5.2 performance testing, a large portion of this section is devoted to its configuration.

This section also describes the volume management software and how it was used with the Sun StorEdge T3b array.

The following basic elements were used in our benchmark configuration:

- Internal SCSI disks were used on the entry-level 280R benchmark configuration for reasons of price.
- The Sun StorEdge T3b arrays were used on all configurations, where the number required was balanced with the available processing power and I/O throughput of the host. The main driver for using Sun StorEdge T3b arrays was price and performance.
- The Sun StorEdge T3b arrays were configured as workgroup arrays. Each array had a single eight-disk hardware RAID 5 layout with 16-Kbyte block size and a hot spare for further resiliency.
- Each array was connected to its own controller at the host machine.
- A software stripe was applied over two or more Sun StorEdge T3b arrays to provide plaiding for better performance.

- Veritas Volume Manager 3.2 for Solaris 9 OE is used for software RAID management because this is most likely to be used by customers.

- UFS was chosen over VxFS as a file system because there are no longer any advantages in using the latter.

- The Network Interconnect was an isolated 100 Mbit/sec switched Ethernet.

The following sections describe how file systems and volumes were laid out on the storage for this benchmark.

Sun™ ONE Directory Server 5.2 Enterprise SCSI Disk Layout

In our performance tests, the following SCSI disks were only used for low-end to mid-range directory server tests:

- Two SCSI disks were used: the root disks which had the directories /ds-data, /ds-logs, /ds-bak and /ds-db directly under root (/). The following describes the purpose of each of the directories created for use with the directory server.

    - /ds-data—Generated LDIF files.

    - /ds-logs—Server logging generates a relatively small amount of write activity, and it is unlikely to saturate any disk. In tests we have performed on understanding the optimal file system layout in the directory server has shown us that there is virtually no difference in performance when placing the logs on a file system shared by other files (the transaction logs) versus isolating them to their own disk. The Sun ONE Directory Server software provides access, error, and audit logs, which feature buffered logging capabilities. Log buffering is only available for the access log. Neither the error log nor the audit log are buffered. As such, enabling audit logging can have a significant impact on update performance.

    - /ds-bak—A backup directory is created, which consists of all the databases, including the changelog database, and the transaction log.

    - /ds-db—Multiple database support, which refers to the database that consists of all .db3 files (id2entry.db3 and index files) for any given suffix (or sub-suffix), allows each database to be put on its own physical disk. The load of the directory server can thus be distributed across multiple sets of database files, which can leverage individual disk subsystems. In order to prevent I/O contention for database operations, place each set of database files, including changelog database files, on a separate disk subsystem.

    - /ds-txnlog—Transaction logs are critical to directory server write performance. The Sun ONE Directory Server software is generally run with Durable Transaction capabilities enabled. When this is the case, a synchronous I/O operation occurs on the transaction log with each add, delete, or modify to the directory. This is a potential I/O bottleneck, as the operation may be blocked when the disk is busy with other directory, application, or Solaris OE operations. Placing transaction logs on an individual disk can provide an increase in write performance to the directory server, especially in high-volume environments. Previous testing has shown us that transaction logging does not incur as much I/O overhead as was previously believed. In fact, it is extremely unlikely that transaction logging will saturate the disk subsystem. However, a database checkpoint can be a very expensive process and can certainly saturate even a T3 array. As such, if only two disks are available, it is much more valuable to isolate the database than to isolate the transaction logs.

- A further disk was partitioned using the format (1M) command to create just one partition. A UFS file system was applied using newfs (1M) command and mounted under /ds-txnlog.

- No volume management was used. The /ds-txnlog partition was separated from the other directories because it was anticipated that most activity would occur in this directory.

Sun™ ONE Directory Server 5.2 Enterprise Volume-Managed Sun StorEdge T3b Array Layout

For low-end to mid-range directory server tests, the following configuration was used:

- Two Sun StorEdge T3b arrays were connected to separate FC-AL controllers on the host.

- A Veritas disk group was created and the hardware RAID 5 LUNs from the arrays were added to it.

- Five striped volumes were created.

- UFS file systems were added to the volumes and the following directories served as mount points: /ds-data, /ds-logs, /ds-bak, /ds-db and /ds-txnlog.

Low-End Configuration

The following diagrams depict the details of how the storage for the E280R/T3b was utilized with the low-end to mid-range servers.

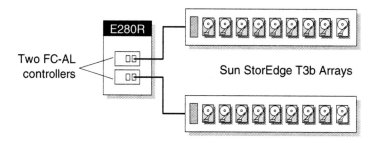

FIGURE 9-1   Cabling of Host Arrays

Mid-Range Configuration

FIGURE 9-2 depicts the details of the logical view of the Sun StorEdge Array Volumes that were utilized with the low-end to mid-range servers.

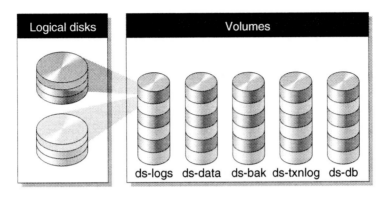

FIGURE 9-2   Logical View of Volumes From the Host

A Veritas disk group was created and the hardware RAID 5 LUNs from the arrays were added. RAID 5 was used because RAID 5 provides redundancy inasmuch as the directory data is still available after a single disk failure. It does this by creating a parity stripe by logically XORing the bytes of the corresponding stripes on the other disks.

In normal operation, RAID 5 is less performant than RAID 0, 1+0, and 0+1. This is because a RAID 5 volume must perform four physical I/O operations for every logical write.

FIGURE 9-3 depicts the details of the physical view of the volume blocks on the Sun StorEdge T3b that were used with the low-end to mid-range servers.

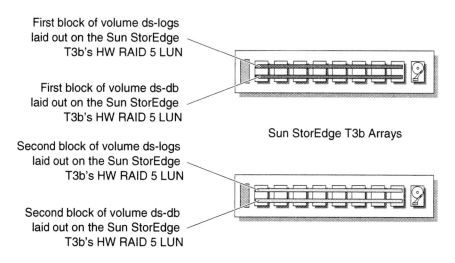

First block of volume ds-logs
laid out on the Sun StorEdge
T3b's HW RAID 5 LUN

First block of volume ds-db
laid out on the Sun StorEdge
T3b's HW RAID 5 LUN

Sun StorEdge T3b Arrays

Second block of volume ds-logs
laid out on the Sun StorEdge
T3b's HW RAID 5 LUN

Second block of volume ds-db
laid out on the Sun StorEdge
T3b's HW RAID 5 LUN

FIGURE 9-3 Physical View of Volume Block on the Sun StorEdge Arrays

The main point to note here is that the volumes are all created from the same two disks, and no attempt is made to separate file systems onto disks with respect to their anticipated loads as per the SCSI disk tests described above. Experience has shown that random data access over aggregated controllers and disks (that is, a stripe) is generally better than that achieved by placing file systems on discrete disks. This makes sense when you consider that not all of the file systems are busy all the time, and any spare capacity in bandwidth and I/O operations can be used for the file systems that are busy.

The Sun Fire v880 Server and Volume-Managed T3b Array Layout

The v880 tests were conducted after the E280R tests. Given that the same (Sun StorEdge T3b array) storage was required, the Sun StorEdge T3b arrays and their associated volumes and file systems were deported from the E280R and imported onto the v880 using Veritas utilities.

FIGURE 9-4 through FIGURE 9-6 show the details of how the storage for the v880/T3b was utilized with the low-end to mid-range servers.

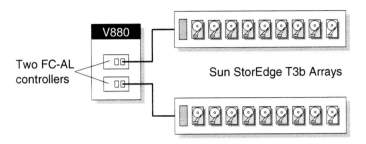

FIGURE 9-4 Cabling of Host Arrays

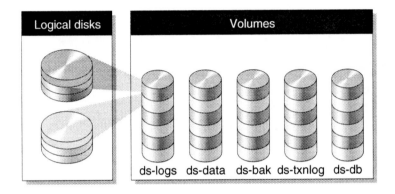

FIGURE 9-5 Logical View of Volumes From the Host

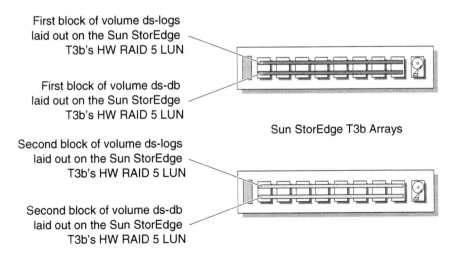

First block of volume ds-logs laid out on the Sun StorEdge T3b's HW RAID 5 LUN

First block of volume ds-db laid out on the Sun StorEdge T3b's HW RAID 5 LUN

Sun StorEdge T3b Arrays

Second block of volume ds-logs laid out on the Sun StorEdge T3b's HW RAID 5 LUN

Second block of volume ds-db laid out on the Sun StorEdge T3b's HW RAID 5 LUN

FIGURE 9-6 Physical View of Volume Blocks on the Sun StorEdge Arrays

E6800 and Volume-Managed T3b Array Layout

The same method of plaiding is used for the E6800 tests, the only difference being that four Sun StorEdge T3b arrays are used instead of two. This means that each software volume comprises blocks from all four arrays. FIGURE 9-7 through FIGURE 9-9 show the details.

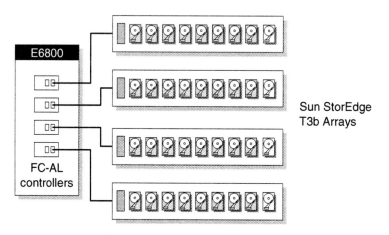

FIGURE 9-7 Cabling of Host Arrays

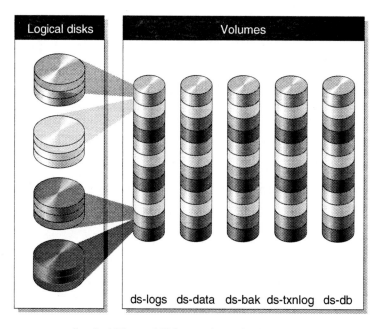

FIGURE 9-8 Logical View of Volumes from the Host

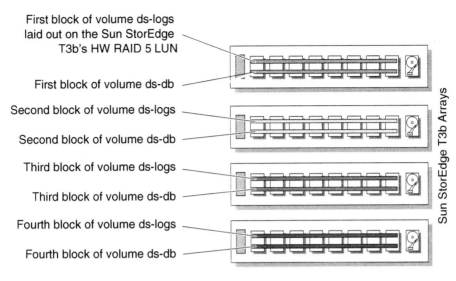

First block of volume ds-logs laid out on the Sun StorEdge T3b's HW RAID 5 LUN

First block of volume ds-db

Second block of volume ds-logs

Second block of volume ds-db

Third block of volume ds-logs

Third block of volume ds-db

Fourth block of volume ds-logs

Fourth block of volume ds-db

Sun StorEdge T3b Arrays

NOte: Other volumes omitted for clarity

FIGURE 9-9 Physical View of Volume Blocks on the Sun StorEdge Arrays

Benchmark DIT Structure and Database Topology

The DIT structure for the benchmark configuration is dc=example,dc=com in which the directory clients and directory server support domain-component-based naming (RFC 2247).

The immediate sub entries of the root suffix are container entries for people and groups. The people branch is loaded with the test data and all performance tests are run against this subtree.

A corresponding database topology consists of one database back end. This holds the people branch, the root suffix and all other branches.

Directory Server Settings

The following directory server options were set:

■ Entries – Each was 2 Kbytes. All were located in a flat entry directory tree that was rooted at
dc=Entries,dc=example,dc=com. The entries are governed by the inetOrgPerson standard ObjectClass.

- Indexing – Enabled for the searchable user attributes (for example, cn, uid, and so forth).

- Bulkload – Import cache set to 2 Gbyte for bulkloading. The bulk load process is not I/O intensive because the cache is heavily used to delay writes to disk. As such, it is unlikely that the addition of RAID will double import times.

- Search – It is good practice to put the entire entry database (if it is able to fit) into the system memory. The in-memory cache is then primed by using the SLAMD LDAP Prime Job, which can use multiple clients and threads per client, as well as priming an attribute into the entry cache. It should be noted that using a subtree "(objectClass=*)" search is an extremely bad method to use when priming the server for a benchmark. It is very slow, uses only a single client and thread, and does not do anything to prime the database cache. To maximize search performance, ensure that sufficient RAM is available for the entries and indexes which are most frequently accessed. The Sun ONE Directory Server 5.2 software supports a 64-bit addressable cache, which makes it potentially possible to use terabytes of memory for caching data.

- Modify – Durability, transactions, referential integrity, and uid uniqueness options are all turned on. These options ensure that all adds, modifies, and deletes are recoverable transactions, and that any DN-valued attributes (pointers) always point to valid entries, and that uniqueness on adds is enforced. These options are recommended for mission critical deployments where disaster recovery is critical. There is a cost associated with these options with regard to write performance when using non-RAID, standard disks. When using high-end disk subsystems, with fast-write caching technology and fast disks, write performance increases significantly. The dominant cost for writing is Database check pointing, which is the most I/O-intensive component and which can saturate a disk. For high performance writes, we always recommend investing in high-end I/O hardware (for example, Sun StorEdge technology, high-end systems from EMC, and so on.) While it is true that you definitely want to have transaction logging and durability enabled, you may find that transaction batching can provide a notable improvement in write performance without any cause for concern about database integrity. It does however introduce a very small chance that changes could be lost in the event of a directory server or system failure (up to transaction-batch-val minus one changes in a maximum of 1000 milliseconds), but in many cases this is an acceptable risk particularly when compared with the performance improvement it can provide. The better the disk subsystem, the higher the write performance. Although disk I/O is generally not the main bottleneck in write performance, spending less time writing data to disk can result in a higher number of updates per second.

Including Directory Server Replication in Your Benchmark

Performing a directory benchmark can be time consuming, and depending on various factors, you may decide not to include directory server replication in your benchmark.

Replication performance is similar to update performance. The dominant issues include disk I/O performance and network bandwidth, end-to-end latency, packet loss, and network congestion. You can consider your modify performance numbers to be similar to the rate for replication over 100 Mbit/sec Ethernet with the same hardware configuration. One very important aspect to note is when performing performance tests involving replication is that it will virtually always be the case that the replication subsystem cannot keep up with the directory server's update rate if you are performing changes as quickly as possible. If you want to prevent divergence, it is recommended that you perform stabilized loads (by inserting a delay between requests) to target a particular number of updates per second at a rate where replication can keep up.

Benchmark Network Topology

An isolated network is used for benchmark best practices; otherwise, you have an unknown variable (network traffic) affecting your test results. For our scenario, a standard 16-port 100 base-T Ethernet hub running at 100 Mbps, full duplex over RJ-45 is used.

Creating LDIF for Benchmarks

The MakeLDIF 1.3 program is an LDIF structure and data generation tool for testing the performance of the Sun™ ONE Directory Server version 5.2. This program provides the ability to generate LDIF files that can be imported into the Sun™ ONE Directory Server for testing purposes. The information that MakeLDIF uses to generate the entries is specified using a template file that can be customized to produce LDIF files that can be used in a test harness for benchmark performance validation tests.

The MakeLDIF program is available for download. See "Obtaining the Downloadable Files for This Book" on page xxvii.

The `MakeLDIF` Program

The MakeLDIF program is a Java-based utility for generating LDIF files. It can be used to generate sample data to import into an LDAP directory server, such as the Sun ONE Directory Server software. Although other utilities exist for this purpose (for example, `dbgen.pl`), `MakeLDIF` offers a number of powerful features not available in other tools:

- `MakeLDIF` is highly customizable. LDIF files are generated based on templates defined by the user. This means that it is easy to include custom attributes, model complex DIT structures, and generate realistic data.

- User-defined templates can use a wide range of tags that make it possible to dynamically generate different kinds of data. In addition, an API is available that makes it possible to define custom tags to handle different kinds of processing not offered by the standard tags.

- `MakeLDIF` is written in Java. This allows it to be used on a wide range of platforms without recompilation like native code, but does not suffer from the lack of large file support in most Perl interpreters.

- `MakeLDIF` makes it possible to provide additional information while it is in the process of generating the LDIF file. For example, you can write an additional file with the list of the DNs of all the entries created, or you can generate a list of potential search filters that can be used to access the data once it has been imported.

`MakeLDIF` can easily be used as a standalone utility for generating LDIF data for a number of purposes. However, because it has been designed for use with the SLAMD distributed load generation engine (covered later in this chapter), it offers a number of features that make it especially useful for generating data to use in a directory server for running many of the SLAMD jobs that work with LDAP directory servers.

Installing `MakeLDIF`

The only requirement for using `MakeLDIF` is that a Java™ runtime environment be present on the target system. `MakeLDIF` has been designed to work with Java versions 1.2 or higher, although Java 1.4 or higher is recommended for best performance.

The following procedure assumes that you have obtained the downloadable `MakeLDIF-1.3.tar.gz` file (see "Obtaining the Downloadable Files for This Book" on page xxvii).

▼ To Install MakeLDIF

1. **Copy the** MakeLDIF-1.3.tar.gz **file onto your system, and into the location in which you wish to install** MakeLDIF.

2. **Uncompress the** MakeLDIF-1.3.tar.gz **file as shown:**

```
$ gunzip MakeLDIF-1.3.tar.gz
```

Note – If the gunzip command is not available on the system, the -d option with the gzip command:
```
$ gzip -d MakeLDIF-1.3.tar.gz
```

3. **Extract the files from the** MakeLDIF-1.3.tar **file as shown:**

This creates a MakeLDIF directory under the current working directory, and all of the associated files are unpacked into that directory.

```
$ /usr/bin/tar -xvf MakeLDIF-1.3.tar
```

Running MakeLDIF

The following examples show you how to run MakeLDIF in various ways, depending on your environment.

The minimum required command line to run MakeLDIF is:

```
$ java -jar MakeLDIF.jar MakeLDIF -t template -o output_filename
```

template is the path to the template file that describes the way in which the LDIF file should be generated and *output_filename* is the path to the output file that is created.

In the following example, the MakeLDIF command uses the template defined in the file example.template and writes the output into the file example.ldif.

```
$ java -jar MakeLDIF.jar -t example.template -o example.ldif
```

If the Java executable is not currently in your path, you can specify the absolute path to the Java executable you wish to use.

```
$ /usr/java/bin/java -jar MakeLDIF.jar -t template -o output_filename
```

If for some reason the Java runtime environment does not support the use of the -jar option, you can instead place the MakeLDIF.jar file in the Java classpath and run it like in the following example:

```
$ java -cp MakeLDIF.jar MakeLDIF -t template -o output_filename
```

Although only the -t and -o options were illustrated, a number of command-line arguments may be used with MakeLDIF to customize its behavior. The full set of supported arguments is shown in TABLE 9-1.

TABLE 9-1 MakeLDIF Options

Option	Description
-f *filename*	Specifies the name of the file containing first names to use in the entry generation process. By default, the MakeLDIF program uses a file named first.names in the current working directory. If a custom first name file is used, it must only contain the first name information with one first name per line.
-l *filename*	Specifies the name of the file containing last names to use in the entry generation process. By default, the MakeLDIF program uses a file named last.names in the current working directory. If a custom last name file is used, it should contain only last name information with one last name per line.
-t *filename*	Specifies the template file that is used to determine how to create the LDIF file. This is a required parameter. The format of the template file is discussed in a later section.
-o *filename*	Specifies the name of the output LDIF file to generate.
-d *filename*	Specifies the name of a file to which the DNs of generated entries are written. This is useful for a number of utilities that can make use of a DN file.
-b *filename*	Specifies the name of a file to which bind information for the generated entries is written. The format requires one user per line, with the DN followed by a tab and the password for the user with that DN.
-L *filename*	Used to specify the name of a file to which login information for the generated entries is written. The format is one user per line, with the login ID followed by a tab and the password for that user.
-i *attr*	Used to specify the name of the attribute that should be used as the login ID. By default, the uid attribute is used as the login ID.
-F *filename*	Specifies that search filters constructed from the generated entries are written to the specified file. You need to use the -T option to specify which filter types to generate.
-T *type*	Specifies the filter types to generate. The format of {type} should be the name of the attribute followed by a colon and a comma-separated list of filter types to create for that attribute. Allowable filter types are eq and sub. Example: -T uid:eq -T cn:eq,sub.
-s *value*	Specifies the seed to use for the random number generator. If no seed is specified, a value is chosen based on the current time. If a positive integer value is given, that is used as the seed to the random number generator. Using the same template file and the same random seed should consistently produce exactly the same LDIF file.

TABLE 9-1   MakeLDIF Options *(Continued)*

Option	Description
-m *value*	Specifies the maximum number of entries that should be written to a single LDIF file. After this number of entries has been written, the current LDIF file is closed and a new file created with a .2 extension. This counter increments sequentially for each new file created.
-x *value*	Specifies the maximum number of entries that should be created for each template below each branch. This can be used to create an example of the LDIF file that would be generated from the provided template to verify that the template syntax is valid.
-w	Specifies that long lines should be wrapped (folded). By default, the entire value of an attribute is written on a single line, which is useful if the LDIF file needs to be processed by another application, but can be difficult to read for long values.
-M	Specifies that a different filter file should be created for each index type for each attribute for which filter information is to be collected.
-S	Specifies that branch entries should be skipped when writing the LDIF information to the requested output file.
-D	Specifies that MakeLDIF should operate in debug mode, which causes it to provide additional debugging information for some errors that may occur while using MakeLDIF.
-H	Displays usage information for the MakeLDIF program.
-V	Displays version information for the MakeLDIF program.

The Template Format

As mentioned earlier, MakeLDIF uses template files to define the way in which the LDIF files should be generated. This is a much more powerful approach than those taken by other LDIF generators, because it allows for a great deal of flexibility without the need to alter any code to produce the desired result.

The template files contain three sections:

- Global replacement variables
- Branch definitions
- Template definitions

The remainder of this section discusses each separately.

Customizing the Template File for `MakeLDIF`

The `MakeLDIF` program uses a template file to customize LDIF files. The use of the template file makes it possible to customize the location and kinds of entries that are generated by the `MakeLDIF` program. Two kinds of entries can be written into a template file: *branch entries* and *template entries*. It is also possible to define variables that may be used throughout the branch and template entries.

Global Replacement Variables

Replacement variables define strings of text that are referenced later in the template file and that are automatically replaced as each line is read into memory.

`MakeLDIF` branch entries example:

```
define suffix=dc=example,dc=com
```

In this example, `define` creates a variable called `suffix` with a value of `dc=example,dc=com` (the first equal sign is the delimiter between the variable name and the value). Once that definition is made, any occurrence of `[suffix]` in the template file is automatically replaced with `dc=example,dc=com`. As noted earlier, this replacement occurs as each line of the token file is read into memory, which means that it is possible to perform these replacements in branch definitions and other places where other tokens are not parsed.

Note – The parsing algorithm used by `MakeLDIF` uses the `[` character to denote the beginning of a replacement variable usage. If it is necessary to have the `[` character included in the template file, but not in the context of a variable reference, it should be escaped with the backslash character (`\ [`). This signifies that the bracket is not to be treated as part of a variable reference. The backslash immediately before the opening bracket is removed.

Branch Entries

Branch entries define a hierarchical branch of a directory server DIT to include in the LDIF file and may be associated with zero or more templates that specify the kinds of entries to create beneath that branch in the hierarchy. A branch entry with no subordinate entries generated by a template might look like:

```
branch: dc=example,dc=com
```

This creates an entry that looks like this:

```
dn: dc=example,dc=com
objectclass: top
objectclass: domain
dc: example
```

The basic structure of the entry is defined by the RDN attribute of dc specified in the DN of the branch definition. MakeLDIF automatically associates the dc RDN attribute with the domain object class. It has similar default definitions for other common RDN attributes in branch entries:

- o -- Creates an entry with the organization object class
- ou -- Creates an entry with the organizationalUnit object class
- c -- Creates an entry with the country object class
- l -- Creates an entry with the locality object class

In addition, it is possible to use any other kind of RDN attribute for a branch entry. For branch entries with an RDN attribute other than one specified above, the entry is created with the extensibleObject object class.

It is possible to customize the information contained in a branch entry by adding the additional information below the branch definition.

Example:

```
branch: dc=example,dc=com
description: This is the description.
```

The preceding example produces an entry that looks like:

```
dn: dc=example,dc=com
objectclass: top
objectclass: domain
dc: example
description: This is the description.
```

Note – All of the branch entries defined so far have created only a single entry in the directory with limited control over the information contained in that entry. However, this does not have to be the case. If one or more subordinateTemplate values are specified, it is possible to create additional entries below this branch.

Example:

```
branch: ou=People,dc=example,dc=com
subordinateTemplate: person:1000
```

The preceding example causes the ou=People,dc=example,dc=com entry to be created, but also creates 1000 entries below it based on the person template. If you wish to have multiple kinds of entries created below a single branch, you can specify each kind of entry with a different subordinateTemplate definition.
For example:

```
branch: ou=People,dc=example,dc=com
subordinateTemplate: person:1000
subordinateTemplate: certificatePerson: 100
```

Branch entries are not limited to just one subordinateTemplate definition. It is possible to specify multiple subordinateTemplate definitions by simply including them on separate lines of the branch definition. The example above creates 1000 entries based on the person template and an additional 100 entries based on the certificatePerson template:

Template Entries

The heart of the MakeLDIF template file are the actual template definitions. Template definitions define the structure of the entries that will be generated. They specify the set of attributes to include in the entries and the types of values that those attributes should contain. The specification of the values is handled through the use of tags that are parsed by MakeLDIF and replaced with the appropriate values for those tags.

A sample template entry might look like this:

```
template: person
rdnAttr: uid
objectclass: top
objectclass: person
objectclass: organizationalPerson
objectclass: inetOrgPerson
givenName: first
sn: last
cn: {givenName} {sn}
initials: {givenName:1}{sn:1}
uid: {givenName}.{sn}
mail: {uid}@[maildomain]
userPassword: <random:alphanumeric:8>
telephoneNumber: <random:telephone>
homePhone: <random:telephone>
pager: <random:telephone>
mobile: <random:telephone>
employeeNumber: <sequential:100000>
street: <random:numeric:5> <file:streets> Street
l: <file:cities>
st: <file:states>
postalCode: <random:numeric:5>
postalAddress: {cn}${street}${l}, {st} {postalCode}
description: This is the description for {cn}.
```

The actual tags that may be included in a template definition are discussed in a later section. However, this example does illustrate some of the flexibility that MakeLDIF offers when generating LDIF data.

The tags contained in this template are parsed and replaced with information appropriate for the specified tag. For example, an entry created using the preceding template might look like this:

```
dn: uid=Neil.Wilson,ou=People,dc=example,dc=com
objectclass: top
objectclass: person
objectclass: organizationalPerson
objectclass: inetOrgPerson
givenName: Neil
sn: Wilson
cn: Neil Wilson
uid: Neil.Wilson
mail: Neil.Wilson@example.com
userPassword: d82fk32n
telephoneNumber: 823-630-8157
```

At the top of the template definition are two lines that provide information about the template itself and are not actually included in entries created from this template. The first line specifies the name of the template. This is the name that is referenced in the subordinateTemplate lines of the branch definition. The second line specifies the name of the attribute that should be used as the RDN attribute for the entry. This attribute must be assigned a value lower in the template definition, and the way in which the value is assigned must ensure that the value is unique.

Note – It is possible to use multivalued RDNs by separating the attribute names with a plus sign, like rdnAttr: uid+employeeNumber.

If multivalued RDNs are used, the combination of RDN attribute values must be unique, but it is possible for one or more of the attributes in the RDN to be non-unique as long as the combination is never duplicated.

In addition to the template and rdnAttr lines, it is also possible to include one or more subordinateTemplate lines. This makes it possible to include dynamically generated entries below other entries that have been dynamically generated (that is, if each user entry has one or more entries below it), and can allow for some rather complex hierarchies. While there is no limit placed on this level of nesting, it is important to ensure that no recursive loops are created by having a subordinateTemplate that either directly or indirectly creates additional entries using the same template.

Template definitions also support the concept of inheritance through the use of the extends keyword. For example, entries generated from the template definition look like this:

```
template: certificatePerson
rdnAttr: uid
extends: person
userCertificate;binary:: <random:base64:1000>
```

Include all of the attributes defined in the person template as well as userCertificate;binary with the specified format. Multiple inheritance is allowed (by including multiple lines with the extends keyword), but as with the subordinateTemplate keyword it is important not to create a recursive loop in which a template could either directly or indirectly extend itself.

Template File Tags

In order to ensure that MakeLDIF provides the ability to generate LDIF files that can be used to simulate a wide variety of deployments, a large number of tags have been defined for use in template definitions. This section describes the standard set of tags that may be used in a MakeLDIF template file. It is possible to use custom tags in template files as well, and the process for developing custom tags is defined in a later section.

Standard Replacement Tags

The tags that may be used in a template file include those in TABLE 9-2:

TABLE 9-2   Supported Tags for MakeLDIF Template Entries

Tag	Description
`<presence:{percent}>`	Indicates how likely the associated attribute value is to be included in any given entry generated from this template. The value specified for {percent} should be an integer between 0 and 100, inclusive. This should only be used with attributes that are not required by the object classes used in the entry. There should also be something included in the value of the attribute that will be present in entries chosen to include this attribute value. The presence tag itself is replaced with an empty string.
`<ifpresent:{attribute}>`	Indicates that this attribute value is to be included in an entry only if the entry contains one or more values for the attribute {attribute}. If this feature is used, {attribute} must be assigned a value in the template before the line that checks for its presence. The ifpresent tag itself is replaced with an empty string.
`<ifpresent:{attribute}:{value}>`	Indicates that this attribute value is to be included in an entry only if the entry contains the attribute {attribute} with a value of {value}. If this feature is used, {attribute} must be assigned a value in the template before the line that checks for its presence. The ifpresent tag itself is replaced with an empty string.
`<ifabsent:{attribute}>`	Indicates that this attribute value is to be included in an entry only if the entry does not contain any values for the attribute {attribute}. If this feature is used, {attribute} must be assigned a value in the template before the line that checks for its presence. The ifabsent tag itself is replaced with an empty string.
`<ifabsent:{attribute}:{value}>`	Indicates that this attribute value is to be included in an entry only if the entry does not contain attribute {attribute} with a value of {value}. If this feature is used, {attribute} must be assigned a value in the template before the line that checks for its presence. The ifabsent tag itself is replaced with an empty string.

TABLE 9-2 Supported Tags for MakeLDIF Template Entries *(Continued)*

Tag	Description
`<first>`	Replaces the tag with a value from the first name file. If both a first name and a last name are included in an entry, the combination of the first and last name is guaranteed to be unique. That is, no two entries in the same LDIF file have the same combination of first and last name values. To guarantee this, it is necessary to ensure that the first name file does not contain any duplicate values, the last name file does not contain any duplicate values, and the first and last name values are used in their entirety. (You cannot use the substring feature of the attribute value replacements of the form {givenName:5} discussed below.)
`<last>`	Replaces the tag with a value from the last name file. If both a first name and a last name are included in an entry, the combination of the first and last name is guaranteed to be unique. That is, no two entries in the same LDIF file have the same combination of first and last name values. To guarantee this, it is necessary to ensure that the first name file does not contain any duplicate values, the last name file does not contain any duplicate values, and the first and last name values are used in their entirety. (You cannot use the substring feature of the attribute value replacements of the form {sn:5} discussed below.)
`<dn>`	Replaces the tag with the distinguished name (DN) of the current entry. For this to work properly, the RDN attribute for the entry must be assigned a value on an earlier line of the template.
`<parentdn>`	Replaced with the DN of the parent entry.
`<ancestordn:{depth}>`	Replaces the tag with the DN of the entry's ancestor at the specified depth. A depth of 1 returns the DN of the entry's immediate parent, a depth of 2 returns the DN of the entry's grandparent, and so on. If the entry does not have an ancestor at the specified depth, the `<ancestordn:{depth}>` tag is replaced with an empty string.
`<exec:{command}>`	Replaces the tag with the information sent to standard output when the command {command} is executed on the system. Because this requires a separate process to be invoked for each entry created using this template, using this tag can make the LDIF generation process proceed much more slowly than if the exec tag is not used.

TABLE 9-2 Supported Tags for MakeLDIF Template Entries *(Continued)*

Tag	Description
`<exec:{command},{arg1},{arg2},...,{argN}>`	Replaces the tag with the information sent to standard output when the command {command} is executed on the system with the provided set of arguments. Because this requires a separate process to be invoked for each entry created using this template, using this tag can make the LDIF generation process proceed much more slowly than if the exec tag is not used.
`<random:chars:{characters}:{length}>`	Replaces the tag with {length} characters from the character set {characters}. The character set {characters} can contain any character other than the colon.
`<random:chars:{characters}:{minLength}:{maxLength}>`	Replaces the tag with between {minLength} and {maxLength} (inclusive) characters from the character set {characters}. The character set {characters} can contain any character other than the colon.
`<random:alpha:{length}>`	Replaces the tag with a string of {length} randomly chosen alphabetic characters.
`<random:alpha:{minLength}:{maxLength}>`	Replaces the tag with a string of between {minLength} and {maxLength} (inclusive) randomly chosen alphabetic characters.
`<random:numeric:{length}>`	Replaces the tag with a string of {length} randomly chosen numeric digits.
`<random:numeric:{minValue}:{maxValue}>`	Replaces the tag with an integer value between {minValue} and {maxValue} (inclusive). The integer value is not padded with leading zeroes, so if that is desired the `<random:numeric:{minValue}:{maxValue}:{minLength}>` tag should be used.
`<random:numeric:{minValue}:{maxValue}:{minLength}>`	Replaces the tag with an integer value between {minValue} and {maxValue} (inclusive). If the integer value chosen contains less than {minLength} digits, it is padded with leading zeroes to the required minimum length.
`<random:numeric:{length}>`	Replaces the tag with {length} randomly chosen alphanumeric characters.
`<random:numeric:{minValue}:{maxValue}>`	Replaces the tag with between {minLength} and {maxLength} (inclusive) randomly chosen alphanumeric characters.
`<random:hex:{length}>`	Replaces the tag with {length} randomly chosen hexadecimal digits.
`<random:hex:{minLength}:{maxLength}>`	Replaces the tag with between {minLength} and {maxLength} (inclusive) randomly chosen hexadecimal digits.

TABLE 9-2   Supported Tags for MakeLDIF Template Entries *(Continued)*

Tag	Description
`<random:base64:{length}>`	Replaces the tag with {length} randomly chosen characters from the base64 character set. If {length} is not a multiple of 4, the generated value is padded with equal signs so that the total length is a multiple of 4 as per the base64 specification.
`<random:base64:{minLength}:` `{maxLength}>`	Replaces the tag with between {minLength} and {maxLength} (inclusive) randomly chosen characters from the base64 character set. If the selected length is not a multiple of 4, the generated value is padded with equal signs so that the total length is a multiple of 4 as per the base64 specification.
`<random:telephone>`	Replaces the tag with a string of randomly chosen numeric digits in the form `123-456-7890`. This uses a U.S.-style telephone number, but it is possible to generate telephone numbers in other formats by combining other kinds of tags (for example, to generate a telephone number in the UK format, you could use +44 `<random:numeric:4>` `<random:numeric:6>`).
`<random:month>`	Replaces the tag with the name of a randomly chosen month.
`<random:month:{length}>`	Replaces the tag with the first {length} characters from the name of a randomly chosen month.
`<guid>`	Replaces the tag with a GUID (globally unique identifier) value containing hexadecimal digits in the form `12345678-90ab-cdef-1234- 567890abcdef`. GUID values should be unique within the same LDIF file.
`<sequential>`	Replaces the tag with a sequentially increasing numeric value. The first entry generated using this tag has a value of 0, the second a value of 1, and so on. Sequential counters are maintained on a per-attribute and per-template basis, so it is possible to use multiple sequential counters in different attributes of the same entry without impacting each other. It is also possible to use sequential counters for the same attribute in different templates without impacting each other. However, it is not possible to use multiple sequential counters for the same attribute in the same template without them impacting each other.

TABLE 9-2 Supported Tags for MakeLDIF Template Entries *(Continued)*

Tag	Description
`<sequential:{initial}>`	Replaces the tag with a sequentially increasing numeric value, starting at specified initial value {initial}. The first entry generated using this tag has a value of {initial}, the second a value of {initial}+1, and so on. Sequential counters are maintained on a per-attribute and per-template basis, so it is possible to use multiple sequential counters in different attributes of the same entry without impacting each other. It is also possible to use sequential counters for the same attribute in different templates without impacting each other. However, it is not possible to use multiple sequential counters for the same attribute in the same template without them impacting each other.
`<list:{value1},{value2},...,{valueN}>`	Replaces the tag with a randomly chosen value from the provided comma-delimited list. Each value in the list provided has an equal chance of being selected.
`<list:{value1}:{weight1},{value2}:{weight2},...,{valueN}:{weightN}>`	Replaces the tag with a randomly chosen value from the provided comma-delimited weighted list. The weight associated with each list item determines how likely that value is to be chosen. A list item with a weight of 2 is twice as likely to be chosen as an item with a weight of 1. The weights specified must be positive integers.
`<file:{filename}>`	Replaces the tag with a randomly chosen value from the specified file. There should be one value per line of the file. It is not possible to assign weights to the values in the file, but a value can be weighted artificially by including it in the file multiple times. For example, a value that appears in the file three times is three times as likely to be chosen as a value that appears only once.
`<base64:{value}>`	Replaces the tag with the base64-encoded representation of {value}. The value {value} is converted into a byte array using the UTF-8 character set, and that byte array is base64 encoded.
`<base64:{charset}:{value}>`	Replaces the tag with the base64-encoded representation of {value}. The value {value} is converted into a byte array using the rules of the Java character set {charset}, and that byte array is base64 encoded. See the Java API documentation to determine the names of the character sets that may be used.

TABLE 9-2   Supported Tags for MakeLDIF Template Entries *(Continued)*

Tag	Description
`<loop:{lowerBound}:{upperBound}>`	Creates (`{upperBound}` - `{lowerBound}` + 1) copies of this line with this tag replaced in each copy with a sequentially incrementing number starting at `{lowerBound}` in the first copy, (`{lowerBound}` + 1) in the second copy, and so on, so that in the last copy this tag is replaced with `{upperBound}`. It is possible to include multiple loop tags on the same line (even with different `{lowerBound}` values), but only the first tag is used to determine the number of copies to create.
`<custom:{class}>`	Replaces the tag with the value generated by invoking the custom tag whose implementation is provided in the class `{class}`. The provided class name `{class}` must be fully qualified (that is, including the package name if applicable), and that class must exist in the classpath used to run MakeLDIF.
`<custom:{class}:{arg1},{arg2},...,{argN}>`	Replaces the tag with the value generated by invoking the custom tag whose implementation is provided in the class `{class}` with the specified argument list. The provided class name `{class}` must be fully qualified (that is, including the package name if applicable), and that class must exist in the classpath used to run MakeLDIF.

Attribute Value Reference Tags

In addition to the standard replacement tags listed in TABLE 9-2, it is possible to use tags that reference the values of other attributes in the same entry. These tags are called attribute value reference tags and they may be used by simply enclosing the name of the desired attribute in curly braces. When these tags are encountered in the template, they are replaced with the value of the specified attribute. If the specified attribute has not been assigned a value for the current entry, this tag is replaced with an empty string.

For example, consider the following excerpt from a template:

```
givenName: <first>
sn: <last>
uid: {givenName}.{sn}
cn: {givenName} {sn}
mail: {uid}@example.com
```

If the value chosen for the first name is `Neil` and the last name is `Wilson`, the following LDIF output would result:

```
givenName: Neil
sn: Wilson
uid: Neil.Wilson
cn: Neil Wilson
mail: Neil.Wilson@example.com
```

Note – In order for this to work properly, it is necessary to assign a value to an attribute before it may be referenced in this manner. If, for example, the definition of the `mail` attribute had appeared before the definition of the `uid` attribute, the resulting email address would have been `@example.com` because the `{uid}` tag would not have a value and therefore would have been replaced with an empty string.

It is also possible to place a colon after the name of the attribute followed by a positive integer value `{length}`. This causes at most the first `{length}` characters of the value from the specified attribute to be used instead of the entire value. For example, the template excerpt:

```
givenName: <first>
sn: <last>
initials: {givenName:1}{sn:1}
```

Would produce the following LDIF for a first name of `Neil` and a last name of `Wilson`:

```
givenName: Neil
sn: Wilson
initials: NW
```

If the specified `{length}` is longer than the value of the named attribute, the entire value of the attribute is used and no padding is added.

Tag Evaluation Order

The order in which tags are evaluated while parsing a template definition is important because changing the evaluation order can change the way that the output is produced. Although it is not possible for the end user to change this evaluation order, it is important to understand how template definitions are processed so that LDIF files are generated in the appropriate manner.

In most cases, it is not possible to nest tags. That is, the output of one tag cannot be used as input to another. For example, consider the following MakeLDIF tag evaluation order:

```
description: <random:alpha:<random:numeric:5:10>>
```

One might hope that this would first evaluate the `<random:numeric:5:10>` tag to create a numeric value between 5 and 10 (for example, 7) and then evaluate the outer tag as `<random:alpha:7>`. However, this is not the case. Because of the way that MakeLDIF parses template definitions, this fails because it tries to interpret `<random>` as an integer value. Fortunately, this is not a problem in most cases because enough variations of the standard replacement tags have been provided to deal with this. For example, to achieve the desired result attempted by the above template line, you can instead use:

```
description: <random:alpha:5:10>
```

For the purposes of this discussion, MakeLDIF parses template files in the following order:

1. All standard replacement tags other than base64, custom, and loop.

2. All attribute value reference tags.

3. The base64 standard replacement tags (`<base64:{value}>` and `<base64:{charset}:{value}>`).

4. The custom standard replacement tags (`<custom:{class}>` and `<custom:{class}: {arg1},{arg2},...,{argN}>`).

5. The loop standard replacement tag (`<loop:{lowerBound}:{upperBound}>`).

Based on this order of operations, any tag at one level may be used as input to any tag at a higher level. For example, the following is legal because base64 standard replacement tags are evaluated after attribute value reference tags:

```
description:: <base64:{givenName}>
```

Defining Custom Tags

One of the benefits of MakeLDIF is the large number of tags it provides that can be used to customize the process of creating LDIF files. However, even with the large set of tags provided, it may be desirable to extend the functionality even further. This is possible through the use of custom tags.

Custom tags can be easily defined by creating a Java class that extends the abstract CustomTag class. This class defines three methods:

- public void initialize() -- Provides the ability to perform any one-time initialization that may be necessary when this tag is first created. This is an optional step, and by default no initialization is performed.

- public void reinitialize() -- Provides the ability to perform additional initialization every time the template is used to start processing a new branch. This is also optional, and by default no reinitialization is performed.

- public String generateOutput(String[] tagArguments) -- Generates the output that should appear whenever this custom tag is invoked in the template. The provided set of arguments can be used to customize the output as necessary. This method must be implemented in all custom tags.

A Sample Custom Tag Implementation

```
# MakeLDIF Custom Tag Usage
#
/**
* This class provides an implementation of a MakeLDIF custom tag
that will be
* used to calculate the sum of all the integer values provided as
arguments to
* the tag.
*/
public class SumCustomTag
extends CustomTag
/**
* Performs any necessary one-time initialization that should be
performed
* when this custom tag is first created. In this case, no
initialization is
* performed.
*/
public void initialize()
{
// No implementation required.
}


/**
* Performs any initialization that should be performed each time
the LDIF
* generation starts working on a new branch (e.g., to reset any
internal
* variables that might have been in use). In this case, no
reinitialization
* is performed.
*/
public void reinitialize()
{
// No implementation required.
}

{
/**
* Parses the list of arguments, converts the values to integers,
and totals
* those values.
*
* @param tagArguments The arguments containing the numeric values
to be
```

```
* totaled.
*
* @return The string representation of the total of all the
argument values.
*/
public String generateOutput(String[] tagArguments)
{
int sum = 0;
for (int i=0; i < tagArguments.length; i++)
{
sum += Integer.parseInt(tagArguments[i]);
}
return String.valueOf(sum);
}
}
```

Using the Example Custom Tag

Once the custom tag class has been implemented and compiles properly, it may be used by specifying that class in a custom tag in the template file. For example, to use the custom tag we just implemented, something like the following could be placed in the template file:

```
cn: <custom:SumCustomTag:1,2>
```

When MakeLDIF is run using a template that contains this definition, the generateOutput method of the SumCustomTag class is invoked and produces output containing:

```
cn: 3
```

Because static values were provided as arguments to the tag, the output is exactly the same every time. This is not all that useful in this case, but it doesn't have to be that way. As indicated earlier, custom tags are parsed after most other kinds of tags. This means that it is possible to use something like:

```
cn: <custom:SumCustomTag:<random:numeric:5>,<random:numeric:5>>
```

There, the output from other tags is used as arguments to the custom tag. In this case, each `<random:numeric:5>` tag generates a five-digit integer, and the custom tag adds those values together. Unlike the previous example, the output in this case may be different for each entry because the arguments are randomly chosen values. Of course, even then this particular custom tag is not very useful, but it is a simple example that can be used as the foundation for creating more useful custom tags for real-world purposes.

Using and Automating `MakeLDIF`

Once you understand how to use the `MakeLDIF` application, you can automate the process of generating test data for a benchmark.

As a summary, the `MakeLDIF` application is recommended for use as an LDIF structure and data generation tool for testing the performance of the Sun™ ONE Directory Server 5.x (or any other directory server for that matter). `MakeLDIF` provides the ability to generate LDIF files that can be imported into the Sun™ ONE Directory Server 5.x environment. The information needed to generate the entries is specified using a template file that can be customized to produce LDIF files for use as a test harness for directory server benchmark performance validation tests.

TABLE 9-3 lists examples of the layout and files that can be used in benchmark performance validation tests. Specific examples follow the table.

TABLE 9-3   BenchMark Performance Validation Tests 250k

Sun ONE Directory Server 5.x Software	Files and LDIF Templates (250 Kbyte Entries)
Makefiles	Makefile
`MakeLDIF` User Defined Template	Template
Sample LDIF Data	`example-data.ldif`

Sample Root Makefile

```
# Copyright © ©2003 Sun Microsystems, Inc.  All rights reserved.
# Use is subject to license terms.
#
#ident "@(#)Makefile    1.0 08/01/03 SMI"
#
# Root Makefile for 250k.ldif file
#
OUTDIR=bp250k-data

TARGET=bp250k

all: output_dir $(TARGET)

clean:  output_dir
        @-if [ -d $(OUTDIR) ]; then \
        /usr/bin/rm -rf $(OUTDIR); fi

bp100k:

@echo Building...
@-#java -cp MakeLDIF.jar MakeLDIF -t bp250k.template -o $@.ldif
@echo Moving LDIF Files...
@echo Please wait...
@-/usr/bin/mv $@.ldif $(OUTDIR)

output_dir:
        @-if [ ! -d $(OUTDIR) ]; then mkdir -p $(OUTDIR); fi
```

Makefile and Generating the Filter File

```
# Copyright © 2003 Sun Microsystems, Inc.  All rights reserved.
# Use is subject to license terms.
#
#ident "@(#)Makefile    1.0 08/01/03 SMI"
#
# Root Makefile for 250k.ldif file
#
OUTDIR=bp250k-data

TARGET=bp250k

all: output_dir $(TARGET)

clean:  output_dir
        @-if [ -d $(OUTDIR) ]; then \
        /usr/bin/rm -rf $(OUTDIR); fi

bp100k:

#
# Generate the filter file with (caution, its VERY slow)
#
@echo Building...
@-#java -cp MakeLDIF.jar MakeLDIF -t bp250k.template -o $@.ldif \
-T uid:eq -T sn:eq -T givenName:eq -T cn:eq -T cn:sub -F $@-filter-
file.ldif
@echo Moving LDIF Files...
@echo Please wait...
@-/usr/bin/mv $@.ldif $(OUTDIR)
@-#/usr/bin/mv $@-filter-file.ldif $(OUTDIR)

output_dir:
        @-if [ ! -d $(OUTDIR) ]; then mkdir -p $(OUTDIR); fi
```

The following code box shows an example of running the Makefile without the filter option and the output:

```
Building 250k LDIF File...
Processed 250000 entries
250000 entries written to bp250k.ldif
Moving LDIF file to bp250k-data location...
Done.
```

The following code box shows an example of running the Makefile with the filter option and the output:

```
Building 250k LDIF File...
Processed 250000 entries
250000 entries written to bp250k.ldif
Writing filters to bp205k-filter-file.ldif
Wrote 250000 equality filters for uid
Wrote 250000 equality filters for givenname
Wrote 250000 equality filters for sn
Wrote 2479 substring filters for cn
Moving LDIF files to bp250k-data location...
Done.
```

The previous examples showed how you can automate the process of generating LDIF data sets. It is also possible to automate the process of building of larger data sets using a global Makefile.

Example:

```
# Copyright © 2003 Sun Microsystems, Inc.  All rights reserved.
# Use is subject to license terms.
#
#ident "@(#)Makefile    1.0 08/01/03 SMI"
#
# Global Makefile
#
SUBDIRS= bp250k-src bp500k-src bp1M-src bp5M-src \
bp10M-src bp25M-src bp50M-src

all:
#all clean:
        @for i in $(SUBDIRS) ; \
        do \
          cd $$i ; \
          echo "=================================" ; \
          echo " Current directory: $$i" ; \
          echo "=================================" ; \
          if [ -f makefile ] ; \
          then \
            $(MAKE) -f makefile $@ ; \
          else \
            $(MAKE) -f Makefile $@ ; \
          fi ; \
          cd .. ; \
        done
```

Below is an example of running the global Makefile and the output:

```
====================================
 Current directory: bp250k-src
====================================
Building 250k LDIF File...
Processed 250000 entries
250000 entries written to bp250k.ldif
Moving LDIF file to bp250k-data location...
Done.
====================================
 Current directory: bp500k-src
====================================
Building 500k LDIF File...
Processed 500000 entries
250000 entries written to bp500k.ldif
Moving LDIF file to bp500k-data location...
Done.
====================================
 Current directory: bp1M-src
====================================
Building 1M LDIF File...
Processed 1000000 entries
250000 entries written to bp1M.ldif
Moving LDIF file to bp1M-data location...
Done.

etc...
etc...
```

Using SLAMD, the Distributed Load Generation Engine

The directory server performance benchmark testing in this section is accomplished using the SLAMD application, which is a tool developed by Sun engineering for benchmarking the Sun™ ONE Directory Server product. It is important to understand that SLAMD was not designed to be used only for testing directory servers. It was intentionally designed in a somewhat abstract manner so that it could be used equally well for load testing and benchmarking virtually any kind of network application. Although most of the jobs provided with SLAMD are intended for use with LDAP directory servers, there are also jobs that can be used for testing the messaging, calendar, portal, identity, and web servers.

The SLAMD environment is in essence a distributed computing system with a primary focus on load generation and performance assessment. Each unit of work is called a job, and a job may be processed concurrently on multiple systems, each of which reports results back to the SLAMD server where those results can be viewed and interpreted in a number of ways. The SLAMD environment comprises many components, each of which has a specific purpose. The components of the SLAMD environment include:

- The core server
- The configuration handler
- The scheduler
- The logger
- The client listener
- The job cache
- SLAMD clients
- The administrative interface
- The access control manager

In this next section we take a look at SLAMD, which is an extremely useful Java application for benchmarking the Sun™ ONE Directory Server 5.x, but not limited to the Sun™ ONE Directory Server. This application is available for download. See "Obtaining the Downloadable Files for This Book" on page xxvii.

SLAMD Overview

The SLAMD Distributed Load Generation Engine is a Java-based application designed for stress testing and performance analysis of network-based applications. Unlike many other load generation utilities, SLAMD provides an easy way to schedule a job for execution, either immediately or at some point in the future, have that job information distributed to a number of client systems, and then executed concurrently on those clients to generate higher levels of load and more realistic usage patterns than a standalone application operating on a single system. Upon completing the assigned task, the clients report the results of their execution back to the server where the data is combined and summarized. Using an HTML-based administrative interface, you can view results, either in summary form or in varying levels of detail. You may also view graphs of the statistics collected and may even export that data into a format that can be imported into spreadsheets or other external applications for further analysis.

The SLAMD environment is highly extensible. Custom jobs that interact with network applications and collect statistics can be developed either by writing Java class files or executed using the embedded scripting engine. The kinds of statistics that are collected while jobs are being executed can also be customized. The kinds of information that can be provided to a job to control the way in which it operates is also configurable. Although it was originally designed for assessing the performance of LDAP directory servers, SLAMD is well suited for interacting with any network-based application that uses either TCP- or UDP-based transport protocols.

This section provides information about installing and running the components of the SLAMD environment. Additional topics, like developing custom jobs for execution in the SLAMD environment, are not covered in this book.

Installation Prerequisites

Before SLAMD may be installed and used, a number of preliminary requirements must be satisfied:

- All components of the SLAMD environment have been written in Java and therefore a Java runtime environment is required to use them. All components have been developed using the Java 1.4.0 specification. Version 1.4.0 or higher of the runtime should be installed on the system that hosts the SLAMD server, as well as all systems used to run the SLAMD client. Any system used to develop custom jobs for execution in the SLAMD environment should have the Java 1.4.0 or higher SDK installed.

Note – Both the Java runtime environment and the Java SDK may be obtained online from `http://java.sun.com/`.

- Some aspects of job execution are time sensitive, and differences in system clocks can cause inaccuracies in the results that they can obtain. Therefore, time synchronization should be used on all systems in the SLAMD environment to ensure that such clock differences do not occur.

- The communication that occurs between clients and the SLAMD server requires that the host name of those systems be available. The addresses of all client systems must be resolvable by both the client and server systems through DNS or some other mechanism like the /etc/hosts file.

- Much of the configuration and all of the job data for the SLAMD environment is stored in an LDAP directory server. Therefore, a directory server must be accessible by the system that acts as the SLAMD server. SLAMD has been designed and tested with the iPlanet Directory Server 5.1 and the Sun ONE Directory Server 5.2 software.

Note – The entries that store information about scheduled jobs may be quite large. It is therefore necessary to ensure that the configuration directory is properly tuned so it can properly handle these entries.

- The HTML that makes up the SLAMD administrative interface is dynamically generated using Java servlet 1.2 technology. A servlet engine is required to provide this capability. By default, SLAMD is provided with the Apache Tomcat servlet engine and this engine is quite capable of providing the administrative interface. However, it should be possible to use any compliant servlet engine to host that interface. In addition to Tomcat, SLAMD has been tested with the Sun™ ONE Web Server 6.0 SP3 software.

- Nearly all interaction with the SLAMD server is performed through an HTML interface. A Web browser must be installed on all systems that access the administration interface. SLAMD has been tested with Netscape and Mozilla, but the administrative interface has been designed in accordance with the HTML 4.01 specification and therefore any browser capable of rending such content may be used. Even text-based browsers are quite capable of performing all administrative tasks.

Note – If SLAMD is to be used in a purely text-based environment, it is recommended that the Links browser be installed on systems that need to access the administration interface. Links is a text-based browser that is similar to the better-known lynx (available at http://lynx.browser.org/), but provides better support for rendering tables, which are used throughout the SLAMD administrative interface. See http://links.sourceforge.net/ for more information.

Installing the SLAMD Server

Once all the prerequisites have been filled, it is possible to install the SLAMD server.

The following procedure assumes that you have acquired the `slamd-1.5.1.tar.gz` file. It is available as a downloadable file for this book (see "Obtaining the Downloadable Files for This Book" on page xxvii).

▼ To Install the SLAMD Server

1. **Copy the `slamd-1.5.1.tar.gz` file onto the server system, and into the location in which you wish to install SLAMD.**

2. **Uncompress the `slamd-1.5.1.tar.gz` file as shown:**

```
$ gunzip slamd-1.5.1.tar.gz
```

Note – If the `gunzip` command is not available on the system, the `-d` option with the `gzip` command:
```
$ gzip -d slamd-1.5.1.tar.gz
```

3. **Extract the files from the `slamd-1.5.1.tar` file as shown:**

```
$ /usr/bin/tar -xvf slamd-1.5.1.tar
```

All files are placed in a subdirectory named `slamd`.

Note – If you wish to use a name other than `slamd` for the base directory, simply rename that directory immediately after extracting the installation archive. However, once the SLAMD server has been started, the path in which it is installed should not be changed.

4. **Change to the newly created `slamd` directory.**

5. **Edit the** `bin/startup.sh` **shell script.**

This shell script is used to start the SLAMD server and the administrative interface, but it must first be edited so that the settings are correct for your system. Set the value of the `JAVA_HOME` variable to the location in which the Java 1.4.0 or higher runtime environment that you have. You may also edit the `INITIAL_MEMORY` and `MAX_MEMORY` variables to specify the amount of memory in megabytes that the SLAMD server and the administrative interface are allowed to consume. Comment out, or remove the two lines at the top of the file that provide the warning message indicating that the startup file has not been configured.

6. **Edit the** `bin/shutdown.sh` **shell script.**

This shell script is used to stop the SLAMD server and the administrative interface. Set the value of the `JAVA_HOME` variable to the location in which the Java 1.4.0 or higher runtime has been installed, and comment out, or remove the two lines at the top of the file that provide the warning message indicating that the shutdown file has not been configured.

7. **Execute the** `bin/startup.sh` **shell script to start the Tomcat servlet engine and make the SLAMD administrative interface available.**

8. **Start a Web browser and access the SLAMD administrative interface.**

The SLAMD administrative interface is available at: `http://`*address*`:8080/slamd`, where *address* is the IP address or DNS host name of the SLAMD server machine. A page is displayed indicating that the SLAMD server is unavailable because it has not yet been configured.

9. **Click on the Initialization Parameters link to a page on which it is possible to specify the configuration directory settings.**

The configuration directory is the LDAP directory server that is used to store much of the configuration and all of the job data for jobs that have been scheduled.

10. **Click on the Config Directory Address link.**

You are presented with a form that allows you to specify the address to use for the configuration directory server.

The address must be entered as either an IP address or a host name, as long as the SLAMD server machine can contact the configuration directory machine using the provided address. Repeat this process for the remaining configuration directory settings. TABLE 9-4 describes the kind of values that should be used by each:

TABLE 9-4   SLAMD Configuration Parameters

Parameter	Description
Config Directory Address	Specifies the address that should be used to contact the configuration directory server.
Config Directory Port	Specifies the port number that should be used to contact the configuration directory server.
Config Directory Bind DN	The DN of the user that should be used to bind to the configuration directory server. This DN must have full read and write permissions (including the ability to add and remove entries) for the portion of the directory that is to hold the SLAMD configuration data.
Config Directory Bind Password	The password for the configuration bind DN.
Configuration Base DN	The location in the configuration directory under which all SLAMD information is stored. If this entry does not exist, the SLAMD server can create it provided that the DN specified is under an existing suffix in the configuration directory.
Use SSL for Config Directory SSL Key Store Location SSL Key Store Password SSL Trust Store Location SSL Trust Store Password	Settings that control whether the communication between the SLAMD server and the configuration directory is encrypted with SSL. It is recommended that the initial configuration be completed without SSL. See a later section for information on configuring SLAMD for use with SSL.

11. **Click the Add SLAMD Schema button at the bottom of the Initialization Settings page.**

This communicates with the configuration directory server, finds the schema subentry, and adds the custom SLAMD schema definitions over LDAP while the server is online. This schema information must be added to the configuration directory before SLAMD can use it to store configuration and job information.

Note – If you prefer, you can add the schema information to the directory manually rather than over LDAP. A file containing the SLAMD schema definitions is included in the installation archive as `conf/98slamd.ldif`.

12. **Click the Add SLAMD Config button at the bottom of the Initialization Settings page.**

    This automatically adds all required entries to allow that directory instance to be used as the configuration directory for SLAMD. All information added to the directory is at or below the configuration base DN.

    Note – At least one entry in the hierarchy of the configuration base DN must already exist in the directory server before the configuration may be added to it. For example, if the directory is configured with a suffix of `dc=example,dc=com` and the configuration base DN is specified as `ou=SLAMD,ou=Applications,dc=example,dc=com`, then at least the `dc=example,dc=com` entry must already be present in the directory server before attempting to add the SLAMD configuration data. Any entries between the directory suffix and the SLAMD configuration base DN that are not present in the directory are automatically added when the Add SLAMD Config button is pressed.

13. **Click the Test Connection button at the bottom of the Initialization Settings page.**

    This establishes a connection to the configuration directory server, verifies that the bind DN and password provided are correct, and verifies that the SLAMD schema and configuration entries have been added to that directory. If all tests succeed, a message is displayed indicating that it is suitable for use as the SLAMD configuration directory. If any failure occurs, details about that failure are displayed so that the problem may be corrected.

14. **Follow the SLAMD Server Status link on the left side of the page.**

    This page normally displays a significant amount of information about the SLAMD server, including the number and types of jobs defined, the number of clients connected, and statistics about the Java environment in which SLAMD is running. However, when the SLAMD server is offline, much of this information is not available.

15. **Click the Start SLAMD button in the Server Status section and when prompted, click Yes to provide confirmation for the startup.**

    If all goes well, the SLAMD server is started properly and the full set of SLAMD functions is made available.

SLAMD Clients

Because SLAMD is a distributed load generation engine, the SLAMD server itself does not execute any of the jobs. Rather, the actual execution is performed by SLAMD clients, and the server merely coordinates the activity of those clients. Therefore, before any jobs can be executed, it is necessary to have clients connected to the server to run those jobs.

The client application communicates with the SLAMD server using a TC-based protocol. Therefore, it is possible to install clients on different machines than the one on which the SLAMD server is installed. In fact, this is recommended so the client and server do not compete for the same system resources, which could interfere with the ability of the client to obtain accurate results. Further, it is possible to connect to the SLAMD server with a large number of clients to process multiple jobs concurrently. In such cases, it is best to have those clients distributed across as many machines as possible to avoid problems in which the clients are competing with each other for system resources.

The following procedure assumes that you have the SLAMD client package called `slamd_client-1.5.1.tar.gz`. This file is available for download in two ways:

- As part of the `slamd-1.5.1.tar.gz` downloadable file
- Downloadable in a compressed file that only contains the SLAMD client software (`slamd_client-1.5.1.tar.gz`)

See "Obtaining the Downloadable Files for This Book" on page xxvii for download information.

▼ To Install the SLAMD Client

1. **Copy the** `slamd-client-1.5.1.tar.gz` **file onto the client system, and into the location in which you wish to install the SLAMD client.**

2. **Uncompress the** `slamd-client-1.5.1.tar.gz` **file as shown:**

```
$ gunzip slamd-client-1.5.1.tar.gz
```

Note – If the `gunzip` command is not available on the system, the `-d` option with the `gzip` command:
`$ gzip -d slamd-client-1.5.1.tar.gz`

3. **Extract the files from the** `slamd-1.5.1.tar` **file as shown:**

```
$ /usr/bin/tar -xvf slamd-client-1.5.1.tar
```

All files are placed in a `slamd_client` subdirectory.

Note – As in the server installation, the directory in which the client files are placed may be modified. However, unlike the server, the client does not store any path information. Therefore, it is possible to move or rename the directory containing the SLAMD client files even after the client has been used.

4. **Edit the** `start_client.sh` **script.**

   This script may be used to start the SLAMD client application, but it must first be edited so that the settings are correct for your system. Set the value of the `JAVA_HOME` variable to the location in which the Java 1.4.0 or higher runtime environment has been installed, and the `SLAMD_HOST` and `SLAMD_PORT` variables to indicate the address and port number that the client should use to communicate with the server.

   You can also edit the `INITIAL_MEMORY` and `MAX_MEMORY` variables to specify the amount of memory in megabytes that the SLAMD client is allowed to consume.

   Finally, comment out or remove the two lines at the top of the file that provide the warning message indicating that the file has not been configured.

▼ To Start the SLAMD Client

● **Use the following command:**

```
$./start_client.sh
```

This starts the client application, connects to the SLAMD server, and indicates that it is ready to accept new job requests. If a problem occurs, an error message is printed that indicates the cause of the problem so that it may be corrected.

While it is not necessary to provide any arguments to this script, there are a couple of options that are supported. One such option is the -a argument. This argument indicates that the client should aggregate all the data collected by each thread into a single set of statistics before sending those results to the SLAMD server. This can significantly reduce the volume of data that the client needs to send to the server and that the server needs to manage, but it does prevent the end user from being able to view performance information about each individual thread on the client (it is still possible to view aggregate data for each client).

It is also possible to use the -v option when starting the client application. This starts the client in verbose mode, which means that it prints additional information that may be useful for debugging problems, including detailed information about the communication between the client and the server. However, using verbose mode might incur a performance penalty in some cases and therefore it is recommended that its use be reserved for troubleshooting problems that cannot be solved with the standard output provided by the client.

The SLAMD Administration Interface

All interaction with the SLAMD server is performed through an HTML administration interface. This interface provides a number of capabilities, including the ability to:

- Schedule new jobs for execution
- View the results of jobs that have completed execution
- View status information about the SLAMD server
- Make new job classes available for use in the SLAMD environment
- Configure the SLAMD server
- Customize the appearance of the HTML interface

This section provides a brief overview of the administrative interface to describe how it can be used.

By default, the administrative interface is accessed through the URL `http://address:8080/slamd`, where *address* is the address of the system on which the SLAMD server is installed. Any browser that supports the HTML 4.01 standard should be able to use this interface, although different browsers may have differences in the way that the content is rendered.

Provided that the SLAMD server is running, the left side of the page contains a navigation bar with links to the various tasks that can be performed. This navigation bar is divided into four major sections:

- Manage Jobs
- Startup Configuration
- SLAMD Configuration
- SLAMD Server Status

Note – If access control is enabled in the administration interface, some sections or options may not be displayed if the current user does not have permission to use those features. Configuring the administrative interface to use access control is documented in a later section.

FIGURE 9-10 illustrates the SLAMD administrative interface.

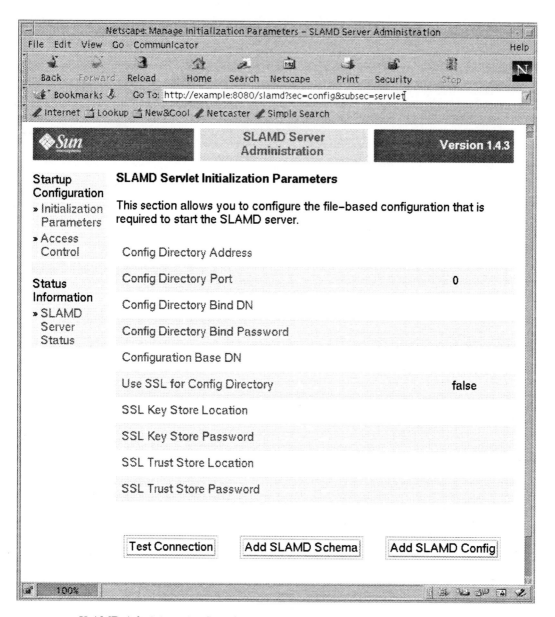

FIGURE 9-10 SLAMD Administrative Interface

The Manage Jobs section provides options to schedule new jobs for execution, view results of jobs that have already been completed, view information about jobs that are currently running or awaiting execution, and view the kinds of jobs that may be executed in the SLAMD environment.

The Startup Configuration section provides options to edit settings in the configuration file that contain the information required to start the SLAMD server (by default, `webapps/slamd/WEB-INF/slamd.conf`). These settings include specifying the settings used for communicating with the configuration directory and the settings used for access control.

The SLAMD Configuration section provides options to edit the SLAMD server settings that are stored in the configuration directory. These settings include options to configure the various components of the SLAMD server, and to customize the appearance of the administrative interface.

The SLAMD Server Status option provides the ability to view information about the current state of the SLAMD environment, including the number of jobs currently running and awaiting execution, the number of clients that are connected and what each of them is doing, and information about the Java™ Virtual Machine (JVM) software in which the SLAMD server is running. This section also provides administrators with the ability to start and stop the SLAMD server, and a means of interacting with the cache used for storing access control information.

Scheduling Jobs for Execution

One of the most important capabilities of the SLAMD server is the ability to schedule jobs for execution. You can schedule them to execute immediately or at some point in the future, on one or more client systems, using one or more threads per client system, and with a number of other options.

For a job to be available for processing, it must first be defined in the SLAMD server. You can develop your own job classes and add them to the SLAMD server so that they are executed by clients. The process for defining new job classes is discussed later, but the SLAMD server is provided with a number of default job classes that can be used to interact with an LDAP directory server.

To schedule a job for execution, you must first follow the Schedule a Job link in the Manage Jobs section of the navigation sidebar. This displays a page containing a list of all job classes that have been defined to the server. To choose the type of job to execute, follow the link for that job class, and a new page is displayed containing a form in which the user may specify how the job is to be executed. Some of the parameters that can be specified are specific to the type of job that was chosen. The parameters specific to the default job classes are documented in a later section. However, some options are the same for every type of job.

The common configuration parameters that are displayed by default are as follows:

- Description – This field allows you to provide a brief description of the job that allows it to be distinguished in a list of completed jobs. This is an optional field. If no description is desired, leave this field blank.

- Start Time – This field allows you to specify the time at which the job should start running. If no value is provided, the job starts running as soon as possible. If a value is provided, it must be in the form YYYYMMDDhhmmss.

- Stop Time – This field allows you to specify the time at which the job should stop running, provided that it has not already stopped for some other reason. If no value is provided, the job is not stopped because of the stop time. If a value is provided, it must be in the form YYYYMMDDhhmmss.

- Duration – This field allows you to specify the maximum length of time in seconds that the job should be allowed to run. This is different from the stop time because it is calculated from the time that the job actually starts running, regardless of the scheduled start time. If no value is provided, there is no maximum duration.

- Number of Clients – This field allows you to specify the number of clients on which the job runs. When the time comes for the job to run, it is sent to the specified number of clients to do the processing. This is a required parameter, and it must be a positive integer.

- Wait for Available Clients – This checkbox allows you to specify what should happen if the time comes for the job to start but there is not an appropriate set of clients available to perform that processing. If this box is not checked, the job is cancelled. If this box is checked, the job is delayed until an appropriate set of clients is available.

- Threads per Client – This field allows you to specify the number of threads that should be created on each client to run the job. Each thread executes the instructions associated with the job at the same time, which allows a single client to perform more work and generate a higher load against the target server. However, specifying too many threads may cause a scenario in which the client system or the target server is overloaded, which could produce inaccurate results.

- Statistics Collection Interval – This field allows you to specify the minimum interval over which statistics are collected while a job is being executed. Statistics are collected for the entire duration of the job, but they are also collected for each interval of the specified duration while that job is active. This is helpful for graphing or otherwise analyzing the results of the job over time.

- Job Comments – This text area allows you to add free-form text that describes additional aspects of the job that cannot be reflected through the other parameters associated with the job. Unlike the other parameters common to all jobs, the job comments field appears at the bottom of the schedule job form. In addition, these comments can be edited after the job has started running or even after the job has completed. This makes it possible to provide comments on the job based on observations gathered during job execution.

In addition to the above parameters, there are a number of other options that are available by clicking on the Show Advanced Scheduling Options button. These options are more specialized than the above parameters, and therefore are not commonly used. However, they are available for use if necessary. These advanced options include:

- Job Is Disabled – This checkbox allows you to specify whether the job should be disabled when it is scheduled. When a job is disabled, it is not considered eligible for execution until it is enabled. This can be beneficial for cases in which it is necessary to make changes to the job after it has been scheduled (for example, if a number of jobs are scheduled at the same time and then individual changes need to be made to each of them).

- Number of Copies – This field allows you to specify the number of copies that are made of the current job when it is scheduled. By default, only a single copy is made, but it is possible to specify any number of copies. This is useful for cases in which a number of jobs of the same type are to be executed with only minor differences between them, since each job can be edited after it is scheduled to make those minor changes.

- Time Between Copy Startups – This field allows you to specify the length of time in seconds that should be left between each job's start time when multiple jobs are scheduled. Note that this is the interval between start times for the jobs, not the time between the end of one job and the beginning of the next. If this is not specified, all copies are scheduled with the same start time.

- Use Specific Clients – This text area allows you to request that the job be executed on a specific set of clients. By default, the clients that are used to run a job cannot be guaranteed. However, if a specific set of addresses are specified, those systems are used to run the job. It is possible to specify either the IP address or DNS host name (as long as those names can be resolved to IP addresses). A separate address must be specified on each line.

- Thread Startup Delay – This field allows you to specify the length of time in milliseconds that each client should wait between starting each thread. This is useful for cases in which there are a number of threads on the client that may be attempting the same operations at the same time in a manner that could lead to resource contention. By introducing a small delay between each thread, that contention might be somewhat reduced for more accurate results.

- Job Dependencies – This field allows you to specify one or more jobs on which the current job is dependent. That is, any job on which the current job is dependent must complete its execution before the current job is considered eligible for execution. When a job is initially scheduled, only a single dependency can be specified. However, by editing the job after it is scheduled, it is possible to add additional dependencies. Only jobs that are currently in the pending or running job queues are possible to specify as dependencies when scheduling or editing a job.

- Notify on Completion - This field allows the user to specify the email addresses of one or more users that should be notified when the job has completed. If multiple addresses are to be included, separate them with commas and/or spaces. This option only appears if the SLAMD mailer has been enabled.

The remaining parameters that appear on the form when scheduling a new job are specific to that job type. The default jobs are described later in this book. Regardless of the job type, following the link at the top of the page in the sentence Click here for help regarding these parameters displays a page with information on each of those parameters.

Once all appropriate parameters are specified for the job, clicking the Schedule Job button causes those parameters to be validated. Provided that all the values provided were acceptable, the jobs are scheduled for execution. If any of the parameters are unacceptable, an error message is displayed indicating the reason that the provided value was inappropriate. A form is displayed allowing you to correct the problem.

Managing Scheduled Jobs

Once a job is scheduled for execution, it is added to the pending jobs queue to await execution. Once all of the criteria required to start the job are met (for example, the start time has arrived, the job is not disabled, all dependencies have been satisfied, and an appropriate set of clients is available), that job is moved from the pending jobs queue into the running jobs queue, and the job is sent out to the clients for processing. When the job completes execution, the job is removed from the running jobs queue, and the job information is updated in the configuration directory.

As described previously, a job can be in one of three stages:

- Pending – The job is awaiting execution and has the potential to be executed once all the appropriate conditions are met. This also includes jobs that are disabled.
- Running – The job information has been sent to at least one client, and the server is currently waiting for results from at least one client.
- Completed – The job has completed all the execution that it is going to do. This could mean any of a range of values, from an indication that the job completed successfully to an indication that a problem occurred that prevented the job from being started.

Viewing Job Execution Results

Once a job is executed and all clients have sent the results back to the SLAMD server, those results are made available through the administration interface. Those results are made available in a variety of forms, and the data collected can even be exported for use with external programs like spreadsheets or databases.

When the job summary page is displayed for a particular job, all of the parameters used to schedule that job are displayed. If that job has completed execution, additional information is available about the results of that execution. That additional information falls into three categories:

- Job Execution Data – This section provides an overview of the execution results and links to obtain more detailed information. This section is described in more detail later.

- Clients Used – This section provides the client IDs of all the clients used to run the job. The client ID contains the address of that client, which makes it possible to determine which systems were used in the job execution.

- Messages Logged – This section provides a list of all messages that were logged while the job was in progress. These messages may provide additional information about problems that occurred while the job was active, or any other significant information that should be known about the job execution. If there are no such messages, this section is not displayed.

Of these three sections, the one of most interest is that containing the job execution data, because it provides the actual results.

Optimizing Jobs

When using SLAMD to run benchmarks against a network application, it is often desirable to find the configuration that yields the best performance. In many cases, this also involves trying different numbers of clients or threads per client to determine the optimal amount of load that can be placed on the server to yield the best results. To help automate this process, SLAMD offers optimizing jobs.

An optimizing job is actually a collection of smaller jobs. It runs the same job repeatedly with increasing numbers of threads per client until it finds the number that yields the best performance for a particular statistic. At the present time, optimizing jobs do not alter the number of clients used to execute the job, although that option may be available in the future.

There are two ways in which an optimizing job may be scheduled:

- View information about a particular completed job that contains the settings you wish to use for the optimizing job. On this page, click the Optimize Results button at the top of the page.

- Follow the View Optimizing Jobs link in the navigation sidebar. Choose the job type from the drop-down list box at the top of that page and click Submit.

Organizing Job Information

After the SLAMD server is used to schedule and run a large number of jobs, the page that stores completed job information can grow quite large, and the process of displaying that page can take more time and consume more server resources. Therefore, for the purposes of both organization and conserving system resources, the server offers the ability to arrange jobs into folders. It is also possible to specify a variety of criteria that can be used to search for job information, regardless of the folder in which it is contained. This section provides information on using job folders and searching for job information.

Real Job Folders

Real job folders correspond to the location of the job information in the configuration directory. As such, it is only possible for a job to exist in a single real folder. Real job folders are used to store information about jobs that have completed execution so that viewing completed job information does not become an expensive process.

Virtual Job Folders

Although real job folders can be very beneficial for a number of reasons, they also have some drawbacks that prevent them from being useful in all circumstances. For that reason, the SLAMD server offers the ability to classify jobs in virtual folders in addition to real folders.

Virtual job folders offer a number of advantages over real job folders:

- A virtual job folder is completely independent of real job folders. That is, a virtual job folder can contain jobs from a number of different real job folders.

- A virtual job folder is not dependent upon the location of the job information in the configuration directory. Therefore, a single job can exist in multiple virtual job folders while it can only exist in a single real job folder.

- A virtual job folder can contain jobs in any state. Real job folders do not display jobs in the pending, running, or disabled states.

- In addition to having a specific list of jobs to include, a virtual job folder can also have a set of search criteria that can be used to dynamically include jobs. This allows newly created jobs to be automatically included in the virtual job folder without requiring any administrative action.

The Default Job Classes

When the SLAMD server is installed, a number of default job classes are registered with the server. The majority of these job classes are used to generate load against LDAP directory servers, because that is the first intended purpose for SLAMD. However, it is quite possible to develop and execute jobs that communicate with any kind of network application that uses a TCP- or UDP-based protocol. The process for adding custom jobs to the SLAMD server is described later. The remainder of this section describes each of the jobs provided with the SLAMD server by default, including the kinds of parameters that are provided to customize their behavior.

Null Job

The null job is a very simple job that does not perform any actual function. Its only purpose is to consume time. When combined with the job dependency feature, it provides the ability to insert a delay between jobs that would otherwise start immediately after the previous job had completed. It does not have any job-specific parameters.

Exec Job

The exec job provides a means of executing a specified command on the client system and optionally capturing the output resulting from the execution of that command. It can be used for any purpose, although its original intent is to be used to execute a script that can perform setup or cleanup before or after processing another job (for example, to restore an LDAP directory server to a known state after a job that may have made changes to it).

HTTP GetRate Job

The HTTP GetRate job is intended to generate load against web servers using the HTTP protocol. It works by repeatedly retrieving a specified URL using the HTTP GET method, and can simulate the kind of load that can be generated when a large number of users attempt to access the server concurrently using web browsers.

LDAP SearchRate Job

The LDAP SearchRate job is intended to generate various kinds of search loads against an LDAP directory server. It is similar to the searchrate command-line utility included in the Sun ONE Directory Server Resource Kit software, but there are some differences in the set of configurable options, and the SLAMD version has support for additional features not included in the command-line version.

Weighted LDAP SearchRate Job

The Weighted LDAP SearchRate job is very similar to the SearchRate job, with two exceptions: it is possible to specify two different filters to use when searching, and also to specify a percentage to use when determining which filter to issue for the search. If this is combined with the ability to use ranges of values in the filter, it is possible to implement a set of searches that conform to the 80/20 rule (80 percent of the searches are targeted at 20 percent of the entries in the directory) or some other ratio. This makes it possible to more accurately simulate real-world search loads on large directories in which it is not possible to cache the entire contents of the directory in memory.

LDAP Prime Job

The LDAP prime job is a specialized kind of SearchRate job that can be used to easily prime an LDAP directory server (retrieve all or a significant part of the entries contained in the directory so that they may be placed in the server's entry cache, allowing them to be retrieved more quickly in the future). It is true that the process of priming a directory server can often be achieved by a whole subtree search with a filter of (objectClass=*). However, this job offers two distinct advantages over using that method. The first is that it allows multiple clients and multiple client threads to be used concurrently to perform the priming, which allows it to complete in significantly less time and with significantly less resource consumption on the directory server system. The second is that this job makes it possible to prime the server with only a subset of the data, whereas an (objectClass=*) filter results in the retrieval of the entire data set.

One requirement of the LDAP prime job is that it requires that the directory server be populated with a somewhat contrived data set. Each entry should contain an attribute (indexed for equality) whose value is a sequentially incrementing integer. As such, while it can easily be used with data sets intended for benchmarking the performance of the directory server, it is probably not adequate for use on a directory loaded with actual production data.

LDAP ModRate Job

The LDAP ModRate job is intended to generate various kinds of modify load against an LDAP directory server. It is similar to the modrate command-line utility included in the Sun ONE Directory Server Resource Kit software, but there are some differences in the set of configurable options. The SLAMD version also has support for additional features not included in the command-line version.

LDAP ModRate with Replica Latency Job

The LDAP ModRate with replica latency job is intended to generate various kinds of modify load against an LDAP directory server while tracking the time required to replicate those changes to another directory server. It accomplishes this by registering a persistent search against the consumer directory server and using it to detect changes to an entry that is periodically modified in the supplier directory. The time between the change made on the supplier and its appearance on the consumer is recorded to the nearest millisecond.

It is important to note that this job works through sampling. The replication latency is not measured for most of the changes made in the supplier server. Rather, updates are periodically made to a separate entry and only changes to that entry are measured. This should allow the change detection to be more accurate for those changes that are measured, and provide a measurement of the overall replication latency. However, it does not measure the latency of changes made to other entries by other worker threads. Therefore, it is not possible to guarantee that the maximum or minimum latency for all changes is measured.

LDAP AddRate Job

The LDAP AddRate job is intended to generate various kinds of add load against an LDAP directory server. It is similar to the `infadd` command-line utility included in the Sun ONE Directory Server Resource Kit software, but there are some differences in the set of configurable options. The SLAMD version also has support for additional features not included in the command-line version, such as the ability to use SSL and the ability to specify additional attributes to include in the generated entries.

Note – Because individual clients are unaware of each other when asked to process a job, this job class should never be run with multiple clients. If this job is run on multiple clients, most operations fail because all clients attempt to add the same entries. However, alternatives do exist. It is possible to use one client with many threads because threads running on the same client can be made aware of each other. Additionally, it is possible to create multiple copies of the same job, each intended to run on one client (with any number of threads) but operating on a different range of entries.

LDAP AddRate with Replica Latency Job

The LDAP AddRate with replica latency job is intended to generate various kinds of add load against an LDAP directory server while measuring the time required to replicate those changes to another directory server. It is very similar to the LDAP AddRate job, although it does not provide support for communicating over SSL.

The process for monitoring replication latency in this job is identical to the method used by the LDAP ModRate job that tests replica latency. That is, a persistent search is registered against a specified entry on the consumer and periodic modifications are performed against that entry on the master directory. The fact that this job performs adds while the test to measure replication latency is based on modify operations is not significant because replicated changes are performed in the order that they occurred regardless of the type of operation (that is, add, modify, delete, and modify RDN operations all have the same priority).

Note – Because individual clients are unaware of each other when asked to process a job, this job class should never be run with multiple clients. If this job is run on multiple clients, most operations fail because all clients attempt to add the same entries. However, alternatives do exist. It is possible to use one client with many threads because threads running on the same client can be made aware of each other. Additionally, it is possible to create multiple copies of the same job, each intended to run on one client (with any number of threads) but operating on a different range of entries.

LDAP DelRate Job

The LDAP DelRate job is intended to generate delete load against an LDAP directory server. It is similar to the `ldapdelete` command-line utility included in the Sun ONE Directory Server Resource Kit software, but it has many additional features, including the ability to use multiple concurrent threads to perform the delete operations.

Note – Because individual clients are unaware of each other when asked to process a job, this job class should never be run with multiple clients. If this job is run on multiple clients, most operations fail because all clients attempt to delete the same entries. However, alternatives do exist. It is possible to use one client with many threads because threads running on the same client can be made aware of each other. Additionally, it is possible to create multiple copies of the same job, each intended to run on one client (with any number of threads) but operating on a different range of entries.

LDAP DelRate with Replica Latency Job

The LDAP DelRate with replica latency job is intended to generate delete load against an LDAP directory server while measuring the time required to replicate those changes to another directory server. It is very similar to the LDAP DelRate job, although it does not provide support for communicating over SSL.

The process for monitoring replication latency in this job is identical to the method used by the LDAP ModRate job that tests replica latency. That is, a persistent search is registered against a specified entry on the consumer and periodic modifications are performed against that entry on the master directory. The fact that this job performs deletes while the test to measure replication latency is based on modify operations is not significant because replicated changes are performed in the order that they occurred regardless of the type of operation (that is, add, modify, delete, and modify RDN operations all have the same priority).

Note – Because individual clients are unaware of each other when asked to process a job, this job class should never be run with multiple clients. If this job is run on multiple clients, most operations fail because all clients attempt to delete the same entries. However, alternatives do exist. It is possible to use one client with many threads because threads running on the same client can be made aware of each other. Additionally, it is possible to create multiple copies of the same job, each intended to run on one client (with any number of threads) but operating on a different range of entries.

LDAP CompRate Job

The LDAP CompRate job is intended to generate various kinds of compare load against an LDAP directory server. The Sun ONE Directory Server Resource Kit software does not have a command-line utility capable of generating load for LDAP compare operations, although it does provide the ldapcmp utility that makes it possible to perform a single compare operation.

LDAP AuthRate Job

The LDAP AuthRate job is intended to simulate the load generated against an LDAP directory server by various kinds of applications that use the directory server for authentication and authorization purposes. It first performs a search operation to find a user's entry based on a login ID value. Once the entry has been found, a bind is performed as that user to verify that the provided password is correct and to verify that the user's account has not been inactivated, that the password is not expired, or that the account is not otherwise inactivated. Upon a successful bind, it might optionally verify whether that user is a member of a specified static group, dynamic group, or role.

Note – The Sun ONE Directory Server Resource Kit software does contain a command-line authrate utility, but the behavior of that utility is significantly different because it only provides the capability to perform repeated bind operations as the same user.

LDAP DIGEST-MD5 AuthRate Job

The LDAP DIGEST-MD5 AuthRate job is very similar to the LDAP AuthRate job, except that instead of binding using Simple authentication, binds are performed using the SASL DIGEST-MD5 mechanism. DIGEST-MD5 is a form of authentication in which a password is used to verify a user's identity, but rather than providing the password itself in the bind response (which could be available in clear text to anyone that might happen to be watching network traffic), the password, along with some other information agreed upon by the client and the server, is hashed in an MD5 digest. This prevents the password from being transferred over the network in clear text, although it does require that the server have access to the clear text password in its own database so that it can perform the same hash to verify the credentials provided by the client.

Because the only difference between this job and the LDAP AuthRate job is the method used to bind to the directory server, all configurable parameters are exactly the same and are provided in exactly the same manner.

LDAP Search and Modify Load Generator Job

The LDAP ModRate job makes it possible to generate modify-type load against an LDAP directory server. To accomplish this, the DNs of the entries to be modified must be explicitly specified, or the DNs of the entries must be constructed from a fixed string and a randomly chosen number. It is possible that neither of these methods are feasible in some environments, and in such cases, the LDAP search and modify job might be more appropriate. Rather than constructing or using an explicit list of DNs, the search and modify job performs searches in the directory server to find entries and performs modifications on the entries returned.

LDAP Load Generator with Multiple Searches Job

The LDAP load generator with multiple searches job provides the capability to perform a number of operations in an LDAP directory server. Specifically, it is able to perform add, compare, delete, modify, modify RDN, and up to six different kinds of search operations in the directory with various relative frequencies. It is very similar to the LDAP load generator job, with the exception that it makes it possible to perform different kinds of searches to better simulate the different kinds of search load that applications can place on the directory.

Note – That the different kinds of searches to be performed should be specified using filter files – it is not possible to specify filter patterns for them.

Solaris OE LDAP Authentication Load Generator Job

The Solaris OE LDAP authentication load generator is a job that simulates the load that Solaris 9 OE clients place on the directory server when they are configured to use pam_ldap for authentication. Although this behavior can vary quite dramatically based on the configuration provided through the idsconfig and ldapclient utilities, many common configurations can be accommodated through the job parameters. In particular, the lookups can be configured to be performed either anonymously or through a proxy user, using either simple or DIGEST-MD5 authentication with or without SSL.

The directory server against which the authentication is to be performed should be configured properly to process authentication requests from Solaris clients. It may be configured in this manner using the idsconfig and ldapaddent tools provided with the Solaris OE, with at least the passwd, shadow, and hosts databases imported into the directory. However, it may be more desirable to simulate this information. The appropriate information may be simulated using the MakeLDIF utility with the solaris.template template file. The data produced in that case is more suited for use by this job because all user accounts can be created with an incrementing numeric value in the user ID and with the same password, which makes it possible to simulate a much broader range of users authenticating to the directory server.

The full set of parameters that may be used to customize the behavior of this job is as follows:

- Directory Server Address – This field allows the user to specify the address that the clients should use when attempting to connect to the LDAP directory server. All clients that may run the job must be able to access the server using this address.

- Directory Server Port – This field allows the user to specify the port number that the clients should use when attempting to connect to the LDAP directory server. If the authentication should be performed over SSL, this should reference the directory server's secure port.

- Directory Base DN – This field allows the user to specify the base DN under which the Solaris OE naming data and user accounts exist. All searches are performed using a subtree scope, so this base DN may be at any level in the directory under which at least the hosts and user account information exist.

- Credential Level – This field allows the user to specify the manner in which clients should bind to the server when finding user accounts and other naming information. The credential level may be either anonymous, in which no authentication is performed and all the user IDs and host information should be available without authentication, or proxy, which means that a third-party account should be used to bind to the directory server to retrieve this information. If the proxy method is selected, a proxy bind DN and password must be specified.

- Proxy User DN – This field allows the user to specify the DN that the client uses to bind to the server when performing lookups to find user entries and to retrieve other naming information. This is only used if the credential level is set to proxy, in which case a proxy user DN and password must be specified. The typical proxy user DN as created by idsconfig is cn=proxyagent, ou= profile, {baseDN}, where {baseDN} is the DN of the entry below which Solaris OE naming information is stored.

- Proxy User Password – This field allows the user to specify the password for the proxy user account. This is only used if the credential level is set to proxy, in which case a proxy user DN and password must be specified.

- Authentication Method – This field allows the user to specify the means by which users authenticate to the directory server. The authentication method may be either simple or DIGEST-MD5 authentication, and it may or may not be configured to use SSL. It should be noted that if DIGEST-MD5 authentication is to be performed, the directory server must be configured to store the passwords for the specified users in clear text.

- User ID – This field allows the user to specify the user ID of the user or users that is used to authenticate to the directory server. It is possible to include a range of numeric values enclosed in brackets that is replaced with a randomly chosen integer from that range. For example, if the value specified for this field is user.[1-1000], a random integer between 1 and 1000 (inclusive) is chosen and used to replace the bracketed range. It is also possible to specify a sequential range of values to use for the user ID values by replacing the dash with a colon. For example, a value of user. [1:1000] results in the first login ID value generated being user.1, the second being user.2, and the one thousandth value being user.1000. If the maximum value is reached, the generation starts over with the minimum value again (so user ID 1001 would be user.1).

- User Password – This field allows the user to specify the password for the user or users that is used to authenticate to the directory server. If the user ID contains a range of values, this password must be the same for all those users. Further, if the job is configured to perform authentication using DIGEST-MD5, the directory must be configured to store this password in clear text for the user or users specified by the user ID.

- Simulated Client Address Range – This field allows the user to specify the IP address or address range from which clients appear to be originating. Whenever a client connects to a Solaris OE system configured to use pam_ldap, the Solaris OE system attempts to find the host name associated with the IP address of that client system, and the value provided for this parameter is used to specify what those addresses should be. The value provided for this field may be either a single IPv4 address (in standard dotted-quad format), or a range of addresses using the classless inter-domain routing (CIDR) format. CIDR is a popular means of expressing contiguous ranges of IP addresses on the same network and is defined in RFC 1519. The format used is a.b.c.d/e, in which a.b.c.d is an IPv4 address and /e specifies the number of bits in the provided IPv4 address that must match a client address to be considered in the range. For example, 192.168.1.0/24 indicates that any IPv4 address that matches the first 24 bits of the address 192.168.1.0 is considered part of the range. Although the number of bits to use may be any integer value between 0 and 32 (inclusive), the most commonly used values are 0 (any address matches), 8 (the first octet must match), 16 (the first two octets must match), 24 (the first three octets must match), and 32 (all four octets must match). See RFC 1519 for further explanation. This parameter does not currently support the use of IPv6 addresses.

- SSL Key Store – This field allows the user to specify the location (on the local file system of the client) of the Java™ Secure Socket Extension (JSSE) key store used to help determine whether to trust the SSL certificate presented by the directory server. It is used if either of the SSL-based authentication methods are chosen.

- SSL Key Store Password – This field allows the user to specify the password that should be used to access the information in the JSSE key store. It is used if either of the SSL-based authentication methods are chosen.

- SSL Trust Store – This field allows the user to specify the location (on the local file system of the client) of the JSSE trust store used to help determine whether to trust the SSL certificate presented by the directory server. It is used if either of the SSL-based authentication methods are chosen.

- SSL Trust Store Password – This field allows the user to specify the password that should be used to access the information in the JSSE trust store. It is used if either of the SSL-based authentication methods are chosen.

SiteMinder LDAP Load Simulator Job

As its name implies, the SiteMinder LDAP load simulation job attempts to simulate the load that Netegrity SiteMinder (with password services enabled) places on a directory server whenever a user authenticates. This simulation was based on information obtained by examining the directory server's access log during a time that SiteMinder was in use.

POP CheckRate Job

The POP CheckRate job provides the capability to generate load against a messaging server that can communicate using POP3. It chooses a user ID, authenticates to the POP server as that user, retrieves a list of the messages in that user's mailbox, and disconnects from the server.

IMAP CheckRate Job

The IMAP CheckRate job is very similar to the POP CheckRate job, except that it communicates with the messaging server over IMAPv4 instead of POP3. Like the POP CheckRate job, it chooses a user ID, authenticates to the POP server as that user, retrieves a list of the messages in that user's INBOX folder, and disconnects from the server.

Calendar Initial Page Rate Job

The Calendar Initial Page Rate job provides the capability to generate load against the Sun ONE Calendar Server version 5.1.1. It does this by communicating with the Calendar Server over HTTP and simulating the interaction that a web-based client would have with the server when a user authenticates to the server and displays the initial schedule page.

It is important to note that because of the way in which this job operates and the specific kinds of requests that are required, it may not work with any version of the Calendar Server other than version 5.1.1. At the time that this job was developed, version 5.1.1 was the most recent release available, but it is not possible to ensure that future versions of the Calendar Server will continue to behave in the same manner.

Adding New Job Classes

The SLAMD server was designed in such a way that it is very extensible. One of the ways this is evident is the ability for an end user to develop a new job class and add that class to the SLAMD server. Once that class has been added to the SLAMD server, it is immediately possible to schedule and run jobs that make use of that job class. It is not necessary to copy that job class to all client systems, as that is done automatically whenever a client is asked to run a job for which it does not have the appropriate job class.

Note – Although job classes are automatically transferred from the SLAMD server to clients as necessary, if a job class uses a Java library that is not already available to those client systems, that library must be manually copied to each client. Libraries in Java™ Archive (JAR) file form should be placed in the lib directory of the client installation, and libraries provided as individual class files should be placed under the classes directory (with all appropriate parent directories created in accordance with the package in which those classes reside).

If any new versions of job classes are installed, it is necessary to manually update each client, as the client has no way of knowing that it would otherwise be using an outdated version of the job class.

Using the Standalone Client

Even though jobs are designed to be scheduled and coordinated by the SLAMD server, it is possible to execute a job as a standalone entity. This is convenient if you want to run a job in an environment where there is no SLAMD server available, if you do not need advanced features like graphing results, or if you are developing a new job for use in the SLAMD environment and wish to test it without scheduling it through the SLAMD server.

The standalone client is similar to the network-based client in that it is included in the same installation package as the network client and requires a Java environment (preferably 1.4.0) installed on the client system. However, because there is no communication with the SLAMD server, it is not necessary that the client address be resolvable or that any SLAMD server be accessible.

Before the standalone client may be used, it is necessary to edit the standalone_client.sh script. This script may be used to run the standalone client, but it must first be edited so that the settings are correct for your system. Set the value of the JAVA_HOME variable to the location in which the Java 1.4.0 or higher runtime environment has been installed. You may also edit the INITIAL_MEMORY and MAX_MEMORY variables to specify the amount of memory in megabytes that the standalone client is allowed to consume. Finally, comment out or remove the two lines at the top of the file that provide the warning message indicating that the file has not been configured.

Since the standalone client operates independently of the SLAMD server, it is not possible to use the administrative interface to define the parameters to use for the job. Instead, the standalone client reads the values of these parameters from a configuration file. In order to generate an appropriate configuration file, issue the command:

```
$./standalone_client.sh -g job_class -f config_file
```

where *job_class* is the fully-qualified name of the job class file (for example, com.example. slamd.example.SearchRateJobClass), and *config_file* is the path and name of the configuration file to create. This creates a configuration file that can be read by the standalone client to execute the job. This configuration file likely needs to be modified before it can actually be used to run a job, but comments in the configuration file should explain the purpose and acceptable values for each parameter.

Once an appropriate configuration file is available, the standalone client may be used to run the job. In its most basic form, it may be executed using the command

```
$./standalone_client.sh -F config_file
```

This reads the configuration file and executes the job defined in that configuration file using a single thread until the job completes. However, this default configuration is not sufficient for many jobs, and therefore there are additional command-line arguments that may be provided to further customize its behavior.

Starting and Stopping SLAMD

The SLAMD server has been designed so that it should not need to be restarted frequently. Most of the configuration parameters that may be specified within the SLAMD server can be customized without the need to restart the server itself or the servlet engine that provides the administrative interface. However, some changes do require that the server be restarted for that change to take effect. This section describes the preferred ways of starting, stopping, and restarting the SLAMD server and the Tomcat servlet engine.

Starting the Tomcat Servlet Engine

By default, SLAMD uses the Tomcat servlet engine to generate the HTML pages used for interacting with the SLAMD server. However, the servlet engine is responsible for not only generating these HTML pages, but actually for running the entire SLAMD server. All components of the server run inside the Java Virtual Machine used by the servlet engine. Therefore, unless the servlet engine is running, the SLAMD server is not available.

As described earlier in this document in the discussion on installing the SLAMD server, the Tomcat servlet engine may be started by using the bin/startup.sh shell script provided in the installation archive. This shell script must be edited to specify the path of the Java installation, the amount of memory to use, and the location of an X server to use when generating graphs. Once that has been done, this shell script may be used to start the Tomcat servlet engine.

Starting SLAMD

By default, the SLAMD server is loaded and started automatically when the servlet engine starts. However, if a problem is encountered when the servlet engine tries to start the SLAMD server (that is, if the configuration directory server is unavailable), the Tomcat servlet engine is started but SLAMD remains offline. If this occurs, a message is displayed indicating that the SLAMD server is unavailable, and this message should also include information that can help administrators diagnose and correct the problem.

When the problem has been corrected, the SLAMD server may be started by following the SLAMD Server Status link at the bottom of the navigation bar and clicking the Start SLAMD button (this button is only visible if the SLAMD server is not running). This attempts to start the SLAMD server. If the attempt is successful, the full user interface is available. If the SLAMD server could not be started for some reason, it remains offline and an informational message describing the problem that occurred is displayed.

Restarting SLAMD

As indicated earlier, a few configuration parameters require the SLAMD server to be restarted in order for changes to take effect. This can be done easily through the administrative interface without the need to restart the servlet engine. To do so, follow the SLAMD Server Status link at the bottom of the navigation bar and click the Restart SLAMD button on the status page (this button is only visible if the SLAMD server is currently running). This causes the SLAMD server to be stopped and immediately restarted.

Stopping SLAMD

Restarting the SLAMD server should be sufficient for cases in which it is only necessary to re-read configuration parameters, but in some cases it may be necessary to stop the SLAMD server and leave it offline for a period of time (for example, if the configuration directory server is taken offline for maintenance). This can be done by following the SLAMD Server Status link at the bottom of the navigation bar and clicking the Stop SLAMD button on the status page. This causes the SLAMD server to be stopped, and it remains offline until the Start SLAMD button is clicked or until the servlet engine is restarted.

Note – Stopping or restarting the SLAMD server (or the servlet engine in which it is running) disconnects all clients currently connected to the server. If any of those clients are actively processing jobs, an attempt is made to cancel those jobs and obtain at least partial results, but this cannot be guaranteed. Any jobs that are in the pending jobs queue are also stored in the configuration directory and are properly re-loaded when the SLAMD server is restarted. However, if the SLAMD server is offline for any significant period of time, the start times for some jobs may have passed, which could cause the pending jobs queue to become backlogged when the server is restarted.

Stopping the Tomcat Servlet Engine

It should be possible to edit all of the SLAMD server's configuration without needing to restart the servlet engine in which SLAMD is running. However, if the configuration of the Tomcat servlet engine itself is to be modified, it is necessary to stop and restart Tomcat for those changes to take effect.

Before stopping Tomcat, it is recommended that the SLAMD server be stopped first. To do this, follow the SLAMD Server Status link and click the Stop SLAMD button. Once the SLAMD server has been stopped, it is possible to stop the Tomcat servlet engine using the bin/shutdown.sh shell script.

If the SLAMD server is not stopped before the attempt to stop the Tomcat servlet engine, it is possible (although unlikely) that the Tomcat servlet engine will not stop properly. If that occurs, the servlet engine may be stopped by killing the Java process in which it is running (note that on Linux systems it may appear as multiple processes). The Tomcat startup scripts have been modified so that the process ID of the Tomcat process should be written into the logs/pid file. If Tomcat does not shut down properly, this PID may be used to determine which process or processes should be killed. If it is necessary to manually kill the Tomcat process, it should be done using the SIGTERM signal (the default signal used when the kill command is issued). A SIGKILL signal should only be used if the Tomcat process or processes do not respond to the SIGTERM signals.

Tuning the Configuration Directory

In addition to storing the SLAMD configuration, the configuration directory is used to store information about all jobs that have been scheduled for execution in the SLAMD environment, including the statistical information gathered from jobs that have completed. Nearly all operations that can be performed in the administrative interface require some kind of interaction with the configuration directory. Therefore, properly tuning the configuration directory can dramatically improve the performance of the administrative interface and the SLAMD server in general. Further, entries that store statistical information may grow quite large and without proper configuration, it may not be possible to store this information in the directory. The changes that should be made to the directory server configuration are described below.

Configuring for Large Entries

All information about scheduled jobs is stored in the configuration directory. For completed jobs, this includes the statistical information gathered while those jobs were running. As a result, these entries can be required to store several megabytes of data, especially for those jobs with a large number of threads, with a long duration, or that maintain statistics for a number of items. This can cause a problem because by default the directory server is configured to allow only approximately two megabytes of information to be sent to the server in a single LDAP message. This limit is controlled by the `nsslapd-maxbersize` configuration attribute, which specifies the maximum allowed message size in bytes. A value of at least 100 megabytes (104857600 bytes) should be specified to prevent updates with large amounts of statistical information from being rejected, although it is possible that a job could return even more than 100 megabytes of data, particularly for jobs that run for a very long period of time and have a relatively short collection interval.

Cache Tuning

The directory server contains two caches that may be utilized to improve overall performance: the entry cache and the database cache. The entry cache holds copies of the most recently used entries in memory so they can be retrieved without having to access the database. The database cache holds pages of the database in memory so it is not necessary to access the data stored on the disk. By default, both of these caches are configured to store approximately ten megabytes of information. Increasing the sizes of these caches increases the amount of information stored in memory and therefore the overall performance when it is necessary to retrieve information from the directory server. Increasing the size of the database cache can also improve the performance of the server when writing information to the database.

Proper Indexing

Whenever the SLAMD server needs to retrieve information from the configuration directory, it issues an LDAP search request to the directory. If the directory server is properly indexed, the server is able to locate the matching entries more quickly. Adding indexes for the following attributes helps the directory server process the queries from SLAMD more efficiently:

- slamdJobActualStopTime -- Presence and equality
- slamdJobClassName -- Equality
- slamdJobID -- Equality
- slamdJobState -- Equality
- slamdOptimizingJobID -- Equality
- slamdParameterName -- Equality

Typical SLAMD Architecture

FIGURE 9-11 shows an example of how you might architect and deploy SLAMD.

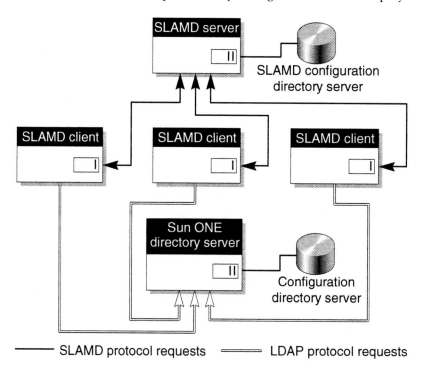

FIGURE 9-11 SLAMD Architecture

The SLAMD Architecture figure depicts how the SLAMD clients are distributed amongst multiple machines, and how the clients receive what is termed as job data, from the SLAMD server. This information is related to how the Sun™ ONE Directory Server should be load tested by the SLAMD server. This results in data being sent as a report back to the SLAMD server when the job is done. This load testing of the Sun™ ONE Directory Server is achieved through LDAP protocol requests. In FIGURE 9-11, the clients are distributed, which means in order to obtain the average results, the SLAMD server must aggregate the results from all participating clients and present the results to the user as one single job. The SLAMD server also requires a directory server to store configuration and result data. A typical SLAMD server and its configuration directory are normally located on the same system, which could be a Sun Enterprise 420R.

Directory Server Performance Tuning

Completing a Sun™ Directory Server performance benchmark is not a simple task, and requires much planning and knowledge to be completed successfully. In any performance benchmark, one of the final phases is the wrap-up phase that consists of specific activities required to collect and analyze data (testing and configuration). This normally includes throughput, latency and utilization. With this in mind, we look now at some pertinent information about tuning the directory server.

One of the main factors limiting server performance is the amount of time it takes to update information in files on the physical disks of the machine on which the directory is running. When a write operation of any type is performed, the directory writes information to files in many different places. Appropriate indexes are updated. The update is noted in the transaction log. The change log is updated if replication is to be performed. In order to guarantee the integrity of its data, the directory never considers a write operation complete until the underlying operating system has confirmed that all of the appropriate files have been updated on physical media. Since disk access is significantly slower than memory access, write operations are often many times slower than reads, as reads are often completed out of the in-memory caches. Therefore, anything that reduces or eliminates disk traffic speeds updates. Although disk configuration (which was covered in Chapter 8 "Selecting Storage for Optimum Directory Server Performance") and other hardware resources play a factor, the configuration of the server can have a huge impact on the performance of the directory server. The tuning parameters listed in TABLE 9-5 through TABLE 9-26 are key to the performance of the directory server.

Core Sun ONE Directory Server Software Configuration

TABLE 9-5   `cn=config`

Attribute	`nsslapd-accesslog`
Default Value	*<ServerRoot>*/*<slapd-serverID>*/`logs/access`
Comment	Used to specify the location of the access log files
Tuning Recommendation(s)	Storing log files on a separate volume can help reduce the I/O overhead associated with logging.

TABLE 9-6   `cn=config`

Attribute	`nsslapd-errorlog`
Default Value	*<ServerRoot>*/*<slapd-serverID>*/`logs/error`
Comment	Used to specify the location of the error log files
Tuning Recommendation(s)	Storing log files on a separate volume can help reduce the I/O overhead associated with logging.

TABLE 9-7   `cn=config`

Attribute	`nsslapd-auditlog`
Default Value	*<ServerRoot>*/*<slapd-serverID>*/`logs/audit`
Comment	Used to specify the location of the audit log files
Tuning Recommendation(s)	Storing log files on a separate volume can help reduce the I/O overhead associated with logging.

TABLE 9-8   `cn=config`

Attribute	`nsslapd-accesslog-logbuffering`
Default Value	on
Comment	Indicates whether the server buffers access log information in memory for delayed writes in bulk, or commits this information immediately to disk.
Tuning Recommendation(s)	Buffering is enabled by default, which provides better performance. However, if the server shuts down abruptly or is killed, it is possible that some log data will not be written.

TABLE 9-9 `cn=config`

Attribute	`nsslapd-maxdescriptors`
Default Value	65536
Comment	Indicates whether the server buffers access log information in memory for delayed writes in bulk, or commits this information immediately to disk.
Tuning Recommendation(s)	Since each connection to the server consumes a file descriptor, this configuration attribute can have an impact on the number of concurrent connections that the server can handle. Note that increasing this value may require changes to the Operating System configuration to support more file descriptors.

TABLE 9-10 `cn=config`

Attribute	`nsslapd-threadnumber`
Default Value	30
Comment	Specifies the number of worker threads that are used by the directory server to handle requests.
Tuning Recommendation(s)	We have found that the directory server exhibits best performance when the number of worker threads is a multiple of the number of CPUs in the system, however it should be at least 16 or 20 to prevent the server from becoming unresponsive if a number of inefficient queries are requested at the same time.

TABLE 9-11 `cn=config`

Attribute	`nsslapd-schemacheck`
Default Value	on
Comment	Specifies whether the directory server enforces schema checking.
Tuning Recommendation(s)	Although disabling this configuration parameter may improve performance for imports and update operations, it also introduces the danger that information added to the database is not valid and possibly may not be able to be found by clients under some circumstances. Therefore, it is recommended that schema checking only be disabled on master servers only for imports, or only for cases in which it is possible to guarantee that all clients accessing the server will always use entries conforming to the server schema definitions (this includes administrators who might make changes using `ldapmodify`, where a typo could easily result in a change that violates schema).

TABLE 9-12 `cn=config, cn=ldbm database,cn=plugins,cn=config`

Attribute	`nsslapd-allidsthreshold`
Default Value	`4000`
Comment	Specifies the maximum number of entries allowed to match any single index key.
Tuning Recommendation(s)	If this value is too high, the server performance can degrade for update operations. If it is too low, valid searches that match more than this number of entries might take significantly longer to complete.

TABLE 9-13 `cn=config, cn=ldbm database,cn=plugins,cn=config`

Attribute	`nsslapd-directory`
Default Value	*<ServerRoot>*/*<slapd-serverID>*/db
Comment	Specifies the base location for the directory server database files.
Tuning Recommendation(s)	In most cases, this can be left unchanged because these files contain only parent information for the database. Each back end makes it possible to specify the location of its own database files.

TABLE 9-14 `cn=config, cn=ldbm database,cn=plugins,cn=config`

Attribute	`nsslapd-dbcachesize`
Default Value	`10485760` (10Mb)
Comment	Specifies the amount of memory (in bytes) allocated for use in caching database information.
Tuning Recommendation(s)	This database cache contains pages of the database files (including indexes and id2entry files). Any time it is necessary to access information in the database, it is significantly faster if this information is in the database cache than if it is necessary to retrieve the information from the disk-based database.

TABLE 9-15 `cn=config, cn=ldbm database,cn=plugins,cn=config`

Attribute	`nsslapd-logdirectory`
Default Value	*<ServerRoot>*/*<slapd-serverID>*/db
Comment	Specifies the location for the database transaction log files.
Tuning Recommendation(s)	The process of writing the transaction log files can be very I/O intensive, so it is highly recommended that these files be separated onto their own disk subsystem for best performance.

TABLE 9-16 `cn=config, cn=ldbm database,cn=plugins,cn=config`

Attribute	`nsslapd-db-home-directory`
Default Value	*\<ServerRoot\>*/*\<slapd-serverID\>*/db
Comment	Specifies the location of the backing files that the database uses to hold the memory-mapped database cache.
Tuning Recommendation(s)	For best performance, these files should be moved to a tempfs file system (for example., a subdirectory under /tmp).

TABLE 9-17 `cn=config, cn=ldbm database,cn=plugins,cn=config`

Attribute	`nsslapd-import-cachesize`
Default Value	20971520 (20Mb)
Comment	Specifies the amount of memory that may be used for caching data during bulk imports (imports performed with `ldif2db` or `ldif2db.pl`).
Tuning Recommendation(s)	Making more memory available (up to some point, which varies based on the server configuration and the data being imported) can improve the performance of the server during a bulk import.

TABLE 9-18 `cn={backend-name},cn=ldbm database,cn=plugins,cn=config`

Attribute	`nsslapd-cachesize`
Default Value	`-1`
Comment	Specifies the maximum number of entries that may be held in the entry cache.
Tuning Recommendation(s)	This is a legacy parameter used primarily for migration from 4.x versions of the server. It is recommended that the default value of `-1` (no limit) be used and that the `nsslapd-cachememsize` be used to specify the amount of memory for use by the entry cache.

TABLE 9-19 `cn={backend-name},cn=ldbm database,cn=plugins,cn=config`

Attribute	`nsslapd-cachememsize`

TABLE 9-19 `cn={backend-name},cn=ldbm database,cn=plugins,cn=config`

Default Value	10485760 (10Mb)
Comment	Specifies the amount of memory that can be used for caching entries from this back end (that is, the entry cache).
Tuning Recommendation(s)	Whenever the server needs to retrieve an entry, it is much faster to do so from the entry cache than if it is necessary to retrieve the information from the database. Therefore, the more memory that can be used for entry caching (up to the point at which all entries are cached), the more likely it is that a given entry is in the cache.

TABLE 9-20 `cn={backend-name},cn=ldbm database,cn=plugins,cn=config`

Attribute	`nsslapd-require-index`
Default Value	`off`
Comment	Specifies whether searches in this back end are required to be indexed. Indexed searches are significantly faster than unindexed searches, and unindexed searches can consume a great deal of CPU and memory.
Tuning Recommendation(s)	It is recommended therefore that appropriate indexes be defined and that the server require indexed searches.

TABLE 9-21 `cn={backend-name},cn=ldbm database,cn=plugins,cn=config`

Attribute	`nsslapd-single-writer`
Default Value	
Comment	Specifies whether a single or multiple threads are used when writing information to the database.
Tuning Recommendation(s)	Although using multiple threads to write to the database can yield significantly better update performance than a single thread, it also introduces a very real risk of corrupting the database. This is an experimental parameter and it should not be set to `off` under any circumstances in a directory deployment.

TABLE 9-22 `cn={backend-name},cn=ldbm database,cn=plugins,cn=config`

Attribute	nsslapd-directory
Default Value	
Comment	Specifies the location of the database files associated with this back end.
Tuning Recommendation(s)	Each back end used to service a large number of requests (either read or write) can benefit greatly from having its database files stored on a different disk subsystem.

Note – The referential integrity plug-in is disabled by default, but it is needed in many environments. If it is used, then the following changes should be made.

TABLE 9-23 `cn=referential integrity postoperation,cn=plugins,cn=config`

Attribute	nsslapd-pluginarg0
Default Value	0
Comment	This parameter specifies the update interval for operations performed by the referential integrity plug-in.
Tuning Recommendation(s)	Its default value of zero is very bad for performance, particularly when several delete and/or modify DN operations are in progress concurrently in the server. A value of around 90 is a much better setting.

TABLE 9-24 `cn=referential integrity postoperation,cn=plugins,cn=config`

Attribute	nsslapd-pluginarg3, nsslapd-pluginarg4, nsslapd-pluginarg5, ...
Default Value	member, uniquemember, owner, ...
Comment	These plug-in arguments specify the attributes for which referential integrity is maintained.
Tuning Recommendation(s)	Equality indexes must be defined for these attributes in all databases. If any of these attributes do not have equality indexes, delete or modify DN operations can cause significant CPU and memory consumption.

TABLE 9-25 `cn={attr-name},cn=index,cn={backend-name},cn=ldbm`
`database,cn=plugins,cn=config`

Attribute	cn
Default Value	N/A
Comment	Specifies the name of the attribute to index. A separate configuration entry is used for each indexed attribute in each back end.
Tuning Recommendation(s)	It is important that attributes referenced in search filters be indexed appropriately to ensure that indexes can be used to perform the searches. Similarly, maintaining indexes for attributes that are not used in search filters can degrade update performance. Note that this applies only to attributes that are not used for system indexes —even though they are not referenced in search filters, having appropriately defined indexes for those attributes is critical to ensuring directory server performance.

TABLE 9-26 `cn={attr-name},cn=index,cn={backend-name},cn=ldbm`
`database,cn=plugins,cn=config`

Attribute	nsIndexType
Default Value	
Comment	Specifies the type(s) of indexes that are maintained for the associated attribute.
Tuning Recommendation(s)	Substring indexes impose the most significant performance penalty and should therefore be limited to only those attributes that absolutely require them.

## CHAPTER 10

Emerging Directory Technologies

Directory technology is dynamic and evolving as more uses are discovered. Sun is embracing evolving directory technology, incorporating new features in its products while following emerging standards.

The information in this chapter is not comprehensive, but instead highlights technology that is likely to impact how LDAP naming services are deployed.

This chapter is organized into the following sections:

- "DSMLv2 Interface" on page 549
- "Sun ONE Identity Synchronization for the Windows Technology" on page 557
- "NIS to LDAP Gateway" on page 561

Note – Appendix A, "LDAP Standards Information" contains a list of most relevant RFCs and lists where to go to find more information about them.

DSMLv2 Interface

In this section, the new DSMLv2 interface for Sun ONE Directory Server 5.2 software is examined. The section addresses the following questions:

- What is DSML?
- How is it used?
- How it is implemented?

What Is DSML?

The Directory Services Markup Language (DSML) provides a means for representing directory information and performing directory operations from an XML document. This means you can search, add, delete, and modify directory data using DSML over HyperText Transport Protocol (HTTP) without the Lightweight Directory Access Protocol. This is important because some clients such as personal digital assistants (PDAs) do not contain a full-blown client.

DSMLv1 focused on how to represent directory structured data. DSMLv2 goes further, providing a method for expressing directory queries and updates (and the results of these operations) as XML documents. DSMLv2 documents can be used in a variety of ways. For instance, they can be written to files so they can be consumed or produced by programs, or they can be transported over HTTP to and from a server that interprets and generates them.

The design approach for DSMLv2 is to express LDAP requests and responses as XML document fragments. For the most part, DSMLv2 is a systematic translation of LDAP's ASN.1 grammar (defined by RFC 2251) into XML-Schema. Thus, when a DSMLv2 element name matches an identifier in LDAP's ASN.1 grammar, the named element means the same thing in DSMLv2 as it does in LDAP.

DSMLv2 is defined in terms of a set of XML fragments that are used as payloads in a binding. A binding defines how the DSMLv2 XML fragments are sent as requests and responses in the context of a specific transport such as SOAP, SMTP, or a simple data file. DSMLv2 defines two types of bindings:

- A SOAP request/response binding
- A file binding that serves as the DSMLv2 analog of LDIF

For the most part, DSML is aligned with LDAP. However there are a few places where it makes sense for DSMLv2 to diverge from LDAP:

- An LDAP application associates a security principal with an LDAP connection by issuing a *bind* request or, in the SASL bind case, by issuing as many successive bind requests as needed to complete the authentication. A DSMLv2 document can be transported through a variety of mechanisms, so the document itself is not used to authenticate the requestor. DSMLv2 includes an *Auth* request that can be used to associate a security principal with a collection of DSMLv2 operations.

- LDAP does not include a method of grouping operations together so they can be expressed in a single request. DSMLv2 allows multiple LDAP operations to be expressed in one request document by specifying a simple positional correspondence between individual requests within a request document.

- In LDAP, a single search request typically generates multiple responses, closed by a `searchResultDone` response. To enable the positional correspondence between requests and responses mentioned above, DSMLv2 provides for a binding to wrap the complete set of related search responses into a single searchResponse element containing the individual LDAP responses to a search request.

- The systematic translation of RFC 2251 results in a redundant level of nested elements, the LDAPMessage. DSMLv2 eliminates this extra level.

- Defaulting works more naturally in XML documents than in ASN.1 structures, so DSMLv2 uses defaulting in a few places where LDAP doesn't. In DSMLv2 the string-valued elements matchedDN and errorMessage (from LDAPResult in LDAP) and attributes (from SearchRequest in LDAP) are optional, and when absent are treated as the empty string. The sizeLimit, timeLimit, and typesOnly elements (from SearchRequest in LDAP) default to 0, 0, and FALSE respectively.

The base Universal Resource Name (URN) for DSMLv2 is:

```
urn:oasis:names:tc:DSML:2:0:core
```

The above URN is used to construct the URN for the core namespace consisting of the individual operations and responses, a request envelope, a response envelope, an envelope grouping the entries, and references and result of a search operation.

An example of using the DSMLv2 URN is:

```
<dsml:batchRequest xmlns:dsml=
"urn:oasis:names:tc:DSML:2:0:core">
```

There are two types of DSMLv2 documents:

- request document
- response document

In a DSMLv2-based interaction between a client and a server, there is a pairing of requests and responses. For each request document submitted by the client, there is one response document produced by the server. In the two bindings defined in the DSMLv2 specification, the top-level element of a request fragment is a BatchRequest and the top-level element of a response fragment is a BatchResponse.

A BatchRequest contains zero, one, or many individual request elements, while a BatchResponse consists of zero, one, or many individual response elements. A BatchRequest containing zero request elements is a valid request; the valid response is a BatchResponse containing zero response elements. Such a batch request-response pair can be used to verify that a server is capable of processing DSMLv2 documents.

The client and server associate an individual response in a BatchResponse with the corresponding individual request in a BatchRequest using one (or both) of the following methods: positional correspondence or RequestID. In a positional correspondence, the nth response element corresponds to the nth request element. For instance, if the third response element is a delete response, it directly corresponds to the third request element, a delete request.

LDAP Operations

With the exception of extendedRequest, each individual request element contains:

- A dn attribute (as in DSMLv1) containing a distinguished name
- Zero or more control elements representing LDAP Controls

Here are a few examples of LDAP request elements:

```
<batchRequest xmlns:xsd="http://www.w3.org/2001/XMLSchema"
xmlns:xsi="http://www.w3.org/2001/XMLSchema-instance"
xmlns="urn:oasis:names:tc:DSML:2:0:core">
<modifyRequest dn="CN=Joe Smith, OU=Dev, DC=Example, DC=Com">
...
</modifyRequest>
<addRequest dn="OU=Sales,DC=Example, DC=Com">
...
</addRequest>
<delRequest dn="CN=Alice,OU=HR,DC=Example,DC=Com">
<control>...</control>
<control>...</control>
</delRequest>
<searchRequest>
<control>...</control>
...
</searchRequest>
</batchRequest>
```

Here is an example of an LDAP Control:

```
<control type="1.2.840.113556.1.4.619" criticality="true">
<controlValue xsi:type=
"xsd:base64Binary">RFNNTHYyLjAgcm9ja3MhIQ==
</controlValue>
```

Here are a few examples of LDAP response elements:

```
<batchResponse xmlns="urn:oasis:names:tc:DSML:2:0:core">
...
<modifyResponse>
<resultCode code="53" descr="unwillingToPerform"/>
<errorMessage>System Attribute may not be
modified</errorMessage>
</modifyResponse>
<resultCode code="0" descr="success"/>
</addResponse>
```

What Can You Use It For?

DSMLv2 functionality is motivated by scenarios such as:

- A smart cell phone or PDA that needs to access directory information but does not contain an LDAP client.
- A program that needs access to a directory through a firewall, but the firewall is not allowed to pass LDAP protocol traffic because it isn't capable of auditing such traffic.
- A programmer is writing an application using XML programming tools and techniques, and the application needs to access a directory.

DSMLv2 Sun ONE Directory Server 5.2 Software Implementation

The DSMLv2 interface is implemented as a front-end plug-in. The plug-in is configured to listen on an encrypted and a non-encrypted port. The configuration data for the service resides at the DN:

cn=DSMLv2-SOAP-HTTP,cn=frontends,cn=plugins,cn=config

The attributes stored here are described in TABLE 10-1.

TABLE 10-1   DSMLv2 Attributes

Attribute	Description
`ds-hdsml-clientauthmethod`	Defines how the server identifies a client on a TLS/SSL connection. Options are: • `clientCertOnly` – the server uses credentials from the client certificate • `httpBasicOnly` – the server uses the credentials from the HTTP authorization header • `clientCertFirst` – tries using the client certificate first, then the HTTP authentication header
`ds-hdsml-dsmlschemalocation`	The path to the DSMLv2 schema. This should not be changed.
`ds-hdsml-iobuffersize`	The size of the buffer where the DSML request is stored. The default is `8192` and must be a multiple of 256.
`ds-hdsml-poolmaxsize`	The maximum size of the pool of parsers. The default is `10`.
`ds-hdsml-poolsize`	The minimum size of the pool of parsers. The default is `5`.
`ds-hdsml-port`	The HTTP port used for unencrypted communications. The default is `80`, but must be changed if that port is in use.
`ds-hdsml-requestmaxsize`	The maximum size of a DSML request allowed by the server. The default is `32768`.
`ds-hdsml-responsemsgsize`	The maximum size of a server response to a DSML request. The default is `65536`.
`ds-hdsml-rooturl`	The root URL that is specified in a DSML request. The default is `/dsml`.
`ds-hdsml-secureport`	The port number used for secure DSML communication over TLS/SSL. There is no default port number.
`ds-hdsml-soapschemalocation`	The path to the SOAP schema. This value should not be changed.

To view these attributes and their values, use the `ldapsearch` command:

```
# ldapsearch -L -D "cn=directory manager" -w mysecret -b \
cn=frontends,cn=plugins,cn=config cn=DSMLv2-SOAP-HTTP
dn: cn=DSMLv2-SOAP-HTTP,cn=frontends,cn=plugins,cn=config
objectClass: top
objectClass: nsSlapdPlugin
objectClass: ds-signedPlugin
objectClass: extensibleObject
cn: DSMLv2-SOAP-HTTP
nsslapd-pluginPath: /var/mps/serverroot/lib/hdsml-plugin.so
nsslapd-pluginInitfunc: hdsml_init
nsslapd-pluginType: frontend
nsslapd-pluginVersion: 5.2
nsslapd-pluginVendor: Sun Microsystems, Inc.
nsslapd-pluginDescription: HTTP/SOAP/DSMLv2 frontend plugin
nsslapd-pluginId: http-soap-dsmlv2-frontend
ds-hdsml-port: 80
ds-hdsml-iobuffersize: 8192
ds-hdsml-requestmaxsize: 32768
ds-hdsml-responsemsgsize: 65536
ds-hdsml-poolsize: 5
ds-hdsml-poolmaxsize: 10
ds-hdsml-clientauthmethod: clientCertFirst
ds-hdsml-rooturl: /dsml
ds-hdsml-soapschemalocation: /var/mps/serverroot/lib/soap-env.xsd
ds-hdsml-dsmlschemalocation: /var/mps/serverroot/lib/DSMLv2.xsd
nsslapd-pluginEnabled: off
#
```

Note – By default, the DSMLv2 plug-in is turned off and no secure port is defined.

Configuring DSML

The Sun ONE Directory Server 5.2 software can be configured to listen to and process DSML requests either through the Console or from the command line. Configuration consists of:

- Enabling the plug-in
- Setting a security policy
- Changing the default values

To enable the plug-in, change the value of the `nsslapd-pluginEnabled` from `off` to `on`. After the attribute value is changed, the directory server must be restarted for the change to take effect.

Example:

```
# ldapmodify -D "cn=directory manager" -w mysecret
dn: cn=DSMLv2-SOAP-HTTP,cn=frontends,cn=plugins,cn=config
changetype: modify
replace: nsslapd-pluginEnabled
nsslapd-pluginEnabled: on
^D
# directoryserver stop
# directoryserver start
```

There are a number of authentication options that can be deployed, such as:

- Anonymous
- Basic HTTP
- Basic HTTP over TLS/SSL
- Client TLS/SSL certificates

Anonymous access is granted if no authorization header or client certificate is submitted with the DSML request. This is the same behavior that is defined in the LDAPv3 specification for normal directory access.

An authentication header can be included with the DSML request. If it is, basic HTTP authentication is performed. A technique called identity mapping is implemented on the directory server. This associates values in the header with user entries in the directory. The values in the header are the user name and password.

Unless a secure port is configured, communication to and from the directory server is sent in clear text. To avoid sending the authorization header in clear text, a secure port must be configured. With basic HTTP authentication over TLS/SSL, the client does not need to have a certificate. Only the server certificate is required.

The following code box shows how to specify a secure DSML port:

```
# ldapmodify -D "cn=directory manager" -w mysecret
dn: cn=DSMLv2-SOAP-HTTP,cn=frontends,cn=plugins,cn=config
changetype: modify
add: ds-hdsml-secureport
ds-hdsml-secureport: 1443
^D
# directoryserver stop
# directoryserver start
```

If the DSML request contains a client certificate, the authentication header is not required. Instead, a mapping of the certificate to one stored in the directory is performed. If a client certificate is found that matches the one sent in the DSML request, the request is authenticated.

Sun ONE Identity Synchronization for the Windows Technology

The Netscape Directory Server 4.1x software provided a facility for synchronizing user account data between a Windows NT Primary Domain Controller (PDC) and the directory. The technology was later bundled into the Sun ONE Meta-directory product. Since this technology was introduced, Microsoft has standardized on user authentication based on their Active Directory (AD) technology. While there might be some enterprises still using the old LAN manger style authentication service for which PDCs were based, most have switched to the new AD technology.

To interoperate in an AD environment, the Active Directory Connector for the Sun ONE Meta-directory Server was introduced. This product synchronizes user profile data for AD to the directory and from the directory to AD. This allows user information such as email addresses, phone numbers, and so on, to be shared between the Sun ONE Directory Server and AD. However, the AD Connector does not support password synchronization.

As an adjunct to Sun ONE Directory Server 5.2 software, the Sun ONE Identity Synchronization for the Windows (ISW) software was introduced. With the addition of this product and underlying technology, user passwords can be synchronized between Windows environments and the Solaris OE. This section describes this product and gives an overview of how it is configured and managed. Because of the complexity of the implementation, only an overview is presented. Full details can be found in the product documentation.

ISW Product Overview

The ISW 1.0 software provides bidirectional synchronization of passwords between Windows directories. This includes both Windows 2000 AD and the NT Security Access Manager (SAM) registry. If passwords are updated on the Sun ONE Directory Server software, they can be propagated to the Windows environment without the addition of software on the Windows system. If you want to update passwords in a Windows NT directory and have the passwords propagated to the Sun ONE Directory Server software, software must be added to the Windows system. No additional software is required to synchronize with AD.

The ISW 1.0 software is implemented primarily as a set of connectors. There is a connector for AD and one for NT SAM. The connectors can be used to connect to more than one controller or domain. To protect the passwords, transfers are made over an encrypted TLS/SSL LDAP channel. Not all passwords need to be synchronized. The administrator has the ability to specify a list of users who will have their passwords synchronized. Attributes other than `userPassword` can be synchronized.

A core component of ISW 1.0 is the Sun ONE Message Queue (MQ) that implements the Java™ Message Service (JMS). The Sun ONE MQ software provides secure and reliable message transfers. This is key because you need to protect the integrity of passwords and do not want password changes to be lost. The Sun MQ software establishes a trust between connectors and ensures that all password update messages are delivered. Another benefit of this approach is ease of system administration.

Deployment Scenarios

The ISW 1.0 software provides a great deal of flexibility. You can deploy unidirectional or bidirectional password synchronization between the Sun ONE Directory Server software and Windows 2000 AD, or between Sun ONE Directory Server software and Windows NT SAM. To understand how these deployment scenarios work, it is helpful to examine how passwords are propagated.

Keep in mind, that for password synchronization to work, updates need to be captured in clear text before they are committed to the directory. This is because passwords are stored in a one-way hash, so once committed cannot be reversed. Windows directories support different hashing algorithms than Sun ONE Directory Server software, so it is not sufficient to simply copy over the hashed version of the password. The directory must be able to capture the password in the clear so it can be hashed.

The following sections describe how password transfers occur with different scenarios.

Scenario 1 – Sun ONE Directory Server Software to Windows 2000 Active Directory

Assuming the user's password is changed from the Secured LDAP Client:

1. A user makes a password change by running the Solaris OE `passwd(1)` command.

2. The new password is passed to the directory as a text string over an encrypted TLS/SSL connection.

3. The Sun ONE Directory Server plug-in detects the change then sends it to the Sun ONE MQ over an encrypted connection. The directory database is updated.

4. The Sun ONE MQ sends the password update message to the AD connector.

5. The AD connector sends the password change to the Windows 2000 AD server, where it is committed.

6. The Sun ONE MQ updates the appropriate log files.

Scenario 2 – Windows 2000 Active Directory to Sun ONE Directory Server Software

Assuming the user password is changed from a Windows client:

1. The password change is sent to the AD, controller where it is committed.

2. The AD Connector detects a password change by monitoring the AD change log.

3. The AD Connector sends a password change event notification to the Sun ONE Directory Server Connector.

4. The corresponding user password in the directory is marked as invalid.

5. The user logs into a Secured LDAP Client

6. The Sun ONE Directory Server software plug-in detects an attempted login with a password marked invalid.

7. The Sun ONE Directory Server software plug-in sends the password to the AD Connector.

8. The AD Connector attempts to log into the AD Controller using the password sent to it.

9. If the login is successful, the user is authenticated and the directory is updated with the new password.

Scenario 3 – Windows NT SAM to Sun ONE Directory Server Software

In this scenario, a Change Detector DLL is installed on the Windows NT PDC.

1. The user makes a password change on a Windows client.

2. The Windows client sends the password change to the Windows PDC.

3. The DLL installed on the PDC detects the change and intercepts it before it is committed to the SAM.

4. The intercepted password is sent to the Sun ONE Directory Server software over an encrypted connection, where it is committed to the directory.

Administration Issues

The ISW 1.0 software is very flexible, offering several deployment options. Because of this flexibility, there are several administration decisions that need to be made. These include:

- Defining what user account entries look like.
- Deciding which users will have their passwords synchronized.
- Implementing either unidirectional or bidirectional synchronization.
- Creating Connector/Sun ONE MQ trust relationships.
- Configuring directories or domains that are to be synchronized.
- Automating the initial population of directories.

Conclusion

The ISW 1.0 software is a sophisticated and comprehensive solution for creating a unified login between the Solaris OE and Windows environments. Providing password synchronization between these two disparate environments is not a trivial task. Security must be maintained at all components and the synchronization must be performed reliably.

One could almost write an entire book based on the ISW 1.0 software. What was presented here is just an overview and a guide to get started. It is strongly recommended that experienced consulting services be enlisted before using this product in production mode.

NIS to LDAP Gateway

The NIS to LDAP Gateway, or NIS to LDAP transition service (N2L service) software, is in the BETA test phase. This software might not be shipping at the time this book is published. Because this software offers a helpful tool for companies migrating from NIS to LDAP, an overview of the service is provided for high-level awareness of this emerging technology.

Note – As with any software that is not officially released, the exact features, implementation techniques, or even the product as a whole is subject to change without notice. Use the following information for general familiarity.

The NIS to LDAP transition service is a service that replaces an NIS master. Instead of maintaining name service data in DBM files, an LDAP directory is used as a back-end store. In many respects, N2L services is similar to the NIS+ Gateway discussed in Chapter 6 "Management Tools and Toolkits." The obvious difference is that native NIS clients are supported instead of native NIS+ clients.

The Directory Information Tree (DIT) that N2L services uses is the same DIT that Secured LDAP Clients use. Therefore, you can set up a single DIT that supports NIS clients accessing the directory through N2L services and clients that access the directory directly through LDAP operations.

The intention of N2L services is not to simply replace NIS. Instead, it is meant to be used as a tool to migrate from NIS to LDAP-based name services. By using N2L transition services, you can begin to deploy LDAP without having to modify client software. This is an important consideration especially if clients are running a version of the operating system earlier than Solaris 8 OE, because these versions do not have a Secured LDAP Client.

Comparison with NIS Extensions

Companion software to the Netscape Directory Server 4.1x, (NsDS 4.1x) software was introduced, called NIS Extension to Netscape Directory Server 4.1x. This software is tightly coupled to NsDS4.1x, and is not available for the Sun ONE Directory Server 5.x software versions. One reason for this is the Extension's reliance on a directory plug-in that was written to an API that changed in newer versions of the Sun ONE Directory Server software.

The purpose of the plug-in is to detect operations performed on the directory that affected name service data. If an entry was added, deleted, or modified the plug-in notifies the dsypserv process running on the same server where the change occurred. The dsypserv process then regenerates the affected NIS DBM files. The problems with the plug-in implementation are:

- There are no standards for directory plug-in APIs, so they are subject to change.
- The plug-in expected the dsypserv to be running on the same server which limited scalability.
- The directory server had to run as root so it could create the NIS DBM files.

The NIS Extensions support bi-directional synchronization. This means you can update the NIS DBM files with NIS tools like makedbm or update the directory data through LDAP operations. While this provides flexibility, inconsistencies can develop if both methods are used concurrently. For this reason, it is recommended that one method be chosen, and only that method used. To implement NIS to LDAP synchronization, modifications to the NIS Makefile are required.

To perform the synchronization from NIS DBM files to LDAP data, a program called dsimport needs to be run. The dsimport program relies on a mapping file to determine how changes should be mapped to LDAP data. The dsimport program also must query the directory to see if an updated entry exists, and if it does, identify which attributes are affected. The mapping file format is very complex and not well documented. While it is possible to create a mapping for custom maps, it is very difficult.

The NIS Extensions are based on a schema that is different than what a Solaris OE LDAP naming client uses. This means that, with this technology, you cannot support both Solaris OE LDAP name clients and NIS clients using the same DIT.

LDAP Standards Information

LDAP, like any other standards-based technology, is defined in great detail in a series of documents which are publicly available. As the technology matures and becomes more popular, requests for enhancements are inevitable, necessitating changes to these documents. We could have included copies of the current revision of LDAP documents, but the dynamic nature of LDAP technology would soon make them outdated so, instead of including these documents, we provide information on them and their location.

The following sections provide guidelines to important documents and pointers to where they can be found.

Locating RFCs and Internet Drafts

To locate the specifics of protocols such as LDAP v3, look at RFCs and Internet Drafts. RFC, which stands for Request for Comments, is where each distinct version of an Internet standards-related specification is published as part of the Request for Comments (RFC) document series. This archival series is the official publication channel for Internet standards documents and other publications of the Internet community.

The sites below do not list all the RFCs defining a particular standard; some, are classified as Experimental, Informational, Historic, or Early (before IETF— standards track). Most RFCs start off as Internet Drafts before being approved as RFCs. When you are searching for a particular RFC or Internet Draft, you will find that it is available at mirrored sites all over the world.

The following sites are not complete but can be used as a starting place for locating your favorite (and most useful) RFCs:

```
http://www.rfc-editor.org/rfcsearch.html
```

```
http://www.ietf.org/rfc/rfc.html
```

```
http://src.doc.ic.ac.uk/computing/internet/rfc/
```

```
ftp://src.doc.ic.ac.uk/computing/internet/rfc/
```

```
http://info.internet.isi.edu:80/in-notes/rfc/files/
```

```
ftp://ds.internic.net/rfc/
```

For example, if you want to access a particular RFC and you know the specific RFC number, say, RFC 2251, you would type 2251 in the box provided. If you do not know the RFC number, use the URL in the following example to locate the RFC you are interested in.

```
http://www.rfc-editor.org/rfcsearch.htm
```

This Web site enables you to specify the RFC number and other information such as the Title. You can enter the word LDAP and, assuming you have set the maximum number of entries returned high enough, all the LDAP-related RFCs will be returned. Be aware that if you search for an Internet Draft and you are unable to find it, it does not mean that the draft does not exist! You may need to refine your search—try searching for the same draft with a higher number.

Life Cycle of an RFC

The first step toward publication of an RFC is publication of the document as an Internet Draft. Internet Drafts are working documents of the IETF, its areas, and its working groups (sometimes ending in ietf-*workinggroupname*). Today, many LDAP related drafts are individual submissions and they do not have an ietf extension.

Once an Internet Draft has been submitted, it has a life span of six months; after that time the Internet Draft expires. Expiration means either that a new draft is submitted (which typically means that a new draft is issued with a higher sequential number) or that the Internet Draft has expired and is no longer available. When an Internet Draft expires, it is deleted. Sometimes, you receive a date and timestamp with the information that a particular Internet Draft was deleted.

When the document reaches consensus of the Internet community, it is published as an RFC. RFCs can be of different types, such as the Standards Tracks RFC which include the Proposed Standard, Draft Standard, and Standard. Not all documents are published in the Standards Track; it is also possible to have the documents published as Historical, Experimental, or Informational; these are not Internet Standards.

You can also find Internet Drafts at these sites:

IETF: `ftp://ftp.ietf.org/internet-drafts/`

Africa: `ftp.is.co.za`

Canada: `ftp.normos.org`

Sweden: `ftp.nordu.net`

Switzerland: `ftp://sunsite.cnlab-switch.ch`

Italy: `ftp.nic.it`

Pacific Rim: `munnari.oz.au`

US West Coast: `ftp.isi.edu`

South America: `ftp.ietf.rnp.br`

LDAP RFCs and Internet Drafts

This section lists some of the LDAP RFCs and provides a sample of LDAP Internet Drafts.

LDAP RFCs

RFC 1823: *The C LDAP Application Program Interface*

RFC 1823 defines the old LDAPv2 interface. This RFC will eventually be replaced by a document that is currently an Internet Draft. This Internet Draft defines the LDAPv3 extensions to the C API for accessing LDAP.

Status: INFORMATIONAL

RFC 2247: *Using Domains in LDAP/X.500 Distinguished Names*

This document defines an algorithm by which a name registered with the Internet Domain Name System (DNS) can be represented as an LDAP-distinguished name.

Status: PROPOSED STANDARD

RFC 2251: *Lightweight Directory Access Protocol (v3)*

This is the main RFC for LDAPv3 and defines the protocol operations, data representation, and data organization.

Status: PROPOSED STANDARD

RFC 2252: *Lightweight Directory Access Protocol (v3): Attribute Syntax Definitions*

LDAP transmits most attribute values as strings, rather than as binary structures. For example, the number 4,000 is transmitted as "4000". This document defines the standard attribute type representations and specifies how attribute values are compared for each standard type during a search operation.

Status: PROPOSED STANDARD

RFC 2253: *Lightweight Directory Access Protocol (v3): UTF-8 String Representation of Distinguished Names*

Each entry in an LDAP directory is uniquely identified by its distinguished name (DN), represented as a string. This document defines the syntax and structure of these names.

Status: PROPOSED STANDARD

RFC 2254: *The String Representation of LDAP Search Filters*

The basic LDAPv3 RFC (RFC 2251) defines a binary format for search expressions passed from a client to a server. However, users of clients compose and submit search requests in an easily readable and printable string format, which is defined in RFC 2254.

Status: PROPOSED STANDARD

RFC 2255: *The LDAP URL Format*

RFC 2255 defines the URL format for expressing an LDAP search. You can enter an LDAP URL in many browsers to perform an LDAP search.

Status: PROPOSED STANDARD

RFC 2256: *A Summary of the X.500(96) User Schema for Use with LDAPv3*

Where possible, LDAP leverages the schema standardization work of X.500, rather than inventing new standards for schema information. This document defines standard attributes for representing a person in an LDAP entry. These attributes are based on the X.500 standard.

Status: PROPOSED STANDARD

RFC 2307: *An Approach for Using LDAP as a Network Information Service*

This document describes an experimental mechanism for mapping entities related to TCP/IP and the UNIX system into X.500 entries so that they can be resolved with the LDAP protocol.

Status: EXPERIMENTAL

RFC 2589: *LDAPv3 Extensions for Dynamic Directory Services*

This document defines extended operations to support dynamic (short-lived) directory data storage.

Status: PROPOSED STANDARD

RFC 2596: *Use of Language Codes in LDAP*

This document describes how language codes as defined in RFC 1766 are carried in LDAP and are to be interpreted by LDAP servers.

Status: PROPOSED STANDARD

RFC 2696: *LDAP Control Extension for Simple Paged Results Manipulation*

This document describes an LDAPv3 control extension for simple paging of search results. This control extension allows a client to control the rate at which an LDAP server returns the results of an LDAP search operation.

Status: INFORMATIONAL

RFC 2713: *Schema for Representing Java™ Objects in an LDAP Directory*

This document defines the schema for representing Java™ objects in an LDAP (v3) directory.

Status: INFORMATIONAL

RFC 2714: *Schema for Representing CORBA Object References in an LDAP Directory*

This document defines the schema for representing CORBA object references in an LDAP (v3) directory.

Status: INFORMATIONAL

RFC 2739: *Calendar Attributes for vCard and LDAP*

This document describes a mechanism to locate (URI) an individual user's calendar and free/busy time.

Status: PROPOSED STANDARD

RFC 2798: *Definition of the inetOrgPerson LDAP Object Class*

This document defines a person object class that meets the requirements found in today's Internet and Intranet directory service deployments.

Status: INFORMATIONAL

RFC 2829: *Authentication Methods for LDAP*

This document specifies particular combinations of security mechanisms which are required and recommended in LDAP implementations.

Status: PROPOSED STANDARD

RFC 2830: *Lightweight Directory Access Protocol (v3) Extension for Transport Layer Security*

This document defines the Start Transport Layer Security (TLS) Operation for LDAP [LDAPv3, TLS]. This operation provides for TLS establishment in an LDAP association and is defined in terms of an LDAP extended request.

Status: PROPOSED STANDARD

RFC 2849: *The LDAP Data Interchange Format (LDIF) - Technical Specification*

This document specifies an Internet standards track protocol for the Internet community and requests discussion and suggestions for improvements.

Status: PROPOSED STANDARD

RFC 2891: *LDAP Control Extension for Server Side Sorting of Search Results*

This document describes two LDAP v3 control extensions for server side sorting of search results. These controls allow a client to specify the attribute types and matching rules a server should use when returning the results to an LDAP search request. The sort controls allow a server to return a result code for the sorting of the results that is independent of the result code returned for the search operation.

Status: PROPOSED STANDARD

RFC 3045: *Storing Vendor Information in the LDAP root DSE*

This document specifies two Lightweight Directory Access Protocol (LDAP) attributes, vendorName and vendorVersion that may be included in the root DSA-specific Entry (DSE) to advertise vendor-specific information. These two attributes supplement the attributes defined in section 3.4 of RFC 2251. The information held in these attributes MAY be used for display and informational purposes and must not be used for feature advertisement or discovery.

Status: INFORMATIONAL

RFC 3296: *Named Subordinate References in Lightweight Directory Access Protocol (LDAP) Directories*

This RFC describes schema and protocol elements for representing and managing named subordinate references in Lightweight Directory Access Protocol (LDAP) Directories.

Status: PROPOSED STANDARD

RFC 3377: *Lightweight Directory Access Protocol (v3): Technical Specification*

This document specifies the set of RFCs comprising the Lightweight Directory Access Protocol Version 3 (LDAPv3), and addresses an *IESG Note* attached to RFCs 2251 through 2256.

Status: PROPOSED STANDARD

LDAP Internet Drafts

Internet Drafts have a set path that they follow every six months. When you start looking at Internet Drafts, you will be amazed by the number of available drafts that are related to LDAP.

The LDAP Bis is a newly created working group whose charter will be to move the LDAP v3 to a Standard, by reissuing the LDAP v3 RFCs and renewing ambiguities.

The LDAPEXT (LDAP Extension) working group is just as important as the LDUP working group by providing LDAP v3 with a standard access control model for the representation and semantic access control information.

The LDUP (LDAP Duplication Replication Update Protocols) working group is a working group for LDAP users. This working group is in its finishing up, and is in the process of publishing most of the work as INFORMATIONAL and EXPERIMENTAL, implying that this working group will not define a standard for LDAP server replication.

Controls and Extended Operations

Persistent Search: A Simple LDAP Change Notification Mechanism, (`draft-ietf-ldapext-psearch-03.txt`)

This document defines two controls that extend the LDAP v3 search operation to provide a simple mechanism by which an LDAP client can receive notification of changes that occur in an LDAP server. The mechanism is designed to be very flexible yet easy for clients and servers to implement. Since the IETF is likely to pursue a different, more comprehensive solution in this area, this document will eventually be published with Informational status in order to document an existing practice.

LDAP Extensions for Scrolling View Browsing of Search Results, (`draft-ietf-ldapext-ldapv3-vlv-09.txt`)

This document describes a Virtual List View (vlv) control extension for the LDAP Search operation. This control is designed to allow the "virtual list box" feature, common in existing commercial email address book applications, to be supported efficiently by LDAP servers. LDAP servers' inability to support this client feature is a significant impediment to LDAP replacing proprietary protocols in commercial email systems. The control allows a client to specify that the server return, for a given LDAP search with associated sort keys, a contiguous subset of the search result set. This subset is specified in terms of offsets into the ordered list, or in terms of a greater than or equal comparison value.

LDAP Control for a Duplicate Entry Representation of Search Results, (`draft-ietf-ldapext-ldapv3-dupent-04.txt`)

This document describes a Duplicate Entry Representation control extension for the LDAP Search operation. By using the control with an LDAP search, a client requests that the server return separate entries for each value held in the specified attributes. For instance, if a specified attribute of an entry holds multiple values, the search operation will return multiple instances of that entry, each instance holding a separate single value in that attribute.

Returning Matched Values with LDAP v3, (`draft-ietf-ldapext-matchedval-02.txt`)

This document describes a control for the LDAP v3 that is used to return a subset of attribute values from an entry, specifically, only those values that match a "values return" filter. Without support for this control, a client must retrieve all of an attribute's values and search for specific values locally.

A Taxonomy of Methods for LDAP Clients Finding Servers, (`draft-ietf-ldapext-ldap-taxonomy-02.txt`)

There are several different methods for an LDAP client to find an LDAP server. This draft discusses these methods and provides pointers for interested parties to learn more about implementing a particular method.

Discovering LDAP Services with DNS, (`draft-ietf-ldapext-locate-03.txt`)

This document specifies a method for discovering such servers using information in the Domain Name System.

Authentication and Security

X.509 Authentication SASL Mechanism, (`draft-ietf-ldapext-x509-sasl-03.txt`)

This document defines a SASL authentication mechanism based on X.509 strong authentication, providing two-way authentication. This mechanism is only for authentication and has no effect on the protocol encodings and is not designed to provide integrity or confidentiality services.

Information and X.500 Documents

A great deal of the LDAP standards are based on the standards model of X.500. As you may have noticed, the LDAP standards documentation is freely available on the Internet today. This is not the case when dealing with the basic X.500 documentation. If you are interested in gaining access to this documentation, then you must purchase it from the International Telecommunication Union (ITU) or International Organization for Standardization (ISO). Here is the location from which the X.500 documentation may be purchased:

http://www.itu.int/itudoc/itu-t/rec/x/x500up/

The following list of documents has been taken from the book *Understanding X.500 The Directory* by David Chadwick.

- The Directory (CCITT REC. X.500-X.521 | ISO/IEC Standard 9594:1993)
- X.500: *Overview of Concepts, Models and Services*
- X.501: *Models*
- X.509: *Authentication Framework*
- X.511: *Abstract Service Definition*
- X.518: *Procedures for Distributed Operations*
- X.519: *Protocol Specifications*
- X.520: *Selected Attribute Types*
- X.521: *Selected Object Classes*
- X.525: *Replication*

The North American Directory Forum (NADF) Documents (April 1993)

- SD-0: *NADF Standing Documents: A Brief Overview*
- SD-1: *Terms of Reference*
- SD-2: *Program Plan*
- SD-3: *Service Description*
- SD-4: *The Directory Schema*
- SD-5: *An X.500 Naming Scheme for National DIT Subtrees and Its Application for C= CA and C=US*
- SD-6: *Guidelines on Naming and Subtrees*
- SD-7: *Mapping the North American DIT onto Directory Management Domains*
- SD-8: *The Experimental Pilot Plan*
- SD-9: *Charter, Procedure, and Operations of the Central Administration for NADF*
- SD-10: *Security and Privacy: Policy and Services*
- SD-11: *Directory Security: Mechanisms and Practicality*
- SD-12: *Registry of ADDMD Names*

EWOS Directory Functional Standards

- A/711 (A/DI1): *Directory Access*, published as ENV 41 210 (also published as ISP 10615 parts 1 and 2)
- A/712 (A/DI2): *Directory System Protocol*, published as ENV 41 212 (also published as ISP 10615 parts 3 and 4)
- A/713 (A/DI32): *Dynamic Behavior of DSAs for Distributed Operations*, published as ENV 41 215 (also published as ISP 10615 part 6)
- A/714 (A/DI31): *Directory User Agents Distributed Operation*, published as ENV 41 217 (also published as ISP 10615 part 5)
- Q/511 (F/DI11): *Common Directory Use*, published as ENV 41 512 (also published as ISP 10616; see also ISO/IEC PDISP)

- Q/512 (F/DI2): *Directory Data Definitions Directory Use by MHS*
- Q/513 (F/DI3): *Directory Data Definitions FTAM Use of the Directory* (to be published as ISP 11190)
- ETG XXX: *Introduction to Directory Profiles* (final draft)
- ETG 017: *Error Handling in the OSI Directory* (final draft, May 1992)
- ETG XXX: *Security Architecture for the Directory* (fifth draft in 1992)

Joint ISO Standards and CCITT Recommendations

- ISO/IEC 8824:1988 | CCITT X.208: *Specification of Abstract Syntax Notation One (ASN.1)*
- ISO/IEC 8824-2 DIS (1993) | CCITT X.208-2: *Abstract Syntax Notation One (ASN.1): Information Object Specification*
- ISO/IEC 8825-1 | CCITT X.209-1: *Part 1: Basic Encoding Rules (BER)*
- ISO/IEC 8825-3 DIS (1993) | CCITT X.209-3: *Part 3: Distinguished Encoding Rules*
- ISO/IEC 9072-1 | CCITT X.219: *Remote Operations Model, Notation and Service Definition*
- ISO 8649:1988 | CCITT X.217: *Service Definition for the Association Control Service Element*

Other ISO Documents

- ISO/IEC JTC 1/SC21 N6063: *Use of Object Identifiers to Access Directory Information* (May 1991)
- ISO 3166:1988: *Codes for the Representation of Names of Countries*
- ISO IS 10162/3: *Documentation Search and Retrieve Service Definition/Protocol Specification*
- ISO 6523:1984: *Data Interchange Structure for the Identification of Organizations*
- ISO/IEC 10646-1:1993: *(E) Information Technology Universal Multiple-Octet Coded Character Set (UCS)*
- ISO/IEC PDISP 10616: *International Standardized Profile FDI11 Directory Data Definitions Common Directory Use* (February 1993)

LDAP v3 Result Codes

This appendix explains some of the LDAP error codes that can be returned by your LDAP server. It is not a complete list and does not discuss the mechanism of why an LDAP server gives a particular error. To find out additional information on error codes refer to RFC 2251, which defines these error codes. Also, as another very useful resource, see Internet Draft `draft-just-ldapv3-rescodes-02.txt`, which details exact descriptions of these error codes. Finally, you may also want to refer to the `ldap.h` file, which in the case of the Solaris Operating Environment can be found in `/usr/include`.

In addition to reviewing the RFC 2251, review the access and error log files, which are located by default under `/var/mps/serverroot/`*slapd-instance*`/logs`. These files can help you debug certain problems with your directory server.

The error codes in TABLE B-1 apply to the iPlanet Directory Server, and possibly to other LDAP servers, but not to all. This list is not comprehensive. Codes without comments in the third column are not currently returned to clients by Netscape Directory Server or generated by the SDK.

TABLE B-1   LDAP Error Codes

0	0x00	LDAP_CONNECTION_SUCCESS	The operation completed successfully.
1	0x01	LDAP_OPERATIONS_ERROR	Invalid syntax for ACI or schema, or inappropriate control for the operation.
2	0x02	LDAP_PROTOCOL_ERROR	Invalid filter expression on search, or DN on add, modify, or delete.
3	0x03	LDAP_TIME_LIMIT_EXCEEDED	Either the server's or the client's specified search time limit was exceeded.

TABLE B-1   LDAP Error Codes *(Continued)*

4	0x04	LDAP_SIZE_LIMIT_EXCEEDED	Either the server's or the client's specified limit on number of search results was exceeded.
5	0x05	LDAP_COMPARE_FALSE	A compare operation returns mismatch.
6	0x06	LDAP_COMPARE_TRUE	A compare operation returns match.
7	0x07	LDAP_STRONG_AUTH_METHOD_NOT_SUPPORTED	The server does not support the requested authentication method.
8	0x08	LDAP_STRONG_AUTH_REQUIRED	The server requires an authentication method stronger than unencrypted user name and password.
9	0x09	LDAP_PARTIAL_RESULTS	The client has bound with LDAP v2, or the server supports only LDAP v2, and the base DN specified by the client is not among the naming contexts of the server.
10	0x0a	LDAP_REFERRAL	The server is configured to return a referral or search reference when an operation is directed toward this DN. This is an LDAP v3 error ONLY.
11	0x0b	LDAP_ADMIN_LIMIT_EXCEEDED	To satisfy the search request, the server would need to process too many entries; the search may need to be narrowed, or the server's lookthrough limit raised.
12	0x0c	LDAP_UNAVAILABLE_CRITICAL_EXTENSION	A control was provided with request; the control was tagged as critical, but the server doesn't support it.

13	**0x0d**	`LDAP_CONFIDENTIALITY_REQUIRED`	This error code is new in LDAPv3. This error code may be returned if the session is not protected by a protocol which provides session confidentiality. For example, if the client did not establish a TLS connection using a cipher suite which provides confidentiality of the session before sending any other requests, and the server requires session confidentiality then the server may reject that request with a result code of `confidentialityRequired`.
14	**0x0e**	`LDAP_SASL_BIND_IN_PROGRESS`	SASL authentication is being negotiated between the client and the server.
16	**0x10**	`LDAP_NO_SUCH_ATTRIBUTE`	An attribute to be modified or deleted was not present in the entry.
17	**0x11**	`LDAP_UNDEFINED_ATTRIBUTE_TYPE`	Applicable operations: Modify, Add. This error may be returned if the specified attribute is unrecognized by the server, since it is not present in the server's defined schema. If the server doesn't recognize an attribute specified in a search request as the attribute to be returned, the server should not return an error in this case - it should just return values for the requested attributes it does recognize. Note that this result code applies only to the Add and Modify operations
18	**0x12**	`LDAP_INAPPROPRIATE_MATCHING`	The value specified doesn't adhere to the syntax definition for that attribute.

19	**0x13**	`LDAP_CONSTRAINT_VIOLATION`	Invalid attribute for this entry, or new password does not meet password policy requirements
20	**0x14**	`LDAP_ATTRIBUTE_OR_VALUE_EXISTS`	Attempt to add an identical attribute value to an existing one.
21	**0x15**	`LDAP_INVALID_ATTRIBUTE_SYNTAX`	
32	**0x20**	`LDAP_NO_SUCH_OBJECT`	Attempt to bind with a nonexistent DN, to search with a nonexistent base DN, or to modify or delete a nonexistent DN.
33	**0x21**	`LDAP_ALIAS_PROBLEM`	Applicable operations: Search. An alias has been dereferenced which names no object.
34	**0x22**	`LDAP_INVALID_DN_SYNTAX`	Invalid DN or RDN specified on adding an entry or modifying an RDN.
35	**0x23**	`LDAP_IS_LEAF`	
36	**0x24**	`LDAP_ALIAS_DEREFERENCING_PROBLEM`	Applicable operations: Search. An alias was encountered in a situation where it was not allowed or where access was denied. For example, if the client does not have read permission for the `aliasedObjectName` attribute and its value, then the error `aliasDereferencing` Problem should be returned.
48	**0x30**	`LDAP_INAPPROPRIATE_AUTHENTICATION`	Applicable operations: Bind. This error should be returned by the server when the client has tried to use a method of authentication that is inappropriate.

49	0x31	LDAP_INVALID_CREDENTIALS	Invalid password or other credentials supplied on bind.
50	0x32	LDAP_INSUFFICIENT_ACCESS_RIGHTS	Give the user the proper privileges. Check the ACL rules to make sure they are correct.
51	0x33	LDAP_BUSY	Applicable operations: All. This error code may be returned if the server is unable to process the client's request at this time. This implies that if the client retries the request shortly, the server will be able to process it then.
52	0x34	LDAP_UNAVAILABLE	Returned by SDK if server is not accessible.
53	0x35	LDAP_UNWILLING_TO_PERFORM	User not allowed to change password, password expired, operation not implemented (moddn), attempt to modify read-only attribute, attempt to delete all schema elements, attempt to delete an object class that has derived object classes, attempt to delete a read-only schema element, the database is read-only, no back end (database) is available for the operation, or other uncategorized error.
54	0x36	LDAP_LOOP_DETECT	Applicable operations: All. This error may be returned by the server if it detects an alias or referral loop and is unable to satisfy the client's request.

64	0x40	LDAP_NAMING_VIOLATION	Applicable operations: Add, ModifyDN.
			The attempted addition or modification would violate the structure rules of the DIT as defined in the directory schema and X.501. That is, it would place an entry as the subordinate of an alias entry, or in a region of the DIT not permitted to a member of its object class, or would define an RDN for an entry to include a forbidden attribute type.
65	0x41	LDAP_OBJECT_CLASS_VIOLATION	Invalid attribute specified for modify operation on an entry. Update the schema.
66	0x42	LDAP_NOT_ALLOWED_ON_NONLEAF	Attempt to delete an entry that has child nodes.
67	0x43	LDAP_NOT_ALLOWED_ON_RDN	Applicable operations: Delete, ModifyDN.
			Attempt to modify the value of the attribute which is the RDN of the entry.
68	0x44	LDAP_ENTRY_ALREADY_EXISTS	No need to update the directory server, since it already has this value/entry.
69	0x45	LDAP_OBJECT_CLASS_MODS_PROHIBITED	Applicable operations: Modify.
			An operation attempted to modify an object class that should not be modified, for example, the structural object class of an entry.
70	0x46	LDAP_RESULTS_TOO_LARGE	

71	0x47	LDAP_AFFECTS_MULTIPLE_DSAS	X.500 restricts the ModifyDN operation to only affect entries that are contained within a single server. If the LDAP server is mapped onto DAP, this restriction will apply and this result code will be returned if this error occurred.
80	0x50	LDAP_OTHER	
81	0x51	LDAP_SERVER_DOWN	SDK could not connect to server. Start the directory server.
82	0x52	LDAP_LOCAL_ERROR	
83	0x53	LDAP_ENCODING_ERROR	
84	0x54	LDAP_DECODING_ERROR	
85	0x55	LDAP_TIMEOUT	
86	0x56	LDAP_AUTH_UNKNOWN	
87	0x57	LDAP_FILTER_ERROR	
88	0x58	LDAP_USER_CANCELLED	
89	0x59	LDAP_PARAM_ERROR	No modifications on a modify operation, no attributes on an add operation, invalid scope or empty search filter on search, or other invalid argument to an SDK method.
90	0x5a	LDAP_NO_MEMORY	
91	0x5b	LDAP_CONNECT_ERROR	SDK reports unexpected error connecting to server.
92	0x5c	LDAP_NOT_SUPPORTED	
93	0x5d	LDAP_CONTROL_NOT_FOUND	
94	0x5e	LDAP_NO_RESULTS_RETURNED	
95	0x5f	LDAP_MORE_RESULTS_TO_RETURN	
96	0x60	LDAP_CLIENT_LOOP	
97	0x61	LDAP_REFERRAL_LIMIT_EXCEEDED	SDK reports hop limit exceeded on referral processing.

Using snoop with LDAP

This appendix discusses the snoop utility and how snoop can be used to debug the Solaris OE Secured LDAP Client.

In particular, this appendix introduces you to the snoop command set and how to get the information you want. This appendix provides common examples of using the LDAP APIs. Finally, snoop is used to analyze the LDAP packet.

Background

Many people think of the OSI seven-layer model. For TCP/IP, it is probably more useful to focus on four layers as described in TABLE C-1:

TABLE C-1   TCP/IP Protocol Suite Layers

OSI Layer	Description
Application Layer (SMTP, TELNET, LDAP)	Application layer protocols such as TELNET and LDAP, use a transport layer (TCP) to send their protocol messages as streams of bytes from one host to another.

TABLE C-1   TCP/IP Protocol Suite Layers *(Continued)*

OSI Layer	Description
Transport Layer (TCP & UDP)	Applications use the transport layer via an API such as sockets. TCP is a connection-orientated transport layer and provides applications a way of sending arbitrary streams of data to each other. UDP Port numbers allows one machine to send datagrams to another machine over IP.
Network Layer (IP, IPX, and so on)	The network layer sends packets of information from one host to another. The packets are often sent via a number of hops across data-link layers. This layer is also responsible for fragmentation, (the splitting of packets into smaller fragments that will fit into a data-link frame) and routing (deciding what the next hop is for any particular packet).
Data Link Layer (Ethernet, Token Ring, FDDI)	The data-link layer transfers frames from the host to another directly connected host.

Each layer has a specific purpose independent of the others, yet each layer talks to the next layer. Data starts at the application layer, works its way down the stack to the data-link layer, and is then sent to the other system. The other system's data-link layer receives the frame, then sends it up the stack.

The snoop utility in the Solaris OE provides you with the ability to debug problems on a network by capturing packets from the network and displaying their contents. snoop uses both the network packet filter and streams buffer modules to provide efficient capture of packets from the network.

Note – The Solaris 8 and 9 OE snoop utility has been enhanced with new options to facilitate both IPv4 and IPv6 protocols.

Having this functionality is very useful in diagnosing and debugging problems. snoop has many features, including the ability to let you to filter Ethernet packets for specific information contained within a specific packet. Using several command-line options, it is possible to use snoop in such a way that you can view specific portions of Ethernet packets as they pass along your network.

If you do not know, or are unsure if you are running the Solaris 8 7/01 OE or above, a recommended approach to finding this out, is to enter the following command:

$ **cat /etc/release**

Running this command shows you the installed version of the Solaris OE. If you are running the Solaris 8 7/01 OE, you will see something similar to the following output:

Solaris 8 Maintenance 7/01 applied

The reason for bringing this to your attention is the fact that there is no visible LDAP specific characteristics to this version of snoop. In addition, no other documentation, apart from a minor change to the snoop (1M) man page exists for this enhanced functionality. In general, the ldap module is just one of several other protocol decoders for snoop.

What is snoop?

The /usr/sbin/snoop utility is an executable that reads frames from your network interface or from a previously saved capture file. In addition, snoop allows you to filter the data it is collecting. For example, you can specify that you want to capture TCP segments to or from port 389 (such as LDAP traffic). You must be root to capture data from a network interface due to the device permissions (for example, permissions on the /dev/hme device). What makes snoop so powerful is the detail of information it provides, and the flexibility of the tool.

Using the snoop command results in one of the following objectives:

- Captures and displays network packets.
- Captures network packets and saves them to a capture file.
- Reads from a capture file and displays the contents
- Reads from one capture file and writes to another capture file (used primarily with filtering to select packets of interest)

When snoop is reading packets (capturing network packets, or reading from a capture file) it allows you to filter specific packets you are interested in. For example: to select the telnet traffic between hosta and hostb you might issue the following command:

snoop port 23 between hosta hostb

How snoop Works

The basic design of snoop is quite simple. If you understand how to use snoop in general, there is no special knowledge required or additional options for the LDAP specific case.

Depending on whether you're reading from a captured file or not, the main function either calls net_read() to begin processing packets off the network or *cap_read()* to begin processing them from a file. Upon completion of being passed to one of the above mentioned functions, the function passes the data to *scan()*.

The function scan() goes through each packet, and depending on whether you want to further interpret the packet or not, calls the process_pkt(), which in turn calls the appropriate protocol decoder function.

Interpreting and displaying each packet depends on what flags are set. The interpreters send the data piece of the packet (a pointer and the length) to the next level interpreter. Most of the actual work decoding the ldap context is done by decpdu which is called from decode_ldap after taking into account a hack to take care of multi-packet PDUs (with some restrictions). This ability to decode multi-packet PDUs is the one feature that sets this module apart from most, if not all of the other snoop modules.

snoop Options

Let's take a look at what options we can use with snoop. TABLE C-2 depicts two columns which describe snoop options.

TABLE C-2   Common snoop Options

Options	Definition
-c maxcount	Exit after capturing maxcounts packets
-C	List the code generated from the filter expression for either the kernel packet filter, or snoop's own filter
-d device	Receive packets from the network using the interface specified by device, usually, le0 or hme0.
-D	Display the number of packets dropped during a capture on the summary line.

TABLE C-2   Common snoop Options *(Continued)*

Options	Definition
-i filename	Display packets previously captured in a filename.
-n filename	Use the filename as an IP address to name mapping table.
-N	Create an IP address to name file from a capture file.
-o filename	Save the captured packets in a filename as they are captured.
-p first, last	Select one or more packets to be displayed from a captured file.
-P	Capture packets in non-promiscuous mode.

Changes to the snoop Utility in the Solaris OE

TABLE C-3 depicts some of the new options that have been added to the Solaris snoop command.

TABLE C-3   New snoop Options

New Solaris OE Options	Definition
-q	When capturing network packets into a file, do not display the packet count.
-r	Do not resolve the IP address to the symbolic name. This option prevents snoop from generating network traffic while capturing and displaying packets.
inet, inet6, inetboth	A qualifier that modifies the host primitive. If you specify inet, then try to resolve the host name to an IPv4 address. If you specify inet6, then try to resolve to an IPv6 address. If you specify inetboth, then try both IP v4 and IPv6, either or none.
slp	Tells snoop to select an SLP packet.

Protocol Decoders for snoop

The snoop utility can understand and decode a large number of protocols. It uses protocol decoder modules to do this. Some of the modules are listed in TABLE C-4:

TABLE C-4   Protocol Decoders Available for snoop

Protocol Decoder	Protocol Decoder	Protocol Decoder
snoop_arp	snoop_nis	snoop_nfs
snoop_bparam	snoop_nisplus	snoop_nfs3
snoop_dhcp	snoop_tcp	snoop_mount
snoop_dns	snoop_rpc	snoop_slp
snoop_ether	snoop_ipsec	snoop_ip
snoop_http	snoop_udp	snoop_ether
snoop_icmp	snoop_ldap	snoop_tftp

Note – This is not an exhaustive list.

Running snoop with LDAP in Mind

Before you run the snoop utility, you must decide if you want real-time data or you'd prefer to capture packets to a snoop-capture file. In most situations, you will want to capture the data to a file. In real-time mode, the data flies across your screen much too fast for you to read. The only real benefit of real-time mode is to give you a quick feel for the traffic that's moving on your network. To do some serious analysis, you'll want to capture packets to a file so you can take your time with them.

snoop syntax:

`/usr/sbin/snoop [options]`

The syntax and complete list of options for snoop are described in snoop (1M) man page. The examples in this article focus on snoop options that are related to LDAP. The examples that follow use the following snoop syntax and options depending on the desired level of tracing:

- For basic tracing:

  `snoop [port portnumber] [LDAPhostname]`

  Where port is the keyword, *portnumber* is the port number obtained from the `/etc/services` file, and *LDAPhostname* is the host name of the host used to capture packets, as either the source or

  destination, and display them as they are received.

- For summary mode (by using the -V option):

  `snoop -V [port portnumber] [LDAPhostname]`

- For detailed snoop trace using the verbose mode (-v option), which provides a detailed packet header trace:

  `snoop -v [port portnumber] [LDAPhostname]`

Note – Instead of using snoop port 389 you could use the name ldap which is the name of the service.

Understanding the LDAP Protocol Exchange

This section is about running the snoop utility with the LDAP protocol in mind. If you are not familiar with LDAP protocol, then tracing the protocol exchange using snoop will not make much sense. In this short section, we will take a look at the basics of the protocol exchange between an LDAP client and a Directory (LDAP) server.

The general model adopted by the LDAP v3 protocol is whereby clients perform protocol operations against a server. Using this model, a client transmits a protocol request describing the operation that needs to be performed on a server. The server is then responsible for performing the necessary operations in the directory. Upon completion of the operations, the server returns a response containing any results or errors to the requesting client, as illustrated in FIGURE C-1.

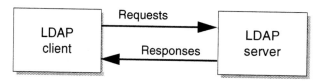

Listens on TCP port
389 for LDAP
636 for LDAPover TLSv1/SSL

FIGURE C-1 LDAP Protocol Big Picture

LDAP Protocol Big Picture

In the first sequence of events, the LDAP session is initialized. LDAP structure is created which contains information about the LDAP server and LDAP session. Initializing this LDAP session uses the ldap-init() function call.

```
if ( (ld = ldap_init( LDAP_HOST, LDAP_PORT )) == NULL) {
    perror ( "ldap_init" );
    return ( 1 );
}
```

Next, the client binds to the Directory (LDAP) Server. The bind request is optional, and is only needed if the client wants to indicate who it is. When connecting to a Directory (LDAP) server, the client must send a bind operation request to the server. This LDAP bind request contains various pieces of information, such as the DN of the client that is attempting to authenticate, and so on. When the client binds to the server in the most basic form, it binds as an anonymous client, whereby NULL values are provided for the DN and password. To be sure that the server responds, I always recommend that you use the synchronous function, `ldap_simple_bind_s()`, which enables you to wait for the bind operation to complete. If this bind operation is successful, the function returns `LDAP_SUCCESS`.

```
if ( ldap_simple_bind_s( ld, NULL, NULL ) != LDAP_SUCCESS) {
      ldap_perror( ld, "ldap_simple_bind_s" );
      ldap_unbind( ld );
      return ( 1 );
}
```

On completion of the binding to the directory server, the client performs LDAP operations. Once the client has initialized a session with the LDAP directory server, and the authentication process is complete, the client performs LDAP operations. The client might use the `ldap_search_s()` function. For Example:

```
if ( ldap_search_s(ld, LDAP_SEARCHBASE, LDAP_SCOPE_SUBTREE,
      MY_FILTER, NULL, 0, &result ) != LDAP_SUCCESS ) {
      ldap_perror( ld, "ldap_search_s" };
      if( result == NULL ) {
          ldap_unbind( ld );
          return( 1 );
      }
}
```

After completing this, the client parses and prints the results. For Example:

```
for (e = ldap_first_entry( ld, result ); e != NULL;
        e = ldap_next_entry( ld, e ) ) {
            if ( (dn = ldap_get_dn( ld, e )) != NULL ) {
                printf("dn: %s\n", dn );
                ldap_memfree(dn);
            }
        for ( a = ldap_first_attribute( ld, e, &ber );
            a != NULL; a = ldap_next_attribute( ld, e, ber ) ) {
                if ((vals = ldap_get_values( ld, e, a)) != NULL) {
                    for ( i = 0; vals[i] != NULL; i++ ) {
                            printf( "%s: %s\n", a, vals[i] );
                    }
                    ldap_value_free( vals );
                }
                ldap_memfree( a );
        }
        if ( ber != NULL ) {
                ber_free( ber, 0 );
        }
        printf( "\n" );
}
```

The client then closes the connection to the LDAP server by calling one of two functions, ldap_unbind() or ldap_unbind_s().

```
ldap_msgfree( result );
ldap_unbind( ld );
return ( 0 );
```

The following code example searches for all entries of `Ruble` and prints every attribute that is a associated with `Ruble` at `example.com`.

```
dn: uid=LRuble,ou=People, dc=sun,dc=com
telephoneNumber: 1-201-513-1084
mail: Lucy.Ruble@example.com
uid: LRuble
givenName: Lucy
uidNumber: 1002
gidNumber: 2002
homeDirectory: /export/home/lruble
loginShell: /usr/bin/sh
gecos: Sun ONE Directory User
objectClass: top
objectClass: person
objectClass: organizationalPerson
objectClass: inetorgperson
objectClass: posixAccount
objectClass: shadowAccount
objectClass: account
sn: Ruble
cn: Lucy Ruble

dn: uid=TRuble,ou=People, dc=sun,dc=com
telephoneNumber: 1-187-244-7705
mail: Chris.Ruble@example.com
givenName: Chris
uid: TRuble
uidNumber: 1001
gidNumber: 2001
homeDirectory: /export/home/truble
loginShell: /usr/bin/ksh
gecos: Sun ONE Directory Administrator
objectClass: top
objectClass: person
objectClass: organizationalPerson
objectClass: inetorgperson
objectClass: posixAccount
objectClass: shadowAccount
objectClass: account
sn: Ruble
cn: Chris Ruble
```

Examples of LDAP Enabled snoop In Action

In the following examples, the protocol exchange between an LDAP client and an LDAP directory server for common LDAP operations is examined. The first example (LDAP search) includes three snoop options. These are:

- Non-verbose
- Verbose summary (-V)
- Verbose (-v)

For the other LDAP operations, only the verbose mode is shown.

LDAP Search Request Example

The following is a simple search for an entry with the uid equal to lruble with a search based of dc=example,dc=com. The output shows the matching entry that is returned to the client.

```
# ldapsearch -h veda.example.com -b "dc=example,dc=com" uid=lruble
uid=LRuble,ou=People,dc=example,dc=com
mail=lruble@example.com
uid=LRuble
givenName=Lucy
objectClass=top
objectClass=person
objectclass=inetorgperson
sn=Ruble
cn=Lucy Ruble
#
```

Non-verbose LDAP snoop Result

The following is the output of snoop when run without specifying the verbose mode when the previous LDAP search was performed.

```
# snoop ldap vipivot
Using device /dev/hme (promiscuous mode)
vipivot -> veda         LDAP C port=32829
        vipivot -> veda           LDAP C port=32829 Search Request
neverDerefAliases
        veda -> vipivot          LDAP R port=32829
        veda -> vipivot          LDAP R port=32829 Search ResEntry
       veda -> vipivot         LDAP R port=32829 Search ResDone Success
    vipivot -> veda             LDAP C port=32829
    vipivot -> veda             LDAP C port=32829
    vipivot -> veda             LDAP C port=32829 Unbind Request
    vipivot -> veda             LDAP C port=32829
        veda -> vipivot          LDAP R port=32829
  .
  .
  .
```

Only the LDAP operation name and result code is displayed as shown in bold. The port number shown is the TCP port, not the LDAP port.

Verbose Summary Mode LDAP Search snoop Result

The following is an abbreviated output when the same search is performed with
snoop in the verbose summary mode.

```
# snoop -V ldap vipivot
Using device /dev/hme (promiscuous mode)

        vipivot -> veda        ETHER Type=0800 (IP), size = 62 bytes
        vipivot -> veda        IP  D=129.148.181.130 S=129.148.181.142
LEN=48, ID=11313
        vipivot -> veda        TCP D=389 S=32849 Syn Seq=2825400714
Len=0 Win=49640 Options=<mss 1460,nop,nop,sackOK>
        vipivot -> veda        LDAP C port=32849
. . .
vipivot -> veda        LDAP C port=32849 Search Request
neverDerefAliases
  .
  .
  .
```

Verbose LDAP Search snoop Result

The following is the output of a verbose snoop when the same LDAP search is
performed. Because of the length of this example, and to show you the different
output in specific sections, the snoop trace is divided into several parts.

Part 1 - Ethernet and TCP/IP Packet Information

```
# snoop -v ldap vipivot
Using device /dev/hme (promiscuous mode)
ETHER:  ----- Ether Header -----
ETHER:
ETHER:  Packet 1 arrived at 14:22:19.03
ETHER:  Packet size = 62 bytes
ETHER:  Destination = 8:0:20:8a:e5:71, Sun
ETHER:  Source      = 8:0:20:ab:be:31, Sun
ETHER:  Ethertype = 0800 (IP)
....
IP:    ----- IP Header -----
IP:    Version = 4
IP:    Header length = 20 bytes
IP:    Protocol = 6 (TCP)
IP:    Header checksum = 9c4b
IP:    Source address = 129.148.181.142, vipivot
IP:    Destination address = 129.148.181.130, veda
IP:    No options
...
TCP:   ----- TCP Header -----
TCP:
TCP:   Source port = 32834
TCP:   Destination port = 389 (LDAP)
TCP:   Sequence number = 3301917698
TCP:   Acknowledgement number = 0
TCP:   Data offset = 28 bytes
```

Part 2 - LDAP Search Request

```
LDAP:   ----- Lightweight Directory Access Protocol Header -----
LDAP:     * [LDAPMessage]
LDAP:        [Message ID]
LDAP:        Operation * [APPL 3: Search Request]
LDAP:           [Base Object]
LDAP:               dc=example,dc=com
LDAP:           [Scope]
LDAP:            wholeSubtree
LDAP:           [DerefAliases]
LDAP:            neverDerefAliases
LDAP:           [SizeLimit]
LDAP:           [TimeLimit]
LDAP:           [TypesOnly]
LDAP:           Equality Match * [3]
LDAP:               [Attr Descr]
LDAP:                   uid
LDAP:               [Value]
LDAP:                   lruble
LDAP:           * [Sequence]
```

Part 3 - LDAP Search Results

```
LDAP:   ----- Lightweight Directory Access Protocol Header -----
LDAP:     *[LDAPMessage]
LDAP:       [Message ID]
LDAP:       Operation *[APPL 4: Search ResEntry]
LDAP:         [Object Name]
LDAP:             uid=LRuble,ou=People,dc=example,
LDAP:             dc=com
LDAP:          *[Partial Attributes]
LDAP:            *[Attribute]
LDAP:               [Type]
LDAP:                     mail
LDAP:              *[Vals]
LDAP:                   [Value]
LDAP:                       lruble@example.com
LDAP:            *[Attribute]
LDAP:               [Type]
LDAP:                   uid
LDAP:              *[Vals]
LDAP:                   [Value]
LDAP:                       LRuble
LDAP:            *[Attribute]
LDAP:               [Type]
LDAP:                     givenName
LDAP:              *[Vals]
LDAP:                   [Value]
LDAP:                       Lucy
```

Part 4 - LDAP Search Results (continued)

```
LDAP:              *[Attribute]
LDAP:                  [Type]
LDAP:                       objectClass
LDAP:                  *[Vals]
LDAP:                      [Value]
LDAP:                          top
LDAP:                      [Value]
LDAP:                          person
LDAP:                      [Value]
LDAP:                          organizationalPerson
LDAP:                      [Value]
LDAP:                          inetorgperson
LDAP:              *[Attribute]
LDAP:                  [Type]
LDAP:                       sn
LDAP:                  *[Vals]
LDAP:                      [Value]
LDAP:                          Ruble
LDAP:              *[Attribute]
LDAP:                  [Type]
LDAP:                       cn
LDAP:                  *[Vals]
LDAP:                      [Value]
LDAP:                          Lucy Ruble
```

Verbose LDAP Add Operation

The following example shows what a verbose snoop of an LDAP add operation would look like.

First, the command that is run:

```
# ldapadd -h veda -D "cn=directory manager" -w dirmanager
dn: uid=truble,ou=people,dc=example,dc=com
objectclass: person
objectclass: inetorgperson
uid: truble
cn: Chris Ruble
sn: Ruble
adding new entry uid=truble,ou=people,dc=example,dc=com
^D
```

Next, the snoop trace shows the BIND request and response:

```
LDAP:  ----- Lightweight Directory Access Protocol Header -----
LDAP:    *[LDAPMessage]
LDAP:       [Message ID]
LDAP:      Operation *[APPL 0: Bind Request]
LDAP:         [Version]
LDAP:         [Object Name]
LDAP:            cn=directory manager
LDAP:        Authentication: Simple  [0]
LDAP:            dirmanager
...
LDAP:  ----- Lightweight Directory Access Protocol Header -----
LDAP:    *[LDAPMessage]
LDAP:       [Message ID]
LDAP:      Operation *[APPL 1: Bind Response]
LDAP:         [Result Code]
LDAP:          Success
LDAP:         [Matched DN]
LDAP:         [Error Message]
```

Then, the actual LDAP operation is performed followed by the unbind operation:

```
LDAP:    ----- Lightweight Directory Access Protocol Header -----
LDAP:     *[LDAPMessage]
LDAP:        [Message ID]
LDAP:         Operation *[APPL 8: Add Request]
LDAP:            [Entry]
LDAP:                uid=truble,ou=people,dc=example,
LDAP:                dc=com
LDAP:             *[Attributes]
LDAP:               *[Attribute]
LDAP:                  [Type]
LDAP:                       objectclass
LDAP:                  *[Vals]
LDAP:                     [Value]
LDAP:                          person
LDAP:                     [Value]
LDAP:                          inetorgperson
LDAP:               *[Attribute]
LDAP:                  [Type]
LDAP:                       uid
LDAP:                  *[Vals]
LDAP:                     [Value]
LDAP:                          truble
LDAP:               *[Attribute]
LDAP:                  [Type]
LDAP:                       cn
LDAP:                  *[Vals]
LDAP:                     [Value]
LDAP:                          Chris Ruble
LDAP:               *[Attribute]
LDAP:                  [Type]
LDAP:                       sn
LDAP:                  *[Vals]
LDAP:                     [Value]
LDAP:                          Ruble
```

```
LDAP:         Operation *[APPL 9: Add Response]
LDAP:            [Result Code]
LDAP:            Success
LDAP:            [Matched DN]
...
LDAP:     *[LDAPMessage]
LDAP:        [Message ID]
LDAP:         Operation  [APPL 2: Unbind Request]
```

Verbose snoop Trace of an LDAP Delete Operation

The following command is issued:

```
# ldapdelete -h veda -D "cn=Directory Manager" -w dirmanager "uid=
truble,ou=people,dc=example,dc=com"
```

The following is the corresponding snoop output:

```
LDAP:  ----- Lightweight Directory Access Protocol Header -----
LDAP:   * [LDAPMessage]
LDAP:      [Message ID]
LDAP:      Operation * [APPL 0: Bind Request]
LDAP:         [Version]
LDAP:         [Object Name]
LDAP:             cn=directory manager
LDAP:         Authentication: Simple  [0]
LDAP:             dirmanager
...
LDAP:  ----- Lightweight Directory Access Protocol Header -----
LDAP:   * [LDAPMessage]
LDAP:      [Message ID]
LDAP:      Operation * [APPL 1: Bind Response]
LDAP:         [Result Code]
LDAP:          Success
LDAP:         [Matched DN]
...
LDAP:  ----- Lightweight Directory Access Protocol Header -----
LDAP:   * [LDAPMessage]
LDAP:      [Message ID]
LDAP:      Operation  [APPL 10: Del Request]
LDAP:          uid=truble,ou=people,dc=example,d
LDAP:          c=com
LDAP:
LDAP:  ----- Lightweight Directory Access Protocol Header -----
LDAP:   * [LDAPMessage]
LDAP:      [Message ID]
LDAP:      Operation * [APPL 11: Del Response]
LDAP:         [Result Code]
LDAP:          Success
LDAP:         [Matched DN]
LDAP:         [Error Message]
LDAP:
...
LDAP:   * [LDAPMessage]
LDAP:      [Message ID]
LDAP:      Operation  [APPL 2: Unbind Request]
```

Solaris OE 9 PAM Architecture

This section describes the PAM application programming interface (API) and the PAM service provider interface (SPI). Also included are procedures on how to effectively write PAM modules when using the Solaris 9 OE. Before we discuss the PAM API and SPI, let us take a brief look at the PAM components:

- PAM API (pam(3PAM)) used by applications to perform authentication and authentication token (password) changes.
- PAM framework used to export the API.
- PAM SPI (pam_sm(3PAM)) used by the PAM framework to call PAM Service Modules.
- PAM service modules (pam_*(5)) used to export the PAM SPI.

By writing these PAM service modules, it is possible to extend the capability of the Solaris 9 OE authentication mechanisms in a number of different ways. The PAM interface in the Solaris 9 OE provides a set of APIs that can be used by third-party applications to extend authentication capabilities. By using the PAM layer, applications authenticate to the system without worrying about what authentication method has been chosen by the system administrator for any given client. For example, it is possible for a system administrator to prevent users from choosing new passwords that resemble their old password.

A PAM module is a shared object that is developed and written using the C programming language. The module is dynamically selected based on the contents of the pam.conf(4) configuration file. This is an extremely efficient mechanism that enables the selection of the most appropriate authentication mechanism for a particular environment—without sacrificing functionality or the need to depend on third-party or unsupported software.

Developing a PAM module is not as difficult as you might think. The PAM API has a rich set of features, and is fairly intuitive to learn and use. Online documentation is also available (see http://docs.sun.com).

This section addresses the following topics:

- Details of the PAM API
- Details of the PAM SPI
- Details on how to write a PAM service module
- Details on how to test a PAM service module

The PAM API

The PAM framework, includes the PAM library (`libpam.so.1`), which consists of an interface library and multiple authentication service modules that are the layer implementing the PAM API.

It is outside the scope of this section to detail every single API and function. However, the most commonly used and well-known APIs are presented here. The PAM API can be grouped into five functional categories:

- PAM framework functions
- Authentication functions
- Account management functions
- Session management function
- Password management functions

These functions enable an application to invoke the PAM service modules and to communicate information to these modules. The functions are described in the following sections.

PAM Framework Functions

These framework functions are PAM transaction routines for establishing and terminating a PAM session.

- `pam_start()` function takes, as arguments, the name of the application calling PAM, the name of the user to be authenticated, and the address of the callback conversation structure provided by the caller. It returns a handle for use with subsequent calls to the PAM library.

- `pam_end()` function is called to terminate the authentication transaction identified by `pamh` and to free any storage area allocated by the authentication module. The argument, `status`, is passed to the `cleanup()` function stored within the PAM handle, and is used to determine what module-specific state must be purged.

- `pam_get_item()` and `pam_set_item()` functions are PAM routines that enable both applications and the PAM service modules to access and update common PAM information such as service name, user name, remote host name, remote user name, and so on, from the PAM handle.

TABLE D-1 details the items that may be manipulated by these functions. This list is exhaustive. These are manifest constants defined by the 'standard'. Others can only be added by amending the 'standard'. This would require a change to *<security/pam_appl.h>* and the `libpam`, which is the Pluggable Authentication Module library.

TABLE D-1 Setting PAM Items

Item Name	Description
PAM_SERVICE	Service (application) name
PAM_USER	User name
PAM_RUSER	Remote user name
PAM_TTY	TTY name
PAM_RHOST	Remote host name
PAM_CONV	pam_conv structure. (register the conversation function)
PAM_AUTHTOK	Authenticated token
PAM_OLDAUTHTOK	Old authentication token
PAM_REPOSITORY	Specifies which repository is to be updated.
PAM_USER_PROMPT	Prompt the module should use if asking for a username.

- `pam_getenv()`, `pam_getenvlist()`, and `pam_putenv()` functions enable applications and PAM modules to set and retrieve environment variables that are to be used for the user session.

- `pam_strerror()` function returns a textual representation of a PAM error, much like the `strerror(3c)` error.

PAM Authentication Functions

These authentication functions are used to authenticate the user and the current process. The term credentials, means whatever the PAM service module stack defines it to mean. That is each of the PAM service modules defines whatcredentials mean to them. In the case of `pam_unix_cred(5)`, it provides functions that establish user credential information. Among other things, `pam_sm_setcred()` initializes the user's privilege sets and initializes or updates the user's audit context if it hasn't already been initialized. And in the case of `pam_krb5(5)`:

`pam_sm_setcred()` creates and modifies the user's credential cache. This function will initialize the user's credential cache, if it doesn't already exist, and store the initial credentials for later use by Kerberized network applications. It is important to understand that the authentication and credential setup are distinct actions. In the case of `pam_krb5`, `pam_sm_authenticate()` performs a Kerberos authentication. `pam_sm_setcred()` sets up the local Kerberos ticket cache as described in kinit(1). The Kerberos credential db is later used by the GSS/Kerberos applications such as telnet and Kerberized NFS to enable single sign-on.

The following flags may be set in the flags field. They are best described by their effect on the user's credential cache.

- `pam_authenticate()` function called to verify the identity of the current user.
- `pam_setcred()` function called to set the credentials of the current process associated with the authentication handle supplied.

Typically, this process is done after the user has been authenticated (after the `pam_authenticate()` function succeeds).

Account Management Function

This account management function is used to validate the users account information. It typically includes checking for password and account expiration, valid login times, and etc.

- `pam_acct_mgmt()`

Session Management Functions

These session management functions are called on the initiation and termination of a login session.

- `pam_open_session()`
- `pam_close_session()`

The `pam_unix_session` module implements these calls to update the `/var/adm/lastlog` information. These functions can also support session auditing.

Password Management Function

This password management function is called to change the authentication token (password) associated with the user.

- `pam_chauthtok()`

The PAM SPI

The PAM service modules are a set of dynamically loadable objects invoked by the PAM SPI to provide a particular type of user authentication. The functions comprising the PAM SPI are provided by the modules called by the PAM infrastructure, and are grouped, in the following sections, on the basis of the module type.

Authentication Module Functions

These authentication module functions are used to authenticate the user and the current process.

- `pam_sm_authenticate()` module function is called to verify the identity of the current user, as specified by the `PAM_USER` item.
- `pam_sm_setcred()` module function is called to set the credentials of the current process associated with the authentication handle supplied. Typically, this process is done after the user has been authenticated.

Note – A service module that is specified as `auth` *must* implement both interfaces. If the module has no credentials to set, the `pam_sm_setcred` function should return the `PAM_IGNORE` value.

Account Management Module Function

This account management module function is used to validate the account of the user when signing on. It is meant to check for password and account expiration, valid login times, and so on.

- `pam_sm_acct_mgmt()`

Session Management Module Functions

These session management module functions are called on the initiation and termination of a login session.

- `pam_sm_open_session()`
- `pam_sm_close_session()`

Password Management Module Function

This password management module function is called to change the authentication token (password) associated with the user.

- `pam_sm_chauthtok()`

Note – For an understanding of the relationship between the different APIs, please refer to the PAM Framework Architecture documentation available at `http://docs.sun.com`.

Writing a PAM Service Module

The easiest way to gain experience writing PAM service modules is to code one. The following example, `pam_compare.so.1`, is a standalone module for the PAM password stack. It enables a system administrator to prevent users from choosing a new password string that resembles their old password string.

The concept for this module is as follows: Each character in the users *new* password is checked against a particular character that may have been present in the users *old* password string. The module is based on the logic that there can only be a configurable number of matching characters between the old and new passwords. If the limit is exceeded, the new password is rejected.

The configuration of the `pam_compare` module is accomplished by adding the following entries to the `/etc/pam.conf(4)` file. These entries need to be placed before the `pam_authtok_store.so.1` definition.

Here is an example of such an entry:

```
other    password required    pam_authtok_get.so.1
other    password requisite pam_authtok_check.so.1
other    password requisite pam_compare.so.1          maxequal=4
other    password required    pam_authtok_store.so.1
```

The pam_compare module accepts two flags:

- debug: Turns on debugging messages through the syslog level LOG_DEBUG value.
- maxequal=n: Configures the maximum number of allowable shared characters.

If the maxequal flag is not specified, old and new passwords will not be allowed to contain any shared characters.

PAM Source Code

The source code consists of a number of files that are available for download (see "Obtaining the Downloadable Files for This Book" on page xxvii). These files are several make files, the C-source pam_compare.c, and the associated man page. Prerequisites are an ANSI C compiler and the make utility found in the /usr/ccs/bin/make utility. All work is performed in the Solaris 9 OE.

Note – The supplied make files create both 32-bit and 64-bit versions of the module. Deployable modules should be compiled for both 32- and 64-bit operation because you cannot make assumptions about whether the application using these modules is a 32-bit or 64-bit application.

Makefiles

A combination of makefiles that have been tested on the Solaris 9 OE are provided. You should not need to modify these files. Included in the makefiles are comments that explain what options are required to compile the PAM module. The following code box is the top-level makefile.

```
SUBDIRS=          sparc sparcv9

all     :=        TARGET= all
clean   :=        TARGET=clean

all clean:        $(SUBDIRS)

$(SUBDIRS): FRC
        @cd $@; pwd; $(MAKE) $(TARGET)

FRC:
```

It contains the various implemented make-targets and a list of subdirectories (conveniently named after the architectures that the modules are being built for). This makefile descends into the architecture subdirectories in order to build the given target.

Each of the architecture subdirectories contain a makefile with declarations that are specific to the target architecture together with an include statement that includes the makefile with declarations common for all architectures, named Makefile.common.

The contents of the sparc/Makefile file are:

```
include ../Makefile.common
```

The contents of the sparcv9/Makefile file are:

```
include ../Makefile.common

CFLAGS  += -xarch=v9
LDFLAGS += -xarch=v9
```

These extra flags instruct the compiler to generate a 64-bit code.

The makefile containing the architecture-independent declarations
(Makefile.common) contains the actual target definitions.

```
# -D_REENTRANT is used when writing multi-threaded code. It
enables
# multi-thread-safe declararions from the system header files.
# -Kpic causes the compiler to generate code that is suitable for
# dynamic loading into an applications address space.

CFLAGS=    -D_REENTRANT -Kpic


#
# The -G option tells the linker to generate a shared object.
#
# The -z defs option forces a fatal error if any undefined
# symbols remain at the end of the link-phase (see ld(1))

LDFLAGS=-G -z defs
LDLIBS=    -lpam -lc

VPATH= ..
SRC=   pam_compare.c
OBJ=   $(SRC:.c=.o)

all: pam_compare.so.1

pam_compare.so.1: $(OBJ)
        $(CC) $(LDFLAGS) -o $@ $(OBJ) $(LDLIBS)
        -@/usr/bin/chgrp bin pam_compare.*

clean:
        $(RM) $(OBJ) pam_compare.so.1
```

There are four Makefiles:

```
./Makefile
./Makefile.common
./sparc/Makefile
./sparcv9/Makefile
```

The actual `compile` commands are executed in the architecture-specific directory, so remember to instruct `make` to look for sources in the parent directory (VPATH). The object- and the resulting library command files are placed in the architecture-specific directory.

pam_compare Source File

This section details the `pam_compare.c` source file, including information on how this specific PAM module is built. Examples present the best way to explain how to write your own PAM service modules, such as the following:

```
1/*
2 * Copyright 2002 Sun Microsystems, Inc.  All rights reserved.
3 * Use is subject to license terms.
4 */
5
6#pragma ident    "@(#)pam_compare.c       1.1     02/09/03 SMI"
7
8 #include <stdarg.h>
9 #include <syslog.h>
10#include <stdio.h>
11#include <stdlib.h>
12#include <string.h>
13#include <security/pam_appl.h>
14#include <security/pam_modules.h>
15
```

In order to write a PAM module, you need to include the `security/pam_appl.h` file, which contains PAM error codes and structures used by the PAM API, and the `security/pam_modules.h` file, which contains the PAM SPI prototypes.

Because PAM service modules can't assume that the interaction with the user is based on a simple terminal-like interface (for example, compare the `telnet` interface and `dtlogin` interface)—the command `printf` or the function `puts` cannot be used to communicate with the user. Therefore, the PAM framework introduces the concept of a *conversation* function.

This function is supplied to the module, by the application. For any interaction with the user, the application's conversation function is called. It is up to the application to make sure that the correct interface is used to communicate with the user. For example, the dtlogin interface draws an alert box to display messages to the user, while the telnetd interface might simply perform a write command on a socket.

The following example module introduces a simple routine (pam_display()) that is used to display a one-line message to the user, using the conversation function present in the PAM handle.

```
16 /*
17  * Display a one-line message to the user
18  */
19  static void
20  pam_display(pam_handle_t *pamh, int style, char *fmt, ...)
21  {
22          struct pam_conv *pam_convp;
23          char buf[512];
24          va_list ap;
25          struct pam_message *msg;
26          struct pam_response *response = NULL;
27
28          va_start(ap, fmt);
29          (void)vsnprintf(buf, sizeof (buf), fmt, ap);
30          va_end(ap);
31
32          if (pam_get_item(pamh, PAM_CONV, (void **)&pam_convp)
             != PAM_SUCCESS) {
33                  syslog(LOG_ERR, "pam_compare: Can't get PAM_CONV
                    item");
34                      return;
35  }
36
(continued on the next page)
```

```
(continued from the previous page)
37          if ((pam_convp == NULL) || (pam_convp->conv == NULL)) {
38                  syslog(LOG_ERR, "pam_compare: no conversation
                    function defined");
39                  return;
40          }
41
42          msg = (struct pam_message *)calloc(1, size of (struct
            pam_message));
43          if (msg == NULL) {
44                  syslog(LOG_ERR, "pam_compare: out of memory");
45                  return;
46 }
47
48          msg->msg_style = style;
49          msg->msg = buf;
50
51 (pam_convp->conv)(1, &msg, &response, pam_convp->appdata_ptr);
52
53          if (response)
54                  free(response);
55
56          free(msg);
57  }
```

In Line 25, the pam_message is the structure used to pass a prompt, an error message, or an informational message from the PAM service modules to the application. The application displays the message to the user. Note that it is the responsibility of the PAM service modules to localize the messages. The memory used by the pam_message must be allocated and freed by the PAM service modules.

In Line 26, the pam_response is a structure used to receive information back from the user. The storage used by the pam_response is allocated by the application, and should be freed by the PAM service modules.

Line 32 obtains the conversation structure, pam_conv, to retrieve the address of the function needed to call and display the information to the user. The pam_conv structure contains two members as illustrated in the following:

```
struct pam_conv {
    int (*conv)(int, struct pam_message **, struct pam_response **,
    void *);
    void *appdata_ptr;
};
```

In Line 48, PAM defines several message styles: PAM_PROMPT_ECHO_ON, PAM_PROMPT_ECHO_OFF, PAM_ERROR_MSG, and PAM_TEXT_INFO. Even though this basic routine only deals with displaying messages (it doesn't deal with input from the user), the style attribute is parameterized as an example.

In Line 49, the application conversation function receives an array of pam_message structures. The function pointer conv contains the address of the input/output function that the service module uses to interact with the user. The extra appdata_ptr element is private to the application. The service module is supposed to supply this pointer when calling the conversation function. Because only a single message is displayed, only one element initializes and passes its address to the conversation function.

Line 51 transfers control to the application conversation function. An array of messages containing just one element are passed. Although the application should not collect any responses (this function only displays information), you should still check for responses and free any memory allocated by the application's conversation function (see line 53—54).

Line 56 frees the space allocated to pass the message to the conversation function.

```
58
59  /*
60   * int compare(old, new, max)
61   *
62   * compare the strings old and new. If more than "max"
     characters of new
63   * also appear in old, return 1 (error). Otherwise return
     0.
64   */
65  static
66  int compare(unsigned char *old, unsigned char *new, int max)
67  {
68          unsigned char in_old[256];
69          int equal = 0;
70
71          (void)memset(in_old, 0, sizeof (in_old));
72
73          while (*old)
74                  in_old[*(old++)]++;
75
76          while (*new) {
77                  if (in_old[*new])
78                          equal++;
79                  new++;
80          }
81
82          if (equal > max)
83                  return (1);
84
85          return (0);
86  }
```

Lines 65—86 define a function used to compare the strings old and new. If more than "max" characters of the old string also appear in the new string, return 1 (error). Otherwise, return 0. Use this function in the PAM module to determine whether the new password chosen by the user is acceptable.

```
88   /*
89    * int pam_sm_chauthtok(pamh, flags, argc, argv)
90    *
91    * Make sure the old and the new password don't share too many
92    * characters.
93    */
94   int
95   pam_sm_chauthtok(pam_handle_t *pamh, int flags, int argc,
     const char **argv)
96   {
97           int i;
98           int debug = 0;
99           int maxequal = 0;
100          int pam_err;
101          char *service;
102          char *user;
103          char *passwd;   /* the newly typed password */
104          char *opasswd;  /* the user's old password */
105
106          for (i = 0; i < argc; i++) {
107                  if (strncmp(argv[i], "debug") == 0)
108                          debug = 1;
109                  else if (strncmp(argv[i], "maxequal=", 9) == 0)
110                          maxequal = atoi(&argv[i][9]);
111          }
112
113          if (debug)
114                  syslog(LOG_DEBUG, "pam_compare: entering
                     pam_sm_chauthtok");
```

Line 95 defines the `pam_sm_chauthtok()` function, part of the PAM SPI definition. Once the module is configured in the `/etc/pam.conf(4)` file, the PAM framework calls this routine when the application calls the `pam_chauthtok()` function. This function is the entry point of the module, but it is always through the PAM framework.

Start the module by interpreting the arguments that have been specified in the `/etc/pam.conf(4)` file. Then accept the two different arguments, or *flags* in PAM terminology, `debug` and `maxequal`. Any arguments specified in the configuration file are handed over by the PAM framework. This is just like the command-line arguments presented to an application's `main()` function receiving an argument count (`argc`), and an array of character pointers (`argv`).

Lines 113—114 log some extra messages if the `debug` flag is specified.

The PAM password management stack is different from the other PAM stacks in that it invokes each of the service modules twice. The first time a service module is invoked, the PAM framework sets the `PAM_PRELIM_CHECK` bit in the `flags`, the second time the service module is invoked, the framework sets the `PAM_UPDATE_AUTHTOK` bit in the `flags` file.

The `PAM_PRELIM_CHECK` flag indicates to the service module that the module should not start updating any passwords, but should make sure that all the module's prerequisites for password updates are met.

The module, in this example, is quite simple because it does not depend on any other services. Be aware that more complex modules might differ in this regard. For example, a module that updates a password in an LDAP server needs to check that the LDAP server is up and running before trying to update any information. This preliminary checking avoids the chance of one module updating the password in a Network Information Service (NIS) server, while the next module fails to update the password in an unavailable LDAP server. Such a scenario would leave one module with two different passwords, and complicates future logins.

Because the PAM framework invokes each of the service modules twice, when should you perform a check? You do have three options:

1. At the time you are called with the `PAM_PRELIM_CHECK` flag

2. At the time you are called with the `PAM_UPDATE_AUTHTOK` flag

3. Both times

Because nothing that is important to the module (old and new passwords) has changed between the first and the second time around, option 3 is not useful.

In option 1, using the `PAM_PRELIM_CHECK` flag, the password service only performs preliminary checks. No passwords should be updated. In option 2, using the `PAM_UPDATE_AUTHTOK` flag, the password service updates passwords.

Performing your checks during the preliminary round makes sure that no module updates any passwords without your consent, for example, without this module returning the `PAM_SUCCESS` value.

The `PAM_IGNORE` value is returned during the second round of calls (the `PAM_PRELIM_CHECK` flag is not set) because you do not actually contribute to the updating process. For example:

```
116          if ((flags & PAM_PRELIM_CHECK) == 0)
117                  return (PAM_IGNORE);
```

It is important to note the difference between returning the `PAM_SUCCESS` value and the `PAM_IGNORE` value. In this case, if the `PAM_SUCCESS` value is returned, it might cause the complete PAM stack to succeed, even if all other modules returned the `PAM_IGNORE` value. You do not want the password management stack to succeed without performing any work, so you want to return the `PAM_IGNORE` value.

```
119 pam_err = pam_get_item(pamh, PAM_SERVICE, (void **)&service);
120 if (pam_err != PAM_SUCCESS) {
121 syslog(LOG_ERR, "pam_compare: error getting service item");
122 return (pam_err);
123 }
124
125 pam_err = pam_get_item(pamh, PAM_USER, (void **)&user);
126 if (pam_err != PAM_SUCCESS) {
127 syslog(LOG_ERR, "pam_compare: can't get user item");
128 return (pam_err);
129 }
130
131 /*
132 * Make sure "user" and "service" are set. Otherwise it might
133 * be misconfigured and dump core when these items are for used
134 * for error reporting.
135 */
136 if (user == NULL || service == NULL) {
137 syslog(LOG_ERR, "pam_compare: %s is NULL",
138 user == NULL ? "PAM_USER" : "PAM_SERVICE");
139 return (PAM_SYSTEM_ERR);
140 }
```

Although you are only interested in the old and the new passwords (the PAM items PAM_OLDAUTHTOK and PAM_AUTHTOK), you must also obtain the two other PAM items: PAM_SERVICE (the name of the application) and PAM_USER (the login name of the user whose password that is about to be updated). This information is used to create error messages.

Note that there is a distinction between the pam_get_item() function returning a value other than PAM_SUCCESS, and the item not being set by the application (for example, user == NULL). The first error indicates a problem with the PAM stack (probably a misconfiguration), while the second condition indicates a malfunctioning application because the user's password cannot be changed without setting the PAM_USER item.

```
142        pam_err = pam_get_item(pamh, PAM_AUTHTOK, (void
           **)&passwd);
143        if (pam_err != PAM_SUCCESS) {
144            syslog(LOG_ERR, "pam_compare: can't get password
                  item");
145                return (pam_err);
146        }
147
148        pam_err = pam_get_item(pamh, PAM_OLDAUTHTOK, (void
           **)&opasswd);
149        if (pam_err != PAM_SUCCESS) {
150                syslog(LOG_ERR, "pam_compare: can't get old
                      password item");
151                return (pam_err);
152        }
153
154        /*
155        * PAM_AUTHTOK should be set. If it is NULL, the check
           can't be performed
156        * so this module should be ignored (another module
           will probably fail)
157        */
158        if (passwd == NULL) {
159                if (debug)
160                        syslog(LOG_DEBUG, "pam_compare:
                          PAM_AUTHTOK = NULL.");
161                return (PAM_IGNORE);
162        }
163
164        /*
```
(continued on next page)

```
(continued from previous page)
165          * If PAM_OLDAUTHTOK is NULL (possible i.e. when root
               executes passwd)
166          * there isn't an old password to compare the new
               with. return
167          * PAM_SUCCESS since there is no reason to reject the
               new password.
168          */
169
170     if (opasswd == NULL)
171             return (PAM_SUCCESS);
```

Lines 142 and 148, respectively, retrieve the old and new password so you can compare them. Before invoking the compare() routine, make sure that both passwords are actually set, because there might be valid reasons for these passwords to not be set.

Line 158 checks the new password. If, for whatever reason, the password is not set, you cannot perform the check. If you cannot perform the check, the result of the module should not contribute to the overall result of the password stack, as configured in /etc/pam.conf(4)file, so the PAM_IGNORE value must be returned.

You can choose to return the PAM_AUTHTOK_ERR value to force an error of the overall stack, but, in general, you should return a PAM_IGNORE value if your module somehow results in a non-operation. This is the case for this module, if you cannot perform a check.

Note – Please remember this about return values; besides the PAM_SUCCESS value being returned on a successful completion, error return values as described in the pam(3PAM) function may also be returned. For example, PAM_AUTHTOK_ERR indicates an authentication token manipulation error.

Also check the old password to see if it is set. There is only one valid reason why the old password might be not set, and that is if the system administrator sets the password for an ordinary user. If that is the case, then the password program doesn't always ask for the old password. So if the old password is not set, accept the new password and return the PAM_SUCCESS value.

```
173          if (compare((unsigned char *)opasswd, (unsigned char
             *)passwd,
174             maxequal)) {
175                pam_display(pamh, PAM_ERROR_MSG,
176                  "%s: Your old and new password can't share
                   more than %d "
177                  "characters.", service, maxequal);
178                syslog(LOG_WARNING, "%s: pam_compare: "
179                  "rejected new password for %s", service,
                   user);
180
181                return (PAM_AUTHTOK_ERR);
182             }
183
184          return (PAM_SUCCESS);
185  }
```

Now that both passwords have been retrieved, and you have made sure they are both set, call the compare() function to see if the new password should be accepted. If the compare() function reports success (returns 0), return the PAM_SUCCESS value to the PAM framework (see line 184).

If however, the compare routine reports failure (the old and new password share more than maxequal characters), inform the user of the problem (using the simple one-line-message-display-routine, pam_display()), and log a system message to record this failure (see lines 178—179). Exit the PAM module by returning the PAM_AUTHTOK_ERROR value which causes the PAM password stack to fail.

Remember that all these checks are done in the PRELIMINARY phase of the password stack traversal. Because any failure detected in this phase prevents the actual update of the password (which should happen in the next traversal), no password is changed if the PAM_AUTHTOK_ERR value is returned.

This concludes the code walkthrough of the example module, pam_compare.

Testing the PAM Module

In order to test the pam_compare.so.1 module, update the /etc/pam.conf(4) file as detailed on page 610, and run the passwd command. With the maxequal variable set to 4, this is what you see in the code box:

```
$ passwd
passwd: Changing password for testuser
Enter existing login password: s3cr3t!
New Password: s3cur3!
passwd: Your old and new password can't share more than 4
characters.

Please try again
New Password: a^_g34.Q
Re-enter new Password: a^_g34.Q
passwd: password successfully changed for testuser
```

PAM provides its services to all applications that perform Password Management, and all these applications benefit from the new module. If you created the local account testuser, you can force a password change when testuser logs in the next time, with the following command:

```
$ passwd -f testuser
```

Here is the example of testuser logging in, (please note that the boldface type is user input):

```
$ rlogin -l testuser localhost
Passwd: a^_g34.Q
Choose a new password.
New Password: 55Q.ga_^
rlogin: Your old and new password can't share more than 4
characters.
Try again

Choose a new password.
New Password:
```

As illustrated, the rlogins password management service benefits immediately from the newly installed module.

By plugging multiple, low-level authentication mechanisms into applications at runtime, PAM integrates them with a single high-level API. These authentication mechanisms, are encapsulated as dynamically loadable, shared software modules. These software modules may be installed independent of applications.

In environments where there is an LDAP directory server, either the pam_unix function or the pam_ldap function can be used to authenticate users. Because of its increased flexibility and support of stronger authentication methods, the use of the pam_ldap function is recommended. For organizations using the Solaris 9 OE, which offers LDAP for naming and directory services, the pam_ldap function offers an ideal way to extend the authentication capabilities.

Note – In the Solaris 9 OE, the pam_unix function does not exist in the same form that it does in the Solaris 8 OE. In order to accommodate proper stacking of the pam_unix function it has been broken up into single service modules. When used together these single service modules provide the same functionality as the existing pam_unix function. For example, some of the service modules are: pam_unix_auth(5), pam_authtok_*(5), and pam_passwd_auth(5). This also applies to the Secured LDAP Client backport patch to the Solaris 8 OE.

Glossary

Access Control Instruction (ACI)	An instruction that grants or denies permissions to entries in the directory server.
Access Control List (ACL)	Data associated with a file, directory, or other resource that defines the permissions that users, groups, processes, and devices have for accessing it.
Access Control Rule (ACR)	Collective permissions and bind rules that are set as a pair.
ACI	See Access Control Instruction.
ACL	See Access Control List.
ACR	See Access Control Rule.
Active Directory	Microsoft's directory service used by the core operating system to store user account and system resource data and by the BackOffice suite of products as their data store.
administration domain	A domain that allows a common login to work across several servers.
AFS	Andrew File System – an enterprise-type file system that enables systems to share files and resources across local and wide area networks. It uses a client-server architecture for file sharing.
ASN.1	Abstract Syntax Notation One (ASN.1) describes objects within a management information database.
attribute	Each LDAP entry consists of a number of named attributes, each of which has one or more values.
authentication	The means by which a server verifies a client's identity.
Backup Domain Controller (BDC)	A backup mechanism that maintains a read-only copy of the SAM database.
base DN	The distinguished name (DN) where part of the directory information tree (DIT) is rooted. Sometimes indicated as baseDN.

BDC	See Backup Domain Controller.
Blowfish cyptography	A secret key cryptography that uses a variable key lengths of 32–448 bits.
Broadcast method	A way in which to locate an NIS server to bind to. The method sends out a broadcast message and binds to the first server that responds.
CA	Certificate Authority. A trusted third party that issues digital certificates.
cipher	Encoded character or characters
cipher text	Data that has been coded (enciphered, encrypted, encoded) for security purposes.
cipher strength	Number of bits in the key used to encrypt data.
Cold Start File method	A way to provide a file to a client. The method contains information about how to locate directory objects and also a set of credentials. This is the preferred NIS+ method because it provides additional security.
CRAM-MD5	One of the SASL mechanisms (RFC 2222) that was at one point proposed as a required mechanism for LDAP v3. CRAM stands for Challenge Response Authentication Mechanism. It uses the MD5 (message digest 5) hash algorithm developed by Ron Rivest for generating a message digest, which in turn is used for authentication.
credentials	Authentication information that the client software sends with each request to a naming server to verify the identity of the user or machine.
cryptography	Conversion of data into a secret code for transmission over a network. The original data is converted into ciphertext (a coded equivalent) with an encryption algorithm. The ciphertext is decoded at the receiving end and turned back into the original form.
DAP	Directory Access Protocol (X.500).
Data Encryption Standard (DES)	A commonly used, highly sophisticated algorithm developed by the U.S. National Bureau of Standards for encrypting and decrypting data.
DEN	Directory Enabled Networks.
DES	See Data Encryption Standard.
DHCP	See Dynamic Host Configuration Protocol.
Diffie-Hellman	Cryptography that enables exchange of public keys using shared secret keys at both ends.
DIGEST-MD5	The Digest-MD5 mechanism is described in RFC 2831. In Digest-MD5, the LDAP server sends data that includes various authentication options that it is willing to support plus a special token to the LDAP client. The client responds

by sending an encrypted response that indicates the authentication options that it has selected. The response is encrypted in such a way that proves that the client knows its password. The LDAP server then decrypts and verifies the client's response.

Directory Information Tree (DIT)	An arrangement of directory entries in a treelike structure.
directory naming context	A method to map to the DNS domain name of a company and its subdomains. Termed *Active Directory* by Microsoft.
directory service	A specific type of naming service in which the objects bound to names are directory entries.
Directory Server Entry (DSE)	A naming context that defines the root entry of the directory server.
Directory System Agent (DSA)	The core program of Microsoft's Active Directory implementation.
Distinguished Name (DN)	A unique identifier of each entry in the DIT.
DIT	See Directory Information Tree.
DN	See Distinguished Name.
DNS	See Domain Name System.
domain forests	A set of domains or domain trees that do *not* form a contiguous namespace, but they do have an implicit trust relationship among them.
Domain Name System (DNS)	A method to solve the problem of locating computers on ArpaNet, the forerunner of the Internet. DNS is the de facto standard naming service of the Internet.
domain trees	A set of domains that form a contiguous namespace through a set of hierarchal relationships.
DSA	Directory Services Agent.
DSE	See Directory Server Entry.
DSML	Directory Service Markup Language – A set of XML tags that define the contents of a directory. Developed by Bowstreet Software, it is designed to allow directories to work together.
Dynamic Host Configuration Protocol (DHCP)	A procedure by which IP-related information is provided to new clients.

entry	A single row of data in a database table, such as an LDAP element in a DIT.
Extensible Storage Engine (ESE)	A database that has built-in indexing features, along with other database features such as transaction logging and recovery. All Active Directory data resides in this database.
flat namespace	An area (domain) in which one NIS domain is not related to another.
Global Catalog	A list that provides a way to centrally maintain information about users and universal groups for access control.
GMT	Greenwich Mean Time.
GSSAPI	Generic Security Service Application Programming Interface. Used to provide a standard interface to different authentication methods.
heartbeat signal	Client access to the directory service itself. If the heartbeat or communication channels fail, then the cluster will not function properly.
HTTP	Hypertext Transport Protocol.
IANA	Internet Assigned Numbers Authority.
Indexed Sequential Access Method (ISAM)	A database modeled after the ESE and similar to the one in which Microsoft Exchange stores data.
IMAP	Internet Message Access Protocol – standard mail service protocol that provides a message store that holds incoming email.
ISO	International Standards Organization.
J.N.D.I.	Java Naming and Directory Interface.
KCC	See Knowledge Consistency Checker.
KDC	See Key Distribution Center.
Kerberos	A network authentication protocol that provides strong authentication for client-server applications by using secret-key cryptography.
Key Distribution Center (KDC)	A clearinghouse required by Kerberos.
KM	See Knowledge Module.
Knowledge Consistency Checker (KCC)	An Active Directory process that is responsible for mapping out the Active Directory domain controller topology and determining how replication should be performed.

Knowledge Module (KM)	A utility that monitors the iPlanet Directory Server. KM continually monitors and automatically reacts to critical infrastructure information.
LAN	Local area network
LDAP	Lightweight Directory Access Protocol. The newest addition to the list of Solaris OE naming services. It is an optional naming service that can coexist with legacy Solaris OE naming services. LDAP shares some characteristics with NIS and NIS+, but it is more sophisticated in how stored data is structured and accessed.
LDAP access model	A model that defines how LDAP clients communicate with LDAP servers.
LDIF	See LDAP Data Interchange Format (LDIF)
LDAP Data Interchange Format (LDIF)	A directory server uses the LDAP Data Interchange Format (LDIF) to describe a directory in text format. LDIF is often used to build a directory database. It is also a common method used for importing data from legacy data sources such as NIS maps, and to add large numbers of entries to the directory all at once.
LDAP information model	A model that defines how entries are organized in a directory.
LDAP naming model	A model that defines how objects are named and the type of information which can be stored in the directory.
LDAP referral	A mechanism used to instruct an LDAP client searching the directory to continue the search on another directory server.
LDAP replication model	The mechanism by which directory data is automatically copied from one directory server to another. Using replication, you can copy everything from entire directory trees to individual directory entries between servers.
LDAP security model	A model that defines how information in the directory is protected from unauthorized access.
LDIF	See LDAP Data Interchange Format.
Lightweight Directory Access Protocol	See LDAP.
Management Information Base (MIB)	A data structure used to define network devices and objects that SNMP accesses.
naming service	In a general sense, a facility that organizes and names objects. It provides an association, often referred to as a binding, between a name and an object.
NDS	Netware Directory Server.

Network Information Service	See NIS.
Network Information Service +	See NIS+.
NIS	The first UNIX-based distributed naming service. It replaced text files as the repository for storing information.
NIS+	A successor to NIS that corrected a number of flaws in the NIS architecture.
NMS	Network Management Servers
NTLM	A SAM agent that provides backward compatibility to Windows clients by using NT Lan Manager (NTLM) style authentication.
Object Identifier	A number assigned to child object classes to ensure they will not conflict with another object class.
OID	See Object identifier.
OSI stack	Open Systems Interconnection that allows network devices to read, write, and act upon management data.
PAM	See Pluggable Authentication Module.
PDC	See Primary Domain Controller.
performant	An adjective meaning good performance potential.
Pluggable Authentication Module (PAM)	A framework that allows new authentication technologies to be "plugged in" without changing commands such as login, ftp, and telnet.
Primary Domain Controller (PDC)	A controller that has write privileges on the SAM database.
private key	The private component of a pair of mathematically generated numbers, which, when combined with a private key, generates the DES key. The DES key in turn is used to encode and decode information. The private key of the sender is only available to the owner of the key.
public key	The public component of a pair of mathematically generated numbers, which, when combined with a private key, generates the DES key. The DES key in turn is used to encode and decode information. The public key is available to all users and machines.
PSL	A language that enables users to write their own KMs.

QFS	Quick File System, a standalone file system that reduces bottlenecks by maximizing the performance of the file system in conjunction with the underlying disk technology. QFS limits the physical head movement of disks, and provides other state-of-the-art storage technologies.
RAID	Redundant Array of Inexpensive (or Independent) Disks – a disk subsystem used to either increase performance, or fault tolerance, or both. RAID is often defined in levels 0 - 6 (plus various level combinations). RAID levels and how they apply to LDAP are covered in Chapter 8 "Selecting Storage for Optimum Directory Server Performance.
RBAC	Role-Based Access Control – a methodology or implementation where security is managed in a way that facilitates more granular control of enterprise systems access. Users are assigned one or more roles, and each role is assigned one or more privileges. Security administration with RBAC consists of determining the operations that must be executed by persons in particular jobs, and assigning employees to the proper roles.
RDN	Relative Distinguished Name. The left-most portion of a directory entry name.
Remote Procedure Calls (RPC)	A programming mechanism that enables NIS clients and servers to communicate with each other.
replication	The mechanism by which directory data is automatically copied from one directory server to another.
RFC	Request for Comments, A means by which each distinct version of an Internet standards-related specification is published as part of the RFC document series.
RPC	See Remote Procedure Calls.
SAM	See Security Account Manager.
SAMFS	Storage and Archive Manager File System, a file system originally intended as a disk storage facility supporting SAM (Storage and Archive Manager, tape-based storage). Today, SAMFS is a versatile software package that provides reliable, high performance storage management, archival and retrieval services.
SASL	See Simple Authentication and Security Layer
schema	A set of rules defining what types of data can be stored in any given LDAP DIT.
SDK	Software Development Kit
Secure Socket Layer (SSL)	An authentication method developed by Netscape as a way to create a secure connection between a web client and a web server. It can be used as a transport-layer security mechanism to make application protocols such as LDAP secure.

Security Account Manager (SAM)	A database of user account information maintained on special Windows NT servers called Domain Controllers, of which there are two varieties: primary (PDC) and backup (BDC).
Service Resource Records (SRV RR)	An Active Directory service that clients search to locate the nearest controller.
Service Search Descriptor (SSD)	SSDs define how and where an LDAP naming service client should search for information for a particular service.
shared nothing architecture	An architecture wherein at any time a resource is owned by only one of the cluster nodes.
SID	Security ID. An identification, the generation of which is specific to Microsoft's Active Directory implementation and not a standard LDAP concept.
Simple Authentication and Security Layer (SASL)	A standard proposed for pluggable authentication methods to be used for adding authentication support to connection-based protocols such as LDAP. SASL allows negotiation about multiple authentication schemes between a client and a server. SASL is beneficial as a modular security layer.
Simple Network Management Protocol (SNMP)	A widely deployed protocol originally designed to manage network devices, SNMP can also be used to manage other items such as applications and services.
Single sign-on	The ability to authenticate a user once upon login so that user is automatically authenticated for all applications the user accesses.
SNMP	See Simple Network Management Protocol.
Solaris OE Naming Service Switch	A tool to cope with the coexistence of multiple directory services present in the Solaris operating environment.
Solaris Resource Manager (SRM)	A utility that assigns shares of system resources to different applications, thereby maintaining a minimum threshold of performance.
Specified Server Method	A mechanism that specifies an NIS server or list of servers to bind to.
SQL	Structured Query Language. Standard used for database queries.
SRV RR	See Service Resource Records.
SSL	See Secure Socket Layer.

SSPI	Security Support Provider Interface.
TCP/IP	Transmission Control Protocol/Internet Protocol.
TGT	See Ticket-Granting Ticket.
Ticket-Granting Ticket (TGT)	A Kerberos method for application servers to grant service tickets to an authenticated user.
TLS	See Transport Layer Security.
Transport Layer Security (TLS)	The new standard for secure socket layers. A public-key-based Transport Layer Security protocol.
URL	Uniform Resource Locator
Wide Area Network (WAN)	Wide area network
X.500	A directory service defined as an Open Systems Interconnection (OSI) standard. A precursor to LDAP.

Index

administration tools, 348, 361
Administration URL, 133
administrative interface (SLAMD), 508, 517
administrative tasks, 399
aggregated controllers, 474
alarms, tools for sending, 405
algorithm directive, 47
alias database example, 298
alias directory, 131
aliases attribute, 9
aliases database, 288
aliases database (NIS/NIS+), 27, 31
alternate pathing software, 452
alternate search path, setting an, 437
alternate search paths with SSDs, 434
alternative method of client failover, 257
alternative to mirroring, 464
analyzing alternative solutions, 4
analyzing benchmark results, 468
anonymous, 38
anonymous bind, 8, 39
anonymous credential level and pam_unix
    authentication, 231
anyone permissions, 189
Apache server, unbundled, 381
Apache Tomcat servlet engine, 509
API, naming service, 32
APIs and toolkits, LDAP, 377
APIs, LDAP, 393
appdefaults section in krb5.conf, 78
appendices, descriptions of, xxvi
architecting an enterprise directory solution, 453
assessing performance of LDAP directory servers, 508
attribute mapping, 180, 412
attribute names, 9
attribute value reference tags, 496
AttributeMap attribute, 438
attributes and objects, 9
attributes for client failover, 257
attributes for loading configuration data, 313
attributes for mapping data, 326
attributes for RBAC-related object classes, 302
attributes requiring configuration, 323
attributes shared by DUAconfigProfile, 322
attributes, adding extended user, 304
attributes, standard profile, 306
audit log, 364

audit_user database (NIS/NIS+), 27, 32
auth qop directive, 46
auth_attr database, 439
auth_attr database (NIS/NIS+), 32
auth_attr RBAC database, 302
authenticating, 52
authenticating a telnet user, 64
authenticating using DIGEST-MD5, 61
authentication and security internet drafts, 571
authentication examples, 272
authentication exchange, 51
authentication ID, 42
authentication levels, 213
authentication mechanisms, 38
authentication mechanisms, certificate-based, 39
authentication mechanisms, PAM, 163
authentication mechanisms, SASL, 39
authentication mechanisms, SASL DIGEST-MD5, 42
authentication mechanisms, SASL EXTERNAL, 95
authentication mechanisms, secure, 63
authentication mechanisms, simple, 39
authentication mechanisms, strong (Kerberos), 64
authentication mechanisms, supported, 179
authentication mechanisms, TLSv1/SSL, 93
Authentication Method field, 532
authentication module functions, PAM, 609
authentication options, 212, 290
authentication problem summary, 275
authentication problems, 270
authentication realm, 42
authentication user types, 213
authentication using a DN, 287
authentication with PAM, 178
authentication with pam_ldap, 274
authentication with pam_unix, 177, 273
authentication, client, 8
authentication, Network Operating System (NOS), 17
authentication, PAM functions for, 607
authentication, pam_unix style, 189
authentication, pluggable (SASL), 39
authenticationMethod attribute, 242
authenticationMethod parameter, 314
authenticity, 43
authid, 42
autho_attr database (NIS/NIS+), 27
authorization (or proxy) ID, 42
authorization descriptions, adding, 306

building an LDAP Gateway, 381
building larger data sets, 505
built-in data replication, 256
business case for LDAP, 15

C

C LDAP API, 393
C LDAP Software Development Kit (SDK), 393
C library, 17
CA certificate module, 109
CA required information, 120
cabling of host arrays, 472, 475
cache consistency, 309
cache hits, 426
cache mirroring, 450, 452
cache mode, 450
cache tuning, 539
cache, refreshing, 416
calculating a new digest, 51
Calendar Initial Page Rate job, 534
capturing sensitive information, 97
cascading replication, 11
case sensitive or insensitive, 9
centralized naming service, the first, 20
cert7.db database, 108, 233
certificate (TLSv1), 97
Certificate Authority (CA), 232
certificate database, 133
certificate database key store, 130
Certificate Install wizard, 122
certificate management system (CMS), 147
certificate name, 109
certificate path, 205
certificate request example, 141
certificate request, generating, 113
Certificate Setup wizard, 132
certificate, digital, 39
certificate-based authentication, 39, 95
certificates, installing, 121
certificates, obtaining server, 113
certificates, working with, 108
certmap.conf file, 136
certutil utility, 108, 109, 124, 125
CGI.pm module, 381
chaining over SSL, 106

challenge stage, digest, 45
change log, 541
changes, packaging, 191
changing an authentication token, 160
changing passwords, enforcement of, 38
changing the realm names, 84
changing user login parameters, 438
chapter descriptions, xxv
characteristics, software, 444
characterizing performance, 465
charset directive, 47
checking for current patches, 216
checking name service containers, 269
checking replication status, 423
checklist, 219
checksum, 224
checksum algorithm, 69
child of an object class, 9
choosing a suffix name, 185
choosing high-availability options, 256
choosing NIS/NIS+ migration tools, 33
cipher policy (Start TLS), 153
cipher spec messages, 104
cipher suites, 47, 100, 101, 109, 149
cipherblock chaining (CBC), 47
cipher-opts directive, 47
classes, password, 75
clear text password (not encrypted), 39
clear text password (table), 178
clear text password, required, 58
clear text passwords, 59, 157, 290
client and server versions, differentiating, 191
client and server versions, mixing, 214
client authentication, 8, 95, 98
client authentication (TLSv1), 104
client cache, adjusting, 416
client cannot access data, 268
client configuration, listing, 357
client data access problems, 269
client failover, 33, 257
client fails to initialize, 268
client listener, 507
client parameters (local), updating, 357
client post-installation issues, 252
client problems, 268
client profiles, 189, 242

control flag for `pam_unix`, 175
control flags, PAM, 165
controller failures, 453
controllers, aggregated, 474
controllers, dual, 446
controlling access, 18
controlling access to directory data, 189
controlling operations, 36
controls and extended operations, 570
controls and extended operations, internet drafts, 570
conversion of NIS+ clients to LDAP clients, 312
core server, 507
corporate phone book, 17
correcting common problems, 260
corrective actions, 275
country code (C=) attribute, 185
CPUs and performance, 443
CPUs, adding additional, 444
CRAM-MD5, 38, 174
CRAM-MD5 login, 40
creating a password hash, 362
creating a stripe, 455
creating a volume, 449
creating additional profiles, 413
creating benchmark configurations, 469
creating client certificate databases, 243
creating clusters, 258
creating configuration entries, 327
creating containers, 186
creating entries in LDAP containers from `/etc`
    files, 288
creating host keys, 73
creating LDIF, 235
creating LDIF for benchmarks, 479
creating master KDC host principals, 88
creating RBAC entries with LDIF, 304
creating replication agreements from scripts, 417
creating stash files, 69
creating suffixes, 186
creating unique entries, 287
creating user accounts, 54
creating VLV indexes, 229
creating your own schema definitions, 441
creation and deletion of entries, 348
credential level, 205
Credential Level field, 532
credentials, 22, 79

credentials and tickets, 66
credentials, binding with, 59
critical messages, PAM, 172
CRYPT, 176
`crypt(3c)`, 155
`crypt(3c)` plug-in framework, 158
`crypt(3c)`, flexible, 158
`crypt_gensalt(3c)`, 158
cryptographic devices, 108
cryptographic token, 109
curly braces, 496
custom attributes, 480
custom jobs (SLAMD), 508
custom standard replacement tags, 498
custom tag implementation, sample, 500
custom tags, 480, 499
customizing creation of LDIF files, 499
customizing LDIF files, 485
cyptograhic keys, 100
Cyrus CMU implementation, 42

D

daemons, PAM, 164
dangerous use of plain text passwords, 42
DAP groups, 403
data access, random, 474
data consolidation issues, 26
Data Encryption Standard (DES) cipher, 47
data generation tool, 479
data migration, two approaches, 285
data replication, 19
data repositories, LDAP servers as, 311
data retrieval parameters, 314
data sets, building larger, 505
data stream encryption, 79
data, using LDAP to store, 320
database files, 37
database key store, 130
database loading, recommended order, 289
databases, importing, 300
databases, security, 108
databases, supported, 288
`db2bak` scripts, 362
`db2index` script, 362
`db2ldif` script, 362

F

failing to authenticate, 38
failover, 19, 21
failover, client, 257
fast disks, 446
FC-AL controllers, separate, 472
FC-AL internal disks, 445
fiber-channel arbitrated loop (FC-AL) controller, 447
fibre-channel arbitrated loop (FC-AL) disks, 446
file binding, 550
file parameter mappings (table), 212
file system type, default, 457
files format, extracting entries, 357
files modified, 238
fingerprint, 43
finish script sample, 246
finish scripts, 255
finished messages, 104
first book, xxiii
flexible crypt(3c), 158
flooding, 453
forcing password changes, 75
format utility, 455, 472
formats for entries, 286
formatting for a request, 151
forming a DNS address, 185
Fortezza cases, 149
Fortezza-compliant hardware, 101
four-way multi-master replication, 445
FQDN hostname, 46
FQN, 257
fragmented data storage, 15
frequently asked questions, 2
fsck(1M), 458
ftp command (secure version), 81
fully qualified host names, 257
Fully Qualified Name (FQN), DNS, 260
functional model, 6
future of NIS/NIS+, 19

G

gateway, 309
gateway deployment (figure), 310
gecos (NIS/NIS+), 28
gecos attributes, 10, 189

general scalability, 466
generated LDIF files (for benchmark), 471
generating a certificate request (Console), 113
generating a self-signed certificate request, 125
generating hashed passwords, 282
generating pre-master secrets, 102
generating sample data for benchmarks, 480
generating TLSv1/SSL client certificates, 137
generating version 2 profiles, 209
generic data services, 259
generic pam.conf file, 166
Generic Security Services Application Program
    Interface (also see GSSAPI), 62
gentent command, 359
GetEffectiveRights features, 37
GetEffectiveRights mechanism, 37
getent command, 357
getpassphrase() routine, 158
getpwenc script, 362
GID numbers, potential for collision, 29
GID numbers, reserved, 29
gidNumber attribute, 10
global Makefile example, 506
global replacement variables, 484
group conflicts, 29
group database, 288
group database (NIS/NIS+), 26, 29
group database entry example, 293
group identifier (GID), 22
grouping, 256
groups and users, provisioning, 401
groups, POSIX, 187
GSSAPI, 35, 38, 42, 62, 90
GSSAPI authentication and Kerberos v5, 62
GSSAPI layers, 63
GSSAPI LDIF file, 92
GSSAPI support in Solaris OE, 62
GSSAPI, benefits of, 64
GSSAPI, configuring, 90
GSSAPI, Diffie-Hellman, 63
GSSAPI, implementing, 81
GSSAPI, testing, 93
GSSAPI, understanding, 62
GUI-based tools, 364
guidelines for choosing hardware, 443
gunzip command, 481, 510, 515

H

Hamming Error Correction Coding (ECC), 464
handshake protocol (TLSv1), 99
hands-off installation of LDAP clients, 253
hardening, server, 74
hardware configuration, benchmark, 469
hardware failover, 259
hardware RAID, 446, 447
hardware RAID device, 445
hardware RAID versus software RAID, 459
hardware switches, alternative, 258
hardware volume, 455
hash, one-way, 558
hash-value of the message, 174
hello messages, 100
heterogeneous systems, 20
hierarchal structure of NIS+, 22
high availability, 19
high-availability considerations (Sun StorEdge), 451
high-availability options, choosing, 256
high-end storage, 445, 446
highly available data services, 258
highly available service, 445
history, password, 75
homegrown services, 31
`homePhone` attribute, 10
horizontal scalability, 19, 444
host arrays, cabling of, 472
host names, 250
`hosts` database, 288
`hosts` database (NIS/NIS+), 23, 26, 29
`hosts` database entry example, 294
`hosts` file, 148
`hosts.equiv` file, 80
hot spare, 449
how a Solaris client is configured, 249
how clients use entry DNs, 287
how NIS+ data is mapped to LDAP, 328
how PAM and LDAP work, 176
HTTP Digest, 47
HTTP GetRate job (SLAMD), 525
HTTPS, 131, 133
hub server, 11
human resource database, 17

I

identifier for the NIS+ Gateway, 334
identifying directory management tasks, 400
identifying secondary groups, 361
identifying the solution, 16
identifying the version, 211
identity mapping, 42, 90, 177
Identity Synchronization for Windows (ISW), 557
`idlist` block size, 449
IDs, unique, 32
`idsconfig` command, 180, 187, 189, 193, 225, 321, 353, 359, 413
`idsconfig` failures, troubleshooting, 266
`idsconfig` tips, 231
`idsktune` sample output, 217
`idsktune` utility, 53, 261
`ifconfig` command, 31
IMAP protocol, 41
implementing client profiles with SSDs, 404
implementing custom password management policies, 168
implementing `netgroups`, 404
implementing the GSSAPI mechanism, 81
import and export keys and certificates, 109
importing a signed certificate, 144
importing other databases, 300
incompatible 64-bit installation, 263
incorrect DN specified, 275
increasing I/O speed (storage), 457
incremental database updates (NIS+), 22
index files, 449
indexing and benchmarks, 478
indexing, SLAMD, 540
`infadd` command, 527
information and X.500 documents, internet drafts, 571
information model, 6, 7
information required by CA, 120
information required to configure LDAP clients, 250
inheritance, 489
initial authentication (SASL DIGEST-MD5), 44
`INITIAL_MEMORY` variable, 511, 535
initialization parameters, 313
initialization problems, 268
initializing a Kerberos session, 66
initializing a Secured LDAP Client, 147, 357
initializing LDAP Clients, 238
initiating diagnostics reporting for PAM, 173

mapping from an attribute, 205, 206, 207, 208
mapping function (rpc.nisd), 328
mapping naming service data to LDAP schemas, 286
mapping NIS+ data to LDAP data, 309, 334
mapping RPCs, 31
mapping, testing, 342
mappings, NIS+ to LDAP defaults, 328
maps, 22
maps, NIS/NIS+, 26
master KDC server, 68
master key, local copy, 69
master secret, 104
master servers, 11
masters and consumers, balancing, 258
matrices for password authentication, 179
max_life parameter, 70
MAX_MEMORY variable, 511, 535
max_renewable_life parameter, 70
maxbuf directive, 47
maximum lifetime of a ticket, 70
MD5, 101
MD5 example, 43
MD5 hash, 48, 50
MD5 hashes, 158
MD5 hashing, 43
measuring the scope, 4
mech file, 86
mechanisms for capturing and displaying information, 97
memory and performance, 443
merging data from an NIS/NIS+ domains, 357
message authentication code (MAC), 100
message digest algorithm (also see MD5), 43
message-digest algorithm (also see MD5), 43
Messages Logged section (SLAMD), 523
method for adding authentication support (SASL), 40
methods for custom tags, 499
methods for expressing directory queries, 550
Microsoft's SSPI, compatibility, 64
migrating from NIS to LDAP-based name services with N2L service, 561
migrating legacy data to LDAP, 285
migration example, 339
migration planning, 26
mirror (RAID 1), 448, 461
mirrored storage, 446
misconfigurations, 269

mismatch between server name and certificate header, 282
missing a critical patch, 260
missing shadowAccount attribute, 276
mistyped passwords, 274
MIT KRB5 Release version 1.0, 65
mixing client and server versions, 214
modeling complex DIT structures, 480
models, LDAP, 6
modification of entries, 348
modified server, 309
modify_policy command, 77
modifying default password policies, 77
modifying rpc.nisd, 328
modprinc command, 76
modrate command, 526
modular PAM service modules, 170
module types, PAM, 164
modules in non-default directories, 168
modutil tool, 109
monitor script, 362
monitoring directory services, 424
monitoring handshake activity, 271
monitoring the KDC, 78
monitoring tools, 405
Mozilla modules, 378
mpsadmserver command, 221, 224, 225
mpxio, 452
multi-homed systems, 29, 294
multi-hosting support, 446
multi-master replication (MMR), 11, 19, 192
multi-master replication example, 418
multi-pathing, 452
multi-pathing support, 450
multiple database technology, 445
multiple databases, 19
multiple directory servers, 7
multiple domains, 30
multiple host names, 287
multiple instances of directory service, 7
multiple IP addresses listed, 257
multiple jobs, concurrent (SLAMD), 514
multiple password policies, 38
multiple password systems, 158
multiple passwords, 159
multi-processor support, 444

N

proxyagent password, 404
proxyDn example, 239
proxypassword example, 239
public key, 97, 299
Public Key Cryptography Standard (PKCS) #11, 108
public key technology, 22
public keys (NIS+), 23
public void initialize() method, 499
publickey database, 289
publickey database (NIS/NIS+), 27, 31
publickey database entry example, 299
pwdhash command, 282

Q

qop-options, 46

R

RAID 0, 448
RAID 0 (stripe), 460
RAID 0+1, 462
RAID 1, 448
RAID 1 (mirror), 461
RAID 1+0, 462
RAID 1/0 (mirroring & striping), 470
RAID 2 and 3, 464
RAID 4, 464
RAID 5, 448, 463
RAID 5 LUN layout of eight disks, 453
RAID 5 LUN with a hot spare, 450
RAID 5 stripe, 457
RAID device, 445
RAID explained, 459
RAID levels, 460
RAID levels, usable, 448
RAID manager device, 459
RAM, adding additional, 444
random data access, 474
random reads, 461
random seed, 156
random writes, 461
RBAC database fields and equivalent attributes, 303
RBAC databases, 439
RBAC databases mapped to LDAP object classes, 302

RBAC entries, creating with LDIF, 304
RBAC-related databases, 300
RBAC-related object classes, attributes for, 302
RC2 and RC4, 101
RC4 encryption, 47, 96
rcp (Kerberos v5 version), 80
read ahead policy, 450
read and search privileges, 270
read and write caching, 446
read-only replicas, 11
reads and writes, 444
real job folders, 524
realm, 46, 49
realm (principal component), 67
realm names, changing, 84
realm, server's specified, 48
realms, 68
receipt of a return code, 467
recommended configurations for Sun ONE Directory
    Server software, 453
recommended transition tasks, 311
record protocol (TLSv1), 99
recovery, backup and, 400
redo logs, 461
reducing load on master server, 11
reducing operational costs, 16
redundancy, 453
redundant array of inexpensive disks (also see
    RAID), 459
redundant power supplies, 451
referrals, LDAP, 7
refreshing cache, 416
registered DNS address, 185
registered DNS name, 185
Registration Authorities (RA), 118
regulations, U.S. government, 38
relationships between NSS and NSPR, 107
Relative Distinguished Name (RDN), 8, 286, 336
remote procedure call (RPC), 155
removing replicas, 422
removing test entries, 344
renaming entries, 348
repairing certificate databases, 109
replacement variables, 485
replcheck.pl tool, 423
repldisc tool, 417
replica servers, managing, 404

words file, 71
workgroup array, standalone, 447
workgroup arrays, 445, 451, 453
wrapper script (directoryserver), 348
writebehind mode, 450
writethrough mode, 450
writing PAM service modules, 610
wrong value for the uid attribute, 276

X

X.500 and X.509 specifications, 185
xhost command, 263
XML documents, performing operations from, 550
XML-Schema, 550
XOR logic engines, 464

Y

Yellow Pages (former name of NIS), 20
ypcat example, 292

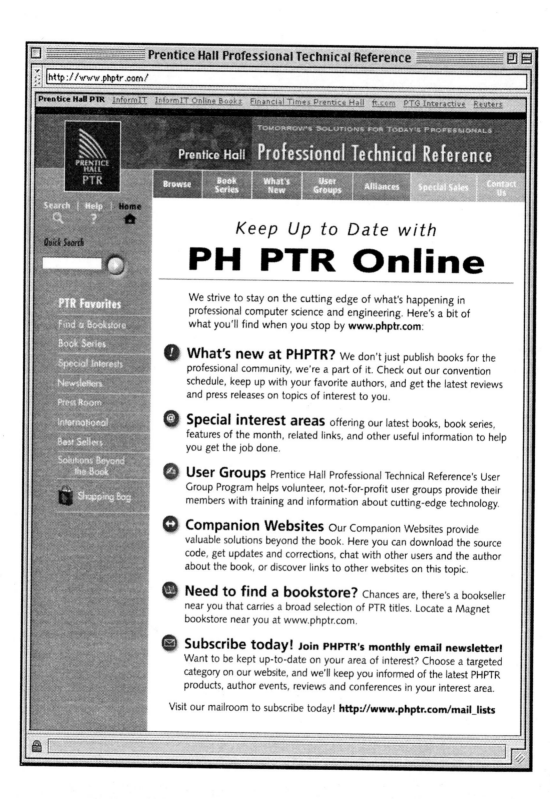

Prentice Hall Professional Technical Reference

http://www.phptr.com/

Prentice Hall PTR   InformIT   InformIT Online Books   Financial Times Prentice Hall   ft.com   PTG Interactive   Reuters

TOMORROW'S SOLUTIONS FOR TODAY'S PROFESSIONALS

Prentice Hall **Professional Technical Reference**

| Browse | Book Series | What's New | User Groups | Alliances | Special Sales | Contact Us |

Search | Help | Home

Quick Search

PTR Favorites
Find a Bookstore
Book Series
Special Interests
Newsletters
Press Room
International
Best Sellers
Solutions Beyond the Book
Shopping Bag

Keep Up to Date with
PH PTR Online

We strive to stay on the cutting edge of what's happening in professional computer science and engineering. Here's a bit of what you'll find when you stop by **www.phptr.com**:

(!) What's new at PHPTR? We don't just publish books for the professional community, we're a part of it. Check out our convention schedule, keep up with your favorite authors, and get the latest reviews and press releases on topics of interest to you.

(@) Special interest areas offering our latest books, book series, features of the month, related links, and other useful information to help you get the job done.

(⊿) User Groups Prentice Hall Professional Technical Reference's User Group Program helps volunteer, not-for-profit user groups provide their members with training and information about cutting-edge technology.

(↔) Companion Websites Our Companion Websites provide valuable solutions beyond the book. Here you can download the source code, get updates and corrections, chat with other users and the author about the book, or discover links to other websites on this topic.

(📖) Need to find a bookstore? Chances are, there's a bookseller near you that carries a broad selection of PTR titles. Locate a Magnet bookstore near you at www.phptr.com.

(✉) Subscribe today! Join PHPTR's monthly email newsletter! Want to be kept up-to-date on your area of interest? Choose a targeted category on our website, and we'll keep you informed of the latest PHPTR products, author events, reviews and conferences in your interest area.

Visit our mailroom to subscribe today! **http://www.phptr.com/mail_lists**